W9-CSK-283

THE
WHOLESALE-
BY-MAIL
CATALOG®
1994

THE WHOLESALE-BY-MAIL Catalog® 1994

BY THE PRINT PROJECT

Lowell Miller, Executive Producer

Prudence McCullough, Executive Editor

HarperPerennial

A Division of HarperCollinsPublishers

The Wholesale-by-Mail Catalog® is a resource for use by the general public. Companies in this catalog are listed at the sole discretion of the editors, and no advertising fees are solicited or accepted. All products and brand names are trademarks of their respective companies or owners.

HarperCollins books may be purchased for educational, business, or sales promotional use. For information, please write to: Special Markets Department, HarperCollins Publishers, Inc., 10 East 53rd Street, New York, NY 10022.

FIRST HARPERPERENNIAL EDITION
ISSN 1049-0116
ISBN 0-06-273161-0
94 95 96 97 ◆/RRD 10 9 8 7 6 5 4 3

CONTENTS

INTRODUCTION

Welcome to *The Wholesale-by-Mail Catalog® 1994*, the eleventh edition of the most popular guide to mail-order values. The word "wholesale" indicates the savings—30% on list or comparable retail on some, if not most, products or services—required to qualify a firm for inclusion here. Although this isn't a directory of wholesalers, some of the firms will sell to craftspersons, small businesses, and others on a wholesale basis. Beginning in this edition, those firms are distinguished with a symbol in the icon line in their listings. For details, see "Wholesale," page xii.

New to this edition, too, are symbols denoting that Spanish-speaking sales representatives are on staff, that the firm has TDD equipment (for the hearing impaired), and that the firm is on America Online, CompuServe, Delphi, GEnie, Prodigy, or another of the online computer services. (See p. xi for more information.) To make room for these new symbols, a few of the old, outdated ones have been jettisoned. Readers of past editions may note the disappearance of the telephone symbol, which showed that a company accepted orders by phone. Since this is now the norm, a special symbol isn't needed. And it's not necessary to "rate" a company's overall worth, since that's determined by its value to you, so the dollar-sign ratings seen in previous editions have been eliminated as well.

Before you send for a catalog or place an order, read the explanation of "The Listing Code" (from p. xi), which will help you get the most from this book. For more detailed information on mail-order shopping, see "The Complete Guide to Buying by Mail," beginning on page 535.

Enjoy *The Wholesale-by-Mail Catalog® 1994*, and please report on your experiences with these firms—see "Feedback," page 572, for address information.

Prudence McCullough, Executive Editor

USING THIS BOOK

The Wholesale-by-Mail Catalog® 1994 is a consumer's guide to buying by mail that's designed to be used by all catalog shoppers, from novice to seasoned veteran. Following is a guide to several of this book's features, which will help you to make the best use of the material.

"FIND IT FAST"

This list, immediately preceding the listings in most chapters, provides an at-a-glance guide to different types of products offered by firms listed in that section. For example, if you're looking for companies selling contact lenses and eyeglasses, check the "Find it Fast" box in the "Medicine and Science" chapter instead of reading through all of the listings. "Find it Fast" supplements the Product Index and the "See Also" section (see below) at the end of each chapter.

"SEE ALSO"

Each firm is listed in the chapter that best reflects its business focus, and *cross-referenced* in the "See Also" sections at the end of other chapters, as appropriate. For example, Gohn Bros. is listed in the "Clothing" chapter, because that's its strong suit. Because Gohn also sells horse blankets, you'll find it cited in the "See Also" section at the end of the "Animal Supplies" chapter. The "See Also" section can often direct you to valuable sources, so don't overlook it.

PATIENCE

Since companies are constantly revising their catalogs and printing new ones, please allow *six to eight weeks* for delivery, unless the listing indicates potential for a longer delay. If the catalog doesn't arrive within the designated period, write or call the company. Please remember that some products, such as flower bulbs and highly perishable foods, can be ordered only at certain times of the year.

PRICE QUOTES

Some firms don't issue catalogs at all. Most of these operate under a price-quote system: You tell them the exact make and model number of the item you want, and they give you the price and shipping cost. Price quotes are given by mail and phone. Businesses that operate this way are clearly indicated in the listings. (Be sure to check the "Special Factors" notes at the end of each listing as well as the core information.) Price-quote firms often have the lowest prices on such goods as appliances, audio and TV components, and furniture; they usually sell well below both the standard manufacturers' suggested list prices and the less-formal minimum prices that some manufacturers try to enforce. Before writing or calling for a price quote or making a purchase in this way, remember to read the "Price Quotes" section of "The Complete Guide to Buying by Mail."

MINIMUM ORDERS

In a few cases, the best buys are available from firms that require a minimum order in dollars or goods. Minimum requirements are usually flexible, and most firms will accept orders below the minimum, although an extra "handling fee" is often imposed. If you want something that's a real bargain, you may have friends who'll want it as well. Even if you can't find a buying partner, remember that a great bargain can also be a great gift.

A CAVEAT

The Wholesale-by-Mail Catalog® 1994 is compiled as a resource for consumers, to help you to find good values available by mail. Never order goods directly from this book, even if prices are given in the listing. Always contact the company first to get a catalog or a current price quote, and follow specific ordering and payment instructions. Do not request extra discounts or wholesale prices, unless the listing states they are available. All of the information in this book is based on research and fact-checking as of press time, and is subject to change.

THE LISTING CODE

Some of the information in the listings is presented in a simple coded form at the head of each entry, formatted as follows:

1) Company name, mailing address, and phone numbers, including 800, fax, and TDD lines
2) Literature form (catalog, brochure, flyer, leaflet, price list, etc.); the price, followed by "refundable" or "deductible" if you can redeem the price by placing an order; SASE: send a long (business-sized), self-addressed envelope with a first-class stamp (unless more postage is stipulated); "Information": price quote or information is given over the phone and/or by letter (when there is no catalog)
3) **Save:** the percentage of savings possible on the "suggested list" or "comparable retail" prices of the goods and/or services. The percentage is often an average and usually applies to some, but not all, goods. Do not deduct this percentage from the order total unless so instructed in the listing text
4) **Pay:** methods of payment accepted for orders (catalog fees should be paid by check or money order unless listing states otherwise):
   - personal check
   - MO: bank or postal money order
   - IMO: bank or postal international money order
   - AE: American Express credit card
   - DC: Diners Club credit card
   - Discover: Discover credit card
   - MC: MasterCard credit card
   - Optima: Optima credit card
   - Universal: AT&T's Universal credit card
   - V: VISA credit card
5) **Sells:** main type of goods sold

6) **Store:** location(s) and hours of the firm's retail site or other outlets, if applicable

✹ THE MAPLE LEAF

This symbol means the firm will ship goods to Canada. Canadian shoppers should check current import restrictions and tariffs before placing an order, and request shipping charges or an estimate before finalizing the order. Please note: U.S. firms generally request payment for goods and catalogs in U.S. funds.

▶ THE FLAG SYMBOL

A small "Old Glory" on the symbol line means the firm will ship goods to APO and FPO (U.S. military) addresses. For more information, see "Shipments Abroad," page 552.

¡Si! SPANISH

This icon means that the firm has Spanish-speaking sales representatives on staff. Before calling a company so indicated, read the listing and the "Special Factors" notes, since the person's availability may be limited to certain hours or days.

▣ THE COMPUTER SYMBOL

A computer on the icon line means the firm is online with America Online, CompuServe, Delphi, GEnie, Prodigy, or another computer-based service. See the "Special Factors" section of the listing for the name of the service; subscription kits are sold at a discount by many of the firms listed in "Office: Computing."

ℭ THE TDD SYMBOL

This symbol indicates that the firm can communicate with a TDD (telecommunication device for the deaf). In most cases, the firm uses a separate phone line for the equipment; sometimes, it's combined with a fax line. Read the listing, and if a separate phone line or other information isn't noted, send for the catalog.

★ THE "WHOLESALE" SYMBOL

Firms so marked will sell at wholesale rates to qualified individuals or other companies. To sell to you at genuine wholesale, most firms require proof that you're running a business—a card, letterhead, resale number, or all three—and may impose different minimum orders and sell under terms different from those that apply to retail. Please note that, unless specified, all information in these listings applies to consumer transactions only.

✔ THE DISCOUNT SYMBOL

If a check mark appears with the listing, the firm is giving a special discount or offer to readers of *The Wholesale-by-Mail Catalog® 1994*. For more information, see "WBMC Reader Offers," page 538.

THE COMPLETE GUIDE TO BUYING BY MAIL

This primer on mail-order shopping, found at the back of the book, can help you with questions on everything from sending for catalogs to interpreting warranties. If a problem arises with a mail-order transaction, look here for help in resolving it. You'll find additional consumer information in the chapter introductions.

THE WHOLESALE-BY-MAIL CATALOG® 1994

ANIMAL SUPPLIES

Livestock and pet supplies and equipment,

veterinary instruments and biologicals,

live-animal referrals, and services

The steady growth of pet ownership testifies to the pleasures of animal companionship, and having a pet can have other pluses: stroking domestic animals seems to have therapeutic benefits for people suffering from a range of maladies. In fact, pets are now widely used in therapy programs for nursing-home patients, hospitalized children, and psychiatric patients.

Most of us, who adopt pets for less pragmatic reasons, are unaware of the long-term costs of ownership: You can spend several thousand dollars in food, health care, and other necessities over the lifetime of the average cat or dog. While buying pet food by mail is seldom cost-effective because of the shipping costs, there are many products you *can* get for less: collars and leashes, cages and carriers, feeding dishes and devices, grooming tools, beds, and even medications. The firms listed here carry products for a wide range of animals—from hamsters and ferrets to horses and barnyard animals—and all can save you money.

Mastering the basics of pet care can save you considerable sums in a variety of ways—in salon costs, the price of obedience school, and sometimes even on vet fees. There's no lack of books and magazines on the topic: *The Common Sense Book of Kitten and Cat Care* and *The Common Sense Book of Puppy and Dog Care* (Bantam Books), by Harry Miller, are excellent reference works. The advice of the late Barbara Woodhouse is especially valuable to owners of uncooperative canines, and can be found in *Encyclopedia of Dogs and Puppies* and *Dog Training My Way* (Berkley Books), as well as *No Bad Dogs* (Summit Books,

I

1982). *The Complete Dog Book,* by the American Kennel Club, Inc., is a highly praised general reference that dog owners may want to add to their own libraries. There are scores of guides to the care of fish, birds, reptiles, and more exotic creatures; the Simon & Schuster Guides (Fireside), on cats, fish, dogs, birds, horses, and other animals, are especially helpful and easy to use. Consult your local library or bookstore for available titles. And the Massachusetts Society for the Prevention of Cruelty to Animals (MSPCA) publishes *Animals,* a terrific magazine that features articles on both household pets and wildlife. Recent issues included a discussion of cat-protection laws, the fate of animals in the former USSR, and useful information for pet owners who are apartment tenants. Proceeds from the magazine benefit the MSPCA's human-education work, and the organization is offering WBMC a year's subscription (six issues) for $14.98, a 25% savings on the regular rate of $19.94. Send payment, or write for a free sample copy, to *Animals* Magazine, Dept. W, 350 S. Huntington Ave., Boston, MA 02130.

If you're among the owners of this country's 50 million pet birds, tell your vet about the Avian Referral Service, which helps vets get advice on bird problems. Your vet should write to AAHA, Avian Referral Service, P.O. Box 15899, Denver, CO 80215, for more information.

Despite the best care, pets invariably succumb to sickness and accidents at some time during their lives, and the ensuing vet bills can be staggering. You might consider insurance: The Animal Health Insurance Agency, 24 Delay St., Danbury, CT 06810, insures cats and dogs under ten years of age against illness and injury. Veterinary Pet Insurance, 400 N. Tustin Ave., Santa Ana, CA 92705, imposes an age limit on new applicants (the animal must be 11 or younger). Write for details, rates, and restrictions.

Several of the firms listed in this chapter retain veterinarians who can answer questions on products and use, but they're not allowed to give specific medical advice. If your pet is ailing, consult a vet, and *always* seek professional guidance if you plan to administer any vaccines or medications to your animal yourself. There are other ways to safeguard your pet's well-being: Keep the number of a local 24-hour service that handles medical emergencies posted near the phone, and become familiar with symptoms and the first-aid measures you may have to take in order to transport the animal to the clinic.

FIND IT FAST

FISH • **Aquatic Supply, Daleco, Pet Warehouse, That Fish Place**
HORSES • **Dairy Association, Econo-Vet, Jeffers, Kennel Vet, Master Animal, UPCO, Wholesale Veterinary**
LIVESTOCK • **Dairy Association, Jeffers, Kansas City, Omaha Vaccine**
PETS (DOGS AND CATS) • **Dog's Outfitter, Kennel Vet, Master Animal, Pet Warehouse, R.C. Steele**
TRAPS • **Tomahawk Live Trap**
VET, KENNEL, AND GROOMER • **Dog's Outfitter, Econo-Vet, J-B Wholesale, Kennel Vet, Master Animal, Omaha Vaccine, R.C. Steele, UPCO**

AQUATIC SUPPLY HOUSE

42 HAYES ST.
ELMSFORD, NY 10523
800-777-7387
914-592-3620
FAX: 914-592-8658

Catalog: $2.50
Save: up to 40%
Pay: check, MO, MC, V, Discover
Sells: freshwater and saltwater fish supplies
Store: same address; Monday, Tuesday, Saturday 10–6, Wednesday, Thursday, and Friday 10–7, Sunday 11–5; also Wappinger Falls, NY

Aquatic Supply House, established in 1975, specializes in products for tropical and saltwater fish. The catalog features a complete line of aquarium supplies and equipment, including air pumps, filters, water pumps, heaters, pond equipment, lighting, tank novelties, chemicals, plants, and fish food and medication. The needs of both freshwater and saltwater fish are covered here. The catalog has a "tropical fish problem solver chart," with advice on troubleshooting fish difficulties. The manufacturers represented here include Aquanetics, Aquarium Products, Coralife Products, Eheim, Hagen, Jungle, Mardel, Marineland, Penn-Plax, Perfecto, Sea Chem, Second Nature, Tetra (including Tetra Press books), Vortex, and Wardley, among others. Prices run up to 50% off list.

Special Factors: Authorized returns are accepted (a 15% restocking fee is charged) within 30 days for exchange, refund, or credit; minimum order is $20 with credit cards; orders are shipped worldwide.

DAIRY ASSOCIATION CO., INC.

DEPT. BI

LYNDONVILLE, VT

   05851-0145

800-232-3610

802-626-3610

FAX: 802-626-3433

Brochure and Price List: free

Save: up to 35%

Pay: check or MO

Sells: livestock treatments and leather balm

Store: mail order only

Generations of herd farmers know Dairy Association Co., Inc., for its Bag Balm ointment. The firm has been in business since 1906, and also sells Hoof Softener and Tackmaster leather conditioner—all at excellent savings.

Bag Balm, formulated to soothe the chapped, sunburned udders of cows, is also recommended by horse trainers for cracked heels, galls, cuts, hobble burns, and other ailments—and is "great as a sweat" as well. Bag Balm can be used on sheep, goats, dogs, and cats, and is touted as a softener for weatherbeaten, chapped hands. A ten-ounce can, over $5 elsewhere, costs $4.75 here; a 4-1/2-pound pail costs $31.90. Green Mt. Horse Products, a division of Dairy Association, produces Hoof Softener—made of petrolatum, lanolin, and vegetable oils, it helps keep hoofs pliable and sound ($5.05 per pint). And Tackmaster—a one-step, all-around conditioner, cleaner, and preservative for leather—is cheaper than similar products at $2.25 for four ounces.

Canadian readers, please note: Contact Dr. A.D. Daniels Co. Ltd., N. Rock Island, Quebec, for prices and ordering information.

Special Factor: Phone orders are accepted for C.O.D. payment.

DALECO MASTER BREEDER PRODUCTS

3340 LAND DR.
FORT WAYNE, IN
46809-1531
219-747-7376
FAX: 219-747-7376

Catalog: $4, refundable (see text)
Save: up to 40%
Pay: check, MO, MC, V
Sells: tropical fish supplies and aquarium specialties
Store: mail order only

 (see text)

Daleco, in business since 1966, publishes the "Aquarists Supply Manual," a catalog/reference book that's packed with information useful to owners of fresh and saltwater fish. The catalog costs $4 (mailed bulk rate, $6 by first-class mail, to U.S. addresses only), and is refundable with a $50 order. Daleco discounts tank filters, aquarium heaters, lights, tank stands, air and water pumps, foods, water test kits, UV water sterilizers, water conditioners, reef trickle filter systems, and related goods. The brands include Aquanetics, Aquarium Products, Aquarium Systems, Eugene Danner, Dupla, Ebo-Jager, Energy Savers, Hagen, Hawaiian Marine, Hikari, Jungle Laboratories, Kordon, Mardel, Marineland, Perfecto, Sees, Tetra, Vortex, and WISA. The catalog is geared to serious hobbyists and breeders, who should find the catalog's "Fish Problem Solver" and "Fish Disease" charts helpful. The Manual is worth the $4 price for the information alone, but the prices are good—savings run up to 40%.

Canadian readers, please note: The Manual costs $6 (in U.S. funds) via surface mail, $9 via airmail.

Special Factors: Shipping included on orders over $25 sent in the contiguous U.S.; authorized returns are accepted; orders are shipped worldwide.

THE DOG'S OUT-FITTER

Catalog: free
Save: up to 50%
Pay: check, MO, MC, V
Sells: vet, kennel, groomer, and pet supplies
Store: mail order only

P.O. BOX 2010
HAZLETON, PA 18201
717-384-5555

Although The Dog's Outfitter catalog is geared to professionals, it has one of the best selections of products for pet owners around. The firm has been in business since 1969, and is exclusive in name only—the 96-page catalog is full of things for cats, and there's even a section devoted to the needs of ferrets. The Dog's Outfitter offers a full range of pet products, including grooming tools, shampoo, flea and tick collars and insecticides, cages, gates and doors, training aids, feeding and watering equipment, nutritional supplements, collars and leads, pet beds, carriers, toys and bones, and even books and gifts. The brands include A & W, Bio-Groom, General Cage, Havahart, Lambert Kay, Oster, PetAg, Resco, Ring 5, Speedy, André Tisserand (shears), Twinco, and Zodiac.

There are a number of items pet owners might appreciate: molting combs for dogs and cats, no-tears pet shampoo, herbal flea collars, pet doors to fit screen doors, a variety of yard scoops, all types of feeding bowls and crocks, "small animal" nurser kits, reflective collars and leads, dog parkas, bulk rawhide bones, and toys in boxes of 50. There are gifts, pet jewelry (for owners), note cards, and books (Arco, Howell, T.F.H.), and grooming videos from Oster and Animal Academy training tapes. And unlike many animal-supply discounters, The Dog's Outfitter has its own warehouse and does not drop ship, paying for shipping on most items.

Special Factors: Satisfaction is guaranteed; shipping is included on most items; authorized returns of new and unused goods are accepted within ten days for exchange, refund, or credit; minimum order is $50; C.O.D. orders are accepted.

ECONO-VET

8687 BLUMENSTEIN RD.
P.O. BOX 1191
MINOCQUA, WI
54548-1191
800-451-4162
715-369-5591

Catalog: free
Save: up to 50%
Pay: check, MO, MC, V, Discover
Sells: vet, kennel, and pet supplies
Store: mail order only

Wholesale prices and no minimum order—that's Econo-Vet's policy, and it means good buys for groomers, vets, kennel operators, and anyone else who cares for dogs, cats, and horses. Save up to 50% on grooming tools and tables, kennels and cages, feeding devices, leashes and leads, muzzles, shampoos, flea and tick treatments, nutritional supplements, biologicals, toys, and books and manuals. The products are from familiar makers—from Allerpet's anti-allergy pet treatment to the Zema flea trap. The prices are as much as 30% lower than other "discount" catalogs, and up to 50% below regular retail.

Special Factors: Satisfaction is guaranteed; returns are accepted within 30 days for exchange, refund, or credit; C.O.D. orders are accepted.

J-B WHOLESALE PET SUPPLIES, INC.

289 WAGARAW RD.,
DEPT. WB
HAWTHORNE, NJ 07506
800-526-0388
201-423-2222
FAX: 201-423-1181

Catalog: free
Save: up to 50%
Pay: check, MO, MC, V, AE, Optima
Sells: vet, kennel, and pet supplies
Store: same address; Monday to Friday 9–6, Thursday 9–9, Saturday 10–5, Sunday 11–4

J-B Wholesale Pet Supplies, in business since 1981, stocks "over 6,500 different items for showing, grooming, training, breeding," and other animal-related functions. J-B is staffed by professional animal handlers who've kennel-tested all of the products the company sells.

The 88-page catalog features a wide range of goods for cats and dogs, with the emphasis on canines: vaccines, remedies for common health problems, vitamins and nutritional supplements, repellents and deodorizers, shampoos and grooming products, beds and mats, flea and tick control products, cages, kennels, pet doors, grooming tables and dryers, leashes and leads, feeding devices, rawhide bones, and rubber toys. Every major manufacturer is represented, and J-B's own line of grooming aids—shampoo and coat conditioners and tints—is also featured. Send for the catalog, or call for prices and availability on specific name-brand items.

Special Factors: Satisfaction is guaranteed; returns are accepted within seven days for exchange, refund, or credit; minimum order is $25; orders are shipped worldwide.

JEFFERS VET SUPPLY

P.O. BOX 100
DOTHAN, AL 36302-0100
800-JEFFERS
FAX: 205-793-5179

Catalog: free
Save: up to 50%
Pay: check, MO, MC, V
Sells: vet and livestock supplies
Store: 419 Inez Rd., Dolthan, AL; also Old Airport Rd., West Plains, MO; every day 7–6, both locations

 ¡Si!

Jeffers Vet Supply, in business since 1976, publishes a 140-page catalog of supplies for livestock farmers and anyone who keeps a horse, as well as goods for cats, dogs, and even rabbits. Livestock farmers who raise cattle (including dairy), swine, sheep, goats, and poultry should see the catalog for antibiotics and sulfa drugs, biologicals, wormers, milking equipment, incubators, and other necessities. A large part of the catalog is devoted to equine supplies—biologicals and nutritional supplements, grooming tools and products, farrier supplies, stable equipment, and tack—including several pages of saddles. Equine videotapes by Al Dunning and Richard Shrake are also available. The line of goods for "companion animals" is likewise geared for professionals, although there are a number of products—training devices, collars, cages, clippers, etc.—that pet owners might find useful.

Special Factors: Satisfaction is guaranteed; quantity discounts are available; returns are accepted for exchange, refund, or credit; orders are shipped worldwide.

KENNEL VET CORP.

DEPT. WBMC
P.O. BOX 835
BELLMORE, NY 11710
516-783-5400
FAX: 516-783-7516

Catalog: $1 (see text)
Save: up to 70%
Pay: check, MO, MC, V, AE, Discover, Optima
Sells: vet, kennel, cattery, and pet supplies
Store: 1811 Newbridge Rd., Bellmore, NY; Monday to Friday 9–6, Saturday 10–4

If you own or raise dogs or cats, you'll find Kennel Vet's compact, 84-page catalog great reading. This firm beats other companies' discount prices on products for horses, as well as house pets, and has been in business since 1971.

Kennel Vet offers vaccines and biologicals, remedies for common health problems, vitamins and nutritional supplements, repellents and deodorizers, and other professional products. Kennel Vet also sells droppings composters, shampoos and grooming products, flea and tick control products, cages, crates, pet doors, dog and cat beds, grooming tables, dryers, leashes, leads, feeding devices, rawhide bones and rubber toys, and other goods. The brands represented include Adams, Classic, Doskocil (carriers), Eight-in-One, Gem-Line, Holiday, Johnson, Lambert Kay, Lawrence (brushes), Mid-West, Mycodex, Natra-Pet, Norden, Oster, Pervinal, Pet Tabs, Redi, Rich Health, Ring 5, Sulfodene, 3M, Vet-Kem, and others. Kennel Vet also sells Eukanuba, Iams, and Science Diet pet food by mail, as well as in the store. And the book department includes veterinary manuals, books on dog breeds, and a selection on cats, birds, and horses—all at a discount. Kennel Vet is offering readers a $2 discount on orders from the first catalog they receive. Identify yourself as a WBMC reader when you send for the catalog, and deduct the discount from the cost of the applicable goods only. This WBMC reader discount expires February 1, 1995.

Special Factors: Authorized returns are accepted; shipping is included on orders of $75 or more (with some exceptions—see the catalog); vaccines and biologicals are sent where ordinances permit; orders are shipped worldwide.

MASTER ANIMAL CARE

Catalog: free
Save: up to 40%
Pay: check, MO, MC, V, Discover
Sells: dog and cat supplies and biologicals
Store: mail order only

LAKE RD.
P.O. BOX 3333
MOUNTAINTOP, PA
18707-0330
717-384-3600
FAX: 717-384-3500

Master Animal Care specializes in dog and cat health supplies, sold at highly competitive prices through the "Master Animal Care" catalog, which includes helpful information on health care and vaccinating procedures, includes products for both cats and dogs. The 72 color pages feature grooming tools, a range of cages, feeding devices, training aids, leashes and leads, and related goods, at prices up to 40% below list. Vet supplies, such as vaccines, biologicals, and medications, are also available. Master Animal Care offers the latest innovations in pet products, such as airline-approved cages in designer colors, timer-operated feeding dishes that keep two meals fresh, natural and biodegradable cleaners and disinfectants, pet car seats and harnesses, and hot-oil skin treatments for dogs and cats. But it's also a good place to save on pet beds and cartons of rawhide bones—and pet-theme gifts and crafts kits.

Special Factors: Satisfaction is guaranteed; returns are accepted for exchange, refund, or credit.

OMAHA VACCINE COMPANY, INC.

3030 L ST.
OMAHA, NE 68107
800-367-4444
402-731-9600
FAX: 402-731-9829

Catalog: free
Save: up to 50%
Pay: check, MO, MC, V, Discover
Sells: dog, cat, and bird supplies
Store: same address; Monday to Friday 7–7,
Saturday 8–5, Sunday 11–5

Omaha Vaccine Company's 264-page "Master Catalog," published several times yearly, offers products for livestock, horses, and household pets. Established in 1965, Omaha Vaccine does much of its business with livestock producers, breeders, and veterinarians, but has branched into the consumer market. The Master Catalog features vaccines and biologicals, medications, surgical instruments, grooming tools, wormers, nutritional supplements, flea and tick products cages and carriers, leads and collars, bird products, and horse tack, among other goods. Omaha also publishes two specialty catalogs: "Best Care," for owners of dogs and cats, and "First Place," for horse and rider. The latter should be useful to the noncommercial owner, since it offers a comprehensive selection of tack, saddles, vet manuals, and a number of videotapes. Whether you're looking for flea treatments for your dog or opening a llama farm, you'll appreciate Omaha's 20,000 products and wholesale pricing.

Omaha Vaccine Company is offering readers a $5 discount on first orders over $50. Identify yourself as a WBMC reader when you order, and deduct the $5 from the total order amount. This offer expires February 1, 1995.

Special Factors: Some pharmaceutical products are available by prescription only (shipment is subject to local ordinances); shipping is included on orders over $50 (except F.O.B. items); C.O.D. orders are accepted; minimum order is $30.

PET WAREHOUSE

DEPT. BMC
P.O. BOX 310
XENIA, OH 45385
800-443-1160
FAX: 513-374-2524

Catalog: free
Save: up to 60%
Pay: check, MO, MC, V, Discover
Sells: pet supplies
Store: mail order only

The 106-page color catalog from Pet Warehouse is one of the best we've seen for the typical pet owner, who probably doesn't need breeding equipment or a wall-sized aquarium. Pet Warehouse has been in business since 1986, selling supplies for cats, dogs, birds, and fish. The catalog even has a page of goodies for "small animals"—hamsters, gerbils, and mice—as well as rabbits and reptiles.

Whether you have a freshwater or marine aquarium, or even a pond, Pet Warehouse can supply you with filters, air pumps, heaters, feeders, lighting, maintenance equipment and water conditioners, tank decorations and plants, fish medication, food, and other fish goods—but no tanks. The brands include Aquarium Pharmaceuticals, Eheim, Hagen, Marineland, Perfecto, Rainbow Lifeguard, and Tetra, among others. Bird owners can choose from over a dozen different Hagen cages, as well as cage accessories and bird toys, nests, feeders, bird food, and dietary supplements and medication. For dogs and cats, there are beds, collars and leashes, feeding devices, grooming supplies and implements, flea and tick repellants, nutritional supplements, cages and carriers, pet doors, litter boxes and scoopers, and toys. And there are rabbit hutches, supplies for reptiles, small animals, and even hermit crabs.If you want to read up on pet care or breeds, Pet Warehouse can provide Barrons and T.F.H. titles on a wide range of topics.

Special Factors: Minimum order is $10; orders are shipped worldwide.

R.C. STEELE CO.

DEPT. WC
P.O. BOX 910
1989 TRANSIT WAY
BROCKPORT, NY
   14420-0910
800-872-3773
FAX: 716-637-8244
TDD: 800-468-8776

Catalog: free
Save: up to 50%
Pay: check, MO, MC, V
Sells: vet, kennel, groomer, and pet supplies
Store: 1989 Transit Way, Brockport, NY;
Monday to Wednesday 9–7:30, Thursday
and Friday 9–8:30, Saturday 9–6, Sunday
12–5

R.C. Steele Co. was founded in 1959 and is the wholesale division of Sporting Dog Specialties, well known as a source for products for hunting dogs. R.C. Steele's prices are excellent—sometimes as much as 50% less than comparable retail—and the only drawback is the $50 minimum order. The 68-page color catalog features products and equipment for canines—cages, pet doors, insecticides, feeding equipment, droppings composters, training dummies and jumps, leashes and leads, grooming supplies and tools, and manuals. There are great buys on rawhide bones, which are sold in case lots at a fraction of full retail, and all types of pet beds, at about half the going rate. A recent catalog featured over two pages of books and tapes from the American Kennel Club (breed shows), Arco, Denlinger, Doral, Howell, Oster, T.F.H., and Volhard (obedience). R.C. Steele also offers a small but well-chosen selection of products for cats, as well as a page of aquarium supplies.

Special Factors: C.O.D. orders are accepted; authorized returns are accepted; minimum order is $50; orders are shipped worldwide.

THAT FISH PLACE

237 CENTERVILLE RD.
LANCASTER, PA 17603
800-733-3829
FAX: 800-786-3829

Catalog: $3 (see text)
Save: up to 50%
Pay: check, MO, MC, V
Sells: aquarium supplies, products for birds, dogs, cats, etc.
Store: same address; Monday to Thursday 10–8, Friday and Saturday 10–9, Sunday 12–5

 (see text)

That Fish Place has been selling aquarium supplies since 1973, and stocks the works: aquariums, air pumps, cleaners, feeders, filters, lighting, heaters, fish food, medication, plants, ornaments, water conditioners, and much more. The 191-page catalog from That Fish Place is packed with everything from acclimators to worm feeders, from scores of manufacturers—from Aquanetics to Zema. The catalog also features several pages of items for ponds—filters, plants, fountains, etc.—as well as supplies for birds, cats, dogs, and reptiles. Scores of books on fish species and care are available, and the catalog includes several pages of charts and information that can help you determine what might be ailing your fish or aquarium. The discounts are excellent—up to 50% on list prices—and the quarterly sales brochures will save you even more.

That Fish Place will send the catalog (usually $3) free of charge to the WBMC readers, so be sure to mention this book when requesting the catalog. This WBMC reader offer expires February 1, 1995.

Special Factors: Authorized, unused returns are accepted (a 15% restocking fee may be charged); minimum order is $15 for dry goods, $25 for live plants; orders are shipped worldwide.

TOMAHAWK LIVE TRAP COMPANY

P.O. BOX 323-WBM
TOMAHAWK, WI 54487
715-453-3550
FAX: 715-453-4326

Brochure: free (see text)
Save: up to 50%
Pay: check, MO, MC, V
Sells: humane animal traps
Store: Tomahawk, WI; Monday to Friday
8–5; also Coburn Company, Whitewater,
WI; and Plow & Hearth, Orange, VA

Tomahawk's box traps are used by the U.S. Army Medical Corps, state and federal conservation departments, dog wardens, universities, and others who want to catch a critter without endangering its pelt or its life. It's somewhat ironical that the founders of this firm once operated a fur farm, and developed the traps to cope with their own runaways. The success of the traps put an end to the farm, a conclusion that should please animal-rights activists.

Tomahawk, which was established in 1930, makes traps for 58 different animals, from mice (about $13) to large dogs (about $173), as well fish and turtles, birds, beavers, grackles, raccoons, skunks, bobcats, jackrabbits, and cats. There are rigid and collapsible styles, transfer cages, station wagon and carrying cages, several with sliding doors (for shipping animals), and special sizes can be made to order. You can order the comprehensive, 56-page catalog ($3.95), which includes tips on trapping animals, a list of common foods that can be used to lure over 20 species, and trap dimensions and specifications. If you're familiar with Tomahawk's traps, *send a self-addressed, stamped envelope for the free brochure and price list only.*

Special Factors: Quantity discounts of 50% are available on orders of six or more of the same trap; orders are shipped worldwide.

UNITED PHARMACAL COMPANY, INC.

P.O. BOX 969,
   DEPT. WBM94
ST. JOSEPH, MO
   64502-0969
816-233-8800
FAX: 816-233-9696

Catalog: free
Save: up to 50%
Pay: check, MO, MC, V, AE, Discover
Sells: vet, kennel, and pet supplies
Store: 3705 Pear St., St. Joseph, MO; Monday to Friday 7:30–6, Saturday 7:30–5

United Pharmacal Company, known as UPCO, offers thousands of products for dogs, cats, birds, and horses in a 160-page catalog that runs from hay racks to catnip-filled fur fish. UPCO's veterinary line includes antibiotics, wormers, medical instruments, nutritional supplements, skin treatments, insecticides, grooming aids, and related goods. Horse owners should check the dozen pages of medications and supplements, farrier supplies, and tack. Dog and cat owners will appreciate the savings on leashes and leads, collars, feeders, books, toys, feeding dishes and stations, pet doors, and other goods. Professional groomers should note the 42 pages of grooming products for show dogs. UPCO also has a selection of bird cages and supplies and products for hamsters, gerbils, guinea pigs, ferrets, and rabbits. The manufacturers include Absorbine, Borden, Dubl Duck, Farnam, Happy Jack, Lambert Kay, Nylabone, Oster, St. Aubrey, and Zema, to note a few. And UPCO offers hundreds of books and manuals that cover the care and breeding of a wide range of animals.

Canadian readers, please note: Payment must be made in U.S. funds, and vaccines are not shipped to Canada.

Special Factors: Quantity discounts are available; C.O.D. orders are accepted; returns are accepted within 20 days; minimum order is $10.

VET EXPRESS, INC.

P.O. BOX 155
HAZELHURST, WI 54531
800-458-7656
715-356-7221

Catalog: free
Save: up to 35%
Pay: check, MO, MC, V, AE, Discover
Sells: vet, kennel, and pet supplies
Store: mail order only

Vet Express answers the needs of animal-care professionals with a wide range of biologicals and medical-care products for horses, cats, dogs, and birds. The manufacturers and brands include Bio-Centic, Coopers, Fort Dodge, Haver, Kenvet, Norden, Pfizer, Pitman Moore, Schering, SmithKline Beecham, Solvay, Summit Hill Labs, Vet A Mix, Vet-Kem, VPL, United Pet Supplies, and many others. Prices are reasonable and drop on quantity orders. If you're looking for something not listed in the catalog, call and ask, since Vet Express may be able to get it for you.

Special Factor: C.O.D. orders are accepted.

SEE ALSO

Cabela's Inc. • dog beds; hunting dog training equipment • **SPORTS**
Defender Industries, Inc. • pet life preservers • **AUTO**
Gander Mountain, Inc. • hunting and fishing gear • **SPORTS**
Gohn Bros. • horse blankets • **CLOTHING**
Mellinger's Inc. • live pest controls, fly traps, bird feeders, etc. • **FARM**
Sharp Bros. Seed Co. • forage and fodder seed • **FARM**
Weston Bowl Mill • bird feeders and bird calls • **GENERAL MERCHANDISE**

APPLIANCES, AUDIO, TV, AND VIDEO

Major, small, and personal-care appliances;

sewing machines and vacuum cleaners;

audio components and personal stereo; TV

and video equipment

The companies here offer the full range of electronic devices, including white goods (washers, dryers, refrigerators, and ranges), brown goods (TVs, air conditioners, etc.), small kitchen and personal-care appliances, pocket calculators, phones and phone machines (autodialers, answerers, line switchers, etc.), sewing machines, vacuum cleaners, and floor machines. Some also sell blank audiotapes and videotapes, luggage, cameras, typewriters, computers, pens, and video games. Thanks to stiff price competition across the country, discounts often run from 15% to 40%—more on extremely popular brands, and less on high-end audio and video components.

The price is important, but it's just one purchase consideration. *Consumer Reports* is an important resource featuring monthly reviews of name-brand products, as is the annual *Buying Guide,* which summarizes scores of the reviews. In addition to dispassionate assessments of product performance and guides to features, the *CR* reviews often include both suggested list and "benchmark" retail selling prices. *Consumer Reports* also publishes news on product recalls, deceptive selling practices, health issues, money management, and related topics of concern to consumers. For subscription information, see the current issue or write to Consumers Union, 256 Washington St., Mount Vernon, NY 10553.

Most appliance and electronics manufacturers will send brochures on specific models upon request. You can often find the manufacturers' address on product packaging, and the consumer contacts and addresses of hundreds of major corporations are listed in *Consumer's Resource Handbook,* which is available from the Consumer Information Center (see the listing in "Books").

Planning to purchase a refrigerator, freezer, or air conditioner? The Association of Home Appliance Manufacturers (AHAM) publishes guides to the features and specifications of refrigerators and freezers in the *Consumer Selection Guide for Refrigerators and Freezers.* Air conditioners are examined in *Consumer Selection Guide for Room Air Conditioners,* which includes the "Cooling Load Estimate Form." This worksheet will help you determine how many BTUs your home or room requires, something you should find out *before* you decide on the model you want. Send a check or money order for $1.50 for each title requested to AHAM, Public and Consumer Relations Dept., 20 N. Wacker Dr., Chicago, IL 60606.

Since even small appliances and light bulbs can consume large amounts of energy over time, determining how much power you're using when you flip the switch will help you figure out wise use of the appliances you own—and help you make energy-efficient purchases in the future. To compute the hourly cost of an appliance, find its *wattage* and divide that figure by 1,000 to find the *kilowattage,* which you can multiply by the price of a *kilowatt hour* (kWh) charged by your utility company. (The wattage of an appliance can usually be found in the same place as its model and serial number, or can be obtained from the manufacturer.) For example, a 600-watt vacuum cleaner has a kilowattage of 0.6 (600 divided by 1,000). Run in New York City, where the price per kilowatt hour is 12.4303¢, the operating cost per hour is 7.46¢. If you have cheaper rates at night, reserve as much high-consumption use (ironing, running the dishwasher and dryer, self-cleaning the oven) for evening hours.

In addition to price and energy consumption, try to find out as much as possible about a product's repair record before you buy. *Consumer Reports* surveys repair shops periodically, and reveals which brands seem to be turning up most frequently. Unfortunately, models in the same line can vary widely in performance, so undifferentiated reviews of brands may not accurately predict how an individual model will behave. You can conduct your own interviews, too, asking your local appliance repair center about lemons and troublesome brands. And don't overlook your friends, who are probably happy to share both their horror stories and the triumphs of their best buys.

The next-best thing to keeping something out of the shop is having it repaired under warranty. The electronics boom of the mid-1980s helped to popularize the sale of service contracts (erroneously termed "extended warranties"), which kick in when the manufacturers' warranties expire. Extended warranties are often pushed on big-ticket items at the point of sale on in-store purchases, but they're also sold by mail-order vendors. (Some credit-card companies provide similar protections, free of charge, for products purchased with their cards. But check the terms of your card's policy before assuming it provides comprehensive coverage.) Extended warranties are honored by the seller, not the manufacturer, at the seller's repair center. Are they worth the money? According to one analyst who examined the warranties, service contracts, and repair records of color TVs, air conditioners, refrigerators, washers, and ranges in a National Science Foundation/MIT study, the answer is no. The bottom line is price: In many cases, the *probable* repair bill is lower than the cost of the service contract. But if you've had a post-warranty appliance breakdown, you may feel that a contract is worthwhile insurance. If you decide to buy one, get answers to these questions:

- Does the service contract duplicate the manufacturer's warranty coverage?
- Does the service contract cover parts and labor?
- Is the company selling the contract stable, and is its service department reputable? (Contact the local Better Business Bureau for information on its record.)
- Could you troubleshoot or repair the appliance yourself? Contact the manufacturer (many have 800 lines staffed by technicians who can provide advice on making repairs) or your local repair center before bringing in a malfunctioning product—it may be something you could fix at home.
- What's your *own* history of appliance and electronics failure? If machines seem to enjoy long and healthy lives in your care, you may not need the insurance.

Good maintenance and care will help extend a product's performance. VCRs, which appear susceptible to breakdown, will work better longer if you keep the heads clean, ease wear and tear by using a rewinder, and follow the manufacturers' use and care instructions carefully. Audio components also reward good treatment, and you'll find a battery of cleaning solutions and devices for LPs and CDs available from Lyle Cartridges and several other firms in this chapter.

If you run into trouble with a *major appliance* and can't get it resolved, you may be able to get help from the Major Appliance Consumer Action Panel (MACAP). MACAP, which is sponsored by AHAM (see above), can request action from a manufacturer and make recommendations for resolution of the complaint. (The Panel's advice is not binding, but it resolves over 80% of the cases it handles.) You can turn to MACAP with problems about dishwashers, ranges, microwave ovens, washers, dryers, refrigerators, freezers, garbage disposals, trash compactors, air conditioners, water heaters, and dehumidifiers. If your complaint concerns one of these appliances, and your attempts to get the problem resolved with the seller and the manufacturer have been futile, write to Major Appliance Consumer Action Panel, 20 N. Wacker Dr., Chicago, IL 60606. Your letter should include the manufacturer's name, model number of the appliance, and date purchased, as well as *copies* of relevant receipts and correspondence. (Call 800-621-0477 for more information.)

For listings of additional firms selling appliances and electronics, see "General Merchandise," "Office and Business" (including the "Computing" subchapter), and "Tools."

FIND IT FAST

APPLIANCES • **Bernie's, Cole's, Dial-a-Brand, Harry's, LVT, Percy's, Irv Wolfson**

AUDIO • **Audio Concepts, Bernie's, Crutchfield, Harry's, Illinois Audio, J & R, Lyle Cartridges, S & S Sound City, Wholesale Tape**

OFFICE MACHINES AND PHONES • **Crutchfield, J & R, LVT, Percy's, S & S Sound City**

SEWING MACHINES • **Derry's, Discount Appliance, LVT, Sewin' in Vermont, Sew Vac City, Suburban Sew 'N Sweep**

TV AND VIDEO • **Bernie's, Cole's, Crutchfield, Dial-a-Brand, Harry's, J & R, LVT, S & S Sound City, Westcoast Discount**

VACUUM CLEANERS • **AAA-Vacuum, ABC Vacuum Cleaner, Bernie's, Derry's, Discount Appliance, Harry's, LVT, Midamerica, Sew Vac City, Irv Wolfson**

AAA-VACUUM CLEANER SERVICE CENTER

1230 N. 3RD.
ABILENE, TX 79601
915-677-1311

Flyer: $2, refundable
Save: up to 75%
Pay: check, MO, MC, V, Discover
Sells: vacuum cleaners, floor shampooers and polishers
Store: same address; Monday to Friday 8:30–5

You can save on some of the best names in the cleaning business at AAA-Vacuum Cleaner, which offers discounts of up to 75% on list prices. The latest models in canister, upright, convertible, and mini vacuums are available, by Bissell, Dirt Devil, Eureka, Hoover, Oreck, Panasonic, Regina, Royal, Sanitaire, Sharp, and Tri-Star. Both home and commercial lines of vacuum cleaners, floor buffers, and rug shampooers are stocked, and AAA-Vacuum Cleaner also sells inexpensive reconditioned Kirby machines. AAA-Vacuum Cleaner has been in business since 1975, and sells supplies and accessories as well as floor machines.

Canadian readers, please note: Only U.S. funds are accepted.

Special Factors: Satisfaction is guaranteed; layaway plan is available; C.O.D. orders are accepted; returns are accepted within ten days; orders are shipped worldwide.

ABC VACUUM CLEANER WAREHOUSE

6720 BURNET RD., WM94
AUSTIN, TX 78757
512-459-7643
FAX: 512-451-2352

Price List: free
Save: up to 50%
Pay: check, MO, MC, V, AE, Discover, Optima
Sells: vacuum cleaners
Store: same address; Monday to Friday 9–6, Saturday 9–5

 ¡Si!

ABC purchases from suppliers who are overstocked or going out of business, and passes the savings—up to 50% on the suggested retail or usual selling price—on to you. ABC has been in business since 1977, and sells machines by Electrolux, Filter Queen, Kirby, Oreck, Panasonic, Riccar, Royal, Sanyo, Sharp, Thermax, and Tri-Star. The popular

Rainbow, by Rexair, is sold at a discount, as well as all of its accessories and parts. And top-of-the-line Eureka and Hoover machines are available, as well as built-in cleaning systems. See the price list for bags, filters, and accessories and attachments for selected models. ABC also offers repair services by mail—call for information if you're having trouble getting your machine repaired locally.

Special Factors: No seconds or rebuilt models are sold; C.O.D. orders are accepted; orders are shipped worldwide.

AUDIO CONCEPTS, INC.

901 S. 4TH ST.
LA CROSSE, WI 54601
800-346-9183
FAX: 608-784-6367

Catalog: free
Save: up to 40% (see text)
Pay: check, MO, MC, V
Sells: speaker kits
Store: mail order only

If you'd like to assemble a good audio system but don't think you can afford it, here's one way to save on the thing that seems to cost the most: the speakers. Audio Concepts invites you to build them yourself, and save up to 40% over the cost of comparable assembled speakers. The kits are sold full with crossovers and cabinets already built, or in parts, with everything except the cabinets. (Audio Concepts makes much of the value of the cabinets created by the craftspeople at the firm; real wood veneers are used, and a number of finish options are available.) The parts kits require no soldering; all connections are made with push-on terminals; and you can create the cabinets yourself (a manual with guidelines is included with your order) or use cabinets you already have.

Audio Concepts' prices begin at $125 for a parts kit for a pair of LX bookshelf speakers, and run to $759 for the full kit (cabinets included) of a pair of Sapphire II speakers. Shipping and handling costs add $20 to $60 to the cost of your order, at this writing, depending on whether you're ordering full or parts kits. If you're a technically proficient audiophile, you'll appreciate all the specifications in the catalog; all the components used in the catalog are available individually, and you can also buy a complete set of manuals that give further specs and advice on maximizing performance for each of the speakers for $10 (refundable with the purchase of a kit). And if you're not a techie, you can bring the catalog to someone who is and get a second opinion—or buy a pair, assemble them, and judge for yourself.

Special Factors: Satisfaction is guaranteed; authorized returns are accepted in new condition in original packaging within 15 days for exchange, refund, or credit; C.O.D. orders are accepted; orders are shipped worldwide.

BERNIE'S DISCOUNT CENTER, INC.

821 SIXTH AVE., D-5
NEW YORK, NY
  10001-6305
212-564-8758, 8582
FAX: 212-564-3894

Catalog: $1, refundable (see text)
Save: 30% average
Pay: check, MO, MC, V, AE, Optima (see text)
Sells: appliances, TV and audio components, office machines
Store: same address; Monday to Friday 9–5:30, Saturday (except July and August) 11–3:30

 ¡Si! (see text)

Bernie's has been in business since 1947, and sells "pluggables"— everything from electric brooms to fax machines—at 10% to 15% above dealers' cost, or an average of 30% off list. The catalog is available for $1 (refundable with a purchase), but it shows just a smattering of the stock at Bernie's, and you're better off calling for a price quote. One of the city's best sources for discounted electronics and appliances, Bernie's tries to carry the top-rated goods listed in popular buying guides, and Bernie's *does not handle grey-market goods.*

Bernie's sells electronics (audio, TV, and video equipment) by Aiwa, Brother, Fisher, JVC, Mitsubishi, Murata, Panasonic, Quasar, RCA, SCM, Sharp, Sony, and Toshiba. White goods (shipped in the New York City area only) are available from Airtemp, Amana, Caloric, G.E., Hotpoint, Jenn-Air, Magic Chef, Maytag, KitchenAid, Tappan, Welbilt, Whirlpool, White-Westinghouse, and other manufacturers. Small and personal-care appliances from Bionaire, Black & Decker, Braun, Clairol, Eureka, Farberware, Hamilton Beach, Hitachi, Hoover, Interplak, KitchenAid, Krups, Norelco, Oster, Panasonic, Presto, Remington, Sanyo, Simac, Sunbeam, Teledyne (Water Pik and Instapure), Toastmaster, Wearever, West Bend, and other brands are available as well.

Please note: Purchases charged to American Express/Optima cards are shipped to billing addresses only, and MasterCard and VISA are accepted for *in-store* purchases only.

Canadian readers, please note: Orders are shipped to Canada via UPS only.

Special Factor: Store is closed Saturdays in July and August.

COLE'S APPLIANCE & FURNITURE CO.

4026 LINCOLN AVE.
CHICAGO, IL 60618-3097
312-525-1797

Information: see text
Save: up to 50%
Pay: check, MO, MC, V, Discover
Sells: appliances and home furnishings
Store: same address; Monday and Thursday 9:30–9, Tuesday, Friday, and Saturday 9:30–5:30 (closed Wednesday and Sunday)

Cole's, founded in 1957, sells electronics (TV and video), appliances, and home furnishings at discounts of up to 50%. If you're pricing something from a major manufacturer, call Cole's for a price quote.

Special Factor: Price quote by phone or letter.

CRUTCHFIELD CORPORATION

1 CRUTCHFIELD PARK,
DEPT. WH
CHARLOTTESVILLE, VA
22906-6020
800-955-9009
TDD: 800-388-9753

Catalog: free (see text)
Save: 10% to 55%
Pay: check, MO, MC, V, AE, DC, Discover, Optima, Crutchfield charge card
Sells: audio and video components, phone equipment, computers, and peripherals
Store: same address; also Market Square East Shopping Center, Harrisonburg, VA; Monday to Saturday 10–6, Friday 10–8, both locations

Crutchfield publishes an informative, 150-page catalog of home and car audio components, video equipment, and computers and peripherals. The catalog is loaded with buying tips and product specifications on featured goods, which are priced from 10% to 55% below list price. The computer section of the catalog is a great resource for anyone doing shopping for a home office or small business. In fact, Crutchfield's catalog can be more helpful in comparing features than the articles in service magazines. And good prices are just one of the pluses—Crutchfield backs everything it sells with a guarantee of satisfaction, and the staff can provide extensive support. Installation walk-throughs over the phone, car stereo kits for genuinely customized audio installation, and informative consumer service manuals are among the available benefits. And all departments employ Spanish-speaking representatives. Crutchfield, which was established in 1974, is a factory-authorized repair station for most of the brands it sells, and *does not sell grey-market goods.*

Crutchfield's car audio components line, which includes equipment for pickup trucks and hatchbacks, features goods by Alphasonik, Blaupunkt, Carver, Cerwin Vega, Clarion, Infinity, JBL, Jensen, JVC, Kenwood, Pioneer, Pyle, Sanyo, Sherwood, and Sony. Crutchfield also sells radar detectors and CB radios by BEL, Midland, and Whistler, as well as dozens of types of car antennas, and Crimestopper and Prestige alarm systems to protect it all.

The home audio portion of the catalog includes pages of features comparisons of current models of receivers, CD players, cassette decks, and speakers, and shows amps, tuners, portable and personal audio, headphones, remote controls, speaker stands, cassette cabinets, and Discwasher maintenance products. The brands include Advent, Bose, Cerwin Vega, Infinity, JVC, Kenwood, NHT, Pioneer, and Sony. You'll also find camcorders, laser disc players, and video components from JVC, Mitsubishi, Panasonic, Pioneer, and Sony offered here. And Crutchfield offers PCs and peripherals, fax machines, software, phone machines, and related office equipment and supplies—all at a discount. The brands include Crutchfield's own line, as well as Canon, Leading Edge, Logitech, Panasonic, Sony, and Toshiba.

Please note: The catalog is free to readers of this book, but be sure to identify yourself as a WBMC reader when you request your copy.

Overseas customers: Request an "International Order Fact Sheet."

Special Factors: Satisfaction is guaranteed;returns are accepted within 30 days; orders are shipped worldwide (via Federal Express).

DERRY'S SEWING CENTER

**430 ST. FERDINAND
FLORISSANT, MO 63031
314-837-6103**

Brochure: $1 and SASE (see text)
Save: up to 40%
Pay: MO, MC, V
Sells: sewing machines and vacuum cleaners
Store: same address; Monday to Friday 10–7, Saturday 10–4

Upgrading your sewing machine may cost less at Derry's, which carries models (sewing and overlock) by Babylock, Necchi, Panasonic, Simplicity, Singer, Viking, and White. Savings run up to 40%, and parts for new and older machines are available, as well as supplies—needles, belts, bobbins, etc. Derry's has been in business since 1979, and provides in-warranty service on the Necchi, Simplicity, and Singer sewing machines. You can request the brochure (send a *$1 bill and a long, stamped, self-addressed envelope*), but if you know the model you want, it's easier to call for a price quote. Derry's also sells Panasonic vacuum cleaners and bags.

Special Factors: Price quote by phone or letter (see above); orders are shipped worldwide.

DIAL-A-BRAND, INC.

57 S. MAIN ST.
FREEPORT, NY 11520
516-378-9694
FAX: 516-867-3447

Information: price quote
Save: 30% average
Pay: check, MO, MC, V, Discover
Sells: appliances, TVs, and video equipment
Store: same address; Monday to Saturday 9–6

¡Si!

Dial-a-Brand, which was founded in 1967, has earned the kudos of institutions and individuals with its wide range of appliances and popular electronics. Dial-a-Brand offers discounts averaging 30%, and does not sell grey-market goods. Call of write for prices on air conditioners, TVs, video equipment, microwave ovens, and large appliances. Dial-a-Brand ships chiefly within the New York/New Jersey/Connecticut area, but deliveries (via UPS) are made nationwide. Freight charges may offset savings on outsized or heavy items shipped long distances, so be sure to get a firm quote or estimate before you place your order.Please note: You *must* call with the manufacturer's name and model number to receive a price quote.

Special Factors: Returns are accepted for exchange if goods are defective or damaged in transit; minimum order is $100.

DISCOUNT APPLIANCE CENTERS

2908 HAMILTON ST.
HYATTSVILLE, MD 20782
301-559-6801
FAX: 301-559-1335

Information: price quote
Save: up to 60%
Pay: check, MO, MC, V, AE
Sells: vacuum cleaners and sewing machines
Store: mail order only

Discount Appliance Centers offers sewing machines, vacuum cleaners, and accessories and supplies for both at good discounts. The firm has been in business since 1965, and doesn't have a catalog—please *write* for prices and availability information, since quotes are given over the phone as staff time permits.

Discount Appliance Centers offers the latest models in vacuum cleaners by Airway, Electrolux, Eureka, Filter Queen, Hoover, Kirby, Mastercraft, Oreck, Panasonic, Royal, Sanitaire, and Tri-Star, as well as bags, belts, and attachments. Write for prices on sewing machines by Bernina, Consew, Elna, Juki, Necchi, New Home, Pfaff, Riccar, Singer, and Viking.

Discount Appliances Centers is offering readers of this book a 10% discount on all orders (deducted from the goods total only). Identify yourself as a WBMC reader when you order. This WBMC reader discount expires February 1, 1995.

Special Factors: Price quote by letter only with SASE; minimum order is $39; orders are shipped worldwide.

ILLINOIS AUDIO, INC.

1284 E. DUNDEE
PALATINE, IL 60067
800-621-8042
708-934-9669

Price List: free
Save: up to 40%
Pay: MO, MC, V
Sells: audio and video equipment and components
Store: mail order only

Illinois Audio discounts audio components 20% to 40%, and publishes a one-page price list that itemizes a fraction of the available goods. Illinois Audio sells car and home components by Aiwa, AKG, Alison, AR, Audio Source, Audio-Technica, Azden, JBL, Jensen (auto audio), JVC,

Kenwood, Koss, Marantz, Monster Cable, Panasonic, Pioneer, Onkyo, Sennheiser, Sherwood, Shure, Sony, Teac, Technics, and Wharfdale. Blank DAT, audiotape, and videotape from Fuji, Maxell, Sony, and TDK are available in cases of ten. Illinois Audio has been in business since 1971, and states the sales policy clearly in the price list.

Special Factors: All goods are new, shipped in factory-sealed cartons with U.S. manufacturers' warranties; authorized returns are accepted (a restocking fee may be charged).

J & R MUSIC WORLD
━━━━━━

59-60 QUEENS-MIDTOWN
*   EXPRESSWAY*
MASPETH, NY 11378
800-221-8180
718-417-3737
212-732-8600
FAX: 718-497-1791

Catalog: free
Save: up to 50%
Pay: check, MO, MC, V, AE, Discover
Sells: audio, video, computers, small appliances, etc.
Store: 23 Park Row, New York, NY; Monday to Saturday 9–6:30, Sunday 10–5

J & R enjoys top billing among New York City electronics discounters for its depth of saving and selection, especially in the audio and video departments. You can call for the catalog or price quotes on current lines of TVs, VCRs and video equipment, audio components and equipment, computers and peripherals, phones, fax machines, radar detectors, cameras, personal appliances, and even pens and watches. All major brand names, from Acoustic Research to Yamaha, are represented here, and everything sold by J & R is guaranteed to be brand new and factory fresh.

Special Factors: Satisfaction is guaranteed; minimum order is $25.

LVT PRICE QUOTE HOTLINE, INC.

**BOX 444-W94
COMMACK, NY
11725-0444
516-234-8884**

Brochure: free
Save: up to 30%
Pay: check or MO
Sells: major appliances, TVs, vacuum cleaners, electronics, and office machines
Store: mail order only

LVT, established in 1976, gives you instant access to over 4,000 products from over 75 manufacturers, at savings of up to 30% on suggested list or full retail prices. The brochure includes a roster of available brands, and price quotes are given on individual items. And LVT does not sell grey-market goods. For information, read LVT's brochure for the sales and shipping policies, then call with the manufacturer's name and exact model number for a price quote on major appliances, bread-making machines, microwave ovens, air conditioners, vacuum cleaners, washers and dryers, TVs, video equipment, phones and phone machines, calculators, typewriters, scanners, radar detectors, copiers, fax machines, and word processors.

The brands available include Admiral, Airtemp, Amana, AT&T, Bearcat, Bell Atlantic, Best, Braun, Brother, Caloric, Canon, Carrier, Casio, Cobra, Code-A-Phone, Creda, Dacor, Eagle, Emerson, Eureka, Fedders, Fisher, Franke, Freedom Phone, Friedrich, Frigidaire, Gaggenau, G.E., Hewlett-Packard, Hitachi, Hoover, Hotpoint, Insinkerator, Jenn-Air, JVC, Kelvinator, KitchenAid, KWC, Magic Chef, Maxon, Maytag, Miami Carey, Miele, Minolta, Mita, Mitsubishi, Modern Maid, Mont Blanc, Murata, Panasonic, Phone-Mate, PSION, Quasar, Rangaire, RCA, Record a Call, Regency, Ricoh, Rolodex, Roper, Samsung, Sanyo, Scotsman, Sharp, Smith Corona, Sony, Southwestern Bell, Speed Queen, Sterling, Sub-Zero, Sylvania, Tappan, Texas Instruments, Thermador, Toshiba, U-Line, Uniden, Victor, Viking, Welbilt, Whirlpool, Whistler, White-Westinghouse, Wolf, and Zenith—see the brands list for others.

Special Factors: Shipping (UPS), handling, and insurance charges included in quotes; all sales are final; all goods are sold with manufacturers' warranties.

LYLE CARTRIDGES

115 SO. CORONA AVE.
VALLEY STREAM, NY 11582
800-221-0906
516-599-1112
FAX: 516-599-2027

Catalog: free with self-addressed, stamped envelope
Save: up to 60%
Pay: check, MO, MC, V, AE, Discover, Optima
Sells: phono cartridges, replacement styli, and accessories
Store: same address; Monday to Friday 9–5

Lyle Cartridges has been in business since 1952 and is a great source for the cartridges and replacement styli (factory original) that bring your music to life. If you're sticking by your LPs despite CDs, you'll really appreciate this reliable, well-informed source.

Lyle stocks phono cartridges and replacement styli by Audioquest, Audio-Technica, Bang & Olufsen, Dynavector, Grado/Signature, Ortofon, Pickering, Shure, Signet, Stanton, and Sumiko. Record-care products by Discwasher, LAST, and Ortofon are stocked, as well as Tweek's contact enhancer. Lyle is the first source to consult if you have to replace arm parts, since you may be able to save on both labor and material costs. Prices of these parts are up to 60% less than list or comparable retail, and orders are shipped worldwide.

Special Factors: Authorized returns are accepted; defective goods are replaced; minimum order is $15, $25 with credit cards.

MIDAMERICA VACUUM CLEANER SUPPLY CO.

666 UNIVERSITY AVE.
ST. PAUL, MN 55104-4896
612-222-0763
FAX: 612-224-2674

Catalog: free (see text)
Save: 25% plus
Pay: check, MO, MC, V, AE, Discover, Optima
Sells: vacuum cleaners, floor machines, and appliance parts
Store: same address; Monday to Friday 9–5:30, Saturday 9–3

Midamerica sells vacuum cleaners and related parts and supplies, as well as floor machines and appliance parts, by and for Beam, Bissell,

Eureka, Hoover, MagNuM, Mastercraft, Optimus, Oreck, Panasonic, Progress Mercedes, Royal, Sanitaire, Sharp, Shop Vac, and Simplicity. In addition, Midamerica offers discount pricing on related products, such as bags, belts, hoses, brushes, and cleaning chemicals.

As a special service to readers of this book, Midamerica has prepared a booklet featuring the most-requested vacuum cleaners and parts. Call or write for your copy—request *The WBMC Booklet*. Price quotes on vacuum cleaners, parts, and supplies not included in the booklet are available on request.

Special Factors: Quantity discounts are available; minimum order is $15; orders are shipped worldwide.

PERCY'S, INC.

19 GLENNIE ST.
WORCESTER, MA 01605
508-755-5334
FAX: 508-797-5578

Information: price quote
Save: up to 40%
Pay: MO, MC, V, Discover
Sells: large appliances, audio and TV components, video, etc.
Store: same address; Monday to Friday 10–9, Saturday 10–5

 ¡Sí! Ⓒ

Percy's has been selling appliances of all types since 1926, at prices 3% above wholesale cost, or up to 40% below list. *Percy's sells no grey-market goods.*

You can call or write for a price quote on washers, dryers, dishwashers, refrigerators, freezers, ranges, standard and microwave ovens, TVs, video equipment and tapes, audio components, copiers, fax machines, radar detectors, dehumidifiers, disposals, and other appliances. The brands available at Percy's include Bose, Caloric, Fisher, Frigidaire, G.E., Hotpoint, Jenn-Air, JVC, Magic Chef, Magnavox, Maytag, Mitsubishi, Panasonic, Quasar, RCA, Sharp, Sony, Sub-Zero, Thermador, Toshiba, Whirlpool, White-Westinghouse, and Zenith. Please note that Percy's *does not sell small appliances,* and *does not publish a catalog.*

Special Factors: Price quote by phone or letter; orders are shipped worldwide.

S & S SOUND CITY

58 W. 45TH ST.,
DEPT. WBMC
NEW YORK, NY
10036-4280
212-575-0210
FAX: 212-221-7907

Brochure: free (see text)
Save: up to 50%
Pay: check, MO, MC, V, Discover
Sells: audio and video, optics, phones, office machines, etc.
Store: same address; Monday to Friday 9–7, Saturday 9–6

S & S Sound City has been in business since 1975, selling TVs and video equipment, audio components, radios, telephones, microwave ovens, air conditioners, and closed-caption decoders. The inventory here includes goods from AT&T, G.E., Harman Kardon, JVC, Minolta, Mitsubishi, Panasonic, Quasar, RCA, Sharp, Sony, Southwestern Bell, and Yamaha. S & S operates a photo department that offers cameras and accessories, binoculars, telescopes, and related goods. A holiday brochure that showcases popular gift selections is available, but call or write for a price quote if you're shopping out of season or don't see the item you want.

Special Factors: Returns are accepted within seven days; special orders are accepted.

SEW VAC CITY

DEPT. WBMC
1667 TEXAS AVE.
COLLEGE STATION, TX
77840
800-338-5672
FAX: 409-696-9262

Brochure: $3 (see text)
Save: 40% average
Pay: MO, MC, V, Discover
Sells: sewing machines, sergers, and vacuum cleaners
Store: same address; Monday to Thursday 10–8, Friday and Saturday 10–5; also Pittsburg Sewing Machine Warehouse, 602 N. Broadway, Pittsburg, KS; Sewing Machine Warehouse, Willowbrook Ct., 17776 Tomball Pkwy., Houston and Sew Vac City, Richland Mall, Waco, TX

Sew Vac City, in business since 1976, sells sewing machines, sergers, and vacuum cleaners. Call for a price quote on sewing machines by

Singer and other manufacturers, or Panasonic, Sharp, and other vacuum cleaners. All of the machines sold here are new, and layaways are accepted—inquire for information.

Special Factors: Layaway plan is available; C.O.D. orders are accepted; minimum parts order is $25; orders are shipped worldwide.

SEWIN' IN VERMONT

84 CONCORD AVE.
ST. JOHNSBURY, VT 05819
800-451-5124
802-748-3803

Information: inquire
Save: 35% average
Pay: check, MO, MC, V
Sells: sewing machines and accessories
Store: same address; Monday to Friday 9–5, Saturday 9–1

If you're shopping for a name-brand sewing machine or serger, but don't want to pay top-of-the-line prices, give Sewin' in Vermont a call. The firm carries several of the best American and European brands at prices 15% to 40% below list: Bernina, Singer, and Viking sewing machines are available, as well as sergers from various manufacturers at savings averaging around 35%. Professional-quality irons and presses by Rowenta, Singer, and Sussman are also carried. The knowledgeable sales staff can help you choose the right equipment for your needs; call the 800 number for information and price quotes.

Special Factors: C.O.D. orders are accepted; orders are shipped worldwide.

SUBURBAN SEW 'N SWEEP, INC.

8814 OGDEN AVE.
BROOKFIELD, IL 60513
800-642-4056
708-485-2834
FAX: 708-387-0500

Information: inquire
Save: up to 50%
Pay: check, MO, MC, V, AE, Discover
Sells: sewing machines and vacuum cleaners
Store: same address; Monday to Saturday 9–5

Suburban Sew 'N Sweep has been selling sewing machines since 1975, and although a brochure is available, you can call for a price quote on sewing and overlock machines by New Home, Singer, White, and other top brands. Discounts vary, but run up to 50%. Suburban Sew 'N Sweep is an authorized dealer for several major sewing machine manufacturers, and also sells Oreck vacuum cleaners.

Special Factors: Price quote by phone; C.O.D. orders are accepted.

WESTCOAST DISCOUNT VIDEO

5201 EASTERN AVE.
BALTIMORE, MD 21224
800-344-7123
410-633-0508

Catalog: $5
Save: up to 35%
Pay: check, MO, MC, V
Sells: camcorders and accessories
Store: mail order only

Westcoast Discount Video is a specialty firm that sells camcorders, attachments, and accessories—for both 8mm and VHS formats. Discounts run up to 35% on models by Canon, G.E., Hitachi, JVC, Magnavox, Panasonic, Quasar, RCA, Sharp, Sony, and Zenith. This is also a good source for auxillary lenses and filters, lighting equipment, power packs, rewinders, mics, tripods, cases, movie and slide converters, and other equipment. The 48-page catalog includes specs on every model Westcoast sells, a list of the optional accessories, and a separate price list. If you don't know much about video equipment, you'll appreciate the three-page glossary of terms and abbreviations in the back of the catalog, and it's nice to know that everything Westcoast Discount Video sells is sent in factory-sealed cartons with the full U.S. manufacturer's warranty.

Special Factors: Price quote by phone; shipping is included on orders over $75; C.O.D. orders are accepted.

WHOLESALE TAPE AND SUPPLY COMPANY

Catalog: free
Save: up to 50%
Pay: check, MO, MC, V, AE, Discover
Sells: audio and video tapes, duplicating services, etc.
Store: 2841 Hickory Valley Rd., Chattanooga, TN

P.O. BOX 8277,
   DEPT. WBM
CHATTANOOGA, TN
   37411
800-251-7228
615-894-9427
FAX: 615-894-7281

Wholesale Tape, which has been selling audio/visual supplies and services worldwide since 1977, publishes a catalog featuring blank audio and video cassettes, reel-to-reel tapes in all configurations, duplicating machines, services, and accessories. The firm manufactures audiotapes for professional duplication and six types of tape are available, in clear, white, and black shells (housing), in standard tape lengths (12 to 122 minutes). Custom tape lengths can be provided, and quantity discounts are offered. Wholesale Tape also sells professional-quality audio and video recording tape from Ampex, Fuji, Maxell, Memorex, and TDK, as well as tape duplication machines by Sony and Telex.

If you need an audiotape or videotape copied but don't have the necessary equipment, you may be interested in Wholesale Tape's duplicating services. Custom labels and shell imprinting can be produced, and cassette boxes, albums, shipping envelopes, and storage units are also sold.

Special Factors: Satisfaction is guaranteed; quantity discounts are offered; C.O.D. orders are accepted; minimum order is $25; orders are shipped worldwide.

SEE ALSO

A Cook's Wares • food processors and other appliances • **HOME: KITCHEN**
Allied Lighting • ceiling fans • **HOME: DECOR**
Atlanta Thread & Supply • commercial sewing machines, sergers, and irons • **CRAFTS**
Cisco • garbage disposals, spas, whirlpools, etc. • **HOME: MAINTENANCE**

Crystal Sonics • auto audio • **AUTO**

Defender Industries, Inc. • marine electronics • **AUTO**

E & B Marine Supply, Inc. • marine electronics • **AUTO**

Ewald-Clark • video cameras • **CAMERAS**

Fan Authority/Lighting Authority • ceiling fans and lighting fixtures • **HOME: DECOR**

Fivenson Food Equipment, Inc. • commercial restaurant equipment • **HOME: KITCHEN**

Goldberg's Marine Distributors • marine electronics • **AUTO**

Kaplan Bros. Blue Flame Corp. • commercial restaurant appliances • **HOME: KITCHEN**

LIBW • bathroom fixtures, whirlpools, and other hardware • **HOME: MAINTE-NANCE**

Main Lamp/Lamp Warehouse • lamps and ceiling fans • **HOME: DECOR**

Peerless Restaurant Supplies • commercial restaurant fixtures, appliances, and supplies • **HOME: KITCHEN**

Solo Slide Fasteners, Inc. • professional pressing and sewing equipment • **CRAFTS**

Thread Discount Sales • sergers, overlock machines, etc. • **CRAFTS**

West Marine • marine electronics • **AUTO**

ART, ANTIQUES, AND COLLECTIBLES

Fine art, limited editions, antiques, and collectibles

The firms listed here offer everything from Victoriana to fruit crate labels, including bronze "art" furniture, vintage advertising ephemera, limited-edition porcelain figures and plates, and contemporary movie posters. Although buying from "dealer" sources means you're usually getting the piece at a lower price than you'd pay at retail, don't buy with the expectation of reselling at a profit, unless you're sure of what you're doing. And be sure to buy antiques from firms that have liberal return policies.

Getting to know the market is one of the pleasures of collecting, and there are hundreds of reference books and guides available to give you the necessary grounding. The guides to prevailing market prices for antiques and collectibles are especially helpful in determining whether you're overpaying—or getting a real buy. But there's no substitute for old-fashioned legwork when it comes to learning about your field of interest. Visit flea markets, antique shops, art galleries, museums, and auction previews, and don't just look—*ask questions.* Dealers enjoy an appreciative customer, and will usually share their valuable tips on the market if you demonstrate interest in their wares.

A collection of any merit usually requires the protection of archival quality materials. University Products, Inc. (in the "Small Business" section of "Office") is an excellent source for display binders, albums, boxes, and restoration materials for art works, books, manuscripts, photographs, textiles, posters, and postcards. The firm's archival products catalog includes goods for mounting, display, and storage.

FIND IT FAST

ANTIQUES • **Antique Imports**
ART BRONZES • **Excalibur**
FINE ART REPRODUCTIONS • **Fine Art Impressions**
FRUIT CRATE LABELS • **Original Paper Collectibles**
LIMITED EDITION COLLECTIBLES • **Art Vest, Atlantic Bridge, Merry-weather, Saxkjaers**
POSTERS • **Cinema City, Miscellaneous Man, Rick's Movie Graphics**

ANTIQUE IMPORTS UNLIMITED

P.O. BOX 2978-WBMC
COVINGTON, LA
70434-2978
PHONE AND FAX: 504-892-0014

Catalog: $3 (see text)
Save: up to 60%
Pay: check, MO, MC, V
Sells: antiques and collectibles
Store: mail order only

Antique Imports, in business since 1981, markets antique jewelry and ephemera through its "Antiques and Collectibles" and "Antiques and Collectible Jewelry" catalogs. The firm sells at "dealer" prices—up to 60% below what's being charged for comparable goods in antique shops. The "Antique and Collectible Jewelry" catalog features old jewelry, charms, and watches, and usually includes exceptional values. A sample copy costs $3, a year's subscription of 10 to 12 issues, $30. The "Antiques and Collectibles" catalog (3 to 5 issues, $3 per copy or $10 for a year of issues), offers glassware, china, metalware, and related miscellany. Past offerings have included a Georgian pewter footed salter ($95), an early Noritake fruit bowl ($60), a Victorian 10K gold ring, set with diamonds and a ruby ($279), and a 14K gold horn brooch ($55). Please note that the catalogs are not illustrated, but Antique Imports accepts returns within two days of receipt.

Special Factors: All goods are one-of-a-kind items, subject to prior sale; listing second choices is recommended; UPS is *not* used; returns are accepted within 2 days for exchange, refund, or credit; minimum order is $110; orders are shipped worldwide.

ART VEST INTERNATIONAL, INC.

190 W. SPANISH RIVER
  BLVD., SUITE 200
BOCA RATON, FL 33431
800-683-4300
407-750-4300
FAX: 407-750-0976

Flyers: free
Save: up to 50%
Pay: check, MO, MC, V, AE
Sells: limited editions
Store: mail order only

Between original art and good prints lies the realm of the limited edition, usually executed as a lithograph or serigraph (silkscreen). Art Vest International sells such works, by a range of artists that include Asaro, Christo, Dine, Erté, Hockney, Morris, and Yamagata, to name just a few. If you collect the work of *any* artist who has authorized limited editions, call Art Vest before you take the plunge with your next acquisition—it may be available here at up to 50% less. (Art Vest even offers the series of hand-inked cels from Warner Brothers, of the immortal Bugs and other Saturday morning favorites.) And if you have an idea of what you'd like to put on the wall, Art Vest will work with you to find the piece that answers your needs.

Special Factor: Price quote by phone or letter.

CINEMA CITY

P.O. BOX 1012-HK
MUSKEGON, MI 49443
616-722-7760
FAX: 616-722-4537

Catalog: $3, refundable
Save: 30% average
Pay: check, MO, MC, V
Sells: movie posters and ephemera
Store: mail order only

Movie posters circa 1975 and later are the specialty at Cinema City, which has been selling to collectors and dealers since 1976. Thousands of movies are listed in the 48-page catalog, from *A Bridge Too Far* ($15 for a set of 12 stills) to *Ziggy Stardust* (27" by 41" poster, $25). Press kits, scripts, and lobby cards are available for some of the titles. The catalog is arranged alphabetically by movie title, and includes a glossary of terms and guide to the poster sizes. (Posters are sent rolled if Cinema City received them "flat," but folded materials are stiffened to minimize damage and shipped that way.) Cinema City adds to its gigantic inventory with each new movie release, and once you're on the mailing list, you'll receive periodic updates—including offerings of autographed posters and photos. Cinema City also handles materials for foreign films and limited-release items. You can send inquiries about these, as well as queries about films made before 1975, but include a self-addressed, stamped envelope if you want to receive a reply.

Canadian readers, please note: Only U.S. funds are accepted.

Special Factor: Orders are shipped worldwide.

EXCALIBUR BRONZE SCULPTURE FOUNDRY

85 ADAMS ST.
BROOKLYN, NY 11201
718-522-3330
FAX: 718-522-0812

Catalog: $10, refundable (see text)
Save: 25% average
Pay: check, MO, MC, V
Sells: art bronze sculptures and furniture
Store: same address

Excalibur Bronze Sculpture Foundry has been casting the works of sculptors and artists across the country since 1967. (Services include mould making, precision sand and ceramic shell casting, enlarging, chasing, patinating, etc.) But the firm is listed here because of its bronze reproductions of renowned sculptures, and its delightful furniture.

The $10 fee brings you three catalogs: "The Excalibur Collection," which includes replicas of works by Rodin, Antoine-Louis Barge, Emile Bourdelle, and other artists. Scores of reproductions of Remingtons, Art Noveau and Art Deco figures, lamps, vases, and mirrors are shown in "The Decorative Arts Collection," at prices beginning at under $200. And the "Hommage à Diego Collection" shows scores of the type of "art" lamps and cocktail tables featured prominently in shelter magazines—wrought metal bases embellished with birds, leaves, hoofs, turtles, and other playful touches, topped with thick slabs of glass—inspired by the work of Diego Giacometti. Please note that the $10 catalog/portfolio fee is refundable only with a purchase, but you can call or write directly about specific pieces or custom work.

Special Factor: Orders are shipped worldwide.

FINE ART IMPRESSIONS

**P.O. BOX 1118
BEVERLY HILLS, CA
90213-1118
800-279-4278**

Brochure: free
Save: up to 50% (see text)
Pay: check, MO, MC, V, AE, Discover, Optima
Sells: fine art reproductions on canvas
Store: mail order only

Fine Art Impressions can put a Monet—or Van Gogh or Picasso—on your living room wall for under $300. It's not quite an original, but is created by transferring an image of the original to artist's canvas, and applying brush strokes to create the most authentic likeness possible. Fine Art Impressions sells the reproductions in gilt frames for $245, or on stretchers, unframed, for $99. Past offerings have included Monet's "Water Lilies," "Camille and Child," and "The Houses of Parliament"; Renoir's "Two Sisters" and "Girl with a Watering Can"; and Van Gogh's "Sunflowers" and "Irises," among others. Over 50 reproductions are offered, including those of works by Matisse, Cezanne, Picasso, Gauguin, Degas, Benson, and Manet. Paying $245 or even $99 for a copy may seem exorbitant, since you can get good prints from museum shops for under $50. But reproductions such as those sold by Fine Art Impressions sell elsewhere for $495 to $1,000 each. Fine Art Impressions also does work to order (see the catalog for information), and all of the reproductions are covered by a complete guarantee of satisfaction.

Special Factors: Satisfaction is guaranteed; returns are accepted within 30 days for exchange, refund, or credit.

MERRYWEATHER IMPORTS, INC.

**6113 JERRY'S DR.
COLUMBIA, MD 21044
800-677-7713
410-730-5333**

Price Lists: SASE
Save: up to 32%
Pay: check, MO, MC, V, Discover
Sells: crystal and cottage collectibles
Store: mail order only

Merryweather Imports specializes in two of today's most popular collectible "smalls": crystal whimsies and miniature cottages. The crystal is

Swarovski, and Merryweather's price list includes nearly 75 of the faceted animals, from a beagle puppy ($30) to a walrus ($95). And anyone who collects David Winter or Lilliput Lane cottages will be delighted with what awaits them here: hundreds of little shops, farmhouses, castles, churches, barns, taverns, and other buildings. The pieces are listed with prices but without illustrations, so you must consult other information sources if you're not sure of your selection— although it's very tempting to order "Stockwell Tenement," "Ugly House," "Ash Nook," "Burns' Reading Room," or "Kennedy Homestead" just to see what they look like.

Special Factor: Price quote by phone or letter.

MISCELLANEOUS MAN

P.O. BOX 1776-W4
NEW FREEDOM, PA 17349
717-235-4766
FAX: 717-235-2853

Catalog: $5
Save: up to 75%
Pay: check, MO, MC, V
Sells: rare and vintage posters and labels
Store: mail order only

George Theofiles, ephemerologist extraordinaire, is the moving force behind Miscellaneous Man. He founded his firm in 1970, trading in vintage posters, handbills, graphics, labels, brochures, and other memorabilia, all of which are original—no reproductions or reprints are sold.

Each Miscellaneous Man catalog offers an average of about a thousand items, including theater and movie publicity materials, collections of colorful product labels, broadsides, and posters. Posters are the strong suit, representing everything from aviation to weaponry: patriotic themes (including both World Wars, other conflicts, and related topics), sports of all sorts, wines and spirits, food advertising, labor, publishing, fashion, African-Americana, the performing arts, and travel, among other themes. Some of the posters are offered mounted on linen or conservation paper, and Mr. Theofiles can give you references for other firms that can mount your poster after purchase (proper backing helps to preserve the poster, and doesn't detract from its value). Collections of unused broom handle labels, antique seed packets, luggage stickers, cigar box labels, and other such detritus have appeared in previous catalogs. Size and condition are noted in the catalog entries, as well as photos; larger shots of individual items may be purchased for $2.

Miscellaneous Man's prices are usually at least 30% below the going rate, and regular customers receive sale catalogs with further reductions. If you're about to purchase a vintage poster elsewhere, give Miscellaneous Man a call first. Although the prices are sometimes comparable (especially on scarce or rare posters), Miscellaneous Man can charge 30% to 75% less than New York City sources—and the selection is always much better.

Special Factors: Layaways are accepted; returns are accepted within three days; minimum order is $50 with credit cards.

ORIGINAL PAPER COLLECTIBLES

700-W CLIPPER GAP RD.
AUBURN, CA 95603
916-878-0296

Brochure, Sample Label: free with *long,* self-addressed, stamped envelope
Save: up to 75%
Pay: check or MO
Sells: original, vintage labels
Store: mail order only

 ¡Si!

William Wauters began his business in 1970, when fruit crate labels were among the hot collectibles in antique and curio shops nationwide. Original Paper Collectibles has thrived over the years, attesting to the enduring appeal of the label designs. At this writing, Mr. Wauters offers labels originally intended for brooms, cigar boxes, soda pop, canned fruits and vegetables, and produce—apples, pears, lettuce, oranges, asparagus, lemons, and other fruits and vegetables. Old used stock certificates, all of which have illustrations, are also sold. And collectors of African-Americana will find a selection of over a dozen labels depicting black characters.

The collections offer the best per-label prices, and Mr. Wauters says that dealers routinely double his prices when they resell. The price list describes the most popular collection of fruit crate labels that include orange, apple, asparagus, lemon, pear, lettuce, cherry, grape, and carrot varieties—150 for $25, postpaid. (A vintage poster gallery in New York City charges that much for a *single* label.) Sliding discounts of 10% to 35% are given on orders of $100, $250, and $500. If you're searching for a specific label, you may find it among the listings of individual labels, which are grouped by size and type. And if you're looking for something out of the ordinary to cover the walls, ask here—the labels can be used as wall treatments. One Detroit pizza parlor even used them in a decoupage treatment on the tabletops!

Please note: Payment for orders should be made to William Wauters, *not* Original Paper Collectibles.

Special Factors: Satisfaction is guaranteed; price quote by letter with SASE; quantity discounts are available; orders are shipped worldwide.

RICK'S MOVIE GRAPHICS, INC.

P.O. BOX 23709-WM
GAINESVILLE, FL
  32602-3709
904-373-7202
FAX: 904-373-2589

Catalog: $3
Save: up to 60%
Pay: check, MO, MC, V
Sells: current and vintage movie posters
Store: mail order only

Today's collectibles can become tomorrow's investments, and although the possibilities of appreciation attract some of the people who buy movie posters, most of us just want mementos of favorite flicks. Rick's Movie Graphics has been serving both interests since 1985, and publishes a 64-page catalog packed with current releases and "vintage" posters dating back to the 1950s. The listings are coded to indicate whether the posters have been rolled or folded. At an average price of $15 (10% to 30% below the going rate), the new releases deliver a lot of visual bang for the buck. Prices of vintage posters are higher here, but dealers usually charge so much more that the savings through Rick's can reach 30% to 65% in this category.

Recent catalogs have offered original releases of *Batman* posters, British posters of *The Rocky Horror Picture Show,* The Who's Italian *Quadrophenia,* and new and advance releases—*A Few Good Men, Wayne's World,* and the black and silver teaser for *Malcolm X.* The catalog shows just a fraction of the inventory, and new titles and collections are constantly added to stock. If you don't see what you're looking for, send your requests with a long, self-addressed, stamped envelope.

Please note: Only U.S. funds are accepted.

Special Factors: Returns are accepted within five days for exchange, refund, or credit; orders are shipped worldwide.

COMPANIES OUTSIDE THE U.S.A.

The following firms are experienced in dealing with customers in the U.S. and Canada. We've included them because they offer goods not widely available at a discount in the U.S., because they have a better selection, or because they may offer the same goods at great savings.

Before ordering from any non-U.S. firm, please consult "The Complete Guide to Buying by Mail," page 535, for helpful tips. Pay for orders from foreign firms with a credit card whenever possible, so you'll have some recourse if you don't receive your order. For more information, see "The Fair Credit Billing Act," page 569.

ATLANTIC BRIDGE COLLECTION CORP. LTD.

DEPT. WBM-94
BALLYBANE
GALWAY
IRELAND
011-353-91-753657
FAX: 011-353-91-753443

Catalog: $3
Save: up to 40%
Pay: check, IMO, MC, V, AE
Sells: porcelain collectibles, tableware, crystal, and handcrafts
Store (warehouse): same address (call for directions); Monday to Friday 9–4

Atlantic Bridge Collection offers some of the most popular porcelain figurines and collectibles, including Belleek, Beswick, Coalport, Hummel, Irish Dresden, Lilliput Lane, Lladró, Royal Doulton, and Wedgwood. Atlantic Bridge, which has been in business since 1972, also sells Royal Crown Derby paperweights and miniature cottages, Beatrix Potter nursery figures, pewter giftware, collectors' teapots, and Peter Rabbit nurseryware. The catalog shows place settings of selected dinnerware patterns from Aynsley, Minton, Royal Albert, Royal Doulton, Royal Worcester, and Wedgwood, as well as crystal giftware and suites by Galway, and Waterford. There are especially good values on Royal Doulton figurines and crystal vases and candlesticks, as well as a delightful collection of Irish specialties and handcrafts—Claddagh jewelry, gifts engraved with coats of arms, and double-damask Irish linen tablecloths. Prices are given in U.S. dollars, and bonuses and special discounts are often featured.

Special Factors: Satisfaction is guaranteed; minimum order is $25 with credit cards; orders are shipped worldwide.

SAXKJAERS

**53 KØBMAGERGADE
1150 COPENHAGEN K
DENMARK
011-45-331-10777
FAX: 011-45-333-27210**

Catalog: $2 (by air), refundable
Save: 40% plus
Pay: check, IMO, MC, V, AE
Sells: collectible porcelain editions and gifts
Store: same address; also Krystalgade 3, 1172, Copenhagen

Saxkjaers, a family business founded in 1904, is the definitive source for collectors' plates and figurines from Bing & Grøndahl, Hummel, and Royal Copenhagen. The yearly issues of Christmas plates will stir even the tamest acquisitive instincts, but it's an affordable habit if indulged in through Saxkjaers. The firm's catalog shows the current Royal Copenhagen Christmas plate (and lists editions as early as 1908), as well as the complementing cup-and-saucer set and Christmas ornament. As Europe's foremost Hummel representative, Saxkjaers sells the Hummel figurines and commemoratives at great discounts—"well below 40% off U.S. prices." The catalog also shows Royal Copenhagen figurines, vases, and dinnerware, Bing & Grøndahl dinnerware, George Jensen silverware and gifts, jewelry, and Christmas ornaments. Prices include surface postage and insurance against all problems; airmail shipping is offered at a surcharge.

The Saxkjaers family runs the entire company, and welcomes all comers with a cup of coffee, so stop by if you find yourself in Copenhagen (downtown, "opposite the old round Tower—impossible to miss"). Saxkjaers is efficient as well as hospitable—letters and inquiries are answered the day they're received, and all efforts are made to ensure your happiness with your order.

Special Factors: Satisfaction is guaranteed; shipping (surface mail) and insurance are included; orders are shipped worldwide.

SEE ALSO

Barrons • *Goebel and Royal Doulton collectibles* • **HOME: TABLE SETTINGS**
Beverly Bremer Silver Shop • *heirloom and estate silver pieces* • **HOME: TABLE SETTINGS**
Caprilands Herb Farm • *collectors' dolls* • **FARM**
Editions • *first editions and rare books* • **BOOKS**
Elderly Instruments • *vintage fretted instruments* • **MUSIC**

Forty-Fives • original 45's from 1950 • **BOOKS**

Mandolin Brothers, Ltd. • vintage fretted instruments • **MUSIC**

Record-Rama Sound Archives • vintage LPs and 45's • **BOOKS**

Rogers & Rosenthal, Inc. • figurines and collectibles • **HOME: TABLE SET-TINGS**

The Scholar's Bookshelf • remaindered university-press art books • **BOOKS**

Skandinavisk Glas • porcelain and crystal collectibles • **HOME: TABLE SET-TINGS**

Strand Book Store, Inc. • books on the fine and applied arts • **BOOKS**

University Products, Inc. • archival-quality collection storage, mounting, and display materials • **OFFICE: SMALL BUSINESS**

ART MATERIALS

Materials, tools, equipment, and supplies for the fine and applied arts

You don't *have* to starve to be an artist, but the cost of good tools and supplies almost guarantees it—unless you can buy them at discount. Small art stores usually sell at list, and seldom knock off more than 10%, except on quantity purchases. But discount mail-order firms routinely offer savings of at least twice that. The firms listed here sell supplies and materials for fine arts and some crafts: pigments, paper, brushes, canvas, frames, stretchers, pads, studio furniture, vehicles and solvents, silk-screening supplies, carving tools, and much more—at great discounts.

Since different materials can profoundly affect the quality and direction of your work, familiarize yourself with what's on the market through catalogs and artists' magazines. The catalog from Daniel Smith, listed in this chapter, provides a wealth of information. For a comprehensive assessment of the properties and uses of almost every medium available today, see *The Artists' Handbook of Materials and Techniques* (Viking Press), which can be found in libraries and is available from several firms in this chapter.

Concern about the safety of art materials has led to the Art Materials Labeling Act of 1988, and Congress has also asked the Consumer Products Safety Commission to create standards for the art materials industry, and banned the use of hazardous materials by children in the sixth grade or younger. This is important legislation, since the list of substances found in widely used materials has included toluene, asbestos, chloroform, xylene, n-hexane, carbolic acid, trichlorethylene, and benzene, to note just a few. Even with reformulation and warnings, art materials can still pose some hazards. Good studio protocol can minimize much of the exposure:

- Select the least toxic and hazardous products available.
- If your work creates dust or fumes, use a quality, OSHA-approved respirator suitable to the task—there are masks to filter organic vapors, ammonia, asbestos, toxic dusts, mists and fumes, and paint spray.
- Use other protective gear as applicable: gloves to reduce the absorption of chemicals through the skin, earplugs to protect against hearing damage from loud machinery, and safety goggles to avoid eye damage from accidents.
- A good window-exhaust system is essential to reducing inhaled vapors. Create a real airflow when working with fume-producing materials—the breeze from an open window isn't enough.
- Keep children and animals out of the workplace, since chemicals reach higher levels of concentration in their systems.
- Don't eat, drink, or smoke in the work area, or before cleaning up.
- Keep appropriate safety equipment on hand to deal with emergencies: an eyewash station if caustics are being used, a first-aid kit, a fire extinguisher if combustible materials are present, etc.
- Ask your school board to make sure the least toxic and hazardous products are used in the classroom.

For further reading, consult *Artist Beware: The Hazards and Precautions in Working with Art and Craft Materials,* by Michael McCann (Watson-Guptill Publications, 1979). *Health Hazards Manual for Artists* (Nick Lyons Books, 1985), a smaller book by Mr. McCann, includes specifics on materials commonly used by children. Both are sold by Ceramic Supply of New York & New Jersey (listed in this chapter). Mr. McCann, who is a chemist and an industrial hygienist, also founded the Center for Safety in the Arts. The organization deals with art-safety issues in *Art Hazards News,* a four-page newsletter published ten times a year. For current subscription rates and more information, write to Center for Safety in the Arts at 5 Beekman St., Suite 1030, New York, NY 10038, or call 212-227-6220.

For firms that sell related products, see "Crafts and Hobbies" and "General Merchandise," and don't overlook the listings in "Surplus."

FIND IT FAST

CERAMICS AND POTTERY • **Ceramic Supply of New York**
CHILDRENS AND EDUCATIONAL ART SUPPLIES • **Dick Blick, Sax**
FINE ARTS • **Art Express, Art Supply Warehouse, Cheap Joe's, Jerry's**

Artarama, Pearl Paint, Daniel Smith, Utrecht
FRAMES • American Frame, Graphik Dimensions, S&W, Daniel Smith,
Stu-Art, Utrecht
GRAPHIC DESIGN • Flax, A.I. Friedman, Utrecht
MAILING TUBES • Yazoo
PAPER AND PRINTMAKING • Daniel Smith
SILKSCREENING • Crown Art

AMERICAN FRAME CORPORATION

1340 TOMAHAWK DR.
MAUMEE, OH 43537-1695
800-537-0944
FAX: 419-893-3553

Catalog: free
Save: up to 50%
Pay: check, MO, MC, V, AE, Discover, Optima
Sells: sectional frames, mat board, acrylic picture glass
Store: same address; Monday to Friday 9–4

American Frame, in business since 1973, sells *wood sectional frames*—a great way to get the look of a custom framing job, at do-it-yourself prices—as well as *metal sectional frames* in a wonderful selection of colors. American Frame's prices were 35% to 50% lower than those charged by other several art-supply firms.

The ten-page catalog features frame sections in basswood, maple, poplar, mahogany, oak, and cherry, in a variety of stains, some with gilding and some with linen liners. The profiles and dimensions of the sections are shown in detail, and each wood frame (two pairs of sections) is sent with corner insets for assembling the sections, spring clips to hold the mounted art work securely in place, and wall protectors. (Assembly requires attaching one end of the spring clips to the frame with screws, which are provided, and gluing the joints. No clamps are required, and instructions are given in the catalog.) The metal frames are offered in a choice of eight profiles, to accommodate ordinary flat work and standard and extra-deep canvases. Ten metallic and 18 enameled colors are available, including pewter, evergreen, copper, salmon, jade, and taupe, among others. The metal frame sections are sold in pairs, and come with assembly hardware.

Crescent board—acid-free mat, mounting, and foam core—is sold in groups of ten or more sheets, depending on the item. The mat board is offered in over 100 colors in the 32" by 40" size; please note that no cutting is done. Rolls of polyester film are available, as well as acid-free acrylic picture "glass" (cut to order in dimensions up to 22" by 28").

Special Factors: Shipping is included on orders over $500; online with CompuServe.

ART EXPRESS

DEPT. C
P.O. BOX 21662
COLUMBIA, SC 29212
800-535-5908
FAX: 803-750-1492

Catalog: $3.50
Save: up to 60%
Pay: check, MO, MC, V, AE, Discover
Sells: art supplies and equipment
Store: mail order only

Art Express publishes a 72-page catalog featuring a well-chosen selection of art tools and equipment, at discounts averaging 40%. The inventory includes papers and board, canvas, brushes, mediums and solvents, pens, portfolios, paint (including casein), Art Bin artists' cases, inks, pastels, pencils, airbrushing equipment, easels by Anco, Best, Martin, and Stanrite; light boxes, Logan mat cutters, and Artograph and Seerite opaque projectors. Among the other names represented are William Alexander, Arches, Berol, Bienfang, Canson, Fabriano, Fredrix, Golden, Grumbacher, Holbein, Isabey, Le Franc & Bourgeois, Liquitex, Luma, Raphaël, Rembrandt, Rives, Rowney, Sennelier, Shiva, Speedball, Strathmore, and Winsor & Newton. Several pages list available books and videotapes on art technique, history, and related topics. If you don't see what you're looking for, write or fax Art Express with product information—the item might be in stock.

Special Factors: Quantity discounts are available; institutional accounts are available; minimum order is $25 on stock paper; orders are shipped worldwide.

ART SUPPLY WAREHOUSE, INC.

360 MAIN AVE.
NORWALK, CT 06851
800-995-6778
FAX: 203-849-0845

Catalog: free
Save: 40% average
Pay: check, MO, MC, V
Sells: art supplies
Store: same address; Monday to Saturday 9:30–5:30; also 14 Imperial Pl., Providence, RI; and 81 45 Baltimore Blvd., College Park, MD

 (see text)

Art Supply Warehouse, founded in 1979, publishes a 76-page catalog of art materials and equipment priced an average of 40% off list. The stock includes oil and acrylic paints, pigments, fixatives, and solvents by Bellini, Blockx, Bocour, Deka, Grumbacher, Holbein, Liquitex, Paasche, Pelikan, Rembrandt, Shiva, Robert Simmons, Weber, Winsor & Newton, and other makers. The catalog shows oil pastels, chalks, colored pencils, markers, inks, pens, brushes, palette knives, and other tools, and paper and board by Bainbridge, Creative Mark, D'Arches, Strathmore, Westport, Whatman, Winsor & Newton, and other firms are offered. Check the prices on stretched and roll canvas by Fredrix, as well as stretchers, easels, art boxes, and related studio gear. Supplies and equipment for other creative pursuits are sold—airbrushing, drafting, sumi-e, silkscreening, and textile arts—and Art Supply Warehouse also carries the Northlight Books series of manuals.

Canadian readers, please note: Payment must be made in U.S. funds.

Special Factors: Satisfaction is guaranteed; returns are accepted; quantity discounts are available; shipping is included on orders sent within the continental U.S.; C.O.D. orders are accepted.

DICK BLICK CO.

P.O. BOX 1267-WM94
GALESBURG, IL 61401
309-343-6181
FAX: 309-343-5785

Catalog: $4
Save: up to 30%
Pay: check, MO, MC, V, AE, Discover, Optima
Sells: art and crafts supplies
Store: 36 locations in CT, GA, IA, IL, IN, KS, MI, MO, MN, NE, NV, OH, and PA
(addresses are listed in the catalog)

Dick Blick, an arts-and-crafts supplier geared to schools, lists tens of thousands of items in a 480-page compendium of supplies and equipment. Blick was established in 1911 and has everything in general art and craft supplies: Liquitex paints, Shiva pigments, Crayola crayons and finger paints, drawing tables and other art furniture, paint brushes, kraft paper, canvas, scissors, and adhesives. The catalog includes silk-screening materials, display lighting, printmaking equipment, wood-carving tools, molding materials, kilns, glazes, copper enamels, decoupage supplies, leather-working kits, dyes, macrame materials, weaving tools and equipment, blackboards, and much more. Over 20 pages are devoted to films, slides, videotapes, manuals, and books on arts and crafts.

Special Factors: Satisfaction is guaranteed; price quote by phone or letter on quantity orders; quantity discounts are available; returns are accepted within 30 days for exchange, refund, or credit; minimum order is $10 with credit cards.

CERAMIC SUPPLY OF NEW YORK & NEW JERSEY, INC.

7 RTE. 46 W.
LODI, NJ 07644
201-340-3005
FAX: 201-340-0089

Catalog: $4
Save: up to 40%
Pay: check, MO, MC, V
Sells: sculpture, pottery, glazing, and crafts supplies and equipment
Store: same address; Monday to Friday 9–5, Saturday 9–1; also 534 La Guardia Pl., New York, NY; Monday to Saturday 9–5

Ceramic Supply of New York & New Jersey serves both its name states with free delivery on orders of $100 or more. The company has been doing business since 1981, and offers good values on glazes, brushes, and a wide range of lightweight ceramics supplies that can be shipped worldwide at nominal expense. The 68-page catalog devotes most of its space to ceramics supplies and equipment: gas and electric kilns (including some that run on household current), raku and fiber kilns, glazes, resists, mediums, brushes, airbrushing tools, slip-casting equipment, potters' wheels, armatures, grinders, and related goods. The manufacturers include Alpine, Amaco, Brent, Kemper, Kimple, North Star, Shimpo, and Skutt, among others. The catalog includes color charts of glazes, underglazes, and other finishes by Duncan and Mayco, glazed and bisqued tiles of varying sizes and shapes, and dozens of types of clay, from white Grolleg porcelain to "economy" clay made of odds and ends of other clays. And there are lots of other modeling materials—FIMO plastic, Sculpey, Van Aken Plastelene, wax, and water-based clay.

Even if you're not a potter or sculptor, the catalog may interest you: music box parts and movements in scores of tunes, lights for ceramic Christmas trees, hard-to-find lamp parts, clock movements and parts, jewelry findings, studio furniture, and safety equipment are all available. Don't overlook the reference section, which features books on sculpture, ceramics, art hazards, and related topics, and videotapes and filmstrips.

Special Factors: Returns are accepted within ten days (a restocking fee may be charged); orders are shipped worldwide.

CHEAP JOE'S ART STUFF

300A INDUSTRIAL PARK RD.
BOONE, NC 28607
800-227-2788
FAX: 800-257-0874

Catalog: free
Save: up to 45%
Pay: check, MO, MC, V, Discover
Sells: art supplies and equipment
Store: Boone Drug Co., 113 E. King St., Boone, NC

There *is* a Joe here at Cheap Joe's, and he makes his voice heard throughout the 36-page catalog in pithy product descriptions and tips on how to make the most of your tools and materials. Only Cheap Joe would use the front inside cover of the catalog (prime selling space) to publish his "Hugging Policy," or turn whole pages over to a *National Enquirer* format in which he reproduces an order from Rodin, and breaks the discovery of Van Gogh's ear, found in the German town of Glockenhammer. Cheap Joe's dream of keeping his company small may be confounded by his great prices—savings of 30% are routine, and quantity pricing deepens the discounts to 70% on at least a few items.

A recent catalog offered Arches and Canson paper, paint from Da Vinci, Holbein, Rembrandt, and Winsor & Newton, paintbrushes from Jack Richeson, Robert Simmons, Whitney, Wilton, and Winsor & Newton, easels, shrink-wrap systems, Logan mat cutters, adhesives, foam-core, Artograph projection equipment, Fredrix canvas, and books and videotapes on painting and art theory. Joe also features his own line of watercolor brushes, as well as Isabey brushes and Daler-Rownay paints and brushes. Cheap Joe set up shop in 1986, and he wants to keep his company from getting too big so he can stay in touch with his artist customers. He's a serious watercolorist, and welcomes your questions and suggestions about materials and equipment.

Special Factors: Satisfaction is guaranteed; shipping is included on orders delivered to U.S. addresses east of the Mississippi River; quantity discounts are available; institutional accounts are available.

CROWN ART PRODUCTS CO., INC.

90 DAYTON AVE.
PASSAIC, NJ 07055
201-777-6010
FAX: 201-777-3088

Catalog: free
Save: up to 50%
Pay: check, MO, MC, V, AE, Discover
Sells: silk-screening supplies and materials
Store: same address; Monday to Friday 9–4:30, Saturday 11:30–6

 ¡Si!

Crown Art has been making and selling silk-screening supplies and equipment since 1974, under the direction of a silk-screen artist who's developed several products for the craft. The 16-page catalog features Crown's products: simple silk-screening kits for textiles and paper ($32), water-based "3-D" paints, Voilà squeeze fabric dyes (nontoxic and air-cured), Crown Aqua and Crown Opaque textile inks, Supertex airbrush ink, Posterelle ink for paper, and even "puffy" and metallic inks. Ready-to-print customized silk screens, screen printing stretcher strips, squeegees, and photo emulsion chemicals are available. Prices are reasonable, and if you're an art teacher, printer, or dealer, contact Crown for information on the special discount program. If you're within commuting distance of the store in New Jersey, you may be interested in taking a silk-screening workshop or lessons at Crown.

Special Factors: Price quote by phone or letter on special sizes and volume orders; minimum order is $25 with credit cards.

FLAX ART & DESIGN

1699 MARKET ST.,
    DEPT. WBM4
P.O. BOX 7216
SAN FRANCISCO, CA
    94120
415-468-7530
FAX: 415-468-1940

Catalog: $6 (see text)
Save: up to 30%
Pay: check, MO, MC, V, AE
Sells: art and graphic design materials and gifts
Store: same address; Monday to Saturday 9:30–6; also 510 East El Camino Real, Sunnyvale, CA; Monday to Saturday 10–6

Flax Art & Design was founded in 1939 by members of the same family that established the Sam Flax art stores that are well known on the East Coast, but it has no affiliation with the Sam Flax business. Though both firms sell supplies and equipment for the fine arts, drafting, and graphic design, Flax Art & Design discounts *everything* it sells in its two California stores.

Flax's big, six-dollar catalog shows goods at list prices, but the free quarterly sales catalogs offer savings of up to 30%. Art professionals should find the investment worthwhile, since there are all sorts of uncommon tools and supplies listed in the big book, in addition to the usual roundup of canvas, pigments, vehicles, brushes, and the like. Flax's strength is graphic design and commercial art products: the newest colors from Pantone, airbrushing supplies and equipment, the sleekest studio furniture and storage units, layout tools and supplies, markers in every conceivable color, professional templates, portfolios and presentation binders, sumi supplies, brushes for decorative paint finishes (graining, mottling, stippling), and even a small selection of conservation supplies are available. Flax has a large offering of ready-made and custom frames, as well as a selection of thousands of hard-to-find and handmade papers. Choice goods and unique gifts show up in the sale catalogs, although not everything is sold at a discount.

Special Factor: Minimum order is $25 from the big catalog.

A.I. FRIEDMAN

44 W. 18TH ST.
NEW YORK, NY 10011
212-243-9000
FAX: 212-929-7320

Catalog: $5 (see text)
Save: up to 40% (see text)
Pay: check, MO, MC, V, AE, Optima
Sells: graphic arts supplies and tools
Store: same address; and 25 W. 45th St.,
New York, NY; Monday to Friday 9–6, both
locations; also Caldor Plaza, Port Chester,
NY; open daily

 ¡Si!

If you're a professional graphic designer or artist, you'll want to add A.I. Friedman to your short list of suppliers. The firm, which has been in business since 1929, serves the creative community with the best in tools and equipment. You can send $5 for the 160-page catalog, but it's free to design professionals requesting it on letterhead.

The catalog itself is an object lesson in good design, making it easy to find what you want amid the equipment for computer graphics, presentation materials, studio furniture, drawing instruments, markers, paint, brushes, paper and board, airbrushing supplies, audio/visual equipment, frames, and reference books. Friedman offers goods not found in every art supply catalog: light boxes, dry-mounting presses, the *complete* Pantone line, precision drawing and drafting tools, a large selection of templates, and complete photostat systems. Among the manufacturers represented are Agfa Gevaert, Bainbridge, Canson, Chartpak, D'Arches, Dr. Ph. Martin's, Grumbacher, Iris, Iwata, Koh-I-Noor, Kolinsky, Lamy, LeRoy, Letraset, Liquitex, Luxo (lamps), Mont Blanc, Mutoh, Osmiroid, Paasche, Pelikan, Stacor, Staedler-Mars, Strathmore, 3M, and Winsor & Newton.

The catalog prices are not discounted, but if your order totals $50 or more, discounts of 20% to 40% are given. (Some items aren't discounted, including the Agfa products.) Call or write for a quote on specific items.

Special Factors: Institutional accounts are available; minimum order is $50 (see text); orders are shipped worldwide.

GRAPHIK DIMENSIONS, LTD.

41-23 HAIGHT ST.
FLUSHING, NY 11355
800-221-0262
718-463-3500
FAX: 718-463-2470

Catalog: free
Save: up to 50%
Pay: check, MO, MC, V
Sells: sectional frames and accessories
Store: mail order only

Every art gallery and museum curator in the world knows the value of a good frame. It serves a practical function—encasing the glass or protecting the edges of an oil painting—but it can also serve as the perfect bridge between the work and the room. The other people who know about frames are professional framers, and they price accordingly.

You can get the frame you want without paying through the nose by making it yourself, with frame sections from Graphik Dimensions. This firm is run by an artist and photographer who have firsthand experience in selecting the right frame for the piece, and finding the best price. Their 32-page color catalog offers the "classic" metal sectional frame you can buy in art-supply stores, in both standard (with glass) and canvas (oil painting) depths, in metallics and enamels. The selection includes frames wrapped in vinyls treated to resemble silk, lizard, parchment, and dulled metals; three-dimensional inset panel molding frames; and wooden gallery frames in plain, gilded, embossed, rustic, and natural finishes. Graphik Dimension's custom line features wood moldings, most of which include linen liners at no extra charge. These are the kinds of frames that you see at framers' shops—rich wood molding with fine gold striping, tapestry insets, and Florentine designs in deep relief. And if the whole prospect of putting a frame together seems too much, there's help: Graphic Dimensions also sells preassembled frames in several different styles. And before you order the frame, order the sample set of corners. These are actual pieces of the frame that show color, depth, and corner joinery style. The cost of the sample sets ($5 to $30, depending on the line) is repaid in the trouble you save if the frame wasn't right for the work and scraps are available free on request.

Special Factors: Quantity discounts are available; authorized returns (except custom frames) are accepted (a 15% restocking fee may be charged); minimum order is $10 with credit cards; C.O.D. orders are accepted.

JERRY'S ARTARAMA, INC.

P.O. BOX 1105-WMC
NEW HYDE PARK, NY
 11040
516-328-6633
FAX: 516-328-6752

Catalog: $2.50
Save: 33% average
Pay: check, MO, MC, V, Discover
Sells: art supplies and equipment
Store: 248-12 Union Tpk., Bellerose, NY; also 270 S. Federal Hwy. (U.S. 1), Deerfield Beach, FL; Monday to Saturday 9:30–6, Sunday 11–5, both locations

Jerry's Artarama publishes a 99-page compendium of materials, tools, and equipment for commercial and fine arts that includes both basics and specialty goods that are seldom discounted elsewhere. Jerry's was established in 1968, and carries over 10,000 different items.

A recent catalog offered pigments, brushes, vehicles and solvents, studio furniture, lighting, visual equipment, canvas and framing supplies, papers, and other goods, with an extensive section of oil, watercolor, and acrylic painting supplies. Jerry's also sells supplies for drawing, graphic arts, drafting, calligraphy, printmaking, sumi-e, airbrushing, fabric painting, marbleizing, and professional framing. There are some "generic" brands, but most are well known: Bill Alexander, Alvin, Badger, Blockx, Conté, Deka, D'Arches, Fabriano, Fredrix, Grumbacher, Holbein, Isabey, Iwata, Koh-I-Noor, Langnickel, Neolt, Paasche, Bob Ross, Robert Simmons, Stabilo, Stacor, Strathmore, Winsor & Newton, and X-Acto are among the many represented. Don't miss the dozen pages of publications, which include technique manuals, color guides and wheels, and workshop videotapes—all of which are discounted.

Special Factors: Satisfaction is unconditionally guaranteed; color charts and product specifications are available on request; quantity discounts are available; minimum order is $20, $50 with phone orders; orders are shipped worldwide.

PEARL PAINT CO., INC.

308 CANAL ST.
NEW YORK, NY
   10013-2572
800-221-6845
212-431-7932
FAX: 212-431-6798

Catalog: $1
Save: up to 70%
Pay: check, MO, MC, V, AE
Sells: art supplies
Store: same address; also 42 Lispenard St., New York, NY (architectural furniture showroom); open daily; also Altamonte Springs, Ft. Lauderdale, Miami, and Tampa, FL; Atlanta, GA; Cambridge, MA; Rockville, MD; Cherry Hill, Paramus, and Woodbridge, NJ; East Meadow, NY; Houston, TX; and Alexandria, VA

Gotham artists have been flocking to Pearl Paint since 1933 for good prices on fine paints, tools, and supplies, and since then Pearl has opened stores in six other states as well (locations are listed in the catalog). Since the catalog represents just 5% of available stock, call, fax, or write if you're looking for something that's not listed. Pearl sells fine-arts materials, tools, equipment, and materials for all kinds of crafts, offering pigments, brushes, vehicles and solvents, stretchers, papers of all kinds, canvas, manuals, studio furniture, and much more. The brands include Aquatec, Bainbridge, Bellini, Caran D'Ache, Deka, Fabriano, Grumbacher, Holbein, Iwata, Koh-I-Noor, Lascaux, Letraset, Liquitex, Paasche, Pantone, Pelikan, Sculpture House, Sennelier, Robert Simmons, Staedtler, and Winsor & Newton, among others. Pearl also stocks fine writing instruments, house paint, tints, and finishes, including gilding and "faux" finishing supplies.

Special Factors: Quantity discounts are available; weekly specials are run on selected items; minimum order is $50.

S&W FRAMING SUPPLIES, INC.

120 BROADWAY
P.O. BOX 340
GARDEN CITY PARK, NY
  11040
800-645-3399
516-746-1000
FAX: 516-746-6877

Catalog: free
Save: up to 40%
Pay: check, MO, MC, V, AE
Sells: professional framing supplies
Store (showroom): same address; by appointment only

Between the low prices and discounts for quantity purchases, you can save up to 40% on the cost of professional-quality framing equipment and supplies at S&W Framing. The catalog is 128 pages of mats, mat cutters and tools, blades, adhesives, films, dry mount equipment and supplies, touch-up materials, books, and much more. Although there are a number of things that anyone hanging pictures might need—screweyes, hangers, picture clips, picture lights, gilt touchup, etc.—it may be difficult to meet the $25 minimum order requirement. But framers will appreciate the depth of selection here, the brands—Bainbridge, Fletcher-Terry, Pistorius, Seal, Deft, Crescent, and Logan, among others—and the good prices.

Canadian and non-U.S. readers, please note: Only U.S. funds are accepted.

Special Factors: Quantity discounts are available; authorized returns (except opened packages of machinery) are accepted (a restocking fee may be charged) within ten days for exchange or merchandise credit; institutional accounts are available; minimum order is $25; orders are shipped worldwide.

SAX ARTS & CRAFTS

DEPT. 94WBMC
2405 S. CALHOUN RD.
NEW BERLIN, WI 53151
414-784-6880
FAX: 414-784-1176

Catalog: $4, refundable
Save: up to 50%
Pay: check, MO, MC, V, AE
Sells: arts and crafts supplies
Store: mail order only

Sax Arts & Crafts publishes a "resource of art and craft materials and equipment for the classroom and studio," a color catalog ($4) of over 500 pages that serves both educator and professional artist. Sax is notable for the range of supplies it offers—everything from craft sticks to kilns—and identifies products that have been certified "safe" or non-toxic by the Art and Craft Materials Institute, a helpful feature if you're buying products for children.

Sax has been in business since 1945, and sells tools and materials for paper lithography, "friendly" plastic for making jewelry, airbrushing, drawing, paper collage and tissue craft, paper sculpture, papermaking, etching, framing and matting, drafting, calligraphy, scratch art, ceramics, copper enameling, engraving, weaving, rug making, bead work, basketry, fabric painting, mosaics, and wood burning. Among the names represented are Amaco, Bockingford, Canson, Chromacryl, Cra-Pas, Crayola, Crescent, D'Arches, Deka, Fabriano, Fimo, Fredrix, Liquitex, Paasche, Pelikan, Pentel, Prang, Prismacolor, Shiva, Speedball, Strathmore, Whatman, and Winsor & Newton. The catalog features a number of unusual items: fluorescent modeling clay, erasable felt-tip pens, balsa foam (cuts with a toothpick, prints like a woodblock), a kiln that works in a microwave oven, silhouette paper, and Venetian glass tile, among others. And there are 40 pages of books, manuals, videotapes, and cards on art-related topics. Prices are competitive, but the real savings are on quantity purchases.

Special Factors: Satisfaction is guaranteed; authorized returns are accepted for exchange, refund, or credit; institutional accounts are available; minimum order is $10.

DANIEL SMITH

P.O. BOX 84268
SEATTLE, WA 98124-5568
800-426-6740 (U.S. AND
   CANADA)
206-223-9599
FAX: 800-238-4065

Catalog: free
Save: 30% average
Pay: check, MO, MC, V, AE
Sells: fine-arts supplies and equipment
Store: 430 First Ave. South, Seattle, WA;
Monday, Tuesday, Thursday 9–6, Wednesday
and Friday 9–8, Sunday 10–6

Daniel Smith's catalogs are designed by artists, for artists, and are appreciated as much for their book reviews, technical discussions, and visual appeal as for their offerings. Daniel Smith has been recommended by artists impressed by the company's line of materials and responsive service department; although the prices aren't rock bottom, sales are run on a regular basis.

The annual Reference Catalog presents an extensive collection of paper from Arches, Canson, Fabriano, Lana, Magnani, Rising, Strathmore, Twinrocker, and other makers, for watercolors, printmaking, drawing, bookmaking, and other applications. This catalog also features uncommon specialty papers, including banana paper from the Philippines, Mexican bark paper, genuine papyrus, and Japanese "fantasy" paper embedded with maple leaves.

Watercolor painters may find inspiration in Daniel Smith's own pigments, as well as dry and moist colors from Grumbacher, Holbein, Schmincke, and Winsor & Newton. Daniel Smith sells acrylic, oil, gouache, and tempera paints from several of these firms, and a complete line of its own oil paints, including luminescent and metallic colors and extra-rich formulations. The brush selection covers all painting media and includes Daniel Smith's own line, as well as brushes by Grumbacher, Isabey, Strathmore, and Winsor & Newton. Canvas, Nielsen sectional metal frames, wood frames, airbrush equipment, solvents, pastels, colored pencils, calligraphy pens, printmaking materials, and other tools and supplies available, rounded out by a fine collection of studio furniture, portfolios, easels, and reference books.

Canadian readers, please note: Only U.S. funds are accepted.

Special Factors: Satisfaction is guaranteed; authorized returns are accepted for exchange, refund, or credit; minimum order of paper is ten sheets; orders are shipped worldwide.

STU-ART SUPPLIES

2045 GRAND AVE.,
   DEPT. W-94
BALDWIN, NY 11510-2999
PHONE AND FAX: 516-
   546-5151

Catalog and Samples: free
Save: up to 50%
Pay: check, MO, MC, V
Sells: sectional frames and framing supplies
Store: same address; Monday to Saturday 9–5

Stu-Art sells sectional frames and framing materials—everything you'll need to do a professional job. The firm has been supplying galleries and institutions since 1970, and it offers the best materials, a range of sizes, and savings of up to 50% on list prices.

Nielsen metal frames are offered in nine profiles, for flat-stretched canvas and dimensional art (deep) mounting, in a stunning array of brushed metallic finishes, soft pastels, and deep decorator colors. Acid-free single and double mats are sold in rectangles and ovals. The catalog includes precise specifications of the frames, and samples of the mats. Stu-Art also sells nonglare and clear plastic (which can be used in place of picture glass), and shrink film and dispensers. If you have to get work framed, see the catalog before handing it over to a professional—you may decide you can do the job yourself.

Special Factors: Shipping is included on UPS-delivered orders over $300 net; authorized returns are accepted (a restocking fee may be charged); minimum order is $15 on sectional frames, $25 on other goods; C.O.D. orders are accepted.

UTRECHT ART AND DRAFTING SUPPLY

33 35TH ST.
BROOKLYN, NY 11232
800-223-9132
718-768-2525
FAX: 718-499-8815

Catalog: free
Save: up to 70%
Pay: check, MO, MC, V
Sells: art supplies
Store: 111 Fourth Ave, New York, NY; Monday to Saturday 9–6; also Berkeley, CA; Washington, DC; Chicago, IL; Boston, MA; Detroit, MI; and Philadelphia, PA

Utrecht has been selling supplies and equipment for painting, sculpture, and printmaking since 1949, and manufactures some of the best-priced oil and acrylic paints on the market. The 48-page catalog describes the manufacturing process and quality controls used to produce Utrecht's paint, and features Utrecht acrylics, oils, watercolors, gesso, and other mediums and solvents. The firm also sells a full line of professional artists' materials and equipment, including canvas, stretchers, frames, pads, paper, brushes, books, easels, flat files, taborets, pencils, drafting tools, and much more. In addition to the Utrecht label, goods by Arches, Bainbridge, Bienfang, Canson, Chartpak, Claessens, D'Arches, Deka, Eberhard Faber, Grumbacher, Koh-I-Noor, Kolinsky, Liquitex, Niji, Pentel, Rembrandt, Speedball, Strathmore, Vermeer, Winsor & Newton, and other manufacturers are available. Utrecht's prices are competitive, and the best buys are on the house brand and quantity purchases.

Special Factors: Institutional accounts are available; quantity discounts are available; minimum order is $40; orders are shipped worldwide.

YAZOO MILLS, INC.

COMMERCE ST.
P.O. BOX 369
NEW OXFORD, PA 17350
717-624-8993
FAX: 717-624-4420

Price List: free
Save: 50% plus
Pay: check, MO, MC, V, AE
Sells: shipping tubes
Store: mail order only

Yazoo Mills takes its name from the Mississippi town where it was founded in 1902, but since moving to Pennsylvania in 1936, Yazoo has run the plant from New Oxford. The firm manufactures paper tubes for shipping and industry—carpet "cores," cable reels, fax paper tubes, even heavy blast casings for the mining industry—Yazoo makes them all. Yazoo also manufactures and sells shipping tubes in the sizes most popular among artists. They're offered in lengths from 12" to 85", in diameters of 2" to 12". (The larger sizes are "heavy duty" or "extra heavy duty.") The tubes are sold by the case—48 in a carton of 2" by 12" tubes, to one of the 12" by 85"—and they come with plastic plug inserts for the ends. The prices, which include shipping, are so low that if all you need are two mid-sized tubes, it's probably worth buying from Yazoo—compared to art-supply houses, you can save as much as 80% by buying here! The tubes can be used for storage as well as shipping art and other objects; although they're made of recycled paperboard, they're not acid-free.

Yazoo does much of its manufacturing to job specifications, and can give you quotes on custom sizes or colors.

Special Factors: Shipping is included; minimum order is one carton of stock tubes; C.O.D. orders are accepted.

SEE ALSO

A to Z Luggage Co., Inc. • artists' portfolios • **LEATHER**
Dharma Trading Co. • tools and materials for fabric painting and dyeing • **CRAFTS**
Plexi-Craft Quality Products Corp. • acrylic display pedestals • **HOME: FURNISHINGS**
The Potters Shop Inc. • books on pottery and ceramics • **BOOKS**
Print's Graphic Design Book Stores • books and manuals on the graphic arts • **BOOKS**
Thai Silks • silk fabrics for fabric painting • **CRAFTS**
Utex Trading Enterprises • silk fabric for fabric painting • **CRAFTS**

AUTO, MARINE, AND AVIATION EQUIPMENT

Parts, supplies, maintenance products, and services

You'll find a wide range of parts and supplies for cars, motorcycles, RVs, trucks, and vans in this chapter—mufflers, shocks, tires, batteries, and much more. Some companies stock products for vintage cars, and one offers products for the "general pilot." You can even buy salvaged parts through several of the firms listed here, priced as much as 70% below the same parts if new. You can also buy cars, trucks, and vans, through services offered by American Auto Brokers. Here are some additional information sources to help you make the best selection when buying a car:

- *The Car Book,* by Jack Gillis (HarperCollins), rates current domestic and imported models on crash-test performance, as well as fuel economy, preventive-maintenance costs, repair costs, and insurance rates. The book also includes valuable information on evaluating warranties, service contracts, insurance, tires, children's car seats, and used cars. The comprehensive, easy-to-understand "Complaint" chapter should help you resolve difficulties, and the "Checklist" at the back of the book will help you ask the right questions. *The Car Book* is available in bookstores or from The Center for Auto Safety, 2001 S St., N.W., Suite 410, Washington, DC 20009. (Send a long, self-addressed, stamped envelope for the publications list and ordering information.)
- *Consumer Reports* publishes reliable vehicle ratings each year, and offers the "Consumer Reports Auto Price Service" as well. The

Auto Price Service provides a computer printout showing both list price and dealer's cost for the model you specify, plus each factory-installed option. If the *CR* Auto Test Division has recommended optional equipment for your model, the options are also listed. And the service also provides guidelines on negotiating the lowest possible price. At this writing, one report costs $11; two are $20; three, $27; and each additional report thereafter, $5. See the current *Consumer Reports* for information, or write to Consumer Reports Auto Price Service, Box 8005, Novi, MI 48376.

- The Better Business Bureau publishes guides to buying cars and tires, as well as other consumer goods. Send a self-addressed, stamped envelope to the Council of Better Business Bureaus, Inc., 4200 Wilson Blvd., Suite 800, Arlington, VA 22203, Attn.: Publications Dept., and request the list of available brochures and ordering information.

You can save hundreds or even thousands of dollars when buying your car, only to squander as much thanks to bad driving habits. The following tips will conserve funds and fuel, keeping your wallet fatter and the air cleaner:

- Drive at 55 miles per hour or less, whenever possible. You'll go about 20% farther on the same tank than you do when traveling at 70 mph.
- Don't burn fuel you don't have to: Don't leave the car in idle for more than a minute (turn it off), don't use air conditioning unless it's really necessary, and keep the car free of excess weight.
- Have the wheels aligned at least once a year, and switch to radials, which maximize mileage.
- Check your tire pressure monthly, using a gauge (the old pencil style is inexpensive and reliable, and stows easily in the glove compartment). If you're driving on underinflated tires, you're using more gas than necessary—as much as 2% of your bill at the pump could be waste. Take the reading when the tires are cold, using guidelines provided by the car manufacturer.
- Follow other care instructions outlined in your car manual, including scheduling tuneups and changing oil and filters.

Fear of getting stranded far from home with a disabled car leads many drivers to join auto clubs. Service and survival are great benefits, but most of the organizations provide far more than emergency towing. The best-known club, the American Automobile Association (AAA), boasts nearly 30 million members among its affiliates and offers a wide range of membership benefits. The AAA of New York, for example, provides travel-planning services, lodging and car rental discounts, no-fee travelers' checks, special services for travel abroad, personal accident insurance, assistance in solving license problems, and other benefits. The package of services varies from affiliate to affiliate; to find the AAA club nearest you, call 800-336-4357. Other clubs worth contacting for rates and services are Amoco Motor Club (800-782-7887) and Exxon Travel Club (713-680-5723).

If your interest is boating, you already know about the expenses—insurance, dock fees, upkeep, and new equipment. You can save 30% *routinely* on the cost of maintenance products, gear, and electronics by buying from the marine suppliers listed here, who sell every type of coating, tool, and device you'll need to keep your vessel afloat. You'll find exhaustive selections of electronics, hardware, and instruments, as well as galley accoutrements and foul-weather clothing. Even landlubbers should see these catalogs for the well-designed slickers and oiled sweaters.

If you're a private pilot who'd like to save on some of the gear and electronics you need while flying high, see the listing Marv Golden, an aviation discounter. Like the marine suppliers, this firm also sells goods of interest to those on terra firma, at savings of up to 35%. And for great leads on good buys in used aircraft, consider subscribing to Trade-A-Plane, a tabloid packed with ads for planes and aviation equipment. For current rates, write to Trade-A-Plane, P.O. Box 509, Crossville, TN 38557-9909.

FIND IT FAST

AVIATION • **Marv Golden**
BOATING SUPPLIES AND EQUIPMENT • **Defender, E & B, Goldbergs', M&E Marine, West Marine, Yachtmail**
CAR AUDIO • **Crystal Sonics**
CAR PARTS • **Cherry Auto, Clark's Corvair, IMPCO, Mill Supply, ProAm**
CARS, TRUCKS, JEEPS • **American Automobile Brokers**
FARM EQUIPMENT PARTS • **Central Michigan**
MOTORCYCLE PARTS • **Capital Cycle**
RACING EQUIPMENT • **ProAm, Racer Wholesale**
TIRES • **Belle Tire, Euro-Tire, Teletire**

AMERICAN AUTO-MOBILE BROKERS, INC.

Information: price quote
Save: see text
Pay: check or MO (see text)
Sells: cars, trucks, vans, and jeeps
Store: same address

24001 SOUTHFIELD RD.,
  SUITE 110
SOUTHFIELD, MI 48075
313-569-5900

When it comes to buying a car, one way to come out on top is to make sure you get a quote from American Automobile Brokers, whose price includes dealer prep, all factory rebates, and delivery from the factory to a dealership near you by train or truck (for domestic vehicles). The savings depend on the prices in your area, but enough customers have been buying cars, trucks, and vans to keep American Automobile Brokers in business since 1972.

If you're shopping for a domestic model, you can buy vehicles by General Motors, Ford/Lincoln-Mercury, and Chrysler/Jeep/Eagle. The foreign makes include Alfa Romeo, BMW, Honda, Isuzu, Mercedes, Mitsubishi, Porsche, Saab, Toyota, and others. (American Automobile Brokers doesn't sell imports to residents of California.) The procedure is simple: Call or write with complete details about the vehicle and options desired, or send a self-addressed, stamped envelope for American Automobile Brokers' price-quote form. You get *one free quote;* extra quotes cost $5 each. Send a self-addressed, stamped envelope both when requesting the form and when sending it back for the quote. You can shop your local dealers, then get a quote here and see what you'll save by buying through American Automobile Brokers.

Special Factors: Price quote by phone, letter, or American Automobile Brokers quote form with SASE; checks and money orders are accepted for deposit only, balance payable by certified check, cashier's check, or wire transfer.

BELLE TIRE
DISTRIBUTORS, INC.

WHOLESALE DIV.
3500 ENTERPRISE DR.
ALLEN PARK, MI 48101
313-271-9200
FAX: 313-271-6793

Catalog: free
Save: up to 35%
Pay: check, MO, MC, V, Discover
Sells: tires, custom wheels, accessories, and parts
Store: same address; also Detroit, Farmington, Grand Rapids, Madison Heights, Novi, Plymouth, Port Huron, Roseville, Sterling Heights, Taylor, Troy, West Bloomfield, and Woodhaven, MI; and Toledo, OH

If you're in the market for tires, Belle Tire can save you up to 35% on the list prices of radials by Bridgestone, Firestone, B.F. Goodrich, Goodyear, Kelly Springfield, Michelin, Pirelli, Uniroyal, and Yokohama. Belle also offers custom wheels, accessories, and auto parts. The firm has been in business since 1922, and charges $5 to $20 per tire for shipping, depending on the destination. Call or write for prices of specific models, or see the brochure.

Special Factors: Price quote by phone, fax, or letter; orders are shipped worldwide.

CAPITAL CYCLE
CORPORATION

P.O. BOX 528
STERLING, VA 20167-0528
703-444-2500
FAX: 703-444-9546

Catalog: free
Save: up to 65%
Pay: check, MO, MC, V, AE
Sells: BMW and European after-market motorcycle parts and accessories
Store: 1508 Moran Rd., Sterling, VA; Monday to Friday 8:30–6, Saturday 9–5

Capital Cycle is the nation's definitive source for replacement parts for BMW motorcycles, with an inventory of over 8,000 genuine, original parts, which are priced up to 65% below what the dealers are charging. Capital Cycle, which has been in business for 20 years, publishes a small, seasonal catalog featuring specials and much-requested items.

Capital offers genuine BMW motorcycle parts, manufactured from 1955 through the current year. The catalog includes only a fraction of the enormous inventory, including engine parts and electronics, carburetors, fuel tanks, mufflers, pipes, clutches, gears, steering bearings, shocks, springs, handlebars, mirrors, brakes, tires, rims, forks, fenders, fairings, locks and keys, paint, seats, switches and relays, tachometers, voltmeters, lights, tools, and decals. Parts books and factory repair manuals for BMW cycles are offered, as well as a selection of BMW car parts. Capital Cycle also sells European after-market parts such as JAMA exhausts at savings.

Canadian readers, please note: Only U.S. funds are accepted.

Special Factors: Quantity discounts are available; UPS ground shipping is included; repair services are available by mail; authorized returns are accepted within 30 days (a 15% restocking fee may be charged); minimum order is $20; orders are shipped worldwide.

CENTRAL MICHIGAN TRACTOR & PARTS

2713 N. U.S. 27
ST. JOHNS, MI 48879
800-248-9263
517-224-6802
FAX: 517-224-6682

Information: price quote
Save: up to 50%
Pay: check, MO, MC, V
Sells: used, new, and rebuilt tractor parts
Store: mail order only

Central Michigan can save you up to 50% on parts for tractors and combines. The company stocks new, used, reconditioned, and rebuilt parts, all of which are backed by a 30-day guarantee. You can buy everything from starters to cylinder blocks for machines made by almost every major manufacturer here—Allis, Case, Chalmers, John Deere, Massey Ferguson, Ford, International, Moline, White/Oliver, and others. The rebuilt parts are overhauled completely, so they should function as well and for as long as new ones. Central Michigan is one of 11 firms that make up the "Parts Express Network," and maintains customers' want lists for parts not in stock. Call between 8 and 5:30, Monday to Friday, or 8 and 3:00 on Saturdays for information.

Special Factors: Price quote by phone or letter; orders are shipped worldwide.

CHERRY AUTO PARTS

5650 N. DETROIT AVE.
TOLEDO, OH 43612
419-476-7222
FAX: 419-470-6388

Information: price quote
Save: up to 70%
Pay: check, MO, MC, V
Sells: used and rebuilt imported-car parts
Store: same address; Monday to Friday
8:30–5, Saturday 8:30–12; also 17770 Tele-
graph Rd., Romulus, MI (Detroit area); Mon-
day to Friday 8:30–5, Saturday 9–12

Why pay top dollar for new car parts if you can get perfectly good ones, used, for up to 70% less? Cherry Auto Parts, "The Midwest's Leading Imported Car Dismantler," can supply you with used and rebuilt imported-car components at sizable savings. Cherry Auto has 45 years of experience in the business, and keeps rebuilt cylinder heads, engines, starters, steering gears, alternators, drive axles, turbos, and other vital parts on hand. If you drive an Acura, Alfa Romeo, Audi, BMW, Chrysler Import (Champ, Colt, Conquest, Raider Vista), Nissan, Eagle, GEO, Honda, Isuzu, Jaguar, Mazda, Mercedes, Merkur, MG, Mitsubishi, Peugeot, Porsche, Renault, Saab, Spectrum, Sprint, Subaru, Toyota, Triumph, Volkswagen, Volvo, or other imported car, you may save up to 70% on your parts bills by getting them here. Cherry can access two nationwide computerized parts-locating networks to trace hard-to-find parts promptly.

Special Factors: Price quote by phone (preferred) or letter; "all parts are guaranteed in stock at the time of quotation, guaranteed to be the correct part, and in good condition as described"; minimum order is $20; orders are shipped worldwide.

CLARK'S CORVAIR PARTS, INC.

RTE. 2
SHELBURNE FALLS, MA
01370
413-625-9776

Catalog: $5
Save: up to 40%
Pay: check, MO, MC, V, Discover
Sells: Corvair parts
Store: mail order only

Every other year, Clark's Corvair Parts publishes an inventory of over 8,000 new Corvair parts in an indexed, 400-page catalog, supplemented by a 50-page Used Parts Catalog (over 2,500 at last count), a 50-page High-Performance Catalog, and 30 pages of extra goodies—all for $5. Clark's, in business since 1973, is an indispensable source for the Corvair owner since it stocks parts available nowhere else. Clark's can save you up to 40% on original and replacement General Motors parts, reproductions, and goods by Champion, Chevrolet, Clevite, Delco, Gabriel, Gates, General Motors, Loctite, Michigan Bearings, Moog, Permatex, Sealed Powers, TRW, and hundreds of other suppliers. The exhaustive inventory includes brakes, cables, lights, air filters, body parts and panels, carburetor and engine parts, gauges, gas tanks, manuals, pistons, points, seals, rims, specialty tools, paint, reproduction upholstery, trim, carpets, and many other parts and supplies. If you're looking for a specific part, you can call for a quote—but the catalogs are valuable reference tools and well worth the $5 to any do-it-yourself Corvair owner.

Special Factors: Price quote by phone or letter; returns are accepted; C.O.D. orders are accepted; minimum order is $10; orders are shipped worldwide.

CRYSTAL SONICS

1638 SOUTH CENTRAL
AVE., #C4
GLENDALE, CA 91204
818-240-7310

Catalog: $2
Save: up to 60%
Pay: check, MO, MC, V, AE
Sells: auto audio
Store: same address; Monday to Friday 9–6, Saturday 10–3

Crystal Sonics, in business since 1977, publishes an informative, 88-page directory of auto audio components that are discounted up to

60%. Past catalogs have featured guides to audio terminology and extensive product specifications, as well as listings of sound systems, amps, speakers, baffles, security devices and alarms, antennas, wires and cables, hardware, installation kits, cellular phones, and related paraphernalia. Crystal Sonics represents Allsop, Alphasonik, Alpine, Art Audio, Audio Control, BEL, Blaupunkt, Boston Acoustics, Clarion, Discwasher, Fujitsu Ten, Harada, Hirschmann, Hot Wires, Infinity, JBL, Klasse, Panasonic, Phoenix Gold, Pioneer, Sony, Streetwires, TDK, Triad, and XTC. Crystal Sonics has a large facility where audio systems can be installed, and if you live within a reasonable distance from Glendale, it's probably worth the trip.

Please note: Not all of the goods shown in the catalog are available by mail.

Special Factors: Authorized returns of new, unaltered, unused goods are accepted within 14 days; minimum order is $50 with credit cards; orders are shipped worldwide.

DEFENDER INDUSTRIES, INC.

255 MAIN ST.

P.O. BOX 820

NEW ROCHELLE, NY

10802-0820

914-632-3001

FAX (U.S. AND CANADA):

800-654-1616

FAX: 914-632-6544

Catalog: free

Save: up to 60%

Pay: check, MO, MC, V, Discover

Sells: marine supplies, gear, equipment, and clothing

Store: The Marine Discount Supermarket, 321 Main St., New Rochelle, NY; Monday to Friday 9–5:45, Thursday 9–8:45, Saturday 9–4:45 (call for hours, October–February)

 ¡Si!

Defender has been selling marine hardware and equipment since 1938, and backs its claim of "the largest selection in the USA at the very lowest prices" with a 252-page catalog that just about proves it. It features page after page of boat maintenance supplies, resins and coatings, winches, windlasses, cordage, communications devices, foul-weather gear, books, tools and hardware, optics, galley fittings, navigation equipment, and electronics. You'll find sailboat hardware from Harken and Schaefer, Barient and Lewmar winches, Evinrude and Tohatsu outboard engines, and lines of marine electronics from Apelco, Hummingbird, ICOM, Impulse, Lowrance, Micrologic, Motorola, Navico,

Raytheon, Signet, Sitex, and Trimble. Also available: Shakespeare antenna, Maxxima and Sony radios, optics from Fujinon, Minolta, and Steiner, Avon and Achilles inflatable boats and life rafts; NYNEX mobile phones, Henri Lloyd, Musto, and Patagonia boating wear, Sebago and Timberland shoes, Force 10 cookers, and Hurricane boat tops and covers—among other items. In addition to equipment, Defender is a national leader in boat-building supplies: fiberglass, xynole, epoxy and polyester resins, and other boat construction and maintenance materials are stocked in depth. Defender also offers a range of custom services, such as life raft repacking and repair, rigging services, and canvas goods to order (seat covers, pool covers, car covers, etc.).

Defender's wholesale affiliate, Atlantic Main Corp., specializes in small boat marine hardware and safety gear. Among other items, Atlantic Main sells the "Horseshoe Harness," an alternative to the Lifesling, at about half the cost. Atlantic Main is also the U.S. agent for Holt Allen sailboat hardware. For details, contact Atlantic Main at 319 Main St., New Rochelle, NY 10801.

Special Factors: Price quote by phone, fax, or letter; returns are accepted within 20 days (a restocking fee may be charged); minimum order is $15, $25 with credit cards; orders are shipped worldwide.

E & B MARINE SUPPLY, INC.

DEPT. WBMC
201 MEADOW RD.
EDISON, NJ 08818
800-533-5007
FAX: 908-819-9222

Catalog: free
Save: up to 60%
Pay: check, MO, MC, V, AE, Discover, Optima
Sells: marine supplies, gear, and equipment
Store: 45 outlets in AL, CT, FL, GA, MA, MD, MI, MS, NJ, NY, PA, RI, and VA (locations are listed in the catalog)

 ¡Si!

E & B Marine, founded in 1946, has a lowest-price policy that assures you great savings on a full range of products for power boating and sailing, boat maintenance and repair, safety, communications, and navigation. The brands include Apelco, Aqua Meter, Boatlife, Bow t' Stern, Chelsea, Eagle, Humminbird, Icom, Igloo, Impulse, Interlux, Kidde, Micrologic, Pettit, Polaris, Ray Jeff, Raytheon, Ritchie, SeaFit, SeaRanger, Standard, and Stearns, among others. Water skis and Achilles inflatables are stocked, as well as boating apparel and sportswear. New products are featured in every catalog, and many items are useful on land as well—clothing, safety equipment, and hardware. Savings vary, but are typically 10% to 25%, and up to 60% on sale items and specials.

Special Factors: Authorized returns are accepted; minimum order is $15, $25 on phone orders; orders are shipped worldwide.

EURO-TIRE, INC.

80 LITTLE FALLS RD.
FAIRFIELD, NJ 07004
800-631-0080
201-575-0080

Brochure: free
Save: up to 50%
Pay: check, MO, MC, V, AE, Optima
Sells: auto tires, wheels, and shocks
Store: 500 Rte. 46 East, Fairfield, NJ; also 290 Rte. 4 East, Paramus, NJ; and 393 West Ave., Stamford, CT

Euro-Tire has been selling tires since 1974, and currently offers Armstrong, Avon, Bridgestone, Continental, Dunlop, Goodyear, Michelin, Pirelli, and Yokohama. The firm's specialty is imported tires and auto components, but domestic lines are also available. Shock absorbers by Bilstein, Boge, and Koni are priced an average of 34% below list, and the brochure lists light alloy wheels by BBS, Centra, MSW, and Ronal. Euro-Tire's concise brochure gives complete details on its sales and warranty policies, as well as services offered at its facilities in Connecticut and New Jersey.

Special Factors: No seconds or retreads are sold; returns are accepted within 30 days (see the catalog for details); minimum order is $25; orders are shipped worldwide.

GOLDBERGS' MARINE DISTRIBUTORS

DEPT. WBMC
201 MEADOW RD.
EDISON, NJ 08818
800-523-2926
FAX: 908-819-9222

Catalog: free
Save: up to 60%
Pay: check, MO, MC, V, AE, Discover, Optima
Sells: marine supplies, gear, and equipment
Store: 12 W. 37th St., New York, NY

 ¡Si!

Goldbergs' has been a marine supplier since 1946, and offers thousands of products at discounts of up to 60%, and even better savings in the sales catalogs. Goldbergs' sells everything from anchors to zinc collars, including rope, bilge pumps, fishing tackle, rigging, knives, lifeboats, life preservers, navigation equipment, boat covers, winches, and even kitchen (galley) sinks. The brands are the best in boating—SeaRanger electronics, Taylor Made buoys, PowerWinch windlasses and winches, motors, and Stearns life preservers are but a few. The emphasis is on pleasure-boat equipment, but much of the sailing apparel—heavy sweaters, sunglasses, boots, Sperry boating shoes, and slickers—has landlubber appeal. A selection of stylish galley gear, teak bulkhead racks, and other yacht accessories rounds out the catalog.

Special Factors: Authorized returns are accepted (policy is stated in the catalog); minimum order is $10; orders are shipped worldwide.

MARV GOLDEN DISCOUNT SALES, INC.

8690 AERO DR., SUITE 102
SAN DIEGO, CA 92123
619-569-5220
FAX: 619-569-4508

Flyer: free
Save: up to 35%
Pay: check, MO, MC, V, AE, Discover, Optima
Sells: equipment for "general aviation" pilots
Store: same address; Monday to Friday 7–6, Saturday 8–3, PST

Marv Golden Discount Sales, in business since 1983, offers the general-aviation pilot savings of up to 35% on headsets, electronics, and accessories. The firm publishes a 16-page catalog of such items as David

Clark headsets, Astrotech digital clocks, Casio pilots' watches, Jeppesen charts and binders, U.S. Air Force kneeboards, Aerox oxygen systems, and flight bags and other accessories. Intercoms by Flightcom, Sigtronics, Soft Comm, Telex, and other manufacturers are available, as well as computers from Jeppesen and Navtronic, and 720-channel transceivers from Icom, King, Narco, and Terra. Call Marv Golden if you don't see what you're looking for, since it may be available.

Special Factors: Satisfaction is guaranteed; shipping is included on prepaid orders delivered in the U.S.; quantity discounts are available; authorized, unused returns in original packaging are accepted within 30 days for credit; C.O.D. orders are accepted; orders are shipped worldwide.

IMPCO, INC.

5300 GLENMONT DR.
DEPT. WBMC
HOUSTON, TX 77081-2002
800-243-1220
713-661-0900
FAX: 713-661-2655

Catalog: free
Save: 30% average
Pay: check, MO, MC, V, Discover
Sells: OEM Mercedes-Benz diesel, 190E, and 190D parts (see text)
Store: same address; Monday to Friday 9–6

IMPCO has been in business since 1984 and sells only first-quality parts through the 60-page color catalog. Whether you're overhauling a wreck, or just want to replace the wiper blades, IMPCO provides everything from front fender moldings to trunk seals, as well as electrical parts and supplies, bulbs, cooling and heating system components, upholstery materials, filters, brake parts, suspension and drive-line parts exhaust systems, window switches, accessories, tools, and Owner's Workshop manuals. If you're overhauling your car, check out IMPCO's engine rebuilding kits. IMPCO also sells Waxshop car-care products, Lexol leather cleaner and conditioner, and engine additives by Lubro Moly. If you're looking for a part or Mercedes-Benz product not listed or have any questions, just call.

Special Factors: Satisfaction is guaranteed; authorized, unused returns (except tools, manuals, and electronics) are accepted within 30 days for exchange, refund, or credit; C.O.D. orders are accepted; orders are shipped worldwide.

M&E MARINE SUPPLY COMPANY, INC.

P.O. BOX 601
CAMDEN, NJ 08101
609-858-1010
FAX: 609-757-9175

Catalog: $2
Save: up to 60%
Pay: check, MO, MC, V
Sells: boating supplies and equipment
Store: Glasgow, DE, and Collingswood and Trenton, NJ

M&E has been serving boaters since 1946 with good prices on everything needed to set sail and stay afloat. The 330-page catalog gives you access to over 30,000 products from anchors to zippers, from well-known manufacturers like Apelco, Aqua Meter, Barient, Harken, Magellan, Maxxima, Schaefer, Signet, Si-Tex, Tasco, and Weems & Plath. If you have a boat or enjoy sailing, you'll appreciate the savings, which average 25% but can reach 80%. A recent sale catalog included navigation equipment, lighting, pumps, electronics, safety equipment, hull repair compounds and finishes, ladders, rope, inflatables (dinghies), horns, bells, and other equipment and supplies. There are lots of products useful on land, like the Sperry Top-Siders, teak boat accessories, acrylic glassware, watches, fishing equipment, and flags. Both list and M & E's discount prices are given, and everything is covered by the blanket guarantee of satisfaction.

Special Factors: Satisfaction is guaranteed; returns are accepted within 30 days for exchange, refund, or credit; minimum order is $15 with credit cards; C.O.D. orders are accepted; orders are shipped worldwide.

MILL SUPPLY, INC.

3241 SUPERIOR AVE.,
  DEPT. WBMC
CLEVELAND, OH 44114
800-888-5072
FAX: 216-241-0425

Catalog: $4
Save: up to 40%
Pay: check, MO, MC, V
Sells: replacement auto panels and hardware
Store: same address; Monday to Friday 8–5

Whether you're just a car nut or you own a body shop, you'll want Mill Supply's 176-page catalog on your shelf. Mill Supply has been selling car parts since 1944, and specializes in replacement panels and supplies for collision and rust repairs. The index runs from Alfa Romeo to Volvo, and the catalog includes all the hardware, tools, finishes, and other shop equipment you need to do installations. You have to have the know-how for certain types of jobs, but even driveway mechanics can install rubber mud flaps and replacement side mirrors, or use the professional brushes and car-washing equipment.

Canadian readers, please note: Only U.S. funds are accepted, paid by postal money order only.

Special Factors: Quantity discounts are available; authorized returns are accepted (a 10% restocking fee may be charged) within 60 days for exchange, refund, or credit; C.O.D. orders are accepted; orders are shipped worldwide.

PROAM SEAT WAREHOUSE

6125 RICHMOND AVE.
HOUSTON, TX 77057
800-847-5712
713-781-7755
FAX: 713-781-8207

Catalog: free
Save: up to 30%
Pay: check, MO, MC, V, AE
Sells: performance driving equipment and accessories
Store: same address; Monday to Friday 8:30–6, Saturday 9:30–4

 ¡Si!

ProAm sells all kinds of accessories to enhance the looks and comfort of high-performance cars—Acuras, Datsuns, Porsches, Jaguars, BMWs, etc. You can upgrade the driver's seat with one from the line of Recaro seats with full recline and full lumbar support, enjoy an anatomically designed steering wheel from ProAm's collection, and replace the stick shift in your car with one made of precious wood. ProAm also carries replacement dashboard covers, wheels by ARE, BBS, MOMO, MSW, and Ronal, and aerodynamically designed panels, spoilers, rear aprons, air dams, skirts, and other products by BBS, Kamei, Kaminari, Mitcom, Pacific, and Zender. (In addition to adding a sporty edge to the looks of the car, these accessories can improve handling and performance.)

ProAm has been in business since 1984, and although the firm serves both amateur and professional drivers with racing suits by Simpson, Shoei helmets, and pit stop accessories, the average car driver will enjoy the good buys on Wolf car covers, Serengeti sunglasses, steering wheel locks, floor mats, and tire gauges.

Please note: Identify yourself as a WBMC reader when you call or write.

Special Factors: C.O.D. orders are accepted; orders are shipped worldwide.

RACER WHOLESALE

DEPT. WBM
1020 SUN VALLEY DR.
ROSWELL, GA 30076
404-998-7777
FAX: 404-993-4417

Catalog: free
Save: up to 70%
Pay: check, MO, MC, V, Discover
Sells: auto racing safety equipment
Store: same address; Monday to Friday 9–6

Racer Wholesale has been serving the serious amateur and professional auto racing markets since 1985, offering safety equipment and accessories at savings of up to 70% on list prices. The 60-page catalog shows professional driving suits from AutoPro, Bell, Pyrotect, Racequip, and other manufacturers, as well as gloves, boots, helmets, belts, harnesses, window nets, arm restraints, Hunsaker racing seats, fire extinguishers, and other safety products. Auto equipment is also available, including K & N filters and accessories, Flowmaster mufflers, Oberg filters and heavy-duty oil, coolers, Aeroquip hoses and connections, fueling accessories, canopies, towing equipment, Wink wide-view mirrors, battery cutoff switches, and related goods. Both list and discounted prices are given in the separate price sheets, and Racer Wholesale has a policy of "guaranteed lowest prices"—see the catalog for details.

Special Factors: Authorized, unused returns (except special orders) are accepted within 15 days for exchange, refund, or credit (a restocking fee may be charged); C.O.D. orders are accepted; orders are shipped worldwide.

TELETIRE

17642 ARMSTRONG AVE.
IRVINE, CA 92714
800-835-8473
714-250-9141
FAX: 714-261-5473

Brochure: free
Save: 30% average
Pay: check, MO, MC, V, Discover
Sells: tires and wheels
Store: mail order only

Past brochures from Teletire have addresseed issues that befuddle many car owners, such as tire rotation, inflation, Plus-1, and the secret meaning of speed ratings. In addition to giving you an education, Teletire offers a great selection of tires and wheels for passenger cars, trucks, vans, and RVs, from Bridgestone, Continental, Michelin, Pirelli, and Yokohama. If what you want isn't listed in the brochure, call or write for a price quote. Teletire, which began doing business in 1969, is affiliated with Telepro (see the listing in "Sports").

Special Factors: Unused, undamaged returns are accepted within 30 days (a restocking fee may be charged).

WAG-AERO, INC.

P.O. BOX 181
1216 NORTH RD.
LYONS, WI 53148
800-766-1216
414-763-9586
FAX: 414-763-7595

Catalog: free
Save: up to 30%
Pay: check, MO, MC, V, Discover
Sells: aircraft parts, supplies, and aviation accessories
Store: same address; Monday to Friday 8–4:30

Wag-Aero is so attuned to the needs of small-aircraft pilots that the catalog includes directions for "fly-in" customers! The firm has been in business for over 30 years, and covers everything from spark plugs and propellers to aircraft decals, aviators' jackets, and manuals. You'll find a full range of piloting instruments, windshields, lorans, lighting, spinner, engine mounts, wheels, and much more, by some major names—Aeronca, Cessna, Grumman, etc. in the 124-page catalog. Many products, however, are sold at great prices under Wag-Aero's own label. Whether you're a dedicated pilot maintaining and aircraft of just dream of taking to the wild blue yonder, you'll find much of interest here.

Special Factors: Satisfaction is guaranteed; authorized returns are accepted within 90 days for exchange, refund, or credit; C.O.D. orders are accepted; orders are shipped worldwide.

WEST MARINE

500 WESTRIDGE DR.
WATSONVILLE, CA 95070
800-538-0775
FAX: 408-728-4360

Catalog: free
Save: up to 50% off list
Pay: check, MC, V, AE, Discover
Sells: marine supplies and equipment
Store: 28 outlets nationwide

West Marine publishes a 104-page color compendium of marine electronics, hardware, and maintenance products for sailboats and powerboats, as well as related goods, such as foul-weather clothing and plumbing supplies. The comprehensive selection of gear and materials includes epoxies and finishes, rope, anchors, windlasses, buoys, horns, seacocks, winches, VHF radios, global positioning systems, navigation instruments, safety equipment, hardware, kerosene lamps, marine optics, inflatable boats, and a complete line of galley gear. There are scores of manufacturers represented, including Apelco, Barient, Harken, Interphase, Lewmar, Magellan, Marinco, Navico, Patagonia, Ritchie, Schaefer, Stearns, Steiner, Taylor Made, and Weems & Plath, as well as the firm's private label. West Marine also offers rope-splicing services at "a reasonable fee." Savings run up to 50%, and West Marine has over 14,000 items in stock, so call and ask if you don't see what you're looking for.

Special Factors: Satisfaction is guaranteed; orders are shipped worldwide.

COMPANIES OUTSIDE THE U.S.A.

Yachtmail, a well-known yacht chandler, is experienced in dealing with customers in the U.S. and Canada. Yachtmail offers goods not widely available at a discount in the U.S. and it has a better selection of certain goods than do domestic discounters.

Before ordering from any non-U.S. firm, please consult "The Complete Guide to Buying by Mail," page 535, for helpful tips. Pay for orders from foreign firms with a credit card whenever possible, so you'll have some recourse if you don't receive your order. For more information, see "The Fair Credit Billing Act," page 569.

YACHTMAIL CO. LTD.

ADMIRAL'S COURT,
  THE QUAY
LYMINGTON, HANTS
  SO41 9ET
UNITED KINGDOM
011-44-590-672784
FAX: 011-44-590-670089

Price List: free
Save: up to 50%
Pay: check, IMO, MC, V, Access
Sells: yachting equipment, clothing, and electronics
Store: same address; Hamble Point Marina, School Lane, Hamble, and Port Hamble Marine, Satchell Lane, Hamble, Hants

Yachtmail was founded in 1966 and specializes in yacht clothing, yacht gear and inflatables, but the firm also sells navigation instruments, winches, pumps, lights, clocks, barometers, and other boating goods. Yachtmail can often beat U.S. discount prices on English brands, even with shipping—so don't overlook this source if you're buying British.

Yachtmail says that the most popular items with U.S. buyers are musto and Henri Lloyd clothing, Autohelm and Navico autopilots, Avon inflatables and life rafts, echo sounders, log speedometers, and sextants. Yachtmail sells Lewmar and S.L. Anchorman winches, EPIRBs, bilge pumps, anchors, compasses, flares, binoculars, life jackets, and other useful goods. The price list includes only a sample of what's available, and if you're looking for a British-made item not mentioned, ask—it may be in stock.

Special Factors: Certain items are unsuitable for mailing; orders are shipped worldwide.

SEE ALSO

Allyn Air Seat Co. • *air-filled seat liners for motorcycles, cars, and trucks* • **SPORTS**
Arctic Sheepskin Outlet • *sheepskin cover steering wheel and seat covers* • **CLOTHING**
Bart's Water Ski Center, Inc. • *boat mounts and hardware for water-skiing equipment* • **SPORTS**
Bennett Brothers, Inc. • *infants' car seats* • **GENERAL MERCHANDISE**
BRE Lumber • *lumber and flooring for marine use* • **HOME: MAINTENANCE**
Cabela's Inc. • *boat seats, covers, electronics, etc.* • **SPORTS**
Camelot Enterprises • *automotive tools* • **TOOLS**

Campmor • *inflatable boats* • **SPORTS**

Crutchfield Corporation • *auto audio and security devices* • **APPLIANCES**

Deerskin Trading Post, Inc. • *shearling car seat covers* • **CLOTHING**

Gander Mountain, Inc. • *boat seats, covers, electronics, motors, etc.* • **SPORTS**

Illinois Audio • *auto audio* • **APPLIANCES**

The Kennel Vet Corp. • *dog seat belts* • **ANIMAL**

LVT Price Quote Hotline, Inc. • *radar detectors, scanners, CBs, etc.* • **APPLIANCES**

Manufacturer's Supply • *parts for motorcycles, snowmobiles, ATVs, etc.* • **TOOLS**

Mardiron Optics • *marine optics* • **CAMERAS**

Northern Hydraulics, Inc. • *wheels and parts for ATVs, minibikes, etc.; auto tools* • **TOOLS**

Overton's Sports Center, Inc. • *marine equipment and electronics* • **SPORTS**

Percy's Inc. • *radar detectors* • **APPLIANCES**

Sailboard Warehouse, Inc. • *sailboard car racks* • **SPORTS**

R.C. Steele Co. • *life preservers and auto safety harnesses for pets* • **ANIMAL**

BOOKS, PERIODICALS, AND RECORDINGS

Publications in all media, cards and stationery, slides, films, videotapes, audiotapes, LPs, and CDs

Why pay list prices for books or tapes, or full rates for magazine subscriptions, when you can get them all by mail at discounts of up to 80%? The firms in this chapter can save you hundreds of dollars a year on your own reading and entertainment buys, as well as on the books, tapes, and movies on your gift list. Looking for stationery, cards, and gift wrapping and ribbon? They're here as well, also competitively priced.

Most of us let our books take care of themselves, but if you have a real collection, you have an investment that requires proper storage and display. University Products (listed in the "Small Business" section of "Office") offers a wide range of conservation supplies, including acid-free book-jacket covers, manuscript cases and folders, rare-book boxes, record sleeves, interleaving sheets, and archival-quality repair materials—and with quantity discounts, it makes sense to take care of your whole library!

Don't overlook the "See Also's," especially if you're looking for a how-to or self-help type of publication. You'll find gardening guides among the firms in "Farm and Garden," cookbooks offered by firms selling gourmet ingredients, books on color theory sold by art-supply houses, and so on. Many of the firms listed in WBMC also offer videotapes on their specialties, usually at competitive prices. And if you're looking for software, see the "Computing" section of the "Office and Business" chapter.

FIND IT FAST

ARTS AND CRAFTS • **Dover, Potters Shop, Print's Graphic Design**
ASTRONOMY • **Astronomical Society**
CARDS AND STATIONERY • **Current, Rocky Mountain**
CHILDREN'S • **Butternut Books**
COOKBOOKS • **Jessica's Biscuit**
GOVERNMENT PUBLICATIONS • **Consumer Information Center, Superintendent of Documents**
MAGAZINE SUBSCRIPTIONS • **American Family, Publishers Clearing House**
PAPERBACKS • **Olde Methuen**
RECORDS, TAPES, CDS • **Adventures in Cassettes, Audio House, Barnes & Noble, Berkshire, Bose Express, Coronet, Forty-Fives, Kicking Mule, Record-Rama, Redding Group**
UNIVERSITY PRESSES • **Scholar's Bookshelf**
USED BOOKS • **Editions, Olde Methuen, Strand, Tartan**
VIDEOTAPES • **Adventures In Cassettes, Astronomical Society, Barnes & Noble, Bose Express, Critics' Choice**

ADVENTURES IN CASSETTES

A DIVISION OF META-COM, INC.
DEPT. WO94
5353 NATHAN LANE
PLYMOUTH, MN 55442
800-328-0108
FAX: 612-553-0424

Catalog: free
Save: up to 30%
Pay: check, MO, MC, V, AE, Discover, Optima
Sells: audiotapes and CDs
Store: mail order only

  ★

Adventures In Cassettes offers hundreds of audiotapes featuring vintage radio classics, including such comedy greats as Amos and Andy, Abbott and Costello, Baby Snooks, The Great Gildersleeve, The Bickersons, Fibber McGee and Molly, Burns and Allen, Jack Benny, Fred Allen, and "My Favorite Husband." If mysteries, thrillers, and crime and punishment are more your line, see the selection of Sherlock Holmes, Arch Oboler's "Lights Out Everybody," Dragnet, This Is Your FBI, The Green Hornet, X-Minus One, and other favorites. And the Western classics are here as well—Hopalong Cassidy, the Lone Ranger, Have Gun Will Travel, and Tales of the Texas Rangers.

The music choices include classical, top-of-the-charts vintage rock and country hits, as well as Broadway's best. The selection of self-help and motivational tapes can help you stop smoking, lose weight, or achieve other goals. Prices of the tapes are comparable to those charged by other discount houses, generally running from $6.98 to $9.98 each.

Adventures In Cassettes is offering readers a discount of 25% on their first order. Be sure to identify yourself as a WBMC reader when you order, and deduct the discount from the cost of the goods only. This WBMC reader discount expires February 1, 1995.

Special Factors: Satisfaction is guaranteed; returns are accepted within 30 days for exchange, refund, or credit; orders are shipped worldwide.

AMERICAN FAMILY PUBLISHERS

P.O. BOX 62111
TAMPA, FL 33662-2111
800-237-2400

Information: inquire
Save: up to 70%
Pay: check or MO
Sells: magazine subscriptions
Store: mail order only

American Family Publishers is a magazine clearinghouse that offers subscriptions to dozens of popular periodicals at rates that are usually much better than those offered by the publishers themselves. In addition to savings, every time you order you'll be entered into the current sweepstakes, which doesn't happen when you buy your magazines at the newsstand. A recent American Family mailing included offers for *Better Homes, Life, People, Golf Digest, TV Guide, Catholic Digest, Time, PC Magazine, Worth,* and *The Family Handyman.* Periodically, American Family features books—*The Columbia University Complete Home Medical Guide,* Rodale's home-improvement series, cookbooks, and other popular reference works have appeared in past mailings, all offered on the company's buying program that allows you to spread payments over four months.

Special Factors: Satisfaction is guaranteed; inquire for information.

THE ASTRONOMICAL SOCIETY

**390 ASHTON AVE.
SAN FRANCISCO, CA
94112
415-337-1100
FAX: 415-337-5205**

Catalog: free
Save: up to 50%
Pay: check, MO, MC, V
Sells: astronomy resources and gifts
Store: mail order only

The Astronomical Society is a not-for-profit organization that was founded in 1889 to support astronomical research and improve the public's appreciation of science, especially astronomy. To further this end, ASP publishes a variety of materials: videotapes, books, charts and maps of the heavens, slides, observing tools, educational items, and astronomy-related gifts. The 48-page catalog features an intriguing collection that includes *The Creation of the Universe,* an enthralling video hosted by Timothy Ferris, Carl Sagan's award-winning *Cosmos* series, the *Starship Earth* 16" celestial globe, and the comprehensive *Norton's 2000.0 Star Atlas and Reference Handbook.* There are breathtaking posters of the planets, a moon phase calendar for the whole year, computer programs that simulate travel through the galaxy, and a number of slide sets covering nebulas and galaxies, the moon, Mars, the solar system, and images of Venus from the voyage of the *Magellan.*

ASP's prices are reasonable but don't seem particularly low ($29.95 for videotapes and $8.95 for posters), until you check the catalogs of supplies for educators selling similar publications. There are school sources charging an astonishing $300-plus for a *single* videotape. So even if you're not in the market for ASP's publications yourself, let your school board or PTA know about this source. Proceeds are used to advance the Society's education programs.

Canadian readers, please note: Only U.S. funds are accepted.

Special Factors: Satisfaction is guaranteed; returns in "as-new" condition are accepted for exchange, refund, or credit; institutional accounts are available; orders are shipped worldwide.

AUDIO HOUSE

4304-G BRAYAN DR.
SWARTZ CREEK, MI 48473
313-655-8639
FAX: 313-655-6817

Catalog: $2, refundable (see text)
Save: up to 50% (see text)
Pay: check, MO, MC, V
Sells: used CDs
Store: mail order only

Audio House has been brokering used CDs to individuals since 1983, and provides you with a great market and great prices—whether you're buying or selling. Audio House publishes a master catalog of CD listings every two months, and releases a ten-page supplement in the off months. A sample costs $2 (refundable with purchase), and a year's subscription is $10 ($12 to Canada). Be sure to request the "$10 in coupons free" (available only to WBMC readers) when you order the subscription, so you can recoup the whole subscription cost when you order. And order you will, because a catalog that opens with 10,000 Maniacs and concludes with Wagner's "Tristan und Isolde" has something for everyone. Audio House offers its stock of 15,000 titles through the catalog only—there is no membership fee. A number of the selections are on more obscure labels, which are generally hard to find anyway. But finding them at an average of about $8 each, guaranteed to play like new, is even better. If you want to cull your own collection, see the catalog for details on selling your used CDs to Audio House.

Canadian readers, please note: Only U.S. funds are accepted, or payment should be made by credit card.

Special Factors: Satisfaction is guaranteed; returns are accepted within 30 days for exchange, refund, or credit; orders are shipped worldwide.

BARNES & NOBLE BOOKSTORES, INC.

126 FIFTH AVE.,
DEPT. 861F
NEW YORK, NY 10011
201-767-7079

Catalog: free
Save: up to 80%
Pay: check, MO, MC, V, AE, DC
Sells: books, tapes, CDs, gifts, etc.
Store: same address; also locations in AZ, CA, CO, CT, FL, IL, MA, MD, MI, MN, NC, NH, NJ, NV, NY, and OH

 (see text)

Barnes & Noble, founded in 1873, considers itself "America's #1 book sale catalog," with prices up to 80% off published rates. In addition, the catalogs feature hundreds of audiotapes, CDs, videotapes, calendars, and other gifts, also at considerable discounts.

The typical Barnes & Noble catalog is 48 to 72 pages of best-sellers, reference works, publishers' overstock, and the firm's own reprints (*The Gentle Art of Verbal Self-Defense* and the collected works of Winston Churchill were among recent offerings). The areas of interest include history, mystery, the arts science, literature, film, medicine, satire, juvenilia, current fiction, linguistics, religion, reference, crafts, and photography. The catalogs also offer a selection of audiotapes and CDs (classical music, jazz, drama, and language tapes), and videotapes from Joseph Campbell's *Transformations of Myth through Time* to *I, Claudius,* from the PBS series. Stunning art books, calendars, lighted globes, beechwood bookshelves, book embossers, statuary, cassette cases and cabinets, and book lights have all appeared in past catalogs.

Canadian and APO/FPO readers, please note: Inquire for shipping charges, and allow extra time for order processing.

Special Factors: Satisfaction is guaranteed; institutional accounts are available; returns are accepted; minimum order is $15 with credit cards

BERKSHIRE RECORD OUTLET, INC.

RR 1, RTE. 102 PLEASANT ST.
LEE, MA 01238-9804
413-243-4080
FAX: 413-243-4340

Catalog: $2
Save: 33% plus
Pay: check, MO, MC, V
Sells: classical recordings
Store: same address; Saturday 11:30–5:30 (call first)

If you're an LP holdout who loves classical music, Berkshire has what you've been looking for. The 182-page catalog lists thousands of classical overstocked and remaindered recordings—LPs, tapes, and compact discs—at savings of 33%-plus on the release prices. It's organized alphabetically by label—from Abbey to Xenophone—and within that, by price groups. Each entry is coded to indicate whether the recording is available in stereo, mono, quadraphonic, or reprocessed stereo (or in digital or analog CD), and the country of origin is noted if the recording is an import. Berkshire is a gold mine for lovers of classical music, although sound tracks, ethnic music, folk songs, and poetry readings also appear. If you're unsure of your choices, find someone who can advise you, since Berkshire isn't keen on second thoughts, stating that "we respectfully ask that you do not attempt to amend your order once it is submitted."

Special Factors: Minimum order is $15 with credit cards; orders are shipped worldwide.

BESTSELLER AUDIO-BOOKS

2302 N. SCOTTSDALE RD.
SCOTTSDALE, AZ 85257
800-BESTSELLER

Catalog: $4.95 (see text)
Save: up to 80% (see text)
Pay: check, MO, MC, V, AE, Discover
Sells: audiotapes
Store: same address; daily 9–9

The growth of the audiotape industry has been a real boon for commuters, persons with impaired vision, and anyone else for whom reading is difficult. But at $10 and up per title, regular listening gets to be pricey fast. And much of what you listen to you'll never feel the urge to hear again. Wouldn't it be nice if you could *rent* audiotapes, like videos?

That's the business of BESTSELLER AUDIOBOOKS, which publishes "The World's Largest Audiobook Catalog," 96 pages with 10,000 audio-tape titles for sale or rent. (A year of monthly issues costs $4.95, which is credited to you with your first order.) The catalog is organized into 94 categories, from "business" to "western," and includes motivational tapes, languages, poetry, politics, smoking cessation, metaphysics, codependency, horror, exercise, tapes for children, and fiction, among others. Each catalog entry includes the title, author, a brief description, purchase and rental prices, tape length, ISBN number, and publisher's name. Rentals begin at just $1.99, though prices generally range from $2.99 to $3.99. Most of the rental rates represent great "buys" compared to the purchase prices: Sidney Sheldon's romantic intrigues rent for $2.99, compared to $15.95 to buy, and Anthony Robbins' motivational "Unlimited Power" home study course rents for $14.99 (purchase price $169.95). The rental fee covers seven or 14 days, clocked from the date you receive the tape by UPS to the date of postmark when you return it (a reusable postpaid mailer is included). A $10 annual membership fee is required to rent the tapes, and because the replacement cost of some runs into three figures, BESTSELLER AUDIOBOOKS also asks for a credit card number. (No deposits or fees are required to purchase tapes.) Your membership fee includes a subscription to the monthly "Listen UpDate," which features new releases and previews of forth-coming publications. And if you have a collection of audiobooks gath-ering dust by your tape deck, you can use them as credit toward your next BESTSELLER AUDIOBOOKS rental or purchase—call for more information.

Special Factor: Returns of defective tapes are accepted within 90 days for exchange.

BOSE® EXPRESS MUSIC®

**THE MOUNTAIN
FRAMINGHAM, MA 01701
800-451-2673
FAX: 508-875-0604**

Catalog: $6, refundable (see text)
Save: see text
Pay: check, MO, MC, V, AE, Discover
Sells: audiotapes, CDs, laser discs, and videotapes
Store: mail order only

Bose® Express Music®, established in 1964, gives you access to virtually every cassette, MD, DCC, and video or laser disc in print. The 288-page catalog includes discount coupons worth about $50 on future orders, and costs $6 (refundable with your first order). As part of your fee, you'll also receive a year of monthly updates and specials. The catalog features extensive listings of rock, pop, R&B, gospel, sound tracks, opera, classical, and Broadway show tunes. Rock videos, workout tapes, and new and old movies are also available, and the selection is diverse—Kiri Te Kanawa shares space with Metallica.

Don't overlook the discount coupons, which reward orders of several items with freebies and extra savings. And regular customers can join the Collectors Club and enjoy bonuses—a free CD, video, or laser disc for every ten purchased at Bose's discount prices (see the catalog for details).

Special Factors: Satisfaction is guaranteed; online with CompuServe; orders are shipped worldwide.

BUTTERNUT BOOKS

**WELL ASSOCIATES, INC.
RD1, BOX 121A
MORRIS, NY 13808
607-263-5620**

Catalog: $2
Save: 15% plus (see text)
Pay: check or MO
Sells: children's books (see text)
Store: mail order only

Butternut Books is a division of WELL Associates, an educational consulting firm that's been in business since 1985. WELL's objectives include the promotion of language development and literacy. Butternut Books—which is devoted to good children's literature—is a natural outgrowth of those goals. The firm's book list represents the choices of the president of the firm, an education professional who's chosen these particular titles because they meet the "Whole Language" approach to learning, are interesting to children, offer appealing story lines, and are well-illustrated. The catalog is organized alphabetically by title, and includes a brief description, as well as noting the author, literary honors, intended age group, and publisher's price for each book. Among those in a recent catalog were several charmers—Vera Williams' *A Chair for My Mother,* Don and Audrey Wood's *Napping House,* and McCloskey's *Blueberries for Sal.* Many of Butternut's choices are winners of Caldecott and Newbery awards, and if you need help with your selection, the staff can advise you and even develop lists of books by theme or idea—a very helpful service for educators. Prices are discounted 15% on orders of $25 or more, and selected sale titles are featured at savings of 30%, 50%, and as much as 70% off list. Butternut is devoted to helping you make the best choices for your needs, whether you're buying for family, friends, play group, or school.

Please note: Orders are shipped via UPS only. Shipping costs in the catalog apply to U.S. orders only.

Special Factors: Institutional accounts are available; quantity discounts are available; minimum order is $25 (see text).

CONSUMER INFOR-MATION CENTER

■■■■■■■■■■

P.O. BOX 100
PUEBLO, CO 81009

Catalog: free
Save: see text
Pay: check or MO
Sells: consumer publications
Store: mail order only

 ¡Si! (see text)

The government's Consumer Information Center was established in 1970 "to help federal agencies promote and distribute useful consumer information." Many of the pamphlets and manuals in the Center's 16-page quarterly catalog are free, and cover such topics as careers and education, child care, federal benefits and laws, food handling and nutrition, health, home building and buying, energy conservation, appliances and electronics, home improvement and safety, travel, hobbies, and money management. You can subscribe to *FDA Consumer* through the Consumer Information Center's catalog, and order pamphlets that help you to learn about ultrasound, find out about Social Security, get tips on buying a mobile home, and obtain government records under the Freedom of Information Act, among other things.

Write for the catalog, if only to order the "Consumer's Resource Handbook," a guide to effective complaint procedures. It lists the best sources of help if you have a problem as a consumer: contacts, addresses, and phone numbers of the customer relations departments of hundreds of major corporations, Better Business Bureau offices worldwide, trade associations, consumer protection offices, and federal agencies. There are over 90 pages of valuable information in the Handbook, at the best possible price—free.

Please note: A Spanish-language catalog of dozens of federal consumer guides in Spanish is also available.

Special Factor: A handling fee is charged on all orders.

CORONET
CDS/CASSETTES
━━━━━━━━━━━

311 BAINBRIDGE ST.
PHILADELPHIA, PA 19147
215-925-2762
FAX: 215-925-1912

Catalog: $2
Save: up to 30% (see text)
Pay: check, MO, MC, V
Sells: CDs, audiotapes, and music videos
Store: mail order only

Coronet sells CDs, audiotapes, and music videos through straightforward catalogs that list the 24,000 available recordings under the artists' names, and includes the manufacturers' code number and Coronet's price. The firm covers the bases, offering rock, pop, rhythm and blues, jazz, country, big bands, movie soundtracks and Broadway shows, and even 1,500 classical music titles. Rock is the featured player, running from ABC and Paula Abdul to ZZ Top. There are lots of great oldies, as well as current releases—Earth, Wind & Fire, Aerosmith, Vanilla Ice, 38 Special, Lou Reed, INXS, Stevie Ray Vaughn, and Indigo Girls are a few of the artists noted in the last catalog, with all or most of their general releases. The performers represent mainstream favorites, and it's hard to resist making out a list while you're reading through the catalog— Coronet has the tapes you always meant to get after you read the reviews, but never did. If world music is more your beat, you'll find it in the catalog supplement, as well as other "alternative" music, imported CDs, and a selection of low-priced CDs and cassettes. Savings generally run up to 30% on list prices.

Special Factor: Orders are shipped worldwide.

CRITICS' CHOICE VIDEO

DEPT. 30058

800 WEST THORNDALE AVE.

ITASCA, IL 60143

800-367-7765

FAX: 708-437-7298

TDD: 800-272-2900

Catalog: free
Save: up to 50% (see text)
Pay: check, MO, MC, V, AE, Discover
Sells: videotapes and laser discs
Store: mail order only

 ¡Si! ©

You don't go to every movie that's released, so why weed through listings of every video in existence just to find what you want? Critics' Choice Video turns something burdensome to your benefit, with a 108-page catalog of over 2,000 titles, culled from tens of thousands. Most of the movies cost under $20, and overstock and sale titles are priced under $10.

Critics' Choice Video has created a good mix of hits, cult favorites, and lesser-known gems, in the categories of movie classics, musicals, drama, foreign films, comedy, family films, action/adventures, great performances, suspense, science fiction, and westerns. Critics' Choice also sells music videos, travel videos, music and dance instruction tapes, classical music and opera performances, fitness tapes, and videos on science, philosophy, language, and even business skills. Disney movies, "Silence of the Lambs," "Backdraft," "Alien 3," "High Society," and "Darkman" are some random picks from a recent catalog; the comprehensive index will help you find exactly what you want. Some of the titles are offered on 8mm video and laser disc as well as VHS video.

Special Factors: Satisfaction is guaranteed; returns are accepted within 30 days for exchange, refund, or credit; Spanish-speaking representatives/TDD service available Monday–Friday 7–7, CST.

CURRENT, INC.

105 EAST WOODMAN RD.
COLORADO SPRINGS, CO
80941
800-525-7170
719-593-5900

Catalog: free
Save: up to 65%
Pay: check or MO
Sells: stationery, wrapping paper, cards, and gifts
Store: outlets in CA, CO, and OR

Current, in business since 1950, publishes a monthly, 60-page color catalog of stationery and cards in appealing designs, many exclusive to Current, ranging from animal and nature scenes to quilt motifs and other Americana. All-occasion and holiday cards are available, as well as notes, stationery, gift wrapping, ribbon, recipe cards and files, toys, games, organizers, calendars, memo boards, mugs, and other gifts. Current's "School Matters" catalog for elementary school teachers offers books, incentives, and classroom decorations. Prices are very reasonable, and discounts are given based on the number of items ordered.

Current's Check Product Division also offers check-printing services: 21 designs, which are priced up to 50% below what your bank probably charges you. And since Current is one of the printers that *banks* use, your checks are guaranteed to be accepted at any U.S. bank. For more information, see the check-printing brochure that's sent with the catalog, or call or write for information.

Special Factors: Satisfaction is guaranteed; sliding discounts of 20% and more are offered on orders of 8 to 12 or more items; returns are accepted.

DAEDALUS BOOKS, INC.

P.O. BOX 9132 (WBM)
HYATTSVILLE, MD
20781-0932
800-395-2665
FAX: 800-866-5578

Catalog: free
Save: up to 90%
Pay: check, MO, MC, V, AE, Discover, Optima
Sells: new and remaindered literary publications
Store: mail order only

Daedalus, founded in 1980, offers fine books from trade publishers and university presses at 50% to 90% off publishers' prices. These remainders have been culled from thousands to appeal to literary readers looking for culture on the cheap. Daedalus isn't *just* remainders, though—about half the catalog is devoted to current titles that are discounted about 20%. And the witty, clearheaded descriptions of each book are reading pleasures in themselves. The categories include literature and general interest, visual and performing arts, philosophy, history, feminism, politics, children's books, travel, cookery, and the social sciences. A gift certificate from Daedalus, presented with the latest edition of the catalog, should delight any serious reader.

Canadian readers, please note: Payment must be made by credit card, a money order drawn in U.S. funds, or a check drawn on a U.S. bank.

Special Factors: Institutional accounts are available; returns are accepted within 30 days; minimum order is $10 with credit cards; orders are shipped worldwide.

DOVER PUBLICATIONS, INC.

DEPT. MC
31 EAST 2ND ST.
MINEOLA, NY 11501-3582
516-294-7000

Catalog: free
Save: up to 50% (see text)
Pay: check or MO
Sells: Dover publications
Store: same address; Monday to Friday 9–3; also 180 Varick St., 9th Floor, New York, NY; Monday to Friday 9–4:30

Many of the firms listed in this book sell selections of Dover books, but if you deal with the publisher directly you can buy any in-print Dover publication. In over half a century of publishing, Dover has built a reputation for books as notable for their quality construction as they are for their content. Dover's catalogs feature paperbacks on crafts and hobbies, Americana, mathematics and physics, American Indian arts, architecture, cooking, games, travel, music, and many other topics. Dover's "Pictorial Archives," featuring designs and graphics, typography, banners and scrolls, borders, etc., and the "Clip-Art Series" are copyright-free art that can be used in newsletters, ads, menus, and the like. Dover's postcard sets run from NASA shots to Tiffany windows, and there are stickers, coloring books, posters, and even gift wrap.

Dover's facsimiles and reprints of rare and valuable texts include a reproduction of an 1864 illustrated catalog of Civil War military goods and the earliest known cookbook, *Cookery and Dining in Imperial Rome,* by Apicius, to cite two. Dover's reprint of the catalog of Gustav Stickley's Mission furniture designs is a standard among antiques dealers, and is probably more widely read now than it was when originally published.

Dover also publishes "Listen & Learn" language tapes, as well as bird song tapes and musical scores by Scriabin, Liszt, Scott Joplin, Couperin, Ravel, Bizet, Brahms, and other greats. The prices are easily up to 50% less than those charged for comparable publications, and there are children's books and literary classics for just $1.

Canadian readers, please note: The shipping surcharge on orders sent to Canada is 20%.

Special Factors: Satisfaction is guaranteed; returns are accepted within ten days for refund; orders are shipped worldwide.

EDITIONS

DESK WM
BOICEVILLE, NY 12412
914-657-7000
FAX: 914-657-8849

Catalog: $2
Save: up to 40%
Pay: check, MO, MC, V
Sells: old, used, and rare books
Store: 153 Rte. 28, Ashokan, NY; daily 10–5; also Rte. 22, Lebanon, NJ; daily 10–6

Editions is a great source for used and out-of-print books, which are often priced 30% to 50% less here than elsewhere. Editions has been selling by mail since 1948, and operates a sprawling store that's stocked with a separate book inventory—worth a stop if you're in the area.

The 64-page monthly catalogs include *partial* listings from a range of categories. For example, the January catalog may list poetry titles from Eliot to Neruda, and February's issue will run from Powys to Wyse. Each catalog lists about 10,000 titles, most priced under $20, from categories that include fiction, literature, history, the social sciences, natural history, travel, women, soldiers and war, the Irish, Americana, British history, theater, philosophy and religion, food, labor, espionage, sports, antiques, gardening, animals, publishing, and Judaica. And it's always interesting to see what ends up in the "Miscellaneous Subjects & Nonsense" section.

Real bargains turn up at Editions, like the collection of Weegee photographs priced at $58 that was offered by a local book dealer for nearly $100, without the dust jacket. The catalogs often list original hardcover titles, in fine condition, at prices lower than those of their paperback editions. Collectors and researchers may wish to see the catalogs for the first editions and books from the Heritage Press and Lakeside Press, as well as the occasional listings of regimental histories, genealogies, and books on local history.

Special Factors: Inquiries by letter only; returns are accepted within three days; orders are shipped worldwide.

FORTY-FIVES

P.O. BOX 358
LEMOYNE, PA 17043-0358

Catalog: $2 and SASE (see text)
Save: up to 50%
Pay: check or MO
Sells: original-label 45rpm records
Store: mail order only

Forty-Fives has been selling vintage and current 45s since 1979, and the firm's closely typed 20-page price list will summon memories you might have thought lost to time. If one of your favorites happened to be "We Gotta Get You a Woman," by Runt, you can get it as a WBMC bonus by ordering just $15 in records here—or you can select one of another of three bonus titles currently available. The catalog lists records released from 1950 through the current year by title and artist and includes a condition rating. Most of the records are Top 40, AM hits of their day, and prices are very low—95% cost $1 to $2 each, and the remainder cost up to about $20. A small selection of LPs is available as well, and a separate country & western price list is available—send $1 and request it by name.

Please note that Forty-Fives asks you to order without enclosing payment; you'll be billed for the records that are still available when your order is received. Orders of $15 or more qualify for the bonus 45—see above. Mention WBMC when you order to be sure to receive the extra record.

Special Factors: Note ordering instructions and pay only when billed for records; minimum order is five records; orders are shipped worldwide.

JESSICA'S BISCUIT

THE COOKBOOK PEOPLE
P.O. BOX 301
NEWTONVILLE, MA 02160
617-965-0530
FAX: 617-527-0113

Catalog: $2, deductible from first order
Save: up to 80% (see text)
Pay: check, MO, MC, V
Sells: cookbooks and food reference
Store: mail order only

Jessica's Biscuit is so discreet about sweetening its luscious catalog with sale books that you might overlook them at first. But they're here—scores of them throughout the 64 color pages of books on cooking, food service, and domestic arts. Jessica's Biscuit is the preeminent catalog for in-print specialty cookbooks and updates on the culinary commandments of the taste dictators. In addition to national cuisines, Jessica's Biscuit offers books with recipes for vegetarian, macrobiotic, microwave, diabetic, gluten-free, low-salt, sugar-free, low-cholesterol, wheat-free, fiber-rich, kosher, and low-cost dishes. There are regional books for everything from soul food to Amish fare, as well as volumes devoted to herbs, muffins, tofu, pizza, biscuits, corn, mushrooms, barbecuing, cheesecake, beans, children's food, chili, garlic, and potatoes. Related topics include professional food service, canning and preserving, outfitting a working kitchen, buffets, wines, and entertaining in style, among others. Savings on the sale titles average 45% and run as high as 80%, and you can deduct the $2 catalog fee from your first order.

Special Factors: Satisfaction is guaranteed; returns are accepted; orders are shipped worldwide.

KICKING MULE RECORDS, INC.

DEPT. W
P.O. BOX 158
ALDERPOINT, CA
  95511-0158
800-262-5312
FAX: 707-926-5250

Catalog: free
Save: up to 85% (see text)
Pay: check, MO, MC, V, Discover
Sells: recordings, music books, videos, etc.
Store: mail order only

Kicking Mule was recommended by a reader for "mostly blues, folk albums with good acoustic guitar, banjo, mandolin, and dulcimer." The firm has been in business since 1972, and features records, tapes, books, and teaching tapes under its own label. Kicking Mule also offers "Lark in the Morning" and other video music lessons and recordings of guitar, banjo, and dulcimer from Flying Fish, Rounder, Schanachie, and Sugar Hill. The 48-page catalog is written by people who really love music—for one, they list all the songs on an album by title. Other catalogs seem to feel that's a waste of space; at Kicking Mule, they know you'll *have* to hear Seth Austen play "Carbolic Rag" as well as the Tennessee Waltz on "Appalachian Fiddle Tunes for Guitar," and Dave Miller's "Star Trek Blues" guitar solo. All this, and prices that average 25% to 40% below list with specials and volume pricing to deepen the discounts to as much as 85% on selected items. (At this writing, records under the firm's label are priced at $2.50, and a grabbag selection of ten guitar LPs costs just $15.)

Kicking Mule is offering readers a discount of 10% on their first order. Be sure to identify yourself as a WBMC reader when you order, and deduct the discount from the cost of the goods only. This WBMC reader discount expires February 1, 1995.

Special Factors: Quantity discounts are available; orders are shipped worldwide.

OLDE METHUEN BOOKSHOPPE

Catalog: $1 each (see text)
Save: up to 50% (see text)
Pay: check, MO, MC, V, AE, Discover
Sells: new and used paperbacks
Store: same address

250 BROADWAY
P.O. BOX 545
METHUEN, MA 01844
508-682-9972

If you like popular fiction but balk at paying $5 for a slim paperback, Olde Methuen Bookshoppe has the answer. This firm's affiliate, Book News, publishes the *Book News* catalog ($1) of historical novels, mysteries and suspense, science fiction, westerns, novels for young adults, romances (including the Harlequin and Silhouette lines), thrillers, and general "contemporary" novels. (Any title in print that's not listed can be special-ordered.) The books are listed at publishers' prices, but you get 10% off when you buy one to nine books, 20% off for orders of ten or more, and 25% on 25 or more books.

You'll save the most, though, with Olde Methuen Bookshoppe, which offers the same range of titles in *used condition,* at prices that run from $1.25 to $6 each, with most books commanding $2 or less. Each of the seven categories has its own catalog ($1), so specify your interest and send proper payment: Used Books—Mystery/Thrillers, Used Books—Romance (Historical and Series), Used Books—Fiction, Used Books—Science Fiction, Used Books—Classics, Used Books—Romance (Regency), and Used Books—Children's titles. To keep prices down, Book News accepts returns under very limited conditions (see below), but will reimburse you for the return postage.

Special Factors: Quantity discounts are available; returns of shipping-damaged, defective, or incorrectly shipped books are accepted for replacement; minimum order is $15 with credit cards; orders are shipped worldwide.

THE POTTERS SHOP INC.

31 THORPE RD.
NEEDHAM HEIGHTS,
  MA 02194
617-449-7687

Catalog: free
Save: up to 75%
Pay: check or MO
Sells: books and videotapes on ceramics and pottery, ceramics tools
Store: same address; Monday to Thursday 9:30–5:30, Friday 9:30–1:30

The Potters Shop, established in 1977, sells books and videotapes on ceramics and pottery at discounts of at least 15%, and as much as 75% on sale titles. The brochure lists hundreds of books and tapes, many of them obscure or hard-to-find imports. You'll find works on pottery technique, historical surveys, profiles of individual potters, ceramics of the East, health and business for the production potter, and even a selection of books for children. Among the videotapes (all VHS) are workshops on raku, form, and technique, and The Potters Shop also sells bamboo and Dolan tools. The firm will search for books, maintains want lists, and buys used books on the pottery and related topics. If you find yourself in Needham Heights, stop in at the shop; the books are there, as well as the pottery of local artisans.
  Special Factors: Orders are shipped worldwide.

PRINT'S GRAPHIC DESIGN BOOK STORE

3200 TOWER OAKS BLVD.
ROCKVILLE, MD
  20852-4216
800-222-2654
301-770-2900
FAX: 301-984-3203

Catalog: free
Save: up to 50% (see text)
Pay: check, MO, MC, V, AE
Sells: books on the graphic arts
Store: mail order only

Print Magazine, which serves the graphic-design community, runs a mail-order bookstore that offers well-chosen manuals, color charts, and other aids and reference materials on a range of design-related topics.

All of the books are discounted, typically 20%, but some are tagged at 30% and 50% below their published prices. The 16-page color catalog offers annuals, clip-art collections, and books on advertising, graphic design, trademarks and logos, computer-based graphics and desktop publishing, illustration, studio protocol, photography, color, and Pantone color manuals and fanfold color guides. You can subscribe to *Print Magazine* through the catalog, and our mailing included an entry form to the magazine's annual regional design competition.

Canadian readers, please note: Only U.S. funds are accepted.

Special Factors: Satisfaction is guaranteed; undamaged returns are accepted within 15 days for exchange, refund, or credit; institutional accounts are available.

PUBLISHERS CLEARING HOUSE

101 WINNERS CIRCLE
PORT WASHINGTON, NY
11050
800-645-9242
516-883-5432

Information: inquire
Save: up to 50%
Pay: check or MO
Sells: magazine subscriptions, books, gifts, etc.
Store: mail order only

Publishers Clearing House primarily acts as an agent for magazine publishers, offering subscriptions to popular and special-interest magazines at savings of up to 50% on regular rates. PCH guarantees lowest to-the-public prices, and a recent mailing featured over 100 periodicals, including *New Woman, Reader's Digest, Consumer Reports, Organic Gardening, Changing Times, Money, TV Guide, Ski, Time,* and *People.* The mailings usually include bonuses, premiums, and sweepstakes, and you can spread payments for your magazines over four months.

Special Factors: Satisfaction is guaranteed; inquire for information; installment plan is available.

PURCHASE FOR LESS

**231 FLORESTA WBM
PORTOLA VALLEY, CA
94028**

Catalog: $2
Save: up to 40%
Pay: check or MO
Sells: books on sewing and quilting
Store: mail order only

Home sewers, and more particularly quilters, will appreciate the collection of pattern books, historical surveys, general reference works, and related titles sold through the 28-page catalog from Purchase for Less. The company's name is based on its other distinguishing feature—discounts of 20% to 40% on publishers' prices. Each book sold here is chosen for its value to the craftsperson who's looking for new designs, techniques, and fresh interpretations of the classics. There are dozens of books on general sewing and serging techniques, fitting clothing, sewing for the home, creating wearable art, and related topics—color harmony, developing a home-based sewing business, and effective time management, for example. And there's one slender $2 volume here that details what's going wrong when the sewing machine "goes crazy"—every sewer on your gift list would appreciate a copy.
Special Factor: Satisfaction is guaranteed.

RECORD-RAMA®
SOUND ARCHIVES

**4981 MCKNIGHT RD.
PITTSBURGH, PA
15237-0595
412-367-7330
FAX: 412-367-7388**

Information: price quote
Save: up to 30%
Pay: check, MO, MC, V, AE, Discover
Sells: vintage 45s, LPs, and CDs
Store: same address; Monday and Thursday 10–9, Tuesday, Wednesday, Friday 10–6, Saturday 10–5

When word reached the Library of Congress that a retired paper goods salesman was claiming to have the country's largest known collection of 45s, a curator was sent over to check it out. Sure enough: Record-Rama Sound Archives, which shares a building with the local Post Office, holds the record with 1.5 *million* oldies on 45s, plus 750,000 LPs. Paul Mawhinney's collection began with his youthful purchase of Frankie Lane's "Jezebel," and an obsession was born.

Mr. Mawhinney isn't sitting on this national treasure; he's created the *MusicMaster®: The 45 RPM Singles Directory,* the ultimate reference on 45's produced from 1947 to 1982. The *MusicMaster,* organized by artist and title, is now the most-used reference in the New York Public Library, and a must-have for any library or serious collector. Record-Rama offers the MusicMaster® Database, and other directories—the *CD-5 Singles Directory* and *The 45 RPM Christmas Singles Directory,* both by artist/title.

Mr. Mawhinney is pragmatic about the changes in the recording industry, and is snapping up CDs with the same dedication he once reserved for 45s. He's already amassed 80,000, and does a tidy business in used CDs. If you're looking for a title, he probably has it—just call and ask, or use his WORLDSEARCH LP and CD locating service.

Please note: Calls are not accepted on the weekends.

Record-Rama is offering readers a discount of 10% on all CDs costing $13.99 or more, except boxed and multiple disks. Be sure to identify yourself as a WBMC reader when you order, and deduct the discount from the cost of the goods only. This WBMC reader discount expires February 1, 1995.

Special Factor: Price quote by phone or letter.

ROCKY MOUNTAIN STATIONERY

11725 CO. RD. 27.3
DOLORES, CO 81323
303-565-8230

Price List: free
Save: up to 50%
Pay: check or MO
Sells: handmade note cards
Store: Piñon Tree, Cortez, and Treasures Unlimited, Ridgeway, CO

Rocky Mountain Stationery is run by Rose Ruland, an artist who presses flowers and leaves from her garden and the surrounding wilds of the Rockies and uses them to create note cards. The cards are small and quite lovely, the flowers artfully arranged on pastel parchment card stock. Ms. Ruland also creates unusual oil "paintings" on cards; the samples we've received show a good eye for color and design.

Rocky Mountain's "Nature" and "Just a Note" series are sold in collections of ten in assorted colors, with envelopes. Each card collection costs $8.95, compared to $2 and up for *individual* cards of the same type sold in gift shops.

Special Factors: Satisfaction is guaranteed; returns are accepted.

THE SCHOLAR'S BOOKSHELF

110 MELRICH RD.
CRANBURY, NJ 08512
609-395-6933
FAX: 609-395-0755

Catalog: free
Save: up to 75%
Pay: check, MO, MC, V
Sells: scholarly and university press books
Store: mail order only

University presses still produce highbrow texts for scholars, but many are of interest—and accessible—to nonprofessionals as well. These books sometimes suffer the same fate as their commercial counterparts—remaindering. The Scholar's Bookshelf, in business since 1974, turns publishing misfortune into intellectual excitement 16 times a year with a wide variety of university press and scholarly imprint remainders. The books are sold at an average of 30% below published prices, although savings can run up to 75%.

The 80-page general sale catalog is packed with concise descriptions of volumes on literature and drama, music, the Civil War, architecture and urban planning, archaeology, art history (ancient to modern), photography, world history and politics, psychology, philosophy, religion, Judaica, and the sciences. Past issues have included *Jane's* reference works on military ships and aircraft, Page Smith's eight-volume history of the United States, the *Atlas of the American Indian,* and other illuminated manuscripts (reproductions) and special editions. History is the strong suit at The Scholar's Bookshelf, and throughout the year the firm produces separate catalogs devoted to world history and militaria, as well as collections of fine art books, literature, and even a four-page broadside of books on baseball!

Special Factors: Returns are accepted within 30 days for exchange, refund, or credit; minimum order is $10, $15 with credit cards; orders are shipped worldwide.

STOREY COMMUNI-
CATIONS, INC.

SCHOOLHOUSE RD.

P.O. BOX 445

POWNAL, VT 05261

802-823-5811

FAX: 802-823-5819

Catalog: $1
Save: up to 30% (see text)
Pay: check, MO, MC, V, AE, Discover
Sells: Country Wisdom Bulletins and books
Store: mail order only

Storey features "books for country living," guides to gardening, cooking, preserving, raising animals, nature appreciation, homesteading, and related topics. Storey can help you learn all about hive management, blacksmithing, composting, organic pest control in the garden, trout fishing, developing a home water supply, raising your own flock of ducks, and outwitting squirrels. The catalog features the Country Wisdom Bulletins, a collection of about 80 manuals that include "all the how-to information you need to easily master dozens of country living skills in 30 minutes or less." The titles illustrate the possibilities of self-reliance: "Building a Solar-Headed Pit Greenhouse," "Drought Gardening," and "Creating a Wildflower Meadow" are examples. The Bulletins are a good buy even at $2.95 each (they're often sold for just $1.50), especially for the person who needs to know the basics, but doesn't have to become an authority on the topic. And even if you're the consummate urbanite, you may find some of the Bulletins of interest, as well as other items—home workshop videos, cookbooks, houseplant guides, and sewing manuals. Prices of the books run from list to 30% off, depending on the title, and the sale items feature further reductions.

Canadian readers, please note: Only U.S. funds are accepted.

Special Factors: Satisfaction is guaranteed; returns are accepted within one year for exchange, refund, or credit; minimum order is $10 with credit cards; C.O.D. orders are accepted; orders are shipped worldwide.

STRAND BOOK STORE, INC.

828 BROADWAY
NEW YORK, NY 10003
212-473-1452
FAX: 212-473-2591

Catalog: free
Save: up to 80%
Pay: check, MO, MC, V, AE, Discover
Sells: new, used, remaindered, and rare books
Store: main store, same address; Monday to Saturday 9:30–9:30, Sunday 11–9:30; also Strand at the Seaport, 159 John St., New York, NY; Monday to Saturday 10–9, Sunday 10–8

Manhattan's legendary Strand Book Store celebrates the printed word with eight miles of books—more than two million volumes—and is believed to be the largest dealer of used and out-of-print books in the U.S. Strand set up shop in 1929, and publishes a number of catalogs that feature samples of its colossal inventory.

The "Specials" catalog, published several times a year, lists thousands of works that run from *The Poetical Works of William Blake* (list price $22.50, Strand's price $5.95) and Irving Penn's *Passage* (list price $100, Strand's price $39.95), to the eight-volume *Le Corbusier's Oeurve Complete* (list price $425, Strand's price $318.95). This catalog includes critique and commentary, biographies, books on art, architecture, philosophy, crafts, politics, food, drama, and other fields of interest. The "Review" catalog, available to institutional accounts, lists new releases at 50% off publishers' prices. (Request this catalog on your institution's letterhead.)

You have to visit to do justice to the Strand, and to find the pricing "accidents"—books ticketed at a few dollars that are worth many times that. (Veteran book collectors who frequent the store can usually produce a few examples.) Strand also has a Rare Books department, with first, fine, and scarce editions, as well as fine bindings and books signed by the author.

Special Factors: Satisfaction is guaranteed; specify catalog desired and request by postcard or letter; want lists are maintained; returns are accepted; orders are shipped worldwide.

SUPERINTENDENT OF DOCUMENTS

U.S. GOVERNMENT PRINTING OFFICE
WASHINGTON, DC
20402-9325
202-783-3238

Catalog: free
Save: up to 30% (see text)
Pay: check, MO, MC, V
Sells: Federal government publications
Store: same address; also U.S. Government bookstores in AL, CA, CO, FL, GA, IL, MA, MD, MI, MO, NY, OH, OR, PA, TX, WA, and WI (see the catalog for locations)

This is probably the only book catalog in the country that could run a subscription offer to *Special Warfare* right before the *1987 Folklife Annual,* followed by *Building a Better America,* George Bush's address to Congress at the beginning of his presidency. These are among past hits from the Superintendent of Documents, whose 48-page catalog offers everything from *Walnut Notes,* a manual for the walnut farmer, to the 54-page *Narcotics Identification Manual.* Back in print is the government's "all time best-seller," *Infant Care,* in an updated edition that costs $4. *The Complete Guide to Home Canning* ($11), *A Citizen's Guide to Radon* ($1), *Health Information for the International Traveler* ($5), and the three-volume *Back-Yard Mechanic* ($7), give you an idea of the government's backlist.

Uncle Sam has taken the time to put together "Making Bag Lunches, Snacks, and Desserts," compile *Letters of Delegates to Congress, 1774–1789,* and help you realize the American dream with the 54-page *Starting and Managing a Business from Your Home* ($1.75). None of the books or pamphlets is free, but many cost under $10 and are real treasure troves of useful information. (Quantity discounts of 25% on orders of 100 of the same title—with some exceptions—are available.) Subscriptions to consumer magazines published by the government can be ordered through the catalog, and there are calendars and a number of posters of American artists' work as well as space shots and maps.

Special Factors: Quantity discounts are available; authorized returns due to Government error are accepted within six months for exchange or credit; institutional accounts are available; orders are shipped worldwide.

TARTAN BOOK SALES

500 ARCH ST., DEPT. N14
WILLIAMSPORT, PA 17705
800-233-8467, EXT. 461
IN CANADA 800-666-9162,
 EXT. 461
FAX: 800-999-6799

Catalog and Brochure: free
Save: up to 74%
Pay: check, MO, MC, V
Sells: new and used books
Store: same address (Brodart Outlet Bookstore); Monday through Friday 10–6, Saturday 10–4

Tartan, a direct-mail division of Brodart Co. that began business in 1960, sells hardbound books that have had short-term library circulation. Only undamaged, popular adult fiction and nonfiction books are offered—no paperbacks, juvenile titles, or reference texts.

Danielle Steele's *Star,* published at $19.95, sold here for $4.49; Philip Roth's *Patrimony* was similarly discounted; and Dr. Stuart Berger's *Forever Young* costs just $4, regularly $17.95. These are a few of many titles listed in the current catalog, which also features other popular fiction, mysteries, romance novels, Westerns, science fiction and adventure, biographies, and self-help books. Tartan provides a great way to get hardbound books for little more than you'd pay for the paperback editions.

Special Factors: Discounts are available; institutional accounts are available; orders are shipped worldwide.

SEE ALSO

A Cook's Wares • cookbooks and videos • **HOME: KITCHEN**
American Musical Supply • books, manuals, and videos on rock & roll technique • **MUSIC**
The American Stationery Co., Inc. • custom-printed stationery, wedding invitations • **GENERAL MERCHANDISE**
Aquatic Supply House • Tetra books on fish topics • **ANIMAL**
Art Express • art-related books, manuals, and videotapes • **ART MATERIALS**
Art Supply Warehouse, Inc. • art-related books and manuals • **ART MATERIALS**
Sam Ash Music Corp. • sheet music • **MUSIC**
Astronomics/Christophers, Ltd. • star charts and manuals on astronomy • **CAMERAS**

Atlanta Thread & Supply • books and manuals on sewing and serging techniques • **CRAFTS**

Bailey's, Inc. • books on logging, chain saw use and maintenance, etc. • **TOOLS**

Baron/Barclay Bridge Supplies • books, cards, and teaching aids for bridge • **TOYS**

Bike Nashbar • manuals on bicycle repair • **SPORTS**

Dick Blick Co. • films, slides, videotapes; arts and crafts manuals • **ART MATERIALS**

Bosom Buddies • books on breastfeeding and maternity topics • **CLOTHING: MOTHER AND CHILD**

Bruce Medical Supply • books on vitamins, health care, and medical topics • **MEDICINE**

Butterbrooke Farm Seed Co-Op • booklets on gardening topics • **FARM**

Campmor • field guides, survival and outdoor guides • **SPORTS**

The Caning Shop • books on seat weaving, upholstery, basketry • **CRAFTS**

Capital Cycle Corporation • factory-repair manuals for BMW cycles • **AUTO**

Caprilands Herb Farm • books on herbs and gardening, making wreaths, and cooking • **FARM**

Ceramic Supply of New York & New Jersey, Inc. • art-related manuals and books on crafts • **ART MATERIALS**

Cheap Joe's Art Stuff • art-related books, manuals, and videotapes • **ART MATERIALS**

Cheap Shot Inc. • reloading manuals • **SPORTS**

Cherry Tree Toys, Inc. • manuals on wood projects and toy making • **CRAFTS**

Clark's Corvair Parts, Inc. • Corvair manuals • **AUTO**

Craft King, Inc. • craft project books • **CRAFTS**

Cycle Goods Corp. • texts on bicycling, repair, and maintenance • **SPORTS**

Daleco Master Breeder Products • books on fish and saltwater fish care and breeding • **ANIMAL**

Defender Industries, Inc. • manuals and videotapes on boating topics • **AUTO**

Dharma Trading Co. • books on textile dyeing, painting, batiking, etc. • **CRAFTS**

The Dog's Outfitter • books and videotapes on dogs, cats, horses, etc. • **ANIMAL**

Econo-Vet • vet and pet manuals • **ANIMAL**

EduCALC Corporation • computer books and programs • **OFFICE: COMPUTING**

Elderly Instruments • folk, rock, and esoteric recordings, songbooks, history, and manuals • **MUSIC**

The Fiber Studio • books on knitting, spinning, dyeing, and weaving • **CRAFTS**

Frank's Cane and Rush Supply • books on basketry, seat weaving, upholstery, etc. • **CRAFTS**

A.I. Friedman • *art-related books, manuals, and videotapes* • **ART MATERIALS**

Gander Mountain, Inc. • *videotapes on hunting and fishing topics* • **SPORTS**

Giardinelli Band Instrument Co., Inc. • *records and books on music* • **MUSIC**

Gohn Bros. • *Amish and country cookbooks, quilting books* • **CLOTHING**

Goldberg's Marine Distributors • *manuals and videotapes on boating topics* • **AUTO**

Marv Golden Discount Sales, Inc. • *aviation flight guides and binders* • **AUTO**

Golfsmith International, Inc. • *texts on golf club making and repair, golfing, etc.* • **SPORTS**

Great Northern Weaving • *books on shirret, rug weaving, and rug braiding* • **CRAFTS**

H & R Company • *reference books on computing and technical topics* • **SURPLUS**

IMPCO, Inc. • *Mercedes-Benz car maintenance manuals* • **AUTO**

Jerry's Artarama, Inc. • *art-related books, manuals, and videotapes* • **ART MATERIALS**

The Kennel Vet Corp. • *manuals and books on dogs, cats, and horses* • **ANIMAL**

E.C. Kraus Wine & Beermaking Supplies • *books on wine- and beer-making* • **FOOD**

Lixx Labelz • *custom-designed bookplates* • **GENERAL MERCHANDISE**

Lone Star Percussion • *books on drumming and percussion recordings* • **MUSIC**

M&E Marine Supply Company, Inc. • *books and manuals on boating* • **AUTO**

Mandolin Brothers, Ltd. • *music books, audiotapes, videotapes, and sheet music* • **MUSIC**

Mass. Army & Navy Store • *survival manuals and outdoor guides* • **SURPLUS**

Master Animal Care • *veterinary handbooks* • **ANIMAL**

Mellinger's Inc. • *books on gardening, farming, landscaping, food preservation, etc.* • **FARM**

Metropolitan Music Co. • *manuals and plans for making and repairing stringed instruments* • **MUSIC**

Model Expo, Inc. • *books on ship models, naval history, maritime topics* • **CRAFTS**

National Educational Music Co., Ltd. • *music software* • **MUSIC**

New England Cheesemaking Supply Company, Inc. • *publications on making cheese* • **HOME: KITCHEN**

Newark Dressmaker Supply, Inc. • *patterns, books, and guides on needlework and other crafts* • **CRAFTS**

Office Depot, Inc. • business manuals • **OFFICE**

Omaha Vaccine Co., Inc. • books on care and breeding of horses, livestock, dogs, and cats • **ANIMAL**

Orion Telescope Center • star charts and manuals on astronomy • **CAMERAS**

Overton's Sports Center, Inc. • windsurfing books and videotapes • **SPORTS**

Patti Music Company • sheet music • **MUSIC**

Pet Warehouse • books and manuals on dogs, cats, birds, and fish • **ANIMAL**

Porter's Camera Store, Inc. • books and videos on photography • **CAMERAS**

ProAm Seat Warehouse • car manuals • **AUTO**

Retired Persons Services, Inc. • health-care manuals • **MEDICINE**

Rick's Movie Graphics • movie posters and ephemera • **ART & ANTIQUES**

S&W Framing Supplies, Inc. • books on framing • **ART MATERIALS**

Sailboard Warehouse, Inc. • windsurfing books and videotapes • **SPORTS**

Sax Arts & Crafts • art-related books, manuals, and videotapes • **ART MATERIALS**

Scope City • star charts, books, manuals • **CAMERAS**

Serge & Sew Notions & Fabrics • books and videos on sewing and serging techniques • **CRAFTS**

Shar Products Company • sheet music, classical music videotapes, and audio cassettes • **MUSIC**

Solar Cine Products, Inc. • books on photography • **CAMERAS**

R.C. Steele Co. • AKC dog show videotapes, manuals for pet professionals • **ANIMAL**

Straw Into Gold, Inc. • Folkwear patterns and books on textile crafts • **CRAFTS**

Sultan's Delight, Inc. • cookbooks featuring Middle Eastern and Greek cuisine • **FOOD**

That Fish Place • books on aquariums, fish, and related topics • **ANIMAL**

Think Ink • guides to Print GOCCO printers • **CRAFTS**

Tool Crib of the North • shop manuals, woodworking guides, and videos • **TOOLS**

Tools on Sale™ • woodworking and construction books, manuals, and videos • **TOOLS**

Turnbaugh Printers Supply Co. • texts on printing • **OFFICE**

Turner Greenhouses • books on gardening • **FARM**

United Pharmacal Company, Inc. • manuals and tapes on animal training and breeds • **ANIMAL**

University Products, Inc. • preservation supplies for book collections, references (books and videos) on archival conservation • **OFFICE: SMALL BUSINESS**

Wag-Aero, Inc. • aviation manuals • **AUTO**

Walnut Acres Organic Farms • *natural foods and vegetarian cookbooks* • **FOOD**

Weinkrantz Musical Supply Co., Inc. • *student music books and cassettes* • **MUSIC**

West Manor Music • *small selection of music manuals* • **MUSIC**

Wholesale Tool Co., Inc. • *shop manuals* • **TOOLS**

CAMERAS, PHOTOGRAPHIC AND DARKROOM EQUIPMENT, OPTICS, FILM, AND SERVICES

Equipment, supplies, and services

In the highly competitive camera market, even major electronics outlets with small camera departments can usually offer good discounts on list price. In addition to cameras, bulbs, and film, large camera houses carry video equipment, lighting equipment, screens, film editors, splicers, batteries, projection tables, lenses, filters, adapters, cases, darkroom outfits, chemicals, and custom photofinishing services—at discounts averaging 40%. Even if you don't need custom work done, you can have your film processed, enlargements made, slides duplicated, and other services done by a discount mail-order lab for half the price often charged by a drugstore or retail outlet.

Even at a discount, photographs cost something—but their value is usually personal. Keep them out of "magnetic" photo albums, which are made with polyvinyl-film that gives off vinyl chloride gas, and cardboard pages that exude peroxide vapors. Both can cause deterioration of slides and prints. Some conservationists believe that an entire generation of family photos is being destroyed by toxic albums and by being stored in garages, attics, and basements. (Photographs should be kept in temperate, relatively dry areas, out of light as much as possible.) To preserve your pictures, use archival-quality materials—acid-free albums and storage boxes, Mylar sheet protectors, "safe" slide sheets, etc. These and other conservation materials are available from University Products, listed in the "Small Business" section of "Office."

THE GREY MARKET

Grey-market goods, also known as "parallel" or "direct" imports, are products intended for sale in other countries. They're usually imported outside manufacturer-approved distribution channels, without authorization of the U.S. trademark owner. Grey-market goods are usually less expensive than their "authorized" counterparts, and although they may be just as good, they may also be produced under different quality-control standards, contain ingredients not approved for such use in the U.S., or have a warranty that is not honored in the U.S.

Many of the firms selling grey-market goods to consumers failed to inform them of the fact, and problems arose when products didn't perform properly, or couldn't be repaired in the U.S. Consumers turned to the U.S. manufacturers, who had no legal obligation to service the goods, but who often tried to make good to preserve a positive image. The manufacturers then turned to the courts to solve the problem.

Grey-market goods are of concern because of potential hazards: The door of a luxury car, "reinforced" by the importer with a broomstick in order to appear to meet U.S. safety standards; the batteries that will leak into the kids' toys because they were left in a hot warehouse for a month; the perfume spray propelled by Freon and the night cream adulterated with an illegal dye—all are examples of grey-market goods that could cause harm.

Champions of parallel imports say they promote competition and keep prices down, but the potential problems make them hard to recommend. So grey-marketers are not knowingly listed in this edition of WBMC. Note that companies can change selling policies, so if you want to be sure a firm is an authorized distributor of a product, call the manufacturer. Ask the mail-order company whether the warranty is honored by the service centers of the *U.S. manufacturer.* And make your purchase by credit card, which gives you certain protections under the Fair Credit Billing Act. See page 569 for more information.

FIND IT FAST

BINOCULARS • *Astronomics/Christophers, Mardiron, Orion, Scope City*
CAMERAS • *Ewald-Clark, Porter's, Solar Cine, Westside Camera*
PHOTO PROCESSING • *Ewald-Clark, Owl Photo, Skyline, Solar Cine*
TELESCOPES • *Astronomics/Christophers, Mardiron, Orion, Scope City*

ASTRONOMICS/ CHRISTOPHERS, LTD.

2401 TEE CIRCLE, SUITE 106-W94
NORMAN, OK 73069
800-422-7876 (TELE-SCOPES)
800-356-6603 (BINOCU-LARS AND SPOTTING SCOPES)

Catalogs: $1 and SASE
Save: up to 50%
Pay: check, MO, MC, V, AE, Discover
Sells: telescopes and optics
Store: same address; Monday to Friday 9:30–5, Saturday by appointment

Astronomics/Christophers sells top names in telescopes and birding equipment, including complete lines for astronomical photography, at up to 50% below list. The firm's information-packed birding and astronomical catalogs are sent free if you specify which one you want, and send $1 and a self-addressed, business-sized envelope. Astronomics/ Christophers was established in 1970, and sells no grey-market goods.

Astronomics sells optics and accessories by Astromedia, Bausch & Lomb, Bushnell, Celestron, DayStar, Dover, Edmund, Fujinon, Kowa, Leica (Leitz), Lumicon, Meade, Mirador, MotoFocus, Nikon, Optolyth, Pentax, Questar, Sky Publishing, Steiner, Swarovski, Swift, TeleVue, Vernonscope, and Zeiss. If you're looking for a telescope, choose from catadioptric, refractor, and reflector models, as well as lenses, mirrors, eyepieces, tripods, photo adapters, visual and photographic filters, equatorial mounts and wedges, spotting scopes for bird watching, and many other items. Astronomical and bird-watching binoculars are also offered, and Astronomics/Christophers offers a great collection of books and star charts, manuals, slides, maps, atlases, and other reference tools.

Special Factors: Shipping is included on prepaid orders delivered within the continental U.S.; minimum order is $25; orders are shipped worldwide.

CLARK COLOR LABS

P.O. BOX 96300
WASHINGTON, DC 20090

Mailers: free
Save: up to 65% (see text)
Pay: check or MO
Sells: film-processing and enlargement services
Store: mail order only

Clark Color Labs is a prominent mail-order film processor that develops 110, 126, 127, 620, disc, 35mm, and disposable cameras, as well as slides and movies. You can also order reprints and enlargements (wallet size to 11" by 14") from negatives and slides, have copy negatives made from prints (color and black-and-white), and buy fresh film (Agfa and Kodak). Clark Color Labs uses the Colorwatch system, which means the paper, chemicals, and quality-control standards are all from Kodak. Clark's prices are much lower than those charged by minilabs, averaging 15¢ for one processed print compared to 40¢ for the same print from a typical minilab. Clark Color Lab has a dozen locations around the country to expedite your order, issues credit for unprintable negatives, and will give you a refund or credit if you're not completely satisfied with your pictures.

Special Factor: Returns are accepted for exchange, refund, or credit.

EWALD-CLARK

ATTN: DON
17 W. CHURCH AVE.
ROANOKE, VA 24011
703-342-1829
FAX: 703-345-9943

Information: price quote (see text)
Save: 30% average
Pay: check, MO, MC, V
Sells: cameras, darkroom equipment, optics, services
Store: same address; Monday to Friday 8:30–5:30; also 2140 Colonial Ave., Roanoke, and 213 Draper Rd., Blacksburg, VA

Ewald-Clark is a full-service photography center that has over 40 years of experience in the field. In addition to cameras, lenses, darkroom equipment, and finishing services, Ewald-Clark sells binoculars and video cameras. Discounts run from 2% to 40%, and average 30% off list prices. Among the available brands are Amphoto, Beseler, Bogen, Bronica, Canon, Fuji Professional, Gitzo, Gossen, Gralab, Hasselblad, Hoya, Ilford, Kodak, Logan, Lumedyne, Mamiya, Minolta, Nikon, Novatron, Pelican, Phillips CDI, Polaroid, Quantum, Ricoh, Samsung, Samyang, Tamrac, Tamron, Tiffen, Tokina, Toyo, and Vivitar. There is no catalog—call or write for a price quote on specific models. You can also inquire for rate and specifications on custom photofinishing services.

Please note: Shipments to non-U.S. destinations are subject to hazardous materials regulations.

Special Factors: Price quote by phone or letter with SASE; orders are shipped worldwide.

MARDIRON OPTICS

THE BINOCULAR PLACE
4 SPARTAN CIRCLE,
  DEPT. WBMC
STONEHAM, MA 02180
617-938-8339

Brochures and Price Lists: 2 first-class stamps
Save: 40% average
Pay: check or MO
Sells: binoculars, spotting and astronomical telescopes, and microscopes
Store: mail order only

Mardiron, in business since 1983, sells binoculars, spotting scopes, astronomical telescopes, night-vision scopes, theater glasses, microscopes, ship's clocks, and nautical instruments from a select group of manufacturers at savings of up to 45% on list prices. Mardiron features goods from Aus Jena, Bausch & Lomb, Bushnell, Kona, Minolta, Pentax, and Swift, and offers Steiner military and fully integrated compass binoculars. To receive the price lists and literature, send two first-class stamps, and please mention the line or model that interests you.

Special Factors: Price quote by phone or letter with SASE; shipping is included.

MYSTIC COLOR LAB

MASON'S ISLAND RD.
P.O. BOX 144
MYSTIC, CT 06355-9987
800-367-6061

Mailers: free
Save: up to 30% (see text)
Pay: check or MO
Sells: film-processing and enlargement services
Store: mail order only

Mail-order film labs abound, but Mystic is one that's gotten good marks in quality comparisons with other labs, and Mystic offers an added benefit: free shipping in postpaid mailers, and no handling charges. Mystic Color Lab's prices on processing film, with one set of standard-size prints, are up to 30% below those of other mail-order labs—and considerably less than the one-hour minilabs. But Mystic does its best to come close to the minilab turnaround time, by pledging to get your processed film and prints in the mail to you within 24 hours of receipt. Mystic not only develops 110, 126, disc, and 35mm color and black-and-white film, but also makes enlargements (to 20" by 30" posters) and slides, and sells its own brand of film: 200 ASA three-packs, 24 exposures each roll, cost $7.95. The ordering instructions are clear and the mailers are easy to use, and Mystic's good picture quality and handling has been established by an independent testing organization.

Special Factor: Shipping is included.

ORION TELESCOPE CENTER

DEPT. WBM
P.O. BOX 1158
SANTA CRUZ, CA
95061-1158
800-447-1001
IN CA 800-443-1001
FAX: 408-464-0466

Catalog: free
Save: up to 40%
Pay: check, MO, MC, V
Sells: telescopes, binoculars, and accessories
Store: 2450 17th Ave., Santa Cruz, CA; Monday to Saturday 10–5:30; also 10555 S. De Anza Blvd., Cupertino, and 3609 Buchanan St., San Francisco, CA

 (see text)

Orion brings you stellar savings on top-quality telescopes and accessories through an informative, 76-page catalog that includes sidebars on telescope selection and sky watching, as well as complete product descriptions. Orion, in business since 1975, stocks astronomical and terrestrial telescopes, including spotting, reflector, refractor, guide, finder, and "deep sky" scopes by Celestron, Orion, and TeleVue. If you visit Orion's stores, you'll also find goods by Bushnell, Fujinon, Minolta, Nikon, Optolyth, Pentax, Swift, and Zeiss. Camera adapters, filters, lenses, optical tubes, tripods, eyepieces, star charts, books, and other accessories are available, and Orion also carries binoculars—deep-sky, sport, folding, waterproof, and armored models—as well as spotting scopes for sport and nature enthusiasts.

Please note: Orion ships only to the U.S. and Canada.

Special Factors: Satisfaction is guaranteed; price quote by phone or letter for institutional orders.

OWL PHOTO CORP.
■■■■■■■■■■

701 E. MAIN ST.
WEATHERFORD, OK 73096
405-772-3353
FAX: 405-772-5804

Mailers: free
Save: up to 40%
Pay: check, MO, MC, V
Sells: film processing and reprinting services
Store: same address; Monday to Friday 7:30–5, Saturday 9–1

Owl Photo offers reasonably priced film processing services by mail, and will send you self-mailers on request. Owl will develop your color and black-and-white film at prices that are competitive with discount drug store processing, and you can also order reprints and fresh film— a price list comes with the mailer. Disc, 110, 120, 126, 127, 135, 616 color (C-41), and 620 film is processed, and reprint sizes run up to 11" by 14". Owl uses Kodak paper and chemicals, and guarantees your satisfaction or your processing costs and postage will be refunded.

Special Factors: Satisfaction is guaranteed; returns are accepted for refund or credit; orders are shipped worldwide.

PORTER'S CAMERA STORE, INC.

**P.O. BOX 628
CEDAR FALLS, IA 50613
FAX: 800-221-5329**

Catalog: free (see text)
Save: 35% average
Pay: check, MO, MC, V, Discover
Sells: cameras and darkroom equipment
Store: 323 Viking Rd., Cedar Falls, IA; Monday to Saturday 9:30–5:30

Porter's has been selling photographic and darkroom equipment since 1914, and publishes a 120-page tabloid catalog packed with an enormous range of photographic products, at prices up to 67% below list. Both amateurs and professionals will appreciate the buys on cameras and lenses, filters, darkroom equipment, film, bags and cases, batteries, studio equipment, chemicals, paper, and much more. The brands run from Agfa to Vivitar, the sales policy is clearly detailed in the catalog, and Porter's has even deputized one of its staff to answer your questions about equipment. A separate video catalog is also available. If you're in Cedar Falls, drop by the warehouse outlet store where you'll find everything tagged at catalog prices—a welcome departure from the two-tier policies prevailing at most discount stores.

Canadian readers, please note: The catalog costs $3 in *Canadian funds,* but orders must be paid in U.S. funds. The catalog describes purchasing procedures and includes a shipping rate chart.

Please note: The catalog costs $10 in U.S. funds if sent to an address without a U.S. or Canadian postal code.

Special Factors: Price quote by phone or letter; authorized returns are accepted; institutional accounts are available; orders are shipped worldwide ($100 minimum order).

SCOPE CITY

679 EASY ST.
SIMI VALLEY, CA 93065
805-522-6646
FAX: 805-582-0292

Catalogs: $7, refundable (see text)
Save: up to 45%
Pay: check, MO, MC, V, AE, Discover, Optima
Sells: telescopes, binoculars, microscopes, and other optics
Store: same address; Monday to Friday 9–6, Saturday 10–6; also Phoenix, AZ; Torrance, Costa Mesa, Riverside, San Diego, and Sherman Oaks, CA; also Las Vegas, NV

Scope City has been selling telescopes, binoculars, spotting scopes, and other optics since 1976. Telescopes and accessories by Celestron, Edmund, Parks, Questar, and TeleVue are available, as well as field and specialty binoculars by Bausch & Lomb, Leica, Optolyth, Parks, Pentax, Swarovski, and other manufacturers. Scope City also offers lenses, eyepieces, adapters, mirrors, star charts, manuals, and other reference tools. Most of the prices are discounted, and savings of up to 45% are possible on selected telescope components. If you know the model you want, you can call for a price quote, or send $7 for the catalog package, which is deductible from your first purchase.

Special Factors: Satisfaction is guaranteed; returns are accepted within 30 days for exchange, refund, or credit; orders are shipped worldwide.

SKRUDLAND PHOTO

5311 FLEMING CT.
AUSTIN, TX 78744
512-444-0958

Mailers: free
Save: up to 50%
Pay: check or MO
Sells: film processing and reprinting services
Store: mail order only

Skrudland Photo has performed well in tests of mail-order film processors, and offers low prices—as little as $2 a roll—for color film processing (with one set of prints, glossy or matte). In addition to developing 110, 126, Disc, and 35mm film, Skrudland can make prints and enlargements from your negatives, and develop your slides and Super 8 movies. The film mailers (available on request) include prices and the standard liability disclaimer used by most mail-order film processors.

Special Factors: Satisfaction is guaranteed; returns are accepted for credit.

SKYLINE COLOR LAB

9016 PRINCE WILLIAM ST.,
   DEPT. WBMC
MANASSAS, VA 22110
703-631-2216
FAX: 703-631-8064

Catalog: free
Save: up to 30%
Pay: check, MO, MC, V, AE
Sells: film processing
Store: same address; Monday to Friday 9–6, Saturday 8–2

 (see text)

Skyline Color Lab, whose parent firm has been in business since 1945, is a full-service professional and commercial mail-order lab that offers film and slide processing, negative duplication and slide copying, prints, and photographic packages (portraits and weddings) at competitive prices. Skyline's 24-page catalog lists the available services and prices, includes directions for cropping, and features a helpful glossary of terms like "internegative," "dodging," and "push/pull processing." Skyline will process your color or black-and-white film (roll or sheet), produce contact sheets, make prints and enlargements (from 3-1/2" by 5" to 48" by 144"), and create murals and photographic displays (from 40" square to 48" by 96"; larger sizes are available on a custom basis). Custom services are offered, including "push" processing to compensate for underexposed film, glass mounts for slides, slide remounting, duplicate negatives and negatives made from slides or transparencies (internegatives), a choice of finishes for enlargements (canvas, pebble, matte, or luster), dry mounting of prints (on art board, foam core, or "gator" foam), mounting on canvas panels or canvas stretchers, and printing for backlit display. Skyline has also put together economical print packages, including a "relative's special"—one 8" by 10", two 5" by 7", and 24 wallet-sized prints—perfect for sending to friends and family—as well as wedding album packages. Complete details of the firm's sales policy and guarantees are given in the catalog.

Special Factors: Liability for damaged or lost film is limited to replacement with unexposed film; minimum order is $25; C.O.D. orders are accepted (for delivery within continental U.S.).

SOLAR CINE PRODUCTS, INC.

4247 SOUTH KEDZIE AVE.
CHICAGO, IL 60632
800-621-8796
312-254-8310
FAX: 312-254-4124

Catalog: free
Save: up to 40%
Pay: check, MO, MC, V, DC, Discover
Sells: photo equipment, supplies, and services
Store: same address; Monday to Friday 8:30–5, Saturday 9–1

 ¡Sí!

Solar Cine's 24-page catalog gives a sample of the thousands of items carried by the company—a full range of photographic equipment and accessories from a large number of manufacturers. Solar Cine has been supplying professionals and serious amateurs since 1937, and stocks a full range of still and movie equipment, including videotapes and video batteries. Range Finder cameras, lenses, studio lights, light meters, tripods, and darkroom materials are available from Canon, Fuji, Kalimar, Kiwi, Kodak, Minolta, Pentax, Polaroid, Smith-Victor, and Vivitar, among others. Scores of books on photography for beginners and professionals are available, as well as electronics and processing services (movies, slides, reprints, and prints). The services are described in the catalog; for more information on cameras and equipment, call or write for a price quote.

Special Factors: Returns (except defective goods) are subject to a restocking fee.

SEE ALSO

Berry Scuba Co. • *underwater cameras* • **SPORTS**
Cabela's Inc. • *binoculars and spotting scopes* • **SPORTS**
Central Skindivers • *underwater cameras* • **SPORTS**
Defender Industries, Inc. • *binoculars and marine optics* • **AUTO**
S & S Sound City • *cameras, accessories, binoculars, telescopes, etc.* • **APPLIANCES**
20th Century Plastics, Inc. • *photo storage sheets and albums* • **OFFICE**
University Products, Inc. • *archival-quality storage materials for photographs, slides, film, negatives, microfiche, etc.* • **OFFICE: SMALL BUSINESS**
Wiley Outdoor Sports, Inc. • *binoculars, spotting scopes, etc.* • **SPORTS**

CLOTHING, FURS, AND ACCESSORIES

Clothing, furs, and accessories for men,

women, and children

The firms listed here sell a wide range of clothing for men, women, and children—Amish clothing from Indiana, lingerie from New York City's Lower East Side, swimsuits that have qualified for the Olympics, executive suiting, custom-made deerskin coats and jackets, and much more—at savings of up to 90%.

Clothing that's made in the U.S.A. must bear labels that provide specific information on cleaning and care. The Federal Trade Commission has compiled "What's New About Care Labels," a booklet defining the terms used in the labeling that answers a number of typical consumer questions. For a copy, request it by title from the Federal Trade Commission, Public Reference Office, Washington, DC 20580. If you want to make the best of what you own, you'll appreciate *Taking Care of Clothes,* by Mablen Jones (St. Martin's Press, 1982). It can help you evaluate clothing before purchase, and gives tips on stain removal, laundering, dry cleaning, ironing and pressing, storage, and caring for leather, fur, and other special materials. You can also get it from the horse's mouth: The Neighborhood Cleaners' Association (NCA) publishes the "Consumer Guide to Clothing Care," a brochure of tips on the care and cleaning of different fabrics and trims. Send a long, self-addressed, stamped envelope to NCA, 116 E. 27th St., New York, NY 10016, for the pamphlet.

FIND IT FAST

HATS • **Manny's Millinery**
MEN'S CLOTHING • **Jos. A Bank, Deerskin Trading Post, Paul Fredrick,**

Huntington, James River, Lee-McClain, Quinn's Shirt Shop
SHEEPSKIN, DEERSKIN, AND FUR • Arctic Sheepskin, Deerskin Place, Deerskin Trading Post, Mid-Western Sport Togs
SPORTSWEAR • L'eggs Catalog, No Nonsense Direct, Sportswear Clearinghouse
UNDERWEAR AND HOSIERY • Chock, Goldman & Cohen, James River, L'eggs Catalog, National Wholesale, No Nonsense Direct, Petticoat Express
UNIFORMS • Tafford
WESTERN WEAR • Vanderbilt's
WOMEN'S CLOTHING • Arielle, Jos. A. Bank, Final Edition, L'eggs Catalog, No Nonsense Direct, Ultimate Outlet
WORK CLOTHING • Cahall's, Gohn, Sara Glove, Todd, Vanderbilt's

---

ARCTIC SHEEPSKIN OUTLET

565 CO. RD. T, BOX WB
HAMMOND, WI 54015
800-428-9276
800-362-9276 (CHIPPEWA
  FALLS)
715-796-2292
FAX: 715-796-2295

Brochure: $2, refundable
Save: up to 60%
Pay: check, MO, MC, V, Discover
Sells: sheepskin clothing and accessories
Store: 30 miles east of St. Paul on I-94 at the Hammond exit; also U.S. Hwy. 53 at Hwy. 124 South, Chippewa Falls, WI; Monday to Saturday 9–5, Thursday 9–8

Arctic Sheepskin Outlet was founded in 1987 by the energetic Joseph Bacon, who's been quite successful with mail-order skylights and insulated glass panels (see the listing of Arctic Glass & Window Outlet in the "Maintenance" chapter of "Home"). His Arctic Sheepskin Outlet features sheepskin favorites—slippers, mittens, hats, car seat covers, rugs, etc.—from the largest sheepskin tannery in the world. Savings vary from item to item; rubber-soled sheepskin moccasins sell here and elsewhere at $49.95, but the car seat covers are real buys at $29.95, as are mittens for $15.95, kids' slippers for $12.95, and deep-pile sheepskin rugs from $39.95—about half the going rate. There are also hats with earflaps, sheepskin headbands, steering wheel covers, and bicycle seat covers. All purchases are covered by Arctic's "money-back guarantee."
  Arctic Sheepskin Outlet is offering readers a discount of 10% on their

first order. Be sure to identify yourself as a WBMC reader when you order, and deduct the discount from the cost of the goods only. This WBMC reader discount expires April 1, 1995.

Special Factors: Satisfaction is guaranteed; returns are accepted for exchange, refund, or credit; minimum order is $5; orders are shipped worldwide.

ARIELLE

3131 RANDALL PKWY.
WILMINGTON, DE 28410
919-251-8555
FAX: 919-343-1971

Catalog: free
Save: up to 35%
Pay: check, MO, MC, V, AE, Discover
Sells: women's clothing and accessories
Store: mail order only

Arielle's 82-page color catalog features good-quality separates for play and work, at prices up to 35% below those charged for comparable styles in other catalogs. The emphasis at Arielle is on casual wear, with relaxed looks dominating the catalog, but there are pages of very attractive outfits for the office—shells, shirts, skirts, blazers, etc.—as well as dresses and suits. The color selection is great, and sizes run from S to XL, 6 to 18 in misses, and 4 to 14 in petite.

Special Factors: Satisfaction is guaranteed; returns are accepted for exchange, refund, or credit.

JOS. A. BANK CLOTHIERS, INC.

500 HANOVER PIKE,
DEPT. WBMC
HAMPSTEAD, MD 21074
800-285-BANK
FAX: 410-239-5911

Catalog: $1
Save: up to 30%
Pay: check, MO, MC, V, AE
Sells: men's and women's career clothing and sportswear
Store: 50 stores in 29 states (locations are listed in the catalog)

Bank's business is executive suiting, which it serves with separate catalogs for men and women. Fine tailoring details and prices up to 30% below comparable goods—but not "discount"—distinguish the company's offerings. The men's catalog features suits, jackets, pants, shirts, ties, accessories, weekend separates, and underwear. The suits are handsomely executed in fine wool worsteds, in pin and chalkline stripes, glen plaids, and herringbones. Chesterfield and cashmere top-coats, tuxedos and formal wear, blazers, tweed jackets, and comple-menting pants and shirts are among the standards, and swatches are available for the suits and sports coats. Braces, silk ties, shoes, and pajamas are sold as well.

The offerings in the women's catalog include fine business ensem-bles in the "relaxed traditional" style—belted suits, double-breasted coatdresses, and wool gabardine skirts paired with Chanel-style jackets are a few examples from past catalogs. Some of the women's clothing is offered in petites and talls, as well as regular sizes. Scarves, belts, jewelry, bags, and coordinated weekend separates are also available. Bank's garments often compare well to similar garments sold elsewhere for more. But note that Bank is recommended more for its selection of fine apparel than for its prices, and *do not ask for discounts*.

Special Factors: Satisfaction is guaranteed; returns are accepted for exchange, refund, or credit.

CAHALL'S BROWN DUCK CATALOG

P.O. BOX 450-WM
MOUNT ORAB, OH 45154
513-444-2094

Catalog: $1
Save: up to 40%
Pay: check, MO, MC, V, Discover
Sells: working clothing and footwear
Store: Cahall's Work Wear Store; 112 S. High St., Mount Orab, OH; Monday to Sat-urday 9–6

The Cahall family opened its department store in 1946, and took the leap into mail order nearly 30 years later with the "Brown Duck Cata-log" of heavy-duty apparel and footwear. You'll find your favorites—jeans, shirts, jackets, and overalls—at savings of up to 40% on suggested list or retail prices. Popular lines from Carhartt, Hanes, Key, Jerzees, Levi, OshKosh, Wolverine, Wrangler, and other well-known manufacturers are available. Cahall's also offers an excellent selection of work shoes and boots for men and women from LaCrosse and other names, in hard-to-find sizes. If you don't see the style or model of a garment or footwear you're looking for in the catalog, call—it may be available. Heavy-duty socks, work gloves, bandannas, T-shirts, hats, and even nail aprons are sold, too.

Special Factors: Satisfaction is guaranteed; returns are accepted for exchange, refund, or credit; orders are shipped worldwide.

CHOCK CATALOG CORP.

74 ORCHARD ST.,
    DEPT. WBMC
NEW YORK, NY
    10002-4594
212-473-1929
FAX: 212-473-6273

Catalog: $1
Save: up to 35%
Pay: check, MO, MC, V
Sells: hosiery, underwear, sleepwear, and infants' clothing
Store: same address; Sunday to Thursday 9–5, Friday 9–1

  ¡Si!

Chock, known to generations of New Yorkers as Louis Chock, is a family operation that's been selling unmentionables since 1921. Chock's 66-page catalog packed with good values on name-brand underthings for men, women, children, and infants: duofold thermal underwear for the whole family, women's stockings and panty hose by Berkshire, Hanes, and Mayer; underpants by Carter's, Danskin, Calvin Klein, Lollipop, and Vanity Fair; and Louis Chock sleepwear for women. The men's department includes lines by BVD, Hanes, Jockey, Calvin Klein, Manshape, and Munsingwear, as well as pajamas and robes from Knothe, Munsingwear, and Oscar de la Renta; and socks by Burlington and Supp-hose. Men's sizes run up to XXXX (58 to 60). Chock's children's department stocks Carter's layette items and nursery needs, baby underwear by Gerber's, bathing necessities, cloth diapers and crib linen, Hanes underwear for boys, Carter's underwear and sleepwear for boys and girls, Trimfit socks for both, and classic wooden toys by Montgomery Schoolhouse. And this is the place for all those well-priced gifts that people really *use,* like Totes umbrellas and other accessories.

Special Factors: Satisfaction is guaranteed; unopened returns with manufacturer's packaging intact are accepted within 30 days; orders are shipped worldwide.

THE DEERSKIN PLACE

283 AKRON RD.
EPHRATA, PA 17522
717-733-7624

Brochure and Price List: $1, refundable (see text)
Save: up to 50%
Pay: check, MO, MC, V
Sells: deerskin clothing and accessories
Store: same address; Monday to Saturday 9–9, Sunday (September–December) 12–5

The Deerskin Place, in business since 1969, features clothing and accessories made of deerskin, cowhide, and sheepskin, at prices up to 50% less than those charged elsewhere for comparable goods. Among the offerings are fingertip-length shearling jackets for $295, fringed buckskin-suede jackets at $179, bomber jackets, and sporty deerskin handbags for about $70. The Deerskin Place offers moccasins and casual shoes, knee-high suede boots, and crepe-soled slip-ons for men and women (from $17), deerskin wallets, clutches, coin purses, and keycases (from about $6), mittens and gloves for the whole family, beaded belts (under $6), and many other accessories.

The Deerskin Place is offering readers of this book a 10% discount on orders of $150 or more. Be sure to identify yourself as a reader when you order, and deduct the discount from the goods total only. This WBMC reader discount expires July 1, 1995.

Special Factors: Satisfaction is guaranteed; inquire before ordering if unsure of color, size, etc.; returns are accepted; C.O.D. orders are accepted; orders are shipped worldwide.

DEERSKIN TRADING POST, INC.

119 FOSTER
PEABODY, MA 01961-6008
508-532-4040
FAX: 508-531-7729

Catalog: $1
Save: up to 30%
Pay: check, MO, MC, V, AE, DC, Discover
Sells: leather clothing and accessories
Store: Rte. 1 South, Danvers, MA

Deerskin Trading Post has been selling leather clothing and accessories since 1944, and offers garments made of lambskin, shearling, and cowhide, as well as deerskin. The 72-page color catalog has up-to-date styles in leatherwear for men and women, and somewhat conservatively styled footwear—walkers, chukka boots, loafers, moccasins, bucks, slippers, boots, scuffs, etc.—for men and women. You'll find all kinds of coat and jacket styles, including bombers, a belted fingertip-length model with shearling collar for men, sportcoats, blazers, blouson jackets for women, baseball styles, washable pigskin suede "jeans" jackets, swing coats for women, car coats, and much more. There are leather pants and skirts, fur hats, shearling car accessories, and good buys on things like deerskin gloves. Deerskin Trading Post features extra-large sizes, running to 10 in women's shoes and 20 dress size, and up to 48 long for men.

Special Factors: Satisfaction is guaranteed; returns of unaltered, unused goods are accepted for exchange, refund, or credit; minimum order is $25 with credit cards; orders are shipped worldwide.

FINAL EDITION

5302 EISENHOWER AVE.
ALEXANDRIA, VA 22304
800-336-0222
FAX: 703-370-0379

Catalog: free
Save: up to 85%
Pay: check, MO, MC, V, AE, Discover
Sells: women's clothing
Store: mail order only

Final Edition brings to women's clothing the same concept that's worked so well with upmarket gift merchandise: A catalog of fine-quality closeouts, overstock, and special buys, at rock-bottom prices. Label names are omitted from most of the catalog descriptions, but Catalina, Jessica Howard, and Joan Leslie have appeared in past issues. Final Edition is exceptional for both its offerings and prices; the clothes are fashion forward and attractive, and although color choice is usually limited at best, what's available is appealing. The offerings range from suits ($58 from $145) to office separates to playwear and swimwear (maillots for $29 from $62 are recent examples) to terrific after-five dresses and evening wear (an off-the-shoulder velvet chemise was priced at $52 from $130 in the last catalog). Because of the extremely limited quantities of many items, call for availability *before* you order.

Special Factor: Quantities are limited, so order promptly.

PAUL FREDRICK SHIRT COMPANY

Catalog: $1
Save: up to 50%
Pay: check, MO, MC, V, AE, DC, Discover
Sells: men's dress shirts and accessories
Store: mail order only

140 W. MAIN ST.,
  DEPT. WM94
FLEETWOOD, PA 19522
215-944-0909
FAX: 215-944-6452

Paul Fredrick is the mail-order division of a shirt manufacturer that's been selling to designers and better stores since 1952. If you're in the market for quality men's shirts or a knockout tie, Paul Fredrick is your source. The 48-page color catalog shows $37 dress shirts that compare favorably in material, construction, and detail to those in other catalogs and stores selling for nearly twice the price. Fredrick's shirts are offered in fine fabrics—pinpoint Oxford cotton, Cambridge Oxford cotton, and Egyptian cotton broadcloth—with a range of tailoring options: French and barrel (buttoned) cuffs, and straight, Windsor, English tab, and buttondown collar styles. Colors and patterns include stripes, plaids, paisleys, madras, and miniature checks, and sizes run from 14-1/2" to 18-1/2" neck, 32" to 37" sleeve. Three-letter monograms (on the left sleeve cuff) cost $5. Complement your new purchases—or existing wardrobe—with an English or Italian silk necktie. The current catalog shows a range of designs, from rep standards in pleasing colors and spiffy small prings on diamantine weaves, to paisleys, florals, polka dots, tumbling dice, and even cowboys. A good selection of men's jewelry—cuff links, studs, tie bars—and leather belts, key rings, and gold-plated collar stays are also available.

Special Factors: Satisfaction is guaranteed; returns are accepted; online with CompuServe and Prodigy; orders are shipped worldwide.

GOHN BROS.

105 S. MAIN
P.O. BOX 111
MIDDLEBURY, IN
46540-0111
219-825-2400

Catalog: $1
Save: up to 40%
Pay: check or MO
Sells: general merchandise and Amish specialties
Store: same address; Monday to Saturday 8–5:30

Other firms add fax machines and 800 lines, but Gohn Bros. remains firmly rooted in a world where bonnet board and work coats were stock items in the general store. Gohn has been in business since 1904, and sells practical goods at prices up to 40% below comparable retail.

Home sewers appreciate Gohn for yard goods staples and notions, such as the all-cotton Sanforized blue denim ($5.98), muslin (as low as $1.39), cotton oxford shirting ($4.59), quilting thread ($1.29), cotton percale and quilting prints, pillow tubing, all-cotton sheeting, tailor's canvas, haircloth, mosquito netting, Coats & Clark embroidery floss (25¢ per skein), and wool overcoating (under $13 per yard, in navy, black, and "Confederate gray").

At least half of Gohn's stock lists are devoted to work-tailored, sturdy Amish clothing, including men's cotton chambray work shirts ($16.98), cotton denim broadfall pants ($14.98), men's underwear, Red Wing shoes, rubber galoshes and footwear by LaCrosse and Tingley, work gloves, felt hats, and handkerchiefs. Much of the clothing is available in large sizes, and many of the items in the men's department are also offered in boys' sizes. If you're assembling a layette, see the catalog for good buys on the basics—diapers, receiving blankets, sleepers, pacifiers, baby pants, and other goods by Curity and Gerber. Nursing bras are available, and women's underwear and hosiery are offered at low prices.

Special Factors: Satisfaction is guaranteed; C.O.D. orders are accepted.

GOLDMAN & COHEN INC.

**55 ORCHARD ST.
NEW YORK, NY 10002
212-966-0737**

Information: price quote
Save: up to 60%
Pay: check, MO, MC, V, AE, Discover
Sells: women's underwear
Store: same address; Monday to Thursday 9–5, Friday 9–3, Sunday 8–5:30

Goldman & Cohen doesn't publish a catalog, but will quote prices on its stock of popular lingerie and hosiery lines. The firm was founded in 1954, and sells at discounts of up to 50% on suggested list prices. Women's intimate apparel is available from Bali, Barbizon, Carnival, Christian Dior, Exquisite Form, Lilyette, Maidenform, Olga, Playtex, Vanity Fair, Warner's, and other well-known manufacturers and designers. You can ask for price quotes on loungewear by these firms, as well as Hanes panty hose. Goldman also carries a full line of nursing and maternity foundations and sleepwear. The firm's experienced saleswomen can help ensure you a proper fit, and choose the garments for your own needs.

Special Factors: No phone orders or inquiries are accepted on Sunday; orders are shipped worldwide.

HUNTINGTON CLOTHIERS

**1285 ALUM CREEK DR.
COLUMBUS, OH
43209-2797
800-848-6203
614-252-4422
FAX: 614-252-3855**

Catalog: free
Save: up to 50% (see text)
Pay: check, MO, MC, V, AE, DC
Sells: executive menswear
Store: same address; Monday to Friday 10–6, Saturday 10–5, Sunday 12–5

The 84-page catalog from Huntington Clothiers illustrates all the basics of a conservative wardrobe, from pinstriped suits to pima boxer shorts, with more fashion-forward accessories and casual attire. Huntington's prices are competitive with those of old-line haberdashers; some items cost up to twice as much elsewhere.

Huntington's own line of shirts are offered in Oxford cloth, pima cotton solids, Sea Island cotton, Egyptian cotton broadcloth, and cotton/poly blends. (Monogramming is available for $5.) Huntington also sells neckwear—foulards, silk regimental stripes, and linen solids and paisley ties—at similar savings, and executive suits that run the gamut from grey chalk stripes and gabardines to poplin and seersucker summer suits to tuxedos. Jackets and blazers are shown, as well as trousers, sportswear separates, walking shorts, lisle cotton polo shirts, rugby shirts, cotton and wool sweaters, belts, suspenders, underwear, and even shoes. Huntington has been in business since 1978, and has added photos to the color illustrations that have been one of the catalog's trademarks.

Special Factors: Satisfaction is guaranteed; returns (except monogrammed goods) are accepted for exchange, refund, or credit.

JAMES RIVER TRADERS

NEW HAMPTON, INC.
JAMES RIVER LANDING
HAMPTON, VA 23631
800-445-2405
804-827-6000
FAX: 800-955-0404

Catalog: free
Save: up to 30%
Pay: check, MO, MC, V, AE, Discover
Sells: casual and career clothing for men and women
Store: mail order only

James River Traders is a standout among catalogs featuring hip, private-label clothing for women. The prices are generally lower at JRT than those charged for similar goods from other catalogs, and there's a good mix of clothing for work and leisure. There are lots of good separates—cotton interlock skirts, updated turtlenecks and tees, blazers, Merino wool knit pants and jewelneck tops, handknitted sweaters, embroidered shirts, and many other versatile pieces have appeared in past catalogs. In addition to playwear, JRT also sells great dresses and soft suits that are perfect for the office. The styles and colors are on the youthful side, and the prices are also down-to-earth. Sales are held on a regular basis, and most catalogs feature a number of items at special discounts.

Special Factors: Satisfaction is guaranteed; returns are accepted for exchange, refund, or credit.

LEE-MCCLAIN CO., INC.

1857 MIDLAND TRAIL

SHELBYVILLE, KY

40065-9035

502-633-3823

Brochure: free

Save: up to 40%

Pay: check, MO, MC, V

Sells: executive menswear

Store: U.S. 60 W., Shelbyville, KY; Monday to Saturday 10–6; also Festival Market, Lexington, KY; Monday to Saturday 10–6, Thursday til 9, Sunday 1–5

Lee-McClain has been manufacturing fine suits and separates for men since 1933, and offers you the same apparel you can find in better stores—at up to 40% below suggested retail prices. Lee-McClain's clothing is sold under the "Strathmore" house label, and the brochure showcases a small collection of suits, and jackets. The conservative, classic styling features slightly fitted, two-button jackets with center vent and straight-leg pants. Suits begin at $195, and fabric choices include cashmere and blends, camel's hair, wool worsted, flannel, gabardine, pinstripes, herringbones, glen plaids, hopsacking, and other weaves. It's hard to beat $225 for a fine camel's hair sports coat, or $55 for slacks in worsted wool. Sizes run from 36 to 52, including short, portly, regular, long, extra-long, and "athletic" cuts.

Special Factors: Swatches are available upon request; list all measurements when ordering

L'EGGS HANES BALI PLAYTEX OUTLET CATALOG

L'EGGS BRANDS, INC.
P.O. BOX 843
RURAL HALL, NC
   27098-0843
919-744-1170
FAX: 919-744-1485
TDD: 919-744-5300

Catalog: free
Save: up to 60%
Pay: check, MO, MC, V, Discover
Sells: first-quality and "slightly imperfect" women's hosiery and underwear
Store: mail order only

C (see text)

The 56-page color L'eggs Bali Playtex Outlet Catalog brings you savings of up to 60% on your favorite panty hose, activewear, and lingerie from Bali, Hanes, Isotoner, L'eggs, Playtex, and Underalls. The best buys are on the "slightly imperfect" irregulars, and the whole range of L'eggs is available, in control-top styles, queen sizes, and a wide range of colors. (Just My Size and Sheer Energy Maternity panty hose are offered, also at savings of up to 60%.) Hanes hosiery—Silk Reflections, Hanes Too!, Hanes Alive, Ultra Silk, etc.—is sold, as well as a wide selection of Bali and Playtex bras and slips, and Hanes socks, underwear, T-shirts, and sweats for the whole family. See the detailed sizing guide in the catalog to be sure you get the best fit.

Special Factors: Satisfaction is guaranteed; "slightly imperfect" goods are clearly identified; returns are accepted; TDD service is available Monday to Friday, 8 A.M. to midnight.

MANNY'S MILLINERY SUPPLY CENTER

26 W. 38TH ST.
NEW YORK, NY 10018
212-840-2253
FAX: 212-944-0178

Catalog: $2
Save: 33% average
Pay: check, MO, MC, V, AE
Sells: hats, millinery supplies, gloves, bridal trimmings
Store: same address; Monday to Friday 9–5:30, Saturday 9–4

 ¡Si!

Manny's is nestled among the shops in New York City's "trimmings" district, which has more sequins, tassels, and decorative add-ons per square foot than a Las Vegas floor show. Manny's offers some of that glitter, but the company's specialty is women's hats, millinery supplies, and bridal accessories.

About half of Manny's 48-page catalog is devoted to headpieces, many of which are trimmed. Hundreds of styles are shown, in parisial, milanette, genuine Milan straw, felt, and fabric. Scores of "frames," or fabric-covered hat forms, are offered. The satin frames are suitable for bridal outfits, and the buckram frames provide a base for limitless flights of fancy. Stunning bridal headpieces, which can be used to decorate the hats and headpieces, are shown in the catalog, as well as lace parasols, fans, satin and velvet gloves, edged veils, and even ring pillows. In addition, Manny's offers over a dozen jeweled or beaded hatpins, pearl and sequin trims, bugle-bead appliqués and trims, fringe, fabric flowers, rhinestone buttons, and even feathers—loose and in boas. Professional millinery supplies and equipment are available, including horsehair braid, hat stretchers, display heads and racks, hat boxes and travel cases, netting, and cleaning products. Savings vary from item to item, but average 33% below regular retail.

Please note: If you're buying hats only, the minimum order is 3; if you buy 1 or 2 hats, you must also buy $15 in assorted items (frames, trims, etc.); if you're buying assorted items only, the minimum order is $25.

Special Factors: Price quote by phone; minimum order on certain items (see text); orders are shipped worldwide.

MIDWESTERN SPORT TOGS

P.O. BOX 230
BERLIN, WI 54923
414-361-5050
FAX: 414-361-5055

Catalog: free
Save: up to 35%
Pay: check, MO, MC, V
Sells: deerskin clothing and tanning services
Store: 227 N. Washington St., Berlin, WI;
Monday to Friday 8–5, Saturday 8–3 (8–12
noon, May–Labor Day

Mid-Western Sport Togs, established in 1869, offers a service useful to hunters: The firm will tan your green hides, color them, and create custom clothing and accessories from the leather. The same items can be made up in stock deerskin, and the prices for the services and finished goods are exceptionally reasonable. The catalog shows deerskin vests, town-and-country jackets and coats, classic wrap coats, safari and bush jackets, Western models, and sports coats, as well as riding, motorcycle, and bomber jackets. The garments can be ordered in custom sizes, lengths, details, and linings. Bags and gloves—driving, shooting, hunting, and dress gloves for men and women—and children's mittens. Change purses, keycases, billfolds, cigarette cases, golf-club covers, and smooth-soled moccasins are also sold. Green deer, elk, and moose hides are accepted for curing and coloring, but no fur work is done.

Special Factors: Tanning rates, guides to shipment of skins, number of hides needed per garment, and other information is listed in the catalog; orders are shipped worldwide.

NATIONAL WHOLESALE CO., INC.

400 NATIONAL BLVD.,
DEPT. WK
LEXINGTON, NC 27292
704-249-0211

Catalog: free
Save: up to 50%
Pay: check, MO, MC, V, AE, Discover
Sells: women's hosiery, underwear, and apparel
Store: National Fashions, Lexington and Wilmington, NC; Monday to Saturday 9–9, Sunday 1–5:30, both locations

National Wholesale's 80-page catalog features a good selection of hosiery in a wide range of sizes—for heights to six feet, and hip sizes to 60". In addition to hosiery, National Wholesale sells bras, girdles, and body shapers by Exquisite Form, Glamorise, and Playtex, slips by Figur-efit and Pinehurst, Models Coat dusters by Swirl, nightgowns and paja-mas, cotton-knit vests, briefs, long-leg underpants, thermal underwear, pants liners, slippers, dickeys, and aprons. And there's a nice selection of blouses, skirts, sweaters, coats, and jackets that are perfect wardrobe staples, and well priced—suit jackets at under $50, denim skirts for $29, and chinos for under $19 are a few examples.

Special Factors: Satisfaction is guaranteed; returns are accepted.

NO NONSENSE DIRECT

P.O. BOX 26095
GREENSBORO, NC
  27420-6095
800-677-5995
FAX: 919-275-9329

Catalog: free
Save: up to 60%
Pay: check, MO, MC, V, AE, Discover
Sells: hosiery
Store: mail order only

If you wear "No nonsense" panty hose or Burlington hosiery, you can save up to 60% on the price of your favorite styles through No Non-sense Direct. This mail-order factory outlet of Kayser Roth has been delivering great buys on pantyhose and socks since 1985. You'll save the most on 12 pairs or more of "Practically Perfect" No nonsense and Burlington panty hose, including Sheer & Silky, Control Top, Light Sup-port, Regular, Great Shapes, Custom Full Figure, A Touch of Silk, and other lines. The "Practically Perfect" goods have "minor, virtually unde-tectable imperfections that do not affect looks or wear," and are cov-ered by the No Nonsense Direct guarantee of satisfaction. In addition to saving you money, you get a full choice of sizes when you buy from the catalog—and that means that unless you're under 4' 11", 85 lb., or over 6', 280 lb., you should find a good fit here.

Please note: Most items are sold in minimum quantities of six.

Special Factors: Satisfaction is guaranteed; quantity discounts are available; returns are accepted for exchange, refund, or credit.

THE PETTICOAT EXPRESS

---

318 W. 39TH ST.
NEW YORK, NY
10018-1407
212-594-1276

Flyer: free
Save: 40% plus
Pay: check or MO
Sells: taffeta slips
Store: mail order only

Petticoat Express offers brides an easy way to cut 40% from the cost of an unseen necessity—the net and taffeta slip that creates the charming silhouette of a full-skirted bridal or attendant's gown. Petticoat Express, which has been in business since 1983, offers white, full-length half-slips: an A-line style for dresses of moderate flare ($21); a flounced, bouffant style for full skirts ($23); a double-ruffle bouffant ($28) for maximum fullness; and a style for tea-length (31") skirts ($20). Sizes run from 3-4 to 19-20. The slips are made of taffeta and net, and are also ideal for full-skirted evening dresses.

Special Factor: C.O.D. orders are accepted.

QUINN'S SHIRT SHOP

RTE. 12
P.O. BOX 131
NORTH
  GROSVENORDALE, CT
  06255
508-943-7183

Price List: $2 and self-addressed, stamped envelope (see text)
Save: up to 50%
Pay: check or MO
Sells: Arrow shirts
Store: 245 W. Main St., Dudley, MA; Monday to Saturday 10–5

Quinn's, a factory outlet for the Arrow Shirt company, offers slightly irregular shirts at up to 60% below the price of first-quality goods. The firm has been in business since 1956, and will send you a price list for $2 and a stamped, self-addressed envelope (the $2 charge is refundable with your first order). You can also call or write for a price quote on your favorite Arrow shirt (you must have the style number or code). Quinn's carries in regular, big, and tall sizes, 14-1/2" to 20" neck, 31" to 38" sleeve. When you order, specify whether you want short sleeves or long, and include the length if long. The shirts may be exchanged if the flaws are too apparent.

Special Factors: Satisfaction is guaranteed; price quote by phone or letter with SASE; returns are accepted for exchange; minimum order is four shirts per order; only C.O.D. orders are accepted.

SARA GLOVE COMPANY, INC.

P.O. BOX 1940
WATERBURY, CT
  06722-1940
800-243-3570
203-574-4090
FAX: 203-574-3500

Catalog: free
Save: up to 30%
Pay: check, MO, MC, V
Sells: work clothing and gloves
Store: same address; Monday to Friday 8:30–4

 ¡Si! ★

Work clothing and safety gear are showcased in the "Worldwide Outfitters" catalog from Sara Glove Company, at savings of up to 30%. Part of the 32 pages are devoted to gloves, gauntlets, and finger cots (tip protectors), including brown jersey and canvas chore gloves, warm fleece gloves, leather-and-canvas work gloves, and heat-resistant gloves of fabric and leather for "dry" work. If you handle solvents, caustics, oil, acids, grease, and chemicals, see the catalog for the line of gloves designed to resist these substances—there are vinyl, neoprene, nitrile, and latex models. Several of the gloves are USDA-approved for food handling, food processing, and related commercial uses. The catalog also features safety glasses and goggles, as well as ear plugs and muffs, respirators and other breathing filters, first-aid kits, and other safety equipment.

Most of the catalog is devoted to clothing, including work shirts in sizes to 5XL, pants, Carhartt work jackets and overalls, Dickies work clothing, lab coats, and boots and footwear by Carolina Boots. Sara Glove's custom department can personalize your work shirts, T-shirts, baseball jackets, and baseball caps with names and corporate logos, at a surcharge.

Special Factors: Satisfaction is guaranteed; quantity discounts are available; C.O.D. orders are accepted; institutional accounts are available; orders are shipped worldwide.

SPORTSWEAR CLEARINGHOUSE

P.O. BOX 317746-E5
CINCINNATI, OH
45231-7746
513-522-3511

Brochure: free
Save: up to 70%
Pay: check, MO, MC, V
Sells: pre-printed sportswear
Store: mail order only

Forget about dayglo cycling shorts and $200 court shoes—you won't find these at Sportswear Clearinghouse. The fare is sportswear basics—T-shirts in sizes from youth to adult XXL, sweats, shorts, night shirts, and hats, already printed with corporate or institutional logos. If you succumb to the brochure, you can wind up wearing a T-shirt printed for the American Embassy at Sanaa Yemen, Notre Dame running shorts, and a hat emblazoned with an advertising message from a local welding shop. The Clearinghouse, which has been in business since 1976, offers T-shirts from *everywhere,* sweatshirts, golf shirts (printed for the "staff" of different institutions), and T-shirts bearing the names of universities, running themes, sports themes, and slogans in foreign languages. Prices are hard to beat; T-shirts and shorts cost a few dollars each, and hats and visors are priced under $2 apiece. Most of these items are sold in lots of three, six, or ten or more, and the Clearinghouse selects the colors, logos, and slogans. First-quality unprinted athletic socks and baseball hats embroidered with the replica logos of major league baseball teams are also available, as well as belly/fanny packs, baseball hats in neon colors, and flowered Hawaiian, zebra-striped, and other non-logo designs.

Sportswear Clearinghouse is offering readers of this book a 7.5% discount on all orders of 12 or more of item #19—"baseball-style hats." Be sure to identify yourself as a reader when you order, and deduct the discount from the goods total only. This WBMC reader discount expires March 1, 1995.

Special Factors: Satisfaction is guaranteed; unused returns are accepted within 30 days for exchange, refund, or credit; C.O.D. orders are accepted (UPS delivery only); orders are shipped worldwide.

TAFFORD MANU-FACTURING, INC.

104 PARK DR.
P.O. BOX 1006
MONTGOMERYVILLE, PA
18936
800-283-0065

Catalog: free
Save: up to 30%
Pay: check, MO, MC, V, AE, Discover
Sells: nurses' uniforms and accessories
Store: mail order only

Compared to the average catalog of uniforms for health-care professionals, Tafford has the best fashion buys for the dollar around. The firm manufactures its own uniforms, which means you beat at least one markup, and the size selection is great—XS to XXXL for women, and S to XXXL for men. The 48-page color catalog shows mostly women's clothing, although there are scrubs and lab coats for men as well. Some of the women's outfits are quite chic, and there are uniforms to suit every figure type, including a maternity style. The catalog also shows cardigans, jackets, shoes, emblem pins, and nursing equipment—stethoscopes, blood pressure kits, scissors, otoscopes, etc. Both the retail and the discount prices of the clothing are given, so you see how much you're saving—usually 20% or 30% on the regular retail. Consult your colleagues before ordering, because if you buy as part of a group, Tafford also offers special services such as swatches and samples, additional sizes if required, and embroidery and silkscreening.

Special Factors: Satisfaction is guaranteed; unworn, undamaged, unwashed returns are accepted within 30 days for exchange, refund, or credit; minimum order is $100 with American Express; orders are shipped worldwide.

TAI, INC.

90 DAYTON AVE.
PASSAIC, NJ 07055
201-777-6010
FAX: 201-777-3088

Catalog: free
Save: quantity discounts (see text)
Pay: check, MO, MC, V, AE, Discover
Sells: silk-screened apparel and accessories
Store: same address; Monday to Friday
9–4:30, Saturday 11–4:30

 ¡Si!

TAI was founded in 1983 by Crown Art Products (see the firm's listing in "Art Materials"), which manufactures silk-screening supplies and equipment. TAI offers a line of clothing and accessories hand-screened with military insignias, at savings that run up to 30% (on goods bought in quantity). The catalog offers a range of items embellished with the motifs of military forces, including aprons, scarves, beach towels, laundry and duffel bags, T-shirts, pennants, decals, and bumper stickers. Choose from insignias of the Airborne divisions, Special Forces groups, the Marines, Rangers, the Foreign Legion, U.S.M.C. Recon, and other forces and divisions.

Special Factors: Quantity discounts are available; minimum order is $25 with credit cards.

TODD UNIFORM, INC.

3668 SOUTH GEYER RD.
ST. LOUIS, MO 63127-1244
314-984-0365
FAX: 314-984-5736

Catalog: free
Save: up to 30%
Pay: check, MO, MC, V, AE, Discover
Sells: work clothing and uniforms
Store: Ripley, TN; Monday to Saturday
9–5:30; also St. Louis, MO, and Louisville, KY

Todd has been manufacturing and selling uniforms and work apparel since 1881, and offers factory-direct prices—up to 30% below the competition. The clothing runs from the classic work shirt for men and women, which is offered in a range of colors, to jumpsuits, pants, jeans, jackets, T-shirts, polo shirts, aprons, rainwear, and caps. Your logo or slogan can be embroidered on the garments or on emblems, and the order form is designed to make it easy to specify even complicated orders.

Special Factors: Satisfaction is guaranteed; minimum order requirements apply to custom work; institutional accounts are available; orders are shipped worldwide.

THE ULTIMATE OUTLET

P.O. BOX 88251

CHICAGO, IL 60680-1251

800-332-6000

TDDL 800-322-1231

Catalog: $2
Save: up to 65%
Pay: check, MO, MC, V, AE, Optima, FCNB Preferred Charge
Sells: clothing, housewares, etc.
Store: seven stores in Chicago area; also Sunrise, FL; Gurnee, IL; and Philadelphia, PA

¡Si! ℂ 🏴 (see text)

The Ultimate Outlet is Spiegel's smart answer to the strong demand for its sales catalogs. An off-price outlet by mail, the upbeat catalog is as jaunty and fresh as the latest Spiegel edition, but The Ultimate Outlet boasts real sale prices on every page. The catalogs usually feature several pages of chic women's shoes, chic separates, flannel blazers, and boardroom-worthy suits. Men are treated to a collection dominated by weekend wear—leather bomber jackets, cotton shirts, and casual and dress pants are typical offerings. Since the stock consists primarily of Spiegel goods, you'll find many of the same brand names here, and The Ultimate Outlet has a similar sales policy.

Please note: Deliveries to Alaska, Hawaii, and APO/FPO addresses are made by the postal service, *not* UPS.

Special Factors: Satisfaction is guaranteed; returns are accepted for refund or credit.

VANDERBILT'S MAIL ORDER, INC.

500 LINCOLN AVE.
WAMEGO, KS 66547
913-456-9199
FAX: 913-456-9599

Catalog: free
Save: up to 45%
Pay: check, MO, MC, V, Discover
Sells: work and Western wear for men, women, and children
Store: same address; ten other locations

If you like real Western working wear, Vanderbilt's offers what you're looking for: Lee, Levi's, and Wrangler jeans, Western-style shirts by Roper, Wahoo, and Wrangler, Dickies overalls and work clothing, and Eddy and Stetson hats. Most of the color catalog is devoted to footwear, including moccasins by Minnetonka, Sioux Mox, and Tru-Stitch, hiking shoes by Hi-Tec and Northlake, jumpboots by Corcoran Force, and work shoes and work boots by Georgia Boot and Vanderbilt's. And there are all kinds of Western boots, from plain ropers to exotic skins by Abilene, Acme, Code West, Dingo, Harley-Davidson, Justin, Laredo, Nocona, Dan Post, Tony Lama, and Walker. Most of the goods are listed with both their regular selling prices and Vanderbilt's prices, so you can see your savings—about 20% to 25% on most of the footwear, and up to 45% on jeans and other popular apparel.

Special Factors: Quantity discounts are available; authorized returns of unworn goods are accepted; orders are shipped worldwide.

COMPANIES OUTSIDE THE U.S.A.

W.S. Robertson, following, is experienced in dealing with customers in the U.S. and Canada. Although ordering from abroad is more demanding, it may be repaid in savings on goods not usually sold at a discount in the U.S. But before ordering from any non-U.S. firm, please consult "The Complete Guide to Buying by Mail," page 535, for helpful tips. It's wise to pay for orders from foreign firms with a credit card whenever possible, so you'll have some recourse if you don't receive your order. For more information, see "The Fair Credit Billing Act," page 569.

W.S. ROBERTSON (OUTFITTERS) LTD.

41 BANK ST.
GALASHIELS TD1 1EP
SCOTLAND
011-44-1-896-2152

Brochures and Price Lists: $5
Save: up to 30%
Pay: check, IMO, MC, V, Access
Sells: Scottish knitwear
Store: same address; Monday to Saturday 9–5:30

W.S. Robertson sells Pringles, the cashmere of cashmeres, which have been Scotland's pride since 1815. Pringle's pullovers, cardigans, and vests are offered here at savings of up to 30% on U.S. prices—and they're also available in lambswool and Shetland wool. Robertson also carries the stylish Lyle & Scott sweaters in cashmere, lambswool, and Botany wool, as well as knits by Ballantyne and Braemar, in cashmere, lambswool, and Shetland wool.

If you're having your order delivered to an address outside the United Kingdom, deduct 15% (the Value Added Tax, not charged on exported goods). The final figure is your cost. Robertson's prices are listed in pounds sterling, and the savings increase when the dollar is strong. If you're not paying in pounds, get the rate of exchange from your local bank on the day you order and use that figure to convert the pounds to dollars. Add shipping costs after you compute the export discount.

Special Factors: Price quote by phone or letter on styles not shown in the brochures; orders are shipped worldwide.

SEE ALSO

Austad's • golf apparel and shoes • **SPORTS**
Bailey's, Inc. • outdoor apparel and footwear • **TOOLS**
Bailey's Wholesale Floral Supply • bridal accessories and floral supplies • **CRAFTS**
Bart's Water Ski Center, Inc. • water-skiing vests, T-shirts, swim trunks, and wet suits • **SPORTS**
Beauty by Spector, Inc. • wigs and hairpieces for men and women • **HEALTH**
Bike Nashbar • bicycling and sports apparel, and sunglasses • **SPORTS**
Bowhunters Warehouse, Inc. • camouflage clothing • **SPORTS**
Bruce Medical Supply • dressing aids for the disabled, stoma scarves, incontinence products • **MEDICINE**

The Button Shop • *replacement zippers for jeans, garment shoulder pads* • CRAFTS

Cabela's Inc. • *hunting and fishing wear, outdoor clothing and footwear* • SPORTS

Campmor • *outdoor clothing and accessories* • **SPORTS**

Clothcrafters, Inc. • *aprons, garment bags, and tote bags* • **GENERAL MER-CHANDISE**

Cycle Goods Corp. • *bicycling apparel and footwear* • **SPORTS**

Defender Industries, Inc. • *foul-weather wear* • **AUTO**

Dharma Trading Co. • *cotton clothing and silk scarves for fabric painting, etc.* • CRAFTS

E & B Marine Supply, Inc. • *foul-weather wear* • **AUTO**

Gander Mountain, Inc. • *hunting and fishing clothing, outdoor wear* • **SPORTS**

Gettinger Feather Corp. • *feather marabous and boas, loose feathers* • CRAFTS

Goldberg's Marine Distributors • *foul-weather wear* • **AUTO**

Golfsmith International, Inc. • *golf clothing and footwear* • **SPORTS**

Las Vegas Discount Golf & Tennis • *tennis and other sports apparel, tennis and golf shoes* • **SPORTS**

Leather Unlimited Corp. • *sheepskin mittens, hats, and bags* • **LEATHER**

M&E Marine Supply Company, Inc. • *foul-weather wear* • **AUTO**

D. MacGillivray & Coy. • *Scottish knitwear, stock and custom-made kilts, etc.* • CRAFTS

Mass. Army & Navy Store • *government surplus clothing and gear, casual wear* • SURPLUS

New England Leather Accessories, Inc. • *leather handbags and accessories* • LEATHER

Northern Hydraulics, Inc. • *work clothing and rugged footwear* • **TOOLS**

Omaha Vaccine Company, Inc. • *Wells Lamont work gloves, Red Ball boots* • ANIMAL

Overton's Sports Center, Inc. • *boating and windsurfing apparel* • **SPORTS**

Performance Bicycle Shop • *cycling clothing, footwear, and helmets* • SPORTS

Performance Golf • *golf clothing and accessories* • **SPORTS**

Pet Warehouse • *dog costumes* • **ANIMAL**

ProAm Seat Warehouse • *sunglasses, car racing suits and helmets* • **AUTO**

Racer Wholesale • *auto racing suits and accessories* • **AUTO**

Retired Persons Services, Inc. • *support hosiery, slippers, socks, etc.* • **MEDI-CINE**

Road Runner Sports • *sports apparel and shoes* • **SPORTS**

Ruvel & Company, Inc. • *government surplus clothing and outdoor wear* • SURPLUS

Sailboard Warehouse, Inc. • *windsurfing apparel* • **SPORTS**

Sierra Trading Post • *outdoor clothing and accessories* • **SPORTS**

Sport Shop • *camouflage clothing* • **SPORTS**

Sultan's Delight, Inc. • *belly-dancing outfits, Arab headdresses and agals* •
FOOD

Support Plus • *support hosiery, comfort-styled shoes, therapeutic apparel* •
MEDICINE

The Tee House • *custom-imprinted golf clothing and accessories* • **SPORTS**

Thai Silks • *silk ties, scarves, handkerchiefs, lingerie, and blouses* • **CRAFTS**

Tool Crib of the North • *work clothing* • **TOOLS**

Utex Trading Enterprises • *silk scarves and ties* • **CRAFTS**

Wag-Aero, Inc. • *aviator clothing and headwear* • **AUTO**

West Marine • *foul-weather wear* • **AUTO**

Wiley Outdoor Sports, Inc. • *hunting (camouflage) clothing and accessories* •
SPORTS

Footwear

Shoes, boots, and slippers for men, women, and children

These firms can help you solve just about all the problems you encounter when buying shoes. They've got selection—they sell everything from arctic boots to moccasins to nurses' shoes. The price is right—you'll find savings of up to 40%. But the biggest problem in buying shoes by mail is getting a good fit. Here are some tips to improve the odds, and to make returns as easy as possible if necessary:

- Have your feet measured at least once a year, and order your true size. (Feet continue to grow and change as you age.)
- Buy from firms with liberal return policies, preferably an unconditional guarantee of satisfaction with a 30-day return period.
- Buy styles and shapes that have fit in the past.
- If the shoes you're buying are also available in a local store, try on a pair before ordering them.
- When the shoes arrive, unwrap them carefully and save the packaging.
- Try them on in the late afternoon, when your feet have swollen slightly.
- Walk around in a carpeted area to avoid scratching the soles.
- Leave the shoes on for at least half an hour, checking for rubbing and pinching after 20 minutes.
- If they fit, consider ordering a second pair *now,* while they're still in stock.
- If the shoes don't fit, return them according to the firm's instructions, indicating whether you want another size or a refund or credit.

Good maintenance is critical in preserving the looks and longevity of your shoes and boots. For helpful tips on caring for all types of footwear, see *The Butler's Guide* (Fireside/Simon & Schuster, 1980), by Stanley Ager and Fiona St. Aubyn, and *Taking Care of Clothes* (St. Martin's Press, 1982), by Mablen Jones. Some of the firms listed in "Leather" sell leather care products, as do a number of companies listed in the "See Also's" of that chapter. If your shoes and boots need professional help and you don't have a good repair service nearby, contact the Houston Shoe Hospital, 5215 Kirby Dr., Houston, TX 77098; 713-528-6268. This firm overhauls worn footwear and handles mail-order repairs.

ALLEN-EDMONDS SHOE CORP.

201 E. SEVEN HILLS RD.
P.O. BOX 998
PORT WASHINGTON, WI
    53074
414-284-7158
FAX: 414-284-7499

Catalog: free
Save: up to 25% on factory seconds
Pay: check, MO, MC, V, AE, Discover, Optima
Sells: Allen-Edmonds shoes and repair services
Store: same address; other stores in AL, AZ, NC, NE, NV, OH, PA, and WI; locations listed in the catalog

Well-made shoes of good design that fit well are worth paying for, but it's even better when you can get them at a discount. Allen-Edmonds shoes are investment dressing for your feet, and the firm's factory seconds are priced 25% less than the same shoes if perfect—and every pair is guaranteed. Both classic and updated models for men are shown in the handsome, 28-page color catalog: tasselled wingtip slip-ons as well as Oxford bluchers, cap-toe Balmoral Oxfords, boarhide chukka boots, handsewn moccasin-style loafers in nubuck, collegiate penny loafers, monk straps, patent evening pumps, and a saddle-style wingtip golf shoe with fringe are a few examples. The shoes are not inexpensive, but the factory seconds begin at $135 for most weekend styles and for handsewn moccasins, and average about $173 for most of the executive styles.

Allen-Edmonds' shoes for women (all flats) parallel the men's line in styling and craftsmanship: loafers with lizard accents, monk-straps with open-weave toes, two-tone wingtip oxfords, kiltie flats with perfed uppers and fringes, tasseled loafer styles, handsome slip-ons with detailing, and Vibram-soled ankle-high boots in Nubuck are among the current offerings.

The size range is amazing—from AAAA to EEE widths, sizes 5 to 18 for men, and AAAA to D, sizes 4 to 12 for women—but please note that not every width or size is offered in every style, and seconds may not be available in all sizes or styles. Accessories and leather-care products are available, as well as recrafting services—from new heels and toplifts to a complete remaking.

Canadian readers, please note: Only U.S. funds are accepted.

Special Factors: Satisfaction is guaranteed; returns are accepted for exchange, refund, or credit; orders are shipped worldwide.

CLOVER NURSING SHOE COMPANY

1948 EAST WHIPP RD.,
  DEPT. WBM
KETTERING, OH
  45440-2921
513-435-0025

Brochure: free
Save: up to 40%
Pay: check, MO, MC, V
Sells: "Nurse Mates" shoes
Store: mail order only

Nurses look for comfort and good fit in their professional shoes, and many find both in Nurse Mates. Clover Nursing Shoe, in business since 1981, specializes in Nurse Mates, and sells them at the best discounts around—up to 40% off regular retail, every day.

The Nurse Mates line includes over a dozen styles, from streamlined T-straps to sturdy blucher models. The shoes are made of soft leather and built up on lightweight wedge soles that sport a little blue heart. Some of the shoes are offered solely in "nurse white," but there are many available in black, navy, wine, brown, and other colors. Clover's prices are great, and the full range of sizes—from 5 to 12, slim (AA) to double-wide (EE)—is carried.

Special Factors: Satisfaction is guaranteed; only first-quality goods are sold; orders are shipped worldwide.

GENE'S SHOES
DISCOUNT CATALOG

126 N. MAIN ST.
ST. CHARLES, MO 63301
314-946-0804

Catalog: free
Save: up to 30% (see text)
Pay: check, MO, MC, V
Sells: dress and casual shoes for men and women
Store: same address

Gene's Discount offers women savings on good, comfortable footwear from Devon Park, Easy Spirit, Hush Puppies, Selby, Soft Spots (including Nurse Mates), and Town & Country. There are a few styles for men, all by Hush Puppies. Most of the shoes are discounted about 17%, but savings run to over 30% on some Soft Spots styles. And you're in luck if you're hard to fit; Gene's offers most of the shoes in AAA to EE widths, sizes 3 to 13 for women, and narrow to extra-wide, size 6-1/2 to 16 for men. The catalog is free on request, but subscriptions (two seasonal issues and notices of interim sales) cost $4 per year.

Please note: The prices in the catalog are good on mail orders only, not on in-store purchases.

Special Factors: Satisfaction is guaranteed; unworn, salable returns are accepted within 30 days for exchange, refund, or credit; orders are shipped worldwide.

JUSTIN DISCOUNT
BOOTS & COWBOY
OUTFITTERS

P.O. BOX 67-JWM
JUSTIN, TX 76247
800-677-BOOT
FAX: 817-648-3282

Catalog: free
Save: 35% average
Pay: check, MO, MC, V
Sells: Western boots and clothing
Store: 101 W. Hwy. 156, Justin, TX; Monday to Saturday 9–6

This firm, although not owned by the Justin Boot Co., sells a number of the Justin boot lines in men's and women's styles. The 56-page color catalog includes "compare at" prices as well as the selling prices for most items—often 20% to 40% less. The footwear choices run from work boots and "ropers," comparatively plain, thick-soled boots with

Western vamps that rise to mid-calf (about $90), to artful creations in exotic skins—ostrich, lizard, bull hide, and alligator. There are several pages of women's styles, including lizard Western boots, "fashion" ropers in Atlantis blue, pink, "gusto green," and "true purple," as well as traditional colors. Children can get their Justin Juniors in red, pink, navy, brown, and other colors, for under $50 a pair. Coordinating belts are available, and the custom embroidery department will embellish your boots with two initials for $6.50 per letter. Justin Discount Boots also sells its own line of straw hats, German silver buckles and belt tips, David James coats, leather-care products, and Wrangler shirts, and Wrangler jeans for men, women, and boys.

Special Factors: Satisfaction is guaranteed; unworn, unscuffed, unaltered returns are accepted for exchange, refund, or credit; C.O.D. orders are accepted; orders are shipped worldwide.

KNAPP SHOES INC.

ONE KNAPP CENTRE
BROCKTON, MA 02401
508-588-9009

Catalog: free
Save: up to 25% (see text)
Pay: check, MO, MC, V
Sells: work shoes for men and women
Store: same address; 28 other stores in CA, GA, IL, MD, ME, MI, NC, NJ, NY, OH, and PA; locations are given in the catalog

Knapp has been keeping America in shoes since 1921, and although the company's discounts don't quite reach 30% (most are between 18% and 25%), there are shoes in the Knapp catalog that aren't easy to find at a discount. The 48-page color catalog shows work shoes and boots for men by Clarino, Knapp, New Generation, Red Label, Rocky, Timberland, and Wrangler; dress shoes and loafers by Dexter and Eagle Rock; casuals by Hush Puppies and Pine Cones; walking shoes by Street Cars; and even slippers. Women can choose from athletic-style service shoes, wedge-sole Oxfords, low-heel pumps, loafers, and slip-ons, all of which are priced under $50 at pair at this writing. If you live near one of the 29 Knapp stores, drop by and try them on; otherwise, anything you buy by mail that doesn't fit can be returned, unworn, for an exchange or refund.

Special Factors: Satisfaction is guaranteed; returns of unworn or defective shoes are accepted for exchange, refund, or credit; C.O.D. orders are accepted.

OKUN BROS. SHOES

356 E. SOUTH ST.-WBM
KALAMAZOO, MI 49007
800-433-6344
FAX: 616-383-3401

Catalog: free
Save: 18% average (see text)
Pay: check, MO, MC, V, Discover
Sells: dress, casual, and work shoes
Store: same address; Monday to Friday 8:30 A.M.–9 P.M., Saturday 8:30–7

Okun Bros. has been serving the footwear needs of Kalamazoo since 1920, and brings its shoe store to the rest of world through a 48-page catalog. Okun maintains that it can fit nearly any foot, and it has the largest stock of men's work and safety shoes available in Michigan. Some of the brands are rarely found sold at less than full retail. The typical discount is 18%, but heavy boots for sub-zero conditions have been sold here at up to 44% off, and specials in the sales flyers further the savings to 50%.

Casual shoes, plain pumps, athletic shoes for several sports, men's dress shoes, sandals, loafers and moccasins, deck shoes, nurses' shoes, bikers' boots, and work shoes and boots are all available through Okun. The brands and lines offered here number over 200, including some of the most popular: Stacy Adams, Adidas, Auditions, Avia, Bates, Brooks, H.H. Brown, Carolina Shoe Co., Champion, Clarks, Converse, Dexter, Dr. Martens, Double H, Drew, Eastland, Easy Spirit, Allen Edmonds, Ellesse, Etonic, Extra Depth, Florsheim, Foot-Joy, Daniel Green, Hi-Tec, Hush Puppies, Johnston & Murphy, K-Swiss, L.A. Gear, La Crosse, Minnetonka, New Balance, Nike, Nunn Bush, Nurse Mates, Propet, Red Bird, Reebok, Rockport, Rocky, Saucony, Sebago, Soft Spots, Sorel, Sperry Top-Sider, Sporto, Timberland, Tingley, Tru-Stitch, and Wolverine. Thor-Lo "padded" specialty sport socks and Spenco insoles are also sold.

Because only a fraction of the stock can be shown in the catalog, inquire about brands and styles not shown—they may be available.

Special Factors: Satisfaction is guaranteed; price quote by phone or letter with SASE; unworn returns are accepted; orders are shipped worldwide.

SEE ALSO

Austad's • *golf apparel and shoes* • **SPORTS**
Jos. A. Bank Clothiers, Inc. • *men's shoes* • **CLOTHING**

Bike Nashbar • *bicycling footwear* • **SPORTS**

Cabela's Inc. • *hunting and fishing wear, outdoor clothing and footwear* • **SPORTS**

Cahall's Brown Duck Catalog • *rugged footwear for men and women* • **CLOTHING**

Campmor • *outdoor footwear* • **SPORTS**

Cycle Goods Corp. • *bicycling apparel and footwear* • **SPORTS**

The Deerskin Place • *suede boots, moccasins, etc.* • **CLOTHING**

Deerskin Trading Post, Inc. • *deerskin and shearling footwear* • **CLOTHING**

Defender Industries, Inc. • *boating shoes* • **AUTO**

Gander Mountain, Inc. • *rugged boots and footwear* • **SPORTS**

Gohn Bros. • *work shoes and boots for men and women* • **CLOTHING**

Goldberg's Marine Distributors • *boating shoes* • **AUTO**

Golf Haus • *golf shoes* • **SPORTS**

Golfsmith International, Inc. • *golf clothing and footwear* • **SPORTS**

Holabird Sports • *shoes for sports activities* • **SPORTS**

Huntington Clothiers • *small selection of men's shoes* • **CLOTHING**

Las Vegas Discount Golf & Tennis • *tennis and other sports apparel; tennis and golf shoes* • **SPORTS**

M&E Marine Supply Company, Inc. • *boating shoes* • **AUTO**

Mid-Western Sport Togs • *deerskin moccasins* • **CLOTHING**

National Wholesale Co., Inc. • *small selection of women's footwear* • **CLOTHING**

Northern Hydraulics, Inc. • *rugged footwear* • **TOOLS**

Omaha Vaccine Company, Inc. • *Red Ball boots* • **ANIMAL**

Performance Bicycle Shop • *cycling clothing, footwear, and helmets* • **SPORTS**

Road Runner Sports • *sports apparel and shoes* • **SPORTS**

Sara Glove Company, Inc. • *work shoes and boots* • **CLOTHING**

Sierra Trading Post • *outdoor shoes* • **SPORTS**

Support Plus • *support hosiery, comfort-styled footwear, therapeutic apparel* • **MEDICINE**

Tafford Manufacturing, Inc. • *nurses' shoes* • **CLOTHING**

Vanderbilt's Mail Order, Inc. • *Western and work boots, hiking boots, etc.* • **CLOTHING**

Wholesale Veterinary Supply, Inc. • *work shoes and boots* • **ANIMAL**

Wiley Outdoor Sports, Inc. • *hunting and outdoor footwear* • **SPORTS**

Mother and Child

Clothing and accessories for babies, children, and expectant and nursing mothers; baby furniture, strollers, and related goods

The firms in this section offer maternity wear, children's clothing and accessories, and even baby furniture—all at savings of up to 60%. In addition, a number of the firms listed throughout this book sell goods for mother and baby. *Chock Catalog Corp.* ("Clothing") features Carter's receiving blankets and crib sets, Curity diapers, and underwear and nightwear for newborn through toddler sizes. *Gohn Bros.* ("Clothing") sells Curity diapers and Gerber bibs, baby sleepers, waterproof pants, and shirts. *Campmor* ("Sports") offers baby buntings, Snuglis, and a diaper-changer backpack for the truly intrepid parent. And the *Consumer Information Center* and *Superintendent of Documents* ("Books") usually offer a number of publications devoted to baby-care advice and related information. For other tips on buying baby goods, see *Guide to Baby Products* and other books from Consumers Union in the current issue of *Consumer Reports*.

THE B2 PRODUCTS

INGRAM DR.
P.O. BOX 1108
HAYMARKET, VA 22069
800-695-7073

Brochure: free with SASE
Save: up to 65%
Pay: check or MO
Sells: infants' clothing
Store: mail order only

After discovering that 85% of parents change their babies' clothing three times a day, the founders of this firm concluded that it would make sense to parents to buy in dozens—for the convenience and for the savings. And you do save when you buy from B2—up to 65% on selected everyday items. B2 sells a selection of baby undershirts, in sizes from newborn to 34 pounds. Once you become a B2 customer, you'll receive a monthly health newsletter, bonus coupons, and other savings.

Please note: Readers in Canada, Alaska, and Hawaii should contact B2 for shipping and handling rates.

Special Factors: Satisfaction is guaranteed; quantity discounts are available; returns are accepted for exchange, refund, or credit.

BABY BUNZ & CO.

P.O. BOX 1717-WB94
SEBASTOPOL, CA 95473
707-829-5347

Catalog: $1
Save: up to 30%
Pay: check, MO, MC, V
Sells: diapering supplies and layette items
Store: mail order only

If you use cloth diapers instead of disposables, you may be over-whelmed by all the prefolded diapers and diaper "systems" on the market. One of the most popular diapering duos among the cloth set is a standard or fitted diaper with a natural-fiber cover. Baby Bunz & Co. has been selling the best-known covers, Nikkys, since 1982. Nikkys are made in soft lambswool, waterproof cotton, "breathable" poly, and vinyl-lined cotton, and are available in sizes from newborn to three years (up to 34 pounds). Training and all-night pants are also offered, and Baby Bunz prices the Nikkys up to 30% below retail.

The Baby Bunz brochure also shows the company's own line of dia-pers in three styles (contour, prefolded, and flat), which are sold at up to 22% below regular retail. (The brochure includes guides to folding diapers and how to use Nikkys.) Dovetails biodegradable diapers are available, as well as Rubber Duckies nylon duffle sacks and pull-on covers, adorable layettewear from Fix of Sweden, lambskin and wool booties, and bedding—pima cotton and Merino wool blankets, and a crib-sized lambskin. The natural theme is carried on with Weleda baby-care products, bath sponges, natural bristle baby brushes, a well-designed potty, and the ideal lovey, "First Doll."

Canadian readers, please note: Only U.S. funds are accepted.

Special Factors: Satisfaction is guaranteed; unused returns are accepted within 30 days for replacement, refund, or credit; minimum order is $15 with credit cards.

BABY CLOTHES WHOLESALE

70 ETHEL RD. WEST
PISCATAWAY, NJ 08854
201-572-9520
201-842-2900

Catalog: $3
Save: up to 50%
Pay: check, MO, MC, V, AE, Discover
Sells: clothing for babies and children
Store: same address; also 70 Apple St., Tinton Falls, NJ

It's a shame to spend lots of money on children's clothing when they grow so quickly, especially when you don't have to: Baby Clothes Wholesale brings you everything from underwear to snowsuits for sizes newborn to seven, at savings of up to 50%. The company's 48-page color catalog features coveralls and rompers, sunsuits, terry sleepers and crawlers, creepers, bibs, receiving blankets, underwear, socks, overalls, party dresses, T-shirts, sweatsuits, turtlenecks, playsuits, cardigans, bonnets and caps, bathing suits, nightwear, vests, and bomber jackets. All of the clothing is first-quality, but some of the layette items (blankets, sheets, bibs, etc.) are irregular, and clearly indicated. Please note that orders under $50 are accepted, but a $5 handling fee is charged.

Canadian readers, please note: Only U.S. funds are accepted.

Special Factors: Satisfaction is guaranteed; quantity discounts are available; returns of unworn, unused, unwashed goods are accepted for exchange, refund, or credit; minimum order is $50.

BOSOM BUDDIES

P.O. BOX 6138,
DEPT. WBM
KINGSTON, NY 12401
914-338-2038

Catalog: free
Save: up to 50% (see text)
Pay: check, MO, MC, V
Sells: nursing bras and clothing
Store: by appointment only

Bosom Buddies was founded in 1983 by a nursing mother who saw a market for "breastfeeding fashions." Nursing bras by Decent Exposures, Leading Lady, and TR Sport are offered, including many all-cotton styles. This is a great source for hard-to-find sizes—the Decent Exposures bras run up to size 46K, and other lines go up to 42H. Nightgowns and other clothing designed to make nursing easy are sold as well. Bosom Buddies also carries nursing pads and a full line of equipment for expressing and storing breast milk, and a number of helpful books. The eight-page catalog includes a guide to taking your measurements, so you're sure to order the right size. Not every item is discounted, but prices are reasonable, and savings run up to 50% on sale items.

Special Factor: Order sale merchandise promptly, since quantities may be limited.

MOTHERS WORK MATERNITY

DEPT. WSBM
1309 NOBLE ST., 5TH FL.
PHILADELPHIA, PA 19123
215-625-4582
FAX: 215-440-9845

Catalog: $3, refundable
Save: up to 30%
Pay: check, MO, MC, V, AE, Optima
Sells: maternity clothing
Store: 60 stores nationwide; four outlet stores: 1714 Walnut St. and Franklin Mills Mall in Philadelphia, PA; Boston Attic, 10 Milk St., Boston, MA; and Potomac Mills Malls, VA

Expectant executives, you can either put your tailor on a retainer as your waistline expands, or look here for suitable maternity wear. The Mothers Work Maternity catalog features business-worthy suits and ensembles designed to take you through every stage of pregnancy: The designs are classy and smart, competitively priced, and half of the 32-

page catalog is devoted to leisure clothes that are just as attractive. Sizes run from 4 to 14.

Special Factors: Satisfaction is guaranteed; returns are accepted within ten days for exchange, refund, or credit; orders are shipped worldwide.

THE NATURAL BABY CO., INC.

114 W. FRANKLIN AVE.,
 SUITE WBM4
PENNINGTON, NJ
 08534-1405
800-388-BABY
FAX: 609-737-7665

Catalog: free
Save: up to 50%
Pay: check, MO, MC, V, Discover
Sells: diapers and infants' clothing, toys, remedies, etc.
Store: mail order only

The people behind The Natural Baby Co. really love children—and their parents. Everything in the firm's catalog has been chosen with an eye to making children comfortable and keeping them healthy, without costing Mom and Dad a bundle. The Natural Baby Co. was established in 1983, and has a policy of supporting home-based businesses—so the quilt you buy here for your own baby may have been made by a mother of nine, and the wood cradles and toys crafted by carpenters "in between pouring out the Cheerios"!

Diapers and covers are the featured items—The Natural Baby's own "Rainbow" diaper, a fitted cloth style (pinless, foldless) made of flannel-lined terrycloth ($28.95 per dozen). If you're on a tight budget, you can get the "Natural Baby Diapers" of birdseye, for $16 a dozen. Nikky diaper covers are available in several styles, as well as The Natural Baby's own waterproof nylon covers, diaper pads, and conventional cloth diapers. The catalog includes helpful sidebars on diapering with pinless covers, the cloth vs. disposables debate, and tips on preventing diaper rash.

There's much more for baby: a line of baby clothing from organically grown cotton, the Cozy Baby Carrier, a versatile baby sling, and sheepskin rugs and play balls, Faribo crib blankets, flannel creepers, and Storkenworks shoes. The catalog offers some clothing for older kids, including long johns, Nikky's heavyweight pants (in sizes to fit children up to 110 pounds), socks, sweaters, turtlenecks, and other goods. Mothers are treated to Leading Lady bras, and sportswear and nightwear designed to make nursing easier. Among the offerings are accupressure wrist bands that help to ease the nausea of morning sickness, a "herbal basket" full of alternative remedies for pregnancy-related conditions, as well as homeopathic treatments and herb-based first-aid cream, tick repellant, and other natural health aids for the whole family. And the catalog also offers wooden toys, dolls, rattles, balls, cradles, and other safe and nontoxic diversions for children. In addition, the firm's ongoing closeout program offers discontinued styles at half the price of *wholesale*.

The Natural Baby Co. is offering readers a discount of $4 on their first order. Be sure to identify yourself as a WBMC reader when you order. This WBMC reader discount expires February 1, 1995.

Special Factors: C.O.D. orders are accepted; orders are shipped worldwide (20% shipping surcharge).

HOLLY NICOLAS
NURSING COLLECTION

DEPT. W
P.O. BOX 7121
ORANGE, CA 92613-7121
714-639-5933

Swatched Catalog: $1
Save: up to 50%
Pay: check, MO, AE
Sells: nursing clothing
Store: mail order only

This business was founded in 1983 by a former fashion model, who began by creating nursing dresses for the mothers of her grandchildren, Holly and Nicolas. The clothes she produces are well designed, incorporating concealed openings for nursing into the lines of the garments.

The catalog shows pretty, feminine blouses, dresses, and nightgowns designed for the nursing mother. The styles are classic: A stylish, sailor-collar dress in dark blue Oxford cloth, a square-neck blouse in blue shirting, and a basic blouse that comes in six colors are among the offerings. Prices are very reasonable: $20 for the nightgown with hidden openings for nursing, to $62 for a long-sleeved, shawl-collared dress in iris. Samples of the actual fabrics are included in the brochure.

Holly Nicolas is offering readers of this book a 20% discount on the "Transition Dress," a flattering style that will see you through the nine months and nursing afterward, thanks to concealed openings. It's self-belted and comes in a wool or cotton/poly blend. Identify yourself as a reader when you order to take the discount. This WBMC reader discount expires February 1, 1995.

Special Factors: Returns are accepted within 30 days for exchange or refund; orders are shipped worldwide.

RUBENS & MARBLE, INC.

P.O. BOX 14900-A
CHICAGO, IL 60614-0900
312-348-6200

Brochure: free with SASE
Save: up to 60%
Pay: check or MO
Sells: infants' clothing and bedding
Store: 2340 N. Racine Ave.; Monday to Friday 9–3

Rubens & Marble has been supplying hospitals with baby clothes since 1890, and sells the same goods to consumers at up to 60% below regular retail prices. The babywear basics include undershirts in sizes from newborn to 36 months, with short, long, and mitten-cuff sleeves; they're offered in snap, tie, plain, and double-breasted slipover styles (many are seconds, with small knitting flaws). First-quality cotton/wool blend and preemie-sized cotton undershirts are available as well. Rubens & Marble also offers fitted bassinet and crib sheets, training and waterproof pants, kimonos, drawstring-bottom baby gowns, and terry bibs.

Special Factors: You *must* send a self-addressed, stamped envelope to receive the price list; seconds are clearly indicated; minimum order is one package (varying number depending on type of item).

THE WABBY COMPANY

3331 GOLD RUN RD.,
    DEPT. W
BOULDER, CO 80302
303-449-2120

Brochure: free
Save: up to 30% (see text)
Pay: check, MO, MC, V
Sells: diapers and covers, long underwear, etc.
Store: mail order only

The Wabby Company sells its own diaper covers, "Wabbies," which are made of "breathable" Gore-Tex fabric. Because Gore-Tex allows vapors to escape but contains actual wetness, the Wabby should help your baby's bottom stay cooler than when it's doing a slow burn in rubber pants. Wabbies can be rinsed out and machine washed and dried (see the brochure for use and care details). They're offered in sizes from newborn (birth to 12 pounds) to XL (29 to 34 pounds), in white, yellow, or a print, and you'll need four or five Wabbies per baby. Wabbies cost $12.25 each, which isn't cheap, but the Wabby is unique in its use of Gore-Tex and may help your baby feel more comfortable and happier. The Wabby Company sells cotton diapers, washcloths, and wet sacks for diapers, as well as hats, booties, and cotton long underwear in sizes from three months to two years.

Special Factors: Quantity discounts are available; orders are shipped worldwide.

SEE ALSO

Alden Comfort Mills • down-filled crib comforters • **HOME: LINEN**
Alfax Wholesale Furniture • institutional nursery and day-care center furniture • **OFFICE**
Butternut Books • children's books • **BOOKS**
Chock Catalog Corp. • baby clothing and bedding • **CLOTHING**
Clothcrafters, Inc. • cloth diapers and crib sheets • **GENERAL MERCHANDISE**
Betty Crocker Enterprises • children's tableware, toys, games, and puzzles • **GENERAL MERCHANDISE**
Michael C. Fina Co. • sterling silver baby gifts • **HOME: TABLE SETTINGS**
Gohn Bros. • nursing bras, layette and baby goods • **CLOTHING**
Goldman & Cohen • nursing and maternity underwear • **CLOTHING**
The Linen Source • crib and juvenile bedding • **HOME: LINEN**
No Nonsense Direct • maternity and nursing underwear • **CLOTHING**
Wicker Warehouse Inc. • wicker nursery furniture, doll buggies • **HOME: FURNISHINGS**

CRAFTS AND HOBBIES

Materials, supplies, tools, and equipment
for crafts and hobbies

The firms here can supply nearly any craft, including the needle arts, marquetry, miniatures, quilting, stenciling, basketry, clock making, wheat weaving, quilling, wood carving, spinning and weaving, batiking, decoy painting, jewelry making, and much more. Some of these companies have been in business for generations and specialize in avocations that your local crafts shop may not even know exist. If you have a problem with a material or technique, most can provide assistance by phone.

Placing an order will usually guarantee you a spot on the mailing list, which means you'll receive the sales flyers with savings of up to 70%. Be sure to save your catalogs—they're invaluable for comparison shopping, and are often good sources of technical information.

Home sewing is enjoying a vogue these days, especially among women who need good business wardrobes, but balk at the ludicrous prices of ready-to-wear. (The do-it-yourself home decorating market has undergone a similar revitalization.) Sewing it yourself can not only save you money, but if you're skilled you'll get a custom tailor job, with the fabric and details *you* want. Every aspect of sewing—from the fabric and notions to the patterns to the machines themselves—has been improved over the past decade. The sources here can help you find the right tools and materials for your clothing project, but see the listings in "Home: Decor" for decorator fabrics.

If you do needlework and use DMC floss, be sure you have the DMC Embroidery Floss Card in your files. This reference includes samples of each DMC floss color and a guide to which colors are available in pearl cotton in sizes 3, 5, and 8. (Most discount sources carry DMC floss, but few include color guides.) The American Needlewoman sells the DMC

Floss Card; request the free catalog from The American Needlewoman, P.O. Box 6472-WBMC, Fort Worth, TX 76115.

If your craft or hobby involves the use of hazardous materials, it's essential to take precautions while you work. For more information, see the introduction to "Art Materials." For wooden toy parts, see the listings in "Tools." For lapidary equipment and findings, see the firms listed in "Jewelry."

FIND IT FAST

BASKETRY AND SEAT REWEAVING • **Caning Shop, Frank's Cane**
BOXES • **Boxes and Bows**
FEATHERS • **Gettinger**
FUN FUR • **Monterey Mills**
GENERAL CRAFTS • **Bailey's Wholesale, Circle Craft, Craft King, Craft Resources, Think Ink, Vanguard**
MODELS • **Model Expo**
NOTIONS AND SEWING TOOLS • **Button Shop, A. Feibusch, Home-Sew, Newark Dressmaker, Solo Slide, Taylor's, Thread Discount Sales**
TEXTILE ARTS, YARN, FABRIC • **Atlanta Thread, Dharma Trading, Fabric Editions, Fashion Fabrics Club, Fiber Studio, Fort Crailo, Global Village, Great Northern Weaving, J & J, Oppenheim's, Serge & Sew, Smiley's Yarn, Straw Into Gold, Thai Silks, Utex, Webs, Babouris, Maurice Brassard, D. MacGillivray**
WOODWORKING PLANS AND PARTS • **Cherry Tree Toys, Meisel Hardware**

ATLANTA THREAD & SUPPLY

695 RED OAK RD.
 DEPT., WBMC 94
STOCKBRIDGE, GA 30281
800-331-7600
404-389-9115
FAX: 404-389-9202

Catalog: $1
Save: up to 50%
Pay: check, MO, MC, V, AE, Discover
Sells: sewing tools, notions, and pressing equipment
Store: mail order only

Atlanta Thread is a division of National Thread & Supply, a major distributor of sewing equipment. Atlanta has been doing business since

1948, and boasts the lowest prices around on Gingher shears, Gosling drapery tapes, Kirsch drapery hardware, YKK zippers, and many other goods. This is a great source for quality supplies and equipment—coned thread, zippers and parts, custom tailoring linings and pads, buttons, Singer's sewing guides and professional tailoring manuals, cords, crinoline stiffening bands, fringe, hook-and-loop tape, professional pressing equipment—tables and boards, irons by Hi-Steam/Naomoto, Rheem, Rowenta, and Sussman—and commercial-quality sewing machines, sergers, and parts. The 64-page catalog is illustrated, but if you need more information on a product, call and ask.

Special Factors: Satisfaction is guaranteed; returns are accepted within 30 days for exchange, refund, or credit; C.O.D. orders are accepted.

BAILEY'S WHOLESALE FLORAL SUPPLY

P.O. BOX 591W
ARCADIA, IN 46030
317-984-3663
FAX: 317-984-3663

Catalog: $3, refundable
Save: up to 50%
Pay: check, MO, MC, V
Sells: silk flowers and bridal accessories
Store: mail order only

Bailey's Wholesale Floral Supply was founded in 1983 by Sharon Bailey, who was then running a part-time business designing silk floral arrangements. After finding that wholesale suppliers were reluctant to fill her small orders for silk flowers, she solved her problem by buying in volume—and sharing the considerable surplus and savings with other small businesses in the same position.

Her 18-page catalog shows a lovely selection of flowers—roses and buds, freesia, carnations, lilies of the valley, orchids, stephanotis, orchids, and more—and a variety of fabric foliage, including ferns, spider plants, Swedish ivy, and geranium leaves. Real dried foliage—baby's breath, eucalyptus, statice, etc.—is available, as well as supplies for wiring and arranging. If you're shopping for bridal accessories, check the savings on fans, lace parasols, ring pillows, tulle, lace, and other items. Most of the flowers are offered in any of dozens of colors, but Bailey's will also dye your flowers to order. A sampler of 32 flowers, one of each, costs $34. And there's *no* minimum order!

Special Factors: Satisfaction is guaranteed; quantity discounts are available; returns are accepted for exchange, refund, or credit; orders are shipped worldwide.

BOXES AND BOWS

**P.O. BOX 773
CANBY, OK 97013
503-651-2500**

Price List: free
Save: up to 50%
Pay: check or MO
Sells: hatboxes and bandboxes
Store: mail order only

Boxes and Bows sells handmade chipboard boxes, both oval band-boxes (from about 3" by 4" by 2-1/2" to about 6" by 8" by 4"), and round hatboxes (from 12" to 18" in diameter). Both kinds of boxes are ready to finish—with paint, fabric, paper, or another covering—and cost from $1.40 for the smallest bandbox to $5.20 for the largest hatbox. (Hatbox sets of similar sizes sell for over twice as much in other catalogs as they do here.) Whether you're interested in decorating them for your own use, as gifts, for resale, or want to sell the unadorned boxes to other craftspersons, you'll get a great deal: Prices are wholesale, but there's no minimum order!

Special Factors: No minimum order is required.

BUFFALO BATT & FELT CORP.

**3307 WALDEN AVE.,
   DEPT. WBMC
DEPEW, NY 14043
716-683-4100
FAX: 716-683-8928**

Brochure and Samples: $1, refundable
Save: 40% plus
Pay: check, MO, MC, V
Sells: fiberfill, quilt batts, and pillow inserts
Store: mail order only

Buffalo Batt's "Super Fluff" polyester stuffing is so springy and resilient, the snowy-white samples nearly bounce out of the brochure. The firm has been in business since 1913, and sells this craft and upholstery stuffing by the case at savings of 40% or more on regular retail prices.

Super Fluff is manufactured in rolls 27" wide by 20 yards long and is the ideal filler for upholstery and crafts in which support and a down-like feel are desired. In addition to having high loft and nonallergenic properties, Super Fluff is machine washable and dryable, mildew resistant, and easy to sew. Buffalo Batt also sells Super Fluff in one- and two-pound bags, bulk rolls, pillow inserts (from 12" square to 24" square), and "traditional" and two-inch-thick "comforter-style" quilt batts. The only negative is the minimum order of any two cases, which may be more than most single projects require. But it's a manageable amount for a home-based crafts business, quilting circle, cooperative, or for a major decorating project. Or you can store the surplus for future use, or share with crafty friends!

Please note: Orders are shipped via UPS within the continental U.S. only.

Special Factors: Quantity discounts are available; minimum order is any two cases; C.O.D. orders are accepted.

THE BUTTON SHOP

P.O. BOX 1065-HM
OAK PARK, IL 60304
708-795-1234

Catalog: free
Save: up to 50%
Pay: check, MO, MC, V
Sells: buttons and sewing supplies
Store: 7023 Roosevelt Rd., Berwyn, IL;
Monday to Friday 9–4, Saturday 10–2

The Button Shop, founded in 1900, stocks closures of all kinds, as well as trims, sewing machine parts, scissors, and other sewing tools and notions at savings of up to 50% on list prices or regular retail. Several pages of the 18-page catalog are devoted to buttons—anonymous white shirt buttons, clear waistband buttons, tiny buttons for doll clothes, classic four-hole coat and suit buttons, gilt heraldic buttons for blazers, designs for dressy clothing, Navy pea coat buttons, braided leather buttons for tweeds, and dozens of others, including baseball gloves and other novelty designs for children's clothing. If you want to custom-cover buttons with your own fabric, you'll find Maxant and Prym kits, as well as make-your-own fabric belt and buckle materials, gripper snaps and grommet sets, hooks and eyes of all types, zippers (including odd sizes to 108"), and Velcro by the inch and by the yard. The Button Shop sells all kinds of ric-rac, bias tape, cording, white and black elastic (from 1/8" to 3"), replacement jacket cuffs, elbow patches, trouser pockets, and other notions and supplies. Thread in cotton, cotton-covered polyester, and polyester is offered; the brands include Dritz, Fiskars, Gingher, Oncore, Prym, Singer, Suisse, Talon, Wiss, and Wrights.

The Button Shop's comparatively deep inventory of sewing machine supplies and parts includes needles, presser feet, bobbins, bobbin cases, needle plates, buttonholers, motors, foot controls, light bulbs, and belts. The catalog descriptions are brief, and line drawings are the only illustrations. If you're not sure an item is the right one and need more information, call or write before ordering. You may also send a fabric swatch for the best color match if you're buying trim, thread, or buttons, and The Button Shop custom-makes zippers in lengths up to 120".

Special Factors: Returns are accepted within 30 days for exchange, refund, or credit; minimum order is $5, $10 with credit cards; orders are shipped worldwide.

THE CANING SHOP

926 GILMAN ST.,
  DEPT. WBM
BERKELEY, CA 94710-1494
510-527-5010

Catalog: $1, refundable
Save: up to 30%
Pay: check, MO, MC, V
Sells: seat-reweaving and basketry supplies
Store: same address; Tuesday to Friday 10–6, Saturday 10–2

 ¡Si!

The Caning Shop stocks the materials, tools, and instructions you'll need to restore your woven-seat chairs—or weave a basket from scratch. The owner of this business coauthored *The Caner's Handbook*, and prides himself on offering the "highest quality materials that can be found in the jungles of Malaysia and Indonesia." Prices are lower here than those charged at some specialty shops, and a little higher than a discount source checked recently. But the selection is excellent, and it's worth paying more if you get materials that last longer.

The Caning Shop, which began business in 1971, carries 15 kinds of prewoven cane webbing, which is used in modern and mass-produced seating. Older chairs, which have holes in the frame around the seat opening, must be rewoven by hand. For these chairs, The Caning Shop offers hanks of cane in a full range of sizes, including binder cane, and also sells Danish seat cord, rawhide lacing, fiber rush, Hong Kong grass (seagrass), ash splint, Shaker tape, whole reed (for wicker), wicker braid, rattan, pressed fiber (imitation leather) seats, and tools to aid in installation. Basketry buffs should look here for kits, materials, hoops, and handles. If you're a novice seat reweaver, there's help here: half of the 40-page catalog is devoted to volumes on caning and seat reweaving, as well as general furniture restoration and basketry. If you live in or near Berkeley, you can get help with your project at the shop, which also gives classes in a variety of crafts—"Seaweed Basketry," "Gourd Crafting," and "Ukrainian Egg Decorating" were among those in a recent brochure.

Canadian readers, please note: Payment for the catalog and goods orders must be in U.S. funds.

Special Factors: Satisfaction is guaranteed; C.O.D. orders are accepted; orders are shipped worldwide.

CHERRY TREE TOYS, INC.

━━━━━━━━

P.O. BOX 369-140
BELMONT, OH 43718
800-848-4363
614-484-4363
FAX: 614-484-4388

Catalog: $1
Save: up to 50%
Pay: check, MO, MC, V, Discover
Sells: woodworking and crafts supplies
Store: I-70, Exit 208, Belmont, OH; Monday to Saturday 9–5, Sunday 11–5

Cherry Tree Toys sells kits for delightful playthings, clocks, and door harps, as well as scores of wooden parts for your own designs. The company was founded in 1981 and prices its goods up to 50% below what toy and gift shops charge for similar items. The 68-page color catalog shows kits for dozens of whirligigs, musical banks, decorative clocks (depicting motifs ranging from trains to football helmets), door harps, wooden wagons and sleds, pull toys, miniatures, dollhouses, and "Wild West" wagons. Clock movements and markers, music boxes, and hundreds of wooden parts—wheels, spindles, smokestacks, beads, knobs, pulls, pegs, etc.—are offered as well. Cherry Tree sells plans, kits, and books on making toys, banks, dollhouses, whirligigs, clocks, and door harps, in addition to the supplies you'll need to finish the projects. See the collection of brass stencils in a range of holiday motifs, and the blank stencil sheets, Dover cut-and-use stencil sets, rubber stamps, paintbrushes and tole paint, and sets of gift tags, cards, and envelopes. If you're able to visit the factory outlet store in Belmont, you'll find discontinued catalog items and seconds at up to 75% off regular prices.

Special Factors: Satisfaction is guaranteed; returns are accepted within 30 days for exchange, refund, or credit; minimum order is $20 with credit cards; C.O.D. orders are accepted ($10 minimum order); orders are shipped worldwide.

CIRCLE CRAFT SUPPLY

P.O. BOX 3000
DOVER, FL 33527-3000
813-659-0992

Catalog: $1
Save: up to 30%
Pay: check or MO
Sells: general crafts supplies
Store: 13295 U.S. Hwy. 92, Dover, FL

The 152-page catalog from Circle Craft Supply lists everything, from "abaca shapes" to zip-lock bags, that you'll need to indulge in any of scores of arts, crafts, and hobbies. Circle Craft was founded in 1982, and sells at discounts that average 20%, and reach 30% on some items. There are tools and materials here for a wide range of crafts and pastimes—beading, jewelry making, basketry, flower making, quick-count plastic canvas crafts, doll making, lamp making, clock making, Christmas ornaments, macrame, chenille crafts, and much more.

Special Factors: Authorized returns are accepted within 10 days; C.O.D. orders are accepted; orders are shipped worldwide.

CRAFT KING, INC.

P.O. BOX 90637, DEPT. W
LAKELAND, FL 33804
813-686-9600
FAX: 813-688-5072

Catalog: $2
Save: up to 60%
Pay: check, MO, MC, V, Discover
Sells: general crafts supplies and projects
Store: 5675 New Tampa Hwy., Lakeland, FL;
Monday to Saturday 9–5

Craft King's 180-page catalog is packed with supplies and kits for the kind of crafts that are popular in schools and camps, which also happen to make great after-school amusements. Craft King was established in 1979, and has no minimum order requirement. The catalog lists tools and materials for every sort of pastime and craft, including painting, macrame, lamp-shade making, cross-stitch, beadwork, Christmas ornaments, felt crafts, pom-poms, doll making, miniatures, plastic canvas crafts, "fashion art," wood burning, punch embroidery, quilting, basketry, candlemaking, dollhouse supplies, and more. Patterns and kits for plastic canvas and beading projects and instruction books for all types of crafts are also available, and prices average 30% to 60% off list.

Special Factors: Satisfaction is guaranteed; authorized returns are accepted for exchange, refund, or credit; orders are shipped worldwide.

CRAFT RESOURCES, INC.

BOX 828
FAIRFIELD, CT 06430-0828
203-254-7702
FAX: 203-255-6456

Catalog: $1
Save: up to 50%
Pay: check, MO, MC, V
Sells: adult-oriented crafts kits
Store: mail order only

Craft Resources, founded in 1972, specializes in needlework projects in kit form and offers "the largest selection of adult-oriented crafts available." The catalog shows kits for projects in latch hooking, needlepoint, long stitch, crewel, stamped and counted cross-stitch, string art, basketry, copper punching, wood crafts, and "stained glass" (sun catchers). The kits range from very basic designs for the beginner to more complex patterns, but a patient novice should be able to tackle any of these projects, with reasonable to impressive results. Most yield purely decorative items, such as the latch-hook blocks, but there are kits to help you create small rugs, afghans, picture frames, baby bibs, pillows, and baskets.

Craft Resources also sells yarn, embroidery floss, needlestitch canvas, knitting needles and crochet hooks, embroidery hoops, pillow forms, fiberfill batts, stencils, picture mats, and frames. The best prices are on the kits sold by the dozen—the per-kit price can drop from $3 to $1.25. Therapists and instructors will find these bargains invaluable, and they provide an ideal way for the rest of us to "try out" a craft without investing much money.

Special Factors: Satisfaction is guaranteed; unused returns are accepted within 60 days; minimum order is $10 with credit cards; orders are shipped worldwide.

DHARMA TRADING CO.

P.O. BOX 150916
SAN RAFAEL, CA
94915-0916
415-456-7657
FAX: 415-456-8747

Catalog: free
Save: up to 50%
Pay: check, MO, MC, V, Discover
Sells: textile art supplies
Store: 1604 Fourth St., San Rafael, CA;
Monday to Friday 8–5

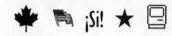

The "whole earth" movement may have peaked in 1969, the year this firm was founded, but Dharma Trading has survived even the pinstripes of the 1980s. The firm sells tools and materials for the textile arts— dyes, paints, resists, and fabrics—and declares, "We are the source for the tie-dye dyes used by most tie-dyers." The informative, 112-page catalog provides helpful tips on the features of the dyes and paints, application techniques and suggested fabrics, and even metric conversion charts and a shrinkage "estimator." Prices are good, running up to 50% off list or comparable retail.

Coloring agents by Deka, Delta/Shiva, Dupont, Jacquard, Pebeo (Orient Express), Peintex, Procion, Sennelier (Super-Tinfix), Setacolor, Versatex, and other firms are offered, as well as color remover, soda ash, urea, Synthrapol, gutta serti, and other resists. The tools include bottles and droppers for dye mixing and application, textile pens, tjantings, brushes (flat, foam, sumi), and steamers for setting dyes. Dharma Trading also offers nearly 40 pages of cotton and silk clothing and accessories; everything from cotton jester hats and silk earring blanks to cotton skirts, jackets, sweats, and more are shown in the current catalog. A list of cotton, rayon, and silk fabrics that have yielded good results with dyeing and painting is included in the catalog; samples (silk or cotton/rayon) are available for 25¢ each. Selected books dealing with fabric design, painting, screening, direct dyeing, batiking, tie-dyeing, and other techniques are also sold.

Special Factors: Quantity discounts are available; institutional accounts are available; C.O.D. orders are accepted; orders are shipped worldwide.

FABRIC EDITIONS LTD.

Catalog: $3
Save: up to 50%
Pay: check, MO, MC, V
Sells: dress, decorating, and craft fabrics
Store: mail order only

25 KENWOOD CIRCLE
FRANKLIN, MA 02038
800-242-5684
508-520-7970
FAX: 508-520-7910

Whether you're a quilter, sew your children's clothing, or enjoy doing your own home decorating, you'll probably welcome a new source for well-priced cottons and blends. Fabric Editions fills the bill with fabric collections that feature wide color choices and well-coordinated patterns, at prices from $3.75 to $6.95 a yard. The firm offers swatch cards ($2 and $4, depending on the collection) and half-yard samples (perfect for quilting and small projects, from $19.95 and up) for all of the collections. Beautifully colored calicos and small designs predominate, but there are striped, gold-enriched patterns (perfect for home decorating and holiday projects), bold animal prints, Victorian florals, and pillow panels (for 16" squares) as well. In addition to fabric, Fairfield poly batts and pillow forms are available.

Fabric Editions responds to the needs of both home sewers and small businesses with quantity discounts (10% on orders of $125 or more, 20% on orders over $200), and if you're buying at least *five* or more 20-yard lengths of fabric, extra savings of up to 45% (inquire for information). And since you want to be able to count on availability, Fabric Editions offers the "Yours for a Year" program, which guarantees that selected fabrics will be available for a whole year (see the current catalog for details).

Special Factors: Satisfaction is guaranteed; quantity discounts are available; uncut returns are accepted for exchange, refund, or credit; minimum order is $20 with credit cards; orders are shipped worldwide.

FASHION FABRICS CLUB

**10490 BAUR BLVD.
ST. LOUIS, MO 63132
314-993-1464**

Membership: $10 (see text)
Save: up to 50%
Pay: check, MO, MC, V
Sells: dress fabrics
Store: mail order only

Fashion Fabrics Club speaks to the needs of home sewers who make their own clothing, but don't have the time to comb yard goods stores for the perfect fabric. Each month, Fashion Fabrics Club sends its members a brochure with over a dozen coordinated fabric swatches, discount coupons, and other offers. The fabrics are chosen to allow you to create coordinated outfits; a recent mailing featured selections from Koret, Tahari, and Eileen West, at $3.99 to $6.99 a yard. Care recommendations and "usual" selling prices are noted for each selection.

If you write to Fashion Fabrics Club, you'll receive the current packet of swatches and descriptions, with an order form; place an order, and you're automatically enrolled in the Club for a year. If nothing strikes your fancy but you'd like to receive the mailings, it will cost you $10 to join. All purchases are covered by the Club's pledge of satisfaction, and you'll receive discount coupons with each order you place, entitling you to savings on future orders.

Special Factors: Satisfaction is guaranteed; returns are accepted for exchange, refund, or credit; minimum order is $5.

A. FEIBUSCH CORPORATION

**30 ALLEN ST.
NEW YORK, NY 10002
212-226-3964
FAX: 212-219-1065**

Information: price quote
Save: up to 50%
Pay: check or MO
Sells: zippers, thread, notions, and garment supplies
Store: same address; Monday to Friday 9:30–5, Sunday 10–5

Feibusch has been helping New Yorkers zip up since 1941, handling requests from the mundane to the exotic. Zippers of every conceivable size, color, and type are sold here—from minuscule dolls' zippers to heavy-duty closures for tents, luggage, and similar applications. If your requirements aren't met by the existing stock, Feibusch can have your zipper made to order. Talon and YKK zippers are available, and Feibusch also carries all-cotton and polyester thread in a full range of colors. There is no catalog, so *write* with your requirements: Describe what you're looking for or send a sample, specifying length desired, nylon or metal teeth, open or closed end, and other details. Enclose a scrap of fabric, if possible, to assure a good color match. Be sure to include a self-addressed, stamped envelope with your correspondence if you want to receive a reply.

Special Factors: Price quote by letter; orders are shipped worldwide.

THE FIBER STUDIO

P.O. BOX 637, DEPT.
WBMC
HENNIKER, NH 03242
603-428-7830

Book and Equipment Catalog: $1 (see text)
Save: up to 40%
Pay: check, MO, MC, V
Sells: knitting, spinning, and weaving equipment and supplies
Store: 9 Foster Hill Rd., Henniker, NH; Tuesday to Saturday 10–4, Sunday by chance

The Fiber Studio has been serving the needs of knitters, spinners, weavers, and doll makers since 1975 with a well-chosen line of tools and supplies, and great prices on yarn. The catalog lists looms, knitting machines, and spinning equipment and accessories by Ashford, Glimarka, Harrisville Design, Kyra, Leclerc, Louet, and Schacht. The prices on these aren't discounted, but shipping is included on some models (see "Special Factors," below). Natural dyes, mordants, and a good selection of spinning fibers—from mohair tops to silk roving—are offered at competitive prices. (The sample card of current spinning fibers costs $4.) And scores of texts on knitting, spinning, and weaving are available.

The bargains here are on yarns, which are sold in two ways: through the stock shown in the yarn sample set ($4), and through the yarn closeouts. The stock yarns include rug wools, natural yarns, Superwash wool, Irish linen, cotton, silk, Shetland wool, mercerized cotton, and more, priced up to 35% less at The Fiber Studio than at other sources. Quantity discounts on these yarns run from 10% on orders over $100 to 20% on orders over $200. *After* you order the yarn card from The Fiber

Studio, you can send $1 and four long, self-addressed envelopes with two stamps each, and ask to be put on the mailing list for the quarterly closeouts. There are outstanding values here, and our mailing included dozens of types of yarns—loop mohair, 8-4 cotton, chenille yarn, silk and blends, bouclé, alpaca, Scottish Shetland, and many others. If you can get to Henniker, you have a treat: the shop offers an extensive selection of beads from around the world, made of semiprecious stones, wood, bone, glass, horn, clay, and other materials, including trade beads. They aren't listed in the catalog, but you can make inquiries and order by phone.

Canadian readers, please note: Only U.S. funds are accepted.

Special Factors: Specify the *spinning fibers* or *yarns* sample set ($4 each); shipping is included on most models of Harrisville Design, Leclerc, and Schacht looms; quantity discounts are available; minimum order is $15 with credit cards; C.O.D. orders are accepted; orders are shipped worldwide.

FORT CRAILO YARNS COMPANY

P.O. BOX G
NEWBURGH, NY 12551
914-562-2698
FAX: 914-561-3623

Brochure and Samples: $2.80
Save: up to 35%
Pay: check, MO, MC, V, Discover
Sells: yarn for handweaving
Store: Broadway and Wisher Ave., Newburgh, NY; Monday to Saturday 9:30–5:30

Fort Crailo Yarns, in business since 1963, sells four kinds of wool yarn and one of cotton, which are especially suited for handweaving. Prices run up to 35% below those of comparable yarns sold elsewhere. The mothproofed, virgin wool yarn includes Crailo Rya (570 yd./lb., 33 colors), Crailo-Spun (700 yd./lb., 30 colors), Crailo Lite-Spun (1,700 yd./lb., 28 colors), and the very fine Crailo Worsted (4,900 yd./lb., 27 colors). Fort Crailo's cotton yarn is sold in 8-2, 3, 4, 5, and 6 ply, in 17 colors, and is suitable for warp or weft, and all the yarns are sold on half-pound cones. The colors are clear and true, and the range of weights makes Fort Crailo a good source for weavers of anything from fine fabrics to rugs.

Special Factors: Quantity discounts are available.

FRANK'S CANE AND RUSH SUPPLY

P.O. BOX 3025
HUNTINGTON BEACH, CA
 92605-3025
714-847-0707
FAX: 714-843-5645

Catalog: free
Save: up to 40% (see text)
Pay: check, MO, MC, V, Discover
Sells: seat-reweaving supplies, furniture, kits, books, etc.
Store: 7252 Heil Ave., Huntington Beach, CA; Monday to Friday 8–5

Frank's has been in business since 1975, and the comprehensive catalog of seat replacement materials includes over a dozen weaves of cane webbing, as well as strand and binding cane, spline, fiber and wire-fiber rush, fiber wicker, Danish cord, oak and ash splints, round and flat reed, and fiber and real reed braid (often used as trim on wicker furniture). Frank's also sells rattan, basketry materials, raffia, seagrass, "tissue flex" (for rag coil baskets), wood hoops and handles, brass hardware, upholstery tools and supplies, dowels and wood crafts parts, and spindles and finials. Prices are competitive on these goods, and there are some bargains—Frank's is selling decorative upholstery nails for $3 per hundred, which are sold locally for $5.25. The catalog also has six pages of books on seat reweaving, woodworking, basketry, and upholstery.

The furniture kits include hardwood Shaker-style arm and side chairs, rocking chairs, and stools. Prices are low: $11.50 for a stool kit, $25 for a child's ladderback chair kit, and $37 for an adult's chair. (The furniture comes with enough fiber rush or flat fiber—your choice—to complete the seat.)

Special Factors: Minimum order is $10 with credit cards; C.O.D. orders are accepted; orders are shipped worldwide.

GETTINGER FEATHER CORP.

16 W. 36TH ST.
NEW YORK, NY 10018
212-695-9470
FAX: 212-695-9471

Price List and Samples: $2, refundable
Save: up to 75%
Pay: check or MO
Sells: feathers
Store: same address (8th floor); Monday to Thursday 9–5:30, Friday 8:30–3

Gettinger has been serving New York City's milliners and craftspersons since 1915 with a marvelous stock of exotic and common feathers. Even if you're not a creative type, you can add cachet to a tired hat with a few ostrich plumes, and Gettinger's feather boas are a dashing alternative to furs for gala occasions.

Pheasant, guinea hen, turkey, duck, goose, rooster, and peacock feathers are available here, loose or sewn (lined up in continuous rows of even length), by the ounce or the pound, beginning at $5 (loose) and $8 (sewn) per ounce. Pheasant tail feathers, 6" to 8" long, cost $13 per hundred; yard-long peacock feathers are priced at $25 per hundred; and pheasant hides cost $9 and up per skin. Feather boas are available, sold in two-yard pieces, as well as ostrich and marabou fans. And if you're reviving old feather pillows, you may be interested in the bedding feathers, which cost $15 to $45 per pound, depending on the quality (minimum five pounds).

Gettinger Feather is offering readers a discount of 10% on their first order. Be sure to identify yourself as a WBMC reader when you order, and deduct the discount from the cost of the goods only. This WBMC reader discount expires February 1, 1995.

Special Factors: Minimum order is $20; orders are shipped worldwide.

GLOBAL VILLAGE IMPORTS

1101 SW WASHINGTON,
 #140-W
PORTLAND, OR
 97205-2313
503-236-9245
FAX: 503-233-0827

Brochure and Swatches: see text
Save: up to 40%
Pay: check or MO
Sells: Guatemalan and Thai ikat fabrics
Store: mail order only

Ikat is a type of weaving that uses tie-dyed warp threads to create striated designs that blend into overall patterns, which may be as subtle as Zen or as colorfully riotous as a Mardi Gras parade. (Double ikats, in which both warp and weft threads are so dyed, represent a further refinement of the art.) Global Village has been selling handwoven Guatemalan ikats since 1988, and has added a line of silk and cotton ikats handwoven by members of the hill tribes of northern Thailand. The Thai fabrics range from traditional ethnic designs dyed with natural indigo, to radiant multicolor silks—some of which feature motifs of elephants and horsemen woven into the material. The sample fees—$5 for the Guatemalan cottons, $7.50 for the Thai fabrics (add $1 for international inquiries), refundable with purchase—bring you an information packet and swatches of what's currently available. All of the fabrics are 36" wide and are woven by hand on large looms. Most of the Guatemalan fabrics run from $9 to $15 per yard; the double ikats, hard to find at any price, are woven by the roll especially for Global Village. The Thai fabrics range from $12 to $32 per yard, depending on the fiber and design. Recent additions include upholstery-weight cottons, embroidered-look and brocade designs, double ikats shot through with Lurex threads, and zarape designs; at $30 a yard, Global Village believes these are the finest handwoven cottons available from Guatemala today. The firm's in-house designers have also created the "Western Star" collection—Navajo and cowboy saddle blanket motifs, redesigned and woven by hand in Guatemala. Global Village's prices are nearly 50% below the rates prevailing in New York City specialty shops. Fabric designers should take note of the company's custom weaving services, and wholesale inquiries are welcomed.

Special Factors: Minimum order is one yard; quantity discounts are available; C.O.D. orders are accepted; orders are shipped worldwide.

GREAT NORTHERN WEAVING

P.O. BOX 361-D
AUGUSTA, MI 49012
616-731-4487

Catalog and Samples: $1
Save: up to 50%
Pay: check, MO, MC, V
Sells: rug-weaving supplies and tools
Store: mail order only

The homey crafts of braiding and weaving rugs are served at Great Northern Weaving, which has been in business since 1985, and prices most items competitively—rags and filler cost up to 50% less here than elsewhere.

The 12-page catalog lists tools and materials for rug weaving, rug braiding, and shirret. Braid-Aids, Braidkins, Braid-Klamps, Fraser rag cutters, reed and heddle hooks, shuttles, and warping boards are all available. The materials include coned cotton warp (8-4 ply) in over two dozen colors, all-cotton rug filler in 15 shades, 16-ply rug roping, new cotton "rags" on rolls, and loopers in bulk. Reference books are also available.

Canadian readers, please note: Shipping charges on orders sent to Canada are paid C.O.D., and order payment must be made in U.S. funds.

Special Factors: Shipping is included on orders over $20; C.O.D. orders are accepted.

HOME-SEW

DEPT. WM4
P.O. BOX 4099
BETHLEHEM, PA 18018-0099
215-867-3833
FAX: 215-867-9717

Catalog: 50¢
Save: up to 70%
Pay: check, MO, MC, V
Sells: sewing and crafts supplies and notions
Store: mail order only

 (see text)

Home-Sew, which has been in business since 1960, offers savings of up to 70% on assorted laces and trims, as well as a wide range of sewing and crafts supplies. Home-Sew's 32-page catalog is well-organized and easy to use, with clear photographs of the trims and notions.

In addition to scores of laces (Cluny, Venice, nylon, poly, eyelet, etc.), Home-Sew offers elastic, satin and velvet ribbon, ricrac, tape, and appliqués. Specialty thread—for general sewing, overlock machines, carpets, and quilting—is available on cones and on spools. There are zippers, snaps, hooks and eyes, buttons, Velcro dots, belts and buckles, pins, needles, and scissors, as well as floss, adhesives, Styrofoam wreaths, spangles, beads, animal and doll parts, interfacings, and related items. If you're making your own curtains or slipcovers, check the prices on shirring and pleater tape, tasseled and moss fringe, cording, and related goods. Home-Sew makes it easy to see the trims before you buy—just join the Sample Club (50¢, order through the catalog), and you'll receive three mailings of lace, trim, ribbon, and elastics samples per year.

Canadian readers, please note: Send $1 (in Canadian funds) to Home-Sew Canada Inc., B.P. Box 1100, Dept. WBMC, Postal Station "E," Montreal, Quebec H2T 3B1, for the bilingual catalog.

Special Factors: Satisfaction is guaranteed; returns are accepted for exchange, refund, or credit; quantity discounts are available; shipping is included on orders over $40; minimum order is $5; orders are shipped worldwide.

J & J PRODUCTS LTD.

117 W. 9TH ST., SUITE 111
LOS ANGELES, CA 90015
213-624-1840
FAX: 213-624-0134

Swatch Cards: $3 each, refundable (see text)
Save: up to 40%
Pay: check, MO, MC, V
Sells: woolen dress goods
Store: mail order only

Here are quality yard goods in beautiful colors, at competitive prices— gabardines, suitings, flannels, and other fine woolens. J & J showcases each type of fabric in a swatch booklet that costs $3, refundable with a purchase from that line.

In each booklet you'll receive a good-sized swatch, with smaller snippets to show the choice of colors. "Gabardine," $18 per yard, is offered in 45 colors; the mid-weight "Flannel" is shown in 17 shades; "Lightweight Wool Suiting" is a wool broadcloth offered in 32 colors, including turquoise and true red; and "Cashmere" features 20 fabrics, including a number of herringbones and tweeds, in beautiful shadings. You can order the swatch booklets by name for $3 each; the cost of each is refundable with a purchase from that particular booklet, and ordering information is included. The fabric is not inexpensive, but it has the luster and hand of fine-quality goods that wear well.

Special Factor: Satisfaction is guaranteed.

MEISEL HARDWARE SPECIALTIES

P.O. BOX 70MW
MOUND, MN 55364-0070
800-441-9870
FAX: 612-471-8579

Catalog: $2
Save: up to 40%
Pay: check, MO, MC, V, Discover
Sells: hardware, wood crafts parts and plans
Store: 4310 Shoreline Dr., Spring Park, MN;
Monday to Friday 9–6, Saturday 9–5

Woodworkers, toy makers, and creative souls should appreciate the 80-page catalog of plans and project ingredients. Meisel has been in business since 1977, and offers a number of items not often seen in other catalogs, in addition to pricing routine items like lamp harps, wood screws, and foam brushes up to 40% below the going rate.

The catalog shows woodworking plans for toys, vehicles, lamps, yard ornaments, door harps, whirligigs, bird houses, useful things for the home, kitchen projects, and dollhouses. There are parts and supplies for many projects, including 13 sizes of wooden wheels, Shaker pegs, dowels, plastic eyes, turned spindles and posts, finials, wood furniture knobs, cork sheets, brass hinges, clock movements and parts, push-button music boxes, and picture-hanging hardware. In addition to plans and parts, Meisel sells brass hardware, sandpaper, glues, stains, acrylic paints, and other finishing touches. The catalog is also a good source for fix-up materials—turned spindles and legs for chairs and small tables, screw-hole buttons and furniture knobs, casters, magnetic cabinet catches, and furniture glides are all available.

Special Factors: Satisfaction is guaranteed; returns are accepted for exchange, refund, or credit; minimum order is $15; orders are shipped worldwide.

MODEL EXPO, INC.

MOUNT POCONO
INDUSTRIAL PARK
P.O. BOX 1000
TOBYHANNA, PA
18366-1000
800-222-3876
FAX: 717-839-2090

Catalog: $3
Save: up to 45%
Pay: check, MO, MC, V
Sells: ship model kits, supplies, books, etc.
Store: mail order only

If you've never considered building a model ship, you probably haven't seen Model Expo's catalog of models, parts, tools, and books. It's 92 pages of full-color photos of beautiful historical ship models, from transport vessels of ancient Egypt to Jacques Costeau's *Calypso*. In addition to the firm's own models (by its manufacturing arm, Model Shipways), the catalog shows lines from Amati, Artesania Latina, Billing, Constructo, Corel, Dumas, Heller (plastic), Mamoli, and Mantua. Each of the featured models is described fully and rated according to difficulty (entry level, intermediate, or advanced). Well over half of the catalog is devoted to books (on model making, ship design and development, maritime history, naval aviation, and military topics), as well as historic and modern fittings, display cases and pedestals, shipwrights' tools, and hand and power tools. Both novice and experienced modelers will find much to interest them, and for those just taking up the hobby, Model Expo's guaranty will be reassuring: If you should break or lose a part during construction, Model Expo will replace it, free of charge!

Special Factors: Satisfaction is guaranteed; returns (except partially built kits) are accepted within 30 days for exchange, refund, or credit; orders are shipped worldwide.

MONTEREY MILLS OUTLET STORE

P.O. BOX 271
JANESVILLE, WI 53547
800-438-6387

Price List: free with SASE (see text)
Save: up to 50%
Pay: check, MO, MC, V
Sells: fake-fur fabric
Store: 1815 E. Delavan Dr., Janesville, WI;
Monday to Friday 8–4:30, Saturday 8–12 noon

Monterey Mills has been manufacturing deep-pile fabrics for a quarter of a century, and sells its deep-pile fabrics, popularly known as "fun fur," at prices up to 50% below the usual retail. The brochure describes the fiber content of the different furs and lists the available colors, pile height, and ounces per yard. In addition to basic plush and shag, you'll find patterns and colors simulating the pelts of bear, fox, seal, calf, tiger, and cheetah. Prices are given per cut yard, per yard on the roll (there are 12 to 15 yards per roll), and for quantity orders. Cut yards run from $7.50 to $12.50 per yard, and prices drop from there. You can buy the fabric in remnants (the Mill will choose the fur type) for $3.50 a pound, or $3 per pound by the carton (35 to 40 pounds). Stuffing for craft projects is available as well, at 59¢ a pound and up.

Please note: A set of samples is offered for $4, a worthwhile investment unless you're buying only remnants.

Special Factors: Minimum yardage order is one yard; minimum order is $25, $100 on orders shipped C.O.D.

NEWARK DRESSMAKER SUPPLY, INC.

Catalog: $1
Save: up to 50%
Pay: check, MO, MC, V, Discover
Sells: sewing notions, crafts, and needework supplies
Store: mail order only

DEPT. WMG
6473 RUCH RD.
P.O. BOX 20730
LEHIGH VALLEY, PA
 18002-0730
215-837-7500
FAX: 215-837-9115

Searching for specialty patterns, smocking guides, bear joints, alphabet beads, silk thread, or toy squeakers? Such requests are routine at Newark Dressmaker Supply, which offers trims, appliqués, scissors, piping, ribbon, lace, braid, twill, zippers, sewing gadgets, knitting supplies, name tapes and woven labels, interfacing, buttons, thread, floss, bias tape, rhinestones, wreath-decorating materials, supplies for making dolls and stuffed bears, fabric, upholstery materials, books and manuals, and much more. Among the brands of goods stocked here, you'll find Boye, Coats & Clark's, Dritz, Lily, Plaid, Sta-Flex, and Talon. "Sew Little" patterns for infants' and children's clothing are stocked, as well as "Great Fit" patterns for women's styles in sizes 38 to 60, and doll patterns from Putnam Pattern and other firms, and Folkwear patterns.

Newark Dressmaker has been in business since 1950 and is a great mail-order source for home sewers, since it offers a huge array of notions and other supplies, from glass-headed pins to yard goods, through the 60-page catalog. The prices are very competitive—up to 50% below regular retail on some items—and that doesn't count the 10% discount you get if your order totals $50 or more.

Canadian readers, please note: Only U.S. funds are accepted.

Special Factors: Satisfaction is guaranteed; minimum order is $20 with credit cards; orders are shipped worldwide.

OPPENHEIM'S

120 E. MAIN ST.
NORTH MANCHESTER, IN
   46962-0052
219-982-6848

Catalog: free
Save: up to 60%
Pay: check, MO, MC, V
Sells: yard goods, notions, crafts materials
Store: mail order only

Oppenheim's has been in business since 1875, and publishes a 48-page newsprint catalog of all kinds of crafts staples and specials. The firm's strength is fabrics, sold in cutaways, remnants, and by-the-yard cuts. The current catalog includes collection of calico, broadcloth, rib knits, Pendleton woolens, fun fur, denim, and other fabrics, in remnants and cutaways (sold by the lot or the pound). The yard goods will appeal to anyone looking for great prices on fabrics for crafts, plain clothing, and home decorating: Onasburg, shirting, sheeting, chambray, flannel, pillow ticking, cheesecloth, Pacific silver cloth, terry cloth, Rembrandt rug canvas and needlepoint canvas, bridal fabrics, velvet, rip-stop nylon, and stretch fabric for exercise wear are all offered in the lists of "staple" fabrics. Some of the fabrics are irregular; Oppenheim's will send you swatches (include a SASE with your request), and returns are accepted.

The catalog also includes an extensive roundup of notions—laces, ribbon, facings, cording, buckles, hook-and-loop tape, and more. Sewing tools, from seam rippers to sleeve boards, are featured, and there are lots of dolls and stuffed toy kits, appliqués, and preprinted quilt tops, pillows, and panels. If you're long on ideas and imagination but short on funds, Oppenheim's will be a welcome addition to your list of sources.

Special Factors: Satisfaction is guaranteed; returns (exceptions noted in catalog) are accepted within ten days for exchange, refund, or credit.

SERGE & SEW NOTIONS & FABRICS

11285 96TH AVE. NORTH
MAPLE GROVE, MN 55369
612-493-2449

Catalog: $2.50
Save: up to 30%
Pay: check, MO, MC, V, Discover
Sells: sewing equipment and notions
Store: Zachary Square Mall, same address; Monday, Wednesday, Friday 9–7, Tuesday and Thursday 9–9, Saturday 9–5, Sunday 12–4

If you enjoy sewing clothes, you'll appreciate the great collection of sewing helpers from Serge & Sew: Rowenta irons, Olfa cutting tools, elastic, serger blades and needles, patterns, measuring tools, coned thread, interfacings, "Little Labels," and fabrics—tricot, Lycra, cotton interlock, sweatshirt fleece, etc.—are a few. Nearly a third of the 80-page catalog is devoted to books and videos on sewing and serging techniques, garment design, home decorating, fabric art, and couture techniques, among other topics. The prices run up to 30% below regular retail, and if you don't see what you want in the catalog, call—Serge & Sew will try to find it.

Canadian and non-U.S. readers, please note: Only U.S. funds are accepted.

Special Factors: Satisfaction is guaranteed; returns (except special orders) are accepted for exchange, refund, or credit; C.O.D. orders are accepted; orders are shipped worldwide.

SMILEY'S YARNS

92-06 JAMAICA AVE.,
  DEPT. W
WOODHAVEN, NY 11421
MAIL ORDER: 718-847-
  2185
STORE: 718-849-9873

Catalog: $2
Save: up to 50% (see text)
Pay: check or MO
Sells: yarn for handknitting and crocheting
Store: same address; Monday to Saturday 10–5:30

Smiley's, where "Yarn Bargains Are Our Business," has been selling first-quality yarns at a discount since 1935. Each month, Smiley's offers a different "Yarn of the Month" selection at discounts from 30% to as much as 80% on list prices. Among the manufacturers represented are Berger du Nord, Bernat, Bouquet, Bucilla, Caron, Coats & Clark's, Grignasco, Hayfield, Ironstone, Ligne Noire, Lion Brand, Melrose, Neveda, Novita, Patons, Phildar, Pingouin, Riviera, Schaffhauser, Scheepjeswool, and Welcomme. You can call or write for a price quote on goods by these firms, or inquire about knitting and crocheting yarns by other manufacturers—they may be available. Smiley's also offers a complete selection of Boye knitting and crocheting accessories at 50% off—knitting needles and crochet hooks, afghan hooks, stitch holders, etc. For samples of the current "Yarn of the Month" offering, send a long, stamped, self-addressed envelope.

Special Factors: Price quote by phone or letter with SASE; quantity discounts are available.

SOLO SLIDE FASTENERS, INC.

P.O. BOX 528
166 TOSCA DR.
STOUGHTON, MA 02072
800-343-9670
FAX: 617-341-4705

Catalog: free
Save: up to 50%
Pay: check, MO, MC, V, AE
Sells: dressmaking and dry-cleaning equipment and sewing supplies
Store: mail order only

 ¡Si!

Solo Slide is a family-run business that's been supplying dressmakers, cleaners, tailors, and other professionals with tools and equipment since 1954. Among the offerings in the firm's 42-page catalog are a number of items found in the "hard-to-find" sections of notions catalogs, at prices as much as 50% less.

Solo offers an extensive selection of zippers by Talon and YKK, zipper parts (slides and stops), straight pins in several sizes, snaps, hooks and eyes, machine and hand needles, buttons (dress, suit, metal, leather, etc.), thread on cones and spools, knit collars and cuffs for jackets, shoulder pads, elbow patches, belting, elastic, and other notions. Fine-quality linings, including Milium and Bemberg, are stocked, as well as pocket material. There are scissors in the most useful models from Gingher, Marks, and Wiss, pressing boards for sleeves and other specialty tasks, Qualitex pressing pads and other hams and rolls, and professional irons, pressers, and steamers by Cissell, Hi-

Steam/Namoto, Rowenta, Panasonic, Spartan, and Sussman. The catalog also shows commercial/industrial sewing machines (blindstitch and lockstitch) and overlock machines by Babylock, Consew, Juki, Singer, and Tacsew.

Special Factors: Authorized, unused returns (except custom-ordered or cut goods) are accepted within 30 days for credit; minimum order is $30; C.O.D. orders are accepted; orders are shipped worldwide.

STRAW INTO GOLD, INC.

████████

3006 SAN PABLO AVE.,
DEPT. WB4
BERKELEY, CA 94702
510-548-5247
FAX: 510-548-3453

Catalog: $1 and a long, double-stamped, self-addressed envelope
Save: up to 30%
Pay: check, MO, MC, V
Sells: textile crafts supplies and books
Store: same address; Tuesday to Friday 12–5:30, Saturday 10–5:30

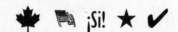

Straw Into Gold, established in 1971, is a well-known mail-order source for textile crafts supplies and equipment, especially exotic and hard-to-find materials for spinners, weavers, and hand and machine knitters. Specials on fibers, yarns, books, and other goods appear regularly in flyers, at savings of up to 30%. The staff is helpful and informed, and classes in the textile arts are given at the shop.

Straw Into Gold offers spinning fibers of silk and silk blends, flax, ramie, wool, alpaca, mohair, camel's hair, goat's hair, and metallic fibers. Ashford spinning equipment and looms (not discounted), bamboo and steel knitting needles, wool winders, umbrella swifts, and other helpful tools are available as well. Straw Into Gold sells yarns by Crystal Palace, Rowan Yarns, and Villawool, and a wide selection of other yarns and spun fibers. If you're a serious textile artist, the sample books and cards represent a worthwhile investment (see the catalog for details). Straw Into Gold's bookshelf includes publications from many museums and publishers of textile-related works, including Interweave Press, Bette Hochberg, and Shire (British), as well as videos and patterns by Rowan, Villawool, and Zimmerman.

Straw Into Gold is offering readers a discount of 10% on their first order. Be sure to identify yourself as a WBMC reader when you order, and deduct the discount from the cost of the goods only. This WBMC reader discount expires February 1, 1995.

Please note: The store is often too busy to accept calls on Saturdays, so please phone during the week, Tuesday to Friday.

Canadian and non-U.S. readers, please note: Only U.S. funds are accepted for catalog and order payments.

Special Factors: Send a double-stamped, self-addressed envelope for future catalog updates and flyers; quantity discounts are offered; Spanish-speaking sales representatives are available Tuesday to Friday noon–4; orders are shipped worldwide.

TAYLOR'S CUTAWAYS AND STUFF

DEPT. WBMC-94
2802 E. WASHINGTON
URBANA, IL 61801-4699

Brochure: $1
Save: up to 75%
Pay: check, MO, MC, V
Sells: cutaways and patterns
Store: mail order only

"Cutaways" are what's left when the pieces of a garment are cut from material. These scraps, sometimes running to a yard long, are perfect for doll clothing, piecework, quilting, and other crafts. Taylor's Cutaways, in business since 1977, offers bundles of polyesters, cottons, blends, calicos, and other assortments, as well as silk, satin, velvet, velour, felt, and fake fur cutaways. The brochure lists a wide variety of patterns and project designs for such items as draft stoppers, puppets, dolls, Teddy bears, pigs, ducks, and other animals. Crocheting patterns for toys and novelties, iron-on transfer patterns, button and trim assortments, and toy eyes, joints, and squeakers are available.

The completely unskilled will appreciate Taylor's for the potpourri, already blended and scented, and the unscented dried flowers and plants, "Potpourri Magic" fixative, essential oils, and satin squares for making sachets. Prices of these and most of the other goods average 50% below comparable retail, and savings can reach as high as 75%. This seems an especially good source for anyone who makes sachets and potpourris, dolls, toys, pieced quilts, and bazaar items.

On the practical side, Taylor's sells "tea baglets," little fiber bags you fill with the tea of your choice and heat-seal with a household iron. (This is a great way to take a favorite loose tea with you when you travel.)

Special Factor: Quantity discounts are available.

THAI SILKS

252-W STATE ST.
LOS ALTOS, CA 94022
800-722-SILK
IN CA: 800-221-SILK
415-948-8611
FAX: 415-948-3426

Brochure: free
Save: up to 50%
Pay: check, MO, MC, V, AE
Sells: silk fabric, scarves, lingerie, etc.
Store: same address; Monday to Saturday
9–5:30

Beautiful, comfortable silk is also affordable at Thai Silks, where the home sewer, decorator, and artist can save up to 50% on yardage and piece goods (compared to average retail prices). Curiously, just 2% of the stock comes from Thailand—China, India, and Korea have contributed to this company's large selection, which includes sueded silk, jacquard weaves, crepe de chine, bouclé, pongee, China silk, silk satin, raw silk, noil, silk velvet, tapestry weaves, silk taffeta, prints, Dupioni silk, and upholstery weights, most of which are offered in a choice of colors. Hemmed white silk scarves and neckties for painting and batiking, Chinese embroidered handkerchiefs, silk lingerie, and blouses are also available.

If you're a serious sewer or textile artist, consider joining Thai Silk's "Silk Fabric Club." For $20 a year, you'll receive four swatched mailings of new silks, and samples of closeouts. Thai Silks has been in business since 1964, and can answer your questions about fabric suitability for dyeing and specific uses.

Thai Silks is offering readers a discount of 10% on their first order, *excluding sale items and books.* Be sure to identify yourself as a WBMC reader when you order, and deduct the discount from the cost of the goods only. This WBMC reader discount expires December 1, 1995.

Special Factors: Satisfaction is guaranteed; quantity discounts are offered to firms and professionals; samples are available (details are given in the brochure); authorized returns are accepted; C.O.D. orders are accepted; minimum order is 1/2 yard of fabric; orders are shipped worldwide.

THINK INK

1452 N.W. 185TH ST.
SEATTLE, WA 98177-3321
206-542-1452

Catalog: long self-addressed envelope with
52¢ postage
Save: up to 45% (see text)
Pay: check or MO
Sells: thermography inks, powders, and
printers
Store: mail order only

Think Ink features Print GOCCO's printing press/thermography silkscreen devices, a great way to get custom prints on the cheap. If you can draw, GOCCOs will enable you to custom-color and print flyers, bulletins, cards, tote bags, T-shirts, and nearly anything else made of paper, fabric, wood, or leather. (And you don't even have to draw: Use clip art—Dover publishes a number of collections of copyright-free images—or use computer graphics, children's drawings, or other sources.) Choose from two Print GOCCO presses, the popular B6 model (with a 3-9/16" by 5-9/16" print area) for $110, and the B5 (with a 5-15/16" by 8-1/16" print area) for $360. Both models are battery-run, and work by creating a master of your design that can be inked like a silkscreen, and printed. Think Ink has been selling the printers and supplies and equipment since 1980, and prices the thermography powder at a discount: $5 for one cup, or $12 per pound—which is as much as 60% less than you'll pay from other vendors. Think Ink also offers a great choice of colors and varieties—sparkle, gold and other metallics, white, fluorescent gold, turquoise, magenta, lavender pearl, and more. The inks are also offered in a wide range of colors and types, including 40cc tubes of textile ink, high-mesh and regular inks (metallics, fluorescents, pastels, pearlescents, and basics are available), and enamel inks for non-porous surfaces. One application of the standard inks yields 80 to 100 prints. If you send a long, double-stamped (52¢), self-addressed envelope, Think Ink will send you a price list and brochure on the Print GOCCO printers, which includes examples of the endless list of things you can create. GOCCO, which means "child's play" in Japanese, is appreciated by graphic artists, craftspersons, small businesses, church groups, and anyone trying to make a great impression at a low cost. And if you're a rubber stamp artist, check the price you're currently paying for embossing powder—Think Ink's thermography powder does the same job, and it's sold at wholesale!

Think Ink is offerings readers of this book a one-time, 5% discount on first orders of the B5 or B6 GOCCO printer. This WBMC reader discount expires February 1, 1995.

Special Factors: C.O.D. orders are accepted; orders are shipped worldwide.

THREAD DISCOUNT SALES

10222 PARAMOUNT BLVD.
DOWNEY, CA 90241
310-928-4029
FAX: 310-928-1064

Catalog: free with long, stamped, self-addressed envelope
Save: up to 50%
Pay: check, MO, MC, V, AE, Discover
Sells: coned thread, sewing machines, and sergers
Store: same address; Monday–Saturday, 10–6

This firm sells machines and supplies for the serious sewer—sewing machines, sergers, overlock machines, and "coned" thread—at savings of up to 50% on list prices. Thread Discount Sales, in business since 1962, offers a batch of photocopied sheets as its catalog; they feature White and Singer sewing and overlock machines at an average 50% discount on list or original prices.

Among the coned thread available is all-purpose polyester thread, 6,000 yards of overlock at under $3 a cone in black and white ($3.49 in any of the 200 colors), and J. & P. Coats general-purpose thread at $1.99 for a 3,000-yard cone, which compares very favorably to spools of just 325 yards selling for $2.99 in fabric shops. Most of the thread is offered in a full range of colors, which are listed by name and number (color charts are available for $1.50). In addition, Thread Discount Sales carries novelty metallics in a variety of colors, two sizes of nylon filament thread for "invisible" work, and "wooly" nylon in 200 colors at $2.88, regularly $5.99.

Please note: A shipping surcharge is imposed on orders sent to Alaska, Hawaii, Puerto Rico, and Canada.

Special Factor: Minimum order is six cones of thread (on thread orders).

UTEX TRADING ENTERPRISES

710 NINTH ST.
NIAGARA FALLS, NY 14301
716-282-4887
FAX: 716-282-8211

Price List: free with SASE
Save: up to 50%
Pay: check or MO
Sells: imported silk fabric
Store: same address; by appointment only

 (see text)

Utex was established in 1980 and offers textile artists, decorators, designers, and home sewers something special—over 200 weights, weaves, and widths of silk. The enormous inventory includes silk shantung, pongee, taffeta, tussah, crepe de chine, brocade, twill, habotai, peau de soie, lamé, and suiting. Most of the fabrics are 100% silk, and the price list includes a guide that recommends appropriate fabrics for specific purposes. Unprinted scarves and ties, silk thread, floss, yarns, and fine brushes and dyes for hand-painting are also stocked.

Canadian readers, please note: Utex's Canadian address is 111 Peter St., Suite 212, Toronto, Ontario, M5V 2H1; the phone number is 416-596-7565.

Utex Trading Enterprises is offering readers a discount of 10% on all orders. Be sure to identify yourself as a WBMC reader when you order, and deduct the discount from the cost of the goods only. This WBMC reader discount expires March 9, 1995.

Special Factors: Volume discounts are available; C.O.D. orders are accepted; orders are shipped worldwide.

VANGUARD CRAFTS, INC.

DEPT. WMC
P.O. BOX 340170
BROOKLYN, NY
11234-0003
718-377-5188
FAX: 718-692-0056

Catalog: $1, refundable
Save: up to 60%
Pay: check, MO, MC, V
Sells: crafts kits and materials
Store: 1081 E. 48th St., Brooklyn, NY; Monday to Friday 10–6, Saturday 10–5

 ¡Si!

Vanguard has been selling fun since 1959 through a 68-page color catalog of crafts kits and projects. Vanguard is geared to educators and others buying for classroom use, but it's a great source for rainy-day project materials at home.

You'll find kits and supplies for hundreds of crafts, including shrink art, foil pictures, grapevine wreaths, mosaic tiling, basic woodworking crafts, suncatchers, Styrofoam crafts, leatherworking, fabric flowers, decoupage, copper enameling, needlepunch, pom-pom crafts, stenciling, string art, crafts sticks projects, Indian crafts, clothespin dolls, calligraphy, and other diversions. Vanguard also features a line of kits inspired by the "spirit of the Southwest"—Santa Fe picture frames, "Pueblo" pottery, concho accessories, bead looms, kachina dolls, and more. Basic art supplies and tools—adhesives, scissors, paper, paint, pastels, hammers, craft knives, etc.—are also available. The prices are *very* reasonable, and the large selection makes it easy to meet the $25 minimum order.

Special Factors: Minimum order is $25; orders are shipped worldwide.

WEBS

**P.O. BOX 147
NORTHAMPTON, MA
01060-0147
413-584-2225
FAX: 413-584-1603**

Price Lists and Samples: $2
Save: up to 80%
Pay: check, MO, MC, V
Sells: yarns and spinning and weaving equipment and books
Store: Service Center Rd. (half a mile off I-91), Northampton, MA; Monday to Saturday 9:30–5:30

Knitters and weavers of all types—production, hand, and machine—will find inspiration in the yarns from Webs, which has been selling natural-fiber yarn for up to 80% below the original prices since 1980. Webs' mailings offer conventional and novelty yarns of cotton, wool, silk, rayon, and blends, sold in bags, coned, wound off, sometimes in balls, and in packs. (The packs come in assortments of 10, 25, and 100 pounds, at outstandingly low prices.)

Each set of samples is folded into a descriptive price sheet, which notes special considerations concerning supply, suitability for knitting or weaving, gauge, length per unit (e.g., yards per ball, cone, or pound), and prices and minimums. There are usually great buys, like mohair in choice colors, ribbon yarn in several hues, fine-quality cotton yarns in different weights and fashion colors, and all-wool rug yarn. The stock includes Webs' own yarns, including mohair, rayon chenille, cotton, and variegated, as well as mill-ends, discontinued lines, and yarn overstocks. Savings can be boosted with an extra 20% discount if your yarn order totals $60 or more, or 25% on orders over $120. (Take note of the exceptions, marked "no further discount" or "NFD" in the price sheets.) Looms, spinning wheels, drum carders, and knitting machines are available at nondiscounted prices, although shipping is free on these items (which can be worth $25 to even $100, depending on where you live and the weight of the article).

Special Factors: Shipping is included on looms, spinning wheels, drum carders, and knitting machines; quantity discounts are available; authorized returns are accepted within 30 days (a 15% restocking fee may be charged); orders are shipped worldwide.

COMPANIES OUTSIDE THE U.S.A.

The following firms are experienced in dealing with customers in the U.S. and Canada. They're included because they offer goods not widely available at a discount in the U.S., because they have a better selection, or because they may offer the same goods at great savings.

Before ordering from any non-U.S. firm, please consult "The Complete Guide to Buying by Mail," page 535, for helpful tips. Pay for orders from foreign firms with a credit card whenever possible, so you'll have some recourse if you don't receive your order. For more information, see "The Fair Credit Billing Act," page 569.

MAURICE BRASSARD & FILS INC.

C.P. 4
PLESSISVILLE, QUEBEC
  G6L 2Y6
CANADA
819-362-2408
FAX: 819-362-2045

Catalog: $8.50 (see text)
Save: 35% average
Pay: check or IMO
Sells: weaving yarns, looms, etc.
Store: 1972 Simoneau, Plessisville, Quebec; Monday to Friday 9–5

Maurice Brassard's catalog is a looseleaf binder packed with two dozen pages of yarn samples, all neatly tied and labeled. Many of the descriptions are in French as well as English, and measurements are mixed—some are in grams, others ounces, some meters, others in feet. The prices translate into savings of 30% and more, on average.

The yarns include cotton warp in 2-8, 2-16, and 4-8, as well as bouclé, pearl cotton, polyester (2-8 and 2-16), Orlon, linen (natural, bleached, and dyed), cotton slub, Superwash wool, and a variety of novelty yarns. The color selection is superb, and the quality of the goods first-rate. Brassard also sells cloth strips for weaving, braiding, and other crafts, in cotton, nylon, acetate, and acrylic. In addition to yarn, Brassard stocks tools and equipment: cloth-cutting machines (to make strips), wool winders, and looms and accessories by Leclerc.

The catalog and ordering instructions have been written for Canadian orders, so if you're buying from the U.S., call or write to get exact shipping costs *before* ordering. If you wish to review Brassard's prices before purchasing the catalog, request the price list, which is free.

Special Factor: Quantity discounts are available.

D. MACGILLIVRAY & COY.

BALIVANICH

BENBECULA

WESTERN ISLES PA88 5LA

SCOTLAND

011-44-870-2525

Price Lists and Catalog: $4
Save: up to 50%
Pay: check, IMO, MC, V, AE
Sells: Scottish fabrics, knitwear, and hand-crafts
Store: Balivanich, Benbecula

Four dollars brings you MacGillivray's assortment of price lists, fabric swatches, and the catalog of everything from Hebridean perfumes to Highland dress accessories, with an emphasis on woven goods. The cream of the crop are the authentic clan tartans in three kinds of wools and weights: fine worsted at £19.50 a yard to the all-wool, heavyweight worsted for £21.50 a yard, in standard, ancient, and reproduction tartan colors. Also sold are many types of Harris tweeds, Scottish tweeds, suitings, coatings, linings, and dress fabrics, all preshrunk, from about £10 a yard.

Once made into garments, you can pair your tweeds with fine sweaters of lambswool, Shetland, or camel's hair, which are available in a palette of colors. Fair Isle sweaters are offered in jumper (pullover) and lumber jacket (high-necked cardigan) styles and as jerseys for children. Hand-knitted Harris wool sweaters for men and women begin at £41. MacGillivray's handknitted Shetland shawls, one of the firm's specialties, have been presented to the Queen, the Duchess of Kent, Princess Margaret, and other members of the royal family. MacGillivray also offers shooting stockings, mohair stoles, heraldic wall shields, Hebridean perfumes, Harris tweed caps and ties, and hand-tailored kilts. Highland dress accessories, from bagpipes and skean dhus to waistcoats and bonnets, can be ordered. And MacGillivray will tailor clothing or make copies from illustrations, at prices as much as 40% less than those charged by most dressmakers. The firm has been mailing orders to customers worldwide since 1942 and lists prices in British pounds. The easiest way to pay for your order is with a credit card.

D. MacGillivray is offering readers a discount of 10% on all orders of $200 or more. Be sure to identify yourself as a WBMC reader when you order, and deduct the discount from the cost of the goods only. This WBMC reader discount expires February 1, 1995.

Special Factors: Satisfaction is guaranteed; returns (except made-to-measure and custom orders) are accepted within 14 days for exchange, refund, or credit; orders are shipped worldwide.

SEE ALSO

The Astronomical Society • *materials on astronomy topics* • **BOOKS**

Baron/Barclay Bridge Supplies • *teaching and playing supplies for bridge* • **TOYS**

The Bevers • *wooden toy wheels, balls, etc.* • **TOOLS**

Dick Blick Co. • *arts and crafts tools and supplies* • **ART MATERIALS**

BRE Lumber • *cabinet-grade lumber* • **HOME: MAINTENANCE**

Campmor • *tent zippers, Eureka yard goods, grommet kits, etc.* • **SPORTS**

Caprilands Herb Farm • *potpourri ingredients, pomanders, essential oils, etc.* • **FARM**

Ceramic Supply of New York & New Jersey, Inc. • *ceramics and sculpting materials, music box parts* • **ART MATERIALS**

Crown Art Products Co., Inc. • *supplies and equipment for silk screening, stained glass, etc.* • **ART MATERIALS**

Daleco Master Breeder Products • *tropical and fresh-water fish supplies and equipment* • **ANIMAL**

Derry's Sewing Center • *sewing machines* • **APPLIANCES**

Discount Appliance Centers • *sewing machines and attachments* • **APPLIANCES**

Eloxite Corporation • *jewelry findings, lapidary equipment, and clock-making supplies* • **JEWELRY**

Gohn Bros. • *sewing and quilting notions and supplies* • **CLOTHING**

Golfsmith International, Inc. • *supplies for making golf clubs, including stains, finishes, etc.* • **SPORTS**

Homespun Fabrics & Draperies • *ultra-wide cotton homespun, curtain sheers, and tow cloth* • **HOME: DECOR**

Hong Kong Lapidaries, Inc. • *scarabs, inlaid intaglios, beads, and other crafts materials* • **JEWELRY**

House of Onyx, Inc. • *semiprecious and precious gems, cabochons* • **JEWELRY**

Leather Unlimited Corp. • *leather, dyes, kits, etc.* • **LEATHER**

Lixx Labelz • *custom-designed labels* • **GENERAL MERCHANDISE**

Manny's Millinery Supply Co. • *millinery supplies, bridal supplies, etc.* • **CLOTHING**

M.C. Limited • *steerhides* • **HOME: DECOR**

Metropolitan Music Co. • *violin wood, stain, varnish, tools, etc.* • **MUSIC**

Original Paper Collectibles • *vintage fruit crate labels* • **ART & ANTIQUES**

The Potters Shop Inc. • *books on pottery and ceramics* • **BOOKS**

Protecto-Pak • *zip-top plastic bags* • **OFFICE: SMALL BUSINESS**

Purchase for Less • *quilting and sewing books* • **BOOKS**

San Francisco Herb Co. • *dried flowers, potpourri ingredients, potpourri recipes, etc.* • **FOOD**

Sew Vac City • *sewing machines and sergers* • **APPLIANCES**

Sewin' in Vermont • *sewing machines and accessories* • **APPLIANCES**

Shama Imports, Inc. • *crewel-embroidered fabric* • **HOME: DECOR**

Storey's Books for Country Living • *books and manuals on country crafts* • **BOOKS**

Suburban Sew 'N Sweep, Inc. • *sewing machines and sergers* • **APPLIANCES**

That Fish Place • *aquarium supplies and equipment* • **ANIMAL**

Triner Scale • *pocket scale* • **OFFICE**

University Products, Inc. • *archival-quality collection storage, mounting, and display materials* • **OFFICE: SMALL BUSINESS**

Weston Bowl Mill • *unfinished wooden boxes, spool holders, etc.* • **GENERAL MERCHANDISE**

Wood's Cider Mill • *natural (undyed) yarns* • **FOOD**

Woodworker's Supply of New Mexico • *woodworking tools and equipment* • **TOOLS**

World Abrasives Company, Inc. • *abrasives of all types for wood, metal, ceramics, etc.* • **TOOLS**

FARM AND GARDEN

Seeds, bulbs, live plants, supplies, tools, and equipment

The choice of plants and bulbs at nurseries tends to be limited, and the prices are usually market rate. Mail order can bring you a fantastic selection of bulbs, plants, flowers, herbs, and other growing things, as well as tools and equipment—often at considerable savings. Before you buy, make sure what you're planting is suitable for your climate or home environment. Many mail-order garden suppliers offer soil test kits; among them the LaMotte kits are highly regarded. LaMotte has been manufacturing test kits, reagents, and apparatus for analyzing water, air, and soil for over 65 years. The best kit for the home gardener costs about $35, and a simplified version that tests just pH levels is available for about $10. The deluxe kit comes with all the reagents and charts you'll need to perform about 30 pH tests and 15 tests for nitrogen, phosphorus, and potassium. The "LaMotte Soil Handbook" that comes with the kit includes a definition of soil nutrients and a "pH preference guide" for over 600 plants, shrubs, and trees. LaMotte's kits can be found in the spring and summer catalogs from Gardener's Supply, 128 Intervale Rd., Burlington, VT 05401. Gardener's Supply isn't a discounter, but offers a wealth of good and useful garden equipment and tools.

The business of preserving old plant varieties is the focus of *The Heirloom Gardener* (Sierra Club Books, 1984), by Carolyn Jabs. This wonderful guide to "living heirlooms"—endangered, rare, and nearly extinct fruit and vegetable varieties—includes a brief history of the business of seeds, information on "seed savers" and seed exchanges, finding lost varieties, capsule histories of some select heirloom varieties, seed research resources, tips on harvesting seeds, and other useful information. For information on this book and other titles, request the publications list from Sierra Club Mail-Order Service, 730 Polk St., San Francisco, CA 94109.

Kent Whealy's 422-page *Garden Seed Inventory* is something of a bible for vegetable seed savers. This book lists varieties alphabetically, describes each (height, appearance, variations, days to maturity), indicates which seed companies offer it, and also shows *how many* firms have offered that variety over the past few years—usually a declining number. The mandate is clear to seed savers: Buy, cultivate, and save those varieties! For price and ordering information on the current edition of the *Garden Seed Inventory,* send a request for the publication list with a long, self-addressed, stamped envelope to Seed Savers Exchange, RR 3, Box 239, Decorah, IA 52101.

If you need farm machinery, see the listing of Central Michigan Tractor & Parts in "Auto." In addition to the Department of Agriculture publications, university cooperative extensions also disseminate technical information of use to farmers and production growers. Among those in the "Small Farms Series," published by the Northeast Regional Agricultural Engineering Service, the 34-page *Used Farm Equipment: Assessing Quality, Safety, and Economics* is a clear and well-illustrated overview of points to consider before making such a purchase. Write to Northeast Regional Agricultural Engineering Service, Cornell University, 152 Riley-Robb Hall, Ithaca, NY 14853 for a list of current publications and prices.

The U.S. government operates an information clearinghouse staffed by agricultural pros who can advise you on technical matters, including how to go organic ("sustainable agriculture" is part of the agency's mandate). Please try other sources, including your local extension agent, before calling; if you can't get help or adequate information, call ATTRA (Appropriate Technology Transfer for Rural Areas), at 800-346-9140, Monday to Friday, 8–5 CST.

If you're building your own greenhouse or cold frames, see Arctic Glass & Window Outlet ("Home: Maintenance") for thermopane panels. Other garden-related products are sold by some of the companies listed in "Tools."

FIND IT FAST

BULBS, SEEDS, PLANTS • *Breck's, Butterbrooke, Caprilands, Carino, Dutch Gardens, Le Jardin, Mellinger's, J.E. Miller, Pinetree Garden, Scheepers, Sharp Bros., R.H. Shumway, Spring Hill, Van Bourgondien, Van Engelen*
GREENHOUSES AND SUPPLIES • *Bob's Superstrong, Turner*

BOB'S SUPERSTRONG GREENHOUSE PLASTIC

BOX 42-WM
NECHE, ND 58265
204-327-5540

Brochure: $1 or two first-class stamps
Save: up to 40%
Pay: check or MO
Sells: greenhouse plastic and fastening systems
Store: same address; by appointment

 ¡Sí! (see text)

Bob Davis and his wife, Margaret Smith-Davis, are resourceful gardeners who experimented with different materials while trying to create an inexpensive greenhouse and discovered that woven polyethylene makes an ideal greenhouse skin, even in harsh climes. Their experiences with the material were so successful that they decided to market it themselves. Their 13-year-old business, Bob's Superstrong Greenhouse Plastic (also known as Northern Greenhouse Sales), is a great source for other innovative gardeners who want to design their own greenhouses. They offer "superstrong" woven poly and two anchoring systems. One is "Cinchstrap," a bright-white, flat, flexible poly strapping material that can be used for permanent anchoring, abrasion reduction in installation, and as a replacement for wood lathing in greenhouse assembly. The other, "Poly-Fastener," is a channel-system anchor that uses a flat spline to secure the poly. Prices for the woven poly run from 15¢ to 23¢ per square foot, depending on the quantity ordered; the standard width is ten feet, but Bob can heat-seal additional widths together to create a wider swath. The Poly-Fastener runs between 53¢ and 58¢ a linear foot in 300' and 100' rolls (or $1 per foot for cut pieces), and the Cinchstrap costs 11¢ a linear foot on 100' rolls.

The literature details several money-saving ideas to help further your savings. One is using rebars ("those long, rusty-colored iron rods placed in concrete to strengthen it"), to create the greenhouse frame. The poly applications aren't limited to greenhouses: solar collectors, vapor barriers, storm windows, pool covers, and tent floors are other possibilities. Send $1 or two first-class stamps—or phone—for the amazingly informative brochure. Or call if you have questions; please note the phone hours, below.

Canadian readers, please note: Write to Box 1450WM, Altona, Manitoba R0G 0B0, for literature.

Special Factors: Calls are taken daily between 6 A.M. and 8 P.M., CST; minimum order is $1; C.O.D. orders are accepted; orders are shipped worldwide.

BRECK'S DUTCH BULBS

DEPT. CA9815A4

U.S. RESERVATION

  CENTER

6523 N. GALENA RD.

PEORIA, IL 61632

309-691-4616

FAX: 309-691-2632

Catalog: free
Save: up to 50%
Pay: check, MO, MC, V, AE, Discover
Sells: Dutch flower bulbs
Store: mail order only

Breck's has been "serving American gardeners since 1818" with a fine selection of flower bulbs, imported directly from Holland. The 52-page catalog is bursting with tulips, crocuses, daffodils, hyacinths, irises, jonquils, anemones, and wind flowers. Blooming period, height, color and markings, petal formation, and scent are all described in the text. Each order is shipped with the Breck's "Dutch Bulb Handbook," which covers naturalizing, planting, indoor growing, bulb care, and related topics. Discounts of up to 50% are offered on orders placed by July 31 for fall delivery and planting, and there are special savings on "samplers" and bulb collections.

Special Factors: Satisfaction is guaranteed; early-order discounts are available; returns are accepted for exchange, replacement, or refund.

BRITTINGHAM PLANT FARM, INC.

P.O. BOX 2538
SALISBURY, MD 21802
410-749-5153
FAX: 410-749-5148

Catalog: free
Save: up to 75% (see text)
Pay: check, MO, MC, V
Sells: berry plants
Store: Rte. 346 and Phillip Morris Dr., Salisbury, MD; Monday to Friday 8–4:30, Saturday 8:30–12

Brittingham, a family business established in 1941, specializes in berries. The firm's 32-page color catalog is packed with cultivation tips and handling guidelines, and details on Brittingham's participation in Maryland's strawberry certification program. (The strict standards assure you virus-free strawberry plants.) Strawberries dominate the offerings, with over two dozen varieties in the current catalog, for early through late yields. Prices begin at $8.65 for 25 plants, and top at $70.50 for 50,000 plants (you may mix up to five varieties; more expensive and patented varieties cost more). In addition to strawberries, Brittingham sells blackberries, raspberries, grapes, blueberries, asparagus, and rhubarb; quantity pricing also applies to these offerings.

Please note: Plants are not shipped to AK, CA, HI, NM, Canada, Mexico, or outside the continental U.S.

Special Factors: Satisfaction is guaranteed; returns are accepted within a specified date (see catalog) for replacement, refund, or credit.

BUTTERBROOKE FARM SEED CO-OP

78 BARRY RD.
OXFORD, CT 06478-1529
203-888-2000

Price List: free with long, self-addressed, stamped envelope
Save: up to 75%
Pay: check or MO
Sells: seeds
Store: mail order only

"Only pure, open-pollinated seeds will produce plants from which you can save seeds for planting another year." So says the straightforward price list from Butterbrooke Farm Seed Co-Op, where becoming "seed self-reliant" is one of several gardening objectives. Butterbrooke's members include organic farmers and seed savers, and the co-op has been in business since 1978. For just $12.50 per year, co-op members receive a 20% order discount, the quarterly Farm newsletter, "Germinations," advisory services, the opportunity to buy rare or heirloom seeds, and other benefits. This is no-frills gardening at its sensible best, from the selection of scores of seeds (a well-rounded kitchen-garden full) to the Farm's own "Home Garden Collection" for first-time planters—a group of vegetable favorites. The packets are measured to reduce waste: the small size (50¢) will plant one to two 20-foot rows, and the large size ($1.25), three to four times that. All of the seeds are fresh, and they've been selected for short growing seasons. Butterbrooke also offers booklets on related topics—composting, making mulch, saving seeds—at nominal sums. You don't have to be a co-op member to buy from Butterbrooke, but the price of membership is low and the advice service alone should justify the expense.

Special Factors: C.O.D. orders are accepted; orders are shipped worldwide.

CAPRILANDS HERB FARM

534 SILVER ST.
COVENTRY, CT 06238
203-742-7244

Brochure: free
Save: see text
Pay: check, MO, MC, V
Sells: live herbs and gifts
Store: same address; daily 9–5 except holidays

Caprilands offers live and dried culinary and medicinal herbs and a potpourri of herbaceous gifts, seasonings, and rite materials. The Farm is run by Mrs. Simmons, a herbalist of sixty years' standing, who provides a legendary luncheon program for visitors to her 18th-century farmhouse. (Reservations are essential; details on the program are given in the brochure.) In the years since its founding in 1929, Caprilands has become a respected source among collectors of hard-to-find herbs and those who dabble in "natural magic." Over 300 kinds of standard culinary herbs and less common plants are available, including Egyptian onions, rue, wormwood, mugwort, monardas, artemisia, santolinas, germander, lamb's ears, nepetas, ajuga, chamomile, woodruff, and many varieties of thyme ($2 to $3 per plant). Scented geraniums, roses, and flowers are also offered. (The plants are available at the Farm only, not by mail.) Packets of seeds for herbs and herbal flowers are available by mail for $1 each. Mrs. Simmons' own guides to the cultivation and use of herbs, including one of the bibles of herbal horticulture—*Herb Gardening in Five Seasons*—are sold through the brochure.

Caprilands offers a marvelous array of related goods: bronze sundials, wooden "good luck crows" for the garden, kitchen witches and costumed collectors' dolls, pomanders and sachet pillows, spice necklaces, wreaths, herbal hot pads, stoneware, note paper and calendars, and much more. Amid this olfactory plenty are two other great buys—rose petals and buds and lavender flowers for $12 per pound, compared to $15 and $22 in other catalogs; essential oils are also sold.

Special Factors: Certain goods listed in the catalog are available only at the Farm; orders are shipped worldwide.

CARINO NURSERIES

DEPT. WBMC
P.O. BOX 538
INDIANA, PA 15701
800-223-7075
FAX: 412-463-3050

Catalog: free
Save: up to 65%
Pay: check, MO, MC, V
Sells: evergreen seedlings and transplants
Store: mail order only

Carino Nurseries has been supplying Christmas tree farmers, nursery owners, and other planters with evergreen seedlings since 1947, and its prices and selection are excellent—savings of 60% are routine. The 36-page color catalog lists varieties of pine (Scotch, white, Mugho, Ponderosa, Japanese black, American red, and Austrian), fir (Douglas, Balsam, Fraser, and Concolor), spruce (Colorado blue, white, Englemann, Black Hills, Norwegian, and Serbian), and white birch, dogwood, olive, black walnut, Chinese chestnut, Canadian hemlock, arborvitae, and other deciduous shrubs and trees.

Each catalog entry includes a description of the variety, age, and approximate height of the plants, and the number of years spent in original and transplant beds. There are specials on ten-plant collections, but most of the seedlings are sold in lots of 100 at prices up to 65% below those of other nurseries. If you're buying 500 or more, Carino's prices drop 50%. Recommendations on selecting, planting, and shearing (for later harvest as Christmas trees) are given, and the shipping methods and schedule policies are detailed in the catalog as well.

Special Factors: Shipments are made by UPS; minimum order is 10 or 100 plants (see text).

DUTCH GARDENS, INC.

DEPT. WMC2
P.O. BOX 200
ADELPHIA, NJ 07710
908-780-2713
FAX: 908-780-7720

Catalog: free
Save: 30% average (see text)
Pay: check, MO, MC, V, AE
Sells: Dutch flower bulbs
Store: mail order only

Dutch Gardens publishes one of the most beautiful bulb catalogs around—over 175 color pages of breathtaking flower "head shots" that approximate perfection. Dutch Gardens has been in business since 1961, and its prices on flower bulbs are solidly below other mail-order firms and garden supply houses—30% less on average, and up to 50% on some bulbs and collections.

The fall planting catalog offers tulip, hyacinth, daffodil, narcissus, crocus, anemone, iris, snowdrop, allium, amaryllis, and other flower bulbs. The tulip selection alone includes single, double, fringed, parrot, lily, and peony types. The spring planting catalog showcases a dazzling array of lilies, begonias, dahlias, gladioli, peonies, tuberoses, anemones, freesia, hostas, and other flowers, and onions and shallots (for planting) are also available. Each Dutch Gardens catalog lists the size of the bulbs and the common and botanical names, height, planting zones, blooming period, and appropriate growing situations of each variety. A zone chart, guide to planting depth and bulb grouping, sun requirements, hints on naturalizing, rock gardening, terrace planting, indoor growing, and forcing are included.

Special Factors: Bulbs are guaranteed to bloom (conditions are stated in the catalog); bulb bonuses or discounts are available on quantity orders; shipping is included on orders over $40; minimum order is $20.

FRED'S PLANT FARM

P.O. BOX 707
DRESDEN, TN 38225-0707
800-243-9377
901-364-5419
FAX: 901-364-3322

Catalog: free
Save: up to 50%
Pay: check, MO, MC, V, Discover
Sells: sweet potato and tobacco plants
Shop (bonded warehouse): Hwy. 89 South, Rte. I, Dresden, TN; Monday to Friday 8–5

Mr. Fred "Famous Since 1940" Stoker presides over "Fred's Plant Farm," which sells eight varieties of yams and sweet potato plants. The plant slips are well-priced—$42 per 1,000 plants in early spring, and from $11 per 50 plants to $300 for 10,000 later in the year. Mr. Stoker estimates typical local yields at an average of 300 bushels an acre, but much depends on the quality of the farming. The "Growers Guide" that accompanies your order gives detailed instructions on handling the slips, planting, cultivating the soil, harvesting, and storage of your crop, so it's well worth studying before you put spade to earth.

Mr. Stoker also sells an extensive line of tobacco—chewing, smoking, twists, and snuffing—at prices up to 50% below the branded versions.

Special Factors: Inquire for information on quantity discounts; shipping is included; plants are shipped April 15 to July 1.

LE JARDIN DU GOURMET

P.O. BOX 75-WC
ST. JOHNSBURY CENTER,
  VT 05863
802-748-1446
FAX: 802-748-9592

Catalog: 50¢
Save: up to 50% (see text)
Pay: check, MO, MC, V
Sells: seeds, plants, and gourmet foods
Store: mail order only

  (see text)

If you like to cook, and if you have even a small patch of land on which you can grow things, you'll appreciated Le Jardin du Gourmet. Founded by a transplanted New York City chef who developed a business from growing his own shallots, Le Jardin is now run by his daughter and her husband. But the same appreciation of fine food is evident in the list of edibles—chestnut spread, chutney, fancy mustards, Pompadour herbal teas from Germany, and snail seasoning are a few. The prices of some of these items are very good—Le Jardin sells four ounces of crystallized ginger for $1.60, for example, while it's sold elsewhere for as much as $4 for just three ounces.

But the firm is listed here for one of the last great mail-order buys—25¢ seed packets. Le Jardin du Gourmet sells seeds for hundreds of herbs, vegetables, peas, beans, and even some flowers. Among the offerings are angelica, bok choi, pennyroyal, milk thistle, kohlrabi, dwarf corn, French endive, mache, salsify, German "beer garden" radishes, African pumpkins, Vidalia onions, fava beans, and forget-me-nots. The 16-page catalog has a few line drawings and growing tips, as well as a huckleberry pie recipe and directions for harvesting flageolets, but brief descriptions of the varieties. If you're a novice gardener, you can invest a few quarters and test a number of "sample" packs of seeds, or play it safe with the live herbs and perennials also available from Le Jardin. The plants are sold in 2-1/4" pots, and suggestions for herb use and growth conditions are given in the catalog. Don't overlook the books on herbs and preserving food (canning, pickling, etc.), and good prices on plain and decorated balsam wreaths, roping, and small cut trees at Christmastime.

Canadian readers, please note: Only U.S. funds are accepted, and plants and bulbs are *not* shipped to Canada.

Special Factors: Minimum order is $15 with credit cards; orders are shipped worldwide.

JACKSON & PERKINS

DEPT. 17C

P.O. BOX 1028

2518 SOUTH PACIFIC
  HWY.

MEDFORD, OR 97501

800-292-4769

FAX: 800-242-0329

Catalog: free
Save: up to 50%
Pay: check, MO, MC, V, AE
Sells: roses and other flowers
Store: mail order only

The subject is roses at Jackson & Perkins, which has been supplying gardeners nationwide since 1872. The horticultural classic absorbs three-fourths of the 58-page catalog—from miniatures and patio roses to classic hybrid teas, floribundas, and grandifloras. Jackson & Perkins is prominent in variety development, and has taken a number of "rose of the year" awards from All-American Rose Selections, an independent organization that ranks entries on how well they grow in diverse settings (they're tested in gardens all over the country).

Unlike many other catalogs, Jackson & Perkins notes the type of fragrance and the bud shapes of the roses, as well as plant height range, blossom size, number of petals, color, variety, patent notes, awards, and other data. In addition to a stunning collection of hybrid tea roses, Jackson & Perkins sells classic and striated floribundas, grandifloras, hedge roses, tree roses, patio roses (2' to 4' tall), and climbers. There are roses selected for their fragrance, exhibition roses, varieties from Germany and Denmark, David Austin's English roses, bush roses, and miniatures. And there are collections of favorites of each type, which are offered at extra savings.

Jackson & Perkins also sells daylilies and hybrid lilies, "garden classics"—hydrangeas, phlox, wisteria, lavender, astilbes, etc.—and begonias, ranunculus, herbs, berries, dwarf fruit trees, garlic, and more. The catalog is peppered throughout with sundials, books, bronze garden plaques, trellises, cast stone sculptures, propagation aids, and lawn games. And "The Basics," a guide to determining what you can plant in your area and how to space your roses, can be found with the order form. Follow the planting directions, and you should enjoy show-worthy roses—your gardening success is guaranteed!

Special Factors: Satisfaction is guaranteed; returns are accepted for exchange, refund, or credit.

MELLINGER'S INC.

━━━━━━

DEPT. WBMC, RANGE RD.
NORTH LIMA, OH
44452-9731
216-549-9861
FAX: 216-549-3716

Catalog: free
Save: up to 45%
Pay: check, MO, MC, V, Discover
Sells: seeds, bulbs, live plants, and home and garden supplies
Store: same address; Monday to Saturday 8:30–5 (June 16 to April); 8–6 (May to June 15)

Mellinger's publishes "the garden catalog for year-round country living," 120 pages of seeds, bulbs, live plants, reference books, greenhouses, garden equipment, and tools. Mellinger's, in business since 1927, has outstandingly low prices on some items, and offers nominal savings on others. The offerings include flower seeds and bulbs, potted trees and shrubs, shade tree and evergreen seedlings, herb plants, fruit trees, vegetable seeds and vines, tropical plants, and seeds for rare and unusual plants. Everything you'll need for successful cultivation is available, from seed flats to greenhouses. You'll find insect and animal repellants, plant fertilizers, soil additives, pruning and grafting tools, spades, cultivators, hoes, seeders, watering systems, cold frames, starter pots, planters and flower boxes, and related goods. In addition to chemical fungicides and insecticides, Mellinger's sells ladybugs, praying mantis egg cases, and other "natural" predators and beneficial parasites. Bird feeders and seed are also stocked.

Mellinger's stocks a wide variety of goods for hydroponic gardening, as well as poly-skin greenhouses in small and commercial sizes. Polyethylene is sold by the foot, and ventilation equipment, heaters, and thermostats are also available. Books on topics from plant propagation and insect control to herbs and cooking are offered, including the Brooklyn Botanic Garden Handbook manuals. The catalog includes a guide to hardiness zones, and a statement of the terms of the warranty covering plant orders.

Special Factors: Plants are warrantied for one year (see the catalog for terms); authorized returns are accepted (a 10% restocking fee may be charged); minimum order is $10 with credit cards; orders are shipped worldwide.

J.E. MILLER NURSERIES, INC.

5060 WEST LAKE RD.
CANANDAIGUA, NY 14424
800-836-9630
716-396-2647
FAX: 716-396-2154

Catalog: free
Save: up to 50%
Pay: check, MO, MC, V, AE, Discover, Optima
Sells: plants, shrubs, trees, and nursery stock
Store: same address; Monday to Friday 8–4:30 (daily during the spring)

Miller's spring and fall catalogs offer a full range of plants, seeds, bulbs, shrubs, and trees, at savings of up to 50%, compared to prices charged by nurseries and garden supply centers. Miller Nurseries has been in business since 1936, and features a fall selection that includes russet apple, golden plum, grapes (including seedless varieties), red raspberry, blueberry, cherry, strawberry, and dozens of other fruit and nut trees, plants, and vines. Shade trees are offered, including poplar, locust, maple, and ash; and there are ornamental grasses and plants for the vegetable garden and some common flower bulbs as well. Garden supplies and equipment, including pruners, animal repellent, soil additives, wheelbarrows, mulch sheeting, etc., are also offered. The catalog includes horticultural tips, and each order is sent with Miller's 32-page planting guide. This firm has gotten rave reviews from several readers of this book, who've praised Miller's service and prices.

Please note: Orders are shipped to U.S. addresses only (not APO/FPO).

Special Factors: Trees and shrubs are sent as plants, guaranteed to grow; minimum order is $10 with credit cards.

NOR'EAST MINIATURE ROSES, INC.

P.O. BOX 307-WB
ROWLEY, MA 01969
508-948-7964
FAX: 508-948-5487

Catalog: free
Save: up to 30%
Pay: check, MO, MC, V
Sells: miniature roses
Store: 58 Hammond St., Rowley, MA; also 955 West Phillips St., Ontario, CA; Monday to Friday 8–4, both locations

 ★

Nor'East publishes a 16-page catalog of its specialty, miniature roses, which are priced at $4.95 each, compared to over $7 for the same varieties sold elsewhere. (Nor'East doesn't tack on a per-plant handling fee, as does some of the competition.) Dozens of types of miniature bush roses are available, including micro-minis (4" to 8" tall at maturity), climbers, and tree roses (miniatures budded to understocks). The varieties are grouped by colors, which include reds, pinks, yellows, oranges, apricots, whites, mauves, and blends. Among the fancifully named specimens are old favorites and new entries: Whoopi (named in honor of Whoopi Goldberg), Good Morning America, Cupcake, Party Girl, Fireworks, and Ice Queen, to name a few. The catalog descriptions include height of the mature plant, blooming pattern and coloring, scent, suitable growth situations, and other information.

Nor'East offers quantity discounts and specially priced bonuses for large orders. "We pick 'em" collections are also offered—prices drop to $3.79 per plant if you let the firm make the selection. Nor'East offers other collections, including easy-to-cultivate choices, fragrant types, and a beginners' kit that includes pots and potting mix. Planting and care directions are sent with each order. And a selection of small vases and Sean McCann's book on miniature roses are available.

Special Factors: Returns of plants that fail to perform are accepted within 90 days for replacement; minimum order is $20 with credit cards.

PINETREE GARDEN SEEDS

P.O. BOX 300
NEW GLOUCESTER, ME
  04260
207-926-3400
FAX: 207-926-3886

Catalog: free
Save: up to 35%
Pay: check, MO, MC, V, AE
Sells: seeds, bulbs, plants, garden equipment, and books
Store: mail order only

Pinetree Garden Seeds was established in 1979 to provide home gardeners with seeds in small packets, suitable for kitchen gardens or horticultural experiments. The firm has long since exceeded its goal, with a 192-page catalog packed with kitchen gadgets, gardening tools and supplies, books and other useful goods. But Pinetree's strength is the stock that built the business—over 650 varieties of vegetable and flower seeds, just a handful of which are treated. Of special interest are the "vegetable favorites from around the world," including radicchio, fava beans, snow peas, entsai, burdock, flageolet, cardoons, epazotes, and chiles. You'll also find plants and tubers for shallots, asparagus, berries, and potatoes. The flower section features seeds, tubers, and bulbs for annuals, perennials, everlastings, and wildflowers.

The tools and equipment run from kitchen and canning helps to hand tools to the well-priced "Easylink" watering system from Suncast. Fertilizers, Havahart traps, netting, and related goods are offered. Over 30 pages of the catalog are devoted to books, including a number of gardening literature classics, cookbooks, garden planners, and many other well-priced titles. Prices are quite competitive, and even the seed packets are backed by Pinetree's ironclad guarantee of satisfaction.

Canadian and non-U.S. readers, please note: The catalog costs U.S. $1.50 if sent to a non-U.S. address.

Special Factors: Satisfaction is guaranteed; returns are accepted for exchange, refund, or credit.

PRENTISS COURT GROUND COVERS

DEPT. WBM

P.O. BOX 8662

GREENVILLE, SC

29604-8662

803-277-4037

Brochure: 50¢
Save: up to 50%
Pay: check, MO, MC, V
Sells: live ground-cover plants
Store: mail order only

Prentiss Court provides an attractive, labor-efficient alternative to a conventional lawn—ground cover. The firm, in business since 1978, offers a wide range of plants at up to 50% below nursery prices, and gives spacing and planting guides in the brochure. The current crop includes varieties of Cotoneaster, crownvetch, daylilies, Euonymus fortunei, fig vine, Hedera canariensis and helix, honeysuckle, hosta, jasmine, hypericum, Ophiopogon japonicus, Pachysandra terminalis, Parthenocissus, Trumpet creeper, and Vinca major and minor. In English, there are over 70 kinds of plants, including many types of ivy and flowering and berry-bearing ground cover. The plants are sold bare-root and/or potted, at an average price of 50¢ each (bare root). The brochure includes tips on planting and caring for ground covers.

Special Factor: Minimum order is 50 plants of the same variety.

ROSEHILL FARM

P.O. BOX 188

GALENA, MD 21635-0188

410-648-5538

Catalog: free
Save: see text
Pay: check, MO, MC, V
Sells: miniature roses
Store: Gregg Neck Rd., Galena, MD; Monday to Saturday 9–5

Rosehill Farm has been selling miniature roses since 1980 and brings out new varieties each year. The color catalog shows standard-size minis, sweetheart sizes, micro-minis, climbers, and hanging basket types, including white, blush, yellow, gold, apricot, lavender, pink, orange, and red varieties. The catalog descriptions note special characteristics of each plant, height of the mature plant, suitable growing situations, color, and other useful information. The roses are sent in 4-3/4" pots, and are guaranteed for one year (replacements are given for plants that fail). If you want to learn about rose cultivation, Rosehill can provide several useful books on related topics.

Rosehill's prices are below those of miniature roses priced in local nurseries and other garden catalogs. Wholesale prices are available to not-for-profit organizations, nurseries, and garden centers, but you must request the wholesale price list on your company letterhead.

Special Factor: Returns are accepted within one year for replacement.

JOHN SCHEEPERS, INC.

▬▬▬▬▬▬▬▬

P.O. BOX 700WBM
BANTAM, CT 06750
203-567-0838
FAX: 203-567-5323

Catalog: free
Save: up to 30%
Pay: check, MO, MC, V
Sells: Dutch flower bulbs
Store: mail order only

John Scheepers has been in business for over 80 years, serving gardeners with premium, exhibition-quality Dutch bulbs of cultivated stock, at very good prices. Scheepers is affiliated with Van Engelen, which offers wholesale pricing on large orders (see that listing if you buy in 100-bulb lots). Scheepers' own prices are lower than market price, but the bulbs themselves—and the plants and blossoms—are significantly bigger.

The 40-page color catalog from Scheepers is heavy on tulips and narcissi: early-flowering Fosterianas, tulips from Asia Minor, trumpet narcissi, peony-like tulips, Giant Darwins, parrot tulips, and more. Like Van Engelen, Scheepers has a good selection of crocus, allium, iris, and other spring flower bulbs, as well as a number for shady, woodsy areas. Bulb food, gifts, and books are available, and cultivating instructions are packed with each order. Most of the bulbs are sold in lots of 6, 12, 24, etc., and the per-bulb price drops the more you order. The sales policy is similar to Van Engelen's, except the minimum order is just $25.

Special Factors: Quantity discounts are available; minimum order is $25.

SHARP BROS.
SEED CO.

Catalog: $1, refundable
Save: up to 30%
Pay: check or MO
Sells: grasses, legumes, and wildflowers
Store: mail order only

P.O. BOX 665
CLINTON, MO 64735
800-451-3779
816-885-8521

Sharp Bros. sells the fruit of the plains—bluegrass and other grasses, prairie wildflowers, legumes, and other field crops. The "Catalog of Wildflowers and Forbs" lists over two dozen flowers by common name, with complete data on habit, color, preferred soil type, exposure, suggestions for use (roadside, cut flowers, etc.), and other characteristics. The seeds can be purchased in a minimum of one ounce per plant species. If you want to cover a larger area, Sharp Bros. has created a number of mixes for mountainous, dry, and moist environments. The catalog has planting directions, but no illustrations—so you'll have to know Sideoats Grama from Dame's Rocket before you order.

If your interests run to grasses and legumes, ask for the "Select Native Grasses" catalog. This is Sharp's own Buffalo Brand seed, and there are 20 different warm-season species and as many cold-season grasses, most of which are offered in a few varieties. Some of the grasses are suited to forage, others erosion control, and general ground cover. Sharp Bros. also sells legumes, lawn grasses, certified field crops—soybeans, wheat, oats, barley, etc.—and shrubs, including sagebrush, mountain mahogany, and saltbrush, to name a few. Both catalogs give planting ratios per 1,000 square feet and by the acre. You have to be familiar with the flowers and grasses to best use the catalog, but Sharp serves all kinds of buyers—"backyard gardeners," farmers, ranchers, conservation agencies, and prairie restoration groups, among others.

Special Factors: Quantity discounts are available; minimum order is one ounce of seed.

R.H. SHUMWAY SEEDSMAN

P.O. BOX 1-WH
GRANITEVILLE, SC 29829
803-663-9771
FAX: 803-663-9772

Catalog: $1, refundable
Save: up to 50%
Pay: check, MO, MC, V, Discover
Sells: seeds, bulbs, and nursery stock
Store: Graniteville, SC; Monday to Saturday 8–4 (open Saturday in spring season only)

 (see text)

"Good Seeds Cheap" declares the cover of R.H. Shumway's catalog, which is full of old-fashioned *engravings* of flowers, fruits, and vegetables—there's not a photograph in sight. Shumway has been "The Pioneer American Seedsman" since 1870, and is notable for the number of old, open-pollinated seeds it carries, as well as new varieties.

The 64-page catalog features spring flower bulbs, many pages of berries, fruit trees, vines, beans, vegetable seeds, corn, onions, squash, tomatoes, and Shumway specialties—lawn grasses, grasses for pasturage and hay, millet and other "forage" seed, sorghums, Sudan grasses, clover, legumes, and alfalfa. Shumway offers over a dozen types of "Oriental greens"—tatsoi, tsoi-sim, mitsuba (a Chinese parsley), several varieties of pak choi, and more. And herb seeds are available, for both culinary and ornamental plants—angelica, coriander, shiso, burnet, pyrethrum, upland cress, and cardoon, as well as the spice rack standards. Market gardeners and other small commercial growers should check Shumway's wholesale prices on bulk seed orders, or get together with gardener friends and combine orders to take advantage of the bulk pricing. Special offers and bonuses are sprinkled liberally throughout the catalog, which also offers a small selection of well-priced garden helpers.

Special Factors: Satisfaction is guaranteed; quantity discounts are available; returns are accepted within 90 days for exchange or replacement; C.O.D. orders are accepted; minimum order is $15 with credit cards.

SPRING HILL NURSERIES

DEPT. NA9816A3
6523 N. GALENA RD.
PEORIA, IL 61632
309-691-4616
FAX: 309-691-2632

Catalog: free
Save: up to 50%
Pay: check, MO, MC, V, AE, Discover
Sells: flowers, bulbs, and shrubs
Store: mail order only

Spring Hill's parent company has been in business since 1849, supplying gardeners across the nation with plants and bulbs at discount prices. The 48-page color catalog is heavy on flower classics—irises, peonies, daffodils, carnations, hydrangeas, daylilies, phlox, and more—as well as ground cover, hostas, ferns, and other perennials. The descriptions include planting guidelines, mature size and characteristics, and site recommendations. Everything Spring Hill sells is backed by the firm's no-quibble guarantee of satisfaction, and the prices are good: specials on collections and quantity discounts bring the savings to as much as 50%, compared to typical nursery stock prices.

Special Factors: Satisfaction is guaranteed; quantity discounts are available.

TURNER EQUIPMENT COMPANY, INC.

DEPT. 131
P.O. BOX 1260
GOLDSBORO, NC
27533-1260
800-672-4770
FAX: 919-736-4550

Catalog: free
Save: up to 35%
Pay: check, MO, MC, V
Sells: greenhouses and accessories
Store: mail order only

Turner Equipment Company was founded in 1939, and has been producing greenhouses since 1957. Turner currently offers three basic series with a choice of options, or a total of 46 models. Prices average 25% less than the competition, and similar greenhouses in other catalogs sell for 35% more.

The three series include a 7'-wide lean-to, and two freestanding lines, 8' and 14' wide. Each greenhouse comes equipped with a ventilating system and aluminum storm door, and can be expanded lengthwise in four-foot increments. You can choose from a 6-mil polyethylene cover or fiberglass (warrantied for 20 years). Turner also sells electric and gas heaters, exhaust fans and air circulators, cooling units, greenhouse benches, thermometers, misters, and sprayers. In addition, the 24-page color catalog features well-chosen books on composting, organic gardening, greenhouse growing, herb cultivation, and related topics.

Special Factors: Satisfaction is guaranteed; authorized returns in original condition are accepted within 30 days for refund or credit (less freight); minimum order is $10.

VAN BOURGONDIEN BROS.

P.O. BOX 1000
BABYLON, NY 11702
800-622-9997
FAX: 516-669-1228

Catalog: free
Save: up to 40%
Pay: check, MO, MC, V, AE, Discover, Optima
Sells: flower bulbs and perennials
Store: mail order only

The 64-page spring and fall catalogs from Van Bourgondien offer a wealth of growing things for home, lawn, and garden at up to 40% less than other suppliers. Both of the catalogs feature hosta and hybrid lilies, ground covers, and a wide range of flowers. Van Bourgondien was founded in 1919, and offers early-order discounts, bonuses, and specials on collections.

Past fall catalogs have shown tulip, daffodil, hyacinth, iris, crocus, narcissus, anemone, allium, fritillaria, and other bulbs. Geraniums, delphiniums, shasta daisies, tiger lilies, lavender, flowering house plants, foxtails, black-eyed Susans, native ferns, and other greenery and flowers are usually offered. If you can't wait for the thaw, you can buy prepotted lilies of the valley, Aztec lily, paperwhites, amaryllis varieties, and crocus bulbs, all of which can be forced. The spring catalog features begonias, gladiolus, dahlias, caladiums, perennials, ferns, cannas, ground cover, and similar goods. Bulb planters and plant supplements are offered as well, and orders are shipped to the 48 contiguous United States.

Special Factors: Goods are guaranteed to be "as described" and to be delivered in perfect condition; quantity discounts are available.

VAN ENGELEN INC.

Catalog: free
Save: up to 50%
Pay: check, MO, MC, V
Sells: flower bulbs
Store: mail order only

STILLBROOK FARM
313 MAPLE ST.,
  DEPT. WBM
LITCHFIELD, CT 06759
203-567-8734, 5662
FAX: 203-567-5323

Van Engelen is the wholesale affiliate of John Scheepers, which also sells Dutch flower bulbs. Scheepers serves the needs of gardeners buying fewer than 50 of the same bulb at the same time, but Van Engelen sells most bulbs in lots of 50 or 100, and requires a $50 minimum order. If you can meet the minimum, you'll have the choice of over 500 different varieties of tulip, narcissus, crocus, daffodil, anemone, allium, freesia, iris, fritillaria, hyacinth, amaryllis, and lilies, all of which are shown in the 26-page catalog. These are Dutch-cultivated bulbs, and while Van Engelen's prices are on a par with those of two other bulb discounters, Van Engelen's plants are taller and have bigger flowers. In addition to buying bulbs a la carte, you can choose from several collections that are priced below listed wholesale. Each has from 215 to 525 bulbs, and if you like the selection of varieties and colors, they're a real buy. Please note that Van Engelen states that, "Complaints may be entertained if made within *10 days* after receipt of goods."

Special Factors: Quantity discounts are available; minimum order is $50.

SEE ALSO

Arctic Glass & Window Outlet • glass panels for cold frames, greenhouses • **HOME: MAINTENANCE**
Central Michigan Tractor & Parts • used and rebuilt parts for tractors and combines • **AUTO**
Clothcrafters, Inc. • knee pads, gardening aprons, porous plastic sheeting • **GENERAL MERCHANDISE**
Dairy Association Co., Inc. • livestock liniment • **ANIMAL**
Daleco Master Breeder Products • kits for yard ponds • **ANIMAL**
Manufacturer's Supply • replacement parts for lawnmowers, rototillers, trimmers, tractors, etc. • **TOOLS**

Northern Hydraulics, Inc. • *trimmers, tractors, lawnmower parts, garden carts, log stackers, lawn sweepers, etc.* • **TOOLS**

Storey's Books for Country Living • *books and manuals on farm and garden topics, homesteading, etc.* • **BOOKS**

That Fish Place • *live aquarium plants* • **ANIMAL**

Zip Power Parts, Inc. • *lawnmower parts* • **TOOLS**

FOOD AND DRINK

Foods, beverages, and condiments

Herbs, spices, coffee, and tea are mail-order naturals, and all of them are available from the firms listed here. You'll also find caviar and Italian truffles, Mexican and Lebanese foods, giant pistachio nuts, Vermont maple syrup, and more—at savings that run to 80%.

When ordering food, be mindful of the weather. Don't purchase highly perishable or temperature-sensitive items—chocolate, soft cheese, fruits, vegetables, and uncured meats—during the summer, unless you have them shipped by an express service and plan to eat them immediately. (Most catalogs include caveats to this effect, and some firms just won't ship certain goods during warm weather under any circumstances.)

Consider the firms listed here when making out gift lists—whether you choose a packet of rare herbs or a year of gustatory delights provided by an "of-the-month" program, your presents will be remembered long after they're consumed. If you want to maximize your savings, choose a popular food gift such as pecans or dried fruit, buy it in bulk, and package it yourself.

FIND IT FAST

CHEESE • **Gibbsville**
COFFEE AND TEA • **Cordon Brew, Festive Foods, Grandma's Spice Shop, The Maples, Northwestern Coffee Mills, Simpson & Vail**
GOURMET FOODS • **Caviarteria, Festive Foods**
HERBS, SPICES, FLAVORINGS • **Bickford, Festive Foods, Grandma's Spice Shop, Karen's Kitchen, E.C. Kraus, Mr. Spiceman, Pendery's, San Francisco Herb, The Spice House**
MAPLE SYRUP • **Palmer's, Elbridge C. Thomas**

NUTS, DRIED FRUITS • Bates Bros., Durey-Libby, The Maples
ORGANIC AND NATURAL FOODS • Deer Valley, Jaffe Bros., Walnut Acres
WINE- AND BEER-MAKING • E.C. Kraus

BATES BROS. NUT FARM, INC.

15954 WOODS VALLEY RD.
VALLEY CENTER, CA 92082
619-749-3333, 3334
FAX: 619-749-9499

Price List: free with self-addressed, stamped envelope
Save: up to 50%
Pay: check, MO, MC, V
Sells: nuts, dried fruits, and candy
Store: same address; daily 8–5; also Terra Nova Plaza, 358 E. H St., #604, Chula Vista, CA; every day, 10–7:30

Nuts are the featured item at Bates, which grows some of what it sells. The nuts and other treats are generally priced below those of a number of Bates' competitors; price checks showed possible savings of almost 50% on selected items.

The four-page brochure lists the standard almonds, walnuts, peanuts, cashews, pecans, and mixes, as well as macadamia nuts, filberts, pignolias, sunflower seeds, and pistachios. You can buy them raw, roasted and salted, smoked, and saltless. The dried fruits include apricots, raisins, dates, papaya, figs, banana chips, pineapple, and coconut, as well as other sweets. These are the ingredients for trail mix, which Bates also sells ready-made, as well as granola, wheat germ snacks, popcorn, and old-fashioned candy—malted milk balls, English toffee, nut brittle, taffy, candy corn, and licorice ropes, among others. And look here for good prices on glacé fruit: fruitcake mix, cherries, colored pineapple wedges, orange and lemon peel, and citron. Gift packs are available year-round.

Special Factors: C.O.D. orders are accepted; orders are shipped worldwide.

BICKFORD FLAVORS

19007 ST. CLAIR AVE.
CLEVELAND, OH
   44117-1001
216-531-6006
FAX: 216-531-2006

Price List: free
Save: up to 40% (see text)
Pay: check, MO, MC, V
Sells: flavorings
Store: same address; Monday to Friday 9–5

Bickford, established in 1914, makes and sells its own concentrated flavorings, from naturally derived oils, leaving out the usual alcohol and sugar that you'll find in other "pure" essences. Over 100 flavorings are offered, from almond to wintergreen. Vanilla is sold here in white, dark, and regular versions. (The white vanilla won't tint your angel food cake or meringues.) All of Bickford's flavorings are sold in one-ounce bottles for $1.99, which is competitive pricing, but the bargain buys are pints ($15.75) and larger sizes. (Vanilla is also sold in bottles of two, four, and eight ounces.) In addition to an unparalleled selection of flavorings, Bickford also sells about 100 exotically flavored oils (ginger, peach, caramel, and sherry oil are all available), food colorings, carob syrup, popcorn popping oil, and dried cranberries.
   Special Factor: Orders are shipped worldwide.

CAVIARTERIA INC.

29 E. 60TH ST.
NEW YORK, NY 10022
800-4-CAVIAR
IN NY 212-759-7410
IN CA 800-287-9773
FAX: 718-482-8985

Catalog: free
Save: up to 30%
Pay: MO, MC, V, AE, Optima
Sells: caviar and gourmet foods
Store: same address; also 247 N. Beverly
Dr., Beverly Hills, CA; Monday to Saturday
9–6, both locations

Caviarteria, established in 1950, brings its line of caviar to the world through an eight-page catalog that's updated with quarterly newsletters. This family-run business stocks every grade of Caspian Beluga, Oscetra, and Sevruga caviar (fresh and vacuum-packed), plus American sturgeon, whitefish, trout, and salmon caviar. Prices begin at about $16 per ounce for Kamchatka bottom-of-the-barrel vacuum-packed and run up to about $275 for 3-1/2 ounces of "Ultra" Beluga. Price comparisons of Caviarteria's Beluga Malassol to those of another caviar-by-mail firm show you can save as much as 40% here, and even the caviar servers are already priced at least 20% off list.

The catalog lists other gourmet treats: whole sides and "center cut" packages of smoked Scottish salmon, Icelandic gravlax, fresh pâté, foie gras from France, tinned white and black Italian truffles, and other delicacies. The Beverly Hills branch features Champagne and wine, and Caviarteria will ship champagne anywhere in California overnight.

Special Factors: Satisfaction is guaranteed; minimum order is $25 with credit cards.

CORDON BREW

■■■■■■■

3339 55TH ST.
SAN DIEGO, CA 92105
800-232-6793
FAX: 619-229-9059

Price List: free
Save: up to 40%
Pay: check, MO, MC, V
Sells: coffee and brewing accessories
Store: mail order only

Cordon Brew, established to cater to the whims of budget-minded coffee connoisseurs, delivers high-altitude Arabica beans in scores of straight and blended coffees, decaffeinated and flavored brews, and even organically grown coffee. The straight coffees run from Brazil Santos to Tanzanian Peaberry and include Ethiopian Sidamo and Maragojipe, which were new to us. Cordon Brew offers blends in roasts from French to Espresso, a good selection of decaffeinated beans, and offers a custom blending service. And the choice of flavored beans is really inspired—or have Hawaiian hazelnut, cookies 'n cream, and pecan coffees become commonplace?

In addition to beans, Cordon Brew sells Krups grinders and coffeemakers, the Bodum "Bistro" plunger-style coffee press, and mugs. All of the equipment is sold at good discounts, and the prices of the coffee beans average $1 to $3 per pound less than those charged by the typical gourmet coffee shop.

Special Factor: Minimum order is 3 lb. coffee or $15 in equipment.

DEER VALLEY FARM

R.D. 1, BOX 173
GUILFORD, NY 13780
607-764-8556

Catalog: 50¢
Save: up to 40% (see text)
Pay: check or MO
Sells: organic and natural foods
Store: Rte. 37, Guilford, NY; Monday to Friday 8–5; 19B Ford Ave., Oneonta, NY; Monday to Saturday 9:30–5:30, Thursday 9:30–8:30; and 64 Main St., Cortland, NY; Monday to Saturday 9:30–5:30, Thursday 9:30–8:30

Deer Valley Farm, which has been in operation since 1947 and is certified organic by the State of New York, sells a full line of foods—from baked bread and cookies to wheat middlings. Whole grains, flours, cereals, nut butters, crackers, fruits, pasta, herbs and spices, tea, soy milk, preserves, and yeast and other baking ingredients are usually available. You can buy "organically grown" meats here at substantial savings: hamburger, typically priced at $4.50 to $6 per pound in health food stores, costs $3.05 per pound, and the trimmed sirloin is $6.19 a pound; veal, pork, lamb, and even fish are also available. Deer Valley sells raw milk cheese, and the cheddar is only $3.29 to $4.39 per pound, less than some of the supermarket varieties. The only drawback here is the minimum order, $150, necessary to reap savings of 25% to 40% on the prices you'd pay if buying the same goods from your local health food store. But if you get your friends together, you can meet that amount easily with a combined order—just be prepared for an impromptu feast when the cartons arrive!

Special Factors: Deliveries are made by Deer Valley truck in the New York City area (elsewhere by UPS); minimum order is $10, $150 for wholesale prices.

DUREY-LIBBY EDIBLE NUTS, INC.

Flyer: free
Save: up to 50%
Pay: check or MO
Sells: nuts
Store: mail order only

100 INDUSTRIAL RD.
P.O. BOX 345
CARLSTADT, NJ 07072
201-939-2775
FAX: 201-939-0386

Durey-Libby, established in 1950, picks and processes "delicious fresh nuts you don't have to shell out a fortune for." You can't eat fancy tins, stoneware crocks, and rattan baskets, so if you're buying nuts, why not *pay* for nuts—and nothing but. Durey-Libby's no-frills price list features walnuts, pecans, cashews, almonds, macadamia nuts, pistachios, and cocktail mixes, packed in bags and vacuum tins. The prices are up to 50% less than those charged by gourmet shops and many food catalogs. The smallest units are three-pound cans, which will give you enough for cooking and snacking.

If you identify yourself as a reader of this book when you order, you may deduct 10% from your order total (computed on the cost of the goods only). This WBMC reader discount expires February 1, 1995.

Special Factors: Satisfaction is guaranteed; shipping is included on orders within the contiguous U.S.; orders are shipped worldwide.

FESTIVE FOODS

Catalog: free
Save: up to 75% (see text)
Pay: check, MO, MC, V, AE
Sells: baking ingredients, fancy foods, herbs and spices, etc.
Store: mail order only

9420 ARROYA LN.
COLORADO SPRINGS, CO
  80908
719-495-2339
FAX: 719-495-2646

Festive Foods has been supplying serious home cooks and bakers with fine ingredients since 1984, and offers a number of items not often seen in other fancy foods catalogs. There are 20 pages of temptations, from

French pastry cream powder to St. Dalfour sugarless fruit conserves. Festive Food's per-ounce prices of the bulk-packed herbs are much lower than those charged at the supermarket: four ounces of dill cost $4.35 here, while just *one ounce* of Spice Island dill weed costs $3.29 locally. The 16-ounce pack of Old Bay seasoning is $4 here, compared to $2.19 for six ounces (30% more), and mild curry powder costs $3.35 for eight ounces here, while one ounce of McCormick's runs $1.79—a difference of over 75%. Savings on the other goods vary, depending on the item and amount ordered.

Festive Foods offers a wide range of products, including pastry and baking ingredients, chocolate and cocoa, extracts, essential oils of plants and spices, a wide variety of herbs and spices in spice-jar "refill" packs as well as the more economical bulk sizes, organic herbs, seasoning blends, tea (black, green, herbal, and flavored), dried mushrooms, maple syrup, sun-dried tomatoes from California, nut oils, flavored champagne vinegars, and dried fruits from Washington State. Among notable products are French coffee extract, Tahitian vanilla beans, lemon grass oil, asafoetida powder, Szechuan peppercorns, horseradish powder, fine sea salt, Cajun seasoning, Chaat Masala, popcorn seasonings, salsa grande instant salsa mix, mushroom powder (porcini or oyster), almond ingot cakes, rice bran oil, and blueberry preserves from northern Maine. If you enjoy cooking and eating, stock up—Festive Foods will pay shipping if your order totals $75 or more.

Special Factors: Satisfaction is guaranteed; shipping is included on orders over $75; returns are accepted for exchange, refund, or credit.

GIBBSVILLE CHEESE SALES

W-2663 CTH-00
SHEBOYGAN FALLS, WI
 53085
414-564-3242
FAX: 414-564-6129

Price List: free
Save: up to 30%
Pay: check or MO
Sells: Wisconsin cheese and summer sausage
Store: same address; Monday to Saturday 7:30–5

 (see text)

Gibbsville Cheese Sales is a standout even in Wisconsin, the Dairy State, where *everyone* produces cheese. The company's prices are appetizingly low—as little as $2.30 a pound for mild cheddar in five-pound bulk packaging. Several types of summer sausage and beef sticks are also offered, in addition to well-priced gift packages for a variety of budgets and tastes.

Gibbsville has been in business since 1933, and produces the most popular kinds of cheese, including Cheddar (mild, medium, aged, super-sharp white, garlic, and caraway), Monterey Jack (including Jacks flavored with salami, hot pepper, dill, and vegetables), and Colby (including salt-free). You can buy Cheddar and Colby in "Economy" boxes of two or ten pounds, or in bulk with as little as a pound. Five pounds of rindless Colby cost $2.30 a pound, and prices of other cheeses are just as reasonable. If you can get to the store in Sheboygan Falls, you can even watch the production process through a viewing window. In addition to the cheeses of its own manufacture, Gibbsville Cheese sells Swiss (baby, medium, aged, and lace), Provolone, Muenster, Parmesan, Romano, Mozzarella, Gouda, Flavored Cold-Pack Cheese Spreads (including Sharp Cheddar, Swiss Almond, Port Wine, French Onion, Horseradish, Garlic, etc.), and Blue, Limburger, and String Cheeses. The price list indicates which cheeses are "lower in fat," and includes several "lite" versions of favorites.

Please note: Shipments are not made during summer months (approximately June to September).

Canadian readers, please note: Deliveries to Canada are made by UPS.

Special Factor: Price quote by letter with SASE.

GRANDMA'S SPICE SHOP

DEPT. B
P.O. BOX 472
ODENTON, MD 21113
410-672-0933

Catalog: free
Save: up to 60%
Pay: check, MO, MC, V
Sells: herbs, spices, coffee, tea, etc.
Store: mail order only

There *is* a Grandma behind this shop: founder Catherine James, pictured in a rocking chair in front of a display of cookie cutters. The enterprise recently changed hands, and hopefully the new owners will maintain Grandma's sophisticated stock lists.

To wit: *Danish* breakfast coffee, Nougatine coffee (flavored with hazelnut oil), Jasmine tea from Fukien province, candied angelica, raspberry leaves, and peach butter are but a few of the uncommon brews and foodstuffs listed in the 16 pages. The inventory includes coffees (regular, flavored, and decaffeinated), loose teas (green, black, flavored, decaffeinated) and rare estate teas, Benchley teabags, a large herb and spice selection, potpourri blends and essential oils, cocoa, herbal vinegars and honeys, hot sauces, McCutcheon preserves, and fruit-sweetened preserves. Spice racks, mortar and pestle sets, gift baskets, and Melitta travel sets are all available. The herbs and spices afford the best savings, up to 60% if bought in bulk (half or full pounds). Coffee and tea connoisseurs should see the catalog for the unusual and rare varieties (which are not sold at a discount).

Grandma's Spice Shop is offering readers of this book a 10% discount on first orders. Identify yourself when your order. This WBMC reader discount expires Feburary 1, 1995.

Special Factor: Orders are shipped worldwide.

JAFFE BROS., INC.

P.O. BOX 636-W
VALLEY CENTER, CA
   92082-0636
619-749-1133
FAX: 619-749-1282

Catalog: free
Save: up to 50%
Pay: check, MO, MC, V, Discover
Sells: organically grown food
Store: (warehouse) 28560 Lilac Rd., Valley Center, CA; Sunday to Thursday 8–5, Friday 8–3

Jaffe Bros., established in 1948, sells organically and naturally grown nuts, seeds, beans, butters, fruit, and honey through its 20-page catalog. The prices average 30% below comparable retail, but there are greater savings on certain items, and quantity discounts are offered on many goods. Jaffe's products are marketed under the Jaybee label, and virtually all of them are grown "organically" (without fumigants or poisonous sprays but with "nonchemical" fertilizers) or "naturally" (similarly treated but not fertilized).

You'll save on wholesome foods here—dried peaches, Black Mission figs, Monukka raisins, papaya, dates of several types, almonds, pine nuts, macadamias, nut butters, brown rice, flours and grains, seeds for eating and sprouting, 15 kinds of peas and beans, unheated honey, coconut, jams, juices, carob powder, salad oil, olives, herb teas, and much more. (Most of the produce is packed in five-pound units or larger.) The catalog also lists dehydrated mushrooms, sun-dried tomatoes, canned olives, organic spaghetti sauce, low-salt dill pickles and sauerkraut, organic whole wheat pasta, kosher maple syrup, organic applesauce, and even a biodegradable peppermint-and-castile soap/shampoo. If you'd like to bestow goodness upon a friend, be sure to see the group of gift assortments—nicely packaged selections of favorites, at reasonable prices.

Special Factors: Quantity discounts are available; problems should be reported to Jaffe within ten days of receipt of goods; store is closed Saturdays; C.O.D. orders are accepted; orders are shipped worldwide.

KAREN'S KITCHEN

43 RANDOLPH RD.,

SUITE 757

SILVER SPRING, MD 20904

301-236-5992

Catalog: $1, deductible
Save: up to 90%
Pay: check or MO
Sells: food and seasonings
Store: mail order only

Karen's Kitchen is the brainchild of a resourceful working mother turned entrepreneur, Karen Nearman, who had to come up with quick, economical, nutritious meals for her hungry family every night. She liked the convenience of mixes like Hamburger Helper, but her family wanted more flavor, so she started doctoring commercial products with her own herbs and spices. The family approved, and when the neighbors asked for the recipes, she knew she was on to something. She went on to create mixes from scratch—using her own noodles, rice, beans, and flavorings. Since she wanted to make them as wholesome and nutritious as possible, she sought out sources for organically grown ingredients. And she turned the entire concept into a business.

Karen's Kitchen publishes a newsletter, which includes recipes for different mixes with cost breakdowns of the from-scratch product and the branded equivalent. They illustrate the savings possible—up to 75% on some mixes—if you do the processing yourself. Past newsletters have included a recipe for creating saucepan stuffing mix and variations, a piece on product "downsizing" deceptions, a guide to making asparagus powder, a comparison of the fat and water content in popular brands of sausage, and notes on keeping a herb garden. Subscribing to the quarterly newsletter is well worth the yearly $14 fee ($17 in Canada, $22 other non-U.S. countries). But the catalog alone ($1) will be appreciated by anyone who enjoys cooking.

There are 18 pages of organic peas and beans, grains and grain products, whole wheat and cornflour pasta, dried fruits, dehydrated vegetables, herbs, spices, seasoning blends, flavors, extracts, and an impressive list of teas. Among the current offerings are anasazi beans, quinoa, whole-wheat artichoke pasta, dried cherries and dried sliced dehydrated Formosan mushrooms, whole white peppercorns, Beau Monde and Souvlaki seasoning blends, Chinese Monastery tea, sherry-flavored black tea, and Benchley tea bags. In the back of the catalog are lists of ingredients of every seasoning blend and herbal tea, so you can customize them to your own taste. And Karen also sells bag sealers and supplies, spice jars and labels, and gift assortments—salad seasonings, peppercorn assortments, chile collections, popcorn seasonings, and others. The best prices are on the one-pound or bulk sizes, although the four-ounce size of Karen's spices beat the supermarket spice prices by up to 90%! If you plan on placing a large order, ask for the "bulk price list," which gives wholesale prices for orders of $100 or more.

Canadian readers, please note: Only U.S. funds are accepted.

Karen's Kitchen is offering readers a 10% discount on first orders from the *retail catalog* only. Be sure to identify yourself as a WBMC reader when you order. This WBMC reader discount expires June 1, 1995.

Special Factors: Satisfaction is guaranteed; quantity discounts are available; minimum order is $10, $100 for bulk.

E.C. KRAUS WINE & BEERMAKING SUPPLIES

P.O. BOX 7850-WC
INDEPENDENCE,
 MO 64054
816-254-7448

Catalog: free
Save: up to 40%
Pay: check, MO, MC, V
Sells: wine- and beer-making supplies
Store: 9001 E. 24 Hwy., Independence, MO; Monday to Friday 8–5:30, Saturday 9–1

E.C. Kraus, founded in 1967, can help you save up to half of the cost of wine, beer, and liqueurs by producing them yourself. The firm's 16-page illustrated catalog features supplies and equipment for the home vintner and brewer, and even includes several beer recipes.

Whether you're a beginner or an experienced vintner, Kraus offers everything you'll need to produce your own beverages: malt and hops, fruit and grape concentrates, yeasts, additives, clarifiers, purifiers and preservatives, fruit acids, acidity indicators, hydrometers, bottle caps, rubber stoppers, corks and corkscrews, barrel spigots and liners, tubing and siphons, Mehu-Maya steam juicers, fermenters, fruit presses, dried botanicals, and much more. The T. Noirot extracts can be used to create low-priced liqueurs, and there are books and manuals to provide help if you want to learn more. If you're just getting started, you may find the Kraus "Necessities Box"—equipment and supplies for making five gallons of wine or four gallons of beer—just what you need.

Special Factors: Local ordinances may regulate production of alcoholic beverages; minimum order is $5 with credit cards.

THE MAPLES FRUIT FARM, INC.

P.O. BOX 167
CHEWSVILLE, MD 21721
301-733-0777

Catalog: free
Save: up to 50%
Pay: check, MO, MC, V
Sells: dried fruit, nuts, coffee, gift baskets, etc.
Store: 13144 Pennsylvania Ave., Hagerstown, MD; Monday to Thursday 9–6, Friday 9–7, Saturday 8–5

The 16-page catalog of dried fruits, nuts, coffee, tea, and sweets from Maples Fruit Farm pictures an early view of the Farm, which has been operated by the same family for 200 years. The prices here are mouthwatering—savings of 25% to 50% were found on selected items. The dried fruits include apricots, dates, pears, peaches, and pineapple. (Fruits prepared with sulphur dioxide are clearly indicated in the catalog.) Raw and roasted (salted and unsalted) nuts are offered, including cashews, almonds, peanuts, pecans, macadamia nuts, filberts, black walnuts, and a number of others, including trail mix. Two pounds of raw pecans from Maples were half as expensive than those from a specialty pecan source, and the roasted macadamia nuts, honey-roasted peanuts, and cashews were all better buys here. Among sweets, Maryland grade-A amber maple syrup costs about 35% less than the syrup offered by competitors (who sell Canadian and New York state products). Maples Fruit Farm also sells 38 kinds of gourmet coffee, roasted fresh at the firm's gourmet shop daily, and tea from Benchley, Celestial Seasonings, and Twinings.

Reasonably priced gift baskets are available, and if you can stock up or share orders, check the *wholesale* prices on cases. Don't miss the store if you're in the Hagerstown area—drop in to smell the coffee roasting, and sample some of the 5,000 gourmet treats on the shelves.

Special Factors: Satisfaction is guaranteed; minimum order is $25; orders are shipped worldwide.

MR. SPICEMAN, INC.

169-06 CROCHERON AVE.,
DEPT. Q-3
AUBURNDALE, NY 11358
718-358-5020

Catalog: $1, deductible
Save: up to 94%
Pay: check, MO, MC, V
Sells: herbs, spices, seasonings, and candy
Store: same address; Friday 8–5 (8–noon in June, July, and August)

Mr. Spiceman publishes a catalog that runs from soup to nuts, but is best known for great buys on herbs, spices, and other seasonings. Founded in 1965, this firm supplies restaurants, delis, and fine food outlets, as well as consumers, at savings that average from 40% to 60%. The catalog lists over 130 herbs and spices, available in small and bulk packaging, including ground allspice, cayenne pepper, ground cumin, curry powder, paprika, and other basics. Mr. Spiceman sells unusual seasonings, such as achiote, juniper berries, cilantro leaves, and freeze-dried shallots, as well as marinade mixes, pasta sauces, barbecue sauces, Tic Tac mints, crystallized ginger, Knorr soup and sauce mixes, Gravy Master flavoring, 4C products, and Virginia Dare extracts and flavorings. A number of kitchen gadgets are available, including a nutmeg grater and a pocket peppermill.

The prices are good, and Mr. Spiceman is bettering them for new customers. As a reader of this book, you may deduct 10% from your first order (computed on the goods total only). This WBMC reader discount expires February 1, 1995.

Special Factors: Call before visiting the retail location; minimum order is $10, $25 with credit cards; orders are shipped worldwide.

NORTHWESTERN COFFEE MILLS

217 N. BROADWAY
MILWAUKEE, WI 53202
800-243-5283
414-276-1031
715-747-5825

Catalog: free
Save: up to 40% (see text)
Pay: check, MO, MC, V, AE
Sells: coffee, tea, herbs, spices, and coffee filters
Store: same address; Monday to Friday 10–5:30, Saturday 10–4

If coffee is America's drink, Wisconsin may be harboring a national treasure. It's the home of Northwestern Coffee Mills, which set up shop in 1875 in a town better known for a different sort of brew. Northwestern begins with top-quality Arabica, and roasts each type of bean separately to develop its optimum flavor.

The catalog describes each of the blends, straights, dark roasts, and decaffeinated coffees, noting relative strength, body, aroma, and flavor. Among the blends are American Breakfast, Fancy Dinner Blend (a strong, after-dinner coffee), Mocha Java, a New Orleans chicory blend, and "Stapleton's 1875 Blend," a favorite of local restaurateurs that "stands up well when heated for hours on end." There are fancy straights, including Brazil Santos (when available), Costa Rica Tarrazu, Kenya AA, Colombia Excelso, and Sumatra Lintong. Fully certified Jamaican Blue Mountain coffee from the Wallenford Estate is available, as well as estate-grown Java and Hawaiian Kona, Yemen Mocha Mattari (the *real* mocha from Yemen), Celebes Kalosi, and other rare straight coffees. Decaf drinkers can choose from solvent-processed or water-processed blends and straights. Coffee filters for all types of drip and percolator systems are sold, including Chemex, Filtropa, and the Wisconsin-made "Natural Brew" unbleached filters. Northwestern also maintains a premium tea department. The catalog describes how tea is grown and processed, tea grading, and the types of teas it Northwestern sells: flavored, black, green, oolong, and decaffeinated. The varieties include Ceylon, Indian Assam, Indian Darjeeling, Irish Breakfast, Russian Caravan, Japan Sencha, "China Dragon Well Panfired Leaf," and Orange Spiced tea, among others. Northwestern's prices on single pounds of coffee or four-ounce packages of tea are market-rate, but the firm will sell both to consumers at bulk rates. There are price breaks at 6 and 24 pounds, and since coffee in whole-bean form will keep well for several months in the freezer, it makes sense to order as much as you can store.

Last but not least, Northwestern sells herbs, spices, and other flavorings in supermarket sizes and in bulk. Several capsicums (peppers) are offered, and dried vegetables (garlic granules, horseradish powder, mushrooms, etc.), blended salt-free and salted seasonings, and natural extracts (vanilla, almond, cocoa, cinnamon, orange, etc.) are also listed. You can use these extracts, says Northwestern, to create flavored coffees (which it does not sell).

Special Factors: Satisfaction is guaranteed; quantity discounts are available; returns are accepted within one year for exchange, refund, or credit; orders are shipped worldwide.

PALMER'S MAPLE SYRUP

████████████

BOX 246
WAITSFIELD, VT
  05673-9711
802-496-3696

Brochure and Price List: free
Save: 33% plus (see text)
Pay: check, MO, AE
Sells: maple syrup, cream, and candy
Store: Mehuron's Market and Bisbee's Hardware, Waitsfield, VT

The Palmers have been sugaring since 1967, and in early spring they head for the woods to draw the sap that will be transformed into a season's worth of maple syrup. Their brochure describes the entire process, including grading and canning, and gives the recipe for the raised doughnuts that Mrs. Palmer serves to visitors who drop by during the sugaring season.

And the Palmers are nice when it comes to the price, which at this writing is $11.40 a quart, compared to $16.95 for the same grade of Vermont syrup sold through another gourmet foods catalog. Even the Palmers' highest per-ounce price, for half pints, is lower by a third than what other mail-order firms are charging. The Palmers sell three grades of syrup—light amber (Fancy), medium amber (A), and dark amber (B)—at the same price. If you like a very delicate flavor, try the Fancy grade; grade B has a strong "mapley" flavor that suits some palates and purposes (cooking and baking) more than the other two grades. Maple cream and candies may also be available; see the price list for information.

Please note: The pint-size "log cabin" tins hold 16.9 ounces, the half-pint tins, 4.5 ounces.

Special Factor: Orders are shipped worldwide.

PENDERY'S INC.

1221 MANUFACTURING ST.
DALLAS, TX 75207
800-533-1870
214-741-1870
FAX: 214-761-1966

Catalog: $2
Save: up to 75%
Pay: check, MO, MC, V, AE, Discover, Optima
Sells: herbs, spices, and Mexican seasonings; teas and botanicals
Store: 304 E. Belknap St., Fort Worth; also Galleria Mall and Inwood Village, 5450 W. Lovers Lane, Dallas, TX

  ¡Si!

Pendery's has been spicing up drab dishes since 1870, and can add the authentic touch of real, full-strength chiles to your Tex-Mex cuisine for a fraction of the prices charged by gourmet shops. The firm's 64-page catalog describes the origins of the company and its contributions to the development of Tex-Mex chile seasonings. It's not a coincidence that "those captivating capsicums" occupy five catalog pages and include pods, ground peppers, and blends. Scores of general and specialty seasonings and flavorings are offered, including fajita seasoning, jalapeño peppers, and spice-rack standards from allspice to white pepper. Among the unusual or hard-to-find ingredients available here are masa harina, Mexican chocolate, annatto, horseradish powder, Worchestershire powder, dehydrated cilantro, corn shucks for tamales and cornhusk dolls, and dried diced tomatoes. The catalog also offers handsome, handblown Mexican glassware, dried flowers and other potpourri ingredients, and related gifts. Prices of the spices are far lower than those charged by gourmet stores and supermarkets—up to 75% less on some of the specialty seasonings.

Special Factor: Orders are shipped worldwide.

PENZEYS' SPICE HOUSE

Catalog: free
Save: 35% average (see text)
Pay: check, MO, MC, V
Sells: seasonings
Store: same address; Tuesday to Saturday 10–5

T921 S. WEST AVE.
WAUKESHA, WI 53186
414-574-0277
FAX: 414-574-0278

Penzeys' Spice House is a family-run firm that "grinds and blends our spices weekly to insure freshness," something no one else in the business seems to be doing. The selection is extraordinary—there are 11 forms and types of cinnamon, for example. Penzeys', established in 1957, prices even one-ounce sizes of seasonings at below-supermarket rates and offers savings of up to 40% on full pounds.

The informative, 26-page catalog begins with adobo seasoning and ends with vanilla beans. In between, you'll find Brady Street Cheese Sprinkle, Bicentennial "Rub" Seasoning (an early American blend), cassia buds from China, cardamom, chili peppers (rated for heat in Skoval units), tandoori chicken seasoning, fenugreek seeds, mulled wine spices, "Old World Seasoning," pot herbs for soups and stews, Spanish saffron, seasonings for salad dressings and homemade sausages, star anise, taco seasoning, French tarragon, and many other straight seasonings and blends. (Nearly three dozen are offered in salt-free versions, and Penzeys' Spice House also offers a line of soup bases.) The descriptions include provenance, ingredients in the blends, and suggested uses.

There are several intriguing gift packages, including "Spicy Wedding," "Great Baker's Assortment," "Indian Curries," and a "Spice Replacement" set (when "the love of your life has left you taking all of your spices, maybe your house burned down or was just swept away by a tornado/hurricane"). Zassenhaus pepper mills and inexpensive jars for herb and spice storage are also available.

Special Factors: Satisfaction is guaranteed; price quote by phone or fax; returns are accepted for exchange, refund, or credit; orders are shipped worldwide.

SAN FRANCISCO HERB CO.

━━━━━━━

250 14TH ST., DEPT. W
SAN FRANCISCO, CA
  94103
800-227-4530
415-861-7174
FAX: 415-861-4440

Catalog with Recipes: free
Save: 50% plus
Pay: check, MO, MC, V
Sells: culinary herbs, teas, spices, and potpourri ingredients
Store (wholesale outlet): same address; Monday to Friday 10–4

Reader-recommended San Francisco Herb is known for excellent prices and a great selection of herbs, spices, potpourri ingredients, fragrance oils, botanicals, and teas. This 21-year-old firm is primarily a wholesaler, but if you can meet the minimum order of $30, you'll find San Francisco Herb a valuable source.

The culinary herbs and spices offered here range from the routine—allspice, cinnamon, marjoram, tarragon—to such uncommon seasonings as spice blends for Greek foods and cilantro leaf. Among the botanicals are alfalfa leaf, balsam fir needles, chamomile, kelp powder, lavender, orris root, pine cones, rosebuds, pennyroyal, spearmint leaf, and yerba maté. (Some of these can be consumed, and others can't; check with a reliable information source before assuming botanicals are safe for food use.) Recipes for mulling spice blend, no-salt flavor enhancers, bouquet garni, and garam masala (a spice blend used in Indian cuisine) are all available on request.

The catalog also features dozens of recipes for sachets and simmering and jar potpourris. The "Hollyberry Christmas Jar Potpourri" has a delectable scent and lovely combination of colors, and "Plantation Peach" is delightfully fruity. If you're not experienced in making potpourri, try some of the recipes to become more familiar with blending colors and fragrances.

The spices and botanicals are sold by the pound (selected items are available in four-ounce units), with quantity discounts of 10% on purchases of five pounds or more of the same item. San Francisco Herb also sells glass vials and spice jars, flavored teas in bulk, dehydrated vegetables, shelled nuts, sprouting seeds, and such miscellaneous food goods as lemon powder, arrowroot powder, bacon bits, pine nuts, and roasted chicory root.

Special Factors: Satisfaction is guaranteed; volume discounts are available; authorized returns are accepted within 15 days (a 15% restocking fee may be charged); minimum order is $30; C.O.D. orders are accepted; online with Prodigy; orders are shipped worldwide.

SIMPSON & VAIL, INC.

P.O. BOX 309
38 CLINTON ST.
PLEASANTVILLE, NY
10570-0309
800-282-TEAS
914-747-1336
FAX: 914-741-6942

Catalog: free
Save: up to 30%
Pay: check, MO, MC, V
Sells: coffees, teas, brewing accessories, and gourmet foods
Store: same address; Monday to Friday 9–5:30. Saturday 9–4:30

Simpson & Vail, established in 1929, sells gourmet coffees at prices lower than those charged by many New York City bean boutiques. Over 50 coffees are offered, including American (brown), French, Viennese, and Italian roasts, Kenya AA, Tanzanian Peaberry, Hawaiian Kona, Sumatra Mandehling Kasho, and other straight coffees and blends. The water-process decaffeinated line includes American-style roast, espresso, Mocha Java, Tip of the Andes, and others. Coffee-making gear and supplies by Krups and Melitta are available.

The tea department features over 80 varieties, among them the classics of England and the East, blends, naturally flavored connoisseur teas (raspberry, vanilla, watermelon, coconut, etc.), and selected decaffeinated teas. You'll also find tea accessories—infusers and balls, strainers, and filters—as well as bone china mugs, tea cozies, warmers, canisters, tea bricks, and tea towels. Simpson & Vail has developed a delightful collection of teapots—fine English bone china, Staffordshire Blue Willow, Chinese terra cotta, German glass, and Irish Parian china are a few. And Simpson & Vail also stocks butter cakes from Vermont, Scottish shortbread, fudge sauces, soups by Abbott's, preserves, jams, marmalades, Patak Indian foods, and the delectable lines of Italian foodstuffs and condiments from Balducci's and Dean & Deluca.

Readers of this book may deduct 10% of the goods total from their first order only. Remember to identify yourself as a WBMC reader when you order. This WBMC reader discount expires February 1, 1995.

Special Factors: All beans are ground to order; gift packages are available; orders are shipped worldwide.

SULTAN'S DELIGHT, INC.

━━━━━━━━

P.O. BOX 140253
STATEN ISLAND, NY
  10314-0014
718-720-1557

Catalog: free with a stamped, self-addressed envelope
Save: up to 50%
Pay: check, MO, MC, V, Discover
Sells: Middle Eastern foods and gifts
Store: mail order only

Sultan's Delight specializes in authentic Middle Eastern food specialties, sold at excellent prices—up to 50% below comparable goods in gourmet shops. The firm was established in 1980, and offers both raw ingredients and prepared specialties, including the Near East and Sahadi lines of foods. See the catalog if you're looking for canned tahini, couscous, tabouleh, fig and apricot jams, stuffed grapevine leaves, bulghur, green wheat, orzo, fava beans, ground sumac, Turkish figs, or pickled okra. You'll also find olives, herbs and spices, jumbo pistachios and other nuts, roasted chick peas, halvah, Turkish delight, marzipan paste, olive oil, Turkish coffee, fruit leather, filo, feta cheese, and other specialties. Cookbooks for Greek, Lebanese, and Middle Eastern cuisine are available, as well as belly-dancing clothing and accessories, Turkish coffee pots, waterpipes, inlaid backgammon sets, and other intriguing items.

Sultan's Delight is offering readers of this book a 10% discount on their first order (computed on the goods total only). Identify yourself as a reader when you order. This WBMC reader discount expires March 31, 1995.

Special Factors: Minimum order is $15; orders are shipped worldwide.

ELBRIDGE C. THOMAS & SONS

RTE. 4, BOX 336
CHESTER, VT 05143
802-263-5680

Brochure: $1
Save: up to 50% (see text)
Pay: check, MO, AE
Sells: Vermont grade-A maple syrup
Store: mail order only

Mr. Thomas makes and sells the nectar of New England—pure, grade-A Vermont maple syrup. He's been in business since 1938, and his prices on large sizes are as much as 50% lower than those of his competitors—and even better than those charged for lesser grades. The stock is pure and simple: Vermont maple syrup, grade A, available in half-pint, pint, quart, half-gallon, and gallon tins. (Plastic containers are available upon request.) Maple sugar cakes, which make irresistible gifts, are also offered (by special order only). The brochure includes a number of suggestions for using maple syrup in your favorite foods—maple milk shakes, maple ham, frosting, and baked beans are just a few examples.

Special Factors: Quantity discounts are available; prices are subject to change without notice; orders are shipped worldwide.

WALNUT ACRES ORGANIC FARMS

DEPT. 3120
WALNUT ACRES RD.
PENNS CREEK, PA 17862
800-433-3998
FAX: 717-837-1146

Catalog: free
Save: up to 40%
Pay: check, MO, MC, V, Discover
Sells: organically grown foods, natural toiletries, cookware, etc.
Store: Penns Creek, PA; Monday to Saturday 9–5

Walnut Acres Organic Farms, in business since 1946, sells organically grown foods, nutritional supplements, cookbooks, and related items. Most of the goods are produced at Walnut Acres, grown on "500 acres of chemical-free soil." The 52-page color catalog presents the bounty in full, appetizing color: grains, cereals, granola, bread and pancake mixes, flours, seeds and nuts, nut butters, soups, salad dressings, sauces, pasta, dried fruits, juices, honeys, and other goods. Herbs and spices, relishes, dehydrated vegetables, canned fruits, vegetables, and beans, powdered milk, crackers, jams and preserves, cheeses, and baked goods are also offered. Walnut Acres sells nutritional supplements and some natural toiletries and unguents as well, and a variety of products "friendly to the environment."

Prices are not uniformly low, but among those spot-checked against two local health-food stores were at least 10% below the going rate for comparable items. Savings of 30% to 40% were possible on the dried fruits and nuts, compared to other mail-order sources. These were pound-for-pound comparisons; Walnut Acres sells its nuts, seeds, grains, cereals, and dried fruits in bulk packages (three and five pounds) at additional savings.

Special Factors: Products are guaranteed to be as represented; orders are shipped worldwide.

WOOD'S CIDER MILL

RD #2, BOX 477
SPRINGFIELD, VT 05156
802-263-5547

Brochure: free with SASE
Save: up to 50% (see text)
Pay: check, MO, MC, V
Sells: cider jelly and syrup
Store (farm): same address; call for appointment

 ¡Si!

The Wood family has maintained a farm in Vermont since 1798 and today produces several wonderful treats for mail-order customers. The prices are better than reasonable—in fact, Wood's cider jelly can be found selling in other catalogs at prices nearly twice as high as those charged by the Woods themselves! And another firm's cider jelly costs over twice as much for the same amount.

The Cider Mill is best known for its jelly, which is made of evaporated apple cider. From 30 to 50 apples are needed to make the cider that's concentrated in just one pound of jelly, but you'll understand why when you taste it on toast or muffins, or try it with pork and other meats as a condiment. Boiled cider is also available; it's a less-concentrated essence that is recommended as a base for a hot drink, as a ham glaze, and as a topping for ice cream and pancakes. For pancakes, however, try the cider syrup, a blend of boiled cider and maple syrup. (It's also outstanding as a basting sauce for Thanksgiving turkeys, and even roast chicken.) Straight maple syrup is also produced on the farm, and even the farm's sheep contribute to the offerings: natural and black two-ply yarns are sold through the brochure as well.

Special Factors: Satisfaction is guaranteed; returns are accepted for exchange or refund; quantity discounts are available; minimum order is four jars; orders are shipped worldwide.

SEE ALSO

A Cook's Wares • gourmet foods and condiments • **HOME: KITCHEN**
Cabela's Inc. • freeze-dried foods, trail packs • **SPORTS**
Campmor • dehydrated camping food, beef jerky, etc. • **SPORTS**
Caprilands Herb Farm • live and dried herbs, herbal vinegars, and teas • **FARM**
Don Gleason's Campers Supply, Inc. • freeze-dried food for camping and survival • **SPORTS**
Le Jardin du Gourmet • gourmet foods, live herb plants, etc. • **FARM**
New England Cheesemaking Supply Company, Inc. • cheese-making supplies and equipment • **HOME: KITCHEN**
The Paper Wholesaler • catering supplies, restaurant paper goods, disposable tableware • **GENERAL MERCHANDISE**
Plastic BagMart • plastic food storage bags • **OFFICE: SMALL BUSINESS**
Protecto-Pak • zip-top plastic bags • **OFFICE: SMALL BUSINESS**
Storey's Books for Country Living • cookbooks and manuals on food preservation • **BOOKS**
Survival Supply Co. • dehydrated and "survival" food • **SPORTS**
Taylor's Cutaways and Stuff • tea "baglets" for making your own teabags • **CRAFTS**
Triner Scale • pocket scale • **OFFICE**
U.S. Toy Company, Inc. • penny candies • **TOYS**
Weston Bowl Mill • sugar buckets and butter churns • **GENERAL MERCHANDISE**
Zabar's & Co., Inc. • gourmet foods and condiments • **HOME: KITCHEN**

GENERAL MERCHANDISE, BUYING CLUBS, AND GOOD VALUES

Firms and buying clubs offering a wide range

of goods and services

Most of the firms listed in this chapter offer such a wide range of products that it might be confusing to put them elsewhere. So you'll find companies here that sell everything from mosquito netting to potpourri. Go through the listings carefully, since there are some real finds here, and countless answers to the question of what to give for Christmas, birthdays, anniversaries, and other occasions.

Shopping has become much easier thanks to 800 lines. Those toll-free numbers also yield travel and lodging reservations, banking and investment assistance, product information and advice, and a wide range of services. The *AT&T Toll-Free 800 Consumer Directory* is a big help in finding 800 numbers quickly; it has over 50,000 listings, from "accountants" to "yarn." The current consumer edition costs $9.95 (plus sales tax and handling), and can be ordered by calling 1-800-426-8686.

If savings are more your concern than are services, you'll appreciate two monthly journals written by and for penny pinchers:

Frugal Times, "dedicated to those of us who want more but have less," is probably the best for working people who, in the words of editor Adrianne Ferree, "don't want to spend all their free time doing things that are time consuming just to save a buck. For example, line drying all your clothes." Common sense—how refreshing. A sample issue of *Frugal Times* covers sticking to New Year's resolutions, buying groceries in bulk, special benefits of all types for seniors, getting justice (and refunds!) when toys break prematurely, saving money on energy bills (chuck the heated waterbed and change those furnace filters), buying checks cheaply, turning junk mail to good use, and much more.

A sample copy costs $1, from The Frugal Times, P.O. Box 2116, Hawthorne, CA 90250.

The Tightwad Gazette is in the business of "Promoting Thrift as an Alternative Lifestyle." Written by Amy Dacyczyn, aka The Frugal Zealot, it also offers down-to-earth advice on things like evaluating old houses as prospective purchases, or whether buying used shoes for children is an acceptable practice. Savvy consumers may wonder, however, why space has been spent noting that you can recycle old kitchen cabinets to the workshop, or find reading material in the local recycling pile. But you be the judge: A sample issue costs $1 from The Tightwad Gazette, RR1, Box 357, Leeds, ME 04263-9710.

AMERICAN ASSOCIATION OF RETIRED PERSONS

Information: inquire
Save: up to 40% (see text)
Pay: check, MO, MC, V
Sells: membership (see text)
Store: mail order only

601 E. ST. N.W.
WASHINGTON, DC 20049
202-434-2277

The American Association of Retired Persons is a not-for-profit organization dedicated to improving the lives of older Americans, especially in the areas of finance and health. Membership is open to anyone aged 50 or older, retired or not, at a cost of just $8 a year. Among the benefits are subscriptions to the bimonthly *Modern Maturity* and the monthly *AARP Bulletin,* the opportunity to buy low-cost supplemental health insurance, auto and homeowner insurance, participation in the AARP Federal Credit Union, the AARP VISA card (15.6% APR, $10 annual fee), the AARP Motoring Plan (affiliated with Amoco Motor Club), group travel programs coordinated with American Express, publications on health topics, discounts on hotels and car rentals, and access to a pharmacy-by-mail. (See the listing for Retired Persons Services in "Medicine" for more details.)

When you write to the AARP for membership information, you can request the group's publication, "Prescription for Action," a 68-page guide to approaching health-care issues on a collective, community level. It gives guidelines and ideas for conducting price-comparison surveys of prescription drugs, compiling directories of physicians in your area who accept Medicare/Medicaid, cataloging services for seniors, having a voice in government, and promoting proven alternative-care options and long-term home care. The book is a compendium of ideas, resources, and references—a great source for health-care activists.

Special Factor: Inquire for information.

THE AMERICAN STATIONERY CO., INC.

100 PARK AVE., DEPT. 4
PERU, IN 46970
800-822-2577
FAX: 317-472-5901

Catalog: free
Save: up to 45%
Pay: check, MO, MC, V, Discover
Sells: personalized stationery
Store: mail order only

The American Stationery Co. offers a good selection of personalized stationery, at prices up to 45% below those charged by other firms for comparable goods and printing. The company has been in business since 1919, and also produces "The American Wedding Album," a 40-page color catalog with actual samples of wedding invitations and accessories.

The correspondence selections include embossed sheets and notes in four colors, deckle-edged and plain sheets and envelopes in white and pastels, and heavyweight Monarch sheets, erasable sheets, business envelopes, and "executive" stationery of heavyweight, chain-laid paper. There are great buys here, including the "Typewriter Box" of 100 printed sheets and the same number of printed envelopes for $16.95. Recent additions to the company's line include informals and notes in contemporary and calligraphic typefaces, notepads in spiffy designs, and a choice of ink colors—peach, gold, teal, and gray, as well as the standard range. Stationery for children, personalized memo pads, bill-paying envelopes, bordered postcards, gummed and self-sticking return-address labels, and related goods are shown in the color catalog.

Special Factors: Satisfaction is guaranteed; returns are accepted for replacement or refund.

ANTICIPATIONS

9 ROSS SIMONS DR.
CRANSTON, RI 02920-4476
800-556-7376
401-463-3100
FAX: 401-463-8599

Catalog: free
Save: up to 50%
Pay: check, MO, MC, V, AE, DC, Discover
Sells: gifts, home accents, etc.
Store: mail order only

Anticipations is 48 pages of treasures to delight your friends and grace your own home, at savings that average 25% on comparable retail. Produced by Ross-Simons (see the listing in "Jewelry"), Anticipations features fine jewelry and baubles, carpets, furnishings, pretty lamps, candlesticks holiday decorations, Mikasa china, mirrors, framed art prints, toys, chinoiserie, statuary, pillows, afghans, Limoges boxes, and much more. Not everything is priced at a discount, but savings on selected furnishings, home accents, and table settings run as high as 45%. Anticipations maintains the same service standards as its parent company, featuring "white glove treatment" (in-home delivery of large pieces of furniture), and a swatching service for the upholstered goods.

Special Factors: Satisfaction is guaranteed; returns are accepted within 30 days.

BENNETT BROTHERS, INC.

30 E. ADAMS ST.
CHICAGO, IL 60603
312-263-4800
FAX: 312-621-1669

Catalog: free
Save: up to 40%
Pay: check, MO, MC, V
Sells: jewelry, appliances, electronics, luggage, furnishings, etc.
Store: same address: Monday to Friday 8:15–5 (see the catalog for holiday shopping hours); also 211 Island Rd., Mahwah, NJ: Monday to Saturday 9–5:30

At the turn of the century, much of Bennett Brothers' business was in jewelry, gems, and watches. They're still a big part of the company's trade, but Bennett's current offerings, shown in the annual "Blue Book," also include furnishings, leather goods, electronics, cameras, sporting goods, and toys.

The Blue Book is 308 color pages of name-brand goods, which helps to make the firm's "Choose-Your-Gift" program one of the easiest ways to deliver presents to employees and business associates. Jewelry takes 115 pages—wedding and engagement bands, pearls, pins and bracelets, necklaces, and other pieces featuring all kinds of precious and semiprecious gems, as well as charms, lockets, medallions, anniversary jewelry, Masonic rings, and crosses and religious jewelry. The watch department offers models from Armitron, Benrus, Casio, Citizen, Gitano, Jules Jurgensen, Pulsar, Seiko, and Timex.

Bennett Brothers offers a fine selection of clocks, timepieces, and weather instrument stations. Silverware and chests, silver giftware, tea sets, pewterware, and fine china are also sold. The catalog shows kitchen cutlery sets, cookware sets, small kitchen appliances, microwave ovens, barbecue grills, vacuum cleaners, air machines, exercise equipment, sewing machines, personal-care appliances, bed linens, towels, tablecloths, and luggage. The leather goods department is especially good, including briefcases and attaché cases and luggage from American Tourister, Elco, Gralnick & Son, Monarch, Samsonite, Skyway, and Winn.

The Blue Book also features a large group of personal electronics and office supplies—clock radios, portable cassette players, stereo systems and components, TVs and video equipment, phones and answering machines, CB equipment, home security systems, cameras, projectors, telescopes, binoculars, microscopes, pens, globes, cash registers, calculators, typewriters, safes, files, and office furnishings. Home furnishings are also available, including patio furniture. The catalog includes Playskool toys, Bachmann and Lionel collectors' trains, Cox radio-controlled cars and planes, playing cards, and board games. There are also exercise machines, golf clubs, basketballs, volleyballs and nets, gun cabinets, hunting knives, fishing rods, bocce ball and croquet game sets, dart boards, and sleeping bags. Metal detectors, flashlights and emergency beams, and even weathervanes, lawnmowers, chain saws, and other power and hand tools are offered.

Bennett's prices are listed next to "suggested retail" prices throughout the book. Price comparisons of several goods substantiated Bennett's guideline prices (suggested retail), and the savings of 30% to 40%.

Special Factors: Authorized returns are accepted within ten days for exchange or credit; orders are shipped worldwide.

CLOTHCRAFTERS, INC.

━━━━━━━━━

P.O. BOX 176, DEPT.
 WM94
ELKHART LAKE, WI 53020
414-876-2112

Catalog: free
Save: up to 40%
Pay: check, MO, MC, V
Sells: home textiles
Store: mail order only

This firm, established in 1936, sells "plain vanilla" textile goods of every sort, from cheesecloth by the yard to flannel patches for cleaning guns. There are many inexpensive, useful items in the 16-page catalog, including a host of practical household goods: pot holders, chefs' hats, bouquet garni bags (12 for $4), salad greens bags, fabric coffee filters, striped denim place mats, cotton napkins ($12 per dozen), hot pads, and aprons. Clothcrafters has a great selection of well-priced kitchen tools, including parchment paper, rubber spatulas, spatter lids, radiant heat plates, and other handy utensils.

You'll also find laundry bags, tote bags, flannel shoe bags, woodpile covers and firewood carriers, garment bags, cider-press liners, computer covers, flannel polishing squares, and mosquito netting. The bed and bath department offers cotton duck shower curtains, lightweight cotton terry towels and bath wraps, terry tunics, beach mats, barbers' capes, cotton flannel sheets, pillowcases, sleeping bag liners, and crib sheets. Three kinds of cloth diapers are available. Textile artists should appreciate this source, since many of these items can be painted, embroidered, dyed, and otherwise embellished.

Gardeners will find the "PlyBan" porous plastic sheeting ideal for protecting newly planted rows from frost and insects ($9 for 4' by 50'). If you garden during the insect high season, you might want to add the mosquito-netting helmet to your order. While you're at it, consider the multi-pocketed apron—it has places for the trowel, seed packets, string, and all those stones that turn up. And don't overlook the denim knee pads—they fasten with Velcro, and are machine washable.

Canadian readers, please note: Only U.S. funds are accepted.

Special Factors: Satisfaction is guaranteed; returns are accepted for exchange, refund, or credit; orders are shipped worldwide.

BETTY CROCKER ENTERPRISES

P.O. BOX 5348
MINNEAPOLIS, MN 55460
612-540-2212
FAX: 612-540-7432

Catalog: 50¢
Save: up to 70% (see text)
Pay: check, MO, MC, V, Discover
Sells: table settings, kitchenware, house-
wares, toys, etc.
Store: mail order only

Betty Crocker, one of the most successful marketing creations in the history of prepared foods, has an image built on helping homemakers make the most of their time and money. All of her mixes and snacks—from Hamburger Helper to Nature Valley Granola Bars—as well as General Mills products bear coupons good for "Betty Crocker Catalog Points," which can be collected and applied toward the purchase of items from the Betty Crocker catalog. And if you've never sent the 50¢ requested for the catalog, do it now—the coupons you've been collecting (or tossing out with the empty packages) are worth big savings on a wide range of goods.

The catalog features tableware, including Oneida Community flatware and china from Franciscan, Johnson Brothers, Pfaltzgraff, and Royal Doulton. Flatware chests are available, as well as Armetale serving pieces, all sorts of bakeware, Betty Crocker, Regal, and T-Fal cookware, cutlery, kitchen gadgets, a line of scissors, and the Betty Crocker cookbook collection. And there are pages of educational toys, games, and puzzles, several patterns of children's tableware, and home entertaining helps like bridge tables and chairs, popcorn bowls, and beechwood accessories and snack tables.

Each item has two prices: the "no points" price (like regular retail), and the "Thrift" price, which you pay if you ante up a lot more Points. For example, a five-piece place setting of Oneida highest-quality 18-8 stainless steel flatware, with a suggested sale price of $32.95, costs just $9.99—plus 65 Betty Crocker Points. The LUX loud-ring kitchen timer costs $8.95 with 20 Points, $11.95 without. And the Points are easy to acquire—they're on all of the over 200 General Mills food products, and the catalog itself comes with 100 free points, plus over $8 in food coupons!

Special Factors: Satisfaction is guaranteed; returns are accepted for exchange, refund, or credit.

GOOSEBERRY PATCH

4 NORTH SANDUSKY ST.
P.O. BOX 190
DELAWARE, OH 43015
614-369-1554
FAX: 614-363-7225

Catalog: $1
Save: up to 30%
Pay: check, MO, MC, V
Sells: "country" gifts and crafts
Store: mail order only

The gift world is divided into two spheres—big and little. It's the "medium" gift, with more impact than a stocking stuffer but not enough to dent your budget, that always eludes. That's what makes Gooseberry Patch such a welcome find, especially if you and your intended recipient like things with a country accent. The firm's 32-page catalog is printed on paper the color of sugar cookies, and its contents are as sweet and wholesome: heart wreaths of canella berries, big bags of potpourri tied with ribbon, gift baskets tailored to specials tastes—filled with herbs, vanilla beans, flower seeds, tea, or bath infusions; wooden watermelon wedges, collectors' dolls, foam eggs and balls wrapped in country fabrics, cookie cutters in the shapes of everything from sunflowers and carrots to angels and crows, and tin cat silhouettes to perch on shelf or windowsill are just a few of the gifts currently available. A number of items cost under $10—a pair of apple candles, potpourri, pierced tin heart nightlights, "patriotic" Teddy bears, and doorknob baskets, for example—and there are dozens of great choices for under $20. And if you're ordering by phone, be sure to ask about specials, and new items that may not be pictured.

Special Factors: Satisfaction is guaranteed; price quote by phone or letter; returns are accepted for exchange, refund, or credit; minimum order is $15 with credit cards; orders are shipped worldwide.

GRAND FINALE

SUBSCRIPTIONS DEPT.
P.O. BOX 620049
DALLAS, TX 75262-0049
800-955-9595

Catalog: $3, year's subscription, refundable on first purchase
Save: 25% to 70%
Pay: MC, V, AE, Discover
Sells: upmarket and name-brand goods
Store: mail order only

Your catalog fee brings you a year of "luxury for less," 40-page catalogs of special values, clearance items, and closeouts from well-known mail-order houses. It's possible to save up to 70% on the original selling or list prices through Grand Finale, which has been in business since 1980.

Past catalogs have featured designer clothing, shoes, handbags, hand-embroidered table linens, Couristan rugs, Lane occasional furniture, cashmere sweaters, ceramic garden seats, needlepoint pillows, quilts, and Christmas decorations. Almost every catalog offers toys, Limoges bibelots, coasters, designer bed linens, rugs, cookware, flatware, fine china and crystal, and women's clothing. There's usually a sale section in the catalog featuring exceptional bargains; quantities of these items are limited, so order promptly. The quality is consistently high, and Grand Finale provides a gift boxing service ($3) and can forward presents to recipients directly.

Special Factors: Satisfaction is guaranteed; quantities are limited, so order promptly; returns are accepted for exchange, refund, or credit; orders are shipped worldwide.

LAND O' LAKES CATALOG

P.O. BOX 1693
CENTER CITY, MN
55012-0993
800-437-5936

Catalog: free
Save: up to 50%
Pay: check or MO
Sells: tableware, kitchenware, gifts, etc.
Store: mail order only

Indulgence pays off with the Land O' Lakes catalog, 48 color pages of attractive table settings, kitchen equipment, cookware, cookbooks, and even toys and crystal vases. Just save the proofs of purchase on Land

O' Lakes dairy products, and you can apply them toward discounts on goods from Reed & Barton, Royal Doulton, Wüstof-Trident, J.G. Durand, and other well-known manufacturers. The current selection is especially appealing, ideal for housewarming, bridal gifts, and other celebrations: Fiesta classic dinnerware in festive colors, matching flatware, Pfaltzgraff's "Arbor Vine" dinnerware, handblown Mexican goblets, Corningware bakeware and serving pieces, Farberware kettles and cookware, Rowenta toasters and irons, Bunnykins children's place settings, and KinderCare toys are among the highlights.

You get the lowest prices with the Super Saver Plan (six or nine points with each product or set), but if you're in a hurry, the Basic Plan requires just three points for each item (but carries a higher price tag). Points run from one on Land O' Lakes margarine to two on Light Sour Cream, to three on Land O' Lakes butter and Country Morning Spread. Although savings on dinnerware sets can reach 50%, most average 20% to 25%—still more than you were getting while you were throwing the coupons out with the packaging!

Please note: Since orders must be accompanied by coupons, only mail orders are accepted—no phone orders. Orders are not shipped outside the U.S., to P.O. Boxes, or to APO/FPO addresses.

Special Factors: Shipping is included.

LIXX LABELZ

BOX 32055K
2619 14TH ST. S.W.
CALGARY, AB T2T 5X0
CANADA
403-245-2331

Catalog: $4
Save: up to 30%
Pay: check or MO
Sells: customized labels and bookplates
Store: mail order only

Put an end to blah correspondence with Lixx Labelz, custom-printed labels for your letters, books, baked goodies, and what-have-you. Other firms put your name on a gummed or self-adhesive label, and some throw in an initial or cute motif, but Lixx Labelz offers you over *150* graphics. The design focus is a meeting of *Wild Kingdom* and modern calligraphy—great hand-lettered type styles and a choice of scores of animals, from giant pandas and other endangered species to geckos, ladybugs, house cats, and otters. Hearts, hydrangeas, maple leaves, piano keyboards, hot-air balloons, stars, Teddy bears, and food and wine designs are also available. The labels are large, running from about 1" by 3" to about 3" by 4". Considering the size, and the custom options, the Lixx Labelz prices of $10.50 for 200 of the smallest size (self-adhesive) to $25 for 200 of the largest bookplate size (self-adhesive) are very reasonable. Lixx Labelz has developed an order form that makes it easy to specify exactly what you want, but if you don't something to your liking among the stock designs, no problem—the firm will work with your own copyright-free art to create the design you had in mind!

U.S. readers, please note: Payment is accepted in U.S. funds.

Special Factors: Phone orders are not accepted; orders take six to eight weeks to arrive.

NEW ENGLAND BASKET CO.

P.O. BOX 1335
N. FALMOUTH, MA 02556
508-759-2000
FAX: 508-295-8299

Catalog: $3
Save: up to 50%
Pay: check, MO, MC, V
Sells: baskets, bows, and ribbons
Store: 19 Patterson Brook Rd., West Wareham, MA

New England Basket Co. sells the kinds of baskets sold at import shops: Tightly woven willow baskets in round, oval, and square shapes; bamboo trays, picnic hampers, rustic rattan baskets, and "country" baskets with a wash of white or soldier blue are among scores shown in the 20-page color catalog. Dimensions of each basket are given, and there are two prices—for one set or piece, or for one case. In addition to their obvious uses as decorative accents and a place for chips or rolls, consider baskets as great gift containers, closet organizers, flowerpot holders, toy catchalls—the list is endless.

New England Basket Co. also offers a great line of ribbon and bows—both satin and curling ribbon, and pom-pom and star bows, in a wide range of colors. These, plus the gift tags (50 per pack for $2.65), are so well priced that it pays to stock up for the holidays. And if you're considering starting a gift-basket business, see the heat sealing machines, cellophane sheets and excelsior, and other supplies—all you add is fruit and cheese!

Special Factors: Satisfaction is guaranteed; quantity discounts are available; authorized returns are accepted (a 15% restocking fee is charged) for exchange, refund, or credit.

THE PAPER WHOLESALER

795 N.W. 72ND ST.
MIAMI, FL 33150
305-836-1400
FAX: 305-836-1410
Catalog: $3

Save: up to 40%
Pay: check, MO, MC, V, Discover
Sells: party supplies, restaurant disposables
Store: (cash and carry warehouses) 2638
S.W. 28th Lane, Coconut Grove; 10101 NW
79th St., Hialeah; 8259 W. Flagler, Miami; and
18329 S. Dixie Hwy., Perrine, FL

The Paper Wholesaler sells restaurant and party and entertaining supplies and related goods in case lots and "retail packs", at discounts of up to 40% on the regular prices. The color catalog is full of table goods, decorations, and the little things that add fun to festive occasions: paper plates and napkins in vibrant colors and snappy designs, including ensembles for children's birthdays, wedding parties, and showers; plastic cutlery and cups, tablecloths, doilies, balloons, crepe paper, party hats, streamers and pennants, favors, and other novelties. Guest towels and toilet paper are sold here, as well as a good selection of candles, hors d'oeuvre picks and drink stirrers, cocktail napkins with amusing slogans, wrapping paper, gift bags, bows and ribbon, and invitations in upbeat designs and colors.

The Paper Wholesaler has a "serious" section for restaurateurs and caterers, which includes a selection of cake-decorating supplies, cake pans, deli and bakery containers, commercial-sized rolls of foil and poly film, ice scoops and bar tools, carafes, syrup pitchers, ash trays, and even the brooms, mops, and buckets you'll need when the guests are gone. And there's food—restaurant-sized containers of Pepperidge Farm Goldfish, Hellmann's mayonnaise, Orville Redenbacher popcorn, Planter's peanuts, and other condiments and snacks. The catalog includes tips on party planning, and the order form even features shopping lists so you don't overlook anything.

Special Factors: Satisfaction is guaranteed; returns of unopened, unused goods are accepted within 30 days for exchange, refund, or credit; orders are shipped worldwide.

THRIFT CLUB

P.O. BOX 9394
MINNEAPOLIS, MN 55440
800-328-0786

Information: inquire
Save: up to 50%
Pay: check, MO, MC, V, AE, Discover
Sells: buying club memberships
Store: mail order only

The Thrift Club can help you save on everything from eyeglasses to your next car through its various programs. Membership costs $49.95 per year, and provides a wide range of benefits: prescription-filling services at a discount, savings on general merchandise (appliances, electronics, home furnishings, computers, tires, musical instruments, and even sports equipment), rebates on Ryder truck rentals, a 15% discount at Pearle Vision Centers, car pricing and dealer referral services, and travel planning services. Discounts on car rentals from several agencies are possible, as well as savings on hotel accommodations, and even a 5% rebate on air travel and Amtrak booked through Thrift Club's travel agency. Membership includes the quarterly *Thrift Magazine,* which features articles on saving time and money and information about new club benefits and services.

Special Factor: Inquire for information.

WESTON BOWL MILL

P.O. BOX 218
WESTON, VT 05161
802-824-6219
FAX: 802-824-4215

Catalog: $1
Save: up to 30%
Pay: check, MO, MC, V
Sells: woodenware and wooden household items
Store: Main St. (Rte. 100), Weston, VT; daily 9–5

Weston Bowl Mill is known for its wooden salad bowls, but the Mill produces hundreds of other wooden items for use throughout the home. Prices of many of the goods run about 25% below comparable retail, and savings are even better on selected goods. Almost everything is available with and without finish (oil or lacquer): The popular salad bowls, thick milled curves of wood, are offered in sizes from 6" to 20" across. You can save a good deal by buying the seconds (with small flaws that should not affect wear), which cost up to 20% less than the first-quality bowls. Weston sells much more for dining table and kitchen, including birch dinner plates and trays, maple lazy Susans, salt-and-pepper shakers, cheese plates, knife racks, tongs, a great selection of carving and cutting boards, and carbon steel knives.

The 16-page catalog offers a wide variety of other home items, including shelves with brackets, towel and tissue holders, spoon racks, pegged coat racks, a large selection of wooden boxes, quilt racks, benches, stools, wooden fruits and vegetables, sugar buckets and churns, and baskets. Weston's bird feeders and whirligigs are well priced; likewise the delightful group of wooden toys—vehicles, tops, puzzles, game boards, cradles, and other classics—that are oil-finished. And the "country store" department includes "magic" massagers, lap boards, door stops and window props, outlet plates, spool holders, bells, yardsticks, and many other useful items.

Special Factors: Minimum order is $5, $20 with credit cards; orders are shipped worldwide.

SEE ALSO

Acme Premium Supply Corp. • premium merchandise • **TOYS**
Baron/Barclay Bridge Supplies • bridge-playing gifts • **TOYS**
Beauty by Spector, Inc. • wigs and hairpieces for men and women • **HEALTH**
Bruce Medical Supply • dining, dressing, bathing, and other aids for the disabled and motor-impaired • **MEDICINE**
Business Technologies, Inc. • cash registers • **OFFICE**
Caprilands Herb Farm • herb charts, note cards, potpourri, pomanders, etc. • **FARM**
Current, Inc. • check-printing services, gifts, cards, stationery, etc. • **BOOKS**
Michael C. Fina Co. • silver and crystal giftware • **HOME: TABLE SETTINGS**
Gohn Bros. • Amish "general store" goods • **CLOTHING**
Kaye's Holiday • holiday ornaments • **TOYS**
D. MacGillivray & Coy. • Scottish tartans, Highland dress accessories, etc. • **CRAFTS**
Merryweather Imports, Inc. • collectible cottages • **ART & ANTIQUES**
Oriental Trading Company, Inc. • gifts, novelties, etc. • **TOYS**
Paradise Products, Inc. • wide variety of party goods • **TOYS**
Pendery's Inc. • potpourri ingredients and gifts • **FOOD**
La Piñata • piñatas • **TOYS**
Plexi-Craft Quality Products Corp. • acrylic furniture, accessories, and gifts • **HOME: FURNISHINGS**

Rapidforms, Inc. • gift boxes and packing and shipping supplies • **OFFICE**

Rocky Mountain Stationery • handmade cards and notes • **BOOKS**

Nat Schwartz & Co., Inc. • bridal registry for gifts • **HOME: TABLE SET-TINGS**

Albert S. Smyth Co., Inc. • giftware, bridal and gift registry • **HOME: TABLE SETTINGS**

Stecher's Limited • clocks, watches, and giftware • **HOME: TABLE SET-TINGS**

Surplus Center • tools, electrical components, security equipment • **SURPLUS**

Survival Supply Co. • "survivalist" gear, books, and food • **SPORTS**

Think Ink • inexpensive thermographic color hand printers • **CRAFTS**

Thurber's • gifts, collectibles, and Christmas ornaments • **HOME: TABLE SET-TINGS**

U.S. Box Corp. • ribbons, bows, gift wrap, etc. • **OFFICE: SMALL BUSINESS**

U.S. Toy Company, Inc. • toys, games, and novelties • **TOYS**

Wag-Aero, Inc. • aviation-related gifts • **AUTO**

HEALTH AND BEAUTY

Cosmetics, perfumes, and toiletries; vitamins and dietary supplements; and wigs and hairpieces

You can save up to 90% on your cosmetic and beauty needs and still get the same name brands featured in beauty emporiums and department stores by buying by mail. For example, if your favorite perfume costs $160 an ounce, consider trying "copycat" scents, which are produced by Essential Products. And since beauty comes from within, firms selling vitamins and dietary supplements are also listed here. (Consult your physician before taking anything to augment your diet.)

For more firms selling related products, see the listings in "Medicine and Science."

FIND IT FAST

EXERCISE EQUIPMENT • **Creative Health**
PERFUME AND BEAUTY PRODUCTS • **Beautiful Visions, Essential Products, Holbrook Wholesalers, Kettle Care**
VITAMINS • **Freeda, Hillestad**
WIGS AND HAIRPIECES • **Beauty by Spector**

BEAUTIFUL VISIONS

1233 MONTAUK HWY.
OAKDALE, NY 11769
516-567-9500

Catalog: free
Save: up to 90%
Pay: check, MO, MC, V
Sells: cosmetics and preparations
Store: same address; Monday to Friday 9–5, Saturday 9–4

 ¡Si!

Beautiful Visions, which has been in business since 1977, sells beauty essentials from top manufacturers at up to 90% off list prices. Each issue of the 80-page catalog brings you cosmetics, skin-care products, and perfumes from Almay, Aziza, Charles of the Ritz, Clarion, Coty, Jōvan, L'Oreal, Max Factor, Maybelline, Prince Matchabelli, Revlon, Vidal Sassoon, Vitabath, and other manufacturers. Current fashion shades are stocked, as well as the basics. The catalog also features vitamins and minerals, grooming tools, fashion jewelry, and gifts, all at very reasonable prices.

Special Factors: Satisfaction is guaranteed; returns are accepted.

BEAUTY BY SPECTOR, INC.

DEPT. WBMC-94
MCKEESPORT, PA
15134-0502
412-673-3259

Catalog: free (see text)
Save: up to 50%
Pay: check, MO, MC, V
Sells: wigs and hairpieces
Store: mail order only

  ★

Beauty by Spector, Inc., founded in 1958, offers the Alan Thomas line of wigs and hairpieces at savings of up to 50% on salon prices. The 30-page "Hairgoods Portfolio" features a number of designer styles for women. The wigs range from neat, softly coiffed heads to "Heavenly," a youthful head of curls falling past the shoulders. These are contemporary styles—pretty, relaxed, and well shaped. Included in the Portfolio are wiglets, cascades, and extensions that are ideal for everyday wear as well as dressy or special occasions, and a special line of "ultra-light-weight" wigs for women. Men's hairpieces, made with thermal-conductive and mesh bases, are offered in 55 base styles. Both wigs and hairpieces are made of several types of synthetic fibers and human hair, and are offered in a choice of dozens of colors and textures. Beauty by Spector, Inc. will match your wig or piece to the closest shade if you provide a hair sample, or you may purchase a set of actual fiber samples. The firm has been in business since 1958, and employs a specialist who can assist customers dealing with chemotherapy's side effects, or scalp problems. (Ask for the "CSD" specialist.)

Beauty by Spector, Inc. offers readers of this book favorable prices (50% off suggested list), so be sure to identify yourself as a WBMC reader when you send for the catalog.

Special Factors: *Specify men's or women's styles when requesting information;* inquiries may be made by phone between 8 A.M. and 10 P.M., EST; orders are shipped worldwide.

CREATIVE HEALTH PRODUCTS

5148 SADDLE RIDGE RD.
PLYMOUTH, MI 48170
800-742-4478
313-996-5900
FAX: 313-996-4650

Catalog: free
Save: 30% average
Pay: check, MO, MC, V, AE
Sells: fitness equipment, related medical devices
Store: mail order only (see text)

Creative Health Products has been selling health, fitness, and exercise equipment since 1976, and carries some of the best product lines available. Savings vary from item to item, but average 30% on list or regular retail prices. The 14-page catalog lists current models of stationary bicycles, ergometers, rowers, treadmills, stair climbers, and accessories by Aerobics, Altero, Avita, Cateye, Marathon, Monark, Oglend-Bodyguard, Pacer, Quinton, Spirit, and Tunturi. There are pulse/heart rate monitors from Biosig Instruments, CIC, Elexis, Nissei, and Polar, and skin-fold calipers, body-fat analyzers, strength and flexibility testers, and professional scales by Detecto, Health-O-Meter, Metro, and Seca. Stethoscopes, blood pressure testers (sphygmomanometers), otoscopes, ophthalmoscopes, and books on health and fitness are also sold, and the catalog includes guides on buying different types of devices. Please note that this is professional equipment and, even with discounts, the prices are not low. Creative Health welcomes questions about any of the products, and can help you find the best equipment for your needs.

Although primarily a mail-order firm, Creative Health welcomes visitors (weekdays, 9–5), so drop by if you're in the area.

Special Factors: Quantity discounts are available; institutional accounts are available; C.O.D. orders are accepted; orders are shipped worldwide.

ESSENTIAL PRODUCTS CO., INC.

90 WATER ST.
NEW YORK, NY
10005-3587
212-344-4288

Price List and Sample Cards: free with SASE (see text)
Save: up to 90% (see text)
Pay: check or MO
Sells: "copycat" fragrances
Store: same address; Monday to Friday 9–6

 ¡Si!

"We offer our versions of the world's most treasured and expensive ladies' perfumes and men's colognes, selling them at a small fraction of the original prices." Essential was founded in 1895 and markets its interpretations of famous perfumes under the brand name of "Naudet."

Essential Products stocks 50 different copies of such costly perfumes as Beautiful, Coco, Eternity, Giorgio, Joy, L'Air du Temps, Obsession, Opium, Passion, Poison, White Diamonds, and Ysatis, as well as 20 "copycat" colognes for men, from Antaeus to Zizanie. A one-ounce bottle of perfume is $20 (1/2 ounce, $11.50), and four ounces of any men's cologne cost $11. When you write to Essential Products, please identify yourself as a WBMC reader, which entitles you to five free "scent cards" of Essential's best-selling fragrances. The sample cards give an idea of how closely the Naudet version replicates the original, but you should try the product to evaluate it properly. You must also enclose a long, stamped, self-addressed envelope for the set of samples.

Special Factors: Satisfaction is guaranteed; returns are accepted within 30 days for refund; minimum order is $20; orders are shipped worldwide.

FREEDA VITAMINS, INC.

36 E. 41ST ST.
NEW YORK, NY
  10017-6203
800-777-3737
212-685-4980
FAX: 212-685-7297

Catalog: free
Save: up to 30%
Pay: check, MO, MC, V
Sells: dietary supplements
Store: Freeda Pharmacy, same address; Monday to Thursday 8:30–6:00, Friday 8:30–4

Freeda, a family-run operation, has been manufacturing vitamins and minerals in its own plant since 1928. Freeda is dedicated to providing the purest possible product, and its formulations are free of coal tar dyes, sulfates, starch, animal stearates, pesticides, sugar, and artificial flavorings, and are suitable for even the strictest vegetarian or Kosher diet. The Zimmermans, who run the firm, put an extra tablet in every bottle just to be nice. There are savings of up to 30% on some of Freeda's supplements—and the WBMC reader discount makes this the best vitamin buy around.

The 36-page catalog lists vitamins, minerals, multivitamins, and nutritional products, which are available in a dizzying choice of combinations and strengths. The vitamin "families" include A and D, B, C, and E; among the minerals are calcium, iron, magnesium, potassium, selenium, and zinc; amino acids, proteins, and other dietary extras are offered. Freeda is listed here not for its megadose formulations, but because of its emphasis on quality production and additive-free goods. It's great to find a source for children's (and adults') vitamins made without sugar, coal tar dyes, sulfiting agents, animal stearates, sulfates, or artificial flavorings..(Freeda's chewable vitamins are naturally flavored, and there is an unflavored version for children on restricted diets. All of the Freeda vitamins are approved by the Feingold Association.) Needless to say, the Freeda catalog is free of the preposterous claims and misleading information often given by supplement sellers. And wonderful as all of this is, it's still important to check with your health-care professional before taking supplements and to avoid megadoses unless they're specifically recommended.

Freeda is offering readers of this book a special discount of 20% on all orders. You must mention WBMC to take the discount, which should be computed on the cost of the goods only, and can't be combined with other discounts and specials. This WBMC reader discount expires December 31, 1995.

Special Factors: Courtesy discounts are given to health-care professionals; C.O.D. orders are accepted; orders are shipped worldwide.

HILLESTAD INTERNATIONAL, INC.

AV 178 U.S. HWY. N.
WOODRUFF, WI 54568
800-535-7742
408-298-0995
FAX: 408-298-0803

Catalog: free
Save: up to 40%
Pay: check, MO, MC, V
Sells: nutritional supplements, toiletries, and cleaning products
Store: same address; Monday to Friday 9–4

You can get "factory-direct" prices on the "Harvest of Values" line of vitamins, minerals, and other supplements by ordering from Hillestad, the manufacturer, which began doing business in 1959. Prices here are up to 40% lower than those charged elsewhere for comparable goods.

Hillestad offers good selection of vitamins and nutritional supplements through a comparatively hype-free, 20-page catalog. There are multivitamin and mineral formulations for adults, chewable versions for children, vitamins A, B-complex, C, and E; a "stress" formula; and chelated iron, bone meal, lecithin, alfalfa, amino acids, and protein. Hillestad also sells pet vitamins, garlic concentrate in capsules, vitamin E cream and aloe body lotion, shampoo, cream rinse, and liquid "soapless" soap, a biodegradable, phosphate-free cleanser for dishes, handwashables, and general cleaning. Complete label data on most products are given in the catalog.

Special Factors: Satisfaction is guaranteed; all goods are guaranteed against defects in manufacturing; shipping is included on orders over $35; returns are accepted within 30 days; orders are shipped worldwide.

KETTLE CARE

1535 EAGLE DR.,
 DEPT. WBMC
KALISPELL, MT 59901
406-756-3485

Catalog: $1, refundable
Save: up to 30% average (see text)
Pay: check, MO, MC, V
Sells: natural skin-care and bath products
Store: mail order only

Every skin-care empire ever built began with someone at the stove, turning improbable ingredients into the stuff of dreams. That's the business of Kettle Care, where natural products and botanicals are combined to create moisturizers, cleansing creams, facial scrubs, lotions, balms, and other things to soothe your skin and spirit. The eight-page catalog features Citrus Facial Cleanser, Worker's Creme, natural facial scrubs, liquid castile-based facial soaps, Limey's Lotion for normal-to-oily complexions, aromatherapy oils, and herbal pillows, to note a few items. The prices are very reasonable: Kettle Care's Overnight Creme with almond oil costs under $6 for two ounces, while Caswell-Massey's Almond Night Cream costs nearly $15 for the same amount. Among the other good buys are quarter ounces of essential and fragrance oils for $4 and jars of naturally flavored lip balm for under $2. You can buy everything individually, or take advantage of the sample sets and discounted "packs" of four or six of the same kind of item. The catalog lists the ingredients of most of the products, and includes directions for use. And there's a guide to which skin-care products suit which complexion types, so you can develop your own treatment line and regimen.

Special Factors: Satisfaction is guaranteed; returns are accepted for exchange, refund, or credit; C.O.D. orders are accepted.

NEW YORK COSMETICS AND FRAGRANCES

318 BRANNAN ST.
SAN FRANCISCO, CA
94107
415-543-3880
FAX: 415-896-0373

Catalog: $2
Save: up to 70%
Pay: check, MO, MC, V, Discover
Sells: fragrances, cosmetics, beauty treatments
Store: same address; also 674 Eighth St., San Francisco, CA; Monday to Friday 11–5:30, Saturday 11–5

Whether you love a perfume that no one seems to carry any more, or just want to save on a fresh bottle of Giorgio, New York Cosmetics and Fragrances is your source. The 34-page catalog lists hundreds of scents in the forms of cologne, eau de toilette, eau de parfum, and perfume. A sampling of names of the women's scents includes Adolfo, Bijan, Decadence, First, Galanos, Knowing, Mad Moments, Montana, Opium, Paris, Private Collection, Red, and White Linen. A comparable selection of men's cologne and eau de toilette is offered as well. Half of the catalog is devoted to cosmetics and beauty products—Lancôme and Elizabeth Arden skin treatments, bath accessories (loofahs, sponges, bath brushes, soaps, etc.), and the firm's private label line of products for skin, hair, and nails. In addition to substantial discounts on most of the name-brand goods, you'll find good prices on the house-label lipstick, eye and lip pencils, eye shadows, blush, foundation, concealer, loose and pressed powder, and nail polish—and a great color selection. Don't overlook this source when you're making gift lists, since a collection of perfume miniatures, a set of makeup brushes, or the 20-color eyeshadow kit are all affordable possibilities.

Special Factors: Authorized returns are accepted; orders are shipped worldwide.

YVES ROCHER

YVES ROCHER CENTER
NO. 2672
WEST CHESTER, PA
19380-9820
215-430-8200

Catalog: $1
Save: up to 50%
Pay: check or MO
Sells: cosmetics and toiletries
Store: mail order only

Yves Rocher's botanically based beauty treatments have been developed to answer the needs of all skin types—normal, combination, oily, sensitive, dehydrated, aged, and sun-exposed. Haircare products, bath and shower treats, scents, nail treatments, and cosmetics are also shown in the 44-page color catalog. Night creams, spot treatments, foaming cleansers, eye creams, masks, after-sun preparations, body contouring gels and creams, bath oils, shower geleés, hand lotions, nail polish and manicure products, and even deodorants and toothpaste are offered. Prices are not low, but the catalog is packed with special offers and bonuses, which easily yield savings of 50% on the regular rates. Yves Rocher notes that its products are safety tested, but not on animals. Your satisfaction is assured with every purchase, and you're billed with each shipment instead of paying with the order.

Special Factors: Satisfaction is guaranteed; shipping is included on orders over $15; quantity discounts are available; returns are accepted for exchange, refund, or credit.

SCENTE PERFUMERIE INC.

1205 BROADWAY, RM. 204
NEW YORK, NY 10001
800-347-3738
212-889-8681
FAX: 212-725-2562

Catalog: free
Save: up to 35%
Pay: check, MO, MC, V
Sells: perfumes and Lancôme products
Store: mail order only

You don't buy fragrances to put a sales commission in a stranger's pocket, you buy them because you like the way they make you—or someone else—smell. So if you don't need the "help" you'll get at the department store counter, skip it: Buy from Scente Perfumerie, and save up to 33% on the prices you usually pay.

This firm's 48-page catalog doesn't have glossy photos or provocative descriptions, it's just a no-frills list of men's and women's scents, their forms (perfume, cologne, after shave, etc.), and the retail and discount prices. The latest edition offered popular and hard-to-find fragrances among the hundreds, including Bibi de Jean Barthet, Decadence, Dunhill, Giorgio, Tea Rose, and Zibeline. If you'd love to have a large "wardrobe" of scents but can't afford it even at a discount, see the listing of about 70 perfumes and colognes that are available in miniature bottles or sample sizes, from under $3. (They're also great for travel, stocking stuffers, and for the person who uses scent too rarely to justify a bigger bottle.)

Please note: All orders are shipped via UPS.

Special Factors: Satisfaction is guaranteed; authorized returns are accepted for exchange, refund, or credit; minimum order is $20.

SEE ALSO

Adventures In Cassettes • motivational audio cassettes • **BOOKS**
Baby Bunz & Co. • natural bathing toiletries for babies • **CLOTHING: MOTHER AND CHILD**
Better Health Fitness • exercise equipment • **SPORTS**
Caprilands Herb Farm • potpourri ingredients, essential oils, etc. • **FARM**
Dairy Association Co., Inc. • Bag Balm liniment • **ANIMAL**
Deer Valley Farm • nutritional supplements and natural toiletries • **FOOD**
Jaffe Bros., Inc. • Jaybee brand soap/shampoo • **FOOD**
D. MacGillivray & Coy. • Hebridean perfume • **CRAFTS**
Mother Hart's Natural Products, Inc. • natural-bristle hair and bath brushes, sponges, soap, etc. • **HOME: LINEN**
The Natural Baby Co., Inc. • homeopathic and natural remedies • **CLOTHING: MOTHER AND CHILD**
Penzeys' Spice House • salt-free seasonings • **FOOD**
Retired Persons Services, Inc. • vitamins, beauty products, shampoo, etc. • **MEDICINE**
Walnut Acres Organic Farms • natural toiletries, nutritional supplements • **FOOD**

HOME

Decor

Floor coverings, wall and window treatments, lighting, upholstery materials, tools, and services

Do-it-yourself home decor has always been an important part of the market, but the distinctions between D-I-Y and trade (professional decorators) are blurring. Products once available to licensed designers exclusively are now offered by discounters and retail decorators, who sell to consumers who've shopped the showrooms and read the shelter magazines, and don't want any less than the best.

Consumers become educated, discounters respond with access to more products. A retailing success? Not according to the manufacturers, some of which threaten to pull their product lines from discounters if the discounters use their brand or trade names in ads, or even in unpaid editorial mentions like the listings in this book. Consequently, some brand names have been deleted from *all* listings. In order to find out whether a firm offers a specific line not mentioned in the listing, please call or write.

DECORATOR FABRIC • **Dorothy's, Fabric Center, Fabrics by Phone, Home Fabric Mills, Homespun Fabrics, Marlene's, Shama, Silk Surplus, Tioga**
LIGHTING • **Allied Lighting, Brass Light Gallery, Golden Valley, King's Chandelier, Luigi Crystal, Main Lamp**
RUGS, CARPETING, FLOORING • **Bearden Bros., Johnson's Carpets, National Carpet, The Rug Store, S & S Mills, Warehouse Carpets**
WINDOW AND WALL TREATMENTS • **American Discount, Benington's, Custom Window, Dorothy's, Hang-It-Now, Harmony, Homespun Fabrics, Robinson's, Shibui, Silver, Style Wallcovering, Wells Interiors**

ALLIED LIGHTING

DRAWER E
TREXLERTOWN, PA 18087
800-241-6111
FAX: 215-366-1909

Brochure: free (see text)
Save: up to 60%
Pay: check, MO, MC, V
Sells: lighting fixtures
Store: mail order only

If you're in the market for light fixtures—lamps, chandeliers, track lights, recessed lighting, porch and outdoor lighting, or any other type—call Allied Lighting for a price quote. Allied represents American Lantern, Baldwin Brass, Frederick Cooper, Nulco, Progress, Stiffel, and World Imports, among others. The brochure includes a partial listing of the manufacturers available, and if you know the style/model number of the fixture you want, you can call for a price quote. Allied Lighting also sells Casablanca ceiling fans. Discounts run up to 60% on list prices, and shipping is included on orders delivered nationwide.

Special Factors: Price quote by phone; shipping is included.

AMERICAN DISCOUNT WALL AND WINDOW COVERINGS

1411 FIFTH AVE.,
  DEPT. WBM
PITTSBURGH, PA 15219
800-777-2737, DEPT. WBM
FAX: 412-471-3347

Information: price quote
Save: up to 70%
Pay: check, MO, MC, V, Discover
Sells: wall coverings, fabrics, and window treatments
Store: same address; Monday to Friday 8:30–5, Saturday 8:30–1

American Discount Wall and Window Coverings, whose parent firm was founded in 1916, offers savings of up to 70% on the best in decorator wall and window treatments. Custom bedspreads and draperies by a prominent manufacturer are also discounted 20%. Most of the wall coverings are discounted 40% to 50%; upholstery and decorator fabrics are priced 10% to 35% below regular retail here.

Among the firms and designers represented are Boussac of France, Carefree, Eisenhart, Essex, Fashon, Greeff, Imperial, Judscott, Katzenbach and Warren, Kravet, Ralph Lauren, Carey Lind, Mirage, Quadrille, Sandpiper, Sanitas, Seabrook, Sunworthy, United, Van Luit, Westgate, Winfield, and York—and there are scores more. Custom window treatments by Bali, Del Mar, Flexalum, Graber, HunterDouglas, Joanna, Kirsch, Levolor, LouverDrape, Nanik, and Verosol are discounted 25% to 70%.

Special Factors: Request order form when obtaining price quotes; all goods are first quality; returns (except cut rolls, borders, custom wall coverings, and custom window treatments) are accepted within 20 days (a 25% restocking fee is charged).

BEARDEN BROS. CARPET & TEXTILES CORP.

DEPT. 4000
3200 A DUG GAP RD.
DALTON, GA 30720
800-433-0074
FAX: 706-277-1754

Catalog: free (see text)
Save: up to 50%
Pay: check, MO, MC, V, AE, DC, Discover, Optima
Sells: carpeting, rugs, padding, and vinyl and wood flooring
Store: same address; Monday to Friday 8:30–5:30

Bearden Bros. set up shop in 1965 in Dalton, "Carpet Capital of the World," joining hundreds of other companies devoted to manufacturing carpet. Bearden sells carpeting and flooring lines from scores of mills, including Aladdin, Armstrong, Beaulieu, Bigelow, Cabin Craft, Citation, Cumberland, Evans and Black, Galaxy, Horizon, Interloom, J.P. Stevens, L.D. Brinkman, Lees, Masland, Mohawk, Philadelphia, Salem, Shaw, and World—and that's just a few of the many brands available.

You can call with the manufacturer's name, style name, and color codes, and number of square yards you plan to buy and ask for a price quote, or send a carpet sample if you don't have that information. (Carpet samples are available from Bearden for $7, refundable with a purchase.) Bearden Bros. also sells its own line of flooring and carpet products, as well as reproduction Oriental, Victorian, and contemporary designs, braided rugs, border designs, and even brass stair rods and vacuum cleaners. Bearden ships carpeting to all 50 states and countries around the world, and offers special discounts to religious institutions and carpet dealers.

Bearden is offering the color catalog, usually $3, free of charge to readers of this book. Be sure to mention WBMC when requesting the catalog.

Special Factors: Satisfaction is guaranteed; written confirmation of phone orders is required; quantity discounts are available; orders are shipped worldwide.

BENINGTON'S

1271 MANHEIM PIKE
LANCASTER, PA 17601
800-252-5060

Information: price quote
Save: up to 50%
Pay: check, MO, MC, V
Sells: carpeting, wall coverings, decorator fabric
Store: same address

Benington's incorporates wall coverings, decorator fabrics, and carpeting under one roof, representing the major names in all three industries. There's no catalog, but you're welcome to call with the name of the mill or maker, the pattern book name or number, style, color, and amount required for a price quote. Prices average at least 40% below list, and if you're ordering large quantities, you may receive deeper discounts.

Special Factors: Price quote by phone or letter; quantity discounts are available.

BRASS LIGHT GALLERY, INC.

131 S. 1ST ST.
MILWAUKEE, WI 53204
414-271-8300
FAX: 414-271-7755

Catalog: $5
Save: 20% average (see text)
Pay: check, MO, MC, V
Sells: lighting fixtures
Store: same address

After you've seen the fixtures from Brass Light Gallery, you'll know why you've held off buying from other sources. Not only are the materials and workmanship here of superior quality, but the designs have that satisfyingly "right" quality that's so often lacking in lighting fixtures. For example, the Mission-style hanging, wall, and table lamps are executed with that odd combination of nearly Japanese proportion and angles and Western rigidity that makes sense of the whole style. (If you're accustomed to "chunky" Stickley-style fixtures, you'll see the difference immediately.) Brass Light Gallery's "Goldenrod" and "Continental" collections include Mission/Prairie styles, chandeliers in polished brass with cased glass shades, double wall sconces, and much more. The alabaster chandeliers, sconces, and table lamps are actually less expensive than comparable fixtures from the 20s and 30s—when you can find them, intact and unchipped, in antiques stores. And the firm's "Prismatics" collection for kitchens and lots features vintage heavy, ribbed glass shades, retrofitted with different styles of brass or metal poles, or other fixtures for low and angled ceiling mounts. The glass and finish options for many of the pieces make it possible to create truly individual fixtures, or faithful interpretations of the originals. The Brass Light Gallery's catalog—40 pages of lighting, 50 pages of technical specifications—has been designed for use by homeowners, interior designers, and architects. Prices average 20% below retail, but the fixtures are much better quality than those being sold for by Brass Light Gallery's competitors—so the values are much better as well.

Special Factor: Satisfaction is guaranteed.

CUSTOM WINDOWS & WALLS

32525 STEPHENSON HWY., DEPT. WM MADISON HEIGHTS, MI 48071
800-772-1947, 7747
FAX: 313-583-2863

Brochure: free
Save: up to 75%
Pay: check, MO, MC, V, Discover
Sells: wall coverings, window treatments, decorator fabrics
Store: mail order only

After deliberating over window treatments and wallpaper patterns, go the final step and get the best price. Custom Windows & Walls, which has been in business since 1908, should definitely be on your list of sources. Upon request, Custom will send you manufacturers' brochures describing the available lines, along with a measuring guide, samples, and a list of discount prices. The firm offers window treatments by Comfortex, Del Mar, Graber, HunterDouglas (Duette), Kirsch, Levolor, and LouverDrape, as well as its own "Window Express" 1" mini and 1/2" micro blinds and vertical blinds in a choice of scores of colors and materials, at 50% to 75% below list price. Wall coverings from Birge, Carefree, Imperial, Sunwall, Van Luit, Warner, York, and other manufacturers are available, as well as coordinating fabrics. Prices are discounted to 50% plus below list, and a price-quote form is included in the information packet. Please note that all of the window treatments are made to order and are not returnable. Measure and *remeasure* carefully before ordering.

Custom Windows & Walls is offering readers a discount of 10% on orders of Window Express mini blinds and verticals. Be sure to identify yourself as a WBMC reader when you order, and deduct the discount from the cost of the goods only. This WBMC reader discount expires February 1, 1995.

Special Factor: Quantity discounts are available.

DOROTHY'S RUFFLED ORIGINALS, INC.

6721 MARKET ST.
WILMINGTON, NC 28405
800-367-6849

Catalog: $4
Save: up to 30% (see text)
Pay: check, MO, MC, V, AE, Discover
Sells: decorator fabrics and custom services
Store: same address; also Roswell, GA; Charlotte, Goldsboro, and Raleigh, NC; Myrtle Beach, SC; and Newport News and Richmond, VA

The popularity of rich, dramatic window treatments and decorative accessories shows no signs of waning, and Dorothy's Ruffled Originals celebrates the swags, poufs, jabots, flounces, and flourishes with a large collection of made-to-measure draperies, bed linens, table toppers, pillows, nursery linens, shower curtains, canopies, and all the hardware and rods you need to put things in place.

Dorothy's has two catalogs, the "Tailored Collection" and the "Ruffled Collection." Both are full-color showcases of Dorothy's designs, coordinated in room settings. Both include a guide to the fabrics Dorothy offers, and detailed price and measurement guides. The "tailored" collection is suited to more traditional, reserved decor, although there are plenty of swags and poufs. If you love the look of deep gathers and wide bows, of double ruffles and butterfly valances (a house specialty), see the "Ruffled Collection." These creations have a Southern glamour and add a distinctly feminine touch to a room. Dorothy uses a generous six-to-one ratio of yardage to finished ruffle in many of her creations in this collection, which produces dense, luxurious gathers—most draperies are half as voluminous.

The prices of the custom work aren't *cheap,* but they're reasonable, compared to local decorating shops. If you don't know how to sew, you could order made-to-order pillows and custom tiebacks or swags to enliven a room without spending a fortune. But if you *can* sew, see the good buys on Dorothy's fabric, which is sold by the full yard. There are all kinds of decorating basics—chintz in dozens of colors, eyelet, moiré, lace, etc.—as well as romantic florals, damask-print solids, stripes and paisleys, "wallpaper" prints on fabric, and more. Most of the fabrics are cotton/poly blend, cotton/linen, or all-cotton, and prices run from about $3 to $11 a yard—about half the going rate for decorator fabric of this type. It's helpful that most of the fabrics are also shown in the room displays, which gives you a good idea of their scale and whether the fabric looks good when it's gathered or pleated. Some of the fabrics have coordinating wallpapers, and don't miss the hardware section in the back of both catalogs, which has an excellent selection of rods, brackets, finials, supports, sashes, shelves, and other drapery fittings.

Special Factors: Satisfaction is guaranteed; returns of defective goods are accepted for exchange, refund, or credit.

THE FABRIC CENTER, INC.

485 ELECTRIC AVE.
FITCHBURG, MA 01420
508-343-4402
FAX: 508-343-8139

Catalog: $2
Save: up to 50%
Pay: check, MO, MC, V
Sells: interior decorator fabrics
Store: (showroom) same address; Monday to Saturday 9–5:30

The Fabric Center has been in business since 1932, selling fine fabrics for home decorating at savings of up to 50% on suggested list prices. Fabrics for upholstery and window treatments are available, including lines from Robert Allen, American Textile, Paul Barrow, Covington, George Harrington, Kravet, Peachtree, Waverly, and many others. The splendid 164-page color catalog ($2) features hundreds of fabrics from a wide range of manufacturers, shown in room settings and grouped with complementary patterns and colorways. The catalog descriptions include fiber content, width, vertical repeat, and a usage code to help you determine if the material is appropriate for the intended use. And The Fabric Center's "Sampling Service" allows you to try the fabric in your home before you order. The 3" by 4" samples cost 15¢, the 8" by 10" pieces are 50¢, and 24" by 27" samples cost $3.95 each. (The price of each $3.95 sample can be credited to each $50 in goods ordered.) In addition to the latest designs in home fashion, The Fabric Center stocks cotton moiré in 26 colors, 60 shades of cotton/poly chintz, dozens of tapestries, cotton/linen-blend solids and prints, and drapery sheers and linings. Prices are very reasonable—solid color chintz costs under $3.98 a yard at this writing.

Special Factors: Minimum order is one yard; orders are shipped worldwide.

FABRICS BY PHONE

P.O. BOX 309, DEPT. 200
WALNUT BOTTOM, PA
17266
800-233-7012, EXT. 25

Brochure and Samples: $3
Save: up to 50%
Pay: check, MO, MC, V
Sells: decorator fabrics and custom window treatments
Store: Fabric Shop, 120 N. Seneca St., Shippensburg, PA

Fabrics by Phone has been doing business since 1937, as the mail-order arm of a decorating store, and suggests that you call with manufacturer's name and fabric colorway for price and availability information. Fabrics by Phone also makes custom draperies and accessories, including bedspreads, coverlets, dust ruffles, pillows, tablecloths, and more. For more on these services, send $3 for the literature, price list, and swatches.

Special Factors: Price quote by phone or letter with SASE; minimum order is three yards (on goods not in stock).

FAN AUTHORITY/ LIGHTING AUTHORITY

31567 U.S. 19 N.
PALM HARBOR, FL 34684
800-521-FANS
813-787-3936
FAX: 813-786-8277

Information: price quote (see text)
Save: up to 75%
Pay: check, MO, MC, V
Sells: ceiling fans and lighting
Store: mail order only

When your needs include overhead cooling and lighting, put this firm on your list of places to call for price quotes. Fan Authority/Lighting Authority covers both bases with fans by Casablanca, Demco, Emerson,

Homestead, Hunter, Quorum, Union, and other firms, and lighting by American Lantern, Georgian Art, Kenroy, Minka, and Fredrick Raymond, among others. If you haven't shopped extensively and want to see what's available, order Fan Authority's 170-page catalog ($9.95, refundable with purchase of a fan), which showcases lines from the top five names in the business. If you know the model you want, or if you're buying lighting, call for a price quote and shipping estimate.

Special Factor: Price quote by phone or letter.

GOLDEN VALLEY LIGHTING

274 EASTCHESTER DRIVE,
#117A
HIGH POINT, NC 27262
800-735-3377
919-882-7330

Catalog: $5, refundable
Save: up to 50%
Pay: check, MO, MC, V
Sells: lighting fixtures, floor and table lamps, and ceiling fans
Store: mail order only

Golden Valley, a company founded in 1989 and run by veterans of the lighting industry, offers savings of up to 50% on ceiling fans, floor and table lamps, and lighting fixtures from over 200 manufacturers. Call when you've decided what you want (have the manufacturer's name, model number, color, finish, and any other details at hand). When you're ready to order, you can make a deposit of 50% of the cost of the fixture, and pay the balance before shipment, or prepay the entire amount and expedite the order (details are given in the brochure).

Special Factors: Price quote by phone or letter with SASE; orders are shipped worldwide.

HANG-IT-NOW WALL-PAPER STORES

10,517F N. MAIN ST.
ARCHDALE, NC 27263
800-325-9494
919-431-6341
FAX: 919-431-0449

Information: price quote
Save: 40% average
Pay: check, MO, MC, V, AE
Sells: wall coverings and decorator fabrics
Store: same address; also 4620 W. Market St., Greensboro, and 759 Silas Creek Pkwy., Winston-Salem, NC; Monday to Friday 9–6, Saturday 9–3, all locations

Hang-It-Now Wallpaper, established in 1981, sells wall coverings at savings of 30% to 65% on list prices. A limited selection of decorator fabrics is also available, at discounts of up to 40%. All major brands of wall coverings (plus strings, grass cloth, and borders) are offered here, including Color House, Crutchfield, Eisenhart, Imperial, Katzenbach & Warren, Carey Lind, Sanitas, Sunwall, United, and Van Luit, among others. Hang-It-Now specializes in providing wall coverings to retail establishments, and has done numerous installations for furniture retailers and decorators.

Special Factors: Only first-quality goods are sold; shipping is included on orders sent within the continental U.S.; orders are shipped worldwide.

HARMONY SUPPLY INC.

P.O. BOX 313
MEDFORD, MA 02155
617-395-2600
FAX: 617-396-8218

Information: price quote
Save: up to 60%
Pay: check, MO, MC, V
Sells: wall coverings, window treatments, decorator fabrics
Store: 18 High St., Medford, MA; Monday to Saturday 8–5:30, Thursday 8 A.M.–9 P.M.

Harmony Supply, in business since 1949, can give your home a face-lift at a discount with savings of up to 60% on wallpaper, coordinating fabrics, and window treatments. Harmony carries over 2,500 designs and patterns of wallpaper, grass cloth, and string cloth, including Laura Ashley, Imperial, Ralph Lauren, Van Luit, and many others. Harmony Supply also sells made-to-measure mini, micro, vertical, and pleated shades and blinds by Bali, Flexalum, HunterDouglas, Kirsch, Levolor, Louverdrape, and Verosol. You'll save the most on goods that are currently in stock, but even special orders are discounted up to 60%, and everything Harmony sells is first quality. Call or write for a price quote, since there's no catalog or price list.

Special Factors: Satisfaction is guaranteed; returns (except custom blinds) are accepted within 30 days (a 25% restocking fee is charged on special-order goods).

HOME FABRIC MILLS, INC.

882 S. MAIN ST.
P.O. BOX 888
CHESHIRE, CT 06410
203-272-3529
FAX: 203-272-6686

Brochure: free
Save: up to 40%
Pay: check, MO, MC, V (see text)
Sells: decorator fabrics and custom services
Store: same address; also Rte. 202, Belchertown, MA; and 443 Saratoga Rd., Rte. 50, Scotia, NY; Monday to Wednesday 10–9, Thursday to Saturday 10–5

The lovely color brochure from Home Fabric Mills comes with samples of some of the firm's most popular upholstery and drapery materials. This company has been in business since 1968 and is a good source for the home decorator who's unsure of what type of fabric is best for a particular project, or the person who's trying to match a color.

The three Home Fabric Mills stores are stocked with thousands of bolts of upholstery and drapery materials, lining, trims, and workroom supplies from Bloomcraft, Conso, Covington, Graber, Kaufmann, Kirsch, Lanscot-Arlen, Waverly, Wolf, and other manufacturers. Only first-quality goods are sold, and Home Fabric Mills will sell in half-yard increments—great to know if you're still deciding on your fabrics. Swatches are also available on request.

Please note: Credit card payments are accepted on out-of-state mail orders only.

Home Fabric Mills is offering readers a discount of 20% on first orders. Be sure to identify yourself as a WBMC reader when you order, and deduct the discount from the cost of the goods only. This WBMC reader discount expires February 1, 1995.

Special Factors: Price quote by phone or letter; minimum order is 1/2 yard; orders are shipped worldwide.

HOMESPUN FABRICS & DRAPERIES

4464 MCGRATH ST.,
  SUITE 109
VENTURA, CA 93003
805-642-8111
FAX: 805-642-0759

Price List and Samples: $2
Save: up to 30%
Pay: check, MO, MC, V
Sells: decorator fabric, draperies, accessories, and services
Store: same address; by appointment only

Homespun Fabrics & Draperies has a solution to some of the biggest drapery headaches—bulkiness, sun rot, the expense of dry cleaning, and the hassle of pleater hooks are among them. Homespun Fabrics sells all-cotton material that's ten feet wide, or about 105" to 109" after shrinkage. The fabric includes homespun (plain weave), hobnail, barley, and monkscloth, in white and natural, but it can be dyed to order for a fee. The width makes the fabric perfect for wide windows, and even eliminates some of the finishing work. Homespun Fabrics can also custom-make "fanpleat" draperies, which use a track system that's hung from the ceiling or mounted on the wall, with a buckram header tape with nylon tabs that engage the track. The drapery folds are four or five inches deep, so the stackback (the area covered by the curtain when it's drawn back) that would be 37" deep with conventional pinch-pleat draperies is only 11" deep with the fanpleat system. Made in Homespun Fabrics' heavyweight cottons, this system produces handsome, neutral window coverings that give you maximum glass exposure. They have a crisp, tailored appearance that's ideal for modern decor and office settings, and are machine washable and dryable, guaranteed against sun rot for seven years. In addition to the heavy cottons, Homespun Fabrics offers openweave casement fabric (tow cloth) and both regular-width and ultra-wide semi-sheers—batiste, voile, and bouclé slub, in lots of colors. And there are helpful books on home decorating and making fanpleat draperies.

Special Factor: Returns are accepted within ten days for exchange, refund, or credit.

JOHNSON'S CARPETS

3239 S. DIXIE HWY.
DALTON, GA 30720
800-235-1079, EXT. 601
706-277-2775
FAX: 706-277-9835

Brochure: free
Save: up to 80%
Pay: check, MO, MC, V, AE, Discover, Optima
Sells: vinyl flooring, carpeting, area rugs, and padding
Store: same address; Monday to Friday 8–5

Johnson's has arrangements with over 40 carpet mills that allow it to offer carpet lines from a wide range of manufacturers, at prices up to 80% below those charged by department stores and other retail outlets. If you've decided on your carpet, call or write with the name of the manufacturer, the style name or number, and the square yardage required. Johnson's also creates its own "custom designer" rugs, and can produce patterns to match wallpaper or furnishings—samples are shown in the catalog (available upon request). Padding, adhesives, and tack strips for installation are also available.

A deposit is required when you place your order, and final payment must be made before shipment (common carrier is used). Both residential and commercial carpeting needs are served here—details on the products and sales policy are given in the brochure.

Special Factor: Orders are shipped worldwide.

KING'S CHANDELIER CO.

DEPT. WBM94
P.O. BOX 667
EDEN, NC 27288
919-623-6188

Catalog: $3.75
Save: up to 50%
Pay: check, MO, MC, V
Sells: Czech, Venetian, and Strass chandeliers
Store: Hwy. 14 (Van Buren Rd.), Eden, NC; Monday to Saturday 10–4:30

The Kings have been designing and producing chandeliers since 1935 and offer their designs through the 100-page catalog. There are light fixtures to suit every taste, at prices for all budgets.

The catalog shows page after page of chandeliers, candelabras, and wall sconces in a range of styles: Victorian, "colonial," contemporary, and many variations on the classic lighting fixture dripping with prisms, pendalogues, faceted balls, and ropes of crystal buttons. Austere styles with brass arms and plain glass shades are also available, as well as the Kings' own magnificent designs made of Strass crystal. Prices begin at about $125 for a brass single sconce, and go up to $14,500 for the palatial Strass Royal Belvedere. Options include different finishes on the metal parts, hurricane shades or candelabra tapers, and candelabra bulb sockets. Replacement parts for these lighting fixtures are stocked as well.

Since a catalog can't show the chandeliers to best advantage, King's will create a videotape of the lighting fixtures that interest you—preferably not more than six models. The VHS tapes are available for a $25 deposit, refundable on return.

Special Factors: Satisfaction is guaranteed; returns are accepted within five days for refund or credit; orders are shipped worldwide.

LUIGI CRYSTAL

7332 FRANKFORD AVE.
PHILADELPHIA, PA 19136
215-338-2978

Catalog: $1.50, refundable
Save: up to 50%
Pay: check, MO, MC, V, AE
Sells: crystal lighting fixtures
Store: same address; Monday to Saturday 9–5:30, Friday 9–8

Luigi Crystal may be located in the land of Main Liners, but its heart belongs to Tara. Luigi has been creating crystal lighting fixtures since 1935, and the prices are surprisingly low—under $200 for a full-sized chandelier, for example. The 44-page catalog shows each candelabra, chandelier, sconce, and hurricane lamp in black-and-white photographs. Many of the styles are formal and ornate, heavily hung with prisms and pendalogues and set in marble or faceted crystal bases. Several lamps feature globe shades, gold cupid bases, "Aurora" crystal prism shades, and even stained glass. At the other end of the spectrum are simple "Williamsburg chimney lamps" for under $50 a pair, and several graceful five-arm chandeliers.

If you're searching for replacement parts for your own fixtures, see the catalog for glass chimneys, bobeches, strung button prisms, drop prisms in several styles (3" to 8" long), and pendalogues. In addition to those models, Luigi's workshops can produce designs to your specifications; call or write to discuss details and prices.

Please note: The minimum order on goods sent outside the U.S. and Canada is $1,000.

Special Factor: Orders are shipped worldwide ($1,000 minimum order).

MAIN LAMP/LAMP WAREHOUSE

1073 39TH ST.
BROOKLYN, NY 11219
800-52-LITES
718-436-8500
FAX: 718-438-6836

Information: price quote
Save: up to 50%
Pay: check, MO, MC, V, Discover
Sells: lighting fixtures and ceiling fans
Store: same address; Monday, Tuesday, and Friday 9–5:30, Thursday 9–8, Saturday and Sunday 10–5

Main Lamp/Lamp Warehouse, established in 1954, is noted for its comprehensive inventory of lamps, lighting fixtures, and ceiling fans, all of which are sold at everyday discounts of up to 50%. Call or write for prices on lighting fixtures, lamps, and track lighting by Fredrick Cooper, Crystal Clear, Halo, George Kovacs, Lenox Lamps, Rembrandt, Schonbek (crystal chandeliers), Stiffel, and other major names. Ceiling fans by Casablanca, Emerson, and other firms are also stocked.

Special Factors: Price quote by phone or letter with SASE; store is closed Wednesdays; minimum order is $50.

MARLENE'S DECORATOR FABRICS

301 BEECH ST., DEPT. 2J
HACKENSACK, NJ 07601
800-992-7325
201-843-0844
FAX: 201-843-5688

Information: price quote
Save: up to 50%
Pay: check, MO, MC, V
Sells: decorator fabrics
Store: mail order only

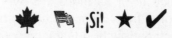

Marlene's Decorator Fabrics has been selling upholstery, slipcover, and drapery goods since 1951, and can save you up to 50% on the list prices of fabrics by Artmark, Paul Barrow, Berger, Brunschwig & Fils, Carole Fabrics, Duralee, Greeff, JAB, Kasmir, Kravet, Lee Jofa, Michaels, Peachtree, Stroheim & Roman, Westgate, and many other names. Write or call for a price quote, or send a sample and a self-addressed, stamped envelope if you're not sure of the manufacturer or pattern. Specify the yardage needed and whether you're interested in upholstery, drapery, or other decorator fabric.

Marlene's Decorator Fabrics is offering readers *free shipping* on first orders, so be sure to mention WBMC when you order. This WBMC reader discount expires February 1, 1995.

Special Factors: Minimum order is four yards retail, 20–25 yards wholesale.

M.C. LIMITED FINE LEATHERS

P.O. BOX 17696
WHITEFISH BAY, WI 53217
414-263-5222
FAX: 414-263-5508

Brochure and Price List: free
Save: up to 40%
Pay: check, MO, MC, V
Sells: steerhides and hide pillows
Store: mail order only

Whether your home style is New Western, chromed modern, 90s eclectic, or Neolithic, there's nothing like steerhide to add decorative depth. M.C. Limited offers processed skins in full hides (36 square feet on average, 5' to 6' wide by 7' to 8' long) in eight natural colors for $235. This is nearly 40% below prices by two New York City leather suppliers for comparable skins. M.C. Limited also makes steerhide pillows backed with pigskin suede, which are offered plain or with fringe, tassels, medallions, or other embellishments. Sizes range from 6" by 13" to 24" square, priced from $35 to $175. Custom options—calf hide, down filling, steerhide backs, special shapes and sizes—are also available. M.C. Limited notes that all of its hides are byproducts of the beef industry, and are not claimed from animals raised primarily for their skins.

Special Factors: Satisfaction is guaranteed; authorized returns (except pillows) are accepted (a percent restocking fee is charged) within 30 days.

NATIONAL CARPET CO., INC.

1384 CONEY ISLAND AVE.
BROOKLYN, NY 11230
800-421-5172
718-253-5700
FAX: 718-692-2363

Catalog: $3 (see text)
Save: 40%
Pay: check, MO, MC, V
Sells: area rugs and carpets
Store: same address; Monday to Wednesday 9–6, Thursday 9–8, Friday 9–4, Sunday 10:30–5

 ¡Si!

National sells Karastan rugs, and sends you the Karastan catalog sampler featuring the different lines for the $3 fee. The rugs include the Karastan Originals Collection—reproductions of Tabriz, Heriz, Bokhara, Kasham, and other classic designs, the Williamsburg Collection, and the Garden of Eden Collection, a line featuring floral motifs. Karastan's Kara Mar and Kara Shah rug collections are available as well. National has over half a century of experience in selling rugs, and offers discounts of 40% on suggested list prices.

Special Factors: Satisfaction is guaranteed; shipping is included on orders delivered in the contiguous United States; store is closed on Saturday; orders are shipped worldwide.

ROBINSON'S WALL-COVERINGS

DEPT. 4LY
225 W. SPRING ST.
P.O. BOX 427
TITUSVILLE, PA 16354-0427
800-458-2426
814-827-1893
FAX: 814-827-1693

Catalog and Samples: $2
Save: up to 50%
Pay: check, MO, MC, V, AE, Discover
Sells: wallpaper, decorator fabrics, and accessories
Store: 339 W. Spring St., Titusville; also 3506 Liberty Plaza, Erie; 1720 Wilmington Rd., New Castle; and 7219 McKnight Rd., Ross Towne Center, Pittsburgh PA

Robinson's has been in business in 1919, and sells both vinyl-coated and solid vinyl wallpaper, coordinating borders, and fabrics that are suitable for use throughout the home. The catalog also offers tools and supplies for installation, as well as decorating accents to complement your scheme. Robinson's provides color photographs that show how different designs look when they're installed—a very helpful feature— as well as samples of selected papers. Prices are competitive—an average of $7.49 for a single roll of wallpaper, and $6.99 for five yards of border trim.

Patterns not shown in the catalog are available through Robinson's Custom Order Department, at savings of 30% off book price. See the catalog for details, or call with manufacturer's name, book name, pattern number, price code, and suggested retail price, to receive a quote.

Special Factors: Satisfaction is guaranteed; returns are accepted within 30 days for exchange or refund; minimum order is $15 with credit cards.

THE RUG STORE

SUITES E AND F
2201 CROWNPOINT
   EXECUTIVE DR.
CHARLOTTE, NC 28227
800-257-5078
704-845-8591

Catalog: $5, refundable
Save: up to 30%
Pay: check, MO, MC, V
Sells: area rugs
Store: mail order only

You've just moved or you're redecorating, and you need an area rug— but you just can't afford to spend $1,000. The Rug Store may have your answer: Antron area rugs, in sizes from approximately 4' by 6' to 10' by 14', in designs and colors to complement just about every decor. Adaptations of carpet classics include "Serabend," an all-over repeat in jewel tones; "Marseille," a Savonnerie style; "Limani," a dhurrie lookalike; "Leah,"inspired by needlepoint block rugs; "Herat," a dense flower-and-vine design; "Lakota," which reflects the patterns of Navajo weaving; and "Aubusson," a tribute to the great French design, are just a few of the choices. Prices for a typical room-size rug—approximately 8' by 11'—begin as low as $289, and top at under $500. Smaller sizes cost much less, and if you need to cover a very large area, you'll find two designs offered in sizes up to 11' by 20'. The cost of the catalog is refundable with the purchase of a rug, and swatches may be ordered ($5 for one, three for $10), so you can sample the color and texture before you buy.

Special Factors: Satisfaction is guaranteed; returns are accepted within seven days for exchange, refund, or credit; orders are shipped worldwide.

S & S MILLS

2650 LAKELAND RD.
P.O. BOX 1568
DALTON, GA 30722
800-848-8114
404-277-3677

Brochure: free
Save: up to 60%
Pay: check, MO, MC, V
Sells: carpeting
Store: mail order only

S & S Carpet Mills manufactures carpeting for commercial and residential installations, and is able to pass on savings of 50%, sometimes more, by selling directly so you bypass the usual markups. S & S offers Saxonies, Berbers, textured loops, velvet cuts, and other carpeting styles, treated with Scotchgard, in over 30 decorator colors. All of the carpeting is covered by a five- or ten-year limited warranty on wear. Send for the brochure, which includes details on the sales policy and information on ordering samples.

Special Factor: Price quote by phone or letter.

SHAMA IMPORTS, INC.

P.O. BOX 2900,
   DEPT. WBM-94
FARMINGTON HILLS, MI
   48333-2900
313-478-7740

Brochure: free
Save: up to 50%
Pay: check, MO, MC, V
Sells: crewel fabrics and home accessories
Store: mail order only

Shama Imports, which began business in 1982, offers excellent prices on Indian crewel fabrics and home accessories. Crewel is hand-embroidered on hand-loomed cotton, offered here in traditional serpentine flower-and-vine motifs and other distinctive designs, in a range of colors. The eight-page color brochure that shows the patterns also includes decorating suggestions. Background (unembroidered) fabric is also available by the yard, and Shama stocks crewel chair and cushion covers, tote bags, bedspreads, and tablecloths as well. All of the fabric is 52" wide and can be washed by hand or dry cleaned. Samples are available for $1 each; those showing one-fourth of the complete pattern cost $5 (refundable). The brochure lists the pattern repeats for all of the designs.

Special Factors: Satisfaction is guaranteed; uncut, undamaged returns are accepted within 30 days for refund or credit; C.O.D. orders are accepted; orders are shipped worldwide.

SHIBUI WALL-COVERINGS

DEPT. WBM-94
P.O. BOX 1268
SANTA ROSA, CA 95402
800-824-3030
707-526-6170
FAX: 707-544-0719

Brochure and Samples: $4
Save: up to 50%
Pay: check, MO, MC, V
Sells: imported grass cloth and "natural" wall coverings
Store: mail order only

Shibui, which has been doing business since 1966, sells fine wall coverings made of natural materials—jute, grasses, strings, and textiles. Shibui stocks imported jute-fiber grass cloth, rush cloth, textile papers, textured weaves, and string wall coverings. The $4 brochure fee includes samples, and larger pieces are available upon request. The string wall coverings include several that look like silk at a fraction of the price, and there are lots of wonderful wall coverings of woven grasses backed by paper of contrasting colors. Paper-hanging tool kits, adhesives, and lining paper are also stocked, and Scotchgard treatment is available.

Special Factors: Satisfaction is guaranteed; shipping is included on orders over $100; single and double rolls can be cut from regular bolts (not returnable); returns are accepted within 30 days; C.O.D. orders are accepted; orders are shipped worldwide.

SILK SURPLUS

235 EAST 58TH ST.
NEW YORK, NY 10022
212-753-6511

Information: price quote
Save: up to 75% (see text)
Pay: check, MO, MC, V
Sells: discontinued decorator fabric and trim (see text)
Store: same address; Monday to Saturday 10–5:30; also 223 E. 58th St., New York; 449 Old Country Rd., Westbury; 1215 Northern Blvd., Manhasset; and 281 Mamaroneck Ave., White Plains, NY

Silk Surplus is well-known to budget-minded New Yorkers who covet luxurious upholstery and drapery fabrics, because it's where they can save up to 75% (and sometimes even more) on sumptuous Scalamandré closeouts and fabrics from other mills. Silks, cottons, velvets, woolens, chintzes, brocades, damasks, and other weaves and finishes are usually available from Silk Surplus, which opened its doors in 1962. Walk-in customers can select from among the bolts in any of the five Silk Surplus shops. But if you're buying by mail, you must know exactly which Scalamandré fabric you want, and in which color. If it's there, you're in luck. You may also send the store a fabric sample with a query. This is a great shopping stop on a trip to New York City, but only serious searchers for Scalamandré closeout fabrics should contact the store intending to buy by mail. If you're a design professional, you may ask for an additional trade discount.

Special Factors: Price quote by phone or letter with SASE; sample cuttings are free; all sales are final; orders are shipped worldwide.

STYLE WALLCOVERING

P.O. BOX 865
SOUTHFIELD, MI 48037
800-627-0400

Information: price quote
Save: up to 50%
Pay: check, MO, MC, V
Sells: wall coverings
Store: mail order only

Style Wallcovering doesn't have a catalog, but it *does* have access to over 100,000 different wall coverings, from every major manufacturer and designer. When you've decided on the pattern, determine the number of rolls you'll need, and call Style for pricing and availability information. Discounts run up to 50%, depending on the amount you're buying, and shipping is included in the price.

Special Factors: Price quote by phone or letter; quantity discounts are available; shipping is included.

TIOGA MILL OUTLET STORES, INC.

DEPT. WBM-94
P.O. BOX 3171
200 S. HARTMAN ST.
YORK, PA 17403
717-843-5139
FAX: 717-854-9223

Brochure: free (see text)
Save: up to 50%
Pay: check, MO, MC, V, Discover
Sells: decorator fabrics
Store: same address; Monday to Thursday 9:30–6, Friday 9:30–8, Saturday 9–5 (9–3 in July and August)

"When you think fabric, think Tioga!" urges the brochure from this firm, where drapery and upholstery fabrics are sold at up to 50% off list prices. Tioga stocks material by Lanscot/Arlen, Bloomcraft, Covington, Fabricut, John Wolf, and many other designers and manufacturers. If you've selected your fabric, you can write or call Tioga for a price quote. If you're still shopping, you can avail yourself of the firm's decorating service by completing the "Special Project/Sample Request" portion of the order form and returning it with the $2 fee. Tioga will send you selected swatches, from which you may select your fabric. If you're looking for "non-designer" fabric—lace panels, crewel embroideries, Haitian cottons, sheeting and muslin, moirés, velvet, and open-weave casements—you'll find them here. Drapery and upholstery supplies are also available, including tools, batting, padding, linings (in widths of 48" and 54"), gimp, burlap, and other goods.

Tioga Mill Outlet has been in business since 1970, and guarantees that all goods are first quality; flawed or damaged goods will be replaced or your money refunded. Returns due to customer error are not accepted, so *measure* and *remeasure* before you order.

Special Factors: Minimum order is 1/4 yard; orders are shipped worldwide.

WAREHOUSE CARPETS, INC.

P.O. BOX 3233
DALTON, GA 30719
800-526-2229
706-226-2229
FAX: 706-278-1008

Brochure: free
Save: up to 50%
Pay: check or MO
Sells: carpeting, vinyl flooring, and padding
Store: Walnut Ave. (Exit 136 off I-75), Dalton, GA; Monday to Friday 8–5

Warehouse Carpets began life in 1977 as a carpeting wholesaler, and has since moved into retail mail order, offering customers savings of as much as 50% on carpeting and floor coverings. Call for a quote if you're shopping for carpeting from Aladdin, Cabin Crafts, Columbus, Coronet, Downs, Galaxy, Horizon, Interloom, Lees, Masland, Mohawk, Philadelphia, Salem, J.P. Stevens, Sutton, World, or Wunda Weave; or vinyl flooring from Armstrong, Congoleum, Mannington, or Tarkett. And if you'd like to save an average of 50% on rug padding, Warehouse Carpets can provide several types.

Can call or write with the names of the manufacturer and style of the carpeting you want, and follow with a 50% deposit (check or money order). The balance is due when the goods are ready for shipment, which is made by common carrier, and the brochure and information sheet include details of the terms.

Special Factors: All goods are first quality; price quote by phone or letter; orders are shipped worldwide (except Canada).

WELLS INTERIORS INC.

7171 AMADOR PLAZA DR.
DUBLIN, CA 94568
800-547-8982

Catalog: free
Save: up to 85%
Pay: check, MO, MC, V
Sells: window treatments and accessories
Store: same address; Monday to Friday 10–6, Saturday 10–5, Sunday 12–4; 19 other stores in CA and OR (see the catalog for locations)

Wells Interiors has been in business since 1980 and guarantees "the lowest prices" on its goods, and will beat any other dealer's price down to cost on a wide range of top brands. Discounts can run up to 85% on retail prices on Levolor's Riviera, Monaco, private-label blinds, and vertical lines (in all fabrics, materials, colors, and options offered by Levolor), blinds by Bali, Graber, HunterDouglas, Joanna, and M&B, LouverDrape vertical blinds, Del Mar woven woods, Duette blinds, Softlight shades, and metal blinds and verticals. Kirsch woven woods, pleated shades, decorator roller shades, verticals, and miniblinds are also available.

The catalog includes a guide to the lines currently available, and includes instructions on measuring your windows and installing the blinds. Details of the firm's warranty are given in the catalog as well.

Special Factors: Written confirmation is required on phone orders; orders are shipped worldwide.

SEE ALSO

American Frame Corporation • sectional frames and mats • **ART MATERIALS**

Anticipations • home accents, furniture, etc. • **GENERAL MERCHANDISE**

Arctic Sheepskin Outlet • sheepskin rugs • **CLOTHING**

Bedroom Secrets • window treatments, home accessories • **HOME: LINEN**

BRE Lumber • flooring, cabinet-grade lumber, decking, and paneling • **HOME: MAINTENANCE**

Buffalo Batt & Felt Corp. • throw pillow inserts and upholstery stuffing • **CRAFTS**

The Caning Shop • seat-weaving materials, replacement seats, upholstery supplies • **CRAFTS**

Cherry Hill Furniture, Carpet & Interiors • rugs, carpeting, and accessories • **HOME: FURNISHINGS**

The Deerskin Place • sheepskin rugs • **CLOTHING**

Defender Industries, Inc. • teak kitchen and bath accessories • **AUTO**

Domestications • home accents, window treatments, etc. • **HOME: LINEN**

Excalibur Bronze Sculpture Foundry • reproduction art lamps, vases, etc. • **ART & ANTIQUES**

Fabric Editions Ltd. • decorating cottons • **CRAFTS**

Frank's Cane and Rush Supply • seat-reweaving materials, upholstery supplies, etc. • **CRAFTS**

The Furniture Showplace • lamps, decorator accessories, etc. • **HOME: FURNISHINGS**

Global Village Imports • upholstery-weight ikat fabrics • **CRAFTS**

Goldberg's Marine Distributors • teak kitchen and bath accessories • **AUTO**

Gooseberry Patch • country crafts and home accents • **GENERAL MERCHANDISE**

Home-Sew • upholstery supplies • **CRAFTS**

Leather Unlimited Corp. • sheepskin rugs • **LEATHER**

The Linen Source • window treatments, home accents • **HOME: LINEN**

Loftin-Black Furniture Company • mirrors • **HOME: FURNISHINGS**

M&E Marine Supply Company, Inc. • teak boat accessories for kitchen and bath • **AUTO**

D. MacGillivray & Coy. • sheepskin rugs • **CRAFTS**

Monarch • radiator enclosures • **HOME: MAINTENANCE**

Murrow Furniture Galleries, Inc. • lamps • **HOME: FURNISHINGS**

The New England Slate Company • salvaged slate for flooring • **HOME: MAINTENANCE**

Newark Dressmaker Supply, Inc. • upholstery supplies • **CRAFTS**

Quality Furniture Market of Lenoir, Inc. • lamps, decorator fabrics, etc. • **HOME: FURNISHINGS**

Saco Manufacturing & Woodworking • wood lampposts, columns, pilasters, etc. • **HOME: MAINTENANCE**

Shuttercraft • interior and exterior wooden window shutters • **HOME: MAINTENANCE**

Stuckey Brothers Furniture Co., Inc. • clocks, mirrors, etc. • **HOME: FURNISHINGS**

Sultan's Delight, Inc. • "leather camel" saddlebag hassocks • **FOOD**

Thai Silks • upholstery-weight silk fabrics • **CRAFTS**

Utex Trading Enterprises • upholstery-weight silk fabric • **CRAFTS**

FURNISHINGS

Household furnishings of all types,

including outdoor furniture, office

furnishings, and services

You can save as much as 50% on suggested retail by ordering your furniture from North Carolina, the manufacturing center of the industry. The discounters don't take the staggering markups that make furnishings and home accessories prohibitively expensive in department and furniture stores. This doesn't endear them to the furniture manufacturers; in fact, it's becoming common for manufacturers to do everything they can to make it difficult for discounters to sell by mail, by forbidding them to trade outside designated "selling areas" and sometimes prohibiting the firms from having 800 phone lines. (Manufacturers elicit compliance by threatening to refuse to fill the discounters' orders.) This practice has the effect of limiting trade and raising the prices we all have to pay. To avoid creating problems for the discounters, while giving access to the best buys possible, all brand names have been *omitted* from these listings. But most of the firms listed here can take orders for furniture and accessories from hundreds of manufacturers, can supply catalogs, brochures, and swatches, and give decorating advice over the phone.

It's advisable to use the "in-home delivery service" when a firm offers it, since your furniture will be uncrated exactly where you want it. If there are any damages, you'll see them right away and can contact the company while the shipper is there to find out what to do.

For listings of other firms that sell furnishings and decorative pieces for the home, see the "Decor" section of "Home" and "General Merchandise." Some of the firms listed here also sell lines of office furniture, but see "Office and Business" for a more comprehensive selection.

BARNES & BARNES FINE FURNITURE

190 COMMERCE AVE.
SOUTHERN PINES, NC
  28387
800-334-8174
919-692-3381
FAX: 919-692-3381

Brochure: free
Save: up to 55%
Pay: check, MO, MC, V, Discover
Sells: home furnishings
Store: same address; Monday to Friday 9–5, Saturday by appointment

Barnes & Barnes has been selling home furnishings and accessories since 1980, and can save you up to 55% on the suggested retail prices on pieces from a long list of manufacturers. In addition to hundreds of furniture lines that include patio furniture, brass beds, and office furniture, Barnes & Barnes sells lamps, mirrors, clocks, and decorator fabric from a number of prominent firms. A deposit of 50% is required to place an order, and the rest is due upon delivery. Shipping charges are collected on delivery. For a roster of the available manufacturers and details on the firm's sales policy, request the free brochure.

Special Factor: Price quote by phone or letter.

CHERRY HILL FURNITURE, CARPET & INTERIORS

DEPT. WBMC94
P.O. BOX 7405, FURNI-
  TURELAND STATION
HIGH POINT, NC 27264
800-328-0933
800-888-0933
919-882-0933
FAX: 919-882-0900

Brochure: free
Save: up to 50%
Pay: check or MO
Sells: home and office furniture and accessories
Store: mail order only

Cherry Hill, in business since 1933, offers a wide range of home and office furnishings, accessories, rugs, and carpeting at prices that average

45% off list. The Contract Division serves the needs of importers, business owners, developers, purchasing directors, architects, and others who are doing residential or commercial installations. Cherry Hill can supply lines from over 500 manufacturers, and will send a brochure upon request.

Special Factors: Price quote by phone or letter with SASE; inquiries are accepted over the 800 lines; shipment is made by common carrier or van line; orders are shipped worldwide.

FACTORY DIRECT TABLE PAD CO.

1501 W. MARKET ST.
INDIANAPOLIS, IN 46222
800-428-4567

Prices and Samples: $1
Save: up to 50%
Pay: check, MO, MC, V, Discover
Sells: custom-made table pads
Store: mail order only

Factory Direct's brochure states that about half of the cost of a custom-made table pad is the fee paid to the person who measures the table. For $1, Factory Direct Table Pad will send you a guide to doing this yourself, as well as a discount coupon for $100 off the normal retail prices. You'll also receive several sample swatches of the table pad top, which can be made in pebble-grain or smooth finish, in plain colors or in wood grain, in different thicknesses. The table pads are warrantied for 7, 15, or 20 years, and complete details of the terms of sale are given in the literature.

Special Factors: Authorized returns are accepted within 15 days; orders are shipped worldwide.

THE FURNITURE SHOWPLACE

1190 HWY. 74 BYPASS
SPINDALE, NC 28160
704-287-7106
FAX: 704-287-8785

Brochure: free with SASE
Save: up to 55%
Pay: check, MO, MC, V
Sells: home furnishings and accessories
Store: same address; Monday to Saturday 9–5

The Furniture Showplace is a family-owned firm that sells fine furnishings and decorative accessories at great prices, and prides itself on prompt handling of orders and excellent delivery service. The Furniture Showplace, established in 1970, represents hundreds of manufacturers that are listed in the brochure, which also includes details on the terms of sale. If you're in the Spindale area, drop by—there's a "mini-barn" for children and a 20,000-square-foot showroom.

Special Factors: Price quote by phone or letter with SASE; shipment is made by "a professional delivery specialist"; a 33% deposit is required on all orders.

GENADA IMPORTS

P.O. BOX 204, DEPT. W-94
TEANECK, NJ 07666
201-790-7522

Catalog: $1
Save: up to 40%
Pay: check, MO, MC, V
Sells: Danish, modern, and traditional furniture
Store: mail order only

Genada has been in business since 1968, selling Danish modern furniture in its most American incarnation: low-slung, teak-finished chairs and couches, with loose-cushion backs and seats of tweed-covered foam. The style has weathered fad and fatigue quite well, and the furniture's basic appeal is only enhanced by its low prices. Armchairs begin at under $100, and couches start at under $170 (armless divans from $120).

Genada isn't limited to Scandinavian design; the catalog shows reproductions of the Eames chair and other modern classics, folding chairs with woven rope seats and backs, knock-down bookcases and cabinets, butcher block table tops and bases, convertible foam-block chairs and sofas, gateleg tables with chairs that store in the base, and bent-wood chairs. The catalog also features modern chairs by Paoli Chair Co., suitable for home of office, as well as several handsome styles in molded teak, walnut, and rosewood finishes, from about $300 and up. Imported armoires, patio furniture, "country" kitchen furniture, free-standing wall units, computer work stations, desks, VCR carts, and bar stools are all available. If you're shopping for a bridge table with folding hardwood chairs, you'll find several reasonably priced styles here.

Special Factors: Price quote by phone or letter; specify upholstery and finish materials when ordering.

HARVEST HOUSE FURNITURE

P.O. BOX 1440
DENTON, NC 27239-1440
704-869-5181
FAX: 704-869-5187

Information: inquire (see text)
Save: up to 52%
Pay: check, MO, MC, V, Discover
Sells: home and office furnishings
Store: Hwy. 109 S., Denton, NC; Monday to Friday 9–5, Saturday 9–1

Harvest House has been doing business since 1977, selling name-brand home and office furnishings at savings averaging 45% to 50% off list. During the periodic "sales," prices are up to 52% off manufacturers' suggested retail (with a minimum order of $600).

If you're deciding which furniture to buy, you can send for the Harvest House brochure that includes a brands list and a questionnaire, which you may complete and return with $7 (refundable with purchase). Harvest House will send you an information packet, with manufacturers' brochures selected to suit your tastes and needs. If you've chosen your furniture and are comparison shopping, you can call or write for a quote. Be sure to ask for the "Sales and Delivery Policy" sheet before you order, since it details the delivery terms and procedures.

Special Factors: Price quote by phone or letter with SASE; orders are shipped worldwide.

HUNT GALLERIES, INC.

2920 HWY. 127 N.
P.O. BOX 2324
HICKORY, NC 28603
800-248-3876
704-324-9934

Catalog: $4
Save: up to 30%
Pay: check, MO, MC, V
Sells: upholstered furniture
Store: same address

Hunt Galleries, a family business that was founded nearly half a century ago, has become a full-fledged manufacturing center for a large line of upholstered furniture. Hunt's 90-page catalog and supplementary price list are models of clarity—every piece is shown in color, fully described with complete measurements. Most of the line is seating—sofas, loveseats, chairs, armchairs, dining room chairs, tuffets, ottomans, benches, vanity stools, etc., most of traditional design—but Hunt Galleries also offers upholstered headboards, mirrors, and even sofa tables. At this writing, half a dozen sofas are offered as sleepers, with seven-inch-thick innerspring mattresses.

The price list specifies charges for your fabric (COM) versus different grades of Hunt's material, as well as options, including leather upholstery, skirt styles, fabric lining, brass nail trim, casters, swivel mechanisms, seat filling choices (poly foam, down and feather blends, blends with innersprings, and foam with springs), Scotchgarding, quilting the fabric, and extra arm protectors. And the catalog shows the quality points of the furniture itself—doweled and glued hardwood frames, tied springs, deep padding, etc. Prices run around 30%-plus below what comparable national brands cost, *without* the custom features. The terms of sale are detailed in the price list, including the shipping alternatives: truck, inside delivery, and UPS. If you still have questions, just give the Hunts a call!

Special Factors: Satisfaction is guaranteed; minimum order is $10 with credit cards.

INTERIOR FURNISHINGS LTD.

P.O. BOX 1644
HICKORY, NC 28603
704-328-5683

Brochure: free
Save: up to 50%
Pay: check or MO
Sells: home furnishings and accessories
Store: 1308 Hwy. 70 S.W., Hickory, NC; Monday to Friday 8:30–5, Saturday 8:30–12 noon

The brands list from Interior Furnishings includes the names of some of North Carolina's best-known manufacturers, who produce home furnishings, bedding, lamps, mirrors, table pads, and other accessories. A deposit of one-third is required to place an order, and the balance is due before shipment is made. Only first-quality goods are sold, and Interior offers both common carrier and van line deliveries.

Special Factor: Orders are shipped worldwide.

DON LAMOR INC.

2220 HWY. 70 EAST
BH9 HICKORY FURNI-
** TURE MART**
HICKORY, NC 28602
704-324-1776

Information: price quote
Save: up to 40%
Pay: check, MO, MC, V
Sells: home and office furnishings
Store: same address; Monday to Friday 9–6, Saturday 9–5

Don Lamor lays claim to "North Carolina's largest display of fine home furnishings," and is an authorized dealer for a number of prominent manufacturers. The sales consultants can assist you in selecting the right furnishings for your needs, and require a 50% deposit on your order (the balance is due before the order can be shipped). Both home and office furnishings, rugs, and accessories and occasional pieces are available.

Special Factor: Price quote by phone or letter.

LOFTIN-BLACK
FURNITURE COMPANY

111 SEDGEHILL DR.
THOMASVILLE, NC 27360
800-334-7398
919-472-6117
FAX: 919-472-2052

Brochure: free
Save: up to 50%
Pay: check, MO, MC, V
Sells: furnishings, bedding, and accessories
Store: same address; Monday to Friday
8:30–5:30, Saturday 8:30–4:30

Loftin-Black, founded in 1948, delivers selection, service, and savings. The firm offers fine home, office, and patio furniture and accessories from hundreds of companies, including the top names in furnishings. Check here before ordering mirrors, table pads, and bedding—they're also available, at sizable savings. The brochure includes a brands listing and general sales information (a 50% deposit is required when ordering, and the balance is due upon delivery). Loftin-Black will provide in-home delivery and setup, although you can engage a common carrier if you prefer. If you're in the Thomasville area, drop in and see Loftin-Black's 14,000 square feet of furniture on display.

Special Factors: Price quote by phone or letter; delivery (in-home) is made by Loftin-Black's van service; orders are shipped worldwide.

MARK SALES CO., INC.

609 E. 81ST ST.
BROOKLYN, NY 11236
718-763-2591

Catalog: $2
Save: up to 30%
Pay: check or MO
Sells: unfinished furniture
Store: mail order only

Two dollars brings you the Mark Sales catalog, 62 pages of clear, sepia-toned photographs of over 100 pieces of furniture that await your finishing hand. The flavor is French provincial—side chairs and armchairs with graceful legs, rush seats, and cane backs, imposing cane-back "tub" chairs with lion's head-arms, settles with serpentine ladderbacks and carved aprons, Chinese Chippendale styles, ornate bombé chests, and even desks and semaniers are among the offerings. Every piece is made in Spain or Italy from beechwood and arrives completely assembled, ready for paint or stain and finish. Seats are rush, cane, or muslin-covered foam. Prices begin at $145 for a simple side chair, and run up to $1,810 for a dramatically carved console table. Furniture of this style and quality is usually priced a good 25% more, and since you finish it yourself you can create a custom look for a more modest investment.

Special Factors: Satisfaction is guaranteed; authorized returns are accepted within 20 days.

EPHRAIM MARSH CO.

DEPT. 362
P.O. BOX 266
CONCORD, NC
 28026-0266
800-992-8322
704-782-0814
FAX: 704-782-0436

Catalog: $5, refundable
Save: up to 40%
Pay: check, MO, MC, V
Sells: fine home and office furnishings
Store: mail order only

Between decorating indecision and budget restraints, furnishing a home can be a daunting affair. What you need is a friend with good taste and a decorator's discount—or Ephraim Marsh.

After surveying the offerings of hundreds of furniture manufacturers nationwide, Ephraim Marsh selects a number of pieces for its own production. Since the furniture is made to order, you can select the finish (depending on the options available), and most of the upholstered furniture can be made with your material (COM), or a choice from Ephraim Marsh's swatches. The 130-page catalog includes straightforward descriptions of the quality points of each group of furniture— whether solid wood or veneers are used, the type of joinery, finish, upholstery details, etc. What distinguishes Ephraim Marsh from other furnishings purveyors is the respect for good design and creature comfort that's shaped the collection. Each piece has been chosen for some combination of utility, charm, and beauty. Unless you're a diehard modernist, you'll find something to enhance your own rooms here: State-occasion mahogany ball-and-claw dining tables, a plain maple "Grandma's Kitchen" breakfront, a lovely yew "drum" table, Chinese Chippendale sofas and wing chairs, and even leather-upholstered furniture for bar and boardroom are just a few of the hundreds of offerings.

The prices are not *cheap*—this is "Furniture for the Long-Term Investor." But pieces of comparable quality sell elsewhere for 25% to

50% more, and it's wonderful to have the option of custom upholstery. Ephraim Marsh has been in business since 1956, and is enjoying a steady trade despite lean times in the home furnishings market—which is the best endorsement possible.

Special Factors: Authorized returns in original condition (except COM upholstery jobs) are accepted; orders are shipped worldwide.

MURROW FURNITURE GALLERIES, INC.

P.O. BOX 4337,
  DEPT. WBMC
WILMINGTON, NC 28406
919-799-4010
FAX: 919-791-2791

Brochure: free
Save: up to 50%
Pay: check, MO, MC, V
Sells: home furnishings, bedding, and accessories
Store: 3514 S. College Rd., Wilmington, NC; Monday to Friday 8:30–5:30, Saturday 9–5:30; also The Furniture Patch of Calabash, 10283 Beach Dr. SW, Calabash, NC; Monday to Saturday 9–5:30

Murrow Furniture Galleries, founded in 1979, sells furnishings, bedding, and accessories from over 500 manufacturers (listed in the brochure; a color catalog showcasing a broad range of styles is also offered). The extensive selection of brands and consistently good savings make this one of the best furniture discounters around. If you're able to visit the store in Wilmington, you'll find five gallery showrooms of 45,000 square feet, with fine furnishings and accessories on display. Delivery options and terms of sale are detailed in the brochure.

Special Factors: Price quote by phone or letter; deposit is required; orders are shipped worldwide.

PLEXI-CRAFT QUALITY PRODUCTS CORP.

**514 W. 24TH ST.
NEW YORK, NY
10011-1179
212-924-3244
FAX: 212-924-3508**

Catalog: $2
Save: up to 50%
Pay: check, MO, MC, V
Sells: acrylic furnishings and accessories
Store: same address; Monday to Friday
9:30–5, Saturday 11–4

Plexi-Craft manufactures its own line of premium acrylic goods, and prices them at up to 50% less than what department and specialty stores charge for comparable items. The 16-page catalog shows acrylic furnishings and accessories of all kinds. There are a number of tables—dining, cocktail, Parsons, TV, snack, and side—and the models with separate bases may be ordered with glass instead of acrylic tops. Several rolling bars are available, as well as chairs, pedestals, computer stands, vanities and stools, luggage racks, magazine units, and telephone tables. Desk sets, kitchen organizers and paper towel holders, and bathroom fixtures round out the selection, and there's an antistatic cleaner and a polish formulated for acrylic to keep everything gleaming. Plexi-Craft, founded in 1972, also accepts orders for custom work.

Special Factor: Price quote by phone or letter on custom work.

QUALITY FURNITURE MARKET OF LENOIR, INC.

**2034 HICKORY BLVD. S.W.
LENOIR, NC 28645
704-728-2946
FAX: 704-726-0226**

Information: price quote
Save: up to 47%
Pay: check, MO, MC, V
Sells: furnishings, bedding, and accessories
Store: same address; Monday to Saturday
8:30–5

Quality Furniture Market, in business since 1953, takes its name seriously: You're invited to check the firm's ratings with Dun and Bradstreet, the Lyons listing, and the Lenoir Chamber of Commerce before you buy. The firm's magnificent selection is offered at prices that are 20% over cost, compared to the usual 110% to 125% markups.

Quality Furniture sells indoor and outdoor furniture, bedding, and home accessories by literally hundreds of firms. The list of brands is given in the brochure, as well as terms of sale and other conditions. Readers have written to say they were very pleased with Quality's prices and the firm's in-home delivery service. If you're traveling near Lenoir, drop by and get lost in the three floors of furniture galleries and display rooms.

Special Factors: Price quote by phone or letter with SASE; all orders must be prepaid before shipment; shipment is made by common carrier or in-home delivery service.

ST. CHARLES FURNITURE CO.

P.O. BOX 2144
GREENSBORO, NC 27261
800-545-3287
919-852-1987
FAX: 919-547-0696

Information: price quote
Save: up to 40%
Pay: check, MO, MC, V
Sells: home and office furnishings and accessories
Store: 5828 High Point Rd., Greensboro, NC; Monday–Friday 9–6, Saturday 10–5

The brochure from St. Charles Furniture lists scores of manufacturers of home and office furnishings, patio furniture, clocks and lamps, table pads, and bedding. You can call for a price quote if you've decided on the line and model, or ask for advice and manufacturers' brochures if you're still shopping. St. Charles offers substantial discounts, and requires a 50% deposit and signature to process your order. Delivery can be made by common carrier (sidewalk) or St. Charles' own truck or Furniture Delivery Systems (in-house, uncrated, with setup). The brochure and order form give complete details of the sales policy.

Special Factor: Price quote by phone or letter.

SHAW FURNITURE GALLERIES, INC.

P.O. BOX 576
RANDLEMAN, NC 27317
919-498-2628
FAX: 919-498-7889

Brochure: free
Save: up to 50%
Pay: check or MO
Sells: home and office furnishings
Store: 131 W. Academy St., Randleman, NC;
Monday to Friday 9–5:30, Saturday 9–5

The Shaw family has been selling furniture at a discount since 1940 and represents over 300 manufacturers; the large inventory can be seen in Shaw's showroom in Randleman. The brochure includes a partial listing of the available brands; inquire if you're pricing a piece of furniture or an item by a manufacturer not mentioned, since it may be carried. Shaw's references and the terms of sale are detailed in the brochure, and please note that final payments must be made by certified check or money order.

Special Factors: Price quote by phone or letter with SASE; shipments are made by Superior Delivery Service (owned by Shaw's management); minimum order is $100; orders are shipped worldwide.

SOBOL HOUSE OF FURNISHINGS

RICHARDSON BLVD.
BLACK MOUNTAIN, NC
28711
704-669-8031

Brochure: free
Save: up to 50%
Pay: check or MO
Sells: home and office furnishings
Store: same address

Sobol House has been saving informed consumers on their furniture purchases since 1970, and the firm's low prices have helped build a clientele worldwide over the years. Sobol's specialty is traditional, 18th century, and country styles, from the most prominent names in the business. Sobol can help you make your selection—with advice and manufacturers' catalogs—and gives price quotes on specific items. Both sidewalk and in-house delivery are available, and details of the sales policy are given in the brochure and order form.

Special Factors: Price quote by phone or letter; orders are shipped worldwide.

STUCKEY BROTHERS FURNITURE CO., INC.

RTE. 1, BOX 527
STUCKEY, SC 29554
803-558-2591
FAX: 803-558-9229

Information: price quote
Save: up to 50%
Pay: check or MO
Sells: indoor and outdoor furnishings and accessories
Store: same address; Monday to Friday 9–6, Saturday 9–5

Stuckey is South Carolina's answer to High Point—it sells a full line of furniture and accessories at North Carolina prices, and has been doing business by mail since 1946. Furnishings and accessories, including patio and office furnishings, are available from over 300 manufacturers. Lines of clocks, lamps, mirrors, and bedding are offered as well. Request the brochure that details the sales terms and shipping options (van line or common carrier).

Special Factors: Price quote by phone or letter with SASE; orders are shipped worldwide.

MARION TRAVIS

P.O. BOX 292
STATESVILLE, NC 28677
704-528-4424

Catalog: $1
Save: up to 50%
Pay: check, MO, MC, V
Sells: country chairs, benches, and tables
Store: 354 South Eastway Dr., Troutman, NC; Monday to Thursday 8–3:30, Friday 8–12 noon

You can pay hundreds of dollars for an oak pedestal table at your local antique shop, and search every tag sale in the state for a matched set of ladder-back chairs. Or you can send $1 to Marion Travis for the catalog that shows these and other furnishings. The ten pages of black-and-white photographs show country furniture, including a large selection of ladder-back chairs with woven cord seats. There are armchair and rocker styles and children's models, beginning at under $25. Plain, slat-seat kitchen chairs and a classic oak kitchen table with utility drawer are shown, as well as a deacon's bench, porch swing, and Kennedy-style rockers with cane backs and seats. The prices cited are for unfinished furniture, but Marion Travis will stain and finish your selection in natural, oak, or walnut for a surcharge.

Special Factor: Authorized returns of defective goods are accepted within 30 days.

TRIAD FURNITURE DISCOUNTERS

P.O. BOX 3429
NORTH MYRTLE BEACH,
  SC 29582
800-323-8469

Information: price quote
Save: up to 50%
Pay: check or MO
Sells: home and office furnishings
Store: mail order only

Triad's brochure lists nearly 100 major manufacturers of home, office, and outdoor furniture, lamps, mirrors, and bedding, which Triad offers at savings of up to 50% on the suggested list prices. Triad's sales policy—50% down on placing the order, the balance before shipment—is standard among Carolina's furniture discounters. Triad gives you a firm delivery charge (not an estimate), and all shipments are delivered in-house with setup. You can write for the brochure, which includes the partial list of manufacturers, or call for a price quote on specific items.

Special Factors: Price quote by phone or letter.

TURNER TOLSON, INC.

P.O. DRAWER 1507
NEW BERN, NC 28563
919-638-2121
FAX: 919-638-3812

Brochure: free
Save: up to 50%
Pay: check, MO, MC, V
Sells: home and office furnishings
Store: Hwy. 17 South, New Bern, NC; Monday to Friday 10–6, Saturday 10–5

Turner Tolson, in business since 1887, is an authorized dealer for prominent names in home and office furnishings. The firm's brochure includes a partial roster of brands, and inquiries are invited on manufacturers not listed. Turner Tolson's prices are 40% to 50% lower than list, and shipping charges include in-home delivery and setup. A 25% deposit is required to place an order, and you're invited to check the company's references with the New Bern Chamber of Commerce and the local bank. And if you make your purchase in person in the 60,000-square-foot showroom, Turner Tolson may pick up the check for your lodgings in New Bern—inquire for details.

Special Factors: Price quote by phone or letter with SASE; orders are shipped worldwide.

WICKER WAREHOUSE INC.

195 S. RIVER ST.
HACKENSACK, NJ 07601
201-342-6709
FAX: 201-342-1495

Catalog: $5, refundable
Save: up to 50%
Pay: check, MO, MC, V, Discover
Sells: wicker furniture and accessories
Store: same address

Why comb antique stores and flea markets for vintage wicker furniture when you can find freshly minted versions of the same styles, in pristine condition, at comparable prices? Wicker Warehouse sells current styles by the top names in the business, including lines treated to withstand the elements—so you don't have to drag everything inside the garage when it starts raining. The 24-page color catalog shows great groupings for sunporch and summer home, and wicker-embellished bedroom furnishings, mirrors, lamps, dining chairs, stools, nursery accoutrements, bathroom accessories, trunks, and even doll buggies. Fabric and finish options are shown as well. The prices are 30% to 50% below list, and orders are shipped anywhere within the continental U.S.

Special Factors: Satisfaction is guaranteed; price quote by phone or letter.

SEE ALSO

Alfax Wholesale Furniture • *office and institutional furnishings* • **OFFICE**
American Discount Wall and Window Coverings • *upholstery and decorator fabrics* • **HOME: DECOR**
Anticipations • *home furnishings and accents* • **GENERAL MERCHANDISE**

Barnes & Noble Bookstores, Inc. • bookshelves • **BOOKS**

Bedroom Secrets • home furnishings • **HOME: LINEN**

Bennett Brothers, Inc. • small selection of home furnishings • **GENERAL MERCHANDISE**

Business & Institutional Furniture Company, Inc. • office and institutional furniture • **OFFICE**

Cole's Appliance & Furniture Co. • home furnishings • **APPLIANCES**

Coppa Woodworking Inc. • Adirondack chairs, screen doors • **HOME: MAINTENANCE**

Custom Windows & Walls • decorator fabrics • **HOME: DECOR**

Excalibur Bronze Sculpture Foundry • "art" furniture • **ART & ANTIQUES**

The Fabric Center, Inc. • upholstery and decorator fabrics • **HOME: DECOR**

Fabrics by Phone • upholstery and decorator fabrics • **HOME: DECOR**

Frank Eastern Co. • office furniture • **OFFICE**

Frank's Cane and Rush Supply • small selection of unfinished furniture kits • **CRAFTS**

Harmony Supply Inc. • decorator fabrics • **HOME: DECOR**

Home Fabric Mills, Inc. • upholstery and drapery fabrics • **HOME: DECOR**

Marlene's Decorator Fabrics • upholstery and drapery fabric • **HOME: DECOR**

Shama Imports, Inc. • crewel upholstery fabric and cushion covers • **HOME: DECOR**

Silk Surplus • upholstery and drapery fabric • **HOME: DECOR**

Tioga Mills Outlet Store • upholstery and drapery fabric and supplies • **HOME: DECOR**

Kitchen

Cookware, bakeware, restaurant equipment, and food storage

This chapter includes companies selling everything from measuring spoons to commercial ranges, frequently at discounts of 30% to 50% on the regular retail prices. For other kitchen electronics, see "Appliances"; for kitchen tools and linens, see the next chapter, "Linen"; and look in "Books" for cookbooks. In addition, a number of firms that sell specialty ingredients and cookware are listed in the "Food and Drink" chapter—including several that offer stupendous buys on herbs, spices, and other flavorings.

FIND IT FAST

CHEESE-MAKING EQUIPMENT • **New England Cheesemaking Supply**
COMMERCIAL FIXTURES • **Fivenson, Kaplan Bros., Peerless**
GOURMET COOKWARE • **A Cook's Wares, Open House, Zabar's**

COLONIAL GARDEN KITCHENS

DEPT. CGM9609
HANOVER, PA 17333-0066
800-323-6000
717-633-3330

Catalog: $2
Save: up to 40%
Pay: check, MO, MC, V, AE, CB, DC, Discover
Sells: kitchen equipment and household helps
Store: mail order only

Colonial Garden Kitchens is one of the Hanover Direct, Inc. companies offering moderately priced gadgets, as well as name-brand appliances, at a discount. A third or more of the goods in the color catalog are usually on "sale," or tagged 20% to 40% below their regular prices. And every catalog features kitchen appliances, specialty cookware and utensils, work units and food storage containers, serving and entertaining equipment, and lots of things handy to have around the house. The Panasonic Bread Bakery, Pasta Express machines, DeLonghi toaster ovens, commercial oven mitts, cactus muffin tins, insulated bakeware, microwave bacon crispers, sock organizers, and cleaning products have appeared in past catalogs. Everything is backed by the firm's no-questions-asked guarantee of satisfaction.

Special Factors: Returns are accepted for exchange, refund, or credit; minimum order is $15 with credit cards.

A COOK'S WARES

211 37TH ST.
BEAVER FALLS, PA
15010-2103
412-846-9490
FAX: 412-846-9562

Catalog: $2
Save: up to 50%
Pay: check, MO, MC, V, AE
Sells: cookware, kitchen utensils, and cookbooks
Store: same address; Monday to Friday 9–4, Saturday 9–1

A Cook's Wares was founded in 1981, and is run by two devoted cooks. They choose the best in cookware and food preparation equipment, and sell it at savings of up to 50% through an informative, 64-page catalog, published four times yearly.

The firm's stock includes cookware lines by Alessi, All-Clad (the Cop-

R Chef, anodized aluminum, stainless steel, and Master Chef lines), Atlas and Joyce Chen woks and accessories, Chantal, Le Creuset, Cuisinart, Farberware (Milennium Series), Roschco, Scanpan, Spring Copper, T-Fal, and Vollrath, and Mauviel's hotel-weight copper pots and pans. The Jacques Pepin Collection from Bourgeat is available, as well as bakeware by Apilco, Chicago Metallic (Village Baker and Silverstone-on-Steel), Isabelle Marique Blue Steel, Kaiser, Pillivuyt, and Rema. Cookie cutters from Ateco and Fox Run are listed in the catalog, as are molds for ladyfingers, petit fours, madeleines, macaroons, and other sweets. The cutlery and food preparation and serving equipment includes KitchenAid mixers and accessories, Hitachi automatic bread machines, Bron and Moha mandolines, barbecue equipment, Bodum infusion coffee makers, Saeco espresso makers, Krups equipment (coffee grinders, coffee makers, mixers, and toasters); John Wright cookie-muffin tins; Cuisinart, Mouli, and Vitantonio appliances; Kenwood toasters, Russell Hobbs tea kettles, J.K. Adams wooden knife blocks, Rosti utensils and storage containers, Cuisinart food processors, and the complete lines of Henckels cutlery and kitchen gadgets. Also offered are goods by Amco, William Bounds, Copco, F. Dick, DMT, Hallen, Lola, Sparta, Taylor, Victorinox, Westmark, Wüsthof-Trident, Zyliss, and other makers. And cookbooks and cooking videotapes have been added to the firm's impressive inventory—classics and the best new releases, 15 pages of titles, all of which are sold at a discount.

A Cook's Wares has brought the same standards to its line of foodstuffs, primarily condiments: Paul Corcellet vinegars and mustards, Classic American mustards, Blanchard & Blanchard condiments, Select Origins herbs and spices, sun-dried tomatoes, olive spread, and other goods are available. Cooking and eating chocolate from Callebaut, Ghirardelli, and Merkens is offered, as well as Clearbrook Farms' dessert sauces, Tiptree preserves, and Vermont maple syrup.

Special Factors: Satisfaction is guaranteed; price quote by phone or letter with SASE on items not listed in the catalog; returns are accepted within 30 days.

FIVENSON FOOD EQUIPMENT, INC.

324 S. UNION ST.
TRAVERSE CITY, MI
49684-2586
616-946-7761
IN MI 800-632-7342
FAX: 616-946-7126

Catalog: $3, refundable
Save: up to 60%
Pay: check, MO, MC, V, AE, Discover
Sells: equipment for restaurant, bar, concession, and office
Store: same address; Monday to Friday 9–5, Saturday 10–12

Fivenson has been selling restaurant equipment to the food-service industry since 1937 and offers consumers the same products at prices up to 60% below list. Fivenson's 8-page catalog features ranges, ovens, steamers, and fryers by Frymaster, Garland, Toastmaster, U.S. Range, and Vulcan, and Amana Radarange microwave ovens. There are mixers from Hamilton Beach, Hobart, and Waring, as well as dishwashers, cooling units of every description from Delfield, Raetone, Traulson, True, and Ultra; and sinks, lunchroom furniture, bakery racks, popcorn and concession equipment, office coffee service, smoke-reduction equipment, icemakers, cleaning tools, chafing dishes, restaurant china, and other supplies. (The china and glassware are sold by the case only.) You can call or write for a price quote on specific models, or send for the catalog.

Special Factors: Price quote by phone or letter with SASE; kitchen layout and design services are available; minimum order is $25; orders are shipped worldwide.

KAPLAN BROS. BLUE FLAME CORP.

523 W. 125TH ST.
NEW YORK, NY
 10027-3498
212-662-6990
FAX: 212-663-2026

Brochure: free with SASE
Save: up to 50%
Pay: check or MO
Sells: commercial restaurant equipment
Store: same address; Monday to Friday 8–5

Kaplan Bros., established in 1953, sells commercial restaurant equipment at discounts of up to 50% on list prices and will send you manufacturers' brochures on request for a self-addressed, stamped envelope. Kaplan is best known as a source for Garland commercial stoves, including the popular six-burner model that costs over $2,300 at list, but $1,150 here. (Garland's Residential Range model is available.) Garland fryers, ovens, griddles, and salamanders are stocked, as well as Frymaster and Pitco fryers, and equipment by Blickman, Blodgett, MagiKitchin, and Vulcan.

Please note: Goods are shipped to "mainland U.S.A." only—no orders can be shipped to Alaska, Hawaii, Canada, or APO/FPO addresses.

Special Factors: Request brochures by name of manufacturer; if purchasing a stove for residential installation, have kitchen flooring, wall insulation, and exhaust system evaluated before ordering and upgrade if necessary.

KITCHEN ETC.

DEPT. WBM94
P.O. BOX 1560
NORTH HAMPTON, NH
 03862-1560
603-964-5174
FAX: 603-964-5123

Catalog: free
Save: 30% average
Pay: check, MO, MC, V
Sells: tableware and kitchenware
Store: Burlington and Natick, MA; Nashua and North Hampton, NH; and South Burlington, VT (see the catalog for locations)

Kitchen Etc. has put together a great catalog of fine and everyday china, cutlery, kitchenware, and serving pieces that brings you helpful buying information, as well as prices that usually run from 20% to 40% below regular retail. The firm has been doing business since 1983, and has five stores in New England.

The catalog features china patterns from Franciscan, Hutschenreuther, International China, Johnson Brothers, Lenox, Mikasa, Nikko, Noritake, Otagiri (Horizon), Pfaltzgraff, Roma, Royal Albert, Royal Doulton, Royal Minton, Studio Nova, and Wedgwood. The catalog lists the available patterns, a guide to the shape of each piece, present and future availability, and suggested retail and discount prices. Stemware from Gorham, Lenox, Mikasa, and Noritake is sold, as well as Oneida and Pfaltzgraff stainless and silverplate.

The catalog offers kitchenware and serving pieces from All-Clad, Calphalon, Circulon, Farberware, Le Creuset, Reverware, and T-Fal as well as selected kitchen appliances. There are spice racks and cookie jars, marble pastry slabs and rolling pins, all sold at a discount. If looking for cutlery, check the prices on knives from Chicago Cutlery, Farberware, Henckels, and Wüstoff-Trident.

Kitchen Etc. also offers a range of kitchen accessories, including pasta bowl sets, woks, pizza stones, glassware, and fajita skillets. Special orders are accepted on some goods, so if you don't see what you're looking for in the catalog, call to see whether the firm can get it. Kitchen Etc. also maintains a bridal registry service.

Special Factors: Satisfaction is guaranteed; price quote by phone or letter; orders are shipped worldwide.

NEW ENGLAND CHEESEMAKING SUPPLY COMPANY, INC.

85 MAIN ST., WBM
ASHFIELD, MA 01330
413-628-3808
FAX: 413-628-4061

Catalog: $1
Save: up to 80% (see text)
Pay: check, MO, MC, V
Sells: cheese-making supplies and equipment
Store: same address; Monday to Friday 8–4 (call first)

Making cheese at home is one of the few do-it-yourself endeavors with a nominal price tag that doesn't require a significant time or skills investment. New England Cheesemaking Supply, in business since 1978, can provide you with all the tools and materials you'll need to produce hard, soft, and semi-soft cheeses, at savings of up to 80% on the prices charged by supermarkets and specialty stores for the same kinds of cheeses.

Soft cheese is the easiest to make, and may be the cheapest, since you can get as much as two pounds of cheese from a gallon of milk. Milk sells for $1.30 a half gallon in some parts of the country, and flavored soft cheeses often cost $4.50 to $7.00 per pound, or as much as $2.80 for packaged, four-ounce varieties. So, by using the "Gourmet Soft Cheese Kit," you can recoup the $15.95 cost, plus the price of the milk, after making as little as two pounds of soft cheese. This kit is designed for the beginner and comes with cheese starter, cheesecloth, a dairy thermometer, and recipes. It can be used to make *crème fraiche* as well as *fromage blanc*—generic soft cheese—in as little as ten minutes. (If you use skim milk, you can produce low-calorie, low-cholesterol cheese, and omit the salt for sodium-restricted diets.)

New England Cheesemaking Supply also sells a "basic" cheese kit (for ricotta, Gouda, Monterey Jack, cheddar, etc.), and others for making mozzarella and goat cheese. Rennet (animal and vegetable), a large selection of starter and direct-set cultures, lipase powders, mold powder, cheese wax, cheesecloth, thermometers, molds for shaping hard and soft cheese, and several books on cheese production are offered. Experienced cheese producers should see the 16-page catalog for the machinery as well: a home milk pasteurizer and Wheeler's hard cheese press are available. The couple who run this firm are experienced cheese producers, and can answer your questions by phone or letter.

Special Factors: Price quote by phone or letter with SASE; minimum order is $20 with credit cards; C.O.D. orders are accepted; online with Prodigy; orders are shipped worldwide.

OPEN HOUSE

200 BALA AVE.

BALA-CYNWYD, PA 19004

215-664-1488

Information: price quote
Save: up to 40%
Pay: check, MO, MC, V
Sells: flatware, stemware, cookware, etc.
Store: same address; Monday to Saturday 10–5

Open House has been doing business since 1960, and prices its collection of tableware, cookware, cutlery, and linens at up to 40% below list or usual retail prices. There is no catalog, but you can call for a price quote on goods from Arabia, Calphalon, Chantal, Fitz & Floyd, Guzzini, Libbey, Mikasa, Nikko, Schott-Zwiesel, Tri-Chef, and other makers. If you're trying to find the best price on name-brand cookware or table settings, give this firm a call—it may be available.

Special Factor: Minimum order is $25.

PEERLESS RESTAURANT SUPPLIES

1124 S. GRAND BLVD.
ST. LOUIS, MO 63104
314-664-0400
FAX: 314-664-8102

Catalog: $6
Save: 40% average
Pay: check or MO
Sells: commercial cookware and restaurant equipment
Store: same address; Monday to Friday 8–5, Saturday 9–12 noon

Six dollars brings you the hefty Peerless catalog, which has everything you need to set up a professional kitchen or restaurant dining room, except the food. Since so many of the appliances and utensils can do double duty in home kitchens, the catalog makes a good investment if you're planning any significant kitchenware purchases.

Peerless represents over 2,000 manufacturers of everything from diner sugar shakers to walk-in refrigerators: tableware, trays and carts, bar accessories, restaurant seating, table linens and kitchen textiles, cookware, ranges and ovens, refrigerators, sinks, work tables, cleaning supplies and equipment, ice machines, dishwashers, and much more. Sample offerings include Libbey glassware, Hall and Buffalo china, cutlery by Chicago Cutlery and Dexter Russell, WearEver pots and pans, Vollrath stainless steel stock pots and chafing dishes, Rubbermaid's professional line of janitorial storage, and food-service containers, Detecto food scales, Hamilton Beach and Waring professional bar appliances, Peerless' own commercial cleaners and polishes, Seco wire shelves, Market Forge steamers, and Robot Coupe food processors. Peerless also sells cooking equipment by Castle, Dean, Frymaster, Hobart, Montague, Southbend, and Vulcan; commercial microwave ovens from MenuMaster and Panasonic; refrigeration from Delfield, Ice-O-Matic, Kelvinator, Raetone, Scotsman, Traulsen, and True; Eagle sinks, In-Sink-Erator commercial disposers, ventilation equipment, and much more.

If you know what you want by manufacturer and model number, you can call or write for a price quote—but the catalog is worth the $6 fee if you're buying more than a couple of items. Food-service professionals should note the services Peerless can provide, including facility design, installation, construction supervision, concept development, and equipment leasing. Used kitchenware is available at big savings, and if you get to St. Louis, stop in and check out the "Bargain Room," which features closeouts.

Special Factors: Quantity discounts are available; authorized returns are accepted within 30 days for exchange, refund, or credit (a 10% restocking fee may be charged, or 20% on special orders).

ZABAR'S & CO., INC.

**2245 BROADWAY
NEW YORK, NY 10024
800-221-3347
212-787-2000**

Catalog: free
Save: up to 50%
Pay: check, MO, MC, V, AE, DC
Sells: gourmet food, cookware, and housewares
Store: same address; Monday to Friday 8–7:30, Saturday 8 A.M.–midnight, Sunday 9–6; housewares mezzanine daily 9–6

Zabar's, thought of by many as New York City's ultimate deli, offers the better part of North America a sampling from its famed counters and housewares mezzanine via a 62-page catalog. Zabar's has been around since 1934, and offers savings of up to 50% on name-brand kitchenware, and competitive prices on foodstuffs.

Past catalogs have offered smoked Scottish, Norwegian, and Irish salmon, plum pudding, peppercorns, Bahlsen cookies and confections, pâtés, mustards, crackers, escargot, Lindt and Droste chocolate, Tiptree preserves, Dresden stollen, olive oil, prosciutto and other deli meats, and similar gourmet fare. The cookware selections include Mauviel hotel-weight copper pots and pans (send a postcard for a price list); Calphalon, Cuisinart Commercial, Le Creuset, Magnalite, and Spring of Switzerland equipment; Krups and Simac machines, DeLonghi, and Melitta coffee makers, KitchenAid food processors, Mouli kitchen tools, and products by Henckels, T-Fal, Wagner, Wüstof-Trident, and other firms. Zabar's distinguishes itself among kitchenware vendors for the enormous selection of goods and the substantial discounts. The catalog features a representative selection from the store, but price quotes aren't given over the phone—if you don't see it in the catalog, you'll have to visit the store.

Special Factors: Phone orders are not recommended; minimum order is $10.

SEE ALSO

Bernie's Discount Center, Inc. • *microwave ovens and kitchen appliances* • **APPLIANCES**

Bruce Medical Supply • *food preparation equipment for those with limited strength and mobility* • **MEDICINE**

Cabela's Inc. • *camping cookware, stoves, implements* • **SPORTS**

CISCO • *garbage disposals, sinks, etc.* • **HOME: MAINTENANCE**

Clothcrafters, Inc. • *kitchen textiles and kitchen utensils* • **GENERAL MERCHANDISE**

Coppa Woodworking Inc. • *butcher block tables* • **HOME: MAINTENANCE**

Cordon Brew • *coffeemakers and brewing equipment* • **FOOD**

Betty Crocker Enterprises • *cutlery, cookware, and kitchen gadgets* • **GENERAL MERCHANDISE**

Current, Inc. • *canning labels, recipe boxes, etc.* • **BOOKS**

Grandma's Spice Shop • *spice racks, wine racks, mortar and pestle sets, teapots, etc.* • **FOOD**

Jessica's Biscuit • *cookbooks* • **BOOKS**

E.C. Kraus Wine & Beermaking Supplies • *bottle washers, cherry pitters, funnels, corkscrews* • **FOOD**

Lixx Labelz • *custom-designed kitchen labels* • **GENERAL MERCHANDISE**

LVT Price Quote Hotline, Inc. • *microwave ovens, major appliances, etc.* • **APPLIANCES**

The New England Slate Company • *salvaged slate for countertops* • **HOME: MAINTENANCE**

The Paper Wholesaler • *disposable bakeware and cake-decorating supplies* • **GENERAL MERCHANDISE**

Penzeys' Spice House • *pepper mills and spice jars* • **FOOD**

Percy's Inc. • *major appliances* • **APPLIANCES**

Plastic BagMart • *garbage can liners* • **OFFICE: SMALL BUSINESS**

Robin Importers, Inc. • *kitchen cutlery, knife blocks, pepper mills, etc.* • **HOME: TABLE SETTINGS**

S & S Sound City • *microwave ovens* • **APPLIANCES**

Simpson & Vail, Inc. • *teapots, coffee makers, grinders, filters, etc.* • **FOOD**

Mr. Spiceman • *kitchen gadgets* • **FOOD**

Sultan's Delight, Inc. • *Turkish coffee pots and cups, mamoul and falafel molds, mortars and pestles* • **FOOD**

Walnut Acres Organic Farms • *cookware, bakeware, serving pieces, etc.* • **FOOD**

West Marine • *galley gear* • **AUTO**

Weston Bowl Mill • *woodenware, knives, and kitchen helpers* • **GENERAL MERCHANDISE**

Linen

Bed, bath, and table textiles, accessories,

and services

Why wait for a white sale, when you can buy your sheets, towels, pillows, and table linens from discounters who sell at savings of up to 60% every day, year-round? Some of the firms listed here offer both first-quality and irregular goods, and some sell only first-quality—ask before placing your order to be sure you're getting what you want. In addition to goods from the major mills, several of these firms provide sheets to fit waterbeds and oddly shaped mattresses, will rejuvenate down pillows and comforters, and make bed ruffles and coordinating lamp shades to match your sheets or bedroom fabric.

Caring for your bed, bath, and table textiles properly can mean they'll give you years more wear, so follow the manufacturers' care instructions. Protect your down-filled bedding with duvets or pillowslips, and when you have to wash it, use mild detergent, warm water, and the gentle cycle. Never store down-filled goods in cedar or camphor, since they'll pick up those odors permanently.

ALDEN COMFORT MILLS

Save: up to 40%
Pay: check, MO, MC, V, AE, Discover, Optima
Sells: down-filled bedding, and custom services
Store: 1708 14th St., Plano, TX; Monday to Friday 8–5, Saturday 9–4

P.O. BOX 75086-0055
PLANO, TX 75086-0055
214-423-4000
Catalog: $2, refundable

Alden Comfort Mills was founded in 1947 by Joe R. Pool, who later went into law and became a Congressional representative. Alden is still run by the Pool family, which offers its own line of down-filled comforters and pillows, as well as custom services.

The 16-page color catalog features six comforter styles and weights, running from a summer-weight, channel-stitched style (full, under $110) to the sumptuous "Newport," 64 ounces of down (full, under $270). Featherbeds, crib comforters, and both bed and accent pillows filled with down and "featherfluff" feather mix are offered, as well as well-priced dust ruffles, shams, cases, and duvet covers.

If your comforter cover has seen better days but the down itself still has good loft, it's a candidate for Alden's custom department, which can recover, refill, and even reconfigure the comforter to create a longer drop than the original (to suit the deeper mattresses being made today; more down will be required). Prices are reasonable for custom work and much lower than the cost of replacing good-quality bedding. Down and feather pillows can also be recovered and restuffed, and even old wool comforters can be given a facelift. Call for details, or see the catalog.

Special Factor: Satisfaction is guaranteed.

BEDROOM SECRETS

310 E. MILITARY
P.O. BOX 529
FREMONT, NE 68025
800-955-2559
402-727-4004
FAX: 402-727-1817

Catalog: $2
Save: up to 40%
Pay: check, MO, MC, V, Discover
Sells: linens for bed and bath
Store: mail order only

Bedroom Secrets specializes in ensemble dressing for the sleeping chamber and bath, for a polished, pulled-together look. The 30-page catalog is heavy on floral motifs, from sedate bouquets on striped grounds to abstract gardens in fully saturated color. Most of the patterns are offered in sheet sets, comforters, accent pillows, window treatments, and many are presented with coordinating bath accoutrements—shower curtains, towels, rugs, hampers, and even matching mirrors and toothbrush holders. Bedroom Secrets represents some of the best-known names, including Laura Ashley, Collier Campbell, Croscill, Gear Club, Di Lewis, Deborah Mallow, Louis Nichole, Revman, Sanderson, and Eileen West. Discounts on many items average 25%, but some lines are priced nearly 40% below regular retail. And there's another advantage to buying here: The custom department can round out your decorating scheme with made-to-order window treatments, dust ruffles, and whatever else you need to complete your rooms. Coordinating fabrics and wall coverings are available, as well as window treatments and home furnishings. Call for more information, or send $2 for the catalog.

Special Factors: Satisfaction is guaranteed; resalable returns are accepted; minimum order is three yards (if fabric).

DOMESTICATIONS

P.O. BOX 41
DEPT. DOM9609
HANOVER, PA 17333-0041
800-782-7722, EXT.
  DOM9609

Catalog: $2
Save: up to 75%
Pay: check, MO, MC, V, AE, CB, DC, Discover
Sells: bed and bath linens
Store: mail order only

Domestications, a company in Hanover Direct's family of catalogs, offers a colorful selection of linens for bed, bath, and table, plus well-priced home decorating items. The 96-page catalog emphasizes sheets and bedding, with everything from paisley prints and florals to cartoon characters and a spectrum of solids. Selections from Cannon, Fieldcrest, Martex, Dan River, Springmaid, J.P. Stevens, Wamsutta, and Domestications' exclusive line, have been offered in the past. All-cotton and blend sheet sets are available, blankets, bedspreads, and comforters as well as pillows, mattress pads, and hard-to-find items like sofa sheets. The rest of the catalog features a variety of fashion-forward home accents—tablecloths, window treatments, lamps, carpets, tableware, and even occasional furniture, and prices run from market rate to bargain basement.

Special Factors: Satisfaction is guaranteed; returns are accepted; minimum order is $20 with credit cards.

ELDRIDGE TEXTILE CO.

277 GRAND ST., DEPT. L
NEW YORK, NY 10002
212-925-1523
FAX: 212-219-9542

Catalog: $3 refundable
Save: up to 40%
Pay: check, MO, MC, V
Sells: bed, bath, and table linens
Store: same address; Sunday to Friday 9–5:30

 ¡Si!

Eldridge has been selling soft goods and housewares since 1940, and offers mail-order customers savings of up to 40% on bed, bath, and table linens. Fully coordinated bed, bath, and window ensembles are available from Laura Ashley, Bill Blass, Cameo, Collier Campbell, Croscill, Crown Crafts, Dakotah, DiLewis, Faribo, Fieldcrest, Home

Innovations, Martex, Newmark (bath rugs), Pacific Designs, Phoenix (down products), Revman, André Richard, Saturday Knight, Springmaid, Utica, Wamsutta, Eileen West, and other firms. Some of the best-selling sheet and towel lines are featured in the 32-page color catalog, as well as upholstered headboards, ottomans, and footstools.

Special Factors: Price quote by phone or letter with SASE; returns of unused goods are accepted for refund or credit; minimum order is $25.

HEAVENLY DOWN

419 ALLAN CT.
HEALDSBURG, CA
95448-9931
707-431-1400
FAX: 707-431-1474

Catalog: free
Save: up to 60%
Pay: check, MO, MC, V
Sells: down-filled bedding and linens
Store: mail order only

Heavenly Down was founded several years ago by a couple who'd shopped for a comforter themselves, and were amazed by the discrepancies between price and quality. Inspired by what they knew they could offer, they went into business themselves. They sell well-priced comforters and pillows, and use 550 to 700 fill-power white goose down, encased in downproof, all-cotton cambric (230 to 312 thread count). Prices begin at under $80 for the twin-sized "Country Classic I" lightweight/summer comforter, with quilted box-stitch construction and 18 ounces of down, and top at about $500 for the king-sized "Royal Plush," with box-baffle construction and 64 ounces of goose down. The catalog descriptions include the fill power, construction method, thread count of the cover, color selection (usually white or bone), and other details. And if you already have the bedding but can't find nice duvet covers and shams at the right price, take heart: Heavenly Down sells not only the classic all-cotton button-closure cover, but also the sort of covers available through upmarket linens catalogs—but for much less. Matching shams are available, and Heavenly Down also sells feather beds, down robes for women, and a down-filled sleeping bag.

Special Factors: Satisfaction is guaranteed; returns are accepted for exchange, refund, or credit.

HARRIS LEVY, INC.

278 GRAND ST.,
 DEPT. WBM
NEW YORK, NY 10002
800-221-7750
212-226-3102
FAX: 212-334-9360

Catalog: free
Save: up to 60%
Pay: check, MO, MC, V, AE, Optima
Sells: bed, bath, and table linens; kitchen and closet accessories
Store: same address; Monday to Thursday 9–5, Friday 9–4, Sunday 9–4:30

 ¡Si!

Levy, established in 1894, is one of the plums of New York City's Lower East Side—a firm that sells the crème de la crème of bed, bath, and table linens at savings of up to 60%. One-of-a-kind and imported items are available in the store, and *none* of the stock is seconds or discontinued merchandise. What makes Levy special are things like heavy Matelasse blanket covers at about half the price charged by luxury linens catalogs, a sleep connoisseur's choice of pillows, and even mundane items like bathmats in fresh designs.

Levy's imports include Egyptian cotton percale and linen sheets, English kitchen towels, Irish damask tablecloths, and bedding from Switzerland, England, France, and Italy—all worth a trip to the store. Mail-order shoppers can call or write for the free catalog or price quotes on bed and bath linens from the major names: Cannon, Croscill, Crown Crafts, Fieldcrest, Martex, Palais Royal, Revman, Dan River, Springmaid, J.P. Stevens, and Wamsutta. The catalog also gives a sampling of Levy's large selection of bath accessories, shower curtains, rugs, towels, closet organizers, hangers, and travel accessories. Levy specializes in custom services and can provide monogramming and sheets in special sizes and shapes, tablecloths, dust ruffles, curtains, pillowcases, and other products from stock sheets or your own fabric.

Please note: Phone orders are accepted Monday to Friday 10–4.

Special Factors: Price quote by phone, fax, or letter with SASE; store is closed Saturdays; orders are shipped worldwide.

THE LINEN SOURCE

5401 HANGAR CT.
P.O. BOX 31151
TAMPA, FL 33631-3151
800-431-2620
FAX: 813-882-4605

Catalog: free
Save: up to 45%
Pay: check, MO, MC, V, AE, Discover
Sells: bed linens, home accessories
Store: mail order only

Why wait for a white sale when you can restyle your bedroom at a discount any day of the year? The 80-page catalog from The Linen Source features the latest fashions in bed dressing, with an emphasis on bold colors and strong graphics, and rich, romantic ensembles. The 80-page catalog shows current designs in sheets, comforters, and accessories by Laura Ashley, Burlington House, Crown Crafts, Dakotah, Fieldcrest/Cannon (Court of Versailles, Adrienne Vittadini). Gear, Martex, Dan River (Alexander Julian), Springmaid, Utica, Wamsutta, and other names. Patchwork quilts, nursery and juvenile bedding, and window treatments are all shown, as well as complementing vases, statuary, framed prints, rugs, lamps, tableware, and even nightwear. The best savings are on sheet sets, but most of the other products are competitively priced—20% to 35% off regular retail.

Special Factors: Satisfaction is guaranteed; returns are accepted.

MOTHER HART'S NATURAL PRODUCTS, INC.

P.O. BOX 4229-WBM
BOYNTON BEACH, FL
  33424-4229
407-738-5866
407-738-0732

Catalog: free
Save: 50% plus
Pay: check, MO, MC, V
Sells: natural-fiber bed and bath linens and clothing
Store: mail order only

It's not uncommon to find savings of 50%-plus on the products at Mother Hart's—chiefly textiles for bed and bath, activewear, and underthings. Past catalogs have offered stunning buys on flannel sheets and sheet blankets, as well as down pillows and comforters, fleece mattress pads, cotton duvet covers in solids and prints, box spring covers and pads, and quilted cotton comforters. Mother Hart's queen-sized, all-cotton, untreated sheets cost $28.80 at this writing, while the same kind of sheet, in the same size, costs *$110* from a luxury linens catalog. (The upmarket firm does give you 210 threads per inch to Mother's 200, but how can ten little threads be worth over $81?)

Other goods that have appeared in past catalogs include canvas luggage, shower curtains, natural-bristle hairbrushes, tote bags, handkerchiefs, cotton throws, and aprons. Note that some items may be available in limited quantities, so order promptly. All irregular goods are clearly indicated.

Special Factors: Satisfaction is guaranteed; unused returns are accepted within 30 days; orders are shipped worldwide.

J. SCHACHTER CORP.

85 LUDLOW ST.
NEW YORK, NY 10002
800-INTO-BED
212-533-1150
FAX: 718-384-7634

Catalog: $1, refundable
Save: up to 40%
Pay: check, MO, MC, V, Discover
Sells: down-filled bedding, linens, and custom services
Store: same address; Sunday to Thursday 9–5, Friday 9–2:30

 ¡Si! (see text)

Schachter has been making comforters and pillows for the bedding industry and recovering old comforters for private customers since 1919. Custom work is featured in the firm's 16-page catalog, but stock goods are also available. Schachter specializes in custom jobs: Comforters, coverlets, bed ruffles, pillow shams, duvets, and shower curtains are popular requests, and Schachter will take your sheets and create quilted blanket covers, or lightweight summer quilts, with them. Filling choices for the comforters include lambswool, polyester, white goose down, and a nonallergenic synthetic down alternative. Schachter carries bed and bath linens by the major mills—Cannon, Croscill, Fieldcrest, Martex, Springs Industries, J.P. Stevens, and Wamsutta—and labels from France, Germany, England, Switzerland, Italy, and Belgium—Bruna, Palais Royal, Peter Reed, Sferra, and Sufolla. Carter cotton bath rugs, and blankets by Atkinson, Chatham, Early's of Whitney, Faribo, and Hudson Bay are offered. Schachter's own stock comforters and accessories are all available, and the firm can recover and sterilize old down pillows and comforters.

Canadian readers, please note: Orders are delivered by UPS only.
Special Factor: Store is closed Saturdays.

SPRINGMAID-WAMSUTTA FACTORY STORE

**HWY. 9 BYPASS WEST
LANCASTER, SC 29720**

Information: price quote
Save: see text
Pay: check, MO, MC, V, AE, Discover
Sells: Springmaid and Wamsutta bed and bath linens and accessories
Store: same address; also Opelika, AL; Casa Grande, AZ; Gilroy, CA; Castle Rock and Loveland, CO; Ellenton, FL; Calhoun and Savannah, GA; Queenstown, MD; Birch Run, MI; Asheville, NC; Tannersville, PA; Fort Mill, and Lyman, SC; Pigeon Forge, TN; Gainesville and San Marcos, TX; and Fredericksburg, VA

Springmaid and Wamsutta, two respected home-textiles names owned by Springs Industries, have 15 factory stores that offer their products at tremendously low prices every day. Discontinued and irregular sheets and bedding are sold at low prices, and the stores carry complementing throw pillows, window treatments, and a range of towels, and kitchen and bath accessories, as well as a good selection of bed pillows, mattress pads, and blankets—also sold at savings.

There is no catalog, and you should call to see if what you want is in stock. Be sure you know the exact name of the style or pattern, the size needed, the color (and an alternative, if possible). The salespeople in the stores pride themselves on their good customer service, and will make every attempt to locate the item you want.

Please note: The outlet stores sell to consumers, and do not wholesale.

Special Factors: Price quote by phone; refunds "cheerfully given"; orders are shipped worldwide.

SEE ALSO

Baby Bunz & Co. • *crib bedding* • **CLOTHING: MOTHER AND CHILD**
Campmor • *sleeping bags, sleeping bag liners* • **SPORTS**

Chock Catalog Corp. • crib and bassinet bedding • **CLOTHING**

Clothcrafters, Inc. • plain cotton sheets, towels, table linens, etc. • **GENERAL MERCHANDISE**

Gettinger Feather Corp. • pillow feathers • **CRAFTS**

Gohn Bros. • sheets and blankets • **CLOTHING**

Kitchen Etc. • table linens • **HOME: KITCHEN**

D. MacGillivray & Coy. • woven blankets and tartan bedspreads • **CRAFTS**

Plexi-Craft Quality Products Corp. • acrylic bathroom accessories • **HOME: FURNISHINGS**

Retired Persons Services, Inc. • waffle-type foam bed pads • **MEDICINE**

Robin Importers, Inc. • table linens • **HOME: TABLE SETTINGS**

Rubens & Marble, Inc. • bassinet and crib sheets • **CLOTHING: MOTHER AND CHILD**

Shama Imports, Inc. • crewel-embroidered bedspreads • **HOME: DECOR**

Maintenance and Building

Hardware, tools, equipment, supplies,
and materials

Maintaining your home—keeping it clean and in good repair—can involve an enormous amount of time and energy. Consumers Union publishes a number of books to help you with everything from buying your next home to cleaning the windows. *Year-Round House Care, How to Buy a House, Condo, or Co-op, The Complete Guide to Home Repair and Maintenance, Home Security* (on locks, alarms, etc.), and *How to Clean Practically Everything* are among the titles available at this writing. See the current issue of *Consumer Reports* to order, or check your local bookstore.

For related sources, see the listings in "Tools."

FIND IT FAST

ARCHITECTURAL DETAILS • **Crawford's, Saco, Shuttercraft**
INSULATED GLASS PANELS • **Arctic Glass**
LUMBER AND FLOORING • **BRE Lumber**
PLUMBING FIXTURES • **CISCO, LIBW**
RADIATOR ENCLOSURES • **Monarch**
SCREEN DOORS AND WINDOWS • **Coppa Woodworking**
SLATE ROOFING • **New England Slate**

ARCTIC GLASS & WINDOW OUTLET

Catalog: $4, refundable
Save: up to 50%
Pay: check, MO, MC, V, Discover
Sells: exterior doors, windows, skylights, glass panels
Store: I-94 at Hammond Exit, 35 miles east of St. Paul, MN; Monday and Thursday 8–8, Tuesday, Wednesday, Friday, and Saturday 8–5; also U.S. Rte. 53 and WI Rte. 124, Chippewa Falls, WI

RTE. I-W
HAMMOND, WI 54015
800-428-9276
715-796-2292
FAX: 715-796-2295

Joseph Bacon began his business after discovering that second-quality patio door panes doubled perfectly as passive solar panels in the greenhouse he was building—and cost up to 50% less. Since founding Arctic Glass in 1979, he's watched it outgrow several facilities, and increase revenues 2,000%.

Arctic Glass sells surplus and second-quality patio door panels from two of the best-known manufacturers in the business. Different types of double and triple panes are available (some with low E coating) and, except for the middle panes of triple-pane panels, most of the glass is 3/16" thick; all of the panes are double-sealed. The flaws of the seconds shouldn't affect the performance of the panes, and suitable applications and uses are listed in the literature. Arctic also stocks Velux skylights and the complete line of Weather Shield skylights, doors, and windows—wood-framed casements, tilts, slider, direct-set, eyebrow, and fanlight windows and a variety of doors. Hurd and Kolbe & Kolbe windows and doors (no skylights) are available, as well as goods from Caradco.

Prices average 10% to 50% below list, and all of the panels are guaranteed against leakage or failure for ten years. The warranty terms and installation instructions, including retrofitting, are detailed in the literature. And if you have any questions, you can talk them over with Mr. Bacon himself.

Special Factors: Shipments are made to 49 of the 50 states; quantity discounts are available; minimum crating charge is $50 for mail orders; returns are accepted within 30 days for exchange, refund, or credit; minimum order is $50; orders are shipped worldwide.

BRE LUMBER

10741 CARTER RD.
TRAVERSE CITY, MI 49684
800-968-0074
616-946-0043
FAX: 616-946-6221

Information: price quote
Save: up to 30%
Pay: check, MO, MC, V
Sells: lumber, flooring, hardwood, etc.
Store: same address; Monday to Friday 8–5,
Saturday 8–12 noon

Home remodeling involves endless dilemmas, like realizing that prefinished parquet floor tiles have their merits, but you want a *real* floor. If that's out of line with the budget, BRE Lumber may be able to help. BRE sells the genuine article, at a price better than those of other specialty dealers (though you won't beat the floor-in-a-box prices). BRE's stock includes cabinet-grade lumber flooring, wide-plank flooring, paneling, molding, stairs, parts, and "dimensional lumber." Dozens of species of flooring woods are available, include maple, Padauk, Cocobolo, Bubinga, Jatoba (Brazilian cherry), Wenge, and teak, among others, and the stock is "long and clear." Tatajuba decking (Brazilian teak), which is said to be five times harder than redwood, is also available. You can save up to 30% on the delivered cost of the flooring, and sometimes more, depending on prices prevailing in your area. If you're planning to build or remodel, get BRE's current price list and samples ($15 plus shipping) and consider all the options before buying veneer-faced particle board. If you can't get what you need from stock, take advantage of BRE's custom millwork services.

Special Factors: Price quote by phone, fax, or letter with SASE; orders are shipped worldwide.

CISCO

**CHANUTE IRON &
SUPPLY CO.**
*1502 W. CHERRY ST.
CHANUTE, KS 66720-1005
316-431-9290
FAX: 316-431-7354*

Information: price quote
Save: up to 40%
Pay: check or MO
Sells: plumbing supplies and fixtures
Store: same address; Monday to Friday 8–5,
Saturday 8–12 noon

CISCO stocks a full range of fixtures and equipment for plumbing, heating, and air conditioning. CISCO has been selling plumbing supplies, fixtures, and tools since 1941, and offers a portion of the inventory by mail, at savings of 25% to 40%. Delta and Moen faucets, Insinkerator garbage disposers, Burnham boilers, Miami Carey medicine chests and accessories, and whirlpools and fixtures by Aqua Glass, Benjamin, Jason, and Passport are available. There are Elkay and Moen sinks, Crane fixtures, spa and swimming pool accessories and parts (no chemicals), tools by Rigid, and the professional line of tools by Makita. Replacement parts for all types of faucets are also stocked.

Please note: No catalog is available.

Special Factors: Price quote by phone, fax, or letter with SASE; minimum order is $10; orders are shipped worldwide.

COPPA WOOD-WORKING INC.

*1231 PARAISO AVE.
SAN PEDRO, CA 90731
310-548-4142
FAX: 310-548-5332*

Catalog: $1
Save: up to 40%
Pay: check, MO, MC, V
Sells: Adirondack furniture, screen doors, windows, etc.
Store: mail order only

Coppa Woodworking is a small firm that manufactures Adirondack-style furniture, screen doors, and windows (nonmovable) in a variety of finishes, woods, and other options, at prices up to 40% below those charged elsewhere for comparable products. (You know you're dealing directly with the people who make the goods when the catalog itself smells of fresh lumber!) Classic low-slung, slat-back Adirondack chair styles are featured, from the children's model for about $30 to the "fan-back" for under $70 to a 51-inch-wide loveseat for about $100. All of the seating and complementing footrests and side tables are made of unfinished pine that can be stained (white, blue, or green) for a small fee. Old-fashioned butcher block tables with 2-1/2" red oak tops begin at $126, and other woods and custom-painted bases are available.

The other side of Coppa's business is screen doors, windows, and sidelights (panels); the doors can be produced in over 100 styles to suit every decor. A number of options are available, including wood choice (Douglas fir, sugar pine, red oak, mahogany), stain and varnish, single or double-door fixtures, custom sizes, built-in pet doors, and a choice of fiberglass screening materials (including heavy-duty cat-proof mesh). Prices begin at a mere $34 for the plainest style in pine, and custom charges are quite reasonable. And if you'd like a feature or detail not mentioned, be sure to ask, since Coppa may be able to provide.

Special Factors: Satisfaction is guaranteed; returns are accepted.

CRAWFORD'S OLD HOUSE STORE

550 ELIZABETH ST.,
    ROOM 105
WAUKESHA, WI
    53186-4575
800-556-7878

Flyer: free
Save: up to 30%
Pay: check, MO, MC, V, AE
Sells: wood doorstops and corner protectors
Store: mail order only

Crawford's Old House Store offers a number of items useful to home renovators: the oak and beech corner beads are quite popular, a welcome alternative to clear plastic corner protectors, and they're priced from under $11. Bullseye-design corner blocks, used at the top corners of door and window frames, cost $3 or less, depending on the quantity ordered. And the solid wood doorstops with rubber bumpers can be stained or painted to match your woodwork; they're as little as $2 each in quantity. The free flyer also lists a number of catalogs of period plumbing fixtures, hardware, and accessories; they're available for specified charges, but you can also call or write with your specific needs.

Special Factors: Minimum order is $5, $15 with credit cards; quantity discounts are available; orders are shipped worldwide.

LIBW

**717 E. JERICHO TPKE.,
SUITE 294
HUNTINGTON STATION,
NY 11746
800-553-0663
FAX: 516-694-3494**

Catalog: $5, credited to order(see text)
Save: up to 33%
Pay: check, MO, MC, V
Sells: bathroom fixtures and accessories
Store: mail order only

Renovating that old bathroom can run into large sums fast, so it's nice to be able to economize on more than just the towels. LIBW helps you save on the fixtures themselves, with discounts averaging 25% to 33% on faucets, medicine cabinets, mirrors, shower doors, whirlpools, and even door and cabinet hardware. LIBW has been in business since 1989, and represents Altmans, American Standard, Artistic Brass, Baldwin, Dornbracht, Eljer, Grohe, Jacuzzi, Jado, Kohler, Omnia, and Pearl, among others. You can send for the catalog ($5, credited to your order), or write or call for quotes and shipping charges on specific items.

Special Factor: A 5% surcharge is added to credit card payments.

MONARCH

**DEPT. WBMC
2744 ARKANSAS DR.
BROOKLYN, NY 11234
201-796-4117
FAX: 201-796-7717**

Brochure: $1, refundable
Save: up to 35%
Pay: check, MO, MC, V
Sells: all-steel radiator enclosures
Store: mail order only

If you've tired of looking at the exposed ribs of the radiators in your home, consider enclosures. They not only render the unsightly heating fixtures more decorative, but also help to direct the heat into the room. Monarch sells enclosures in two dozen styles, ranging from simple models with plain grilles to designs that incorporate built-in cabinets and bookshelves. Unlike cheaper enclosures, Monarch's are constructed of heavy steel and come with closed backs, and price comparisons show savings of up to 35%. The tops of some of the models are insulated, all of the joints are welded, and the finishes include four stock semi-gloss enamel colors. Custom sizes and other colors, including woodgrain finishes, are available for a surcharge. Monarch's literature includes a guide to measuring your radiator prior to ordering. (Please note that, like window treatments and other goods ordered to measure, the enclosures are not returnable.)

Special Factor: Inquiries from contractors and institutions are welcomed.

THE NEW ENGLAND SLATE COMPANY

R.D. #1, BURR POND RD.
SUDBURY, VT 05733
802-247-8809
FAX: 802-247-0089

Brochure: free
Save: up to 50%
Pay: check or MO
Sells: new and recycled roofing and flooring slate
Store: same address; Monday to Friday 8–4:30

The Taconic Overthrust, an area running along the Vermont–New York border, holds this country's only major deposits of colored slate. Chuck Smid founded The New England Slate Company in 1975, after he had roofed his newly built home in slate salvaged from a nearby barn and figured there was a market in recycled (salvaged) slate.

The New England Slate Company sells both the slate of the area, and reclaimed slate salvaged from buildings all over the Eastern seaboard. Grey, green, purple, brown, and the highly coveted red slate are available, as well as black slate from Maine, Vermont, and Pennsylvania. (The Maine slate, known as "monson" slate, is no longer actively quarried and can be obtained only through recyclers.) Slate is pricier than more commonly used roofing materials such as asphalt and fiberglass tile, but its 100-year-plus lifespan makes it much more cost effective. It's also the only appropriate choice for many historic properties, as well as universities and other public buildings. New England Slate's roofing line features new and salvaged slate in random widths and standard 3/16" to 1/4" thicknesses, in 12" to 24" lengths. Prices at this writing run from $195 for a square (100 square feet) of "semi-weathering green" in 12" lengths, to $1,300 for a square of new, "unfading red" in 24" lengths. (Salvaged slate, when available, costs 20% to 25% less than newly quarried material.) Do-it-yourselfers can also buy the slate hammers, cutters, and rippers needed for the job from New England Slate, as well as copper roofing nails, snow guards, roofing gloves, and even "the slater's bible," *Slate Roofs*. Custom cutting and color matching services can be provided.

The New England Slate Company runs another firm, Vermont Cobble Slate, that offers salvaged slate for use in flooring, hearths, kitchen counters, bathrooms, and as veneer on vertical surfaces. Vermont Cobble's brochure shows several installations in which the rich texture of the material and the interplay of colors are used to maximum effect, and includes guidelines for setting and grouting the flooring and veneer. Boxes of ten square feet of random-sized pieces cost $55, offered in black, purple, green, grey, and mixed colors. The prices for salvaged materials are the best, but New England Slate is very competitive on newly quarried slate as well.

Special Factors: Satisfaction is guaranteed; orders are shipped worldwide.

SACO MANUFACTURING & WOODWORKING

P.O. BOX 149-WBM
SACO, ME 04072
207-284-6613
FAX: 207-284-9707

Flyers: free with SASE (see text)
Save: up to 50%
Pay: check or MO
Sells: hand-turned newel posts and lampposts
Store: 39 Lincoln St., Saco, ME; Monday to Friday 7–3:30

Saco Manufacturing has been doing business since 1872, and it still sells some of the same things it offered at the turn of the century. One is turned lampposts. These are center-bored, unfinished pine posts that are ready to be finished, wired, fitted with a lighting fixture, and installed outside your home. The posts are available in heights from 8' to 12', and are priced from $75 for the 8' length. Saco sells newel, porch, and mailbox posts in pine and other woods, in a choice of several finial styles. "Colonial Columns" and pilasters are also available; these custom-made supports can be created in Doric or Tuscan styles, or to the specifications of your contractor or architect.

Please specify the literature you want when you send your self-addressed, stamped envelope: the flyer on lampposts, Colonial Columns, or newel posts and finials.

Special Factor: Price quote by letter with SASE (include dimension requirements).

SHUTTERCRAFT

282 STEPSTONE HILL RD.
GUILFORD, CT 06437
203-453-1973

Brochure: free with SASE
Save: up to 30%
Pay: check, MO, MC, V
Sells: interior and exterior house shutters and hardware
Store: same address; Monday to Friday 9–5

Authentic, "historic" exterior wood shutters with movable louvers are sold here at prices well below those charged for custom-milled shutters. An added advantage: They look more substantial than the vinyl versions, and the firm's literature points out that "real wood shutters are naturally ventillating and do not cause the wood siding behind them to rot." Shuttercraft's white pine and cedar shutters can be bought in widths up to 30", and in lengths to 144", in shapes that include half-circle tops, Gothic arches, and cutouts in the raised panels. (A pine tree is shown, but Shuttercraft will execute your pattern for $7 per pair of shutters.) Also available are fixed-louver shutters, exterior raised-panel shutters in Western cedar, interior styles, S-shaped holdbacks, and shutter hinges. Shuttercraft will prime, paint, trim, and rabbet your shutters for a fee; details are given in the brochure.

Special Factor: Shipping is included on shutters up to 60" long and on orders totaling $400 or more; orders are shipped worldwide.

SEE ALSO

AAA-Vacuum Cleaner Service Center • *floor-care machines and supplies* • **APPLIANCES**
ABC Vacuum Cleaner Warehouse • *floor-care machines and supplies* • **APPLIANCES**
Bob's Superstrong Greenhouse Plastic • *woven polyethylene and anchoring straps* • **FARM**
Clegg's Handyman Supply • *home fix-up items, plumbing and electrical supplies, etc.* • **TOOLS**
Clothcrafters, Inc. • *mosquito netting and flannel polishing cloths* • **GENERAL MERCHANDISE**
Discount Appliance Centers • *floor-care machines and supplies* • **APPLIANCES**
Fan Authority/Lighting Authority • *ceiling fans and lighting* • **HOME: DECOR**

King's Chandelier Co. • replacement parts for chandeliers • **HOME: DECOR**

LPI Discount Pool & Spa Co. • swimming pool maintenance equipment and supplies • **SPORTS**

Manufacturer's Supply • woodburning furnaces and heaters • **TOOLS**

Midamerica Vacuum Cleaner Supply Co. • floor-care machines, supplies, and parts • **APPLIANCES**

Percy's Inc. • garbage disposals • **APPLIANCES**

Safe Specialties, Inc. • safes for home, office, and business • **OFFICE**

Sewin' in Vermont • floor-care machines • **APPLIANCES**

Staples, Inc. • cleaning products, janitorial supplies, paper towels, brooms, trash bags, etc. • **OFFICE**

Value-tique, Inc. • safes for home, office, and business • **OFFICE**

Table Settings

China, crystal, glass, flatware, woodenware,
and related goods

Buying active patterns of tableware is as easy as picking up the phone and calling one of the firms listed here. But if your pattern—in china, crystal, or silver—is discontinued, you'll have to turn to a specialist. Two of these firms—Beverly Bremer and Buschemeyers—sell discontinued silver flatware (also called "estate" silver). If you're missing pieces of a china or crystal pattern, write to Replacements, Ltd., 302 Gallimore Dairy Rd., Greensboro, NC 27400-9723, or call 919-275-7224. Replacements has over 250,000 pieces in stock, and can help you identify your pattern if you're not sure of the name. The China Connection is another such source for discontinued china patterns, by such manufacturers as Castleton, Haviland, Lenox, and Noritake. Send details on the maker, pattern, and piece you're trying to match to The China Connection, 329 Main St., P.O. Box 972, Pineville, NC 28134.

BARRONS

22790 HESLOP DR.
NOVI, MI 48050
800-538-6340
313-348-0816
FAX: 313-344-4342

Catalog: free
Save: up to 40%
Pay: check, MO, MC, V, Discover
Sells: tableware and giftware
Store: mail order only

Barrons has been selling fine tableware since 1975, and while there is no store, Barrons does offer savings of up to 40% on the list prices of china, crystal, flatware, and gifts, and stocks over 1,500 patterns. Past catalogs have showcased popular lines of china from Block, Fitz & Floyd, Franciscan, Gorham, Hutschenreuther, Johnson Brothers, Lenox, Mikasa, Minton, Nikko, Noritake, Royal Albert, Royal Doulton, Royal Worcester, Spode, and Wedgwood. Crystal from Atlantis, Gorham, Lenox, and Mikasa is offered, and you can save on stainless steel, silver plate, and sterling flatware from Dansk, Gorham, International, Kirk-Stieff, Lunt, Mikasa, Oneida, Reed & Barton, Towle, Wallace, and Yamazaki. Goebel and Royal Doulton figurines, Gorham crystal gifts, Towle silver serving pieces, and other collectibles and accessories are also sold at a discount.

Special Factors: Satisfaction is guaranteed; returns are accepted within 30 days for exchange, refund, or credit; orders are shipped worldwide.

BEVERLY BREMER SILVER SHOP

DEPT. WBMC
3164 PEACHTREE RD., N.E.
ATLANTA, GA 30305
404-261-4009

Information: inquire (see text)
Save: up to 75%
Pay: check, MC, V, AE, Discover
Sells: new and estate silver flatware, holloware, gifts, etc.
Store: same address; Monday to Saturday 10–5

Beverly Bremer herself and her daughter Mimi preside over this shop, which has an astounding inventory of sterling, from new flatware to old loving cups. "The store with the silver lining," which opened in 1975, is worth a detour if you're traveling anywhere around Atlanta. But if you can't get there, call or write with your needs—Beverly Bremer does nearly half her business by mail. The briskest trade is done in supplying missing pieces of sterling silverware, in new, discontinued, and hard-to-find patterns. If you know the pattern name, call to see whether the piece you want is in stock; you can also send a photocopy of both sides of a sample piece if you're unsure of the pattern.

Although the shop's specialty is flatware, the shelves and cases sparkle with vases, epergnes, picture frames, candlesticks, jewelry, christening cups, thimbles, and other treasures. Silver collectors should note that over 1,000 patterns are carried in stock here, "beautiful as new," and Ms. Bremer tells us that, unless noted, there are no monograms on the old silver. (She doesn't sell silver on which monograms have been *removed,* either.) Request a current inventory list of your flatware pattern.

Special Factors: Sterling silver pieces are bought; appraisals are performed; orders are shipped worldwide.

BUSCHEMEYERS SILVER EXCHANGE

515 S. FOURTH AVE.
LOUISVILLE, KY 40202
800-626-4555
FAX: 502-589-9628

Information: price quote (see text)
Save: up to 40%
Pay: check, MO, MC, V, AE, DC, Discover, Optima
Sells: new and discontinued flatware
Store: same address; Monday to Friday 10–5, Saturday 10–4

Buschemeyers can help you save on purchases of new flatware—sterling, silverplate, and holloware. If you're looking for a discontinued pattern, Buschemeyers may have what you need. The firm stocks "all active and inactive sterling and silverplate flatware," including all current American-made sterling patterns, and will put your name on a want list if what you want isn't available. You can call, write, or fax for a price quote on active silver lines, and call (if you know the pattern) about discontinued pieces, or send a photocopy of the front of a teaspoon or fork if you're not sure of the name. Please remember to include your name, address, phone number, and any other information you have about the piece with your query.

Special Factor: Orders are shipped worldwide.

CHINA CABINET, INC.

24 WASHINGTON ST.
TENAFLY, NJ 07670
201-567-2711

Information: price quote
Save: up to 50%
Pay: check, MO, MC, V, Discover, Optima
Sells: tableware
Store: same address; Monday to Saturday 10–6, Thursday 10–8

China Cabinet, in business since 1988, represents scores of manufacturers of fine china, crystal, and flatware. In addition to such widely available brands as Dansk, Gorham, Orrefors, Royal Doulton, and Wedgwood, China Cabinet offers goods from Baccarat, Ceralene Limoges, Arthur Court, Gien, Godinger, Haviland Limoges, Jacques Jugeat, Silvestri, and Wilton, among others. Savings run up to 50%, and giftware from selected manufacturers is offered as well as place settings and serving pieces.

Special Factors: Minimum order is $25 with credit cards; orders are shipped worldwide.

THE CHINA WAREHOUSE

P.O. BOX 21797
CLEVELAND, OH 44121
800-321-3212
216-831-2557

Catalog: free
Save: up to 40%
Pay: check, MO, MC, V
Sells: tableware and gifts
Store: mail order only

The China Warehouse has been in business since 1983 and offers "all major china and crystal lines," as well as flatware, decorative accessories, giftware, and collectible figurines. The brands include Armetale, Block, Gorham, Lenox, Noritake, Orrefors, Reed & Barton, Riedel, Royal Copenhagen, Royal Doulton, Sasaki, Spode, Towle, Wallace, Waterford, Wedgwood, and dozens of others, in china, crystal, and stainless and sterling flatware. A catalog is available, but you can also call or write for a price quote.

Special Factors: Orders are shipped worldwide.

COINWAYS/ANTIQUES LTD.

---

136 CEDARHURST AVE.
CEDARHURST, NY 11516
800-645-2102
516-374-1970
FAX: 516-374-3218

Information: price quote
Save: up to 75%
Pay: check, MO, MC, V, AE, DC, Discover, Optima
Sells: new and used sterling flatware
Store: same address; Monday to Friday 10–5:30, Wednesday 10–7:30, Saturday 10–4

Coinways/Antiques Ltd. should be on your list of firms to call when the garbage disposer claims one of your good teaspoons—especially if it's from an old or discontinued pattern. Coinways, which has been in business since 1979, sells both new and used ("estate") sterling flatware, by the piece or in full sets.

You'll save up to 75% on the suggested retail or market prices of silver manufactured by Alvin, Amston, Dominick & Haff, Durgin, Easterling, Gorham, International, Kirk-Stieff, Lunt, Manchester, National, Oneida, Reed & Barton, Royal Crest, State House, Tiffany, Towle, Tuttle, Wallace, Westmoreland, F.M. Whiting, and other firms. If you're replacing a piece in an old pattern that's still active, try to find a piece of the same vintage. (Over the years, some manufacturers have reduced the amount of silver they use in each piece, so that a fork made today will be lighter and feel less substantial than the same piece, circa 1930.) If you write to Coinways for a quote, note the name of the piece, its length and shape, and include a rubbing of the design if you don't know the pattern name.

Coinways/Antiques Ltd. is offering readers a discount of 5% on all orders. Be sure to identify yourself as a WBMC reader when you order, and deduct the discount from the cost of the goods only. This WBMC reader discount expires February 1, 1995.

Special Factor: Orders are shipped worldwide.

MICHAEL C. FINA CO.

580 FIFTH AVE.
NEW YORK, NY 10036
800-BUY-FINA
718-937-8484
FAX: 718-937-7193

Catalog: free
Save: up to 60%
Pay: check, MO, MC, V, Discover
Sells: jewelry, tableware, and giftware
Store: 3 W. 47th St., New York, NY; Monday to Friday 9:30–6, Thursday 9:30–7, Saturday 10:30–6

Nearly half of Michael C. Fina's holiday catalog is devoted to jewelry—rings embedded with diamonds and emeralds, strands of pearls and gold link necklaces, wedding bands, and modern silver jewelry and accessories are representative of the selection. Fina, which has been in business since 1935, is well known to New Yorkers for its great prices on jewelry.

Fina also offers an impressive line of tableware, including china by Aynsley, Bernardaud Limoges, Ceralene Raynaud Limoges, Dansk, Fitz and Floyd, Franciscan, Ginori, Gorham, Haviland Limoges, Johnson Brothers, Lenox, Mikasa, Minton, Noritake, Portmeirion, Rosenthal, Royal Crown Derby, Royal Doulton, Royal Worcester, Spode, Thomas, Villeroy & Boch, and Wedgwood. Crystal stemware from Atlantis, Baccarat, Gorham, Lenox, Miller Rogaska, Noritake, Orrefors, Royal Doulton, Sasaki, Stuart, and Waterford is available. Fina also sells flatware from Dansk, Gorham, International, Kirk-Stieff, Lunt, Mikasa, Oneida, Reed & Barton, Retroneu, Towle, Wallace, and Yamazaki. Sterling silver baby gifts, picture frames, carriage clocks, and silver dressing table accessories are usually available, and Fina maintains a bridal registry.

Special Factors: Satisfaction is guaranteed; returns (except engraved or personalized items) are accepted within three weeks for exchange, refund, or credit.

FORTUNOFF FINE JEWELRY & SILVER-WARE, INC.

P.O. BOX 1550
WESTBURY, NY 11590
516-294-3300
FAX: 516-873-6984

Catalog: $2
Save: up to 50%
Pay: check, MO, MC, V, AE, DC
Sells: jewelry, tableware, and giftware
Store: 681 Fifth Ave., New York, and 1300 Old Country Rd., Westbury, NY; also Paramus Park Mall, Paramus, West Belt Mall, Wayne, and 441 Woodbridge Center Dr., Woodbridge, NJ

In addition to spectacular buys on fine jewelry and watches, Fortunoff is a top source for place settings in stainless, silverplate, and sterling silver. Attractive groups of silver giftware—chafing dishes, tea and coffee services, candlesticks, ice buckets, picture frames, and antique vanity accessories—appear frequently in the catalogs. Flatware from Empire Silver, International, Kirk-Stieff, Lauffer, Mikasa, Oneida, Reed & Barton, Retroneu, Roberts & Belk, Supreme, Towle, C.J. Vander, and Yamazaki is available—call for prices on specific patterns. Some of the Fortunoff stores carry a broader variety of products, including outdoor furniture, leather goods, decorative accents for the home, linens for bed and bath, organizers, and similar items.

Special Factors: Price quote on flatware by letter with self-addressed, stamped envelope; minimum order is $25; orders are not shipped outside the U.S.

THE JOMPOLE COMPANY, INC.

330 SEVENTH AVE.
NEW YORK, NY 10001
212-594-0440
FAX: 212-594-0444

Information: price quote
Save: up to 50%
Pay: check or MO
Sells: tableware, figurines, watches, and pens
Store: same address; Monday to Friday 9–5

Jompole has been in business since 1913 and offers a fine selection of table settings, giftware, and writing instruments, at savings of up to 50%. The china lines include Bernardaud Limoges, Coalport, Denby, Franciscan, Hutschenreuther, Lenox, Mikasa, Minton, Pickard, Royal

Copenhagen, Spode, and Wedgwood, among others. Crystal stemware is available from Baccarat, Fostoria, Gorham, Kosta Boda, Orrefors, Rosenthal, Val St. Lambert, and Waterford, and there's flatware from Alvin, Community, Fraser, International, Georg Jensen, Kirk-Stieff, Lauffer, Lunt, Oneida, Reed & Barton, Supreme Cutlery, Towle, Tuttle, Wallace, and other firms. Jompole may have figurines and collectibles by some of the same firms, as well as Hummel, Lladró, Norman Rockwell, and Swarovski. Call or write for prices on these, as well as on pens and pencils from Cross, Mont Blanc, Parker, and Waterman, and watches by Borel, Cartier, Heuer, Patek-Philippe, Rolex, and Seiko. Jompole also carries premium items for businesses—"from balloons and lollipops to diamonds and furs"—and invites inquiries from interested firms.

Special Factors: Price quote by phone or letter with SASE; institutional accounts are available; orders are shipped worldwide.

KAISER CROW INC.

3545 G. SO. PLATTE RIVER DR.
ENGLEWOOD, CO 80110
303-781-6888
FAX: 303-781-5982

Brochure: free
Save: up to 55%
Pay: check, MO, MC, V
Sells: flatware
Store: mail order only

Kaiser Crow's business is flatware—stainless, silverplate, and sterling silver—from Gorham, International, Lunt, Oneida, Reed & Barton, Towle, Wallace, and other major manufacturers. Kaiser Crow has been in business since 1985, and sells at discounts of up to 55%. The brochure shows specials on Oneida's Community, Heirloom, and gold-accented stainless flatware lines, at savings of more than 50% on list prices. Call or write for a price quote if you don't see what you're looking for.

Special Factors: Satisfaction is guaranteed; orders are shipped worldwide.

MESSINA GLASS & CHINA CO. INC.

P.O. BOX 307
ELWOOD, NJ 08217
609-561-1474

Information: price quote
Save: up to 50%
Pay: check, MO, MC, V, AE, Optima
Sells: tableware and collectibles
Store: Rte. 30 (White Horse Pike), Elwood, NJ; Monday to Friday (except Thursday) 10–5, Saturday 10–4 (closed Thursday and Sunday)

Fine china and stoneware, stainless and sterling flatware, crystal stemware, and collectibles are among the offerings at Messina Glass & China, which has been in business since 1959. Please request specific manufacturers' catalogs, or a price quote if you know the pattern/piece you want. Messina carries tableware and gifts by Atlantis, Block, Fitz & Floyd, Franciscan, Galway, Gorham, Hummel, Johnson Brothers, Lenox (including lamps), Miller Rogaska, Minton, Noritake, Oneida, Pfaltzgraff (china only), Reed & Barton, Retroneu, Royal Albert, Royal Crown Derby, Royal Doulton, Royal Worcester, Schmid, Spode, Wedgwood, and Yamazaki, among others. If you're looking for a piece in a recently discontinued pattern, try here—it may be available. Messina also sells monogrammed barware, stemware, and crystal serving trays.

Messina is offering readers free shipping on orders of $100 or more sent within the 48 contiguous states. Be sure to identify yourself as a WBMC reader when you order to claim the exemption. This WBMC reader offer expires February 1, 1995.

Special Factor: Orders are shipped worldwide.

ROBIN IMPORTERS, INC.

510 MADISON AVE.,
   DEPT. WBM
NEW YORK, NY 10022
800-223-3373
212-753-6475
FAX: 212-753-6480

Brands List: free with SASE
Save: up to 50%
Pay: check, MO, MC, V, AE, DC, Optima
Sells: tableware, giftware, and kitchenware
Store: same address; Monday to Friday
9:30–6, Saturday 10–5

 ¡Si!

Robin Importers, which was founded in 1957, offers an exhaustive range of tableware, kitchenware, and table and kitchen linens at prices up to 50% below list. The brochure lists the available brands, but no prices are given—call or write for a quote.

Robin carries china place settings and serving pieces by Adams, Arabia, Arzberg, Bernardaud Limoges, Block, Cartier, Coalport, Denby, Fitz and Floyd, Franciscan, Heinrich, Hutschenreuther, Mikasa, Rosenthal, Spode, Villeroy & Boch, and other firms. Crystal stemware and gifts from Atlantis, Baccarat, Daum, Gorham, Iittala, Kosta Boda, Lalique, Orrefors, Riedel, Sasaki, Val St. Lambert, and Waterford are available. And the flatware and cutlery lines include Alessi, Dansk, W.M.F. Fraser, Georgian House, Gorham, Henckels, Lauffer, Lunt, Oneida, Retroneu, Ricci, Stanley Roberts, Supreme, Towle, Wallace, and Yamazaki. Robin completes the table with linens—Carefree cloths and napkins, in all sizes and colors, at 50% off list. Knives by Henckels, and Wusthof-Trident are also sold at savings, as well as knife blocks, salt-and-pepper mills, and other useful kitchen items.

Special Factor: Orders are shipped worldwide.

ROGERS & ROSENTHAL, INC.

22 W. 48TH ST.,
  SUITE 1102
NEW YORK, NY 10036
212-827-0115
FAX: 212-768-4049

Information: price quote
Save: up to 50%
Pay: check or MO
Sells: tableware
Store: same address; Monday to Friday 10–3

 (see text)

Rogers and Rosenthal, two old names in the silver and china trade, represent the business of this firm: the best in table settings at up to 60% below list prices. Rogers & Rosenthal has been in business since 1960, selling flatware (stainless, plate, and sterling) by top manufacturers. The brands include 1847 Rogers, 1881 Rogers, Fraser, Gerber, Gorham, International, Jensen, Kirk-Stieff, Lauffer, Lunt, Oneida, Reed & Barton, Sasaki, Frank Smith, Supreme, Towle, Tuttle, Wallace, and Yamazaki. There are china and crystal lines by Arabia, Aynsley, Bernardaud Limoges, Block, Coalport, Fitz and Floyd, Franciscan, Gorham, Haviland Limoges, Hornsea, Hutschenreuther, Lauffer, Lenox, Mikasa, Noritake, Pickard, Portmeirion, Rosenthal, Royal Copenhagen, Royal Doulton, Royal Worcester, Spode, and Wedgwood. Silver baby gifts, Lladró and Norman Rockwell figurines, and pewter holloware are also stocked. Please write or call for a price quote—*there is no catalog.*

Canadian readers, please note: Only special orders are shipped to Canada.

Special Factors: Price quote by phone or letter with SASE; returns are accepted for exchange; special orders are shipped worldwide.

RUDI'S POTTERY, SILVER & CHINA

176 RTE. 17
PARAMUS, NJ 07652
800-631-2526
201-265-6096
FAX: 265-2086

Information: price quote
Save: up to 50%
Pay: check, MO, MC, V, AE, Optima
Sells: tableware
Store: same address; Monday and Saturday 10–5:30, Tuesday to Friday 10–9

Rudi's has been in business for 25 years, and in that time has expanded the stock to include some of the finest goods available, at savings of up to 60% on list. China, crystal, and flatware are stocked here; the silverware brands include Buccellati, Gorham, International, Kirk-Stieff, Lunt, Reed & Barton, Towle, Tuttle, and Wallace. Rudi's china dinnerware and crystal stemware lines include Arzberg, Baccarat, Belleek, Bernardaud Limoges, Coalport, Fitz and Floyd, Galway, Gorham, Kosta Boda, Lalique, Lenox, Mikasa, Minton, Noritake, Orrefors, Rosenthal, Royal Copenhagen, Royal Doulton, Royal Worcester, Sasaki, Spode, Stuart, Wedgwood, and Yamazaki. Call or write for a price quote on your pattern or suite.

Special Factors: Price quote by phone or letter with SASE; orders are shipped worldwide.

NAT SCHWARTZ & CO., INC.

549 BROADWAY
BAYONNE, NJ 07002
800-526-1440

Information: inquire
Save: up to 50%
Pay: check, MO, MC, V, Discover
Sells: tableware and giftware
Store: same address; Monday to Friday 10–6, Thursday 10–8, Saturday 10–5

Nat Schwartz & Co., established in 1967, publishes a 48-page color catalog filled with fine china, crystal, flatware, and gifts that represent just a fraction of the firm's inventory. Schwartz's china and giftware department offers Aynsley, Belleek, Bernardaud, Bing & Grøndahl, Block, Edward Marshall Boehm, Ceralene Limoges, Dansk, Fitz and Floyd, Ginori, Haviland Limoges, Hermes, Hutschenreuther, Lenox, Lladró,

Mikasa, Minton, Mottahedah, Nikko, Noritake, Pfaltzgraff, Pickard, Port-meirion, Rosenthal, Royal Copenhagen, Royal Crown Derby, Royal Doulton, Royal Worcester, Sasaki, Spode, Villeroy & Boch, and Wedgwood. Crystal suites and gifts by Atlantis, Baccarat, Galway, Gorham, Hummel, Lenox, Lladro, Miller/Rogaska, Rosenthal, St. Louis, Sasaki, Stuart, Waterford, and Wedgwood are available. Also featured are flatware and holloware by Buccellati, Dansk, Empire, W.M.F. Fraser, Gorham, International, Kirk-Stieff, Lunt, Oneida, Reed & Barton, Retroneu, Ricci, Towle, Tuttle, Wallace, and Yamazaki. Schwartz offers a number of valuable services, including coordination of silver, crystal, and china patterns, gift and bridal registry, and a corporate gift program.

Special Factors: Satisfaction is guaranteed; price quote by phone; special orders are accepted with a nonrefundable 20% deposit (unless the order is canceled while still on back order); undamaged returns are accepted within 30 days (a restocking fee may be charged).

ALBERT S. SMYTH CO., INC.

DEPT. WM94
29 GREENMEADOW DR.
TIMONIUM, MD 21093
800-638-3333
410-252-6666
FAX: 410-252-2355

Catalog: free
Save: up to 65%
Pay: check, MO, MC, V, AE
Sells: tableware, giftware, and jewelry
Store: same address; Monday to Saturday 9–5, Thursday 9–9

All that gleams and glitters can be found at Smyth, at savings of up to 65% on comparable retail and list prices. Smyth has been doing business since 1914, and has a well-regarded customer service department. The 24-page color catalog features a wide range of jewelry, including diamonds, strands of semiprecious beads, colored stone jewelry, and pearls. Watches by Krieger, Movado, Omega, Rado, Seiko, Universal Geneve, and Raymond Weil have been offered in the past, as well as Mont Blanc pens, mahogany jewelry chests, Royal Doulton figurines, Virginia Metalcrafters gifts, and Kirk-Stieff pewter and silver gifts.

Tableware and home decorative accents are sold here at impressive savings, including such items as British carriage clocks, Baldwin brass gifts, and fine picture frames. You'll find pewter candlesticks, coffee sets, punch bowls, and place settings by Aynsley, Gorham, Kirk-Stieff,

Lenox, Noritake, Reed & Barton, Royal Doulton, Spode, Towle, Villeroy & Boch, Wallace, Waterford, and Wedgwood among the offerings.

Smyth maintains a bridal registry and provides gift consultations and a gift-forwarding service. The catalog shows a fraction of the inventory, so write or call for a price quote if you don't see what you're looking for.

Special Factors: Satisfaction is guaranteed; returns (except personalized and custom-ordered goods) are accepted within 30 days.

THURBER'S

14 MINNESOTA AVE.
WARWICK, RI 02888
800-848-7237
FAX: 401-732-4124

Catalog: free
Save: up to 50%
Pay: check, MO, MC, V, AE, Discover, Optima
Sells: tableware, giftware, and Christmas ornaments
Store: same address

The 24-page color catalog from Thurber's showcases both fine tableware and gifts, but you can call or write year-round for quotes on specific items. Thurber's has been in business since 1985, selling gifts and the accoutrements of gracious living at up to 50% off list prices. Place settings and other tableware by Gorham, International, Kirk-Stieff, Lenox, Lunt, Minton, Noritake, Oneida, Reed & Barton, Royal Doulton, Royal Worcester, Spode, Tirschenreuth, Towle, Wallace, Wedgwood, and Yamazaki are available as well, at savings of up to 50%. And the holiday catalog features a lovely selection of limited-edition Christmas ornaments, and plates.

Special Factors: Satisfaction is guaranteed; returns are accepted within 30 days for exchange, refund, or credit; orders are shipped worldwide.

COMPANIES OUTSIDE THE U.S.A.

The following firms are experienced in dealing with customers in the U.S. and Canada. They're included because they offer goods not widely available at a discount in the U.S., because they have a better selection, or because they may offer the same goods at great savings. Before ordering from any non-U.S. firm, please consult "The Complete Guide to Buying by Mail," page 535, for helpful tips. Pay for orders from foreign firms with a credit card whenever possible, so you'll have some recourse if you don't receive your order. For more information, see "The Fair Credit Billing Act," page 569.

SKANDINAVISK GLAS

4 NY ØSTERGADE
1101 COPENHAGEN K
DENMARK
011-45-3313-8095
FAX: 011-45-3332-3335

Brochure and Price Lists: $4, refundable
Save: up to 40%
Pay: check, MO, MC, V, AE, DC
Sells: crystal and china table settings and giftware
Store: same address; Monday to Friday 9:30–5:30, Saturday 9:30–2

Skandinavisk Glas was founded in 1920 and sells the finest European crystal and porcelain: Herend, Hummel, Lladró, NAO, Royal Copenhagen, Royal Doulton, Wedgwood, and David Winter. The prices at Skandinavisk Glas, which *include* postage (surface) and insurance, are good: place settings are priced 25% to 33% below New York City rates, and Lladró figurines cost about 30% below retail. The crystal collection is comparable; in addition to a comprehensive listing of Waterford stemware, vases, and giftware, Skandinavisk Glas sells decorative and service pieces by Baccarat, Iittala, Mats Jonassen, Kosta Boda, Nachtmann, Orrefors, and Swarovski.

Canadian readers, please note: Prices are listed in U.S. dollars. Add 25% to the prices if you're paying in Canadian funds.

Special Factors: Shipping and insurance are included; orders are shipped worldwide.

STECHER'S LIMITED

27 FREDERICK ST.
PORT-OF-SPAIN
TRINIDAD, WEST INDIES
809-62-35912, 32586
FAX: 809-627-8444

Brands List: free
Save: up to 40%
Pay: check or IMO
Sells: tableware, watches, jewelry, and giftware
Store: same address; Piarco International Airport; also Hilton Hotel, Long Circular Mall, and Westmall in Port-of-Spain; Gulf City Mall, San Fernando; Carrington Street, Scarborough, Tobago; and Arnos Vale Airport and Cobblestone Inn, Bay Street, Kingston in St. Vincent

Here in Trinidad is one of the world's best sources of luxury goods, which are sold at impressive discounts. Stecher's has been doing business since 1946 and has satisfied the whims of such shoppers as Tony Curtis and Lena Horne. The firm carries the best of the best in tableware, watches, clocks, pens, and lighters, at savings of up to 40%: crystal by Baccarat, Dartington, Daum, Hoya, Iittala, Kosta Boda, Lalique, Nybro, Orrefors, Riedel, Rosenthal, Royales de Champagne, St. Louis, Schott-Zwiesel, Sevres, Swarovski, Val St. Lambert, Vannes Le Chatel, and Waterford. Place settings, gifts, and figurines from Aynsley, Bing & Grøndahl, Capodimonte, Coalport, Hutschenreuther, Kaiser, Lladró, Minton, Noritake, Rosenthal, Royal Albert, Royal Copenhagen, Royal Crown Derby, Royal Doulton, Royal Worcester, Spode, Wedgwood, and David Winter Cottages are available. The flatware lines include Christofle, Georg Jensen, and Wallace, among others.

This is an impressive list, but Stecher's is more frequently cited for its bargains on watches, clocks, jewelry, pens, and lighters. Again, the goods are first-rate: timepieces by Audemars Piguet, Cartier, Consul, Girard-Perregaux, Tag-Heuer (chronographs), Patek-Philippe, Seiko, and similar firms are offered, in addition to pens and lighters from Pierre Cardin, Cartier, Cross, Dunhill, Dupont, Lamy, Mont Blanc, Parker, Sheaffer, and Waterman, as well as a wide variety of fine jewelry (including cultured pearls) and leather goods, pipes, Swiss Army knives, sunglasses by Artie, Christian Dior, Christian La Croix, Porsche Carrera, and Ray-Ban, and a wide variety of perfume is available in Stecher's two Airport Shops.

Stecher's doesn't have a catalog, but will send a list of brands and lines of merchandise currently available. The firm invites written inquiries concerning specific goods and manufacturers, and will send specific brochures and prices upon request.

Special Factor: Price quote by letter.

SEE ALSO

A Cook's Wares • *cutlery and serving pieces* • **HOME: KITCHEN**

Atlantic Bridge Collection Corp. Ltd. • *china and crystal tableware* • **ART & ANTIQUES**

Bruce Medical Supply • *dining aids and cutlery for those with limited strength or muscle control* • **MEDICINE**

Betty Crocker Enterprises • *china, stemware, and flatware* • **GENERAL MERCHANDISE**

Fivenson Food Equipment, Inc. • *restaurant appliances, tableware, and serving pieces* • **HOME: KITCHEN**

Kitchen Etc. • *tableware* • **HOME: KITCHEN**

Harris Levy, Inc. • *table linens* • **HOME: LINEN**

Paradise Products, Inc. • *party supplies, doilies, disposables, etc.* • **TOYS**

Pendery's Inc. • *Mexican glassware* • **FOOD**

Ross-Simons Jewelers • *china, crystal, and silver tableware* • **JEWELRY**

Saxkjaers • *china and silver* • **ART & ANTIQUES**

Weston Bowl Mill • *wooden plates, trays, and tableware* • **GENERAL MERCHANDISE**

JEWELRY, GEMS, AND WATCHES

Fine, fashion, and costume jewelry; loose stones, watches, and services

Whether you're looking for flea-market neck chains or investment-grade gems, you'll find them here, at savings of 20% to 75%. Before making a financial commitment of any magnitude, make sure you know what you're buying:

All About Jewelry: The One Indispensable Guide for Buyers, Wearers, Lovers, Investors, by Rose Leiman Goldenberg (Arbor House Publishing Co., 1983), covers precious and semiprecious stones, pearls, metals, and other materials used in jewelry. For an inside look at the business, try *Modern Jeweler's Consumer Guide to Colored Gemstones,* by David Federman (Modern Jeweler Magazine, 1990), with dazzling color photographs by Tino Hammid. A gemlike production in its own right, it reveals the intrigue and chicanery that shape each stone's market, and discusses irradiation and heat treatment of gems. Write to Modern Jeweler, Vance Publishing Corporation, P.O. Box 1416, Lincolnshire, IL 60069-9958 for the current price and ordering information if you can't find it in a bookstore.

The FTC has established guidelines for the jewelry trade and publishes pamphlets for consumers that discuss the meanings of terms, stamps and quality marks, and related matters. Request "Gold Jewelry," "Bargain Jewelry," and "Guidelines for the Jewelry Industry" from the Federal Trade Commission, Public Reference Office, Washington, DC 20580.

If you need help in finding an appraiser, contact the American Society of Appraisers at 212-687-6305. The Society will locate an appraiser in your area and have that person contact you, at no charge. (The Society's senior members have at least five years of experience and are required to pass an exam; they handle all "appraisables," not just jewelry.)

The Gemological Institute of America can tell you what should appear on a GIA report and confirm whether an appraiser has been trained by the organization. For more information, write to the Gemological Institute of America, Inc., 1180 Avenue of the Americas, New York, NY 10036. There is also a GIA office in California, at P.O. Box 2110, 1660 Stewart St., Santa Monica, CA 90406.

The Jewelers' Vigilance Committee can tell you whether your dealer is among the good, the bad, or the ugly. This trade association monitors the industry and promotes ethical business practices. For more information, write to the Jewelers' Vigilance Committee, 1180 Avenue of the Americas, 8th Fl., New York, NY 10036.

ACCESSORIES U.S.A.

229 CARPENTER ST.

P.O. BOX 105

PROVIDENCE, RI 02909

401-421-0652

FAX: 401-272-7450

Catalog: $1
Save: up to 50%
Pay: check, MO, MC, V
Sells: costume jewelry
Store: mail order only

By the time you've saved up enough for the real thing, you could have bought the average bauble from Accessories U.S.A. about 20 times over. The 12-page color catalog features some of the prettiest, least expensive jewelry around—perfect for those whose taste errs on the conservative side, but with enough fun pieces to please everyone. Among the cutest items in the current selection is a charm necklace and matching bracelet that alternate gold wire figures with brightly colored, pearlized beads—under $25 for each. There are large twisted gold-hoop earrings for $11.99, substantial pieces embedded with Austrian crystal for the popular handmade look (from under $12), and tennis bracelets for under $7. This is a great source for lovely, inexpensive gifts, but it's also a good place to pick up a few pieces to take with you when you're traveling—if anything happens to them, at least you know they won't cost much to replace!

Special Factors: Satisfaction is guaranteed; returns are accepted for exchange, refund, or credit.

DIAMONDS BY RENNIE ELLEN

15 W. 47TH ST., RM. 401
NEW YORK, NY 10036
212-869-5525

Catalog: $2
Save: up to 75%
Pay: check, MO, teller's check, bank draft
Sells: stock and custom-made jewelry
Store (factory): by appointment only

It's hard to believe that you can buy diamond engagement rings wholesale, but that's Rennie Ellen's business. You can save up to 75% on the price of similar jewelry sold elsewhere by buying here. Rennie Ellen is honest, reputable, and personable, and she's been cutting gems since 1966.

Rennie Ellen sells diamonds of all shapes, sizes, and qualities, set to order in platinum or gold. The color catalog shows samples of Ms. Ellen's design work, including rings, pendants, and earrings set with diamonds. The factory is open to customers by appointment only. Please note that the catalog ($2) includes information on both Diamonds by Rennie Ellen and her other concern, R/E Kane Enterprises (see that listing in this chapter).

Special Factors: A detailed bill of sale is included with each purchase; returns are accepted within five working days; minimum shipping, handling, and insurance charge is $15.

ELOXITE CORPORATION

DEPT. 4
P.O. BOX 729
WHEATLAND, WY 82201
307-322-3050
FAX: 307-322-3055

Catalog: $1
Save: up to 75%
Pay: check, MO, MC, V
Sells: jewelry findings
Store: 806 Tenth St., Wheatland, WY; Monday to Friday 8:30–4, Saturday 8:30–3

Eloxite has been selling jewelry findings, cabochons, beads, and other lapidary supplies since 1955. Prices here are up to 75% below those charged by other crafts sources for findings and jewelry components, and Eloxite also sells Crystalite cutting and grinding equipment for professional jewelers.

Jewelry findings with a Western flair are featured here: bola ties and slide medallions, belt buckles and inserts, and coin jewelry are prominent offerings. Also shown are pendants, rings, earrings, lockets, tie tacks, and pins made to be set with cabochons or cut stones, as well as jump rings, chains, pillboxes, screw eyes, and ear wires. The stones themselves are sold—cut cubic zirconia and synthetic gemstones and oval cabochons of abalone, agate, black onyx, garnet, opal, obsidian, jasper, and malachite. A recent catalog included loosely strung gemstone bead necklaces and jewelers' tools and supplies.

Sandwiched between the pages of jewelry components are quartz clock movements and blanks for clock faces, clock hands, oil paints and palettes, and ballpoint pens and letter openers for desk sets. Discounts are available on most items, and specials are usually offered with orders of specified amounts.

Special Factors: Quantity discounts are available; undamaged returns are accepted within 15 days for exchange or refund (a $2 restocking fee may be charged); minimum order is $15; C.O.D. orders are accepted; orders are shipped worldwide.

HONG KONG LAPIDARIES, INC.

2801 UNIVERSITY DR.
CORAL SPRINGS, FL 33065
305-755-8777
FAX: 305-755-8780

Catalog: $3, refundable
Save: up to 50%
Pay: check, MO, MC, V
Sells: jewelry supplies and loose stones
Store: mail order only

Hong Kong Lapidaries, established in 1978, sells a wide range of precious and semiprecious stones in a variety of forms. The 42-page catalog lists items of interest to hobbyists as well, and the prices run as much as 70% below comparable retail.

Thousands of cabochons, beads, loose faceted and cut stones, and strung chips of pearl, garnet, amethyst, onyx, abalone, and other kinds of semiprecious stones are offered through the catalog, which comes with a separate 12-page color brochure that shows representative pieces. Egyptian clay scarabs, coral, cameos, cubic zirconia, yellow jade, cloisonné jewelry and objets d'art, 14K gold-filled and sterling silver beads, and ball earrings are available. Hobbyists should note the necklace thread—100% silk or nylon—in a score of colors and 16 *sizes*—plus stringing needles.

Special Factors: Satisfaction is guaranteed; price quote by fax; quantity discounts are available; returns are accepted within 12 days; minimum order is $25; C.O.D. orders are accepted; orders are shipped worldwide.

HOUSE OF ONYX, INC.

THE AARON BUILDING
GREENVILLE, KY
  42345-0261
800-844-3100
502-338-2363
FAX: 502-338-9605

Catalog: free
Save: up to 60%
Pay: check, MO, MC, V, Discover
Sells: investment-grade stones, jewelry, and gifts
Store: 120 Main St., Greenville, KY; Monday to Friday 9–4

The House of Onyx publishes a large tabloid catalog filled with reports on the gem industry and listings of diamonds and other precious stones, as well as specials on gifts and jewelry. Imported gifts and jewelry from Mexico, China, and India have been offered in the past, including Aztec onyx chess sets, ashtrays, bookends, vases, statuettes, and candlesticks. Cloisonné and vermeil beads, jewelry, and artware, and carvings of soapstone, rose quartz, tiger's eye, Burmese jadeite, lapis lazuli, carnelian, turquoise, and agate are usually available. The jewelry includes semiprecious bead necklaces, freshwater and cultured pearls, and diamond and gemstone rings, earrings, and pendants, from department-store grade to fine one-of-a-kind pieces. Collectors of crystals and mineral specimens should check here for amethyst, fluorite, quartz, pyrite, and other geodes and samples.

House of Onyx has been in business since 1967, and offers a wide range of investment-quality stones, with discounts of 50% and 60% offered on parcels of $2,000 to $12,500. The investment stones account for much of the business here, and the catalog is packed with useful information and commentary on gems and investing.

Special Factors: Satisfaction is guaranteed; investment gemstones are sold with an unlimited time return guarantee and "100% purchase price refund" pledge; other returns are accepted within 30 days; minimum order is $25; orders are shipped worldwide.

INTERNATIONAL GEM CORPORATION

3601 HEMPSTEAD TPK.
LEVITTOWN, NY 11756
516-796-0200
FAX: 516-796-0285

Catalog: $1, refundable
Save: up to 40%
Pay: check or MO
Sells: semiprecious stone jewelry
Store: mail order only

International Gem Corporation, which has been selling to the trade since 1950, offers consumers the opportunity to buy jewelry and beads at wholesale prices—up to 40% below comparable retail. The IGC catalog and price list feature hand-knotted strands of 8mm balls of a variety of gemstones, in everything from amethyst to unikite. There is a collection of scarab jewelry, fashion pins with Austrian crystal accents, strands of beads and freshwater pearls, with gold bead and cloisonné spacers in a choice of sizes and arrangements, and drop and stud earrings to match. Black onyx jewelry, beggars' beads, sumptuous ropes made of several strands of 4mm balls and pearls twisted together, and cloisonné jewelry and accessories are also offered. Options include the addition of gold spacer beads to some strands, custom lengths, and hand-knotting of loose strands.

Special Factors: Price quote by phone or letter with SASE on quantity orders; minimum order is $25; orders are shipped worldwide.

NATURE'S JEWELRY

27 INDUSTRIAL AVE.,
   DEPT. NJ-106E
CHELMSFORD, MA
   01824-3692
800-333-3235
FAX: 800-866-3235

Catalog: free
Save: up to 40% (see text)
Pay: check, MO, MC, V, AE, Discover
Sells: fashion and novelty jewelry
Store: mail order only

No matter what your personal style, taste, or budget, you'll find a bauble to suit your fancy in the Nature's Jewelry catalog. Each issue has nearly 100 pages of classic, theme, and holiday jewelry and accessories, including strands of semiprecious stones, preserved wildflower jewelry, pins and watches with environmental themes, jewelry for the season—from "star" bow earrings in red and green for Christmas to a cuff of enamelled hearts for Valentine's Day—and much more, at very affordable prices. Many of the designs are exclusives, so they're hard to compare to other jewelry, but prices on items at Nature's Jewelry are up to 50% lower than those charged elsewhere for similar pieces. Many of the pierced earrings are priced under $10, and a large proportion of other pieces cost under $20.

If you'd like to be able to wear fresh flowers every day, you'll love the collection of handmade, handpainted stone-and-resin buds and blossoms. Past catalogs have shown lilacs, roses, irises, pansies, poppies, and other flowers, and there's even a line of *preserved* blossoms in earrings, pins, and pendants. Love pigs? They're here, to adorn your ears or dress, as well as cows, sheep, lots of cats, horses, dinosaurs, dolphins, whales, pandas, fish, birds, dragonflies, coyotes, frogs, and many other animals. Nature's Jewelry sells dozens of pierced ear "illusions," figures and animals that appear to go *through* the earlobe. There are $10 tennis bracelets, golf-motif jewelry, pieces of nature (real parsley, four-leaf clovers, maple leaves, etc.) dipped in 24K gold, and chunks of "beach glass" made into beautiful, jewel-like necklaces and earrings. Every catalog has much more, with lots of new additions in each issue, and sale pages with dozens of pieces at 50% off.

Special Factors: Satisfaction is guaranteed; returns are accepted for exchange, refund, or credit; orders are shipped worldwide.

R/E KANE ENTERPRISES

P.O. BOX 1745, ROCKE-
FELLER PLAZA
NEW YORK, NY 10185
212-869-5525

Catalog: see text
Save: up to 75%
Pay: check, MO, teller's check
Sells: stock and custom-made cubic zirconia jewelry
Store: mail order only

If you have diamond tastes but a rhinestone budget, consider the best alternative to the natural stone—cubic zirconia. Also known as C.Z., it's a synthetic stone, is the best impostor on the market. C.Z. weighs 80% more than diamonds; a 1.80-carat C.Z. stone is about the same size as a one-carat diamond.

This division of "Diamonds by Rennie Ellen" sells stock and custom-made C.Z. jewelry at just $10 a carat (plus the cost of the 14K gold mountings), including rings, earrings, bracelets, and necklaces, in both stock and custom designs. Please note that the catalog for R/E Kane is combined with the "Diamonds by Rennie Ellen" catalog. See the listing for that firm in this chapter for information on the catalog price.

Special Factor: Minimum shipping, handling, and insurance charge is $10.

ROSS-SIMONS
JEWELERS

9 ROSS-SIMONS DR.,
  DEPT. TWBMC
CRANSTON, RI
  02920-4476
800-556-7376
401-463-3100
FAX: 401-463-8599

Catalog: free
Save: up to 40%
Pay: check, MO, MC, V, AE, DC, Discover, Optima
Sells: jewelry, tableware, and giftware
Store: Kittery, ME; also Atlanta, GA; and Barrington, Providence, and Warwick, RI

Ross-Simons has 41 years of experience in the jewelry business, and the firm's color catalog showcases a selection of gems and baubles. Half of each issue is also devoted to fine china, flatware, and gifts. Prices are discounted up to 40% below suggested list and regular retail, and you can call directly for a quote if you're shopping for a specific item.

Stylish jewelry is the strong suit here: Diamond-encrusted necklaces and pins are prominent in the holiday catalog, as well as gold bands with cabochon gems, gold mesh bracelets and chokers, necklaces of semiprecious gems, clasp bracelets of diamonds and rubies, a large collection of stud jackets, strands of cultured pearls, and more affordable versions in cubic zirconia, sterling silver, and 18K gold plate. Ross-Simons also sells watches, and you can call for a price quote if you're looking for a model by Audemars-Piguet, Bertolucci, Concord, Corum, Chopard, Ebel, Geneva, Movado, Omega, Piaget, Rado, Tissot, or Raymond Weil.

Fine china, crystal, silver, and gifts complete the catalog, which features patterns from Aynsley, Bernardaud Limoges, Block, Ceralene Limoges, Coalport, Fitz & Floyd, Gorham, Haviland, Johnson Brothers,

Lenox, Mikasa, Minton, Noritake, Royal Copenhagen, Royal Doulton, Royal Worcester, Sasaki, Tirschenreuth, Villeroy & Boch, and Wedgwood. Crystal is available from some of the same manufacturers, as well as Atlantis, Baccarat, Miller Rogaska, Orrefors, St. Louis, and Waterford. And Ross-Simons sells flatware—stainless, silverplate, and new sterling—by Dansk, Fraser, Gorham, International, Kirk-Stieff, Lunt, Mikasa, Oneida, Reed & Barton, Retroneu, Sasaki, Towle, Wallace, and Yamazaki. Commemoratives by Bing & Grøndahl and other makers, music boxes, jewelry chests, and other gifts are also offered.

Special Factors: Satisfaction is guaranteed; returns (except personalized items) are accepted within 30 days for exchange, refund, or credit; orders are shipped worldwide.

SEE ALSO

Antique Imports Unlimited • vintage jewelry and watches • **ART & ANTIQUES**
Beautiful Visions • fashion jewelry • **HEALTH**
Bennett Brothers, Inc. • costume and fine jewelry and watches • **GENERAL MERCHANDISE**
Berry Scuba Co. • underwater timepieces • **SPORTS**
Central Skindivers • underwater timepieces • **SPORTS**
Ceramic Supply of New York & New Jersey, Inc. • jewelry findings • **ART MATERIALS**
Circle Craft Supply • economy jewelry findings, boxes, etc. • **CRAFTS**
Michael C. Fina Co. • fine jewelry and watches • **HOME: TABLE SETTINGS**
Fortunoff Fine Jewelry & Silverware, Inc. • fine jewelry and watches • **HOME: TABLE SETTINGS**
Paul Fredrick Shirt Company • men's jewelry • **CLOTHING**
Marv Golden Discount Sales, Inc. • pilots' watches • **AUTO**
The Jompole Company, Inc. • fine watches • **HOME: TABLE SETTINGS**
Manny's Millinery Supply Co. • hat pins • **CLOTHING**
Saxkjaers • Bing & Grøndahl and Georg Jensen pendants • **ART & ANTIQUES**
Nat Schwartz & Co., Inc. • fine jewelry • **HOME: TABLE SETTINGS**
Albert S. Smyth Co., Inc. • fine jewelry and watches • **HOME: TABLE SETTINGS**
Stecher's Limited • fine watches and clocks • **HOME: TABLE SETTINGS**

LEATHER GOODS

Small leather goods, handbags, briefcases, attaché cases, luggage, trunks, and services

The firms listed here stock everything you should need to tote your effects around town, to the office, and farther afield. In addition to handbags, briefcases, suitcases, steamer and camp trunks, and small leather goods, some of the firms also sell cases for musical instruments and portfolios for models and artists.

If you're buying luggage, consider the different luggage materials available and the pros and cons of each before making your purchase. It's not advisable to buy luggage with attached wheels if you're doing any flying. The wheels tend to jam in conveyor systems and are usually ripped off by the time you've taken a few trips. Collapsible luggage carriers, which can be taken with you as hand baggage, solve the problem of getting bags around in huge, porterless terminals.

Companies that sell small leather goods and handbags are also listed in "Clothing," portfolios and display cases and binders are available from a number of the companies listed in "Art Materials," and companies selling travel accessories are listed in "Travel."

ACE LEATHER PRODUCTS, INC.

2211 AVE. U
BROOKLYN, NY 11229
800-DIAL ACE
718-891-9713
FAX: 718-891-3878

Catalog: $1 (see text)
Save: up to 40%
Pay: check, MO, MC, V, AE, Optima
Sells: luggage and leather goods
Store: 2211 and 2122 Ave. U, Brooklyn, NY; Monday to Saturday 10–6, Thursday 10–8 (extended hours in December)

 (see text)

Ace, which was established in 1961, sells luggage by American Tourister, Andiamo, Boyt, Delsey, Amelia Earhart, French, Hartmann, Lark, Lucas, Samsonite, Scully, Skyway, LeSport Sac, Tumi, and Ventura at discounts of up to 40%. Briefcases and attaché cases by Atlas, Boyt, Eagle Creek, Hartmann, Jansport, Lodis, Schlesinger, Scully, and Tumi, are available, as well as handbags and small leather goods by Etienne Aigner, Bosca, and Garys. You'll find travel alarms, Swiss Army knives, lighters, pens, and other small luxuries by Colibri, Cross, Mont Blanc, Seiko, and Waterman in the store. The catalog that's published during the holiday season features gift merchandise, but catalogs and price quotes on the luggage and leather goods are available throughout the year.

Canadian readers, please note: Orders to Canada are shipped via UPS.

Special Factor: Price quote by phone or letter with SASE.

AL'S LUGGAGE

2134 LARIMER ST.
DENVER, CO 80205
303-295-9009
303-294-9045
FAX: 303-296-8769

Catalog: $2, refundable
Save: up to 50%
Pay: check, MO, MC, V, AE, Discover
Sells: leather goods and luggage
Store: same address; Monday to Saturday 9–5

 (see text)

The $2 catalog fee (refundable with purchase) brings you a sheaf of photocopied materials from Samsonite, including price lists, ordering instructions, and shipping rate charts. Al's Luggage has been selling leather goods and luggage since 1946, and carries Diane Von Furstenberg, Jordache, Lion Leather, London Fog Luggage, Members Only, Platt, Stebco, Winn, and WK. In addition to current lines of suitcases, overnight bags, cosmetics cases, totes, wardrobes, duffels, and garment bags, Al's offers business cases, portfolios, and even camcorder carrying cases. The catalog shows only Samsonite models, which are sold here for 30% to 50% below list prices. If you're shopping for an item by another manufacturer, call or write for a price quote.

Canadian readers, please note: A minimum-order requirement may be imposed on orders to Canada; write for a shipping quote before ordering.

Special Factors: Price quote by phone or letter with SASE; C.O.D. orders are accepted; orders are shipped worldwide.

A TO Z LUGGAGE CO., INC.

━━━━━━━━━

4627 NEW UTRECHT AVE.
BROOKLYN, NY 11219
800-342-5011
718-435-2880
FAX: 718-435-6317

Catalog: free
Save: up to 50%
Pay: check, MO, MC, V, AE, DC, Optima
Sells: luggage, leather goods, and pens
Store: same address; Sunday to Friday 9–6; also 425 Fifth Ave., New York, NY; Sunday to Friday 9–6; and 7 other New York City locations

A to Z Luggage has been supplying New Yorkers with luggage and leather goods since 1945, discounting prices up to 50%. The firm sells luggage, briefcases and attaché cases, and other leather goods by Adolfo, American Tourister, Andiamo, Boyt, Delsey, Amelia Earhart, Hartmann, Lark, Lucas, Members Only, Samsonite, Tumi, Zero Halliburton, and other designers and manufacturers. Artists' portfolios, steamer trunks, and related gifts are also available, and A to Z Luggage also discounts pens by Cross, Mont Blanc, and Waterman. The 28-page holiday catalog has dozens of gift ideas—desk and travel accessories, executive novelties, etc.—in addition to leather goods, but you can call or write for price quotes throughout the year.

Special Factors: Price quote by phone or letter with SASE; service and repairs are available; orders are shipped worldwide.

LEATHER UNLIMITED CORP.

DEPT. WBMC94

7155 CTY. HWY. B

BELGIUM, WI 53004-9990

414-994-9464

FAX: 414-994-4099

Catalog: $2, refundable

Save: up to 50%

Pay: check, MO, MC, V

Sells: leathercraft supplies and equipment and finished products

Store: same address; Monday to Friday 7–3:30

Here's a catalog for the beginner, the seasoned leather worker, and the rest of us. It offers all sorts of leathercrafting supplies, from kits to raw materials, as well as leather cleaners and conditioners, a line of bags, business cases, small leather goods, and even blackpowder (shooting) supplies. Leather Unlimited has been in business since 1971, and offers substantial savings on crafts supplies, beginning with leather—sold by the hide, or in pieces. The weights run from fine lining grade to heavy belting leather, in a variety of finishes and colors. There are laces, belt blanks, key tabs, and dozens of undyed embossed belt strips; these are matched by hundreds of belt buckles, which run from embossed leather buckles to a line with organization logos and sporting themes. The 72-page catalog features dozens of kits for making all sorts of finished goods, plus stamping tools, punches, carvers, rivets, screws, snaps, zippers, lacing needles, sundry findings, leather-care products and dyes by Fiebing's, and Missouri River patterns for making authentic Native American and frontier-style clothing.

Among the finished products available here are sheepskin rugs, slippers, mittens, hats, and purses made of sheepskin and deerskin, duffels and sports bags, leather totes, and wineskins. Leather Unlimited is an authorized dealer for Harley-Davidson accessories, and offers truckers' wallets, belts, keyrings, and other items. You'll also find top-grain belt leather business cases, portfolios, wallets, and other small leather goods listed in the catalog. And the firm recently added a line of books on Indian lore, crafts, and related topics. The prices are outstandingly low—up to 50% below comparable retail on some items—and extra discounts are given on quantity or volume purchases.

Special Factors: Satisfaction is guaranteed; authorized returns are accepted within ten days; minimum order is $30; orders are shipped worldwide.

THE LUGGAGE CENTER

960 REMILLARD CT.
SAN JOSE, CA 95122
800-626-6789

Information: price quote
Save: see text
Pay: MO, MC, V, AE
Sells: luggage, business cases, and travel accessories
Store: locations in Bakersfield, Berkeley, Burlingame, Citrus Heights, Dublin, Emeryville, Fresno, Los Gatos, Mountain View, Pleasant Hill, Redwood City, Sacramento, San Francisco, San Jose (four), San Rafael, Visalia, and Walnut Creek, CA

  (see text)

The Luggage Center can save you up to 50% off the manufacturers' suggested list prices on the top names in luggage, and even more when the firm is running a sale. The the latest lines from well-known makers are available, including Atlantic, Atlas, Caribou, Halliburton, High Sierra, Lark, London Fog, Members Only, Pegasus, Ricardo, Samsonite, and Skyway. Business cases, garment bags, and travel accessories are carried as well; call or write for a price quote.

Canadian readers, please note: Orders to Canada are shipped via UPS.

Special Factor: Returns are accepted within 30 days.

NEW ENGLAND LEATHER ACCESSORIES, INC.

11 PORTLAND ST.
ROCHESTER, NH 03867
603-332-0707
FAX: 603-332-4526

Catalog and Samples: $5, refundable
Save: up to 30%
Pay: check, MO, MC, V, AE
Sells: leather handbags and accessories
Store: same address; Monday to Saturday 9–5; also North Country Leather, Rte. 1, Tidewater Mall, Kittery, ME; Monday to Saturday 10–6

The 12-page catalog from New England Leather is illustrated with line drawings of its handsome leather bags and accessories, which are priced up to 30% below comparable leather goods. The $5 catalog fee also brings you a handful of butter-soft leather samples that show you the color range—cobalt blue, hunter green, brown, wine, black—and the textures of the two leathers used here, deerskin and goatskin.

Dozens of handbags and small leather items are available, mainly classic envelopes, hobo bags, knapsacks, and variations on simple pouch designs. The bags are lined, constructed with brass and pewter hardware, treated to repel rain, and some styles are trimmed in cowhide. Prices run from under $20 for a clutch purse to $170 for an enormous "mailbag." New England Leather has been in business since 1976, continuing on in the tradition of the region, which was once the leatherworking capital of the country. Everything produced by the firm is 100% American made.

Special Factors: Returns are accepted; orders are shipped worldwide.

THE OMNISOL COLLECTION

1555 SHERMAN AVE.,
SUITE 236
EVANSTON, IL 60201
708-328-9926
FAX: 708-869-0312

Price List: $3
Save: up to 60%
Pay: check, MO, MC, V, Discover
Sells: Givenchy luggage
Store: mail order only

The Omnisol Collection offers considerable savings on Givenchy's Signature lines of luggage, in both leather and in ballistic nylon. The firm's literature includes product descriptions, price sheets, details of the sales policy, and order forms, which make it easy to buy here *without* having to find the luggage in a nearby store—a departure from the usual procedure among luggage discounters. The pieces available at this writing include everything from tie cases to 48" garment carriers, from about $56 and up, and the savings on comparable retail run up to 60%.

Special Factors: Satisfaction is guaranteed; price quote by phone or letter; returns are accepted within 15 days for exchange, refund, or credit; orders are shipped worldwide.

SEE ALSO

Bennett Brothers, Inc. • *small leather goods, luggage, and luggage carts* • **GENERAL MERCHANDISE**

Dairy Association Co., Inc. • *Tackmaster leather balm* • **ANIMAL**

The Deerskin Place • *deerskin leather goods* • **CLOTHING**

A. Feibusch Corporation • *replacement luggage-weight zippers* • **CRAFTS**

Gander Mountain, Inc. • *backpacks and lightweight luggage* • **SPORTS**

Holabird Sports • *racquet-sports bags* • **SPORTS**

IMPCO, Inc. • *leather conditioner* • **AUTO**

Justin Discount Boots & Cowboy Outfitters • *leather-care preparations* • **CLOTHING: FOOTWEAR**

M.C. Limited • *steerhides and hide pillows* • **HOME: DECOR**

Mid-Western Sport Togs • *deerskin handbags, gloves, billfolds, etc.* • **CLOTHING**

Office Depot, Inc. • *attaché cases and portfolios* • **OFFICE**

United Pharmacal Company, Inc. • *leather-care products* • **ANIMAL**

MEDICINE AND SCIENCE

Prescription and over-the-counter drugs,

hearing aids, contact lenses and eyeglasses,

and post-surgery supplies and equipment

Buying medication by mail is convenient, and it can be less expensive than having prescriptions filled at the local drugstore. Even generic drugs may be cheaper by mail, affording you savings of up to 60% on some commonly prescribed remedies. But not all medications are discounted, so price out each prescription you have filled. You can also save up to half of the usual cost of hearing aids, contact lenses, breast forms, and products for ostomates, diabetics, and convalescent patients by buying them from the firms listed here.

For related products, see the listings in "Health and Beauty."

FIND IT FAST

BREAST FORMS • **B & B Company**
CONTACT LENSES AND SUPPLIES • **Contact Lens Replacement Center, National Contact Lens Center**
EYEGLASSES AND FRAMES • **Hidalgo, Precision Optical, Prism Optical**
FIRST-AID KITS • **Masuen**
HEARING AIDS • **Ric Clark**
INCONTINENCE PRODUCTS • **Medical Supply**
OSTOMY AND TRACHEOSTOMY SUPPLIES • **Bruce Medical**
PRESCRIPTION DRUGS • **Family Pharmaceuticals, Medi-Mail, Pharmail, Retired Persons Services**

B & B COMPANY, INC.

2417 BANK DR., SUITE 201
P.O. BOX 5731,
   DEPT. WC01
BOISE, ID 83705
208-343-9696

Brochure: free
Save: up to 50% (see text)
Pay: check, MO, MC, V, Discover
Sells: breast forms
Store: mail order only

B & B produces a comfortable, reasonably priced external breast form, weighted and shaped to ideal dimensions with cushioned pillows, each of which contains 1-1/2 ounces of tiny glass beads. (The weight may be adjusted by adding or removing pillows.) The form itself is all-fabric (no silicone is used), made of nylon softened with fiberfill, with an all-cotton backing that rests next to your skin. Bosom Buddy is interchangeable (fits both left and right sides), available in sizes from 32AAA to 46DDD, and it costs $60 ($65 for sizes DD and DDD). These prices are about 50% below silicone models. The brochure gives complete details, and B & B's staff can answer any questions you may have by phone.

   Special Factors: Satisfaction is guaranteed; returns are accepted; C.O.D. orders are accepted; orders are shipped worldwide.

BRUCE MEDICAL SUPPLY

411 WAVERLY OAKS RD.,
   DEPT. 10736
WALTHAM, MA 02154
800-225-8446
FAX: 617-894-9519

Catalog: free
Save: up to 60%
Pay: check, MO, MC, V
Sells: ostomy, tracheostomy, diabetic, and general medical products
Store: mail order only

The Bruce Medical Supply catalog is a valuable aid to persons who are in need of home health products, including those needing goods for laryngectomies, colostomies, ileostomies, urostomies, or mastectomies, as well as diabetes, arthritis, incontinence, or special dietary restrictions. Bruce Medical Supply, which has been in business since 1978, also stocks products designed to make all sorts of routine tasks easier.

The 64-page catalog offers a comprehensive range of ostomy supplies, diabetes monitoring supplies and equipment, bathtub safety benches, tub grips, wheelchairs, walkers, canes, crutches, magnifying glasses, reading glasses, blood pressure kits, stethoscopes, compresses, and similar products. Most of the goods are from well-known firms, including Ames, Amoena, Convatec, Hollister, Johnson & Johnson, Kimberly Clark, Mentor, Procter & Gamble, and 3M.

Books on related topics, and general nursing and caretaker supplies are available. The catalog also features a good selection of dining, food preparation, dressing, grooming, and bathing aids for persons whose range of movement or strength is limited.

Special Factors: Satisfaction is guaranteed; price quote by phone or letter; goods are shipped in unmarked boxes; C.O.D. orders are accepted.

RIC CLARK COMPANY

**36658 APACHE PLUME DR.
PALMDALE, CA 93550
805-947-8598**

Catalog: free
Save: 50% plus
Pay: check or MO
Sells: hearing aids
Store: mail order only

Ric Clark Company's catalog features six hearing aid models, designed for varying degrees of hearing loss. Ric Clark's aids are suitable for losses from mild to severe and include in-the-ear models, "compression" aids designed to "cushion" sudden loud noises, and standard models. Prices are about half those charged by hearing-aid dealers, and a $10 deposit entitles you to a month's free trial, after which you may return the aid for a complete refund or keep it and pay the balance. Batteries and repairs are also available. Ric Clark Company recommends that you see a physician before buying an aid; you must sign a waiver if you don't provide a physician's note stating that you need an aid.

Special Factors: Satisfaction is guaranteed; all aids are warrantied; a budget payment plan is available; orders are shipped worldwide.

CONTACT LENS REPLACEMENT CENTER, INC.

Price List: free with SASE
Save: up to 70%
Pay: check or MO
Sells: contact lenses and sunglasses
Store: mail order only

P.O. BOX 1489, DEPT. 94
MELVILLE, NY 11747
800-779-2654
516-491-7763

Contact Lens Replacement Center, in business since 1986, sells contact lenses of every type at savings of up to 70%. The replacement lenses include hard, soft, disposable, and gas-permeable types. Toric, bifocal, and aphakic lenses are also available. The brands include Allergan Hydron, Barnes Hind/Hydrocurve, Bausch & Lomb, Boston, Ciba, Coopervision, CSI, Fluorex, Fluoroperm, Johnson & Johnson, Ocular Sciences, Paraperm, Sunsoft, and Wesley-Jessen. All soft and disposable lenses are shipped in factory-sealed containers. Hard and gas-permeable lenses are made to order. Please note: This is a *replacement* service—not for first-time lens wearers—and you must supply a current prescription for the lenses you are now wearing. The prices are so low that it may make sense to discontinue your lens insurance and rely on this service if you lose or damage your contacts—the Center's staff can help you determine the least expensive way to replace your prescribed lenses. And there are *no* membership fees of any kind. Sunglasses by Randolph Engineering, Ray-Ban, Revo, Serengeti, and Vuarnet are also available, at discount prices. Call with the specific model name and number for a price quote.

Special Factors: Price quote by phone or letter with SASE; orders are shipped worldwide.

FAMILY PHARMA-CEUTICALS OF AMERICA, INC.

P.O. BOX 1288
MT. PLEASANT, SC
  29465-1288
800-922-3444
FAX: 803-849-1035

Price List: free
Save: up to 30% (see text)
Pay: check, MO, MC, V
Sells: prescription drugs
Store: 966 H. Northcutt Blvd., Suite E, Mt. Pleasant, SC; Monday to Friday 9–6, Saturday 9–1

Family Pharmaceuticals has been helping Americans save money on prescription drugs since 1981, and will send you a price list of 100 frequently prescribed medications—just a sample of the available drugs. But Family offers more: To quote the president of the firm, "The thing that sets FPA apart. . . is our emphasis on providing medications to those who have catastrophic illnesses, such as AIDS, cancer and organ transplants. Many of these patients are required to take medications that cost hundreds to thousands of dollars each month (e.g., Retrovir, ddI, alpha interferon, Diflucan). Our invoices are specifically designed to facilitate the reimbursement by their insurance company. We do, of course, also serve the medication needs of folk with common medical problems as well." Family Pharmaceuticals screens all prescriptions for possible interactions, and each order is invoiced, which can make it easier to track costs. The price list includes an order form, and you can write or call for a quote on your next prescription. The branded drugs are discounted 10% to 20% off the full price, and generics (when available) can save you up to 50%.

Special Factors: Price quote by phone or letter; shipping is $1.50 per order, sent via first-class mail.

HIDALGO, INC.

DEPT. WB
45 LA BUENA VISTA
WIMBERLEY, TX 78676
512-847-5571
FAX: 512-847-2393

Catalog: free
Save: up to 60%
Pay: check, MO, MC, V, AE, DC, Discover, Optima
Sells: prescription eyeglasses and sunglasses
Store: Wimberley North Too Shopping Center, Wimberley, TX; Monday to Friday 9–5, closed Saturday

Hidalgo's 48-page catalog makes ordering your eyeglasses by mail seem so easy, you'll wonder why you haven't tried it before. Hidalgo has been in business since 1967 and understands the concerns of the person who's buying glasses by mail. The catalog includes detailed descriptions of the frames, lenses, and special coatings, and includes a "Consumers' Guide to Sunglasses" that answers just about every question you can think of. There are instructions on taking your "pupil distance" measurements, and a chart that shows the light transmission data on the lenses sold by Hidalgo. The "try-on program" allows you to order up to three frames and try them out *before* ordering your glasses—a great feature for people who have a hard time finding frames that fit or flatter.

Hidalgo's own frames dominate the selection, and there are sunglasses by Bausch & Lomb and Ray-Ban, as well as replacement parts for the latter. The lens options include a choice of materials (glass, plastic, etc.), colors, coatings, and UV protection. Terms of Hidalgo's warranty are stated clearly in the catalog, as well as details of the "try-on" program. The prices are as much as 40% less than regular retail on the nonprescription eyewear, and 50% or more below customary charges for prescription glasses.

Special Factors: Returns in new, unused condition are accepted within 30 days for exchange, refund, or credit; orders are shipped worldwide.

MASUEN FIRST AID & SAFETY

P.O. BOX 901
TONAWANDA, NY 14151
800-831-0894
FAX: 800-222-1934

Catalog: free
Save: up to 30%
Pay: check, MO, MC, V, AE, Discover
Sells: first-aid kits, medical supplies
Store: mail order only

 ¡Si!

Masuen, "Your First Aid Supply Source," publishes a 64-page catalog that's full of stock items for the medicine chest. Masuen's specialty is first-aid kits, and over a dozen are shown in the catalog, from small kits for the glove compartment to the "Masuen Portable First Aid Cabinet," which provides treatment for up to 120 persons. Masuen also sells resuscitators, blood-pressure kits, thermometers, all kinds of adhesive bandages and dressings, swabs, cotton balls, splints, braces, antibiotic creams, soaps, analgesics, infection-control supplies, and protective clothing, eyewear, and gloves. Some of the prices are higher than those charged in local drugstores, but with quantity discounts you can realize savings of up to 30% on other items—be sure to price carefully before you buy.

Special Factors: Price quote by phone or letter; quantity discounts are available; minimum order is $25; orders are shipped worldwide.

MEDICAL SUPPLY CO., INC.

P.O. BOX 250
HAMBURG, NJ 07419-0250
800-323-9664
201-209-8448
FAX: 201-209-4799

Price List: free with SASE
Save: 30% average
Pay: check or MO
Sells: diapers, underpads, disposable briefs
Store: mail order only

Coping with incontinence is easier now that Attends, Depends, and similar products have come onto the market. But these products aren't cheap, so it's great to find a source for incontinence products at a discount. Medical Supply Co. has been in business since 1977, selling

Depends briefs and Chux underpads at savings of up to 50%. For example, Depends selling for 90¢ each in a local drugstore are sold here as "Incontinence Pants" at 50¢ each (in cases of 50). The Chux underpads run from 13¢ to 41¢ each (sold in cases), depending on the size. Medical Supply accepts Medicaid (in Delaware and New Jersey only) and does not charge shipping on orders delivered in Connecticut, New Jersey, New York, and Pennsylvania. (Customers in other states pay UPS charges collect.)

Medical Supply Co. is offering readers of this book a 10% discount on first orders. Be sure to identify yourself when you order, and take the discount on the goods total. This WBMC reader discount expires February 1, 1995.

Special Factors: Shipping is included on deliveries to CT, NJ, NY, and PA; minimum order is one case; orders are shipped worldwide.

MEDI-MAIL, INC.

P.O. BOX 98520
LAS VEGAS, NV 89193-8520
800-793-4726

Brochure: free
Save: see text
Pay: check, MO, MC, V
Sells: prescription drugs and health-care products
Store: mail order only

Medi-Mail is a national membership pharmacy-by-mail/phone that offers name-brand prescription drugs and over-the-counter health products at competitive prices. The firm's 48-page catalog answers general questions on buying prescription drugs by mail, and lists scores of generic over-the-counter remedies, nutritional supplements, and beauty preparations. Among other services, Medi-Mail provides a refill slip (when appropriate) and an itemized receipt with each prescription, and will send you a printout of your past orders on request.

Special Factors: For group buying information, call 619-232-2300.

NATIONAL CONTACT LENS CENTER

3527 BONITA VISTA DR.

SANTA ROSA, CA

95404-1506

800-326-6352

707-545-6352

FAX: 707-545-6353

Brochure: free
Save: up to 75%
Pay: check, MO, MC, V
Sells: soft and gas-permeable contact lenses
Store: same address (Santa Rosa Optometry Center); Monday to Friday 9–5

The Santa Rosa Optometry Center runs this lens-by-mail service, which can save you up to 75% on your next pair of contact lenses. You must be an experienced lens wearer to buy here, since National Contact Lens Center can't provide, through the mail, the fitting and monitoring services needed by first-time wearers.

National Contact Lens Center was established in 1974 and sells all the major soft contact lens brands, including lines by American Hydron, Aquaflex, Bausch & Lomb, Boston, Ciba, Coopervision, CTL, Hydrocurve, Johnson & Johnson, Sola/Barnes Hind, Syntex, Vistakon, and Wesley-Jessen. Colored, standard, and extended-wear lenses are offered, as well as toric (for astigmatism), bifocal, and aphakic (for cataracts) lenses. Hard and gas-permeable lenses are also available. Savings can reach 75%, depending on the lens and manufacturer, and every lens is backed by National Contact Lens Center's 30-day replacement guarantee.

Special Factors: Satisfaction is guaranteed; returns are accepted within 30 days for replacement, exchange, refund, or credit; orders are shipped worldwide.

PHARMAIL CORPORATION

87 MAIN ST.
P.O. BOX 1466
CHAMPLAIN, NY
12919-1466
800-237-8927
518-298-4922

Information: inquire
Save: 50% average
Pay: check, MO, MC, V
Sells: prescription drugs, vitamins, and health-care products
Store: same address; Monday to Friday 9–5

Pharmail wants you to be able to "pay 'insurance plan prices' for prescription drugs and enjoy benefits of scale on quantity purchases." This pharmacy has been dispensing prescription drugs, both name-brand and generic, since 1988. Pharmail's eight-page catalog is a partial list of the available drugs; you can also call for prices. Pharmail must have your physician's signed prescription to fill orders (authorized refills may be requested by phone), and birth date information is also required. There are no membership requirements, and groups are served under preferential arrangements. Quantity prices are lower, and if you're on a maintenance medication and can order a six-month supply, you'll save on the per-dose cost and spare yourself price increases. (Make sure the shelf life of your medication safely permits this economy.) Pharmail can also provide a list of your purchases for the year, which is helpful at tax time. Request the catalog and literature for complete details and prices of commonly used name-brand and generic medications.

Special Factors: Shipping is included; quantity discounts are available; minimum order is $4.99 per prescription, $25 per order.

PRECISION OPTICAL

DEPT. WBMC
ROCHELLE, IL 61068-0380
815-562-2174

Catalog: free
Save: up to 30%
Pay: check, MO, MC, V, AE
Sells: nonprescription reading glasses
Store: mail order only

If you're having trouble seeing the fine—or not so fine—print, see your eye doctor. *Then* get the catalog from Precision Optical. In it, you'll find about 20 eyeglass styles for men and women, all with nonprescription magnifying lenses (what are usually known as "reading glasses"). The catalog includes a guide to finding the strength you need; Precision Optical offers eight levels, or diopters, from 1.25 to 3.25. The glasses are covered by the firm's guarantee, so if they're not right, check the catalog (it has a guide to diagnosing strength problems), and exchange them until you get a pair that works for you. The frames are contemporary and attractive, and both full- and half-lens styles are available. Precision Optical also sells eyeglass cases, magnifying lenses, loupes, and eyeglass repair kits.

Special Factors: Satisfaction is guaranteed; returns are accepted within 30 days for exchange, refund, or credit.

PRISM OPTICAL, INC.

P.O. BOX 680030
10992 N.W. 7TH AVE.,
** DEPT. WC94**
NORTH MIAMI, FL 33168
305-754-5894
FAX: 305-754-7352

Catalog: $2, refundable
Save: up to 70% (see text)
Pay: check, MO, MC, V, AE, Discover
Sells: prescription eyeglasses and contact lenses
Store: same address; Monday to Friday 9–5

 ¡Si!

Prism Optical has been selling prescription eyeglasses by mail since 1959, and publishes a 16-page catalog that shows dozens of eyeglass frames for men, women, and children, discounted an average of 30% to 50%. Frames (and designer sunglasses) from Armani, Bollé, Carrera, Cazal, Christian Dior, Gucci, Anne Klein, Neostyle, Polo, Ray-Ban, Revo, and Serengeti are available. One of the benefits of ordering from Prism is being able to choose from a number of lens options, including photochromic lenses, polycarbonate (ultra-thin) lenses, permanently tinted lenses, lenses with grey mirror-finish, and UV-filtering coating and scratch-resistant coating. The lens styles include single-vision and bifocal lenses, trifocals, and "invisible" bifocals, among others. Prism guarantees that the glasses will fit correctly, and the catalog provides guides to gauging the correct size of the temple and bridge pieces.

Prism Optical also sells prescription contact lenses at prices up to 70% below those charged elsewhere. The firm sells "all brands," factory-sealed and guaranteed against defects. Call Prism with your prescription information for availability and price informationn.

Special Factors: Satisfaction is guaranteed; returns are accepted within 30 days for refund or credit; C.O.D. orders are accepted; orders are shipped worldwide.

RETIRED PERSONS SERVICES, INC.

DEPT. 493000
500 MONTGOMERY ST.
ALEXANDRIA, VA
 22314-1563
ORDERS AND INFO:
 800-456-2277
FAX: 800-456-7631
TDD: 800-933-4327

Catalog: free
Save: up to 80%
Pay: check, MO, MC, V, Discover
Sells: drugs, health and beauty aids, etc.
Store: stores in CA, CT, DC, FL, IN, MO, NV, NY, OR, PA, TX, and VA; locations are listed in the catalog

Retired Persons Services, Inc., is the mail-order pharmacy of the American Association of Retired Persons (AARP). Ordering from the AARP Pharmacy is a benefit of membership in the AARP, which may be the smartest $8 you ever spend (see the listing for the AARP in "General Merchandise"). The 72-page catalog offers nutritional supplements, over-the-counter remedies, analgesics, supplies for diabetics, nail clippers and scissors, magnifying glasses, perfumes and products for skin and hair, sun blockers, liniments, razor blades, blood-pressure kits, support hosiery and foot-care products, dental-care items, hearing aid batteries, and much more. Prices of generic and branded prescription drugs are given by phone (800-456-2226) Monday through Friday, 8

A.M. to 6 P.M. You may also speak directly with a pharmacist (800-456-4635) if you have questions. Medical information leaflets for seniors are provided with most prescriptions, and computerized prescription histories are available for tax and insurance purposes. RPS will call your doctor for you on prescription drug refills, and the AARP Pharmacy also participates in major prescription drug insurance plans. Orders are filled on an invoice basis—you'll be billed, instead of paying when you place the order.

Special Factors: Satisfaction is guaranteed; returns (except prescription drugs) are accepted for exchange, refund, or credit; orders are shipped worldwide.

SUPPORT PLUS

99 WEST ST.,
  DEPT. WBM94
P.O. BOX 500
MEDFIELD, MA 02052
800-229-2910
508-359-2910
FAX: 508-359-0139

Catalog: free
Save: up to 30%
Pay: check, MO, MC, V, AE, Discover
Sells: support hosiery and therapeutic apparel
Store: same address; Tuesday, Thursday, Saturday 10–1

Support Plus has been in business since 1972, and offers an extensive selection of supportive hosiery and undergarments for men and women, as well as comfortable leather footwear. Discounts average about 15%, but we found some items selling for 30% less than regular retail.

If your physician recommends or prescribes support (elastic) hosiery, you'll find this catalog a helpful guide to what's available. Support Plus offers panty hose, stockings, knee-highs, and men's dress socks in different support strengths. (The compression rating for each style is given in the catalog descriptions.) Among the brands sold here are Bauer & Black, Berkshire, Futuro, Hanes, T.E.D., and Support Plus' own line. Maternity, cotton-soled, control-top, open-toe, and irregular styles are available.

Support Plus also sells posture pads for chairs and beds, joint "wraps" for applications of heat and cold, Dale abdominal and lumbrosacral supports, Futuro braces and joint supports, and personal-care products and bathing aids—eating and dressing implements, bedding, underpads and disposable pants, bath seats and rails, and toilet guard rails. The catalog also features a collection of comfort-styled shoes and slippers for women by Clinic Shoe, Drew, and Daniel Green, in standard and hard-to-fit sizes.

Special Factors: Price quote by phone; unworn returns are accepted; orders are shipped worldwide.

SEE ALSO

Allyn Air Seat Co. • *air-filled seats for wheelchairs* • **SPORTS**

The Astronomical Society • *publications on astronomy topics* • **BOOKS**

Astronomics/Christophers, Ltd. • *telescopes* • **CAMERAS**

Bailey's, Inc. • *first-aid kits* • **TOOLS**

Bennett Brothers, Inc. • *microscopes and telescopes* • **GENERAL MERCHANDISE**

Campmor • *snake bite kits, variety of first-aid kits* • **SPORTS**

Clover Nursing Shoe Company • *Nurse Mates nurses' shoes* • **CLOTHING: FOOTWEAR**

Creative Health Products • *fitness equipment, blood pressure kits, skinfold calipers, etc.* • **HEALTH**

Defender Industries, Inc. • *first-aid kits, marine safety gear* • **AUTO**

Freeda Vitamins, Inc. • *dietary supplements* • **HEALTH**

Goldberg's Marine Distributors • *first-aid kits, marine safety gear* • **AUTO**

Hillestad International, Inc. • *dietary supplements* • **HEALTH**

Mardiron Optics • *telescopes and microscopes* • **CAMERAS**

No Nonsense Direct • *nurses' hosiery* • **CLOTHING**

Okun Bros. Shoes • *nurses' shoes* • **CLOTHING: FOOTWEAR**

Omaha Vaccine Company, Inc. • *biologicals and pharmaceuticals for livestock* • **ANIMAL**

Orion Telescope Center • *telescopes* • **CAMERAS**

Plastic BagMart • *zip-top plastic bags* • **OFFICE: SMALL BUSINESS**

S & S Sound City • *closed-caption decoders* • **APPLIANCES**

Scope City • *telescopes* • **CAMERAS**

United Pharmacal Company, Inc. • *animal biologicals and vet instruments* • **ANIMAL**

MUSIC

Instruments, supplies, and services

Professional musicians rarely pay full price for their instruments, and if you buy from the same sources they use, neither will you. The firms listed here sell top-quality instruments, electronics, and supplies, and while they usually serve the knowledgeable, they can assist you even if you're a musical neophyte. If you catch the clerks during a lull in store trade, you can usually get the same kind of help over the phone—but please understand that they're usually very busy. Some of the stores take trade-ins, some rent instruments, and most sell used equipment.

By purchasing from these sources, you can save hundreds of dollars on top-rate equipment, and if you're equipping a band, you might save enough money to buy the van and pay the roadies. Get the best equipment you can—instruments can last a lifetime, and the resale market for quality pieces is good. Buy wisely today and you may be selling your "vintage" ax to Elderly Instruments or Mandolin Brothers 20 years down the road for several times what you paid!

FIND IT FAST

ACCORDIONS • *A.L.A.S.*
DRUMS • *American Musical, Sam Ash, Lone Star*
FRETTED INSTRUMENTS • *American Musical, Metropolitan Music, Shar, Weinkrantz*
GENERAL, SCHOOL, AND MARCHING BAND INSTRUMENTS • *Giardinelli, Interstate Music, Kennelly Keys, National Educational Music, West Manor*
GUITARS AND ELECTRONICS • *American Musical, Sam Ash, Carvin, Discount Music, Kennelly Keys, Manny's*

PIANOS AND ORGANS • *Altenburg*
REEDS • *Discount Reed*
SHEET MUSIC • *Patti Music*
STRINGS • *Fred's String Warehouse*
VINTAGE INSTRUMENTS • *Elderly Instruments, Mandolin Brothers*

A.L.A.S. ACCORDION-O-RAMA

16 W. 19TH ST.
NEW YORK, NY 10011
212-675-9089
212-206-8344

Catalog: $1 (see text)
Save: up to 40%
Pay: check, MO, MC, V
Sells: accordions, accessories, and services
Store: same address (11th Floor); Tuesday to Friday 9–4, Saturday 11–3

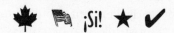

A.L.A.S., in business since 1950, has an extensive inventory of new and rebuilt accordions and concertinas that are all sold at a discount. A.L.A.S. is an authorized dealer and factory-service center for several leading brands, and can customize your instrument to meet your requirements—including MIDI. Concertinas and accordions—electronic, chromatic, diatonic, and piano—are offered here at considerable savings. A.L.A.S. carries its own line, as well as instruments by Arpeggio, Avanti, Cordovox, Crumar, Dallape, Elka, Excelsior, Farfisa, Ferrari, Gabbanelli, Galanti, Guerrini, Hohner, Polytone, Sano, Scandalli, Solton, Sonola, Paolo Soprani, Vox, and other firms. The catalog features color photos of individual models with specifications. New and reconditioned models are stocked, and accordion synthesizers, amps, speakers, generators, organ-accordions, and accordion stands are available.

When you write for information, be sure to describe the type of accordion that interests you. In addition to the color catalog ($1), you can request the black-and-white catalog, which is free, or order a video: The "Demonstration" video provides a tour of Accordion-O-Rama and the "Basics of MIDI" tape gives an introduction to MIDI. Either tape can be purchased for $25 or both for $45 (postpaid in the U.S.).

A.L.A.S. is offering readers of this book an extra 2% discount on purchases of new, full-size models. Identify yourself as a reader when you order. This WBMC reader discount expires February 1, 1995.

Special Factors: Trade-ins are welcomed; orders are shipped worldwide.

ALTENBURG PIANO HOUSE, INC.

1150 EAST JERSEY ST.
ELIZABETH, NJ 07201
800-526-6979
IN NJ 800-492-4040
FAX: 908-527-9210

Brochure: free
Save: 35% minimum
Pay: check, MO, MC, V, AE
Sells: pianos and organs
Store: same address; Monday to Friday 9–9, Saturday 9–6, Sunday 12–5; also Asbury Park, Atlantic City, Cherry Hill, Edison, Montclair, Paramus, Toms River, Totowa, and Trenton

The Altenburg Piano House has been doing business since 1847, and it's run today by a descendant of the founder. Altenburg sells pianos and organs by "almost all" manufacturers, including lines by Baldwin, Hammond, Kawai, Kimball, Mason, and Yamaha. Prices are at least 35% below list or suggested retail, and if you write to Altenburg for literature, you'll receive information on its own line of pianos—upright, grand, and console models. Complete specifications are listed for each piano, including details on the encasing, keys, pinblock, bridges, soundboard, action, strings, hammer felt, and warranty. If you're in the area of Elizabeth, New Jersey, drop by the Art Deco showroom and hear an Altenburg—they've been recommended by no less than Franz Liszt! And if you're pricing a name-brand model, call or write with the name of the piano or organ for price and shipping details.

Special Factor: Orders are shipped worldwide.

AMERICAN MUSICAL SUPPLY

235 FRANKLIN AVE.
RIDGEWOOD, NJ
07450-3295
800-458-4076

Catalog: free
Save: up to 40%
Pay: check, MO, MC, V, Discover
Sells: musical instruments and recording equipment
Store: Victor's House of Music; same address

Forget the brass and woodwinds—American Musical Supply is rock & roll all the way. The 96-page catalog opens with Shure and Audio-Technica mics, and ends with Roland mixers. Recorders, speakers, amps, headsets, signal processors, monitors, DAT and CD players and recorders, equalizers, mastering decks, pedals and effects boxes, cables, pickups, tuners, and other accessories are offered. Guitars are featured as well—the latest acoustic and electric models from Charvel, Fender, Gibson, Ibanez, Martin, and Washburn. The percussion section includes drums by Pearl and Tama, as well as cymbals, chimes, cowbells, and other esoteric instruments. American Musical Supply sells electronic keyboards and accessories, books, manuals, and videos on technique, making music with MIDI, Recorded Versions Guitar transcriptions, and much more. Prices run up to 40% below list, although discounts vary from item to item. AMS is the mail-order division of Victor's House of Music, a third-generation family business. If you need advice on the best equipment for your music, they should be able to help.

Special Factors: Minimum order is $10; C.O.D. orders are accepted; orders are shipped worldwide.

SAM ASH MUSIC CORP.

DEPT. WBMC
P.O. BOX 9047
HICKSVILLE, NY 11802
800-4-SAM ASH
IN CANADA 800-726-2740
516-333-8700
FAX: 516-333-8767

Information: inquire
Save: up to 50%
Pay: check, MO, MC, V, AE, DC, Discover, Optima
Sells: instruments and electronics
Store: 401 Old Country Rd., Carle Place, NY; Monday and Friday 10–9, Tuesday to Thursday, and Saturday 10–6; also Forest Hills, Huntington Station, White Plains, Brooklyn, and New York, NY; and Cherry Hill, Edison, and Paramus, NJ

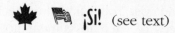 ¡Si! (see text)

In 1924, violinist and bandleader Sam Ash opened a musical-instruments shop in Brooklyn. The company is still family-run, but now boasts nine stores and patronage by superstars, schools and institutions, and the military, as well as the music-making general public. Regular half-off specials are a feature here, so don't buy anywhere else until you've given Sam Ash a call.

Musical instruments, musical electronics, karaoke, software, sound systems, home audio, electronic keyboards, recording equipment, disk jockey equipment, digital home pianos, specialized lighting, and accessories are available from hundreds manufacturers,including Akai, AKG, Armstrong, Audio-Technica, Bach, Benge, Bose, Buffet, Bundy, Casio, Cerwin-Vega, Charvel, Conn, dbx, DigiTech, DOD, Electro-Voice, E-Mu, Ensoniq, Fender, Gemeinhardt, Gibson, Guild, Harmon Kardon, Hartke, Ibanez, Jackson, JBL, JVC, Karaoke (sing-along machines), Kawai, Kenwood, King, Klipsch, Kurzweil, Leblanc, Ludwig, Marshall, Martin, Mesa-Boogie, Noble & Cooley, Ovation, Paiste, Pearl, Rickenbacker, Roland, Sabian, Samson, Selmer, Sennheiser, Shure, Paul Reed Smith, Sony, Suzuki, SWR, Tama, Takamine, Tascam, Technics, Toa, Yamaha, and Zildjian. Sheet music is stocked, repairs and service are performed, and trade-ins are accepted at the stores.

Please note: For a Spanish-speaking sales representative, call 212-719-2299.

Special Factors: Minimum order is $25; orders are shipped world-wide.

CARVIN CORP.

1155 INDUSTRIAL AVE.
ESCONDIDO, CA 92029
800-854-2235
FAX: 619-747-0743

Catalog: free
Save: up to 40%
Pay: check, MO, MC, V
Sells: Carvin instruments and accessories
Store: same address; Monday to Friday 8:30–4:30; also 7414 Sunset Blvd., Hollywood, and 1907 N. Main St., Santa Ana, CA; Monday to Friday 10:30–7, Saturday 10–6, both locations

 ¡Si!

Carvin manufactures its own line of instruments and equipment, made to exacting standards. You'll find the specifications, features, and individual guarantees of each instrument noted in the full-color catalog; prices are up to 40% less than those of comparable models. You'll also find luminaries of the pop and jazz music world shown throughout the catalog, alongside Carvin equipment—Chet Atkins, The Oak Ridge Boys, Bunny Brunel, and Stanley Clarke are a few.

Mixers, amps, mikes, monitor systems, and electric guitars are offered here, as well as professional-quality guitars designed for the requirements of professional musicians. All of Carvin's instruments and equipment are sold under a ten-day free trial arrangement. Servicing and performance testing is done free of charge during the warranty period, and warranties range from one to five years, depending on the item.

Special Factors: Satisfaction is guaranteed; returns are accepted for refund; minimum order is $15 with credit cards.

DISCOUNT MUSIC SUPPLY

41 VREELAND AVE.,
  DEPT. WB
TOTOWA, NJ 07512-1120
201-942-9411
FAX: 201-890-7922

Catalog: free
Save: 35% average
Pay: check, MO, MC, V
Sells: musical accessories
Store: mail order only

Rock guitarists should get to know Discount Music Supply, whose 40-page catalog is packed with guitars, electronics, strings, and other the accessories you need to make music. Discount Music, in business since 1986, can save you an average of 35% on list prices, and much more on selected items and lines. Quantity discounts on strings, for example, can reduce list prices by nearly 70%.

DMS sells guitars by Fender, speakers by Celestion, amps by Gorilla and Hondo; the Pignose amp, DiMarzio and Seymour Duncan, Fender, and Select pickups, Audio-Technica and Shure mikes, Sabine's Chromatic Autotuner, Conquest and SpectraFlex cables, Nady devices, Hamilton stands, guitar cleaning products, and effects boxes by Arion, Boss, DOD, Dunlop, Ibanez, and Rocktek. Studio systems and components by Boss and DigiTech are offered, as well as Hohner and Huang harmonicas and Fender picks. If you use strings by Augustine, Ernie Ball, La Bella, D'Addario, D'Angelico, Darco, Fender, GHS, Gibson, Guild, Kaman, Dean Markley, Martin, Maxima, S.I.T., or Vinci, see the catalog for enormous savings. Discount Music Supply doesn't list the entire inventory, so if you don't see what you're looking for, call, write, or fax your inquiry.

Special Factors: Quantity discounts are available; authorized returns are accepted within 14 days for exchange, refund, or credit; minimum order is $10; C.O.D. orders are accepted; orders are shipped worldwide.

DISCOUNT REED COMPANY

24307 MAGIC MOUNTAIN
  PKWY.
BOX 181
VALENCIA, CA 91355
800-428-5993
805-294-9437
FAX: 805-294-9762

Price List: free
Save: up to 45%
Pay: check, MO, MC, V
Sells: reeds for musical instruments
Store: mail order only

Discount Reed sells just that—"mail order reeds at fantastic savings"—through the four-page price list. The firm, which began business in 1980, sells woodwind reeds by the box, priced up to 45% less than the list prices—which represents really big savings if you're used to buying reeds one at a time. Reeds for all types of clarinets and saxophones are stocked, as well as reeds for oboes and bassoons, in strengths from 1 to 5-1/2 (soft to hard). The names include Grand Concert, Dave Guardala, Fred Hemke, Java, Jones (double reeds), Marca, Mitchell Lurie, La Mode, Olivieri, Rico, V-12, Vandoren, and La Voz. (If you're looking for a reed not listed in the flyer, call or write, since it may be available.) In addition, Discount Reed sells Harrison and Vandoren reed cases, reed trimmers, La Voz reed guards, Blue Note sax straps, swabs, and other accessories.

Special Factors: Satisfaction is guaranteed; minumum order is $20 with credit cards; orders are shipped worldwide.

ELDERLY INSTRUMENTS

P.O. BOX 14210-WM94
LANSING, MI 48901
517-372-7890, EXT. 123
FAX: 517-372-5155

Catalog: free (see text)
Save: 33% average
Pay: check, MO, MC, V, Discover
Sells: new and vintage musical instruments, books, videotapes, and recordings
Store: 1100 North Washington, Lansing, MI; Monday to Wednesday 11–7, Thursday 11–9, Friday and Saturday 10–6

 ¡Si!

Elderly Instruments has an extraordinary selection of in-print, hard-to-find recordings of all types of music, from folk and bluegrass to jazz and classical, listed in the closely printed 96-page "Recordings" catalog. (For a sample of Elderly's picks, call "Dial-a-Ditty-a-Day," several minutes of an Elderly selection: 517-372-1212, touch-tone phones only.) Elderly Instruments also sells books on dance, repair and construction of instruments, music history, folklore, and even songbooks and videotapes (request the "Books" catalog).

Despite the impressive publication department, this firm has built 22 years of business on vintage instruments. Fenders, Martins, Dobros, Gibsons, Rickenbackers, and other electric and acoustic guitars have been offered in the past, as well as banjos, violins, mandolins, and other fretted instruments. (There are two additional catalogs—one for electric guitars and effects, and another for acoustic guitars and accessories. Request the catalog that best answers your needs.) Elderly Instruments also sells new instruments, lays claim to the title of world's largest dealer of new Martin guitars, and is among the top 20 Gibson dealers. You'll find a good selection of equipment here by Alvarez-Yairi, Boss, Collings, Crate, DiMarzio, Dobro, DOD, E.S.P., Fender, Gibson, Guild, Martin, Sigma, Steinlinger, Stelling, Taylor, and Yamaha, among other names. The monthly "used instruments list" is sent free with catalog orders, or you may subscribe for $5 ($10 outside the U.S. and Canada). Prices are as low as 50% off list, and everything is covered by the Elderly Instruments guarantee of satisfaction (see the catalog for details).

Please note: Mail-order hours are Monday to Saturday, 9–5.

Special Factors: Satisfaction is guaranteed; unused, authorized returns are accepted within five days for exchange, refund, or credit; minimum order is $5; orders are shipped worldwide.

FRED'S STRING WAREHOUSE

212 W. LANCASTER,
   DEPT. WM
P.O. BOX 328
SHILLINGTON, PA 19607
800-677-2882
215-777-3733
FAX: 215-777-1007

Catalog: $1
Save: up to 40%
Pay: check, MO, MC, V, Discover
Sells: replacement strings for fretted instruments
Store: same address; Monday to Thursday 2–7, Friday 12–8, Saturday 9–5

This firm, also known as Fred's Music Shop, offers strings for almost every sort of fretted instrument at savings of up to 40% off list or comparable retail. The catalog lists steel, brass, bright-bronze, and phosphor-bronze strings for all guitars, as well as a selection for pedal steel, mandolin, bass, banjo, violin, sitar, autoharp, and bouzouki. The brands include Aranjuez, Ernie Ball, Black Diamond, D'Addario, Darco, Fender, GHS, Gibson, Guild, Martin, John Pearse, Savarez, Dr. Thomastick-Infeld, and Vega. Picks, cables, harmonicas, DiMarzio pickups, Ibanez effects boxes, the Crybaby and other electronics, mikes, and capos are also available at a discount.

Special Factors: Authorized returns are accepted within 14 days; orders are shipped worldwide.

GIARDINELLI BAND INSTRUMENT CO., INC.

7845 MALTLAGE DR.
LIVERPOOL, NY 13090
800-288-2334
315-652-4792
FAX: 315-652-4534

Catalog: free
Save: up to 50%
Pay: check, MO, MC, V, AE, Discover
Sells: brasses, woodwinds, and accessories
Store: same address; Monday to Friday 9–7

Giardinelli has been selling fine brasses and woodwinds since 1948, and publishes a 125-page catalog with an exhaustive listing of brass instruments, woodwinds, and accessories for both. Trumpets, flugelhorns, trombones, French horns, euphoniums, tubas, clarinets, flutes, piccolos, saxophones, oboes, and bassoons are all available. The brands include Bach, Besson, Buffet, Bundy, Courtois, DEG, Emerson, Farkas, Gemeinhardt, Getzen, Holton, Humes & Berg, Leblanc, Mercedes, Schilke, Selmer, Signet, Denis Wick, Yamaha, Yanigasawa, and others. Mouthpieces, mutes, reeds, metronomes, tuners, cases, stands, cleaning supplies, and books round out the catalog, and Giardinelli features its own line of fine stock and custom mouthpieces for brasses. Savings run up to 50%, and the customer service department can assist you if you have questions or need advice.

Special Factors: Satisfaction is guaranteed; returns are accepted for exchange, refund, or credit; institutional accounts are available; orders are shipped worldwide.

INTERSTATE MUSIC SUPPLY

P.O. BOX 315
NEW BERLIN, WI 53151
800-982-BAND
FAX: 414-786-6840

Catalog: free
Save: up to 60%
Pay: check, MO, MC, V
Sells: instruments, electronics, and accessories
Store: Cascio Music Co., 13819 W. National Ave., New Berlin, WI; Monday to Thursday 10–8, Friday 10–5, Saturday 10–2

 ¡Si!

Interstate Music Supply is a division of Cascio Music Company, which has been in business since 1949. IMS serves the needs of schools and music teachers with a wide range of equipment, listed in the 160-page catalog, at savings of up to 60%. Everything from woodwind reeds and corks to full lines of brass, woodwind, percussion, and stringed instruments is available, including repair kits and parts, cleaning supplies, neckstraps, cases, storage units, music stands, stage lighting, sound systems, piano labs, and even riser setups for bands and orchestras. There are great buys on goods from Anvil, Bach, Blessing, Buffet, Bundy, Dynamic, Emerson, Engelhardt, Fender, Fostex, Franz, Gemeinhardt, Gibson, Holton, Korg, Kramer, Leblanc, Ludwig, Mesa-Boogie, Orff, Ovation, Pearl, Peavey, Roland, Sansui, Schilke, Seiko, Selmer, Trace-Elliot, Vandoren, Vito, Yamaha, and Zildjian. The catalog shows a fraction of the inventory, so call or write if you don't see what you're looking for.

Special Factors: Satisfaction is guaranteed; price quote by phone or letter with SASE; returns are accepted within ten days for exchange, refund, or credit; institutional accounts are available; minimum order is $25; orders are shipped worldwide.

KENNELLY KEYS MUSIC, INC.

5030 208TH ST., S.W.
LYNNWOOD, WA 98036
800-426-6409
206-771-7020

Catalog: free with SASE (see text)
Save: up to 50%
Pay: check, MO, MC, V, AE, Discover
Sells: musical instruments and accessories
Store: same address; Monday to Friday 8–5; also Bellevue, Everett, Mill Creek, Redmond, and Seattle, WA

Marching bands, student musicians, guitarists—take note: Kennelly Keys has an excellent selection of instruments and equipment for all of you, at savings of up to 50% on suggested list prices. Kennelly has been in business since 1960 and runs a repair department that offers its services to mail-order customers.

Woodwind, brass, and percussion instruments are available here, as well as guitars, speakers, amps, tuners, effects boxes, autoharps, mics, stage lighting, instrument cables, and more. The brands include Altus, Armstrong, Artley, Atlas, Bach, Blessing, Brilhart, Bose, Buffet, Bundy, DEG, Emerson, Getzen, Gibson, Haynes, Kawai, King, Korg, Larilee, Latin Percussion, Leblanc, Mitchell Lurie, Manhasset, Martin, McCormicks, Meyer, Mirafone, Muramatsu, Musser, Pearl, Polytone, Remo, Rico, Roland, Seagul, Selmer, Shure, Soldano, Studio 49, Vandoren, Vito, Yanagisawa, and Zildjian. When you request the catalog, include a stamped, self-addressed envelope and indicate your area of interest.

Special Factors: Institutional accounts are available; authorized returns are accepted; minimum order is $25.

LONE STAR PERCUSSION

10611 CONTROL PL.
DALLAS, TX 75238
214-340-0835
FAX: 214-340-0861

Catalog: free with a long, self-addressed, stamped envelope
Save: 40% average
Pay: check, MO, MC, V
Sells: percussion instruments
Store: same address; Tuesday to Friday 9:30–5:30, Saturday 9:30–2

Concert, marching, jazz, and rock percussion—Lone Star stocks it all. This firm has been doing business with individuals and institutions worldwide since 1978, and publishes a 48-page catalog that lists drums and heads, cases, drumsticks, keyboard mallets, cymbals, castanets, gongs, tambourines, triangles, wood blocks, bells, percussion for Latin music, and much more. The brands include American Drum, Balter, Deschler, Vic Firth, Gambal, Tom Gauger, Goodman, Grover, Hinger, R. Holmes, Holt, Latin Percussion, Linwood, Ludwig, Malletech, Musser (Ludwig), Payson, Pearl, Premier, Pro-Mark, Regal Tip, Remo, Ross, Sabian, Silverfox, Spectrasound, Tama, Yamaha, Zildjian, etc. In the unlikely event you don't see what you're looking for among the thousands of items listed, call or write—it's probably available.

Special Factors: Satisfaction is guaranteed; authorized returns are accepted within two weeks (a restocking fee of up to 20% may be charged); institutional accounts are available; orders are shipped worldwide.

MANDOLIN BROTHERS, LTD.

**629 FOREST AVE.
STATEN ISLAND, NY
10310-2576
718-981-3226
718-981-8585
FAX: 718-816-4416**

Catalog: free
Save: up to 35%
Pay: check, MO, MC, V, AE, Discover, Optima
Sells: new and vintage fretted instruments, electronics, and accessories
Store: same address; Monday to Saturday 10–6

Mandolin Brothers has been selling vintage fretted instruments at good prices since 1971, and offers select new instruments at a standard discount of 35% from list prices. The 72-page catalog is packed with listings of vintage guitars, mandolins, mandolas, banjos, electric basses, and other stringed instruments. Part of the catalog is devoted to new equipment—guitars, mandolins, banjos, electronics, and accessories. The instruments carried include Benedetto, Breedlove, Collings, D'Angelico, D'Aquisto, Deering, Dobro, Epiphone, Flatiron, Franklin, Gibson, Guild, Heritage, Hofner Basses, Kentucky, Lowden, Martin, National Reso-Phonic, OME, Ovation, M.V. Pedulla, Jose Ramirez, Bart Reiter, Rickenbacker, Santa Cruz, Sigma, Steinberger, Stelling, Taylor, Wildwood, and Yamaha. There are pickups by DeArmond, DiMarzio, and Seymour Duncan; Fostex multitrack tape decks, and cables, strings, straps, frets, mutes, capos, books, videos, and more. Written instrument appraisals and repairs are available, and Mandolin Brothers ships in-stock instruments on a three-day approval basis—and that includes vintage equipment. If you're in the Staten Island area, you can visit the well-stocked showroom and try out any of the instruments.

Special Factors: Satisfaction is guaranteed; returns are accepted within three days; orders are shipped worldwide.

MANNY'S MUSICAL INSTRUMENTS & ACCESSORIES, INC.

156 W. 48TH ST.
NEW YORK, NY 10036
212-819-0576
FAX: 212-391-9250

Information: price quote
Save: up to 50%
Pay: check, MO, MC, V, AE, DC, Discover, Optima
Sells: instruments, electronics, and accessories
Store: same address; Monday to Saturday 10–6

Manny's has been selling musical instruments since 1935, and it's rare that this store on New York City's "Music Row" doesn't have a rock luminary or two checking out the equipment. Sales are run on a regular basis, bringing the standard 30% discounts up to 50%. Call for a price quote on instruments, electronics, and accessories, from amps and mixers to fine woodwinds and brass instruments, by Bach, Bose, Buffet, Casio, Digitech, EMG, Fender, King, Gibson, Hohner, Ibanez, JBL, Korg, Leblanc, Ludwig, Marshall, Martin, Ovation, Pearl, Peavey, Roland, Shilke, Soundtech, Stewburger, Tascam, Washburn, and Yamaha. You'll find just about anything you need here (except grand pianos, accordions, and sheet music), and if an item isn't stocked, Manny's can probably get it for you.

Special Factors: Price quote by phone, fax, or letter with SASE; orders are shipped worldwide.

METROPOLITAN MUSIC CO.

P.O. BOX 1415
STOWE, VT 05672
802-253-4814
FAX: 802-253-9834

Catalog: $1.25
Save: up to 50%
Pay: check or MO
Sells: stringed instruments and accessories
Store: mail order only

Metropolitan Music Co., in business since 1928, sells stringed instruments and accessories through the 40-page catalog, and maintains a workshop for repairs and adjustments. There are some "student" quality instruments here, but most of the models are chosen for professional musicians. Metropolitan carries John Juzek violins, violas, cellos, and basses, and bows by F.N. Voirin, Glasser, and Emile Dupree. Bridges, pegs by Taperfit and other firms, bow hair and parts, fingerboards, necks, chin rests, Resonans shoulder rests, Ibex tools, strings, cases, and bags are all stocked. This is an excellent source for the experienced musician who is familiar with the instruments and accessories. Books on instrument repair and construction are available, as well as a fine selection of wood, parts, and tools. The prices listed in the catalog are subject to discounts of 30% to 50%.

Special Factors: Price quote by phone or letter with SASE; minimum order is $15.

NATIONAL EDUCATIONAL MUSIC CO., LTD.

Catalog: free
Save: up to 60%
Pay: check, MO, MC, V, AE
Sells: instruments and accessories
Store: mail order only

DEPT. M
P.O. BOX 1130
MOUNTAINSIDE, NJ 07092
908-232-6700
FAX: 908-789-3025

 ¡Si!

NEMC has been supplying schools with new band and orchestra instruments since 1957, at savings of up to 60% on list prices. NEMC sells brass, woodwind, stringed, and percussion instruments by Alpine, Amati, Bach, Blessing, Buffet, Bundy, Decatur, DEG, F.E. Olds, Fox, Gemeinhardt, Getzen, Holton, International Strings, John Juzek, Korg, Larilee, Leblanc, Lewis, Ludwig, Meisel, Mirafone, Pearl, Ross, Schreiber, Selmer, Signet, Vito, and other makers. The 50-page catalog also offers imported master violins and violas, as well as cases, stands, strings, bows, and other accessories. NEMC provides "the longest warranty in the industry" on woodwinds, drums, and brass and stringed (except fretted) instruments.

Canadian readers, please note: Only U.S. funds are accepted.

Special Factors: Returns (of instruments) are accepted within seven days (a restocking fee may be charged); minimum order is $50; orders are shipped worldwide.

PATTI MUSIC COMPANY

414 STATE ST., DEPT. WC
MADISON, WI 53703
608-257-8829
FAX: 608-257-5847

Catalog: free
Save: 20% average
Pay: check, MO, MC, V, Discover
Sells: sheet music, music books, teaching aids, and metronomes
Store: same address; Monday to Saturday 9:30–5:30

One of the hardest items to find at a discount is sheet music, but that's the raison d'être of Patti Music Company's mail-order department. Patti Music has been in business since 1936, and publishes an 82-page catalog of sheet music and books for piano and organ, and a selection of metronomes and tuners. Savings on the sheet music run around 15%, and the metronomes are discounted up to 33%.

Piano methods, ensembles, and solos are featured, from scores of music publishers from Alfred to Yorktown Music Press. The catalog lists organ music for religious holidays, Christmas music and Broadway shoes, and flashcards, manuscript paper, theory books, and other teaching aids. The proficiency levels of the music and instructional material run from beginner to advanced. In addition to sheet music, there are key-wound, quartz, and electronic metronomes from Franz, Matrix, Seiko, and Wittner, and chromatic tuners by Seiko.

Special Factors: Discounts are available through the catalog only, not in the store; orders are shipped worldwide.

SHAR PRODUCTS COMPANY

P.O. BOX 1411
ANN ARBOR, MI 48106
800-248-7427
FAX: 313-665-0829

Catalog: free
Save: up to 50%
Pay: check, MO, MC, V, Discover
Sells: sheet music, stringed instruments, accessories
Store: 2465 S. Industrial Hwy., Ann Arbor, MI; Tuesday to Saturday 9–5

  (see text)

"Shar is managed by knowledgeable string players and teachers, who are sympathetic to the needs of the string community" states the firm, which has been in business since 1962, and prices its goods up to 50%

below list or full retail prices. The 64-page general catalog gives equal time to stringed instruments and to the firm's extensive collection of classical music recordings and sheet music. If you play violin, viola, cello, or bass, see the catalog for the cases, bows, chin and shoulder rests, strings, bridges, tailpieces, pegs, music stands, humidifying tubes, endpins, and other supplies and equipment. Student violins by Fischer, Schneider, and Suzuki are available, as well as a large collection of new, old, and rare violins by master violin makers.

The accessories catalog features hundreds of books of sheet music, manuals, videotapes, and audio cassettes. (The separate sheet music catalog, with thousands of titles, is available for $2.) Shar sells the Suzuki books and records line, videotapes of master artists (Casals, Segovia, Pavarotti, Heifetz, and others) in performance, classical recordings on CD, and sheet music for a wide range of instruments. Not all goods are discounted, but savings overall average 30%, and selected lines are offered at further savings periodically.

Canadian readers, please note: Personal checks are not accepted.

Special Factors: Satisfaction is guaranteed; C.O.D. orders are accepted; orders are shipped worldwide.

WEINKRANTZ MUSICAL SUPPLY CO., INC.

████████████

870 MARKET ST.,
 SUITE 1265
SAN FRANCISCO, CA
 94102-2907
415-399-1201
FAX: 415-399-1705

Catalog: free
Save: up to 50%
Pay: check, MO, MC, V
Sells: stringed instruments and accessories
Store: same address; Monday to Friday 9–5, PST

Stringed instruments are the whole of Weinkrantz's business—violins, violas, cellos, and basses. Weinkrantz, founded in 1975, prices the instruments and parts 30% to 50% below suggested retail. The 40-page catalog lists the available instruments and outfits, cases, music stands, metronomes, bows, strings, and other supplies. There are several pages of strings alone, including Jargar, Kaplan, Pirastro, Prim, and Thomastik. Weinkrantz carries violins and violas by Helmut Meyer, T.G. Pfretzschner, Ernst Heinrich Roth, Nagoya Suzuki, and Roman Teller. Cellos by these firms and Karl Hauser, Wenzel Kohler, and Anton Stohr are cataloged, as well as basses from Enesco, Roth, and Emanuel Wilfer. Instruments from well-known smaller workshops are also in stock, but not cataloged because of limited production. Call or write with specific requests.

If you don't want to buy an outfit, you can order the bow, case or bag, rosin, string adjusters, and other equipment à la carte. Strings, bow hair, chin rests, bridges, metronomes, and tuners are all sold at a discount. Instrument bags and cases by Gewa, Gordge, Jaeger, Reunion Blues, and Winter are also available.

Canadian readers, please note: Only U.S. funds are accepted.

Special Factors: Satisfaction guaranteed (see the catalog for the policy on strings); minimum order is $10 with credit cards.

WEST MANOR MUSIC

831 EAST GUN HILL RD.
BRONX, NY 10467
718-655-5400

Price List: free
Save: 45% average
Pay: check, MO, MC, V
Sells: musical instruments
Store: same address; Monday to Friday 9–4, Saturday 10–3 (in June and Sept.)

 ¡Si!

West Manor Music has been supplying schools and institutions with musical instruments since 1952 and offers a wide range of equipment at an average discount of 45%. The 16-page catalog lists clarinets, flutes, piccolos, saxophones, oboes, trumpets, trombones, French horns, cornets, flugelhorns, euphoniums, Sousaphones, violas, violins, cellos, guitars, pianos, drums, cymbals, xylophones, glockenspiels, and other instruments. Drum stands and heads, strings, reeds, cases, music stands, metronomes, mouthpieces, and other accessories are sold. The brands represented include Alpine, Amati, Armstrong, Artley, Benge, Besson, Blessing, Buffet, Bundy, Conn, DEG, Fender, Fox, Gemeinhardt, Holton, King, Leblanc, Ludwig, Meisel, Noblet, Olds, Premier, Sabian, Selmer, Signet, Vito, and Zildjian, among others. All of the instruments sold are new, guaranteed for one year. West Manor also offers an "overhaul" service for popular woodwinds and brasses, and can perform repairs as well.

Special Factors: Quantity discounts are available; minimum order is $25, $100 with credit cards; orders are shipped worldwide.

SEE ALSO

Adventures In Cassettes • *greatest hits compilations* • **BOOKS**

Audio House • *used CDs* • **BOOKS**

Barnes & Noble Bookstores, Inc. • *CD and tape cases and accessories* • **BOOKS**

Bennett Brothers, Inc. • *Casio keyboards, small selection of other instruments* • **GENERAL MERCHANDISE**

Berkshire Record Outlet, Inc. • *classical recordings* • **BOOKS**

Bose Express Music • *all in-print recordings* • **BOOKS**

Cherry Tree Toys, Inc. • *music box parts* • **CRAFTS**

Coronet CDs/Cassettes • *music tapes, CDs, and videos* • **BOOKS**

Dover Publications, Inc. • *classical music scores* • **BOOKS**

Forty-Fives • *original 45s from 1950* • **BOOKS**

Kicking Mule Records, Inc. • *video music lessons* • **BOOKS**

D. MacGillivray & Coy. • *bagpipes* • **CRAFTS**

Wholesale Tape and Supply Company • *tape duplicating machines and equipment* • **APPLIANCES**

OFFICE AND BUSINESS

Office machines, furniture, and supplies; printing and related services

If you're using a single source for your office needs, chances are good you're not getting the best prices on supplies, printing, furnishings, and the countless things you need to keep your business going. You can begin a cost-control program by having your buyer send for the catalogs listed here, so you can build a file of discount sources for all of your needs. And to avoid problems with questionable firms, consider making one simple rule: Don't buy from suppliers who solicit your firm by phone or fax.

If you're the head of a small business, consider buying printed envelopes from the U.S. Postal Service. The USPS and the Stamped Envelope Agency, a private concern, offer envelopes with embossed stamps (postage) in windowed or plain styles, size 6-3/4 or 10, with up to seven lines of printing (maximum of 47 characters per line), at about the cost of the postage and a box of envelopes—which is like getting the printing free. Ask for PS Form 3203 from your local post office. You can also order stamps by mail or phone, from sheets of 25 to coils of 500. Ask for PS Form 3227 at your local post office, or call 800-STAMP-24 to order by phone (Discover, MasterCard, and VISA are accepted).

Several of the firms listed here sell computers and supplies, but hardware and software specialists are listed in the next section, "Computing." Look there for vendors of computers, peripherals, programs, furniture, paper goods, supplies, and services.

For bulk pricing on garbage bags, mailroom supplies, and other packaging materials, see the listings in "Office: Small Business," following "Computing."

FIND IT FAST

BUSINESS CARDS, STATIONERY, FORMS • **Brown Print, Business Envelope**
CASH REGISTERS • **Business Technologies, Quill**
GENERAL OFFICE SUPPLIES • **Mail Center USA, Office Depot, Quill, Reliable, Schiller, Viking**
OFFICE FURNITURE • **Alfax, Business & Institutional Furniture, Factory Direct Furniture, Frank Eastern, National Business Furniture, Office Furniture Center, Quill, Viking**
OFFICE MACHINES • **Quill, Schiller**
POSTAL SCALES • **Triner Scale**
RECYCLED GOODS AND RECYCLING CONTAINERS • **Business & Institutional Furniture, Factory Direct Furniture, Quill, Viking**
SAFES • **Safe Specialties, Value-tique**

ALFAX WHOLESALE FURNITURE

370 SEVENTH AVE.,
  SUITE 1101
NEW YORK, NY
  10001-3981
800-221-5710
212-947-9560
FAX: 212-947-4734

Catalog: free
Save: up to 50%
Pay: check, MO, MC, V
Sells: office and institutional furniture
Store: mail order only

 ¡Si!

Alfax has been selling office furnishings since 1946 and does a brisk business with institutional and commercial buyers, especially schools and churches. The best discounts are given on quantity purchases, but even individual items are reasonably priced.

The 92-page color catalog shows furnishings for offices, cafeterias, libraries, and conference rooms. Tables and chairs are offered in several styles, as well as a range of files and literature storage systems. There are several pages of institutional nursery and child-care furnishings, play centers, cots, and accessories. P.A. systems, trophy cases, carpet mats, lockers, hat racks, park benches, heavy steel shelving, prefabricated office and computer stations and work stations are just a few of the institutional furnishings and fixtures available. Representative brands include Bevis, Bretford, D.M.I., Global, Harvard, High Point,

Krueger, Lyon Metal, Samsonite, and Sauder. Many products have home applications, and all of the equipment is designed for years of heavy use.

Special Factors: Satisfaction is guaranteed; institutional accounts are available.

BROWN PRINT & CO.

P.O. BOX 935
TEMPLE CITY, CA 91780
818-286-2106

Price List and Samples: $2
Save: up to 40%
Pay: check or MO
Sells: custom-designed business cards
Store: mail order only

Brown Print & Co. has been designing and printing business cards and stationery since 1966 and offers the person looking for something different just that. Mr. Brown, the proprietor, will send you a generous assortment of actual samples, ranging from black glossy stock and gold foil with iridescent metallic colors, to standard black and white cards with raised inks and artwork. Foldovers and other unusual formats are also available. Mr. Brown's talents would be wasted on someone who wanted a conventional card; his specialty is unusual design, and he enjoys working with his customers to create "the amusing, the novel, and other effective visual concepts."

Special Factors: Quantity discounts are available; minimum order is 500 cards; online with Prodigy.

BUSINESS & INSTITUTIONAL FURNITURE COMPANY, INC.

Catalog: free
Save: up to 50%
Pay: check, MO, MC, V, Discover
Sells: office and institutional furnishings
Store: same address; Monday to Friday 9–5

611 N. BROADWAY
MILWAUKEE, WI 53202
414-272-6080
FAX: 414-272-0248

Although the best prices at B & I are found on quantity purchases, even individual pieces of furniture and office equipment are competitively priced. The 80-page catalog is geared for those who are furnishing offices, but many items are appropriate for home use as well. B & I has been in business since 1960, and offers a lowest-price guarantee (see the catalog for terms). Office furniture is featured, including desks, files, bookcases, credenzas, and panels and panel systems (for office partitioning). The seating runs from stacking lunchroom chairs to leather-upholstered ergonomic executive thrones—reception, clerical, specialty, folding—they're all here. There are data and literature storage units, computer work stations, waste cans, mats, announcement boards, outdoor furniture, energy-saving devices, and much more. Over 250 brands are represented, and B & I can provide space planning and design services, free of charge.

Special Factors: "15-year, no-risk guarantee"; quantity discounts are available; orders are shipped worldwide.

BUSINESS TECHNOLOGIES, INC.

**426 W. FIFTH ST.
DUBUQUE, IA 52001
800-397-5633
FAX: 319-556-2512**

Catalog: free
Save: 33% average
Pay: company check, MO, MC, V
Sells: cash registers and related supplies
Store: same address

Business Technologies makes ringing up sales its business, selling Sharp cash registers, and supplies for virtually all makes of cash register. The firm was established in 1985, and will send you manufacturers' brochures, a guide to selecting the right register for your needs, and a roster of optional accessories that will help you customize the register to the needs of your business. Even the "simple" machines have programmable tax and percentage capabilities, and the top-of-the-line models are built-in bookkeepers and go-fers: one system can enable a restaurant to keep track of employees' tips, track its guests' balances, and even transmit an order to a kitchen printer. Management reports, credit authorization, currency conversion, scanner functions, and other features are available, depending on the model. Prices at Business Technologies are an average of 33% below list, and the firm provides technical support, a one-year warranty, and free programming.

Special Factors: Price quote by phone, fax, or letter; minimum order is $10; orders are shipped worldwide.

FACTORY DIRECT FURNITURE

225 E. MICHIGAN ST.,
  SUITE 11
MILWAUKEE, WI
  53202-4911
800-972-6570
414-289-9770
FAX: 414-289-9946

Catalog: free
Save: up to 70%
Pay: check, MO, MC, V
Sells: office furniture and institutional equipment
Store: mail order only

The 64-page catalog from Factory Direct Furniture features some of the best buys around on office furniture, filing cabinets, bookcases, seating, work stations, storage units, office panel systems, and institutional furnishings. Savings of 40% are routine, and a number of items are tagged 70% below manufacturers' list prices.

Factory Direct Furniture has been in business since 1974, and carries ergonomic seating for the executive as well as support staff, "barrister" bookcases, a full range of files, wood-veneer wall systems, computer work stations and work centers, bulletin and announcement boards, reception furniture, lockers, stacking chairs, and conference furniture. The manufacturers represented include Balt, Bevis, BPI (office panels), Buddy Products, Bush, Diversified, DMI, Edsal, Excel, FireKing, Ghent, Global Furniture, Globe, Hale, Harvard, Jefsteel, Krueger, La-Z-Boy, Lee, MBF, Mill, MLP, National, O'Sullivan, Planto, SafCo, Samsonite, Sauder, Sentry (safes), Signore, Sirco, Stylex, and Virco, among others.

Please note: Factory Direct Furniture offers a seven-year guarantee on everything it sells, normal wear and tear excepted. See the catalog for details on the warranty and the firm's "meet or beat" pricing policy.

Special Factors: Satisfaction is guaranteed; quantity discounts are available; institutional accounts are available.

FRANK EASTERN CO.

599 BROADWAY
NEW YORK, NY
   10012-3258
212-219-0007
FAX: 212-219-0722

Catalog: $1
Save: up to 50%
Pay: check, MO, MC, V
Sells: office, institutional, and computer furniture
Store (showroom): same address; Monday to Friday 9–5

 ¡Sí!

Frank Eastern, in business since 1946, offers furnishings and equipment for business and home offices at discounts of up to 50% on list and comparable retail. Specials are run in every 72-page catalog. Eastern's offerings include desks, chairs, filing cabinets, bookcases, storage units, computer work stations, and wall systems and panels. Seating is especially well represented: ergonomic, executive, clerical, drafting, waiting room, conference, folding, and stacking models in wood, leather, chrome, and plastic were all shown in the most recent catalog. Ergonomic seating is a Frank Eastern specialty, and the prices here are a good 25% less than those listed in two comparable office-supply catalogs. Manufacturers represented include Allied, Business Panels, Global Furniture, Globe Business, Jefsteel, Sauder, and Sirco. Don't overlook good buys on solid oak bookcases, wall organizers, lateral filing cabinets, and mobile computer work stations.

Special Factors: Satisfaction is guaranteed; quantity discounts are available; returns are accepted; minimum order is $75 with credit cards; orders are shipped worldwide.

MAIL CENTER USA

KYLE CENTER
4702 RESEARCH DR.,
  SUITE 140
SAN ANTONIO, TX 78240
512-699-3933
FAX: 512-699-6772

Catalog: $5 (see text)
Save: up to 40% (see text)
Pay: check, MO, MC, V, AE, Discover
Sells: office supplies and equipment, mail-room supplies, etc.
Store: 32 locations in Austin and San Antonio, TX

Mail Center USA runs a fleet of mailing centers in San Antonio and Austin, but is listed here for its mail-order office-supply business. You'll save 30% to 40% on *everything* in the big catalog ($5), and up to 70% on products featured in the quarterly sales catalogs, which are free.

The big catalog runs to 328 pages and offers everything in office needs, from accordion files to ZIP-code directories. The manufacturers represented include AccuFax, Bates, Canon, Curtis, Day Runner, Fellowes, G.E., Hewlett Packard, ITT, Ledu, Maxell, Mont Blanc, Panasonic, Pollenex, Qume, Rolodex, Stabilo, 3M, Trend Enterprises, and Verbatim, among others. Mail Center USA offers great discounts: 30% on goods totals of $15 to $50, 35% on $50.01 to $100, and 40% on orders over $100. The discounts are computed on the catalog prices, which are not inflated, and cover printing services as well (greeting cards, order forms, checks, labels, business stationery, etc.).

Mail Center USA also publishes 78-page sale catalogs that feature closeouts of seasonal goods and office supplies at savings of up to 75%. You can request the current sale catalog, which is free; if you order from it, you'll receive the big catalog free.

Special Factors: Satisfaction is guaranteed; authorized returns are accepted for exchange, refund, or credit; institutional accounts are available; minimum order is $15; online with Prodigy; orders are shipped worldwide.

NATIONAL BUSINESS FURNITURE, INC.

222 E. MICHIGAN ST.
MILWAUKEE, WI 53202
414-276-8511
FAX: 414-276-8371

Catalog: free
Save: 31% to 64%
Pay: check, MO, MC, V
Sells: office and computer furnishings
Store: mail order only

You can furnish your office for less through the 112-page catalog from National Business Furniture, which offers everything from announcement boards to portable offices at savings of up to 64%. NBF has been in business since 1975 and sells office systems, desks and tables for every purpose, credenzas, bookcases, shelving, computer work stations, desk organizers, literature racks, service carts, lockers, floor mats, reception furniture, and much more. The selection is super: There's a range of filing cabinets, and an extensive line of seating, including executive, clerical, luxury, ergonomic, conference, folding, stacking, and reception chairs. The manufacturers include Chairworld, DMI, Fire King, Global, Globe, Harvard, High Point Furniture, Krueger, La-Z-Boy Chair, National Office Furniture, O'Sullivan, Rubbermaid, Safco, Samsonite, Sauder, Signore, and Stylex, among others.

Special Factors: Price quote by phone or letter with SASE; quantity discounts are available; orders are shipped worldwide.

NEONAMERICA

P.O. BOX 67
LEONIA, NJ 07605
201-461-6500

Catalog: free
Save: 25% plus
Pay: check, MO, MC, V
Sells: neon signs
Store: mail order only

Why pay to have a neon store sign made to order, when NeonAmerica can sell you one that may fit your needs exactly—at a far better price? NeonAmerica sells self-contained neon signs with red or red/green lettering and accents and a black background, which increases the contrast and visibility of the message. The signs hang up like pictures, and are delivered ready to use. NeonAmerica's current line includes "Open," "Pizza," "Deli," "Nails," "Fresh Flowers," "Cold Beer," "Lotto," and "Lottery," among others. The price per sign is $219, shipping included, compared to a regular selling price of $295 for the sign alone. If you want a message that's not listed, call—it may be available.

Special Factor: Shipping is included.

OFFICE DEPOT, INC.

2200 OLD GERMANTOWN RD.
DELRAY BEACH, FL 33445
800-685-8800
FAX: 800-685-5010

Catalog: free
Save: up to 75%
Pay: check, MO, MC, V
Sells: office supplies and equipment
Store: over 300 stores in AL, CO, DC, FL, GA, IA, ID, IL, IN, KS, KY, LA, MA, MO, MS, NC, ME, OH, OK, PA, SC, TN, TX, VA, and WI (see catalog for locations)

Everyday office needs at extraordinary savings is the business of Office Depot, which has over 300 stores nationwide and a thriving mail-order trade. Warehouse pricing pushes savings to 75% on regular retail, and even special orders are subject to 25% off list prices. The 240-page catalog runs from accordion files to yardsticks, with the usual stock—copy paper, filing aids, desk accessories, pens, binders, office furniture, and mailroom supplies—as well as electronic organizers, portfolios and attaché cases, business manuals, safes, computers and software, janitorial supplies, fire extinguishers, and even food and drink for the canteen. Office Depot sells only current, first-quality goods by the best names in the business—Apple, AT&T, Brother, DayRunner, Eldon, Global, Hewlett-Packard, IBM, O'Sullivan, Pelikan, Polaroid, Sauder, Sharp, and Verbatim, to cite just a few. Office Depot gives you every option in ordering—by phone or fax, for pickup or delivery. If an item's out of stock, you're advised to reorder—there are no back orders to track, or odd invoices to reconcile!

Special Factors: Satisfaction is guaranteed; price quote by phone or letter; shipping is included on orders over $140 (except furniture); quantity discounts are available; authorized returns are accepted within 30 days for exchange, refund, or credit; institutional accounts are available.

OFFICE FURNITURE CENTER

322 MOODY ST.,
DEPT. 6001
WALTHAM, MA 02154
617-893-7300
FAX: 617-893-1505

Catalog: free
Save: up to 50%
Pay: check, MO, MC, V
Sells: office furnishings and accessories
Store: same address; also 1400 Devon Ave., Elk Grove, IL; Waltham, MA; and 370 Seventh Ave., Suite 1101, New York, NY

The 48-page catalog from Office Furniture Center offers attractive chairs, desks, work stations, filing cabinets, bookcases, partition systems, and other business furniture and equipment. Office Furniture has been in business since 1985, and sells at discounts that average about 35%, and reach 50% on some goods. The brands include Belcino, Bevis, Bush, DMI, Globe, Haskell, High Point, Lee, Meilink, Signore, Stacor, and Stylex, among others. Office Furniture Center's arrangements with over 250 manufacturers help ensure prompt shipment of your order.

Special Factor: Quantity discounts are available.

QUILL CORPORATION

100 SCHELTER RD.
LINCOLNSHIRE, IL
60197-4700
708-634-4800
FAX: 708-634-5708

Catalog: free (see text)
Save: up to 80%
Pay: check, MO, MC, V (see text)
Sells: office supplies and equipment
Store: mail order only

Quill, founded in 1956, offers businesses, institutions, and professionals savings of up to 80% on a wide range of office supplies and equipment. There are real buys on Quill's house brand of office and computer supplies, which are comparable in performance and quality to name brands costing much more. The monthly 56-page catalogs feature general office supplies and equipment, including files, envelopes, mailers, and ribbons and elements for typewriters, word processors, and computer printers. In addition to everyday needs—labels, scissors, paper trimmers, pens and pencils, etc.—Quill sells copiers and supplies, word processors, telephones, fax machines, binders and machines, dictating machines, accounting supplies, chairs, and much more. The computer lines include computers and peripherals, disk drives, network products, software, surge suppressors, disks, and storage units. The brands available through Quill include Ashton-Tate, Citizen, Diablo, Epson, Everex, Hammermill, Hewlett Packard, Honeywell, IBM, Logitech, Lotus, Olivetti, Panasonic, Sanyo, Star, Texas Instruments, Ventura, and WordPerfect, among others. Quill also runs a stationery department with great prices on custom-imprinted business stationery, labels, and forms.

Please note: Quill does business with companies and professionals. Terms (30 days net) are available to qualified businesses.

Special Factors: Satisfaction is guaranteed; institutional accounts are available; returns are accepted.

RAPIDFORMS, INC.

**301 GROVE RD.
THOROFARE, NJ 08086
800-257-8354
FAX: 800-422-8113**

Catalog: free (see text)
Save: up to 40%
Pay: check, MO, MC, V
Sells: business forms and products
Store: mail order only

Rapidforms offers four different specialty catalogs featuring a wide range of business forms designed for every commercial purpose, which are formatted to expedite routine transactions. The firm has been doing business since 1939, and emphasizes commitment to service and quality products.

The "Manufacturing and Wholesale" catalog features invoices, purchase orders, bills of lading, export forms, shipping products, checks, stationery, and labels in various sizes, shapes, and designs. In the "Retail" catalog, you'll find a complete line of sales slips, plastic and paper bags, gift certificates, pricing guns and labels, garment tags, security systems, and other retail merchandising products. The "Contractor" catalog offers specialty forms and products, such as proposals, job invoices, work orders, estimating forms, change orders, and subcontractor agreements. The "Omni," or full-line catalog, is a collection of forms and products from each of the specialty catalogs, as well as forms for the repair service and automotive trades. Each catalog also includes a line of continuous computer forms, with a compatibility index for numerous software programs.

Special Factors: Request the catalog desired *by title;* shipping is included on prepaid orders; C.O.D. orders are accepted; orders are shipped worldwide.

RELIABLE CORP.

■■■■■■■■

1001 W. VAN BUREN ST.
CHICAGO, IL 60607
800-359-5000
FAX: 800-326-3233

Catalog: free
Save: up to 80%
Pay: check, MO, MC, V, AE
Sells: office supplies and equipment
Store: mail order only

Reliable's commitment to giving deep discounts to small businesses has kept it going strong since it was founded in 1918. The firm's big catalog, published twice a year, feature 8,500 products from Reliable's 30,000-plus item stock. Everything is from nationally known manufacturers, from the Ampad legal tablets to the Waber surge suppressors. Savings on list run to 80%, and you *don't* have to buy in huge quantities. And Reliable backs everything it sells with an unconditional assurance of satisfaction.

Special Factors: Satisfaction is guaranteed; institutional accounts are available; minimum order is $25.

RELIABLE HOME-OFFICE

■■■■■■■■

P.O. BOX 804117
CHICAGO, IL 60680-9968
800-869-6000
FAX: 800-326-3233

Catalog: $2
Save: up to 50%
Pay: check, MO, MC, V, AE, DC, Discover
Sells: home office equipment and supplies
Store: mail order only

The handsome, 60-page color catalog from Reliable HomeOffice delivers a design statement seldom seen from discount suppliers. Reliable has been recommended for its good prices, which are up to 50% below retail, and attention to service. The glossy color catalog focuses on the home office, featuring products that have been chosen for their visual impact as well as function and price: ergonomic chairs, compact file/desk units, halogen and fluorescent desk and floor lamps, oak computer carts, sleek filing cabinets, "barrister" bookcases, drafting tables, wire grid organizers and wall units, travel accessories, room intercoms, fax supplies, and even luggage and briefcases. Reliable has expanded the line of electronics and equipment to include desk and laptop computers, copiers, fax machines, calculators, state-of-the-art phones and communications devices, paper shredders, hand-held electronic translators and dictionaries, dictating machines, compact TVs and tape players, and much more. The catalog usually features a number of "fun" items—novelty phones, unusual desk organizers, keyless door locks, etc.—that help make this a great source for gifts and indulgences, at good prices.

Special Factors: Satisfaction is guaranteed; price quote by phone; minimum order is $15 with credit cards.

SAFE SPECIALTIES, INC.

█████████████

215 CENTER PARK DR.,
   SUITE 650
W. 40 TRADE CENTER
KNOXVILLE, TN 37922
800-695-2815
IN TN 615-675-2815
FAX: 615-675-2850

Catalog: $2
Save: 30% average
Pay: check, MO, MC, V, Discover
Sells: home and office safes
Store: same address; Monday to Friday 9–6

Safe Specialties, Inc., has been selling home and office safes since 1989, and offers popular home and office models at an average of 30% off list prices. SSI also manufactures the "Lockette Lockbox," a lockbox ideal for use in homes, office, hotel and hospital rooms, mobile homes, etc. (SSI can paint the box to blend with your existing decor, and produce custom sizes—call or write for information.) And if you're shopping for a safe made by any major manufacturer, give SSI a call. Depository safes, pistol boxes, gun safes, secured boxes for RVs and trucks, data and diskette safes, in-wall and in-floor safes, fire-resistant file cabinets, and other models are available at competitive prices, from Amsec, FireKing, Ft. Knox, Hayman, Homak, Liberty, Meilink, Star, Stowline, Treadlok, and other firms. If you live on the East Coast, SSI can have your safe installed for you, or provide directions on how to do it. Call or write if you're looking for a size or style not shown in the catalog.

Safe Specialties is offering readers a discount of 2% on their first order paid by check or money order, not credit card. Be sure to identify yourself as a WBMC reader when you order, and deduct the discount from the cost of the goods only. This WBMC reader discount expires February 1, 1995.

Special Factor: Shipping is included on some models.

SCHILLER & SCHMIDT INC.

3100 N. ELSTON AVE.
CHICAGO, IL 60618-7191
800-621-1503
312-463-1060
FAX: 312-588-6875

Catalog: $3.50, deductible (see text)
Save: up to 65%
Pay: check, MO, MC, V
Sells: office supplies and equipment
Store: mail order only

Schiller & Schmidt has been selling office supplies since 1927, and offers some great deals on such everyday office needs as printer ribbons and toner cartridges, computer disks, envelopes and mailers, file folders and archive boxes, and chairs. Schiller & Schmidt is a good source for anyone outfitting a small company or a home office, because the firm gives good "volume" prices on single items. The office "superstores" usually sells by the box or multiple, and if you've ever been stuck with half a dozen bottle of white-out that dried up before you got to use them, you'll appreciate being able to buy by the "each." The $3.50 catalog fee can be deducted from your first order of $100 or more.

Special Factors: Shipping is included on orders over $50 to $150, depending on the delivery address; quantity discounts are available; authorized returns are accepted for exchange, refund, or credit; minimum order is $25.

STAPLES, INC.

ATTN: MARKETING
   SERVICES
100 PENNSYLVANIA AVE.
P.O. BOX 9328
FRAMINGHAM, MA
   01701-9328
800-333-3330
FAX: 508-370-8750

Catalog: free
Save: 50% average
Pay: check, MO, MC, V, AE, Discover, Staples Charge
Sells: office supplies, furniture, and business machines
Store: 130 stores in CA, CT, DC, DE, MA, MD, NH, NJ, NY, OH, PA, RI, and VA (locations are listed in the catalog)

Staples delivers "The Price Revolution in Office Products," an office superstore with deep discounts on every item. Staples was founded in 1986 and has earned a loyal following among buyers for small and home offices, as well as larger firms. Staples publishes a 200-page catalog of products with the "catalog list" prices and the Staples price. These are no closeouts, seconds, or unbranded goods, but first-quality products from Acco, Adams (forms), Alvin, Apple Computer, AT&T, Bates, Brother, Canon, Casio, Cross, Curtis, Dell, Dennison Carter's, Eldon, Esselte, Faber Castell, GBC, Globe-Weis, Hammermill, Hewlett Packard, IBM, Maxell, Mont Blanc, Murata, Olympus (recorders), Panasonic, Parker, Phone-Mate, Ricoh, Rolodex, Rubbermaid, SCM, Sentry (safes), Sharp, Sony, Southworth (paper), Texas Instruments, 3M, Vanguard, Velobind, Verbatim, Waterman (pens), and Wilson Jones, among others. You can order office furniture, computers and supplies, paper and forms, filing supplies, business cases, calendars, pens and pencils, adhesives, mailing room supplies, janitorial products, fax machines, copiers, phones and phone machines, and much more through the catalog or by phone. If there's a tradeoff for the savings and product choice, it's in *options*, like color or odd sizes.

Staples offers a free, no-obligation membership card that entitles you to extra savings on selected items. A separate Staples charge card is also available, and you can apply for either through the catalog. Please note that delivery charges are $15 for orders under $150, and free on orders above that amount.

Special Factors: Returns in original packaging are accepted within 30 days for exchange, refund, or credit; minimum order is $15 with credit cards.

TRINER SCALE

2842 SANDERWOOD
MEMPHIS, TN 38118
901-795-0746
FAX: 901-363-3114

Flyer: free
Save: 30% (see text)
Pay: check or MO
Sells: pocket scale
Store: same address; Monday to Friday
8–4:30

Triner Scale, which was founded in 1897, sells a pocket scale with all sorts of uses. It's a precision instrument that measures things that weight up to four ounces, and it comes packed in a pocket-sized case with a list of current postal rates tucked inside. A finger ring allows the scale to hang while measurements are taken; the thing to be weighed is secured with an alligator clip. Suggested uses include postage determination, food measurement, lab use, craft and hobby use, and weighing herbs. It's a useful item to have on hand, and it can give you accurate readings of postage costs. Triner also sells a full line of mechanical and electronic postal scales that are competitively priced; inquire for information.

Special Factors: Shipping is included; orders are shipped worldwide.

TURNBAUGH PRINTERS SUPPLY CO.

104 S. SPORTING HILL RD.
MECHANICSBURG, PA
17055-3057
717-737-5637

Catalog: $1
Save: see text
Pay: check or MO
Sells: printing supplies and new and used equipment
Store: same address; Monday to Friday 8–4

Turnbaugh offers the printer working in the manner of Gutenberg new and used presses, type, and related equipment and supplies. Savings on used equipment are as much as 70%, compared to the prices of new goods. Turnbaugh's stock is listed in *Printer's Bargain News,* a broadside that is published every two years.

Turnbaugh has been in business since 1931, and sells printing presses of every vintage, including hand, antique, treadle, and power (but not computerized) presses; offset machines, paper trimmers, stapling machines, folders, booklet stitchers, punching machines, numbering machines, and related equipment. Goods by Baltimore, Chandler & Price, Gordon, and Kelsey show up frequently. The catalog descriptions include the general condition and bed dimensions of the presses. Type, leads, rules, leaders, quoins, keys, spacers, gauge pins, printers' saws, composing sticks, cold padding cement, ink, type cleaner, rollers, type cabinets and cases, engraving tools, bone paper folders, embossing powder, paper stock, shipping tags, and other goods are offered as well.

Special Factors: Price quote by letter with SASE; *no printing services are available;* minimum order is $10; orders are shipped worldwide.

20TH CENTURY PLASTICS, INC.

3628 CRENSHAW BLVD.
LOS ANGELES, CA 90016
213-731-0900
FAX: 213-735-9901

Catalog: free
Save: up to 35%
Pay: check, MO, MC, V, AE, Discover, Optima
Sells: photo albums and accessories, binders, organizers, etc.
Store: mail order only

 ¡Si!

20th Century Plastics helps you save your memories with a wide selection of archival photo and slide storage sheets and albums, as well as safekeepers for your collections of stamps, baseball cards, recipes, and periodicals. The 48-page, color catalog also features a variety of binders and report covers, as well as photo albums, video and audio cassette portfolios, static-proof floppy disk storage, and business-card files. The prices of the archival quality photo storage products are excellent, and there are especially good prices on the albums. Whether you're organizing snapshots at home or creating a storage and filing system for a large office, you'll find solutions at 20th Century Plastics.

Special Factors: Satisfaction is guaranteed; returns are accepted within 30 days for exchange, refund, or credit; orders are shipped worldwide.

VALUE-TIQUE, INC.

**P.O. BOX 67, DEPT. WBM
LEONIA, NJ 07605
201-461-6500**

Catalog: $1 (see text)
Save: 25% plus
Pay: check, MO, MC, V, AE, DC, Discover, Optima
Sells: Sentry safes, fireproof files, EDP media safes
Store: Discount Safe Outlet, 117 Grand Ave., Palisades Park, NJ; Monday to Friday 9–5, Saturday 9–1

Value-tique has been selling home and office safes since 1968, and offers a range of well-known brands at discounts of 25% and more. Your savings are actually greater, because Value-tique also pays for shipping. And the $1 catalog fee (requested in cash by the owner) buys a $5 credit certificate, good on any purchase. Value-tique sells Sentry Safes, including a model camouflaged as a furniture cabinet, the Media-Safe for computer disk storage, a standard home and office safe, and different wall safes. Elsafe, Fichet-Bauche, Gardall, Knight, and Star safes are also available, as well as Pro-Steel gun safes. Models include wall and in-floor safes, cash-drop safes, and many others for home and business use. If you're not sure of the best type for your security purposes, call Value-tique to discuss your needs. Before ordering, *measure* to be sure the safe will fit the intended location.

Special Factor: Shipping is free in the 48 contiguous United States.

VIKING OFFICE PRODUCTS

**13809 SO. FIGUEROA ST.
LOS ANGELES, CA 90061
800-421-1222
FAX: 800-SNAPFAX**

Catalog: free (see text)
Save: up to 69%
Pay: check, MO, MC, V
Sells: office supplies, furniture, and computer supplies
Store: mail order only

Viking Office Products began business in 1960, and sells office supplies, furnishings, and computer supplies at discounts of up to 69%. The semi-annual, 302-page general catalog features daily office needs, from pens and markers to ergonomic seating and filing cabinets, all of which are sold at a discount. The brands represented include Avery, BIC, Boston, Canon, Eaton, Faber Castell, IBM, La-Z-Boy, Pendaflex,

Pentel, Rubbermaid, Smead, Sony, 3M, Toshiba, and Wilson Jones, as well as Viking's own label. Specials on selected goods are offered in the monthly sale catalogs.

Special Factors: Satisfaction is guaranteed; institutional accounts are available; shipping is free on orders over $25 (to the contiguous 48 United States).

VULCAN BINDER & COVER

KEY WBM
BOX 29
VINCENT, AL 35178
800-633-4526
205-672-2241
FAX: 205-672-7159

Catalog: free
Save: up to 40%
Pay: check, MO, MC, V, AE
Sells: binders and supplies
Store: mail order only

Three-ring binders can be quite pricey at stationery stores, which is why it makes sense to buy from the manufacturer. Vulcan can save you up to 40% on all of your binder needs, from light-duty models with flexible covers to heavy-duty binders with 3" D-rings. Vulcan's 48-page catalog also shows magazine files, zippered binders, catalog binders, 19-ring styles, pocket sizes, tabbed inserts, notepad holders, report covers, page protectors, cassette cases, and business cases and leather luggage. Custom imprinting is available on the binders and tabbed dividers.

Special Factors: Satisfaction is guaranteed; quantity discounts are available; returns are accepted within 15 days for exchange, refund, or credit; minimum order is $25.

SEE ALSO

A to Z Luggage Co., Inc. • *attaché cases and briefcases* • **LEATHER**
Ace Leather Products, Inc. • *attaché cases and briefcases* • **LEATHER**
The American Stationery Co., Inc. • *custom-printed stationery, notepads, and envelopes* • **GENERAL MERCHANDISE**
Barnes & Barnes • *office furnishings* • **HOME: FURNISHINGS**
Bernie's Discount Center, Inc. • *phones, phone machines, fax machines, copiers, calculators, etc.* • **APPLIANCES**

Dick Blick Co. • *flat files and display equipment* • **ART MATERIALS**

Cherry Hill Furniture, Carpet & Interiors • *office furnishings* • **HOME: FURNISHINGS**

Cornell Paper & Box Co., Inc. • *mailers, shipping cartons, tape, etc.* • **OFFICE: SMALL BUSINESS**

Crutchfield Corporation • *copiers, phone machines, fax machines, etc.* • **APPLIANCES**

Current, Inc. • *check-printing services* • **BOOKS**

Dinn Bros., Inc. • *recognition and achievement awards* • **SPORTS**

Flax Art & Design • *drafting furniture, supplies, and equipment* • **ART MATERIALS**

Jerry's Artarama, Inc. • *ergonomic chairs and flat files* • **ART MATERIALS**

The Jompole Company, Inc. • *pen and pencil sets, premiums, etc.* • **HOME: TABLE SETTINGS**

Don Lamor Inc. • *office furnishings* • **IN HOME: FURNISHINGS**

Leather Unlimited Corp. • *leather attaché cases, card cases, portfolios, etc.* • **LEATHER**

Loftin-Black Furniture Company • *office furnishings* • **HOME: FURNISHINGS**

The Luggage Center • *business cases* • **LEATHER**

LVT Price Quote Hotline, Inc. • *calculators, typewriters, phones, fax machines, pens, etc.* • **APPLIANCES**

Ephraim Marsh Co. • *fine executive furnishings* • **HOME: FURNISHINGS**

Plastic BagMart • *trash can liners* • **OFFICE: SMALL BUSINESS**

Plexi-Craft Quality Products Corp. • *acrylic racks, desk accessories, etc.* • **HOME: FURNISHINGS**

Protecto-Pak • *zip-top plastic bags* • **OFFICE: SMALL BUSINESS**

S & S Sound City • *phones and phone machines* • **APPLIANCES**

Sobol House of Furnishings • *contract furnishings* • **HOME: FURNISHINGS**

St. Charles Furniture Co. • *office furnishings* • **HOME: FURNISHINGS**

Stuckey Brothers Furniture Co., Inc. • *office furnishings* • **HOME: FURNISHINGS**

Think Ink • *inexpensive thermographic color hand printers* • **CRAFTS**

Triad Furniture Discounters • *office furnishings* • **HOME: FURNISHINGS**

Turner Tolson, Inc. • *office furnishings* • **HOME: FURNISHINGS**

Turnkey Material Handling, Inc. • *parts bins, office and institutional furnishings, and fixtures* • **TOOLS**

U.S. Box Corp. • *product packaging for resale* • **OFFICE: SMALL BUSINESS**

University Products, Inc. • *archival-quality storage supplies for microfiche and microfilm; library supplies and equipment* • **OFFICE: SMALL BUSINESS**

Wholesale Tape and Supply Company • *mailing supplies for tapes* • **APPLIANCES**

Computing

Computers, peripherals, software, supplies, furniture, and accessories

If you're a first-time computer buyer or want to upgrade your current system, learn as much as you can from as many sources as possible. Attend demonstrations of new products, watch colleagues at work with different systems and programs, and ask questions. Don't assume that any software will perform as promised, no matter who's vouching for it. Evaluate your current and anticipated requirements as carefully as possible, since buying the right equipment and software the first time is the best money spent. Determine what you'll be doing with the computer, and what you'd like to be able to do in six months. How much RAM will the software and operating system require to make that possible? Are you buying for individuals who travel, desk-bound workers, or both? Is a combination of separate notebooks and desktop systems practical, or would docking stations work best? Consult the repair shop of a large computer outlet to get an idea of how much repairs run on different types of equipment, and evaluate manufacturers' warranties and service contracts offered by the resellers *before* committing yourself to added expense. Whatever you decide, use a good-quality surge suppressor, and back up your disks!

COMPUADD CORPORATION

12303 TECHNOLOGY BLVD.
AUSTIN, TX 78727
800-627-1967
FAX: 512-335-6236

Catalog: free
Save: up to 50%
Pay: check, MO, MC, V, AE, Discover
Sells: computers, peripherals, accessories, software, etc.
Store: over 90 locations (see text)

CompuAdd operates nearly 100 superstores nationwide and one in Ontario, Canada, which offer the CompuAdd combination of service, convenience, price, professional setup, on-site repairs, system design, and more. You can enjoy many of the same benefits when you buy through the 64-page catalog, which features CompuAdd's own computers, as well as other hardware, add-ons, software, and accessories. CompuAdd offers multimedia hardware, Ethernet LANs, networks, and other equipment—monitors, graphics cards, printers, scanners, modems, fax/modems, CD ROM, expansion boards and drives, coprocessors, backup systems, power conditioners (surge suppressors and UPS equipment), and goods by American Power Conversion, Canon, DFI, Epson, Everex, Intel, Kodak, Logitech, Mitsubishi, Okidata, Orchid, Panasonic, Proxima, Qtronix, Seiko, Sigma Designs, Texas Instruments, and other firms. You'll also find maintenance and repair equipment, dust covers, cleaning systems, disks and disk storage units, and software—hundreds of popular programs for everything from business productivity to utilities are available at a discount. CompuAdd has one of the best guarantees in the business, which is spelled out in detail in the catalog. The catalog also lists the store locations, but you can call 800-999-9901 for the address of the one nearest to you. In addition to the general catalog of IBM-compatible equipment, there's one devoted exclusively to software (call 800-477-4717), and another for Mac users (call 800-888-6221 for a copy).

Special Factors: Satisfaction is guaranteed; quantity discounts are available; authorized returns are accepted within 30 days for exchange, refund, or credit; institutional accounts are available; C.O.D. orders ($50 minimum) are accepted.

COMPUTER DISCOUNT WAREHOUSE

**CDW COMPUTER
  CENTERS, INC.
2840 MARIA AVE.
NORTHBROOK, IL
  60062-2026
800-597-4239
708-498-1426
FAX: 708-291-1737**

Catalog: free
Save: up to 50%
Pay: check, MO, MC, V, Discover
Sells: computers, peripherals, software, etc.
Store: same address; also 315 W. Grand
Ave., Chicago, IL

   (see text)

CDW is one of the country's top sellers of AST computers, but also sells products by everyone else, from Aldus to Wyse: Borland, Canon, Epson, Hayes, Hewlett-Packard, IBM, Intel, Logitech, Maxtor, Motorola, NEC, Pacific Data, Toshiba, UDS, and WordPerfect, among others. CDW has been in business since 1982 and publishes a 40-page catalog, but you can call for price quotes on desktops, towers, notebooks, hard drives, memory upgrades, coprocessors, monitors, printers, scanners, UPS systems, and popular software—utilities, spreadsheets, graphics, data management, communications, and networking programs. The catalog details the sales policy (including returns), so it's a good idea to request it before placing an order.

Please note: A $25 handling fee is charged on orders shipped outside the United States.

Special Factors: Price quote by phone or letter; C.O.D. orders are accepted; orders are shipped worldwide.

DARTEK COMPUTER SUPPLY CORP.

**949 LARCH AVE.,
DEPT. WBMC
ELMHURST, IL 60126
800-832-7835
708-832-2100
FAX: 708-941-1106**

Catalog: free
Save: up to 60%
Pay: check, MO, MC, V, AE, Discover
Sells: Macintosh supplies and equipment
Store: mail order only

Dartek can save you on the equipment you need to make the most of your Mac, up to 60% on the regular or list prices on many products. Dartek has been serving the industry since 1980 and offers everything from software to work stations. The 76-page color catalog shows both handheld and desktop scanners and accessories, projection equipment, fax modems, hard and CD ROM drives, Bernoulli boxes, keyboards, printers and accessories, Mac cases, monitor arms, mice, joysticks, and much more, by Appoint, CMS, Felix, Hewlett Packard, IOMEGA, Logitech, MicroCentre, Microtek, NEC, O'Sullivan, Seikosha, and 3M among others. Dartek sells a wide range of software, including desktop publishing (type, layout, clip art, photography, graphics, etc.), word processing, time management, accounting, spreadsheet, legal, mailing list and database, virus detection, utilities, disk management, communications, information/reference, languages, and Mac tutorials. And there are all the supplies you'll need to stay productive—cables, power conditioners, disks and disk storage, data cartridges, toner cartridges for laser printers (regular, refillable, and remanufactured), ribbons, banner paper, labels, binding equipment, computer care and maintenance equipment, security devices, and device connections (fax switches, music on hold, phone interruption blockers, etc.), also at savings.

Special Factors: Satisfaction is guaranteed; quantity discounts are available; authorized returns are accepted (a restocking fee may be charged) within 45 days for exchange, refund, or credit; institutional accounts are available; minimum order is $25; C.O.D. orders are accepted.

DAYTON COMPUTER SUPPLY

6501 STATE RTE. 123 N.
FRANKLIN, OH 45005
800-735-3272
513-743-4060
FAX: 513-743-4056

Catalog: free
Save: up to 50%
Pay: MC, V, Discover
Sells: disks, printer ribbons, toner cartridges, etc.
Store: same address; Monday to Friday 8–5

Dayton Computer Supply can save you up to 50% on ribbons for typewriters and printers by everyone from Apple to Xerox, and offers a comprehensive selection of new and recharged toner cartridges, ink jet supplies, copier supplies, cables, surge protectors, gender changers, adapters, mice, switchboxes, disks, data cartridges, continuous-feed paper, labels, fax paper, and more. Dayton Computer Supply has been in business since 1979, and invites you to call with the model number of your machine for current prices of supplies, or see the catalog.

Special Factors: Satisfaction is guaranteed; price quote by phone; quantity discounts are available; institutional accounts are available.

DISK WORLD, INC.

DEPT. WBMC4
4215 MAIN ST.
SKOKIE, IL 60076-2046
800-255-5874
FAX: 708-673-6038

Catalog: free
Save: up to 60%
Pay: check, MO, MC, V, Discover
Sells: data storage media, printing supplies, software, etc.
Store: mail order only

Disk World has been in business since 1983, and stocks 3-1/2", 5-1/4", and 8" disks (as available) from Athana, BASF, Dysan, Fuji, Maxell, Nashua, Sony, and 3M, data cartridges from BASF and 3M, and rewritable optical disks. Prices average 45% to 55% off list, and Disk World also sells toner cartridges and scores of printer ribbons, disk sleeves, labels, mailers, disk storage units, fax paper, and continuous-feed computer paper. A selection of software standards—database, spreadsheet, word processing, utilities, desktop publishing, networking, communications—are also sold at a discount. See the eight-page catalog, or call for a price quote.

Disk World is offering readers of WBMC a 4% discount on *first orders only,* so remember to mention this book when you place your first order. This WBMC reader discount expires February 1, 1995.

Special Factors: Satisfaction is guaranteed; returns are accepted within 30 days for exchange, refund, or credit; C.O.D. orders are accepted.

EDUCALC
CORPORATION

27953 CABOT RD.
LAGUNA NIGUEL, CA
  92677
714-582-2637
FAX: 714-582-1445

Catalog: free
Save: up to 40%
Pay: check, MO, MC, V, AE, Discover, Optima
Sells: calculators, computer peripherals, books, and software
Store: same address; Monday to Friday 8–5

EduCALC, in business since 1976, specializes in calculators and peripherals that maximize the functions of the Hewlett Packard 48SX series and 95LX palmtop computer/calculators. Canon, Casio, Franklin, Sharp, and Texas Instruments calculators are also carried, and used calculators are available. The savings average 25%, but some items are discounted up to 40%.

When hooked up to the appropriate peripherals, the HP calculators can be linked to PCs, receive messages by satellite, edit programs, save data on RAM cards, develop programs, perform language translations, and analyze mathematical, scientific, engineering, and business data with the aid of software cards. The equipment currently available includes printer/plotters, modules, interface units, RAM/ROM cards, disk drives, adapters, and personal (portable) diaries. Stands, covers, keyboard overlay systems, ribbons, printing paper, disks, plotter pens, and other supplies are offered as well. The 75-page catalog should be noted for its comprehensive bookshelf—both general and calculator-related reference texts on astronomy, navigation, engineering, higher mathematics and statistics, programming, and computer systems and languages are listed. The catalog descriptions are comprehensive, easy to understand, and include product specifications.

Special Factors: Satisfaction is guaranteed; returns are accepted within 30 days; orders are shipped worldwide.

EDUCORP COMPUTER SERVICES

7434 TRADE ST.
SAN DIEGO, CA
92121-2410
800-843-9497
619-536-9999
FAX: 619-536-2345

Catalog: $2.95
Save: up to 75%
Pay: check, MO, MC, V, AE, Discover
Sells: Macintosh shareware and CD-ROM titles
Store: mail order only

If you've been looking for a reason to take the plunge into CD-ROM technology, you've got it in the compact, 144-page catalog from EDUCORP. The nature of the technology makes it possible to store graphics, animation, and sound that eat up conventional hard disk space in nothing flat. Since CD-ROM has been the province of art techies until recently, you have a lot of things like semi-psychedelic versions of Alice in Wonderland and underground comic books, side by side with mega-works on American history, the fascinating "Dental Age Evaluation," and other highly educational topics. College board exams, language-learning programs, major collections of art images and backgrounds, fonts, and much more are available.

But CD-ROM represents only half of the business at EDUCORP, which has been serving the Macintosh world since 1984. The rest of the stock here is an enormous collection of shareware, priced from $3.99 to $6.99 per disk, depending on the quantity ordered. The shareware library includes clip art and fonts, laser arts, utilities, DAs, games, HyperCard stacks, and more, from an init file that says "bye bye" when you shut down your Mac, to MacPorkBarrel, a game that involves catching bills dropped from the Capitol building while dodging (and bribing) IRS auditors. (There are lots of practical things, too, but with After Dark's flying toasters at the top of the software chart nationwide, fun seems to have the edge these days.) In addition to shareware and CD-ROM collections, EDUCORP also sells disk storage units, blank disks in bulk, CD-ROM drives, mouse pads, cables, cleaning kits, and other maintenance products. The firm's policy, to "meet or beat" advertised prices on CD-ROM goods, ensures discounts of up to 65%.

Special Factors: Quantity discounts are available; authorized returns are accepted (a 25% restocking fee may be charged); institutional accounts are available; minimum order is $20 with credit cards; orders are shipped worldwide.

EGGHEAD DISCOUNT SOFTWARE

P.O. BOX 185
ISSAQUAH, WA
  98027-7007
800-EGGHEAD
TDD: 800-949-3447

Catalog: free
Save: up to 65%
Pay: check, MO, MC, V, AE, Discover
Sells: software and computer accessories
Store: 78 stores in CT, DC, FL, GA, MA, MD, NC, NJ, NY, PA, RI, and VA; locations are listed in the catalog

If you live in the Northeast, you probably know Egghead Discount from its stores, which offer a broad selection of software for IBM-compatible and Macintosh systems, at savings of up to 60%. Egghead's frequent two-week sale catalogs feature over 70 pages of extra discounts on popular programs and things like joysticks, mice, toner cartridges, and other necessities. But you don't have to go to the store for the savings, or limit yourself to the 1,400 or so programs on the shelves there: Egghead will give you the same good deals on mail and phone orders, as well as access to over 20,000 other programs and 40,000 other items. For an extra 5% discount on everything you buy, become a "CUE" member—it's free, and you'll receive a membership card entitling you to the 5% discount, plus a quarterly newsletter filled with tips and savings. In addition to the exhaustive selection and good prices, Egghead usually has the latest releases as soon as they're available. Call for a price and shipping quote if you know exactly what you want, or request a catalog for the current specials.

Special Factors: Satisfaction is guaranteed; returns are accepted within 30 days for exchange, refund, or credit; institutional accounts are available.

800-SOFTWARE, INC.

———

1003 CANAL BLVD.
RICHMOND, CA 94804
510-412-9020
FAX: 510-412-1550

Catalog: free
Save: up to 50%
Pay: check, MO, MC, V, AE
Sells: software, hardware, and network products
Store: same address; Monday to Friday 9–5, Saturday 10–2

800-Software has won recommendations from computer users who appreciate 800's prices, selection, and technical support. The company's well-designed, 154-page catalog lists programs for PCs, Macintosh computers, and some UNIX products, including databases, graphics, utilities, operating systems, personal finance programs, spreadsheets, desktop publishing programs, and word processing software. There are lines and products by Alpha, Amdek, Apple, Ashton-Tate, AST Research, Borland, Central Point Software, Computer Associates, Digital Research, Fox & Geller, Funk Software, Hayes, IMSI, Intel, Lotus, Micropro, Microsoft, Novell, Oasis Systems, Paperback Software, Quadram, Revelation Technology, Software Solutions, Toshiba, Word Perfect, XyQuest, and many others. You'll also find boards, buffers, graphics cards, keyboards, mice, monitors, printers, surge suppressors, modems, and other peripherals and accessories for PCs. Specials are run on a frequent basis, and the catalog is a great source for information on what's new in word processing, spreadsheet, data management, educational, and other types of programs.

Corporate and government buyers, please note: Free post-sale technical support is provided.

Special Factors: Authorized returns are accepted within 30 days (a 10% restocking fee may be charged); institutional accounts are available; quantity discounts are available; orders are shipped worldwide.

LYBEN COMPUTER SYSTEMS, INC.

P.O. BOX 130
STERLING HEIGHTS, MI
48311
313-268-8100
FAX: 313-268-8899

Catalog: free
Save: up to 70%
Pay: check, MO, MC, V
Sells: computer supplies
Store: 5545 Bridgewood, Sterling Heights, MI; Monday to Thursday 8:30–6, Friday 8:30–5, Saturday 9:30–2:30

Lyben Computer Systems, Inc. has been in business since 1982 and offers a full range of computer accessories, supplies, and peripherals. Lyben can save you up to 70% on the suggested retail price on goods from such companies as Boca, Panasonic, Sony, 3M, and Tripplite, to name a few. The color catalog includes a sampling of the over 3,000 different items Lyben stocks, and if you don't see what you're looking for, call or write—it may be available.

Special Factors: Minimum order is $15; C.O.D. orders are accepted; orders are shipped worldwide.

MACCONNECTION

14 MILL ST.
MARLOW, NH 03456
800-800-0002
FAX: 603-446-7791

Catalog: free
Save: 25% to 40% average
Pay: check, MO, MC, V
Sells: Macintosh computer hardware, software, and accessories
Store: mail order only

MacConnection was founded in 1984 by the same people who established PC Connection two years earlier. (See PC Connection's listing in this section.) MacConnection stocks the latest versions of business, entertainment, and other programs by scores of publishers, as well as hardware and accessories. MacConnection is praised for its commitment to service—it provides warranty backup and technical support for everything it sells, and a 30- or 60-day money-back guarantee on many products. You can call or write for a price quote or the catalog, or see the ads in *MacUser* and *MacWorld* for current specials.

Special Factors: Minimum order is $100 on "international" orders (except APO/FPO); institutional accounts are available; orders are shipped worldwide.

MACWAREHOUSE

P.O. BOX 3013
1720 OAK ST.
LAKEWOOD, NJ
  08701-3013
800-255-6227
FAX: 908-905-9279

Catalog: free
Save: up to 50%
Pay: check, MO, MC, V, AE, Discover
Sells: Macintosh software and peripherals
Store: mail order only

Whether you're a dedicated Macintosh user or are toying with making a cross-platform leap, you'll want to see the 136-page catalog from MacWarehouse. More than a roundup of current releases and enhancements, MacWarehouse offers an upgrade service (competitive and live) for a wide range of programs, an extensive line of enhancements and memory upgrades, network media, monitors, video cards, online service packages, and a broad range of accessories, tools, cables, hardware, and little things to make your Mac sing—including MIDI connections, video imaging kits, and sound-recording systems! And MacWarehouse has an equally impressive selection of software and programs: word processing, database systems, utilities, accounting, graphics, project managers, spreadsheets, fonts, multimedia packages, security systems, and much more. The products run from Access PC to Zephyr Palettes, and the discounts are a satisfying 25% to 50%—and even more on specials and bundled software.

Special Factors: Price quote by phone or letter; authorized returns are accepted; institutional accounts are available; C.O.D. orders are accepted; online with CompuServe; orders are shipped worldwide.

MARYMAC INDUSTRIES, INC.

22511 KATY FRWY.
KATY, TX 77450-1598
713-392-0747
800-231-3680
FAX: 713-574-4567

Information: see text
Save: 15% plus
Pay: check, MO, MC, V, AE, DC, Discover, Optima, Radio Shack card
Sells: Radio Shack and Tandy products
Store: same address; Monday to Friday 8–6

Marymac lays claim to title of "world's largest independent authorized computer dealer," and is able to offer discounts of 15% and more on *anything* in the Radio Shack/Tandy catalog. (Get a copy from your local dealer, or request one from Tandy Catalog, 300 One Tandy Center, Fort Worth, TX 76102—Marymac doesn't mail the catalog.) Price quotes are given on computers, peripherals, fax machines, cellular phones, phone machines, TVs, audio components, scanners, and other goods under the Radio Shack and Tandy labels. Marymac has a "meet or beat" pricing policy, and will pay shipping and insurance on most items delivered within the continental U.S.

Special Factors: Shipping and insurance are included on most items sent within the contiguous 48 United States; C.O.D. orders are accepted; online with GEnie; orders are shipped worldwide.

MEI/MICRO CENTER

1555 WEST LANE AVE.
COLUMBUS, OH 43221
800-634-3478
FAX: 614-486-6417

Catalog: free
Save: up to 75%
Pay: check, MO, MC, V
Sells: data storage, ribbons, paper, etc.
Store: mail order only

MEI/Micro's 28-page catalog brings the prices of computer disks into the realm of reason, even on small orders—and if you buy in bulk, the prices of even double-density disks can drop to under 19¢ each. MEI/Micro has been in business since 1986, and backs everything it sells with an unconditional guarantee of satisfaction.

MEI/Micro's own disks, which are certified to meet or exceed ANSI standards, include both 3.5" and 5.25" disks in all formats, and in colors. Disks by Dysan, Sony, 3M, and Verbatim are also available at a discount, as well as bulk and name-brand data cartridges, labels, sleeves, and mailers. You'll find well-priced disk cases and bulk storage units, head-cleaning kits, surge suppressors, and stands for keyboards, monitors, and printers. Ribbons are sold at rock-bottom prices in packs of six, prices on Hewlett Packard laser and inkjet toner cartridges are among the best around, and paper and labels are also available in bulk.

Please note: MEI/Micro doesn't ship goods outside the U.S. and Canada, and does not ship boxes of paper by the U.S. Postal Service.

Special Factors: Satisfaction is guaranteed; returns are accepted for exchange, refund, or credit; C.O.D. orders are accepted.

MICRO WAREHOUSE, INC.

P.O. BOX 3014
1690 OAK ST.
LAKEWOOD, NJ
08701-9823
800-367-7080
FAX: 908-905-5245

Catalog: free
Save: up to 59%
Pay: check, MO MC, V, Discover
Sells: computers, software, and peripherals
Store: mail order only

There's one way to keep up with the new releases, upgrades, innovations in peripherals, and other developments in computing—find a source to do it for you. MicroWarehouse not only leads with the latest releases, it also gives you great prices on everything it sells. The current catalog is over 90 pages, packed with software for DOS, Windows, OS/2, and other environments, as well as modems, fax machines, scanners, disk drives, expansion devices, printers, monitors, memory upgrades, and much more. The software runs the gamut, from word processing and integrated communications to databases, utilities, graphics, and more—you'll find everything from Act! contact management software to Zoom fax modems. The "Upgrade Warehouse" division can handle both live and competitive upgrades, making it easy to keep on top of changes as they're released. And if you want more information on a given product, the Fax Facts service will send it directly to your fax. All if this, and savings of up to 50%, have helped establish MicroWarehouse as a leading supplier—along with its MacWarehouse division, which handles the needs of Apple owners.

Special Factors: Authorized returns of defective items are accepted within 120 days for exchange, refund, or credit; institutional accounts are available; C.O.D. orders are accepted.

NEW MMI CORP.

DEPT. WBMC01
2400 REACH RD.
WILLIAMSPORT, PA 17701
800-233-8950
FAX: 717-327-1217

Catalog: free
Save: up to 40%
Pay: check, MO, MC, V, Discover
Sells: computers, peripherals, and software
Store: New MMI Corp., 2400 Reach Rd., Williamsport, PA; Monday to Friday 9–6, Saturday 10–3

New MMI Corp. has been in business since 1987, selling computer systems, disk drives, boards, monitors, printers, modems, software, and accessories by a number of manufacturers, at savings of up to 40%. New MMI provides technical assistance before and after the sale, is an authorized dealer for everything it sells, and an authorized repair center for AST, Compaq, Epson, Hewlett-Packard, Okidata, and Panasonic. The 40-page color catalog shows a wide selection of current releases and includes specifications; eight-page flyers with extra savings are mailed regularly. If you don't see what you're looking for in the catalog, call, fax, or write for a price quote—it may be available. The firm's bulletin board service can be accessed by dialing 717-327-9952 (2400 baud and up), or 717-327-9953 (1200 to 2400 baud).

Special Factors: Authorized returns are accepted (a restocking fee may be charged); C.O.D. orders are accepted.

PC CONNECTION

6 MILL ST.
MARLOW, NH 03456
800-800-0005
FAX: 603-446-7791

Catalog: free
Save: 25% to 40% average
Pay: check, MO, MC, V
Sells: IBM-compatible hardware, software, and supplies
Store: mail order only

 ¡Si!

The people who operate MacConnection (see the listing in this section) actually began with IBM-compatible systems in 1982, when they founded PC Connection—and they run both with the same commitment to selection and service.

PC Connection offers the latest versions of software, hardware, and accessories by hundreds of manufacturers, including customized Compaq computers. PC Connection provides warranty backup and technical support for everything it sells, and is a factory-authorized repair center for Canon, Compaq, Epson, IOMEGA, and Okidata products. You can call or write for the current catalog, or see the ads in *PC Magazine, PC World,* or *Windows Magazine.*

Special Factors: Minimum order is $100 on "international" orders (except Canada and APO/FPO); institutional accounts are available; orders are shipped worldwide.

THE PC ZONE

18005 N.E. 68TH ST.,
  SUITE A-110
REDMOND, WA
  98052-9904
800-258-2088
206-883-3088
FAX: 206-881-3421

Catalog: free
Save: up to 50%
Pay: check, MO, MC, V, AE, Discover
Sells: DOS and Windows software and hardware
Store: mail order only

The PC Zone combines two lines in one 48-page catalog: DOS Zone and the Windows Zone (a separate Mac Zone catalog is also available). Software stars here—the latest releases for personal productivity, communications, networking, databasing, desktop publishing, utilities, spreadsheets, word processing, graphics, fonts, multimedia, and more—over 2,000 products at last count. PC Zone includes a number of entertainment and games packages, and a minutely printed list of software that's available but not featured. In addition, PC Zone sells memory upgrades of different types, CD-ROM drives, OCR devices and scanners, monitors, mice, modems, backup devices, printers, other peripherals and accessories, and much more. If you don't see what you're looking for in the catalog, call—it may be available but not listed.

Special Factors: Authorized returns are accepted; institutional accounts are available; C.O.D. orders are accepted; orders are shipped worldwide.

BEN TORRES RIBBON COMPANY

590 E. INDUSTRIAL RD.,
  UNIT 15
SAN BERNARDINO, CA
  92408
909-796-5559

Price List: free
Save: up to 40%
Pay: check or MO
Sells: refilled and new printer ribbons and toner cartridges
Store: same address; Monday to Friday 9:30–4:30

 ¡Si!

Ben Torres can sell you the company's own printer ribbons at prices about 40% below the going rate, or refill your used ribbon cartridges at savings of over 50%. Torres' ribbon price list runs from Anadex to Toshiba, and includes scores of printer models. New ribbons are available for most models, and all of the Torres ribbon cases are refillable (please note that some cartridges can't be opened without breaking them). Laser cartridges for Apple, Canon, Hewlett Packard, and other printers are refilled as well. (Check your printer's warranty or service contract before sending in your empties, to make sure using reconditioned cartridges doesn't violate its terms.) The firm uses only the original cartridge you send (no substitutes), refills with extra toner, includes a test-pattern printout using the refilled cartridge, and guarantees your satisfaction. Torres has been in business since 1979, and guarantees your "satisfaction with impressions" of the ribbons—whether new or refilled.

Canadian readers, please note: Only U.S. funds are accepted.

Special Factors: Satisfaction is guaranteed; returns are accepted within 30 days for exchange, refund, or credit.

RICHARD YOUNG
PRODUCTS

508 S. MILITARY TRAIL
DEERFIELD BEACH, FL
  33442
800-828-9949
305-426-8100
FAX: 305-421-4654

Catalog: free
Save: up to 50%
Pay: check, MO, MC, V
Sells: computer supplies and peripherals
Store: Gold River, San Diego, and Torrance, CA; and Philadelphia, PA

Richard Young's tony, 156-page catalog of computer accessories, supplies, data storage, and office products combines full-page ads for national brands with illuminating discussions of how ink jet printers work, or *why* you can safely use another manufacturer's toner (and save money). Although it's directed to corporate buyers, the catalog will prove useful to anyone ordering at least $50 in printer supplies, data storage media (disks, tapes, etc.), storage units (cases, trays, and racks), plotter supplies, presentation materials, cables, surge protection devices, noise filters, desktop organizers (monitor arms, keyboard drawers, wrist rests, printer stands, etc.), or even the office itself—modular units that can be combined to create different kinds of work stations. Every major brand name is represented, from Alps America to Wang, and savings run up to 50% on suggested retail, depending on the quantity you're buying. If you're unsure of the suitability of a product (a refill or substitute toner, for example), don't hesitate to contact the service department for assistance.

Special Factors: Authorized returns are accepted within 30 days for exchange, refund, or credit; institutional accounts are available; minimum order is $50.

SEE ALSO

The Astronomical Society • astronomy-related computer programs • **BOOKS**
Business & Institutional Furniture Company, Inc. • computer work stations
• **OFFICE**
Clothcrafters, Inc. • cotton computer covers • **GENERAL MERCHANDISE**
Crutchfield Corporation • **PCs,** word processors, software, and supplies •
APPLIANCES

Frank Eastern Co. • *computer work stations* • **OFFICE**
Genada Imports • *computer work stations* • **HOME: FURNISHINGS**
Marv Golden Discount Sales, Inc. • *aviation computers* • **AUTO**
Jerry's Artarama, Inc. • *computer work stations* • **ART MATERIALS**
Mail Center USA • *computer peripherals, disks, and accessories* • **OFFICE**
National Business Furniture, Inc. • *computer work stations* • **OFFICE**
Office Depot, Inc. • *computers and peripherals* • **OFFICE**
Plexi-Craft Quality Products Corp. • *acrylic computer stands* • **HOME: FURNISHINGS**
Quill Corporation • *computers, peripherals, software, etc.* • **OFFICE**
Rapidforms, Inc. • *continuous forms* • **OFFICE**
Reliable HomeOffice • *computer accessories, work stations, etc.* • **OFFICE**
Safe Sepcialties, Inc. • *data and diskette safes, lockboxes, etc.* • **OFFICE**
Staples, Inc. • *computer disks, data binders, work stations, software, etc.* • **OFFICE**
20th Century Plastics, Inc. • *static-proof disk storage* • **OFFICE**
Viking Office Products • *computer supplies, peripherals, and furniture* • **OFFICE**

Small Business

Products and services for businesses

Whether you're running a small office or just drafting the plans for your first venture, maximize every dollar you spend by buying from firms that will sell to you at "bulk" discounts, or wholesale. The companies listed here can help you hold down costs, even if you can't compete with the buying power of the Fortune 500. None of the firms requires a resale certificate—at most, they ask you to send your catalog request on letterhead, or enclose your business card. But many impose minimum orders and have less generous return policies than those offered by consumer-oriented mail-order firms, so order accordingly.

Over the past few years, there's been enormous growth in "alternative" purchasing—buying clubs, members-only warehouses, barter organizations, and co-ops. Explore the options available to you and find the right combination of vendors and services for your needs; there's usually no single "right" source, and it's up to you to determine the balance between paying list price and pushing for the deepest discounts on *everything*.

CORNELL PAPER AND BOX CO. INC.

162 VAN DYKE ST.
BROOKLYN, NY 11231
718-875-3202
FAX: 718-797-3529

Catalog: free
Save: up to 50%
Pay: check or MO
Sells: packaging and resale supplies
Store: mail order only

If you shop by mail frequently, you've probably handled Cornell's goods. This firm sells everything catalogers need to pack and ship your order—boxes and cartons, jiffy bags, bubble pack, mailers, kraft paper, reinforced sealing tape, and much more. Individuals who do a lot of mailing themselves may find use for these supplies, but if you meet the $50 minimum order, you can also scoop up savings on things like toilet paper (33¢ a roll by the 96-roll case) and paper cups ($38 per thousand). Cornell sells storage boxes for archived files at $1.50 each when you buy six, or as little as 85¢ each if you order two dozen. Corrugated cardboard magazine files are also well-priced, from 50¢ to $1 each, depending on the quantity.

If you buy for a business, you'll appreciate the good prices on white mailers and cartons that are offered in hundreds of sizes, floppy disk mailers, Eco-Lite bubble shipping bags made of 100% recycled kraft and poly, clear or tan sealing tape for 50¢ a roll, and ten-pound cartons of poly twine for $17.50. Most of the quantity price breaks are listed in the catalog, and orders are sent freight collect.

Special Factors: Quantity discounts are available; authorized returns are accepted (a restocking fee is charged) for exchange, refund, or credit; institutional accounts are available; minimum order is $50.

PLASTIC BAGMART

904 OLD COUNTRY RD.
WESTBURY, NY 11590
516-997-3355

Price List: free with SASE
Save: up to 60%
Pay: check, MO, MC, V
Sells: plastic bags
Store: same address; Monday to Friday 9–5, Saturday 9–3

 (see text)

Plastic BagMart, established in 1980, offers plastic bags in sizes most frequently used in homes, offices, and industry. Prices are up to 60%

lower than those charged by supermarkets and variety stores for smaller lots. The BagMart stocks plastic bags in sizes from 2" square to 50" by 48", one to four mils thick. Garbage and trash cleanup bags, kitchen and office waste-can bags, food-storage bags, large industrial-type bags, zip-top styles, plastic shopping bags, and other types are available. The bags are sold in case lots only (100 to 1,000 bags per case, depending on the size). The price list features the most popular lines, but if you don't see what you need, write with particulars.

Plastic BagMart is offering readers of this book a 5% discount on their *first* order (computed on the goods total only). This WBMC reader discount expires February 1, 1995.

Canadian readers, please note: Orders are shipped by UPS only.

Special Factors: Satisfaction is guaranteed; price quote by letter with SASE; returns are accepted within ten days; minimum order is one case.

PROTECTO-PAK

P.O. BOX 5096, DEPT. A
LONGVIEW, TX 75608
903-757-6092
903-297-3985
FAX: 903-236-3654

Price List and Samples: $2, refundable
Save: up to 50%
Pay: check or MO
Sells: zip-top plastic bags
Store: mail order only

Protecto-Pak, established in 1983, offers heavy-duty plastic zip-top bags at savings that average 40% below comparable retail. The bags run from 2" square to 13" by 15"; their seals make them relatively water-tight. The suggested uses include storage of crafts supplies, spare parts from kits, polished silverware (wrapped in treated cloth), buttons and surplus trim for different garments, daily doses of medications and dietary supplements, office supplies, photographs, hosiery and clothing in luggage and drawers, hardware, jewelry, and other items. Special sizes and thicknesses are available, and printing services are offered (minimum order 10,000). All of the bags are approved for food storage.

Special Factors: Quantity discounts are available; minimum order is $10.

UNIVERSITY PRODUCTS, INC.

DEPT. F132
P.O. BOX 101
HOLYOKE, MA 01041
800-628-1912
FAX: 800-532-9281

Catalog: free (see text)
Save: up to 40%
Pay: check, MO, MC, V, AE. DC, Discover
Sells: archival-quality materials
Store: mail order only

You may not know it, but anarchy reigns on your bookshelves, in the pages of your photo albums, and among the works of art on your walls. It's sad, but true: most of us store and display our precious belongings in materials and under conditions that damage them, sometimes irreparably.

Help is available from University Products, which publishes the comprehensive "Archival Quality Materials Catalog." University Products has been selling conservation and library supplies to institutions since 1968 and does business with preservation-minded individuals and institutions who want to protect their collectibles and other treasures. Both the materials used in display and storage, and the conditions under which we keep them affect the long-term "health" of many collectibles. Problems with spotting, discoloration, and damage may be seen in stamps, antique textiles, comic books, baseball trading cards, postcards, scrapbooks, photographs, sheet music, and even currency. To meet the need for safe storage of these goods, University Products makes acid-free manuscript boxes and interleaving pages, files, photo albums and Mylar page protectors, archival storage tubes, slide and microfiche storage materials, mounting materials and adhesives, an extensive selection of acid-free papers of all types, and related tools and supplies. The catalog includes valuable information on conservation basics for a range of materials and collectibles. Since a "basic retouching" of an old photograph can cost over $100, each dollar spent in preservation can save a hundred in restoration—*if* restoration is possible.

Special Factors: Satisfaction is guaranteed; quantity discounts are available; institutional accounts are available; orders are shipped worldwide.

U.S. BOX CORP.

1296 MCCARTER HWY.
NEWARK, NJ 07104
201-481-2000
718-387-1510
FAX: 718-384-3756

Catalog: $3
Save: up to 60%
Pay: check, MO, MC, V, AE
Sells: resale packaging
Store: mail order only

 ¡Si!

U.S. Box Corp. has been selling packaging—boxes, bags, canisters, and displays—since 1948. This is primarily a business-to-business firm, but it offers products that consumers use routinely: wrapping paper, tape, gift boxes, ribbon, and mailing bags, for example. Prices are as much as 60% lower here than those charged for comparable items in variety and stationery stores. Volume discounts run from 5% on orders over $500 up to 15% on totals of $2,500 plus. Samples of the goods may be purchased at unit cost plus $2 shipping; this is recommended, since returns are not accepted.

U.S. Box Corp.'s 88-page color catalog shows plain and decorated corrugated cardboard mailers, boxes, shopping bags, gift and presentation boxes, poly bags, rigid plastic boxes, plastic display cases, showcase and window displays, and a full line of velvet boxes, inserts, and stands for jewelry sale and display. Both consumers and businesses should see the selection—and prices—of U.S. Box Corp.'s colorful excelsior, cellophane, gift wrap and gift tins, bows and package decorations, ribbons, and tissue paper. Consolidate your packaging needs and you'll easily meet the $150 minimum order—the current catalog includes computer disk mailers, all-purpose gift stickers (just 5¢ each), gold and silver cord-handled bags, gold folding gift candy boxes, hatbox sets, hinged partitioned plastic boxes (perfect for notions, hardware, and small parts), and jewelry display pieces, many of which could double as jewelry collection organizers. If you're looking for dramatic home accents, see the line of "classical displays." These are cast stone figures that are modeled after Michelangelo's David, Diana, Apollo, and even King Tut. There are also Corinthian column pedestals, lions, and cherubs. Prices are reasonable, beginning at under $25.

Special Factors: Returns are not accepted; minimum order is $150; orders are shipped worldwide.

SEE ALSO

Business Technologies, Inc. • *cash registers* • **OFFICE**

Cherry Hill Furniture, Carpet & Interiors • *contract furnishings* • **HOME: FURNISHINGS**

Current, Inc. • *gift wrapping paper and ribbon* • **BOOKS**

Hunt Galleries, Inc. • *custom-upholstered furnishings for institutions, designers, etc.* • **HOME: FURNISHINGS**

The Jompole Company, Inc. • *pen and pencil sets, premiums, etc.* • **HOME: TABLE SETTINGS**

New England Basket Co. • *ribbon, bows, gift tags, baskets, etc.* • **GENERAL MERCHANDISE**

Oriental Trading Company, Inc. • *fundraising and promotional items* • **TOYS**

Rapidforms, Inc. • *gift boxes and packing and shipping supplies* • **OFFICE**

Turnkey Material Handling Co. • *industrial containers and storage systems* • **TOOLS**

Turnkey Material Handling, Inc. • *parts bins, office and institutional furnishings, and fixtures* • **TOOLS**

U.S. Toy Company, Inc. • *gifts, premiums, fundraising items* • **TOYS**

Yazoo Mills, Inc. • *shipping tubes* • **ART MATERIALS**

Richard Young Inc. • *POS and ATM machine ribbons and supplies* • **OFFICE**

SPORTS AND RECREATION

Equipment, clothing, supplies, and services
for recreational activities

If the high price of recreation equipment seems unsporting to you, you've turned to the right place. Discounts of 30% are standard among many of the suppliers listed here, who sell clothing and equipment for cycling, running, golfing, skiing, aerobics, racquet sports, skin and scuba diving, camping, hunting, hiking, basketball, triathloning, soccer, and other endeavors. Racquet stringing, club repairs, and other services are usually priced competitively as well. Buying your gear by mail may be the only sport that repays a nominal expenditure of energy with such an enhanced sense of well-being.

If you've been sedentary for some time, have a complete physical before beginning any workout program or sport. Stop and cool down if you're in pain, but don't give up. You can make running, aerobics, and racquet sports easier on your joints by wearing properly fitted shoes, learning correct foot placement, and working out on a resilient surface. Low-impact aerobics, fast-paced walking, and swimming are less stressful than running, calisthenics, and traditional sports. Getting fit should be a pleasure, and if you take the time to find an enjoyable, challenging sport or workout routine, cardiovascular health and vigor will be more easily won.

FIND IT FAST

CAMPING • *Campmor, Gander Mountain, Survival Supply*
CYCLING • *Bike Nashbar, Cycle Goods, Performance Bicycle Shop*
EXERCISE EQUIPMENT • *Better Health*

GOLF • *Austad's, Custom Golf Clubs, Golf Haus, Las Vegas, Performance Golf, Tee House, Telepro*
HUNTING • *Bowhunters Warehouse, Cabela's, Cheap Shot, Gander Mountain, Sport Shop, Wiley's*
RACQUET SPORTS • *Holabird, Las Vegas*
SOCCER • *Soccer International*
SWIMMING POOL SUPPLIES • *LPI*
TROPHIES • *Dinn Bros.*
VOLLEYBALL • *Spike Nashbar*
WALKING • *Walk USA*
WATER SPORTS • *Bart's, Berry Scuba, Central Skindivers, Overton's, Sailboard Warehouse*

ALLYN AIR SEAT CO.

18 MILLSTREAM RD.,
  DEPT. WBMC
WOODSTOCK, NY 12498
914-679-2051

Flyer: free with SASE
Save: up to 50%
Pay: check or MO
Sells: air-filled vehicle seat cushions
Store: mail order only

Allyn Air Seat sells air-filled cushions that help you go the distance, whether you're traveling by bike, car, plane, truck, or wheelchair. The cushions help absorb road vibration and bumps, making travel easier and less wearying. The stock includes heavy-duty, air-filled seats for bicycles ($13), motorcycles ($35), standard and bucket auto seats, aircraft seats, wheelchairs, and trucks ($35). Allyn Air Seat also sells covers for lawn and garden tractors, ATVs, snowmobiles, and motorcycles. Allyn Air was established in 1979 and prices some of its goods 30% below the competition.

Special Factors: C.O.D. orders are accepted; orders are shipped worldwide.

AUSTAD'S

DEPT. 30113
P.O. BOX 1428
SIOUX FALLS, SD
  57196-1428
800-759-4653, EXT. 30113

Catalog: free
Save: up to 30%
Pay: check, MO, MC, V, AE, DC, Discover, Optima
Sells: golf equipment and apparel
Store: 1600 Rte. 83, Oak Brook, IL; 7485 France Ave. South, Edina, and 648 NE Hwy. 10, Blaine, MN; also Tenth and Cleveland, Sioux Falls, SD

Austad's, established in 1963, features clubs and other equipment designed to meet the golfing needs and fit the budgets of all kinds of golfers. Training aids, accessories, carts—everything to help you enjoy your game can be found in the full-color catalog. And Austad's own clothing line, Linksport, will keep you fashion-forward on the course, without costing you a fortune.

Special Factors: Satisfaction is guaranteed; orders are shipped world-wide.

BART'S WATER SKI CENTER, INC.

HWY. 13
P.O. BOX 294-WBM
NORTH WEBSTER, IN
  46555
800-348-5016
FAX: 219-834-4246

Catalog: free
Save: up to 40%
Pay: check, MO, MC, V, AE, Discover, Optima
Sells: water-sports gear, equipment, and accessories
Store: same address; Monday to Saturday 9–6

The thrills of water skiing are cheaper at Bart's, where wet suits and skis cost up to 40% below list, and clearance items are offered at even greater savings. Bart's has been in business since 1971, and backs every sale with a guarantee of satisfaction. The 48-page color catalog features water skis that range from beginners' to tournament models by Connelly, EP, Jobe, Kidder, and O'Brien. Kneeboarders can choose from pages of boards and accessories, and there's a large selection of floats, tubes, and other inflatables. Ski vests and wet suits for men, women, and children are offered, in addition to wet suit accessories, swimwear for men and women, T-shirts, and sunglasses. Gloves, slalom (tow) lines, boat hardware and accessories, and manuals and videotapes on water skiing are also available.

Special Factors: Satisfaction is guaranteed; quantity discounts are available; returns are accepted within 60 days; orders are shipped worldwide.

BERRY SCUBA CO.

DEPT. WBMC
6674 N. NORTHWEST
  HWY.
CHICAGO, IL 60631
800-621-6019
312-763-1626
FAX: 312-775-1815

Catalog: free
Save: up to 40%
Pay: check, MO, MC, V, AE, Discover, Optima
Sells: scuba-diving gear
Store: same address; also North Pier Mall, Chicago; Lombard and Palatine, IL; and Atlanta, GA

Berry, "the oldest, largest, and best-known direct-mail scuba firm in the country," carries a wide range of equipment and accessories for diving and related activities. Shop here for regulators, masks, wet suits, fins, tanks, diving lights, strobes, underwater cameras and housing, Citizen diving watches, pole spears, and other gear and accessories for underwater use. The brands include Arena, Bay Side, Chronosport, Citizen, Cyalume, Dacor, Deep Sea, Desco, Global, Henderson, Ikelite, Mako, Mares, Nikon, Parkway, Pennform, Poseidon, Princeton, Scuba Systems, Sea & Sea, Seatec, Sherwood, T.U.S.A., Timex, Trident, Undersea Guns, Underwater Kinetics, U.S. Divers, U.S. Tech, Viking, and Wenoka. Berry does business on a price-quote basis, but will send you the 64-page catalog, on request.

Special Factor: Orders are shipped worldwide.

BETTER HEALTH FITNESS

**5201 NEW UTRECHT AVE.
BROOKLYN, NY 11219
718-436-4693
FAX: 718-854-3381**

Information: inquire
Save: up to 20%
Pay: check, MO, MC, V, AE, Optima
Sells: exercise equipment
Store: same address; Monday to Wednesday
10–6, Thursday 10–8, Sunday 12–5 (closed
Friday and Saturday)

Whether you're buying a stationary bicycle for rainy-day workouts or outfitting an entire gym, you'll get it for less at Better Health. The firm has been selling top-of-the-line models since 1977, including Alva (barres), Barracuda, Bodyguard, Cal-Gym, Cat-Eye, Everlast, Fitness Master, Healthometer, H.W.E. Massage, Life Fitness, Marcy Fitness, Monark (cycles), Pacemaster (treadmills), Parabody, Penco (lockers), Precor, Pro-Tec, Quinton, Rollerblade, Titan, Trotter (treadmills), Tunturi, and Vectra. You can save up to 20% on the regular prices of equipment by these and other manufacturers. Call or write for quotes on multi-station units, free-weight benches, mats, dance studio equipment, hot tubs, saunas, locker room equipment, and related goods. Better Health also carries sportswear by Danskin, Everlast, and Gold's Gym, and gym layout and design services are available to local customers.

Special Factors: Satisfaction is guaranteed; price quote by phone or letter with SASE; authorized returns are accepted within 15 days for exchange, refund, or credit; minimum order is $50; orders are shipped worldwide.

BIKE NASHBAR

4111 SIMON RD.,
DEPT. WBM4
YOUNGSTOWN, OH
44512-1343
800-NASHBAR
FAX: 800-456-1223

Catalog: free
Save: up to 30%
Pay: check, MO, MC, V, Discover
Sells: bicycles, accessories, apparel, and equipment
Store: same address; also three other locations (listed in the catalog)

Bike Nashbar, one of the country's top sources for the serious cyclist, publishes an 84-page catalog that runs from rain parkas to panniers, sold at "guaranteed lowest prices." Bike Nashbar has been in business since 1972 and sells its own line of road, touring, ATB, and racing bikes, which have features usually found on more expensive models. There are full lines of parts and accessories, including saddles from Avocet, Sella Italia, and Vetta, gears, brakes, chain wheels, hubs, pedals, derailleurs, handlebars, and other parts by Campagnolo, Dura-Ace, Shimano, SR, Suntour, and other firms. Panniers and bags, racks, helmets, protective eyewear, gloves, tires and tubes, wheels, toe clips, locks (Nashbar and Kryptonite), handlebar tape, grips, tire pumps, lights, and other accessories are offered. Bike Nashbar also features a large selection of cycling clothing, both its own label and Descente, Hind, and Tinley, as well as shoes by Aria, Avocet, Etonic, Look, Saucony, Sidi, Specialized, and Time.

Special Factor: Satisfaction is guaranteed.

BOWHUNTERS WAREHOUSE, INC.

1045 ZIEGLER RD.
P.O. BOX 158
WELLSVILLE, PA 17365
717-432-8611
FAX: 717-432-2683

Catalog: free
Save: up to 40%
Pay: check, MO, MC, V
Sells: equipment for bow hunting, hunting, and archery
Store: same address; Monday to Friday 9–5, Wednesday 9–9, Saturday 9–1

You can save up to 40% on a complete range of supplies for bow hunting, bow fishing, archery, and hunting through the 136-page catalog from Bowhunters Warehouse, which has been in business since 1974. The catalog features a large selection of bows and arrows, as well as points, feathers, bow sights, rests, quivers, targets, bowhunting books and videotapes, game calls, camouflage clothing and supplies, shooting equipment, and other gear for outdoor sports. Accra, Bear, Beman, Browning, Darton, Delta, Easton, Golden Eagle, Hoyt, Martin, PSE, Saunders, and other manufacturers are represented. Bowhunters Discount Warehouse also builds arrows to order, and the catalog includes a complete description of the features and available options for custom arrows. Specifications are included with the information on the hunting equipment, making this a good reference as well as a source for real savings.

Special Factors: Authorized returns are accepted (a restocking fee may be charged); minimum order is $15; C.O.D. orders are accepted; orders are shipped worldwide.

CABELA'S INC.

812 13TH AVE.
SIDNEY, NE 69160
308-254-5505

Catalog: free
Save: up to 40% on list prices
Pay: check, MO, MC, V, AE, Discover
Sells: hunting, fishing, and camping gear
Store: I-80, Exit #59, Sidney, NE; also E. Hwy. 30, Kearney, NE; Monday to Saturday 8–8, Sunday 12 noon–5:30, both locations

Cabela's, the "world's foremost outfitter" of fishing, hunting, and outdoor enthusiasts, has been praised by several readers. Cabela's catalog pricing represents savings of up to 40% on regular retail on some goods, but *do not ask for discounts.*

Cabela's sells rods, reels, and tackle from well-known manufacturers, including Berkley, Blue Fox, Daiwa, Fenwick, Abu Garcia, G. Loomis, Mitchell, Shakespeare, and Shimano. There's an extensive selection of lures, line, tackle boxes, hooks, nets, and other fishing gear, and pages of Minn Kota electric boat motors, electronics by Eagle, Humminbird, Interphase, and Seacom, boat covers, boat seats, Sea Eagle dinghies, Starcraft fishing boats, downriggers, winches, batteries, and trailer parts. Fishing is the strong suit in the spring and summer catalogs, but a comparable range of hunting equipment is offered in other issues.

General outdoor needs are served by the camping department: Eureka tents, sleeping bags and mats, gear bags, backpacks, cookware and kitchen equipment, heavy-duty flashlights, Pentax and Tasco binoculars, Hobie and Ray-Ban sunglasses, hunting knives, and related products are offered. And there's a good selection of outdoor clothing, including waders, camouflage wear, fishing vests and hunting jackets, snakeproof boots, moccasins, bush jackets, parkas, jeans, and more. The 210-page color catalog includes complete product descriptions and specifications, but if you need help with your selection or are buying for someone else, the customer service department can assist you.

Special Factors: Satisfaction is guaranteed; returns are accepted for exchange, refund, or credit; orders are shipped worldwide.

CAMPMOR

P.O. BOX 997
PARAMUS, NJ 07653-0997
201-445-5000

Catalog: free
Save: up to 50%
Pay: check, MO, MC, V, AE, Discover
Sells: camping gear and supplies
Store: Rte. 17 N., Paramus, NJ; Monday to Friday 9:30–9, Saturday 9:30–6

Campmor's 144-page catalog is full of great buys on camping goods, bike touring accessories, and clothing. You'll save up to 50% on clothing by Borglite Pile, Columbia Interchange System, Sierra Designs, Thinsulate, and Woolrich, as well as duofold and Polypro underwear, Sorel and Timberland boots, and other outerwear. Swiss Victorinox knives are offered at 30% off list, and Buck knives, Coleman cooking equipment, Sherpa snowshoes, Silva compasses, Edelrid climbing ropes, and books and manuals on camping and survival are available. You'll also find tents and sleeping bags by Coleman, Eureka, Moonstone, The North Face, Sierra Designs, Slumberjack, Wenzel, and Campmor's own lines, as well as backpacks by JanSport, Kelly Camp Trails, and Peak. Campmor has been in business since 1946, and is worth a trip if you're in the Paramus area.

Special Factors: Returns are accepted for exchange, refund, or credit; minimum order is $20 on phone orders.

CENTRAL SKINDIVERS

160-09 JAMAICA AVE.
JAMAICA, NY 11432-6111
718-739-5772

Information: price quote
Save: up to 40%
Pay: check, MO, MC, V, AE, Discover
Sells: scuba-diving gear
Store: same address; Monday to Saturday
10–6:30

Central Skindivers, in business since 1952, sells diving gear at savings of up to 40%, including tanks from Dacor, Sherwood, and U.S. Divers, and a full range of regulators, masks, fins, gauges, computers, suits, and other gear. There are buoyancy jackets from Beuchat, Dacor, Seaquest, Seatec, Sherwood, Tabata, and U.S. Divers, and watches and timers from Chronosport, Citizen, Heuer, and Tekna. Central Skindivers has no catalog, so call for a price quote.

Special Factors: Shipping is included; minimum order is $50, $75 with credit cards.

CHEAP SHOT, INC.

294 RTE. 980
CANONSBURG, PA 15317
412-745-2658
FAX: 412-745-4265

Catalog: free
Save: 33% plus
Pay: check or MO
Sells: ammunition
Store: Gun Runner, 950 S. Central Ave.,
Canonsburg, PA; Monday to Friday 8–8, Saturday 8–5, Sunday 10–4

Cheap Shot, "shooters serving shooters since 1976," offers savings of 33% and more on the usual prices of ammo and reloading components from CCI, Federal, Hornady, Nosler, Remington, and Winchester. The 16-page catalog also offers a "reloading library," with several manuals on the subject. Because Cheap Shot specializes in ammo and buys in volume, the discounts are better than those offered by many hunting catalogs.

Please note: Federal regulations on age and identification requirements are stated in the catalog, and you must provide signature and drivers' license number in order to purchase ammunition.

Special Factors: Authorized returns are accepted (a 20% restocking fee may be charged); C.O.D. orders are accepted (a 25% deposit is required).

CYCLE GOODS CORP.

2801 HENNEPIN AVE. SO.
MINNEAPOLIS, MN 55408
612-872-7600
800-328-5213

Catalog: free
Save: up to 30%
Pay: check, MO, MC, V, AE, DC, Optima
Sells: cycling gear and equipment
Store: 2801 Hennepin Ave., Minneapolis, MN; Monday to Thursday 10–8, Friday 10–6, Saturday 10–5, Sunday 12–4

Cycle Goods, which is also known as Cycl-Ology, publishes a 76-page catalog of cycling gear and supplies that includes detailed product information and valuable tips for improved performance and routine maintenance. Cycle Goods has been doing business since 1979 and stocks a wide selection of racing and touring equipment, plus parts, tools, and clothing. Among the manufacturers represented are Araya, Atom, Avocet, Berec, Blackburn, Bollé, Campagnolo, Cinelli, Citadel, Columbus, Descente, Guerciotti, Kingsbridge, Kryptonite, LeMond, Maillard, Mavic, Michelin, Nike, Oakley, Park, Rhode Gear, Scott, Shimano, Sidi, Specialized, Suntour, Wheel Smith, and Weinmann. In addition to frames and complete bicycles, Cycle Goods carries an extensive range of components and parts, car racks and child carriers (seats), training gear, lubricants, helmets, gloves, packs, and books and manuals. And if you want to get closer to the road, see the two pages of in-line skates (Rollerblades) and accessories. Everything is priced up to 30% below full retail, and more on specials and sales.

Special Factor: Orders are shipped worldwide.

DINN BROS., INC.
THE TROPHY PEOPLE

68 WINTER ST.
P.O. BOX 111
HOLYOKE, MA 01041-0111
413-536-3816

Catalog: $1
Save: up to 70%
Pay: check, MO, MC, V
Sells: trophies and awards
Store: same address; also 505 Chapel St., New Haven, CT; and 31 Kingston St., Boston, MA

Sports leagues, civic groups, and personnel directors all know the value of an engraved award. Unfortunately, trophies are usually expensive when they're bought from sports centers and other dealers. But when you buy from Dinn Bros., you're ordering directly from the factory, which can make anything from a figure-topped column for a Little League MVP to a bronze tablet dedicating a building. Prices are up to 70% below those charged by trophy and plaque dealers, and 36 years in the business gives Dinn expertise in selecting the right trophy to suit the budget and the occasion.

Dinn's 48-page color catalog features the classic trophy for athletic events—a gold or silver figure or symbol atop a gilt and marble column. There are lots of variations on this motif, and a lengthy index of figures that can be provided—from "Achievement—Female" to "Wrestler." Dinn sells recognition clutch pins, medals in gold, silver, and bronze metal, and engravable plaques, scrolls, and memorial tablets. And the catalog also features a wide variety of silver-plated trays, Revere bowls, loving cups, and goblets. Engraved plaques cost as little as $15 (7" by 9"), 25 certificates of recognition are just $2.50, awards ribbons cost $1.50 each, and a 5-1/2" figure trophy on a marble base costs under $5. Engraving services are also available.

Special Factors: Satisfaction is guaranteed; minimum order is $10 with credit cards; C.O.D. orders are accepted.

GANDER MOUNTAIN, INC.

P.O. BOX 6
WILMOT, WI 53192
800-558-9410

Catalog: free
Save: up to 35%
Pay: check, MO, MC, V, Discover
Sells: hunting, fishing, camping, reloading, archery, and boating gear
Store: Appleton, Brookfield, Eau Claire, Madison, and Wilmot, WI

Gander Mountain is reader-recommended as a great source for outdoor sports gear and clothing, getting high marks for selection and service. Prices are also reliably good—savings of up to 35% can be found on different items, although not everything is discounted. Fishing and hunting are Gander Mountain's focus, served through the 216-page color catalog of equipment and clothing. The rod and reel department offers gear by Berkley, Browning, Daiwa, Eagle Claw, Fenwick, Abu Garcia, Johnson, Liberty, Mitchell, Quantum, Ryobi, Shakespeare, Shimano, Sigma, and Zebco. There are lures by Bagley's, Mepps, Normark, and many other firms, and fishing line, nets, tackle boxes, rod cases, and other gear. Boat seats, covers, winches, bilge pumps, Minn Kota and other motors, Cannon downriggers, depth finders, recorders, radios, sonar devices, and Humminbird electronics are all offered as well.

Hunters will find a similar range of products for their sport: CVA blackpowder rifles, Lyman and MEC reloaders, Ram-line magazines, Hastings replacement parts for shotguns, Gun Guard gun cases, Tread-lok gun safes, Michaels holsters, practice equipment, shell boxes, and related goods. Spotting scopes, hunting binoculars, mounts, and tripods by Bushnell, Leupold, and Tasco are also available.

Gander's video department offers Warburton and other tapes on big game hunting, shooting and handling guns, game calls and hunting techniques, training hunting dogs, hunting wild birds, and fishing for bass, walleye, and trout. Specialty clothing for both hunting and fishing—waders, hunting and shooting jackets, camouflage wear—is carried, as well as rugged clothing. Chamois cloth shirts, rain suits, leather jackets, and footwear from American Eagle, Browning, Coleman, Danner, Hi-Tec, Long Haul, Tony Lama, Maine Classic, Minnetonka, Rocky, Sorel, and other firms is available, plus Bushnell sunglasses, backpacks and luggage, camp cookware, sleeping bags, tents, Buck knives, and other outdoor gear.

Special Factors: Satisfaction is guaranteed; orders are shipped worldwide.

DON GLEASON'S CAMPERS SUPPLY, INC.

▬▬▬▬▬

9 PEARL ST.
P.O. BOX 87
NORTHAMPTON, MA
  01061-0087
413-584-4895

Catalog: free
Save: up to 50%
Pay: check, MO, MC, V
Sells: camping supplies and equipment
Store: same address; Monday to Friday 9–5:30, Saturday 9–5

Don Gleason has been helping America hit the trail since 1957, with everything from tents to trowels. The firm's 80-page catalog is packed with good buys on equipment—tents and screen houses by Comet, Eureka, The North Face, Sierra Designs, and Walrus, sleeping bags by The North Face, Slumberjack, and White Stag, Winnebago air mattresses, tarps, blankets, primus stoves and cookware, Coleman and Gott coolers, first aid kits, Buck knives, duffles, and backpacks and rucksacks by Camp Trails, Caribou, Eagle Creek, JanSport, and The North Face. Don Gleason has an excellent selection of tent stakes and grommet kits, seals and other tent-mending supplies, hook-and-loop fastening, bungee cords and bungee-by-the-yard, camp toilets, cots, compasses, flashlights, insect repellents, axes, picks, and even gold-panning equipment. Savings run up to 50%, and there are volume discounts of 10% and 15% on the freeze-dried food from Alpine Aire, Backpacker's Pantry, Dri-Lite Foods, and Mountain House. See the catalog for details of the no-hassle warranty.

Special Factors: Satisfaction is guaranteed; quantity discounts are available; returns are accepted for exchange, refund, or credit; minimum order is $10 with credit cards; orders are shipped worldwide.

GOLF HAUS

**700 N. PENNSYLVANIA
LANSING, MI 48906
517-482-8842**

Price List: free
Save: up to 60%
Pay: check, MO, MC, V,
Sells: golf clubs, apparel, and accessories
Store: same address; Monday to Saturday 9–5:30

 (see text)

Golf Haus has "the absolute lowest prices on pro golf clubs" anywhere—up to 60% below list—and stocks goods by every major manufacturer. All of the models sold here are available nationwide, which means that, unlike the "exclusive models" offered by a number of discounters, the goods at Golf Haus can be price-shopped fairly. There are clubs, bags, putters, balls, and other golf equipment and supplies by Dunlop, Hogan, Lynx, MacGregor, Ping, PowerBilt, Ram, Spalding, Tiger Shark, Titleist, Wilson, and other firms. There are Bag Boy carts, Etonic shoes, gloves, umbrellas, spikes, scorekeepers, visors, rainsuits, tote bags, socks, and much more.

Golf Haus is offering readers of this book a gift of knit club head covers (for woods), with each purchase of a complete set of clubs (woods and irons). Identify yourself as a reader when you order. This WBMC reader discount expires February 1, 1995.

Special Factors: Shipping and insurance are included on orders shipped within the continental U.S.; minimum order is $50; orders are shipped worldwide.

GOLFSMITH INTER-NATIONAL, INC.

11000 N. IH35
AUSTIN, TX 78753
800-456-3344
512-837-4810
FAX: 512-837-1245

Catalog: free
Save: up to 50%
Pay: check, MO, MC, V, Discover
Sells: customized golf clubs, accessories, and repair equipment
Store: same address; Monday to Friday 7–7, Saturday 8–4, Sunday 9–5

 ¡Si! ★

The "Accessories" catalog from Golfsmith International features the firm's own line of Golfsmith clubs, which are all made to order, and a full line of golfing accessories. The "Club Components" catalog shows over 200 pages of replacement parts and repair supplies. Golfsmith, which opened its doors in 1967, offers savings of up to 50% on the cost of comparable name-brand products.

The custom department can make golfing woods and irons in a choice of left- or right-handed models, men's or women's styles, in any flex, length, weight, or grip size. Other professional, national brands of golf clubs are available as well. Golfsmith's Accessories catalog also features clothing, footwear, bags, carts, gloves, balls, club covers, and other golfing essentials, plus instructional videotapes and books. The Club Components catalog offers a line of replacement club heads, grips, refinishing supplies, and tools, as well as instruction manuals. Service and repairs are also available to mail-order customers, and if you'd like to learn how to become a professional club maker, check into the Golfsmith Clubmakers Training Program.

Canadian readers, please note: Orders must be paid in U.S. funds.

Special Factors: Request each catalog desired by name; C.O.D. orders are accepted; orders are shipped worldwide.

HOLABIRD SPORTS

9008 YELLOW BRICK RD.
BALTIMORE, MD 21237
410-687-6400
FAX: 410-687-7311

Brochure: free
Save: up to 40%
Pay: check, MO, MC, V
Sells: racquet sports equipment and athletic footwear
Store: same address

Buy here and get the "Holabird Advantage": equipment for racquet sports at up to 40% below list prices, service on manufacturers' warranties, and free stringing with tournament nylon on all racquets.

Holabird has been in business since 1981 and carries tennis racquets by scores of firms, including Donnay, Dunlop, Estusa, Fin, Fischer, Fox, Head, Mizuno, Prince, Pro-Kennex, Rossignol, Slazenger, Spalding, Wilson, Wimbledon, Yamaha, and Yonex. There are tennis balls by Dunlop, Penn, and Wilson, ball machines by Lobster and Tennis Tutor, and footwear by makers from Adidas to Wilson.

Racquetball players should check the prices on racquets by E-Force, Ektelon, Head, Pro-Kennex, Spalding, and Wilson. The squash department features racquets by Black Knight, Donnay, Dunlop, Ektelon, Estca, Fox, Head, Pro-Kennex, Prince, Slazenger, Spalding, and Wilson, and eye guards by Bausch & Lomb, Ektelon, Leader, and Pro-Kennex. Pros can save their clubs sizable sums on court equipment and maintenance supplies, such as court dryers, tennis nets, ball hoppers, and stringing machines.

Holabird also stocks a full line of tournament-level badminton racquets, basketball, cross-training, aerobic, running, and walking shoes, as well as T-shirts, socks, caps, sunglasses from Ray-Ban and Serengeti, Casio and Timex sport watches, and table tennis (ping pong) supplies and equipment. See the monthly eight-page catalog for specials, or call or write for a price quote.

Special Factors: Authorized returns (except used items) are accepted within seven days; online with CompuServe and Prodigy; orders are shipped worldwide.

LAS VEGAS DISCOUNT GOLF & TENNIS

4405 PARADISE RD.,
  WBM-1
LAS VEGAS, NV 89109
702-892-9999
FAX: 702-798-1045

Catalog: free
Save: up to 40%
Pay: check, MO, MC, V, AE, Discover
Sells: golf and tennis gear
Store: same address; also 2200 S. Rainbow Blvd., Las Vegas, NV

Las Vegas Discount Golf & Tennis sells gear and equipment for golf and tennis at savings of up to 40%, through a 40-page catalog that features the latest styles and models: golf clubs (drivers, putters, wedges, chippers), bags, and balls by Callaway, Cleveland Classics, Hogan, Lynx, MacGregor, Ping, Powerbilt, Ram, Spalding, Titleist, Wilson, Yamaha, and Yonex. Clothing and footwear from Dexter, Etonic, Foot-Joy, Hogan, Nike, PGA Tour, and other names are available, as well as instructional books and videotapes. Las Vegas Discount also carries tennis racquets by Ektelon, Head, Mizuno, Prince, Wilson, and Yonex, as well as racquet strings and balls. If you don't see what you want in the catalog, call or write for a price quote.

Special Factors: Authorized returns are accepted for exchange, refund, or credit; orders are shipped worldwide.

LPI DISCOUNT POOL & SPA CO.

801 LUNT AVE.
ELK GROVE VILLAGE, IL
  60007
800-323-5930
FAX: 708-952-8754

Catalog: $2
Save: up to 50%
Pay: check, MO, MC, V, Discover
Sells: swimming pool supplies and equipment
Store: mail order only

Swimming pools have two lives—summer and winter—and LPI sells supplies and equipment for both seasons, at savings of up to 50% on list or comparable retail. Here are all the chemicals you need to keep the water safe, and cut down on maintenance: Monarc chlorinating tabs, oxidizers (shocks), rust and scale preventers, algaecides, pH balancers, and other agents. You'll also find water-testing kits, pool skimmers, vacuums, thermometers, filters, and brushes, and the tools for enjoying the fruits of your labor—inflatable loungers, sport tubes, kiddie "riders," flippers, water balls, and diving games. When the weather turns cool, LPI helps out with high-speed pool pumps (for quick draining), repair kits for vinyl liners, winterizing plugs (to save the skimmer), covers for all pool shapes and sizes, and water sleeves to hold the covers down. The 52-page color catalog features these products and more, from names like Arneson, Polaris, Teledyne, and Weber, and there are seasonable sales that lower the discount prices even further.

Special Factors: Satisfaction is guaranteed; returns are accepted within 30 days for exchange, refund, or credit.

OVERTON'S SPORTS CENTER, INC.

DEPT. 57612
P.O. BOX 8228
GREENVILLE, NC 27835
800-334-6541
919-355-7600
FAX: 919-355-2923

Catalog: free
Save: up to 40%
Pay: check, MO, MC, V, AE, Discover
Sells: marine and water sports goods
Store: 5343 South Boulevard, Charlotte;
111 Red Banks Rd., Greenville; and 1331
Buck Jones Rd., Raleigh, NC

Overton's lays claim to title of "world's largest water sports dealer," selling a wide range of equipment for boating, water skiing, snorkeling, and other avocations at up to 40% off list. Overton's was established in 1975, and publishes three catalogs: The 128-page, color Water Sports catalog features skis and accessories ranging from junior trainers to experts' tricks, jumpers and slaloms by Connelly, EP, Jobe, Kidder, O'Brien, and other firms. Wetsuits, apparel, kneeboards, water toys, inflatables, snorkeling accessories, boating accessories, books, videotapes, and other goods are also offered. The 48-page swimwear and apparel catalog, "Kristi's," features such names as De La Mer, Bendigo, Venus, Solar Tan Thru, Point Conception, OP, O'Neill, Take Cover, Club Sportwear, and many more. The look is California young, with eye-popping prints dominating the collection.

The 148-page Discount Marine Catalog answers your boating needs with a wide range of products: boat seats and covers, safety equipment, instruments, electronics, hardware, cleaners, fishing equipment, clothing, fuel tanks, and performance accessories. The brands include Apelco, Aqua Meter, Brinkman, Eagle, Humminbird, Interphase, Ray Jefferson, Maxxima, Newmar, PowerWinch, Shakespeare, and Si-Tex, among others. The equipment catalogs give both the list or comparable retail, and Overton's discount prices.

Canadian readers, please note: Only U.S. funds are accepted.

Special Factors: Satisfaction is guaranteed; quantity discounts are available; unused returns are accepted within 30 days for exchange, refund, or credit; C.O.D. orders are accepted; orders are shipped worldwide.

PERFORMANCE BICYCLE SHOP

P.O. BOX 2741

CHAPEL HILL, NC

27515-2741

800-727-2453

FAX: 800-727-3291

Catalog: free
Save: up to 40%
Pay: check, MO, MC, V, Discover
Sells: bicycle parts and cycling apparel
Store: 24 stores in CA, CO, IL, MD, NC, PA, VA, and WA

Serious cyclists are familiar with Performance Bicycle Shop for the company's line of high-end road and mountain bikes, which run from under $300 to about $1,300. The firm's parts department is well stocked with components by Campagnolo, Look, Mavic, Shimano, Time, and other firms. Performance offers a complete line of cycling clothing, as well as riding helmets, cycling shoes, gloves, panniers, and hundreds of products to enhance cycling performance. The brands represented in the 80-page color catalog include Avocet, Bell, Dia Compe, Giro, Nike, Profile, Scott USA, Shimano, Specialized, Thule, and Vetta, among others. In-line skates (Rollerblades) and camping gear are also available.

Special Factors: Satisfaction is guaranteed; orders are shipped worldwide.

PERFORMANCE GOLF

P.O. BOX 2741

CHAPEL HILL, NC

27514-2741

919-933-9113

FAX: 919-967-3979

Catalog: free
Save: up to 50%
Pay: check, MO, MC, V
Sells: golf equipment and apparel
Store: mail order only

Performance Golf brings to the green the same standards it's held in the world of cycling (see "Performance Bicycle Shop" in this chapter), with a full line of golf equipment, accessories, and apparel. You'll find steel, carbon graphite, and woven graphite shafted club sets here from about $170, as well as bags, carts, gloves, and apparel for men and women. The brands include Adidas, Aureus, Etonic, Powerbilt, Slotline, Spalding, Sun Mountain, Michael Thomas, and Stan Thompson, among others. The 36-page catalog features a number of products sold under the Performance label, with an emphasis on technologically advanced materials and design, all at savings of up to 50% on list or comparable retail.

Special Factors: Satisfaction is guaranteed; returns are accepted for exchange, refund, or credit.

ROAD RUNNER SPORTS

6310 NANCY RIDGE RD.,

SUITE 107

SAN DIEGO, CA

92121-9486

800-551-5558

FAX: 800-421-0551

TDD: 800-421-0551

Catalog: free
Save: up to 35%
Pay: check, MO, MC, V, AE, Discover
Sells: running shoes and apparel
Store: 9020-B Activity Rd., San Diego, CA; Monday to Friday 10–7, Saturday 10–5, Sunday 12–5

Road Runner Sports publishes a 120-page color catalog of clothing and footwear for running, walking, aerobics, swimming, volleyball, soccer, and cycling. Sizes and styles for both men and women dominate, although there are some separates and shoes in children's sizes. The brands include Adidas, Avia, Brooks, Converse, Etonic, Everlast, Hi-Tec, InSport, Ironman, K-Swiss, LIFA, Medalist, Mizuno, Moving Comfort, New Balance, Prince, Rockport, Russell, Rykä, Saucony, Sideout, Frank Shorter Sports, Speedo, Thor-Lo, Timex, Turntec, and Umbro. The stock includes running suits, singlets, shorts, socks, leggings, tights, shimmel tops, and supportive underwear for men and women. Road Runner Sports also gives you a great selection of accessories—gloves, bicycling helmets, Sorbothane inserts and orthotics, water bottles, Liquipak canteens, gear and locker bags, safety vests and bands, watches and timers, pulse monitors, goggles, swim caps, aerobic steps, exercise manuals and videos, and exercise equipment—dumbbell benches, stair machines, pushup stands, and more. Road Runner Sports has been in business since 1984, and offers an unconditional guarantee of satisfaction.

Special Factors: Price quote by phone or letter with SASE; orders are shipped worldwide.

SAILBOARD WARE-HOUSE, INC.

300 S. OWASSO BLVD.,
  DEPT. WBMC
ST. PAUL, MN 55117
800-992-SAIL
FAX: 612-482-1353

Catalog: free
Save: 35% average
Pay: check, MO, MC, V, AE, Discover
Sells: windsurfing equipment
Store: same address; Monday to Friday 10–8, Saturday 9–2; also Hood River, Oregon; Monday to Saturday 9–9, Sunday 9–6 (April 1–October 1)

Put wind and water together, and you have the prime ingredients for the thrilling sport of windsurfing, also known as sailboarding. The right equipment helps, which is what you'll find at Sailboard Warehouse—at discounts that average 35%, but run much deeper on sale items and special purchases. Sailboard Warehouse has been in business since 1982, selling light to heavy wind sailboards, sails, masts, harnesses, fins, and a broad selection of windsurfing apparel. The 64-page color catalog features equipment by Bailey, BIC, DaKine, Fanatic, F2, Freedom Maui, Gaastra, Maui Magic, Mistral, NeilPryde, O'Brien, SeaTrend, Simmer, Tiga, Topsails, Weichart, Windcatcher, Windsurfing Hawaii, and other manufacturers. The boards run from entry-level to custom models for pros, and the catalog includes numerous informative sidebars on choosing equipment and evaluating construction and materials. Automaxi car racks, windsurfing books and videos, and wet suits, dry-suits, harnesses and other accessories by Bare, Body Glove, O'Neill, and Ronny are also available.

Please note: Phone hours are Monday to Friday 8–6, Saturday 9–1, CST.

Sailboard Warehouse is offering readers a discount of 5% on first orders. Identify yourself as a WBMC reader when you order, and deduct the discount from the cost of the goods only. This WBMC reader discount expires February 1, 1995.

Special Factors: Satisfaction is guaranteed; shipping is included on orders of two or more boards; authorized returns are accepted within 20 days for exchange, refund, or credit; orders are shipped worldwide.

SIERRA TRADING POST

DEPT. WBMC-94
5025 CAMPSTOOL RD.
CHEYENNE, WY 82007-
  1802
307-775-8000
FAX: 307-775-8088

Catalog: free
Save: up to 70%
Pay: check, MO, MC, V, Discover
Sells: outdoor clothing and equipment
Store: same address; also Factory Outlets of Nevada, 105 Sparks Blvd., Sparks, NV

Sierra Trading Post, established in 1986, offers casual and outdoor clothing and camping gear in a charming catalog illustrated with drawings. Sierra is essentially a mail-order outlet store that sells closeouts, overruns, and special purchases at savings of up to 70%. Rugged clothing and outerwear, shoes for hiking and running, great pants and shorts, socks, sweaters, underwear, and even comfortable dresses are among the offerings. Name brands pepper the catalog—Caribou, Columbia, Hanes, Hind, Kelty, Marmot, New Balance, The North Face, Rockport, Sportif USA, and Woolrich are among the manufacturers represented in past mailings. Sleeping bags, backpacks, and tents are also available.

Canadian readers, please note: Orders shipped to Canada are sent by U.S. Postal Service Parcel Post only.

Special Factors: Satisfaction is guaranteed; returns are accepted for exchange, refund, or credit.

SOCCER INTER-NATIONAL, INC.

Catalog: $2
Save: up to 30%
Pay: check or MO
Sells: soccer gear, accessories, and gifts
Store: mail order only

P.O. BOX 7222,
  DEPT. WBM-94
ARLINGTON, VA
  22207-0222
703-524-4333

    (see text)

Soccer International, founded in 1976 by a rabid soccer buff, publishes an 18-page color catalog of game-related items ranging from professional equipment to novelties. The savings run up to 30% on some goods, compared to the prices charged by other firms, but generally average about 20% less. The catalog is a must-see for any soccer enthusiast or friend of one, since it's a great resource for gifts as well as gear.

You'll find a number of balls here from Brine, Mikasa, and Umbro, plus a variety of jerseys and shorts. PVC leg shields and ankle guards, a ball inflator, nets and goals, practice aids, and a great selection of books and videotapes on coaching, game strategy, and soccer rules are available. If you're stuck on the sidelines, you'll want Lava Buns, the stadium cushion: Pop it in the microwave for a few minutes, and it will keep your backside warm for hours. Soccer International also sells soccer-design pillows, a soccer-theme game, radio, door mat, mugs, ties, and dozens of embroidered patches, and bumper stickers. This is where you'll find World Cup 1994 official T-shirts and pins, as well as replica team jerseys of five of the top soccer-playing countries. Soccer-loving puzzle buffs will enjoy the challenge of Mordillo jigsaw puzzles from Germany, which run from 500 to 2,000 pieces. (Mordillo's book of soccer cartoons, also available, is a classic.) And younger soccer diehards will be tickled by the rubber soccer ball noses, and the full-face soccer ball helmet/mask, which makes the wearer look like an android from the Planet Pelé.

Canadian readers, please note: Orders must be paid in U.S. funds.

APO/FPO readers, please note: Orders are not shipped to APO/FPO addresses during November or December.

Special Factors: Minimum order is $15; shipping is included on orders over $35 sent within the contiguous 48 United States.

SPIKE NASHBAR

4111 SIMON RD.,
DEPT. WBM-4
YOUNGSTOWN, OH 44512
216-788-0525
FAX: 216-782-2856

Catalog: free
Save: up to 40%
Pay: check, MO, MC, V, Discover
Sells: volleyball gear and apparel
Store: mail order only

Spike Nashbar, an affiliate of Bike Nashbar (also listed in this chapter), offers savings of up to 40% on competition volleyball gear, clothing, and accessories. The 40-page color catalog offers over two dozen balls for indoor and outdoor play, from Mikasa, Molten, Spalding, and Tachikara. Over two dozen lines of clothing are offered, and several nets and net systems are available, including one from Park and Sun for under $96 and "the best portable net system available," the Spectrum series, which costs about $236. There are volleyball shoes for men and women by Asics, Kaepa, Mizuno, and Reebok beginning at under $40. Sportbras, socks, T-shirts, shorts, duffels, sport watches, and sun shields from Bausch & Lomb and Bollé are also sold, as well as vital knee protection from Asics and Body Glove. If you've ever watched or played serious volleyball, you'll know why they're part of the standard uniform of the game. Spike Nashbar has a "lowest price" guarantee; see the catalog for details.

Canadian readers, please note: Only U.S. funds are accepted.

Special Factors: Satisfaction is guaranteed; returns are accepted for exchange, refund, or credit.

SPORT SHOP

DEPT. WBMC
P.O. BOX 340
GRIFTON, NC 28530
919-746-8288
FAX: 919-746-8296

Catalog: $1
Save: up to 50%
Pay: check, MO, MC, V, Discover
Sells: hunting gear and accessories
Store: Hwy. 11 N., Grifton, NC; Monday to Saturday 8–5

Hunting is the sport served here, with bowhunting and bowfishing equipment and accessories, blackpowder rifles and supplies, and much more offered through a 64-page catalog. Sport Shop has been in business since 1955, and sells at discounts of up to 50% off suggested list or regular retail.

Bowhunters enjoy a wide selection of bows for all ages and abilities, including models by Bear, Darton, Pearson, and PSE. Arrows and shafts from Berman and Easton are available, as well as arrow cases, quivers, arrow-making supplies, archery tools, Cobra bow sights, scopes, releases, arrow rests and plungers, arm guards, gloves, and other equipment for the serious hunter. Sport Shop sells both bullseye and animal (picture) targets, and arrow broadheads and points by Muzzy, Wasp, and Zwickey. Tree stands, camouflage paint, scent killer and dispensers, turkey and deer calls, and camouflage headgear, Rocky boots, and Walls camo pants and jackets are available, and Sport Shop also sells bowfishing supplies, Daisy airguns, Thompson Center blackpowder rifles, and accessories. Nearly two dozen videos on hunting technique are offered.

If you foresee buying more than $400 in hunting gear over the next two years, consider joining Sport Shop's Frequent Buyer club. The $20 fee entitles you to a 5% merchandise discount on all orders you place for two years.

Special Factors: Returns are accepted for exchange, refund, or credit; minimum order is $15 with credit cards; orders are shipped worldwide.

SURVIVAL SUPPLY CO.

P.O. BOX 1745-WM
SHINGLE SPRINGS, CA
95682
916-621-3836
FAX: 916-621-0928

Catalog: $1
Save: up to 30% (see text)
Pay: check, MO, MC, V
Sells: camping and outdoor gear, survival supplies, etc.
Store: mail order only

Survival Supply serves two distinct but overlapping markets: outdoors enthusiasts and survivalists. The firm's 52-page catalog is heavy on emergency food and gear, and there are books on everything from combat ammunition to Caribbean tax havens. Everything is offered at prices that average 25% below regular retail, and quantity discounts are available on food items.

Survival Supply began business in 1987 and offers an extensive selection of dehydrated foods, including goods from Backpackers Pantry,

Ready Reserves, and Stone Mill Farms. Survival Supply's survival kits can keep one or two persons going for 3 to 30 days, or a party of four sustained for up to a year. A seven-day food kit for four costs about $250 at this writing, and includes water purification tablets, stoves and fuel, a cooking kit, 30 candles and waterproof matches, and much more, besides the food. In addition, Survival Supply offers a small selection of tents and sleeping bags, camp stoves and lanterns, mess kits, flashlights, camp saws and shovels, gas masks, knives, first-aid kits, solar-powered batteries and chargers, duffels, some military surplus clothing and camouflage BDU's, and survival guides—from genuine military manuals to handbooks on poaching.

If you do the purchasing for an institution or corporation with an emergency preparedness program, you can call, fax, or write for the corporate price list. It features a number of kits for large-scale emergencies—the "five member search and rescue" and "25 person disaster & trauma first aid" kits are examples. Water pouches and drums and nitrogen-packed dehydrated foods are available, as well as MRE rations, or Meals Ready to Eat. Please note that you must be from a *qualifying group* to receive the price list.

Survival Supply is offering readers a discount of 5% on first orders. Identify yourself as a WBMC reader when you order, and deduct the discount from the cost of the goods only. This WBMC reader discount expires February 1, 1995.

Special Factors: Quantity discounts are available; orders are shipped worldwide.

THE TEE HOUSE

7825 HOLLYWOOD BLVD.
PEMBROKE PINES, FL
33024
305-981-0155
FAX: 305-983-7033

Brochure: free
Save: up to 40%
Pay: check, MO, MC, V, AE, DC, Discover, Optima
Sells: imprinted golf items
Store: same address

The specialty of The Tee House is custom imprinting on golf equipment and apparel. Whether you're buying for yourself or the whole golf club, you'll save up to 40% on tees, golf balls, divot tools, T-shirts, golf caps and visors, towels, and more. If you don't see what you're looking for in the brochure, call and ask—it may be available.

Special Factor: Orders are shipped worldwide.

TELEPRO GOLF SHOP

17622 ARMSTRONG AVE.
IRVINE, CA 92714-5791
800-333-9903
FAX: 714-261-5473

Brochure: free
Save: up to 40%
Pay: check, MO, MC, V, Discover
Sells: golf clubs
Store: Shamrock Golf Shops in Lakewood, Los Angeles, Palos Verdes, Pasadena, and Santa Ana, CA; addresses are listed in the brochure

Telepro, a division of Shamrock Golf Shops and an affiliate of Teletire (see "Auto"), sells first-quality golf clubs and accessories at savings of up to 40%. Telepro's brochure lists clubs by Callaway, Cobra, Hogan, Lynx, Mizuno, Ping, Shamrock, Slotline, Taylormade, Titleist, Wilson, Yonex, and other manufacturers. There are Wilson golf gloves, bags, and other accessories, which are sold at varing discounts. The brochure includes a questionnaire on your golfing style, which helps Telepro determine the best clubs for your game.

Special Factors: Satisfaction is guaranteed; returns (except special orders) are accepted within 30 days (a 15% restocking fee may be charged).

WALK USA

6310 NANCY RIDGE. RD.,
SUITE 101
SAN DIEGO, CA
92121-3209
800-255-6422

Catalog: free
Save: up to 50%
Pay: check, MO, MC, V, AE
Sells: walking clothing, shoes, and accessories
Store: mail order only

If you've had it with shin splints and runner's knee, it's time to slow it down. Mother was right—walking *is* good exercise—and because it's much easier on your joints, it's become very popular over the last few years. Walk USA serves both dedicated strollers and rabid racewalkers with easy-fitting sport suits, lightweight fleece separates, Supplex shorts, Woolrich nylon raincoats, Supplex stirrup and Lycra ankle-length tights, Helly Hansen's Prolite tights, Jogbra sports bras, athletic socks, and accessories. Walking shoe models from Adidas, Asics, Avia, Brooks, Easy Spirit, K-Swiss, New Balance, Rockport, and Saucony are sold at an average discount of 30% off list, and the 40-page color catalog also shows hats and gloves for winter workouts, mesh safety vests with reflective stripes, sunshields and watches with lap monitors, and the ice/heat packs, joint supports, and Sorbothane insoles you may need if you get carried away. And you may do just that after mastering world-class racewalking techniques with the help of one of Walk USA's videos, or reading *America's Greatest Walks,* 100 of the nation's most "scenic adventures." If you need background music but find your running tapes are too fast, you can take your pick tapes mixed for different walking speeds and styles. Not everything is discounted, but the prices are competitive with those charged for comparable private-label work-out wear elsewhere.

Special Factors: Satisfaction is guaranteed; returns are accepted for exchange, refund, or credit; C.O.D. orders are accepted.

WILEY OUTDOOR SPORTS, INC.

DEPT. WBMC 1994
1808 SPORTSMAN LN.
HUNTSVILLE, AL 35816
205-837-3982
FAX: 205-837-4017

Catalog: $3, refundable
Save: 30% average
Pay: check, MO, MC, V
Sells: hunting gear and equipment
Store: 1808 Sportsman Lane, Huntsville, AL; Monday to Friday 9–6, Saturday 9–4:30

This family-run business has been outfitting hunters with a full range of equipment and gear since 1953, and offers savings that average 30%, but can run as high as 50% on certain items and lines. Hunters will find everything from boots to blackpowder supplies in the 192-page catalog, including scopes, binoculars, and other optics from Burris, Bushnell, J.B. Holden, Leupold, Nikon, Pentax, Simmons, Steiner, Swarovski, Tasco, and Zeiss. Blackpowder rifles by Lyman and Thompson Center are available, as well as reloading and bullet-casting equipment by Forster Products, Hornady, Lee, and Lyman. Holsters, gun maintenance products, gun slings, tree stands, and related hunting accessories are stocked, and there are game calls of all types, game scents, compasses, airguns for adults, and camping accessories. Clothing by Browning, Carhartt, Columbia, LaCrosse, Mossy Oak, and Walls is sold, as well as duofold thermal underwear and footwear from Rocky Boots. In addition to hunting needs, Wiley carries bowhunting gear, and an excellent selection of hunting and specialty knives by Al Mar, Browning, Buck, Case, Cold Steel, Gerber, Victorinox, and Wyoming Knife.

Special Factors: Satisfaction is guaranteed; unused returns are accepted within ten days (a 15% restocking fee may be charged) for exchange, refund, or credit; minimum order is $25; C.O.D. orders (via UPS only) are accepted; orders are shipped worldwide.

SEE ALSO

Allen-Edmonds Shoe Corp. • wing-tip golf shoes • **CLOTHING: FOOTWEAR**

Astronomics/Christophers, Ltd. • spotting scopes for bird watching • **CAMERAS**

Bruce Medical Supply • small selection of fitness equipment • **MEDICINE**

The Button Shop • zippers for tents and sleeping bags • **CRAFTS**

CISCO • swimming pool accessories and parts • **HOME: MAINTENANCE**

Clothcrafters, Inc. • flannel gun-cleaning patches, mosquito netting, sleeping bag liners • **GENERAL MERCHANDISE**

Creative Health Products • exercise equipment • **HEALTH**

Defender Industries, Inc. • water sports accessories • **AUTO**

E & B Marine Supply, Inc. • water skis • **AUTO**

Ewald-Clark • binoculars • **CAMERAS**

A. Feibusch Corporation • replacement tent zippers • **CRAFTS**

Leather Unlimited Corp. • black powder supplies, suede duffel bags • **LEATHER**

Mardiron Optics • binoculars and spotting scopes • **CAMERAS**

Mass. Army & Navy Store • government surplus camping and survival gear • **SURPLUS**

Mid-Western Sport Togs • custom tanning, dyeing, and tailoring of green hides • **CLOTHING**

Newark Dressmaker Supply, Inc. • replacement zippers for sleeping bags and tents • **CRAFTS**

Okun Bros. Shoes • sports shoes • **CLOTHING: FOOTWEAR**

Orion Telescope Center • binoculars • **CAMERAS**

Racer Wholesale • auto racing safety equipment and accessories • **AUTO**

Ruvel & Company, Inc. • government surplus camping supplies and survival goods • **SURPLUS**

Safe Specialties, Inc. • gun safes and pistol boxes • **OFFICE**

Scope City • field binoculars, spotting scopes • **CAMERAS**

Sportswear Clearinghouse • athletic apparel • **CLOTHING**

Yachtmail Co. Ltd. • dinghies and boating equipment • **AUTO**

SURPLUS

Surplus and used goods

This is the world of military overstock, obsolete electronics, and the 90% discount. Many of these dealers accept inquiries for goods not listed in their catalogs, but most people don't know what's available. *The Army/Navy Store Catalog* (Penguin Books, 1982), by Andrew I. Adler, Roger Adler, and William G. Thompson, provides a good guide to a wide range of popular items. It's illustrated with line drawings and features extensive listings of surplus suppliers in the U.S. and abroad. If you have any questions about what a cataloger's item is, though, call and ask before you order—you'll save yourself the hassle and expense of a return.

AMERICAN SCIENCE & SURPLUS

3605 HOWARD ST.,
  DEPT. WBM-94
SKOKIE, IL 60076
708-982-0870
FAX: 800-934-0732

Catalog: $1
Save: up to 95%
Pay: check, MO, MC, V
Sells: industrial and scientific surplus goods
Store: 5696 Northwest Hwy., Chicago, IL; also Rte. 38, East of Kirk Rd., Geneva, IL; 5430 W. Layton Ave., Milwaukee, WI; Monday to Friday 10–6, Thursday 10–9, Saturday 9–5, Sunday 11–5

American Science & Surplus offers a wide variety of surplus wares through witty catalogs that are published about seven times yearly. The firm has been selling surplus since 1937, and offers that blend of the strange and useful that is catnip to fans of surplus goods: everything from "humongo scissors and son" (a big and a small pair of scissors), to a baggie sized to fit a motorcycle.

Past catalogs have shown small DC motors, staplers, heat guns, microscopes, farriers' tools, magnets, pharmaceutical bottles, collections of drive belts, drill bits, dozens of kinds of tape, whet stones, silk suturing thread, a Swedish steel helmet, telescoping antennas, pumps, casters, gray cue balls, piano hinges, Chinese riffler tools, aircraft drill bits, and magnifying lenses. (Please *don't* expect to find these particular items in the catalogs you receive—these are surplus goods, and stock is limited.) The descriptions, which are droll and explicit, note the original and possible uses for the products, as well as technical data, when available. Savings on original and if-new prices can reach 95%.

Special Factors: Satisfaction is guaranteed; returns are accepted within 15 days; minimum order is $10 in goods.

H & R COMPANY

18 CANAL ST.
P.O. BOX 122
BRISTOL, PA 19007-0122
215-788-5583
FAX: 215-788-9577

Catalog: free
Save: up to 50%
Pay: check, MO, MC, V, Discover
Sells: new and surplus electro-mechanical, robotic, and optical components
Store: same address; Monday to Friday 12:30–5

H & R Company, formerly known as Herbach & Rademan, was established in 1934 and offers surplus bargains—chiefly electronics, robotics, optics, and intriguing mechanical devices. Past catalogs have offered capacitors, lasers, motors, power supplies, compressors, fans, test equipment, relays, resistors, air and hydraulic cylinders, solenoids, transformers, and similar equipment. Computer components, including monitors, keyboards, cables, and power line filters, are usually available.

H & R sells goods that nearly anyone, electro-mechanically inclined or not, can use: educational kits, phone accessories, digital scales, heavy-duty outlet strips and surge suppressors, model trains and cars, closed-circuit TV components, goggles, robotics components, compasses, cabinet slides, tool cases and cabinets, magnets, weather balloons, and reference books on technical topics. Product specifications are given in the catalog.

Special Factors: Satisfaction is guaranteed; price quote by phone, fax, or letter; returns with original packing materials are accepted within 30 days; minimum order is $25; orders are shipped worldwide.

MASS. ARMY & NAVY STORE

DEPT. WBMC
15 FORDHAM RD.
BOSTON, MA 02134
617-783-1250
FAX: 617-254-6607

Catalog: free
Save: 25% average
Pay: check, MO, MC, V, AE, Optima
Sells: government surplus apparel and accessories
Store: 895 Boylston St., Boston, and 1436 Massachusetts Ave., Cambridge, MA

 ¡Si!

Mass. Army & Navy offers both reproduction and genuine government surplus, presented as a fashion statement. The 48-page color catalog features camouflage clothing, Australian outback coats, U.S. and European battle dress uniforms, field and flight jackets, East German guards' boots, U.S. Air Force sunglasses, survival manuals, and similar surplus. Mass. Army & Navy also offers casual footwear, bandannas, gloves, Levi's jeans, Dockers, bomber jackets, pea coats, knapsacks, sleeping bags, air mattresses, backpacks, duffel bags, tents, mess kits, security products, and insignias and patches, among other useful items.

Special Factors: Satisfaction is guaranteed; returns are accepted for exchange, refund, or credit; orders are shipped worldwide.

RUVEL & COMPANY, INC.

4128-30 W. BELMONT
AVE., DEPT. WBMC
CHICAGO, IL 60641
312-286-9494

Catalog: $2
Save: up to 70%
Pay: check, MO, MC, V
Sells: government surplus
Store: same address; Monday to Friday 10–4:30, Saturday 10–2

Ruvel, established in 1965, is the source to check for good buys on government-surplus camping and field goods. U.S. Army and Navy surplus goods are featured in the 64-page catalog, including G.I. duffel bags, high-powered binoculars, leather flying jackets, mosquito netting, M65 field jackets, U.S. Marine Corps shooting jackets, dummy grenades, U.S. Army technical manuals, and similar items. Past catalogs have offered Israeli and M9 gas masks, Kevlar helmets, hammocks, snowshoes, strobe lights, mess kits, dinghies, night sticks, snowshoes, U.S. Army blankets, parade gloves, first-aid kits, packboards, and duffel bags. Ruvel is noteworthy for its low prices and extensive stock of real surplus—there are hundreds of "genuine" government-issue items available here, and many intriguing, useful surplus things that are increasingly hard to find these days.

Special Factors: Order promptly, since stock moves quickly; orders are shipped worldwide.

SURPLUS CENTER

P.O. BOX 82209
LINCOLN, NE 68501-2209
800-488-3407
FAX: 402-474-5198

Catalog: free
Save: up to 85%
Pay: check, MO, MC, V, AE, Discover
Sells: new and surplus industrial goods, hardware, etc.
Store: 1015 W. "O" St., Lincoln, NE; Monday to Saturday 9–5

Surplus Center, established in 1933, publishes a 148-page catalog that's a treasury of parts for the "build-it-yourselfer." The offerings are heavy on hydraulic equipment of all types, including cylinders, valves, pumps, and motors, as well as hoses, filters, and tanks. Also featured are pressure washers, blowers, winches, electrical motors of all kinds, electrical generators, air compressors, surveying equipment, well pumps, vacuum pumps, gearboxes, gas engines, and even a backhoe that mounts on a pickup truck. Heavy-duty 400-amp DC welders are available, as well as sandblasters, inverters, multimeters, battery chargers, and a full line of residential and commercial burglar alarms. Some of the goods are real government surplus, but most are brand new bargains. If you have any questions about an item, you can call Surplus Center's staff technicians for information.

Special Factors: Authorized returns are accepted (a restocking fee may be charged); C.O.D. orders are accepted; orders are shipped worldwide.

SEE ALSO

All Electronics Corp. • *surplus electrical components* • **TOOLS**
Survival Supply Co. • *surplus goods, survival gear and food, etc.* • **SPORTS**

TOOLS, HARDWARE, ELECTRONICS, ENERGY, SAFETY, SECURITY, AND INDUSTRIAL GOODS

Materials, supplies, equipment, and services

This chapter offers the do-it-yourselfer, woodworker, hobbyist, woodcutter, and small-time mechanic a wealth of tools and hardware, some of it at rock-bottom prices. Replacement parts for lawnmowers, trimmers, garden tractors, snowmobiles, snow throwers, blowers, go-carts, minibikes, and even plumbing and electrical systems are available from these companies. The tools run from hex wrenches and fine wood chisels to complete work benches and professional machinery, and the hardware includes hard-to-find specialty items as well as nuts and bolts.

When you're working, observe safety precautions and use goggles, dust masks, respirators, earplugs, gloves, and other protective gear as appropriate. (A number of these firms sells safety equipment.) Keep your blades sharpened and make sure your tools, hardware, and chemicals are kept out of the reach of children and pets. If you're using a chain saw, make sure it's fitted with an approved anti-kickback device (contact the manufacturer for recommendations).

For more tools and related products, see "Crafts and Hobbies," "General Merchandise," the "Maintenance" section of "Home," and "Surplus."

FIND IT FAST

ABRASIVES • **Red Hill, World Abrasives**
LOGGING EQUIPMENT • **Bailey's, H & H, Zip Power Parts**
SAFETY GEAR • **Bailey's**

497

ALL ELECTRONICS CORP.

DEPT. WBMC
P.O. BOX 567
VAN NUYS, CA 91408
800-826-5432
818-904-0524
FAX: 818-781-2653

Catalog: free
Save: up to 60%
Pay: check, MO, MC, V, Discover
Sells: surplus electronics and tools
Store: 905 S. Vermont Ave., Los Angeles, CA; Monday to Friday 9–5, Saturday 9–4; also 14928 Oxnard St., Van Nuys, CA; Monday to Friday 9–6:30, Saturday 9–5

 ¡Si!

Electronics hobbyists will appreciate the 64-page catalog from All Electronics, which has been in business since 1967. Every issue features a huge number of surplus parts, hardware items, and tools: semiconductors, transducers, heat sinks, sockets, cables and adapters, fans, plugs, switches, solenoids, relays, capacitors, piezoelectric elements, fuses, resistors, transformers, potentiometers, keyboards, computer fans, PC boards, and hard-to-find and one-of-a-kind items are typical offerings. While much of the stock is for electronics hobbyists, the catalogs usually offer such items as telephone cords and jacks, TV and video accessories, screwdrivers, soldering irons, hemostats, and rechargable batteries.

Special Factors: All parts are guaranteed to be in working order; returns are accepted within 30 days; minimum order is $10; orders are shipped worldwide.

BAILEY'S

44650 HWY. 101
P.O. BOX 550
LAYTONVILLE, CA 95454
707-984-6133
OR
1520 S. HIGHLAND AVE.
P.O. BOX 9088
JACKSON, TN 38314
901-422-1300
OR
3 SELINA DR.
P.O. BOX 14020
ALBANY, NY 12212
518-869-2131

Catalog: free (see text)
Save: up to 70%
Pay: check, MO, MC, V, AE, Discover
Sells: woodcutting and reforestation sup-
plies; outdoor and work clothing
Store: same addresses; Monday to Friday 6
A.M.–9 P.M., Saturday 8–5 (CA); Monday to
Friday 6–6, Saturday 8–5 (TN); and Monday
to Friday 6–6, Saturday 8–5 (NY)

Bailey's, one of the country's best sources for chain-saw parts and other woodcutting supplies, stocks a large number of goods everyone will find useful—specialty boots, leather conditioners, outdoor clothing, and safety gear. Campers and even urbanites will appreciate the well-priced outerwear (Filson jackets and pants, flannel shirts, rain slickers, shearling jackets, etc.), and the first-aid kits and portable fire extinguishers. In addition, there are boot dryers, E.A.R. plugs and headset noise mufflers, and work gloves.

The 68-page color catalog (free on request, $2 for a year's subscription) features woodcutting equipment, and lists Oregon chain reels and bars for saws by Homelite, Husqvarna, McCulloch, Pioneer, and Stihl. Silvey chain grinders, spark plugs, tape, guide bars, bar and chain oil, bar wrenches and files, and other tools are available. Calked and heavy-duty boots by Chippewa and Wesco are stocked, as well as climbing gear, log splitters, Alaskan saw mills, winches, firefighting equipment, and reforestation supplies (including seedlings). Bailey's is the place to call if you have questions about your chain saw. (Check for details on the firm's "Chain Saw Safety Awareness Program.") Savings run as high as 60% on goods in the general catalog, and even more on items offered in the sales flyers.

Special Factors: Quantity discounts are available; C.O.D. orders are accepted; orders are shipped worldwide.

THE BEVERS

P.O. BOX 12
WILLS POINT, TX
75169-0012
214-272-8370

Catalog: $2, refundable
Save: up to 50%
Pay: check or MO
Sells: hardware and woodworking parts
Store: mail order only

The Bevers have been selling hardware and parts for household use and crafts projects since 1977, offering a useful mix of items for the hobbyist and do-it-yourselfer. The 52-page catalog offers goods for woodworking, construction, and household repairs: steel and brass wood screws with round and flat heads, lock and flat washers, a full range of eye bolts and squared screw hooks, Tap-Lok threads, machine screws with a choice of head styles, hex heads and carriage bolts, cotter pins, brass-plated hinges, picture hangers, lag screws, countersinks, doweling drill bits, clamps, and rotary and sandpaper drums for drills. There's a good selection of wooden parts for making toys and repairing furniture. including wood balls, toy wheels, Shaker pegs, peg boards, game pieces, golf tees, screw-hole buttons, knobs and pulls, and turned finials and spindles. Unfinished candle cups, napkin rings, honey dippers, egg cups, round boxes, blocks, and balls await the finishing touch of the craftsperson. The Bevers carry a number of hard-to-find items, so consult the catalog if you're having trouble locating a special screw or toy part.

Special Factor: Price quote by letter with SASE on quantity orders.

CAMELOT ENTERPRISES

P.O. BOX 65, DEPT. W
BRISTOL, WI 53104-0065
414-857-2695

Catalog: $2, refundable
Save: up to 60%
Pay: check, MO, MC, V
Sells: fasteners, tools, and hardware
Store: 8234 199 Ave. (facing Hwy. AH), Bristol, WI; Tuesday and Thursday 8–7; other hours by appointment only

Camelot, founded in 1983, sells "quality fasteners, hardware, and tools direct to the craftsman" at savings of up to 60%, through a 29-page catalog that's jam-packed with garage and workshop necessities. Camelot carries a full range of nuts (hex, K-lock, wing, stop, etc.), bolts (hex-head, machine, carriage), screws (wood, lag, drywall, machine), washers, thread fittings, cotter pins, anchors, and other hardware. And you don't have to buy by the pound to get wholesale prices—Camelot packages the hardware in counts of 10, 25, 50, 100, etc. Camelot's tools include screwdrivers, punches, air tools, pliers, snips, rasps, and other hand and power tools for hobbyist and machinist by Astro, Best Tool, Cal-Van, Camelot, Chicago Pneumatic, Excalibur, General, Ingersoll Rand, Lisle, Milton, Milwaukee, and Truecraft, among others. Shop equipment, Excalibur fastener sets, Marson pop rivets, and Camelot's own twist drills and fasteners are also sold at competitive prices.

Camelot is offering readers of this book a 5% discount on orders of $50 or more (excluding shipping and sales tax) *except* from the "Customer Only" sales flyers. Please identify yourself as a reader when you order. This WBMC reader discount expires February 1, 1995.

Special Factors: Satisfaction is guaranteed; price quote by letter only; returns are accepted within ten days for replacement, refund, or credit; no collect calls are accepted.

CLEGG'S HANDYMAN SUPPLY

P.O. BOX 2177
PROVO, UT 84603-2177
801-374-1242

Catalog: $2, refundable
Save: 30% average
Pay: check or MO
Sells: hardware, home fixtures, etc.
Store: mail order only

Clegg's is a family-run firm, dedicated to the "frugal home handyperson," offering a wide variety of hardware, plumbing and electrical products, and sundry home fix-up items. These are the kinds of things that drive you to the hardware store in the middle of Saturday afternoons—cord switches, wood toilet seats, faucet parts, door stops, deadbolt locks, flashlights, molly bolts, switch boxes, augers, phone jacks, and much more—over 800 items at this writing. The prices average 30%-plus below suggested or regular retail, and if your order totals $50 or more, shipping is free. Clegg's prides itself on responding to the needs of its customers, and the firm's 40-page catalog should prove a great help to any do-it-yourselfer with limited access to a good hardware store.

Special Factors: Satisfaction is guaranteed; shipping is included on orders over $50; returns are accepted within 90 days; phone orders are not accepted.

ENCO MANUFAC-TURING COMPANY

5000 W. BLOOMINGDALE AVE.
CHICAGO, IL 60639
800-860-3400
312-745-1500
FAX: 800-860-3500

Catalog: free
Save: up to 50%
Pay: check, MO, MC, V, Discover
Sells: machining tools and hardware
Store: same address; also AZ, CA, FL, GA, IL, MA, MN, OH, TX, and WA (see catalog for locations)

If the notion of saving big on collet closers has you riveted, read on. Enco, one of the country's biggest suppliers of machine shop equipment, gives you access to lathes, grinders, cutting tools, woodworking equipment, fabricating equipment, hand tools, air compressors, measuring tools, manuals, and more. Enco has 53 years of experience in manufacturing and distributing shop equipment, and the 300-page catalog is a valuable reference—and prices are routinely 30% to 50% below list or comparable retail here.

Special Factors: Quantity discounts are available; institutional accounts are available; minimum order is $25; C.O.D. orders are accepted.

H & H MANUFAC-TURING & SUPPLY CO.

P.O. BOX 692
SELMA, AL 36701-0692
205-872-6067

Catalog: free
Save: up to 50%
Pay: check or MO
Sells: chain-saw parts and logging equipment
Store: 111 Hwy. 80 E., Selma, AL; Monday to Friday 7–5, Wednesday 8–12 noon

H & H Manufacturing runs a mail-order firm known as "Saw Chain" that's been offering savings of up to 50% on saw chain and other logging needs since 1965. You can buy the chain, guide bars, and sprockets here for chain saws by Craftsman, John Deere, Echo, Homelite, Husqvarna, Jonsered, Lombard, McCulloch, Olympic, Pioneer, Poulan, Remington, Stihl, and other firms. The chain is sold in a range of pitches and gauges, and both gear-drive and direct-drive sprockets to fit all models are stocked. Swedish double-cut files, Esco rigging products, Windsor and Tilton saw chain and bars, wire rope, logging chokers, slings, and other logging equipment is also available. Remember to include all requested information when ordering chain and sprockets— make and model, chain pitch, gauge, number of drive links, type of bar, and length.

Special Factors: Chains, bars, files, and sprockets are guaranteed to last as long as or longer than any other make; returns are accepted for replacement; C.O.D. orders are accepted.

HARBOR FREIGHT TOOLS

3491 MISSION OAKS BLVD.
P.O. BOX 6010
CAMARILLO, CA 93011
800-423-2567
FAX: 805-388-0760

Catalog: free
Save: up to 80%
Pay: check, MO, MC, V, AE, Discover, Optima
Sells: tools, hardware, industrial equipment, machinery
Store: same address; also Bakersfield, El Cajon, Chula Vista, Escondido, Fresno, Hemet, Hesperia, Lancaster, Modesto, Ridgecrest, Sacramento, Salinas, Santa Maria, Santa Rosa, Stockton, Vallejo, and Visalia, CA; Lexington, KY; and Las Vegas, NV

Great prices on everything from air compressors to woodworking equipment is what you'll find in the 116-page catalog from Harbor Freight Tools, which offers workshop necessities at savings of up to 80% on list and comparable retail. Specials are run frequently, making this a valuable source for the hobbyist, do-it-yourselfer, and professional shop.

The latest catalog offered air tools, compressors, hand tools for all kinds of work, automotive repair and maintenance equipment, shop equipment, power tools and supplies, metalworking, welding and plasma cutting tools, woodworking machines and tools, generators, engines, pumps, and even a roundup of useful things for home and garden—post hole diggers, stud sensors, push brooms, ladders, paint sprayers, and more. AEG, Black & Decker, Bosch, Campbell Hausfeld, Central Forge, Central Pneumatic, Chicago Electric, Cummins, Makita, Master Pneumatic, Milwaukee, Pittsburgh, Porter-Cable, Ryobi, Sentry, Skil, Stanley, Wayne, and WEN are among the brands represented.

Special Factor: Shipping is free on orders over $50 delivered within the continental U.S.

MANUFACTURER'S SUPPLY

DEPT. WBMC-94

P.O. BOX 167

DORCHESTER, WI

   54425-0167

800-826-8563

Catalog: free
Save: up to 50%
Pay: check, MO, MC, V
Sells: replacement parts for lawnmowers, snowmobiles, chain saws, etc.
Store: mail order only

Manufacturer's Supply is the source for the parts you'll need to get all kinds of things functioning again, at prices up to 50% below list or comparable retail. Consult the firm's 52-page catalog for original replacement parts for equipment by Arctic Cat, Briggs & Stratton, Comet, Dayco, Hahn, Hoffco, Husqvarna, Oregon, Tecumseh, Toro, and other makers, for chain saws, lawnmowers, motorcycles, snowmobiles, ATVs, snow throwers, trimmers, trailers, and rototillers. There are sprockets and nose assemblies, chains, grinders, files, air filters, T-wrenches, starter springs, carburetor parts, and guide bars (for dozens of saw brands). Manufacturer's also sells parts for standard and riding lawnmowers, as well as semi-pneumatic tires for mowers and shopping carts, wheelbarrows, and hand trucks.

In addition, Manufacturer's Supply stocks wheels, hubs, bearing kits, roller chains, sprockets, clutches, belts, and other goods for trailers, minibikes, go-carts, riding mowers, snow throwers, rototillers, garden tractors, and ATVs. The snowmobile parts include everything from lubricants to windshields—carburetors, fuel filters, cleats, tracks, pistons, gaskets, fan belts, suspension springs, and engines, among other items. Also available are wood-chopping tools, Woodchuck wood-burning furnaces, and Magic Heat air circulators and chimney-cleaning brushes.

Special Factors: Authorized, unused returns are accepted within 30 days (a 20% restocking fee may be charged); minimum order is $10; C.O.D. orders are accepted; orders are shipped worldwide.

NORTHERN HYDRAULICS, INC.

P.O. BOX 1499,
  DEPT. 17806
BURNSVILLE, MN 55337
800-533-5545
FAX: 612-894-0083

Catalog: free
Save: up to 50%
Pay: check, MO, MC, V, Discover
Sells: do-it-yourself items, garden tools, etc.
Store: Jonesboro, Marietta, and Norcross, GA; Burnsville, Fridley, Maplewood, Minnetonka, Rochester, and Rogers, MN; Charlotte, Greensboro, Matthew, and Raleigh, NC; Greenville, SC; and Richmond, VA

Northern Hydraulics makes it easy to save up to 50% on gas engines, logging equipment, trailer parts, air tools and compressors, winches, hand tools, farm and garden equipment, and much more. The 136-page catalog offers an enormous selection of log splitters, wedges, Homelite and McCulloch chain saws, Oregon chain, files, and other logging gear. The hydraulic pumps include lines by J.S. Barnes and Parker, and there are hydraulic motors, motor valves, hydraulic tanks, strainers, hoses, and other parts and equipment. Gas engines for use with log splitters, lawn and riding mowers, rototillers, and other machines are stocked, including vertical- and horizontal-shaft models by Briggs & Stratton, Honda, Kohler, and Tecumseh. Air compressors and related equipment by American IMC and Campbell Hausfeld are offered, as well as air tools from Chicago Pneumatic, Ingersoll-Rand, and other firms.

Northern Hydraulics also sells go-cart parts and accessories, minibike parts, ATV tires and wheels, halogen tractor lamps, sandblasting equipment, pressure washers, trailer parts, small hand tools, and power tools by Black & Decker, Bosch, Makita, Skil, and other manufacturers. The farm and garden equipment includes gas trimmers, cultivators, 31 hp NorTrac tractors, garden carts, agricultural pumps, mower tires, blowers, sprayers, tillers, and much more. And Dickies overalls, Northlake boots, and other useful items are available as well.

Special Factor: Authorized returns are accepted for exchange, refund, or credit.

RED HILL CORPORATION

P.O. BOX 4234
GETTYSBURG, PA 17325
800-822-4003
717-337-1419
FAX: 717-337-3936

Catalog: free
Save: up to 50%
Pay: check, MO, MC, V
Sells: abrasives
Store: Chuck's Sporting Goods, 39 W. York St., Biglerville, PA

Red Hill's business is the rough stuff that gets things smooth—abrasives. The company was founded in 1978 and offers a wide range of abrasives and refinishing products at prices up to 50% below regular retail. The 20-page catalog includes belts (aluminum oxide on cloth backing) in 13 sizes, plain-back and pressure-sensitive sanding disks, paper disks for orbital sanders, sheets, sleeve and drums, sanding screens, rolls, and foam-core sanding blocks. Red Hill's "Perma Sand," tungsten carbide grit bonded to a metal substrate, promises to last up to 100 times longer than conventional papers. In addition, the catalog offers abrasives for vibrating hand sanders, RASKO's paper-backed steel wool sheets (to mount on sanders, for finishing work), felt-backed sanding disks that work with a hook-and-loop fastening system, abrasive cords and tapes (for getting into crevices), wool buffing pads and bonnets, auto-body refinishing products, tack cloths, and a stick for cleaning sanding belts when the grit gets clogged—a money saver in itself. Red Hill also carries glue guns and glue sticks—and at $5 a pound for five pounds of sticks (white clear, amber clear, and amber super), they cost just a third of the going rate at the typical hardware store, and the savings increase on larger quantities.

Special Factors: Price quote by phone or letter on special order sizes; quantity discounts are available; minimum order is $25; C.O.D. orders are accepted; orders are shipped worldwide.

TOOL CRIB OF THE NORTH

P.O. BOX 1716
GRAND FORKS, ND
   58206-1716
800-358-3096
FAX: 701-746-2857

Catalog: $3
Save: up to 50%
Pay: check, MO, MC, V, Discover
Sells: tools and hardware
Store: Bismarck, Fargo, Grand Forks, and
Minot, ND; locations are given in the catalog

Do-it-yourselfers, hobbyists, contractors, and industrial buyers are among the numerous customers of Tool Crib, which has been in business since 1948. The firm offers a broad range of tools, industrial and shop equipment, and supplies—ladders, pumps, generators, motors, woodworking equipment, saws, compressors, abrasives, concrete-handling equipment, trailers, and much more. You can send $3 for the 208-page catalog, or call or write for price quotes on items by Black & Decker, Bosch, Delta, Emglo, Freud, Hitachi, Kawasaki, Makita, Milwaukee, Porter-Cable, Powermatic, Ryobi, Senco, Skil, Stanley, Target, David White, and any other major manufacturer. Whether you're shopping for a circular saw or an adjustable scaffold system, you'll find it at Tool Crib—at up to 50% off list price. The catalog includes line drawings, products specifications, and both list and discount prices for most items, which makes it a good reference as well as a buying tool.

Canadian readers, please note: Only U.S. funds are accepted.

Special Factors: Satisfaction is guaranteed; shipping is included (with some exceptions) on orders over $75; orders are shipped worldwide.

TOOLHAUZ CORP.

122 E. GROVE ST.
P.O. BOX 1288
MIDDLEBORO, MA
   02346-1288
   800-533-6135
   508-946-4800
FAX: 508-947-7050

Brochure: free
Save: up to 50%
Pay: check, MO, MC, V
Sells: tools and hardware
Store: same address and 57 Crawford St., Needham, MA

The six-page "bargain list" from Toolhauz Corp. features the best names in woodworking and power tools, at discounts that sometimes beat even those of the "wholesale" sources. You'll find everything from Estwing hammers and Stabila levels to Greenbull ladders and Rosseau saw stands—routers, drills, screwguns, disc sanders, and power saws all types, by Delta, Hitachi, Jepson, Makita, Metabo, Milwaukee, Panasonic, Porter-Cable, Ryobi, and Skil. Supplies and hardware, including abrasives, saw blades, hole saws, screws, drill bits, tarps, tool aprons, and related goods are stocked as well. Call for the price list, or a price quote if you know the model you're looking for.

   Special Factors: C.O.D. orders are accepted.

TOOLS ON SALE™

SEVEN CORNERS ACE
  HARDWARE, INC.
216 W. SEVENTH ST.
ST. PAUL, MN 55102
800-328-0457
FAX: 612-224-8263

Catalog: free
Save: up to 50%
Pay: check, MO, MC, V, Discover
Sells: tools for contractors, masons, and woodworkers
Store: same address; Monday to Friday 7–5:30, Saturday 7–1

If you can't get to St. Paul to visit Seven Corners Ace Hardware, where there are "over 35,000 items on the floor," you can do business with the firm's mail-order division, Tools on Sale™. The parent company was founded in 1933, and specializes in tools for contractors and woodworkers.

The Tools on Sale™ catalog is one of the last great freebies in America—500 pages of name-brand tools, at discounts of up to 50%. You'll find everything from air compressors to work benches here, from manufacturers that include Black & Decker (Elu), Bosch, Delta, Dremel, Freud, Hitachi, Jet, Jorgensen, Makita, Milwaukee, Porter-Cable, Rigid, Ryobi, Senco, Skil, 3M, and David White, among others. If you're looking for stair templets, demolition hammers, moisture meters, water stones, mechanics' cabinets, or just want to *see* 20 pages of construction aprons and nail bags, look no farther. And there are ten pages of books, videos, and manuals on everything from making a hobbyhorse to building a home. Free freight on orders shipped to the U.S. (except Alaska and Hawaii) is an added bonus.

Special Factors: Shipping is included on orders shipped within the contiguous U.S.; authorized returns are accepted for exchange, refund, or credit (a 15% restocking fee may be charged); orders are shipped worldwide.

TURNKEY MATERIAL HANDLING CO.

P.O. BOX 1050
TONAWANDA, NY
   14151-1050
800-828-7540
FAX: 800-222-1934

Catalog: free
Save: up to 50%
Pay: check, MO, MC, V, AE, Discover
Sells: commercial and industrial furnishings, storage units, etc.
Store: mail order only

  ¡Sí!

Turnkey's line is geared for industrial and commercial applications, but the sturdy storage units and other equipment sold here has home applications as well. Turnkey has been doing business since 1946, and publishes a 132-page catalog that features shelving and storage bins in a huge selection of sizes and styles. You'll find everything from small parts bins, ideal for hardware storage, to 108-drawer steel wall cabinets, plus plastic bin-and-frame arrangements. The catalog also shows mats and runners, work benches, stainless-steel rolling carts, folding chairs, suspension files, lockers, flat and roll files, moving pads, canvas tarps, security gates, hand trucks, rolling ladders, trash cans, hydraulic lifts, first-aid kits and protective gear, power-failure lights, pumps, recycling centers, and many other products.

Special Factors: Satisfaction is guaranteed; authorized returns (except custom-made items) are accepted (a 20% restocking fee may be charged); minimum order is $25; orders are shipped worldwide.

WHOLE EARTH ACCESS

822 ANTHONY ST.
BERKELEY, CA 94710
800-829-6300
FAX: 510-845-8846

Catalog: free
Save: up to 40%
Pay: check, MO, MC, V, Discover
Sells: hand and power tools and equipment
Store: same address; also Concord, San Francisco, San Mateo, and San Rafael, CA

Whole Earth Access was established in 1969 and offers woodworking tools and equipment at savings of up to 40% on list, with a "lowest prices nationwide" guarantee. See the catalog for details on the sales policy, and 48 pages of hand and power tools for woodworking—saws and sanders of all types, drills, routers, planers, and related machines. The brands include AEG, Black & Decker, Bosch, Clifton (planes), Delta, Freud, Hitachi, Jorgensen, Makita, Milwaukee, Panasonic, Norton (abrasives), Porter-Cable, Ryobi, Senco, Skil, among others. Whole Earth Access sells Emglo air compressors, surveying equipment by David White Instruments, Bosch finish nailers, Lamello hand joining machines, Willson safety products, Two Cherries chisels, and Japanese woodworking tools, among other specialty items. Throughout the catalog you'll find manuals and guides to remodeling, woodworking, using tools, and even building houses—perfect for do-it-yourselfers who want to make more of their efforts.

Special Factors: Authorized returns are accepted; orders are shipped worldwide.

WHOLESALE TOOL CO., INC.

P.O. BOX 68
WARREN, MI 48090
313-754-9270

Catalog: free
Save: 30% average
Pay: check, MO, MC, V, Discover
Sells: tools, hardware, and machinery
Store: 12155 Stephen Dr., Warren, MI; also Tampa, FL; Stoughton, MA; Charlotte, NC; Tulsa, OK; and Houston, TX (see catalog for locations)

Wholesale Tool has been bringing good prices and a great tool selection to hobbyists and industry since 1960, through the 608-page "Full-Line Catalog." This hefty tome runs from Toyota forklifts to Disston trowels, and is a treasury for do-it-yourselfers as well as woodworkers, machinists, contractors, and surveyors. Wholesale Tool is geared to the professional, as you can see from the collection of reference works—no Sunset guides to building decks, but *Die Design Fundamentals,* the 24th edition of *The Machinery Handbook,* a guide to world screw threads, and *Creep Feed Grinding* are here, among others. Wholesale Tool represents both popular commercial brands and industrial suppliers: Black & Decker, Brown & Sharpe, Brubaker Tool, Chicago Pneumatic, Desmond, Dorian Tool, Dremel, Florida Pneumatic, Fowler, General, G.E., Hanson, Heinrich, Jorgensen, Lufkin, Master, Merit, Milwaukee, Minute Man, Mitutoyo, Norton, Porter-Cable, Rigid, Ryobi, Shop-Vac, Starrett, 3M, Vise-Grip, Wesco, and Yuasa, among others. The comprehensive product descriptions include model number, technical specifications, Wholesale Tool's price, and sometimes the list price. Savings average 30%, and the catalog features several pages of clearance and odd-lot items, which are sold below cost.

Special Factors: Authorized returns are accepted within 30 days (a 10% restocking fee may be charged); minimum order is $25.

WOODWORKER'S SUPPLY, INC.

5604 ALAMEDA PL. N.E.
ALBUQUERQUE, NM
87113
505-821-0500
FAX: 505-821-7331

Catalog: $2
Save: up to 30%
Pay: check, MO, MC, V, Discover
Sells: woodworking tools and equipment
Store: same address; Monday to Friday 8–5:30, Saturday 9–1; also 1125 Jay Ln., Graham, NC; and 1108 N. Glenn Rd., Casper, WY

Woodworker's Supply publishes a 144-page, full-color catalog of woodworking tools and hardware, priced up to 30% below comparable goods sold elsewhere. The company has been in business since 1972, selling basics—from abrasives to rolling table shapers—as well as a number of hard-to-find items. Typical offerings include drills (including cordless models), power screwdrivers, routers, saws (circular, jig, orbital, table, band, etc.), sanders (finish, belt, orbital, etc.), laminate trimmers, heat guns, biscuit joiners, power planes, grinders, jointers, drill presses, shapers, and other tools. The manufacturers represented include Bosch, Delta, Freud, Gerstner, Glit, Jorgensen, Porter-Cable, Ryobi, Sioux, Skil, and Woodtek, among others. Drawer slides by Alfit, Delta, and Knape & Vogt are carried, as well as Hettich hinges, coated-wire fixtures for custom kitchen cabinets, furniture and cabinet levelers, cassette storage tracks, halogen canister lights, wood project parts, veneers, butcher block, locks and latches, glue scrapers and injectors, steel wool-backed sheets for finish sanders, Preserve nontoxic wood finish, and Haas knock-down joint fasteners. Like the best of such catalogs, Woodworker's Supply can give you as many ideas for new projects as it provides solutions to old woodworking problems.

Special Factors: Satisfaction is guaranteed; returns are accepted; minimum order is $5 ($25 to Canada); orders are shipped worldwide.

WORLD ABRASIVES COMPANY, INC.

P.O. BOX 5266
OLD BRIDGE, NJ
08857-5266
908-583-9700

Catalog: $1.25, refundable
Save: up to 60%
Pay: check or MO
Sells: abrasives and sanding materials
Store: mail order only

World Abrasives sells all kinds of sanding products and related goods, including hard-to-find sizes and types of abrasives. The firm has been in business since 1972 and can answer just about any question you may have on abrasives. World Abrasives stocks sanding belts for wood, metal, and plastic, as well as waterproof belts for wet grinding glass and ceramics, in grits from 16 to 1000, in a wide range of sizes. There are sanding discs, sheets, rolls of sanding materials, grinding wheels and points, wire wheels, and buffing wheels. The belts are sold in lots of ten, discs in lots of 25, and sheets in packages of 25, but there are small assortments for single jobs as well. Carborundum, Midwest, 3M, and World's own line are represented, and polishing compounds, oil and honing stones, 3M dust masks, goggles, disc adhesives, and belt cleaners are stocked. World Abrasives also sells tubing cutters, hack saws, utility knives, punches, chisels, files, X-Acto knives, drill bits and burs, gloves, and other handy tools. Prices are low, even in small quantities, and custom abrasives can be produced for special applications.

Special Factors: Satisfaction is guaranteed; minimum order is $20; orders are shipped worldwide.

ZIP POWER PARTS, INC.

DEPT. WBM
P.O. BOX 10308
ERIE, PA 16514-0308
800-824-8521
FAX: 814-898-0275

Catalog: free
Save: up to 45%
Pay: check, MO, MC, V, Discover
Sells: parts for chain saws, lawnmowers, snowmobiles, etc.
Store: 2008 E. 33rd St., Erie, PA; Monday to Friday 8–5, Saturday 9–1

If you own a chain saw, Zip Power Parts may be an old friend. In business since 1962, Zip Power Parts is one of the country's best sources for chain-saw parts, with a 32-page catalog of saw chain, bars, bar guards, and sprockets to fit all makes and models of chain saws. Saw chain grinders, chain saw repair parts, and small engine parts are all available, and there are shop tools for filing and grinding, wedges, lubricants, "mini-mills," hand tools, manuals, safety clothing and equipment, and woodcutting accessories. Additional parts for lawnmowers—mufflers, air filters, blades, starter rope and handles, fuel lines and filters, points, condensers, electronic ignitions, etc.—are listed in the catalog.

Special Factors: All products are guaranteed against defects in materials and workmanship; returns are accepted; C.O.D. orders are accepted; orders are shipped worldwide.

SEE ALSO

Alfax Wholesale Furniture • *institutional furnishings and fixtures* • **OFFICE**
American Science & Surplus • *surplus tools, electronics, etc.* • **SURPLUS**
Arctic Glass & Window Outlet • *replacement patio door panes and passive solar panels* • **HOME: MAINTENANCE**
Bennett Brothers, Inc. • *home-security equipment* • **GENERAL MERCHANDISE**
Cahall's Brown Duck Catalog • *work clothing and rugged footwear* • **CLOTHING**
Cherry Tree Toys, Inc. • *wooden toy parts, hardware, etc.* • **CRAFTS**
CISCO • *professional power tools* • **HOME: MAINTENANCE**
Clothcrafters, Inc. • *shop aprons, woodpile covers, tool holders* • **GENERAL MERCHANDISE**

Crutchfield Corporation • security systems for car and home • **APPLIANCES**

Crystal Sonics • auto security devices • **AUTO**

Cycle Goods Corp. • bicycle repair tools • **SPORTS**

Defender Industries, Inc. • wood treatment products, marine hardware • **AUTO**

Frank Eastern Co. • industrial and institutional supplies and furnishings • **OFFICE**

Goldberg's Marine Distributors • wood treatment products, marine hardware • **AUTO**

H & R Company • electrical and electronics components • **SURPLUS**

Knapp Shoes Inc. • work shoes and boots • **CLOTHING: FOOTWEAR**

LIBW • bathroom fixtures, cabinet and door hardware • **HOME: MAINTENANCE**

Meisel Hardware Specialties • wooden craft parts and brass hardware, woodworking plans • **TOOLS**

Metropolitan Music Co. • tools and supplies for making musical instruments • **MUSIC**

Okun Bros. Shoes • work and safety footwear • **CLOTHING: FOOTWEAR**

S & S Sound City • surveillance equipment • **APPLIANCES**

Sara Glove Company, Inc. • work clothing, safety gear • **CLOTHING**

Shuttercraft • shutter-hanging hardware • **HOME: MAINTENANCE**

Staples, Inc. • fire extinguishers • **OFFICE**

Todd Uniform, Inc. • work clothing and footwear • **CLOTHING**

TOYS AND GAMES

Juvenile and adult diversions

This isn't a large chapter, thanks to the fact that it's a seller's market and the big discounters don't have much interest in entering the mail-order field. Perhaps, instead of finding the latest thing on the cheap, you might try reducing demand. Consider limiting the number of ads your children see—by reducing their exposure to commercial television. Foster interests in activities that are built around imagination, instead of gimmicks and props. Encourage reading. And build on your efforts by teaching your children about the marketplace. *Zillions,* published by Consumers Union, is a "Consumer Reports for Kids": an ad-free guide to products, money management, and smart buying for shoppers from 8 to 13 years old. Help educate the next generation— buy a young friend a subscription. Write to Zillions, Subscription Dept., Box 51777, Boulder, CO 80322-0777, for rate information, or see the current issue of *Consumer Reports.*

ACME PREMIUM SUPPLY CORP.

DEPT. WBM
4100 FOREST PARK BLVD.
ST. LOUIS, MO 63108-2899
800-325-7888
314-531-8880
FAX: 800-999-5799

Catalog: free
Save: up to 50%
Pay: check, MO, MC, V, Discover
Sells: toys, novelties, and premium goods
Store (showroom): same address

 ★ ¡Si!

Acme Premium is listed here because so much of what it offers is toys, games, and novelties. The 80-page color catalog is bursting with stuffed animals, balloons, games, and other diversions, but please note that Acme's targeted customers are businesses, clubs, churches, and carnivals. Acme also states that its merchandise "is not intended for use by children under five years of age," a caveat well worth noting.

But Acme offers a number of items everyone can use, at very good prices—tumblers, flashlights, and pens and pencils, for example. If you're throwing a party or organizing a bazaar, call for the expanded, 144-page "OAB Amusement Merchandise" catalog instead. It has a wide selection of dart games, ball toss and hoop game equipment, bingo supplies and equipment, and similar goods. Imprinting is offered on T-shirts and windbreakers, visors, balloons, buttons, key rings, mugs, pens, and pencils. And of course, there are all kinds of stuffed toys: naturalistic animals, Troll-kins®, wizards, and dogs with sunglasses, to name just a few. Complete details of the sales policy are given in the catalog.

Special Factors: Authorized returns are accepted (a restocking fee may be charged); orders are shipped worldwide.

CONSTRUCTIVE PLAYTHINGS

U.S. TOY COMPANY, INC.
1227 E. 119TH ST.
GRANDVIEW, MO
  64030-1117
816-761-5900
FAX: 816-761-9295

Catalog: free
Save: up to 30% (see text)
Pay: check, MO, MC, V
Sells: toys and educational products
Store: Garden Grove, CA; Apopka, FL; Skokie, IL; Leawood, KS; North Wales, PA; and Carrollton, TX

Constructive Playthings sells wholesome, growth-oriented diversions for children, and makes a "lowest price guarantee" on everything it carries (see the catalog for details). Constructive Playthings has been in business since 1954, and features brightly colored, washable, durable toys, from activity centers and baby's first music box to teepees for backyard fun and a scaled-down kitchen, complete with sink. A recent catalog showed "My First Doctor Kit," a hand-puppet family in a choice of ethnic characteristics, black-and-white "see-alongs" (a panel of black and white animals to hang in the crib—the high contrast stimulates the baby); brightly colored bite-proof foam building blocks, activity mats, dollhouses, and arts and crafts kits, to cite a few items. These toys are made to withstand lots of play; in fact, Constructive Playthings also sells directly to schools and child-care institutions. Before giving in to this year's TV spinoff character, see if you can't get your children interested in these games and diversions instead—they'll outlast seasonal fads, and they're easier on your budget.

Special Factors: Satisfaction is guaranteed; returns are accepted for exchange, refund, or credit; institutional accounts are available; C.O.D. orders are accepted.

BARON/BARCLAY BRIDGE SUPPLIES

3600 CHAMBERLAIN
  LANE, SUITE 230
LOUISVILLE, KY
  40241-1989
800-274-2221
502-426-0410
FAX: 502-426-2044

Catalog: free
Save: up to 50% (see text)
Pay: check, MO, MC, V
Sells: bridge playing and teaching materials
Store: mail order only

Baron/Barclay Bridge Supplies carries materials and equipment for every kind of bridge player, from novice to old hand. Baron/Barclay was established in 1946, and stocks hundreds of books on bridge, and sells them at quantity discounts of up to 50%. Over half of the 64-page color catalog is devoted to teaching manuals and texts, books on strategy and bidding, bridge history and reference texts, and complete courses in bridge. Videotapes and instructional software are also available, as well as playing cards, scoring cards and club forms, recap sheets, and a variety of gifts and equipment—bridge-motif china, magnetic card sets, games, jewelry, pens and pencils, and even electronic bridge games.

Special Factors: Satisfaction is guaranteed; quantity discounts are available; returns are accepted within 30 days for exchange, refund, or credit (videotapes and software for exchange only); C.O.D. orders are accepted; orders are shipped worldwide.

KAYE'S HOLIDAY

6N021 MEREDITH RD.
MAPLE PATH, IL 60151
708-365-2224

Catalog: free (see text)
Save: up to 75%+
Pay: check or MO
Sells: holiday ornaments
Store: mail order only

Tired of missing those post-Christmas clearances with the half-price buys on ornaments? Here's a sale that never stops: Kaye's Holiday, where decorations for Christmas, Easter, Halloween, and other holidays are priced from 20% to 75% below regular retail (and sometimes well below *wholesale*) every day. Kaye has been in business since 1982, and sends out a workmanlike set of photocopies showing handmade ornaments of fabric, straw, and wood, tagged at $1 to $5 each. These are the same ornaments that can be found in import shops and gift catalogs selling for three times as much. Ornaments make wonderful gifts and keepsakes, and they're great to give when you're dropping in on people during the holidays.

Special Factor: Shipping is included.

ORIENTAL TRADING COMPANY, INC.

P.O. BOX 3407
OMAHA, NE 68103
800-327-9678
402-331-6800
FAX: 800-327-8904

Catalog: $1
Save: up to 75%
Pay: check, MO, MC, V, Discover
Sells: party goods, novelties, etc.
Store: mail order only

¡Sí! ★

Before you throw another party or plan a single fundraising event, see the catalog from Oriental Trading. It's a novelty shop in 144 pages, crammed with everything from balloons and stickers to spun glass bridal favors, resin animals and figurines, party favors, tickets, bingo supplies, penny candies, ribbon, inflatables, stuffed toys, masks, glow-in-the-dark jewelry, tropical drink stirrers, stars and stripes yoyos, costumes, card assortments, and lots more. Most of the products are sold by the dozen, gross, pound, or other multiple, at prices that are easily 50% below what individual items cost in party goods stores—and often even cheaper. Seasonal catalogs with special holiday selections are released regularly. Oriental Trading has been in business since 1932, and has a separate department devoted to fundraising activities that can help you make the most of your event.

Special Factors: Quantity discounts are available; authorized returns (except food, candy, and costumes) are accepted within five days for exchange, refund, or credit.

PARADISE PRODUCTS, INC.

DEPT. WBMC
P.O. BOX 568
EL CERRITO, CA
94530-0568
510-524-8300
FAX: 510-524-8165

Catalog: $2
Save: up to 50%
Pay: check, MO, MC, V
Sells: party paraphernalia
Store: mail order only

Paradise Products has been sponsoring bashes, wingdings, and festive events since 1962, when it began selling party products by mail. The 88-page catalog is a must-see for anyone throwing a theme event. The firm sells materials and supplies for over 100 different kinds of events, including celebrations of Oktoberfest, the 50s, Mother Nature, the Gold Rush, Presidents' Day, St. Patrick's Day, fiestas, "Las Vegas Night," Hawaiian luaus, pirate parties, Super Bowl celebrations, and July Fourth parties. Balloons, streamers, tissue balls and bells, party hats, banquet table coverings, crepe paper by the roll, pennants, garlands, and novelties are among the items available. Paradise's prices are as much as 50% below those charged by other party-supply stores, depending on the item and the quantity ordered.

Special Factors: Goods are guaranteed to be as represented in the catalog; shipments are guaranteed to arrive in time for the party date specified (terms are stated in catalog); minimum order is $30.

LA PIÑATA

NO. 2 PATIO MARKET,
OLD TOWN
ALBUQUERQUE, NM
87104
505-242-2400

Brochure: $1, refundable (no checks, please)
Save: up to 30%
Pay: check, MO, MC, V
Sells: piñatas and paper flowers
Store: same address; Monday to Saturday
10:30–5, Sunday 12–5 (winter); Monday to
Saturday 9:30–9, Sunday 12–5 (summer)

La Piñata is a marvelous source for piñatas, the hollow papier-mâché animals and characters that are traditionally filled with candy and broken by a blindfolded party guest. Prices here are low, running from $3.50 to $20 each. The stock includes superheroes like Batman and Superman, Sesame Street characters, Spiderman, pumpkins, Santa, snowmen, witches, stars, reindeer, and other seasonal characters. And there are all sorts of animals, including bears, burros, cats, elephants, unicorns, frogs, pigs, kangaroos, and penguins. La Piñata, which has been in business since 1955, also carries inexpensive, colorful paper flowers in several sizes.

La Piñata is offering readers a discount of 10% on all orders of piñatas only. Be sure to identify yourself as a WBMC reader when you order, and deduct the discount from the cost of the goods only. This WBMC reader discount expires February 1, 1995.

Special Factors: Price quote by phone or letter; C.O.D. orders are accepted; orders are shipped worldwide.

U.S. TOY CO., INC.

1227 E. 119TH ST.
GRANDVIEW, MO 64030
800-255-6124
816-761-5900
FAX: 816-761-9295

Catalog: $3
Save: up to 70%
Pay: check, MO, MC, V
Sells: novelties and fundraising items
Store: Garden Grove, CA; Apoka, FL; Skokie, IL; Leawood, KS; North Wales, PA; and Carrollton, TX (see catalog for locations)

It's always party time at the U.S. Toy Company, where masks, costumes, favors, festive tableware, streamers and decorations, games, grabbag prizes, little toys and novelties, penny candy, jewelry, stuffed animals, inflatables, balloons, hats, crowns, and other fun things are available at discounts of up to 70% on regular retail. In addition to party goods grouped by theme—Halloween, St. Patrick's Day, Easter, Mardi Gras, etc.—U.S. Toy has everything you need for your own carnival (except the rides), bingo hall, casino (play money included), or other fundraising event. Some products are sold in cases or large lots, but much is available in small quantities—making this a great source for parents, teachers, camp directors, and anyone else looking for inexpensive party materials.

Special Factors: Institutional accounts are available; minimum order is $25.

SEE ALSO

American Science & Surplus • *educational materials for elementary-grade sciences* • **SURPLUS**

Bennett Brothers, Inc. • *small selection of children's toys, board games, and cards* • **GENERAL MERCHANDISE**

The Bevers • *wooden wheels, balls, and other components for toy making* • **TOOLS**

Butternut Books • *children's books* • **BOOKS**

Cherry Tree Toys, Inc. • *wooden toy kits, parts, and plans* • **CRAFTS**

Betty Crocker Enterprises • *educational toys, games, and puzzles* • **GENERAL MERCHANDISE**

Dover Publications, Inc. • *cut-and-assemble projects, stickers, dioramas, etc.* • **BOOKS**

A. Feibusch Corporation • *zippers for doll clothing* • **CRAFTS**

The Fiber Studio • *doll-making fibers* • **CRAFTS**

Gohn Bros. • *dominos, "Dutch blitz," and other games* • **CLOTHING**

Gooseberry Patch • *collectors' country dolls* • **GENERAL MERCHANDISE**

Home-Sew • *doll and stuffed animal parts* • **CRAFTS**

Land O' Lakes Catalog • **KinderCare** *educational toys* • **GENERAL MERCHANDISE**

Meisel Hardware Specialties • *wooden wheels and other toy parts, toy plans* • **CRAFTS**

Monterey Mills Outlet Store • *fun fur yardage and remnants for toys* • **CRAFTS**

The Natural Baby Co., Inc. • *wooden toys* • **CLOTHING: MOTHER AND CHILD**

Newark Dressmaker Supply, Inc. • *supplies for making dolls and toys* • **CRAFTS**

The Paper Wholesaler • party supplies • **GENERAL MERCHANDISE**

R.C. Steele Co. • dog trivia, dog-breed playing cards, etc. • **ANIMAL**

Taylor's Cutaways and Stuff • kits and patterns for making dolls and toys • **CRAFTS**

Wicker Warehouse Inc. • wicker doll buggies, reproduction miniatures • **HOME: FURNISHINGS**

Woodworker's Supply • wooden toy parts, plans, and dollhouse plans • **TOOLS**

TRAVEL

There are all kinds of ways to save on travel, depending upon the nature of the traveler and the trip. This chapter includes listings of information sources, discount travel brokers, money-saving accommodations, and travel-related services. In addition, membership in professional organizations, unions, buying clubs, and other groups may entitle you to travel discounts and services—check your benefits package to find out.

CONSOLIDATORS/BUCKET SHOPS

Consolidators, also known as bucket shops, are travel wholesalers who buy cruise slots, blocks of rooms, and plane seats from airlines, hotels, and charter agents, and resell them for less than the hotels, airlines, or often the charter operators themselves are willing to accept for individual tickets or rooms. Travel agents are big customers of consolidators, but individuals may buy from them too, which will often save them 20% to 30% on APEX fares and much more on full economy tickets.

Unitravel Corporation, one of the oldest consolidators in the business, books flights in the U.S. and Europe and sells directly to individuals. Contact Unitravel about a month before you anticipate traveling, and allow for some uncertainty, since tickets might not be available until shortly before the day of departure. Call 800-325-2222 or 314-727-8888 for more information.

Council Charter, another consolidator, has been in business for over 40 years and is affiliated with the Council on International Educational Exchange, a not-for-profit travel concern. For information on Council Charter's current offerings, call 800-223-7402 or 212-661-0311.

Nouvelle Frontiers is an off-price travel broker that sells to consumers as well as to travel agencies. For information, call 212-779-0600 or 800-366-6387. You can also try *Travac Tours and Charters,* at 212-563-3303 or 800-872-8800, and *European-American Travel,* at 800-848-6789 or 202-789-2255.

DISCOUNT TRAVEL AGENTS

Simple common sense tells you that commissions pegged to the selling price of a ticket may be something of a disincentive to getting travel agents to find you the lowest fare. On top of this problem is the real difficulty in getting "hard" information in a market that literally changes overnight, every night. Inexperienced and undermotivated travel agents can be impaired on both counts, for which you pay the price.

You can improve the odds of getting the lowest rate by pricing your trip with at least three travel agents and asking for the cheapest fare. Make sure you know just what you're buying *before* you buy it. Ask for a statement of the agency's cancellation policy, and get it in writing if the travel agent is booking your trip through a tour operator.

The problems with agents make *Travel World* (also known as *Fare-finders*) worth checking before your next trip. This travel agency is run by Annette Forest, who's been in the business for over a decade and uses a wide range of information sources to find the lowest fares. Travel World will search for the best rates on travel by air, train, or ship, as well as cruises and tours to any destination worldwide. You can buy your tickets and book reservations through Travel World, but it's optional—there's no obligation for the fare-finding services. Ms. Forest also teaches hands-on college classes for aspiring travel agents at Travel Smart, and invites inquiries on her course. Write to Travel World, 11899 West Pico Blvd., West Los Angeles, CA 90064, or call 213-479-6313 for information.

If you're just interested in the best price on a cruise, give *Cruises Worldwide* a call. This travel agency will send you a printout of last-minute opportunities (from three-day getaways to 14 days on the high seas), as well as cruises scheduled up to a year from now. Discounts run from 5% to 50% on the published rates, and major lines are well represented—Carnival Princess, and Royal Viking were among those we saw in the listing we received. For information or the current print-out, call 800-6-CRUISE, fax 714-975-1211, or write to Cruises World-wide, 16585 Von Karman, Irvine, CA 92714 (there is a $1 fee for the information).

STANDBY TRAVEL

If you can be flexible in your plans, consider the world of standby travel. It really is a last-minute affair, but it can be one of the cheapest ways to fly.

Airhitch is an old friend among travelers who favor 11th-hour departures. The firm has offices in several large cities, but does most of its business by mail. You first phone for information, have a registration form sent to you, apply for the desired dates or range, send in a fee of $25, and then start calling for availability three days before your desired departure dates. The procedure is involved, but it works. The friendly phone system at Airhitch has been programmed to dispense all the details of the standby program. Make sure you have pen and paper at hand before calling 800-372-1234 or 212-864-2000.

Access International also books standby flights from New York to points in Europe. It works on a registration/fee basis, and publishes a brochure that describes the services. Call 212-333-7280 for information.

LODGING AND DINING DISCOUNTS

Entertainment Publications runs very successful programs featuring accommodations and meals at discounts, in the U.S. and abroad. To join, you purchase the directory suited to your travel and entertainment needs; the directory comes with a membership card, which is presented to validate the offer. At this writing, *Travel America at HalfPrice* costs $32.95; the *National/International Edition,* covering the U.S. and Canada, is $52; and there are 115 other guides for individual cities and different regions of the country and Canada. The potential savings are enough to justify getting a directory if you travel at all, since the big guides cover over 1,200 hotels and motels in the U.S., and entitle you to 25% price breaks on meals in some 1,300 restaurants around the country. And *Half-Price Europe,* features coupon offers on dining and hotels in nearly 150 cities. For more information and prices, write to Entertainment Publications, Inc., 2125 Butterfield Rd., Troy, MI 48084, or call 800-477-3234 (313-637-8400 in MI).

Taste Publications runs another popular program that nets savings on dining, entertainment, and accommodations. *America at 50% Discount,* $49.95 yearly, offers savings of up to 25% on rack rates at participating hotels, discounted meals at selected locations, plus reduced-price movie passes (offered by mail for United Artists, Loews, and other major chains). For more information, call 410-882-9726, or write to Taste Publications, 1031 Cromwell Bridge Rd., Baltimore, MD 21202.

Membership in the *International Travel Card,* also known as ITC, costs $36 a year and features savings of up to 50% on over 1,500 hotels nationwide. For more information, call 800-342-0558, or write to ITC, 6001 N. Clark St., Chicago, IL 60660.

And as a general tip on saving money when booking hotel accommodations, always ask whether a special rate is available. You can often take advantage of promotions as nebulous as a "shopper's special" that one Chicago hotel holds regularly; anyone who claims to be in Chicago to shop is entitled to 50% off—but you have to know about the program to claim the discount!

CONNECTIONS

Most travelers insist on the lowest possible prices for airline tickets, but squander comparatively large sums on the last leg of the journey—the trip from the airport to the hotel. Avoid this pitfall with the help of *Crampton's International Airport Transit Guide,* which lists schedules and rates of taxis, car services, trains, buses, car-rental agencies, and other connections from airports worldwide to nearby cities. The pocket-sized guide costs under $5, is updated yearly, and is sold by The Complete Traveller Bookstore (see "Other Resources," following). You may also contact the publisher, Salk International Travel Premiums, Inc., at P.O. Box 1388, Sunset Beach, CA 90742, or 213-592-3315, for more information.

EDUCATIONAL TRAVEL

Combining education with travel isn't a new concept, but *Elderhostel* brings it to a specific group—those 60 and over—and does it so successfully that it's created a loyal group of followers who plan their travel around Elderhostel programs. The organization was founded in 1981 and currently offers programs in hundreds of colleges in the U.S., Canada, and overseas—from Australia to Germany. There are study cruises, "RV" programs for hostelers who are bringing their own accommodations (tent or RV), and "Intensive Studies" programs that offer more in-depth courses, as well as the popular courses held on campuses around the country. Previous catalogs have offered programs as diverse as "Christmas Around the World" at Lakeland Community College, "The Role of the U.S. Intelligence in a Democracy" at Southern Utah University, "The Magic of Opera" at Eckerd College in St. Petersburg, Forida, and "Cults in America" at the Cape May Institute in New Jersey. The price is right: Programs in the U.S. currently run about $250 to $295 each, and include everything except transportation—classes, meals, lodging, and even entertainment. (The overseas programs cost more, since they include round-trip airfare, sightseeing, transfers, and all other costs.) Even the RV hostelers are bussed to the campus or course site, where they receive all their meals. Please note that you, or your spouse, must be at least 60 to participate, but there is no membership fee. Elderhostel's programs provide a wonderful avenue to new interests, friends, and travels, at a very reasonable price. For information, write to Elderhostel, 75 Federal St., 3rd Fl., Boston, MA 02110.

Imagine taking up painting on the coast of Cornwall, or embarking on a safari by jeep in New Mexico. These are two of hundreds of educational opportunities that have been enjoyed through *Learning Vacations* (Peterson's Guides, 1986), by Gerson G. Eisenberg. Although some of the programs are limited to enrolled students, most are extension courses taught on campuses in the U.S., Canada, Europe, and as far afield as Tanzania. Prices for the courses vary considerably from program to program, usually depending on the type of accommodations. *Learning Vacations* is available from The Complete Traveller Bookstore, listed in the "Other Resources" section at the end of this chapter.

STUDENT TRAVEL

Like seniors, students can benefit from a variety of travel opportunities and savings. One of the best-known names in this field is the *Council on International Educational Exchange (CIEE),* which also runs Council Charter (see the previous section, "Consolidators/Bucket Shops"). If you're a high school or college student working toward a degree, CIEE can issue you an International Student Identity Card (ISIS), which you'll need to qualify for discounts on train and plane travel, admission to cultural and entertainment centers, and CIEE's own travel programs. The card costs $14, and comes with the *Student Travel Guide.* CIEE also publishes the highly recommended *Work, Study, Travel Abroad: The Whole World Handbook,* by Marjorie Cohen and Margaret Sherman ($10.95). For the *Student Travel Catalog* with details on the card and the program, write to Council on International Educational Exchange, 205 E. 42nd St., New York, NY 10017, or call 212-661-1414.

CAMPUS ACCOMMODATIONS

Staying on campus *sans* academics is often the cheapest alternative to everything but budget hotels. Rooms are usually available during college vacation periods, at prices as low as $19 a night. Amenities vary widely, but the rates are so good that it makes sense to consider this alternative when you're planning a trip.

Campus Holidays USA, Inc. has been arranging campus accommodations and other travel services since 1975. You can call or write for a list of the U.S. and British accommodations currently on offer, and purchase a book of coupons that can be used to pay for your stay. Campus Holidays can provide "lower-cost youth/student and teacher airfares," and tours of Europe, Asia, Africa, South America, and Australia for travelers who are 18 to 35 years old. Among these trips, its "Top Deck" tours are quite popular: British double-decker buses, which have been converted to hotels (sleeping quarters on top, dining and kitchen facilities below), take intrepid travelers on jaunts of 2 to 20 weeks. (The overland trek from London to Katmandu is a standout.) For information on what's currently available, write to Campus Holidays USA, Inc., 242 Bellevue Ave., Upper Montclair, NJ 07043; you can also call 201-744-8724, or fax 201-744-0531.

If you're interested in exploring the university option, don't miss the directory published by *Campus Travel Service*, "U.S. and Worldwide Travel Accommodations Guide." This 76-page book lists 600 universities in the U.S., and others in Canada, Australia, Ireland, England, Wales, Scotland, Scandinavia, Europe, Israel, Japan, Mexico, New Zealand, Africa, Asia, and Yugoslavia. The name, address, and phone number of each institution are given, as well as rates for singles and doubles, open dates, food service availability, nearby cultural and entertainment opportunities, whether children are accommodated, etc. The guide features listings of YMCA residences (51 in the U.S., 67 in Canada, and 23 overseas), including prices, amenities, restrictions, and booking policies. There are also several pages of valuable tips and references—on travel overseas, information on youth hostels, bargains for those under 30, travel opportunities for educators, toll-free airline numbers, bed-and-breakfast reservation services worldwide, home-exchange services, addresses of U.S. and foreign tourist offices, and some excellent health advice for travelers. All of this costs $13 ($11.95 plus $1.05 shipping); send a check or money order for the "Travel Accommodations Guide" to Campus Travel Service, P.O. Box 5007, Laguna Beach, CA 92652.

HOME EXCHANGES

One of the cheapest ways to save on hotel bills, especially if you're quartering a family, is to billet in someone else's home. There are a number of organizations that can help you effect a trade, either by arranging it or by providing a directory of like-minded parties with whom you negotiate.

Home Exchange International arranges the trades of homes of persons in the U.S., France, Italy, England, and other locations. To register, you pay a one-time fee of $50 and supply photographs of your home. When you've planned your vacation or narrowed your choices, contact the agency with details. Once a trade is arranged, you also pay a "closing fee" that runs from about $150 to $500, depending on the length of stay planned, type of home, etc. For more information, request a brochure from the Home Exchange International office nearer you: 185 Park Row, P.O. Box 878, New York, NY 10038 (212-349-5340); or 22458

Ventura Blvd., Suite E, Woodland Hills, CA 91364-1581 (818-992-8990).

Do-it-yourselfers may prefer dealing with *International Home Exchange Service/Intervac,* an organization that compiles three directories a year listing over 9,000 homes worldwide (most are outside the U.S.). A year's subscription costs $44 ($35 plus $9 for postage), and entitles you to one free listing. The apartments and houses in this directory are available for exchange *and* rent, so you don't necessarily have to exchange your own home to take advantage of a good deal. For more information, write to International Home Exchange Service/Intervac, P.O. Box 190070, San Francisco, CA 94119, or call 415-435-3497.

THE TRAVELER WITH DISABILITIES

Travel can be especially trying for persons with disabilities, which is why *Access to the World* (Henry Holt and Company, 1986), by Louise Weiss, is such an important book. It lists hotels with accommodations for the handicapped, covers all aspects of travel by plane, bus, train, ship, car, and RV, and gives hundreds of references to *other* access guides, travel services for the disabled, and travel tips. *Access to the World* is available from The Complete Traveller Bookstore, listed in the "Other Resources" section at the end of this chapter.

Whole Person Tours, an enterprise providing tours for the disabled in Europe and the U.S., also publishes *The Itinerary,* a bimonthly magazine for the disabled traveler. The cost is $10 for one year, or $18 for two, from The Itinerary, P.O. Box 1084, Bayonne, NJ 07002.

DEALING WITH PROBLEMS ABROAD

No one plans to fall ill while traveling, but it happens. If you travel abroad frequently or want to play it safe on your vacation, consider becoming a member of the *International Association for Medical Assistance to Travelers (IAMAT).* Your $10 contribution to this not-for-profit organization nets you membership and a roster of English-speaking doctors in hundreds of foreign cities, as well as tips on staying healthy during your trip. For more information, write to IAMAT, 736 Center St., Lewiston, NY 14092.

The State Department "assists Americans in distress abroad," and may be able to provide information about the arrest, welfare, or whereabouts of a traveler through its Overseas Citizens Emergency Center. The State Department also issues travel advisories for countries afflicted by civil unrest, natural disasters, or outbreaks of serious diseases. All of this information, as well as visa requirements for travel to specific countries, may be obtained by calling 202-647-5225.

Planning the problems *out* of your trip is the best way to avoid them. Here are some pamphlets that can help ensure a pleasant experience: "Your Trip Abroad," "Travel Tips for Senior Citizens," "A Safe Trip Abroad," and "Tips for Americans Residing Abroad." Each booklet costs $1; request them by title from The Superintendent of Documents, U.S. Government Printing Office, Washington, DC 20402.

NEWSLETTERS

If you travel frequently, or would like to be able to afford to, you'll find the following newsletters of interest:

Consumer Reports Travel Letter, produced by Consumers Union, is a well-regarded "consumerist" publication for both business and recreational travelers. *CRTL* conducts in-depth comparisons of accommodations and prices in the U.S. and abroad, scrutinizes airline food, investigates travel scams, recommends methods of screening travel agents, and has probed the mare's nest of airline booking systems. Each monthly issue of *CRTL* runs around 12 pages; a year's subscription costs $37 at this writing. See the current *Consumer Reports* for an order form, or write to Circulation Department, Consumer Reports Travel Letter, 256 Washington St., Mount Vernon, NY 10553, for information. Single copies of back issues are available for $5 each.

Travel Smart is another newsletter that stays current with travel opportunities of all types, including discount fares and rates (including specials for seniors). Subscribers are offered deals on car rentals, cruises, accommodations, and air travel. And Travel Smart is full of great tips especially valuable to frequent travelers: A recent issue cited the end of an encephalitis alert in Florida, listed a number of short-term hotel bargains that were linked with bonus mileage offers, recommended restaurants in several cities for their moderately priced meals, and featured a two-season guide to cruises—along with the 800 numbers of dozens of cruise lines. A year of monthly issues costs $37; for more information, write to Travel Smart, 40 Beechdale Rd., Dobbs Ferry, NY 10522-9989.

OTHER RESOURCES

Whether your travels are confined to your armchair or you actually get up and go, you'll find travel guides a great help in planning your trip. The best-known series are *Fodor's, Fielding's, Frommer's, Baedeker's,* and *Birnbaum's.* These are reliable, general-purpose guide books to whole countries and major cities. The Frommer "$-A-Day" series is especially helpful if you're pinching pennies, but don't overlook the other books. If you're traveling abroad and want an informed guide to culturally and historically significant sites, see the *Blue Guide* series, which is highly recommended. The Zagats have entered the fray stateside with *Zagat's United States Hotel Survey,* a compilation on accommodations nationwide that have been rated by the Zagats' corps of paying guests and diners.

Many of the firms in "Books" sell travel guides and related literature, but specialty bookstores have far better stock and selection, and the staff can usually provide personal assistance in selecting the right book for your needs, even by mail.

The Complete Traveller Bookstore does a brisk mail-order trade through its 48-page catalog, which lists all the major guides, as well as *Insider's Guides,* the *Michelin* green and red guides, *Crown Insider's Guides* (written by expatriate Americans), the fascinating *Lonely Planet* books, which take you to the Cook Islands as well as Canada, and scores of specialty guides that cover everything from Alaskan hideaways to shopping in Seoul. Maps, foreign language tapes, and travel accessories are sold through the catalog as well. Store shoppers can peruse the collection of antiquarian travel books, including some early Baedekers, which are perched at the tops of the bookcases. For a copy of the catalog, send $1 to The Complete Traveller Bookstore, 199 Madison Ave., New York, NY 10016. Please note: This is *not* a discount bookseller.

The Forsyth Travel Library has an extensive selection of popular guides, road maps to cities and countries around the world, Berlitz phrase books, Audio-Forum language tapes, and Thomas Cook surface transit timetables. Through Forsyth, you can order rail passes to Europe and Britain (including "The Britainshrinkers" sightseeing tours), join American Youth Hostels (an application form is provided in Forsyth's brochure), and even subscribe to over a dozen travel publications, including *Consumer Reports Travel Letter.* Voltage converters and plug adapters, money belts, and other travel accessories are also available. Send 50¢ for the current brochure to Forsyth Travel Library, Inc., 9154 W. 57th St., Shawnee Mission, KS 66201-1375. Forsyth does *not* sell at a discount.

Book Passage publishes a 44-page catalog full of tantalizing reads: *Underwater Paradise: The World's Best Diving Sites, Muddling Through in Madagascar,* and *Doing Children's Museums* were just a few of the hundreds that caught our attention. In addition to the major travel guides and several language courses on tape, Book Passage offers titles on family travel, menu converters, railway timetables, shopping guides, maps, a number of guides to doing business abroad, and accessories— overnight bags, pocket-sized computer translators, fanny packs, etc. Request the catalog from Book Passage, 51 Tamal Vista Blvd., Corte Madera, CA 94925. Book Passage does *not* sell at a discount.

TravelBooks bills itself as "the compleat travel bookstore for domestic or international travel literature," and offers publications on adventure travel, trekking, hiking, student opportunities, and hundreds of maps. Write for the free catalog from TravelBooks, 113 Corporation Rd., Hyannis, MA 02601-2204, or call 800-869-3535.

Traveler's Checklist specializes in travel accessories, including money converters, adaptors and plugs, personal-care items, and related goods. Request a catalog from Traveler's Checklist, Cornwall Bridge Rd., Sharon, CT 06069. Please note that Traveler's Checklist does *not* sell at a discount.

Travel Accessories & Things has just that—those little items that can make life away from home a little easier. Inflatable pillows, personal "safes" of several types, eye masks, a folding cane, world-time alarm clocks, currency converters, and other useful travel aids have been offered in the past. Write to Travel Accessories & Things, P.O. Box 1178, Agoura Hills, CA 91301 for the current catalog.

SEE ALSO

Ace Leather Products, Inc. • *travel clocks, gift items* • **LEATHER**
American Association of Retired Persons • *car rental and lodging discounts* • **GENERAL MERCHANDISE**
Consumer Information Center • *travel tips and related information* • **BOOKS**
Grandma's Spice Shop • *Melitta coffee travel kit* • **FOOD**
The Kennel Vet Corp. • *airline animal carriers* • **ANIMAL**
The Luggage Center • *travel accessories* • **LEATHER**
Reliable HomeOffice • *pocket translators, luggage, travel plugs, etc.* • **OFFICE**
Superintendent of Documents • *travel tips and related information* • **BOOKS**
Thrift Club • *travel discounts* • **GENERAL MERCHANDISE**

THE COMPLETE GUIDE TO BUYING BY MAIL

CATALOGS AND PRICE QUOTES

CATALOGS

Most of the companies in this book publish catalogs, which usually cost between $1 and $5. Firms sometimes ask for a SASE, which is a long (#10), self-addressed with one first-class stamp. If a SASE is requested and you don't send one, don't expect a response.

You'll need stamps to mail all those catalog requests, and you can order them, by mail, directly from the U.S. Postal Service. Both stamps and stamped envelopes are available; ask your postmaster or carrier for PS Form 3227, "Stamps by Mail," or request it from the Consumer Advocate, U.S. Postal Service, Washington, DC 20260. You can also call 800-STAMP-24 and charge your order to your MasterCard or VISA. The stamps are usually delivered within a few days.

"Refundable" Catalogs: Companies whose catalog fee is "refundable" allow you to recoup the cost of the catalog when you place an order. Please note: If you don't place an order, you won't get the refund. Procedures for reimbursement vary, but many firms send a coupon with instructions to enclose it with your order and *deduct* the amount from the total. (A company will often date the coupon, which means that you must order within a limited time period in order to recoup the fee.) If there's no coupon in the catalog, deduct the amount from the order total *after* adding tax, shipping, and other surcharges, and note the reason for the deduction on the order form.

Sending for Catalogs Write a letter or postcard requesting the catalog you want (some firms have several), mention any enclosures, include your return address in the letter, and please refer to WBMC as your source. If the catalog costs up to $1, you can send a dollar bill or coins taped securely between thick pieces of cardboard. For catalogs costing over a dollar, send a check or money order. Never send stamps unless asked, and don't use a credit card to pay for a catalog or a subscription unless the listing advises it.

Catalogs from Foreign Firms When ordering a catalog from a foreign firm, use an international money order (IMO) or personal check if the catalog costs $5 or more, and cash or International Reply Coupons (see below) if it costs less than that. Money orders can be purchased at a bank or post office.

International Reply Coupons (IRCs) are certificates that can be exchanged for units of surface postage in foreign countries. They're available at the post office for 95¢ each, and are recommended when the catalog costs 75¢ or less.

You can save handling charges if the catalog costs $5 or less by sending cash through the mail. (In fact, several firms have requested it.) Technically it's risky and should be used only when you're dealing with currency. To conceal money and enclosures and remain within the half-ounce weight limit of a 50¢ stamp, slip the currency inside a piece of lacquered wrapping paper, or other kind of lightweight, opaque paper. This will camouflage the enclosure completely. Remember to mention enclosures in your letter.

Receiving Catalogs Catalog publication schedules vary widely, and when firms run out of catalogs, are between printings, or issue catalogs seasonally, there can be a delay of months before you receive your copy. Some firms notify customers when this occurs, but most don't. Please allow six to eight weeks to receive your catalog, and contact us if you have a problem (see "Feedback," page 572).

PRICE QUOTES

Some mail-order firms don't publish catalogs, but sell their goods on a price-quote basis. Their name-brand goods can be identified by manufacturer's name, stock or model number, and color or pattern name or code. Cameras, appliances, audio and TV/video components, tableware, furniture, and sporting goods are commonly sold by discounters on a price-quote basis.

A price quote is simply the statement of the cost of that item from that firm. The company may guarantee that price for a limited period of time, or until stock is depleted. Some firms include tax, shipping charges, insurance, and handling in their price quotes, giving you one figure for the final cost.

Finding the Information Before writing or calling for a price quote, have the manufacturer's name, product code (model or style number or pattern name), and size and color information, if applicable. You'll find this information on the factory cartons or tags of goods in stores and in manufacturers' brochures. If you're pricing an item you found in a catalog, remember to look for the manufacturer's data, not the vendor's catalog code numbers. If you're using a buying guide or magazine as a source for information, verify the information before requesting price quotes—it may be out of date or contain typos.

Price Quotes by Letter Most of the firms listed in this book will give quotes over the phone—in fact, many prefer it. When you write requesting price quotes, include all of the available information about the item or items. Leave blanks next to each item so the person giving the quote can enter the price, shipping cost or estimate, and related charges. Ask the firm to note how long it will honor the given prices, and ask for prices of no more than three items at a time. And you *must* include a SASE with your request if you want a response.

Price Quotes by Phone Have all of the information in front of you when you call. *Don't* make collect calls, and don't use the "800" number for price quotes unless the listing recommends it. To avoid problems later, ask to speak to the manager, take down his or her complete name, and make notes of the conversation.

NOTE: If you order over the phone using a credit card, some aspects of the transaction are not currently protected by the laws that regulate mail orders. For more information, see "The FTC Mail Order Rule," on page 555.

HOW TO ORDER

Before ordering, make sure you're getting the best deal:

COST COMPARISONS

Your chief consideration is the *delivered* price of the product. Compute this from your price quotes and/or catalogs, then compare the figure to the *delivered* cost of the item if purchased from a local supplier. Consider mileage costs if you must drive to the local source, parking fees, sales and use tax, shipping and trucking, installation, etc. If you're buying a gift, compare the costs of having the mail-order firm wrap and send the item to the value of your own time, and materials and mailing costs. Finally, weigh the intangibles—return policies, the prospect of waiting for a mail delivery versus getting the item immediately, the guarantees offered by the retailer and mail-order firm, etc. After contemplating costs and variables, you'll reach the bottom line and best buying option.

Before ordering any large item, measure all of the doorways through which the article must pass, allowing for narrow hallways, stairs, and the like. Some savvy shoppers even construct a carton dummy of the item by taping boxes together, and maneuver that through a dry-run delivery before ordering.

ORDERING

If the catalog is more than six months old, request a new edition and order from that (unless it's an annual)—prices can change without notice. (You may find yourself billed for the difference between the old price and the new if you order from an out-of-date catalog.) Use the catalog order form, along with the self-sticking address label on the catalog. If there's no order blank, use one from another catalog as a guide. Transcribe the code numbers, names of items, number of items ordered, units, prices, tax, and shipping charges—onto a separate piece of paper. Include your name, address, and phone number, the firm's name and address, and appropriate information if you're having the order sent to another address. Note any minimum-order requirements. Make a copy of the order, and file it with the catalog.

Second Choices and Substitutions When the firm advises it and you're willing to accept them, give *second choices*. These usually refer to differences in color, not product. If you'll accept *substitutions,* which may be different products that the firm considers comparable to what you ordered, you must give permission in writing on the order form. It's unlawful for a firm to make substitutions without written authorization from the buyer. If you don't want second choices and want to be sure the firm knows this, write "NO SECOND CHOICES OR SUBSTITUTIONS ACCEPTED" in red on the order form.

WBMC Reader Offers If you want to take advantage of a WBMC reader discount, rebate, bonus, or other special, be sure to comply with the conditions stated in the listing. Unless otherwise indicated, calculate discounts on the total cost of the *goods only,* not from the total that includes shipping, handling, insurance, and tax.

PHONE ORDERS

Many of the firms listed in this book take orders over the phone and have toll-free "800" numbers. Here's a brief description of how they work:

WATS Lines The phone numbers with "800" area codes are WATS (Wide Area Telecommunication Service) lines. When you call a firm on its 800 line, no charge is made to your phone bill, even though the call *originated* from your phone. Instead, the cost of the call is billed (in terms of prepriced minutes) to the 800 number, where the call *terminates.*

A firm that wants to offer WATS to its customers chooses the calling areas it wants to serve from areas determined by the phone company. Some firms have their own "in-house" 800 line, but others hire telemarketing firms to handle the orders, inquiries, and complaints. Telemarketers offer companies new to phone selling an opportunity to test the power of an 800 number without investing in line installation and operator training. Although telemarketing operators may not be able to give you information on the products, they should be able to give you the order total, including the shipping and tax, and a good telemarketing service will have a statement of the firm's return policy in its data bank. *Don't* order from a firm whose service representative can't describe the terms of the policy, or when you're told that returns are not accepted under any circumstances—unless you're willing to take the gamble.

ORDERING

Before picking up the phone to place your order, follow this procedure:

1) Have your credit card ready
2) Make sure the card is one that's accepted by the firm, has not expired, and has a credit line sufficient for the purchase
3) Have the delivery name, address, and ZIP code available
4) Fill out the order form to use as a guide, and a record of the transaction. Include the catalog code numbers, units, colors, sizes, etc.
5) Have the catalog from which you're ordering at hand—the operator may ask for encoded information on the address label

When you place the call, ask the operator the following:

1) What is your name or operator number? (Operators are not a subspecies; they do have last names, and should provide them. If they won't, ask why—and reconsider purchasing from the firm if there is hesitation on this point.)
2) Are any of the items you're ordering out of stock? If yes, when is new stock expected?
3) When will the order be shipped?
4) Will any of the items be shipped separately?
5) What is the total, including shipping and tax, that will be charged to my account?
6) What are the terms of the return policy?

Every operator should answer questions 1, 5, and 6. Only those operators with stock information will be able to answer question 2, and, in all likelihood, only in-house operators can answer 3 and 4.

Many operators are required to ask for your home phone number, and sometimes your office number as well. This is done so they can verify that you are the person placing the order rather than a criminal who's obtained your card information from a carbon slip or stolen card. Since the firm may have to absorb the losses arising from fraud, it may refuse your order if you won't divulge your number, especially if you're buying certain types of goods and your order total is high.

While you're on the phone, the operator may try to "upsell" you, or get you to buy more goods. Beware of such unplanned purchases if you're trying to stick to a budget. On the other hand, you may be offered a real bargain on goods the firm wants to clear out. When this happens, the company's loss is your gain. Just make sure you really want the item—a bargain you'll never use is no bargain at all.

Once the transaction is completed and you've noted the operator's name or number, checked off the items you ordered, struck off those you didn't, entered the billing amount, and noted the time and date of the call, put this record in your file with the catalog. They may prove valuable later, if you have problems with your order.

The Pros and Cons of Phone Orders Phone orders have certain advantages over mail orders. They're usually processed more quickly and, when the phone operator has stock information, you'll know right away whether an item is available. There are disadvantages, however, which relate to regulations governing shipment of goods. For more information, see "The FTC Mail Order Rule" on page 555.

ORDERING FROM FOREIGN FIRMS

Despite the fact that the world was supposed to be switching to the metric scale, many of the catalogs from Europe and elsewhere use the U.S. system—inches and pounds—in measurements. Converting metric measurements to U.S. equivalents is easy, though. Use the chart you'll find in any good dictionary.

There are confusing differences in sizing systems, color descriptions, and generic terms from one country to another. Sizes fall into three categories: U.S., British, and Continental, and the sizing chart on page 573 can be used as a general guide to equivalents. Always measure yourself before ordering clothing, and list the measurements on the order form if you're unsure of the proper size.

Color descriptions and terms are usually more poetic than precise, in both U.S. and foreign catalogs. Remember that color charts can resolve these questions, but you must allow for variations between photographic reproductions and the product itself. For a true match, write to the firm and ask for samples *before* you order, or at least make sure the firm will make refunds on returns.

The majority of foreign firms listed in this book give their prices in U.S. dollars. If they don't, you'll have to convert the firm's currency when you order. First, compute the total, including shipping, insurance, and other charges (but do not include duty). Next, convert this figure to dollars using the rate of exchange prevailing on the day you send the order. Get the rate from a bank, business newspaper, or the American Express office nearest you.

Before ordering, determine the rate of duty you'll be charged when the goods arrive and any shipping or transportation costs not included in the order total. See these sections for more information: "Paying for Goods from Foreign Firms," page 544; "Shipments from Foreign Countries," page 549; "Duty," page 551; and "Deliveries from Foreign Firms," page 558.

PAYMENT

There are two basic ways to pay for your order: now or later. You can *prepay,* using a check, money order, or debit card, or buy on *credit.* The distinction between these types of payments is based on the rules that apply to refunds under the FTC Mail Order Rule, but some methods have characteristics of both categories.

Prepaid Orders Payments made by check or money order are sometimes called "cash" by catalogers, since the firm receives dollars instead of extending credit on the basis of a promise to pay.

Personal checks, accepted by most firms, are inexpensive and can be sent without going to the bank or post office. Since some firms wait until your check has cleared before sending your order, shipment may be delayed by as much as two weeks. Checks do provide you with a receipt (the canceled check), which is returned with your monthly statement. Use the "memo" space on your checks to jot down the firm's address, so if you lose track of the company in the future, you'll have a way to find it again.

Certified checks are guaranteed personal checks. You bring your check to the bank on which it's drawn, and pay a fee of about $5 to $9. The bank marks the check "certified" and freezes that sum in your account. Every company that accepts personal checks will accept a certified check, and the guarantee of funds should obviate the delay for clearance. The canceled certified check is returned with the other canceled checks in your statement. Firms that request certified checks for payment will usually accept a *bank check,* a *teller's check,* or a *cashier's check* instead.

Bank money orders are issued by banks for a fee, usually $1 to $3. Ask the teller for a money order in the desired amount and fill in the firm's name and your name and address. If the order isn't dated mechanically, insert the date. Most come with a carbon receipt; some have stubs that should be filled in on the spot before you forget the information.

Bank money orders are generally treated as certified checks (i.e., no waiting for clearance). If necessary, you can have the order traced, payment stopped, and a refund issued. You'll find this vital if your order is lost in the mail, since there's always a chance it's been intercepted.

Postal money orders, sold at the post office, are available in amounts up to $700 and cost 75¢. They're self-receipting and dated, and can be replaced if the order is lost or stolen. Copies of the cashed money order can be obtained through the post office for up to two years after it's paid. This can prove helpful in settling disputes with firms that claim nonreceipt of payment. And, like stamped envelopes and stamps, money orders can be bought from postal carriers by customers who live on rural routes, or have limited access to the post office.

Bank international money orders, issued by banks, are used to pay foreign firms. You complete a form at the bank and, if the catalog prices are listed in foreign currency, the bank computes the amount in dollars based on the day's exchange rate. These orders cost a few dollars or more, and they are receipted. Like domestic money orders, you send them to the firm yourself with the order. They are usually treated as immediate payment.

Postal international money orders are used to pay foreign firms; their cost varies, depending on the amount of the order. (For example, the service charge on a $200 postal IMO sent to Britain is $3 at this writing.) They're not for every transaction: ceilings on amounts to different nations vary from $200 to $500, they can't be sent to every country, and amounts of $400 or more must be registered. When you buy a postal IMO, you fill out a form with your name and address and the name and address of the firm, and you pay the order amount and surcharge. The post office forwards the information to the International Exchange Office in St. Louis, Missouri, which sends a receipt to you and forwards the money order, in native currency, directly to the firm (or to the post office nearest it, which sends it on). The entire procedure takes few weeks; if you use postal IMOs, allow for this delay.

Bank drafts, or transfer checks, are the closest you can come to sending cash to a foreign firm through the mail. You pay the order amount, a mailing fee, and a service charge to your bank, then send one copy of the draft form to the firm and another to the firm's bank. You must have the name and address of the company's bank to do this. When the firm receives the form, it takes it to the bank, matches it to the other copy, and collects the funds. The forms will take five to ten days to reach the foreign country, provided they're sent airmail. Most banks charge $5 or more for bank drafts, depending on the amount of the check, but all foreign firms accept them.

Debit cards, which look like credit cards, are actually more like remote-control cash cards that are hooked into your checking account. See the following section for special caveats that apply to the use of debit cards when buying by mail.

Credit, Charge, and Debit Cards Those wafers of plastic in your wallet have been important factors in the mail-order boom, and the pairing of 800 lines and credit cards has proven an irresistible combination for millions of consumers, creating phenomenal growth in phone orders.

Paying for an order with a credit card is simplicity itself—use a card accepted by the firm, make out the order form, and provide your account number, card expiration date, phone number, and signature in the blanks. If you're ordering from a catalog without a form, supply the same information on a sheet of paper. Using credit cards can make life easier if the shipping costs aren't given or are difficult to calculate— they'll be added to the order total, and the order won't be held up as it might be if you paid by check or with a money order. Always check the minimum-order requirements when using a card, since they're often higher than those imposed on prepaid orders.

If you're low on cash but determined to order from a firm that doesn't accept cards, you can have Western Union send the company a money order and charge it to your MasterCard or VISA account. The surcharge is high—$14 to $37, and higher if you call in the order instead of placing it in person at a Western Union office. But it can be worth the expense if you might otherwise miss the buy of a lifetime.

The card companies, banks, and financial institutions that issue credit cards consider your past credit history, your current salary, and the length of time you've been at your current job when reviewing your application for a card. Minimums are raised when the interest rate climbs, but at this writing, a salary of about $20,000 and two years' employment with the same firm should net you a MasterCard or VISA account, provided you're credit-worthy in other respects. Getting an American Express, Diners Club, or debit card usually requires a higher salary and an excellent credit rating, and the issuers of "gold" accounts that offer larger credit lines and special programs geared for business and travel use usually look for an income of at least $40,000 and an excellent credit history.

Since there are thousands of card issuers and the market is considered saturated, the consumer is being wooed with reduced yearly fees and APRs, extended warranties, tie-ins with frequent-flyer programs, personal and auto insurance, discounts on lodging, and other benefits. If you need help comparing cards, Bankcard Holders of America, a not-for-profit consumer advocacy organization, can help you compare cards and find the one that best suits your buying habits. BHA publishes a list of banks with low APRs, and its bimonthly newsletters have useful information and updates on pending legislation that will affect bank card holders. For membership information and a publications list, write to Bankcard Holders of America, 560 Herndon Parkway, Suite 120, Herndon, VA 22070.

"Debit" cards deserve a special mention because they *look* like regular credit cards, but when the issuing bank receives the invoices for purchases, it *deducts* those amounts from your checking, savings, or money management account. This makes the debit card an electronic, instantly debited check, not a credit card, and it's important to know that the FTC views debit-card payments as *cash* payments. See the discussion of the FTC Mail Order Rule for more information on the debit-card issue.

Paying for Goods from Foreign Firms You can usually pay for goods from foreign firms with a personal check, bank draft, or credit card. Using a credit card is advisable (see "The Fair Credit Billing Act, page 569, for an explanation), but keep the following caution in mind:

If you use a credit card, the card issuer will charge you for the currency-conversion expense—a surcharge of 0.25% to 1%. The methods used to determine the rate of exchange vary widely, and are subject to the regulations existing in each foreign country. Your credit card statement should tell you the date the conversion was made and the surcharge. Check it carefully; the foreign currency total should be the same as your original order total, unless there was a price increase, short shipment, or shipping costs were higher than originally calculated. Check the *interbank* rate of exchange valid on the day the money was converted or the invoice was processed by the card company (your bank should be able to quote this). If there's a significant discrepancy between the interbank rate and the one the card firm used, write or call the customer-service department for an explanation.

Please read "Ordering from Foreign Firms," page 540, before ordering.

RETURN POLICIES

Most catalog firms guarantee satisfaction and will accept returns within 10, 14, or 30 days after you've received the order. Firms selling on a price-quote basis usually accept returns only if the product is defective. There are companies that don't accept any returns under any circumstances, but they're not listed in this book.

Some goods—personalized or monogrammed, custom-made, surplus, and sale items—are routinely exempted from full return policies. (If a firm has to special order an item for you, it may refuse to accept returns on that item—and may require you to buy a minimum number.) Health regulations usually prohibit returns of intimate apparel and bathing suits, but some companies will accept them. For more information, see "Returns," page 560.

Check the company's return policy before ordering. If you're shopping for a big-ticket item that carries a manufacturer's warranty, ask the mail-order firm for a copy *before* you buy, and see "Evaluating Warranties," page 564, for determining its value.

For more information, see "Returns," page 560.

CANCELING YOUR ORDER

When you order goods or services from a firm, whether by phone or mail, you enter into a contract of sale. You don't have the right to call the firm and rescind an order, nor do you have the right to stop payment on a check or money order on the basis of what an FTC staffer described as "buyer's remorse." (This term seems almost poetic in an industry that thrives on impulse purchases.) Different states have different laws governing matters of contract, but your second thoughts might give the firm cause to bring legal action against you. This is especially true if the company has undertaken action on an order, in what is termed "constructive acceptance of payment."

But if, after placing an order, you learn that the firm is in financial trouble or has a bad business record, stopping payment might be worth the possible risks. If you try to cancel, check the terms of the offer first. Magazine and book subscriptions are often sent on an approval basis, giving you a cancellation option. Goods offered with an unconditional guarantee of satisfaction can be sent back when they arrive. If these terms aren't offered and you're determined to cancel, contact the firm to discuss the matter.

SHIPPING, HANDLING, INSURANCE, SALES TAX, DUTY, AND SHIPMENTS ABROAD

When comparison shopping, consider shipping, insurance, tax, and handling as part of the total. (See "Cost Comparisons," page 537, for more information.) If you're having goods sent to Canada, an APO or FPO address, or another country, see "Shipments Abroad," page 552, for more information.

SHIPPING

This section addresses the concerns of consumers buying from U.S. firms who are having goods delivered to addresses in the U.S.

Shipping Computations The largest ancillary cost of an order is usually shipping, which is calculated in a variety of methods:

Postpaid item prices, which include shipping charges, are popular because there's no math for customers to do. The shipping and packing costs are passed along in the item price, however.

Itemized shipping costs are often seen as amounts in parentheses after the product price or code number. If you compare the UPS or USPS tape on the delivered parcel, you may find that the shipping fee you paid the firm is higher than what it really cost. But your fee may include the cost of packing and materials, or it may be prorated. (A California firm might compute all shipping charges based on the price of sending goods to Kansas, midway across the country, making up on local deliveries what it loses on shipments to the East Coast.) And there are some firms that, quite simply, seem to be gouging the consumer with shipping charges that are far higher than their real costs. If you feel charges are exorbitant, contact the company and protest—or take your business elsewhere.

Numeric charges are based on the number of items you're ordering, as in "$2.50 for the first item; 75¢ each additional item." Companies often limit these kinds of charges, so additional purchases made after you reach a certain number of items are exempted from shipping charges entirely.

Flat order fees are simple dollar amounts charged on all orders, usually regardless of the number of items or weight. (Extra charges may apply if part of the order is shipped to another address.) A flat fee may represent a bargain if you're placing a large order, but note that some firms selling this way will charge extra for heavy, outsized, or fragile items. Check the catalog carefully before ordering.

Free shipping is offered, often by smaller companies, on large orders. Customarily, orders under a certain dollar or item amount are charged shipping on some basis, but if your order exceeds a certain amount, no shipping is charged. The fact is often noted on the order blank—"on orders $100 and over, WE pay postage," or "free shipping on three dozen pairs or more same size, style, & color"—usually with the proviso that the order must be sent to one address.

Sliding scales, tied to the cost of the order, are used by many companies. For example, if the goods total $15.00, you pay $2.75 for shipping; from $15.01 to $30.00, the charge is $3.50, etc. This is great if you're ordering many inexpensive, heavy items, but seems unfair when you're buying one, expensive thing. Some firms remedy this by using itemized shipping charges for small, high-ticket goods, and most limit the shipping charges to a maximum dollar amount, usually $7 to $12.

Tables, based on the weight and sometimes delivery distance of the order, require the most work on your part: You must tally the shipping weights given with the item prices, find your zone or area on the rate chart, and then compute the shipping charges. Outsized goods will have to be shipped by truck; their catalog code numbers often have a suffix letter indicating this. Some firms include in their catalogs all the rate charts you'll need to figure exact costs; others state at the bottom of the order form, "Add enough for postage and insurance. We will refund overpayment." In this case, the best solution is to pay by credit card, or call the firm itself and ask the shipping department to give you a quick calculation over the phone. If you're paying by check, you could send in the order without adding anything for shipping and ask the firm to bill you, but this may delay delivery.

Saving on Shipping Costs When you have a chance to save on shipping by placing a large order, consult friends and coworkers to see if they want to combine orders with you. But count the time spent conferring, consolidating orders, and distributing the goods as part of the cost of the order.

Carriers No matter which method a firm uses to calculate shipping, it will usually send your goods by USPS, UPS, truck, or an overnight delivery service.

United Parcel Service (UPS): UPS is the delivery system many businesses prefer for mail order. UPS is cheaper, all costs considered, than USPS; it automatically insures each package for up to $100; and it also picks up the packages at the firm's office or warehouse.

Under its Common Carrier Service, UPS handles packages weighing up to 70 pounds with a combined girth and length measurement of up to 108" (with some qualifications). If your package exceeds the size/weight restrictions, it will be transported by a private trucking firm. UPS offers overnight delivery to certain states and ZIP codes through its Next Day Air service, and 2nd Day Air delivery to the 48 contiguous states and some parts of Hawaii. The delivery fee charged by UPS is determined by the delivery address, pickup location, the dimensions and weight of the package, and the service used.

United States Postal Service (USPS)—Parcel Post (PP): The costs for Parcel Post, or fourth-class mail, are somewhat higher than UPS charges, but Parcel Post offers one distinct advantage: *only packages sent by the U.S. Postal Service can be delivered to a post-office box.* (UPS must have a street address to deliver goods, although carriers will usually deliver to rural routes.) If you're having a package sent to a post-office box, write "DELIVERY BY PARCEL POST ONLY; UPS NOT ACCEPTABLE" in bold red letters on the order form, unless there's a box to check to indicate your preference. On the check, write "GOODS TO BE DELIVERED BY PARCEL POST ONLY." When the firm cashes the check, it's agreeing implicitly to this arrangement and should send the goods by Parcel Post.

While postal rates escalate by leaps and bounds, the size/weight restrictions remain relatively constant. USPS accepts parcels with a combined girth and length measurement of up to 84" that weigh up to 70 pounds. Packages weighing under 15 pounds, with a combined girth/length measurement over 84", are accepted at rates for 15-pound packages.

Truckers: When the firm specifies that an item must be sent by truck, or if you've ordered both mailable and nonmailable (outsized) goods, the entire order may be sent by truck. Sometimes firms indicate that goods are to be trucked with the term "FOB" or "freight," followed by the word "warehouse," "manufacturer," or the name of the city from which the goods are trucked. "FOB" stands for "free on board," and it means that the trucking charges will be billed from that point. When "manufacturer" follows FOB in the catalog, it means that the mail-order firm is probably having that item "drop-shipped," or sent from the manufacturer, instead of maintaining its own warehouse inventories of the product. If you're ordering nonmailable goods that you think will be drop-shipped, ask for the location of the manufacturer's warehouse so you can estimate the trucking costs. If you want the item quickly, or ask the mail-order company to verify that the manufacturer has the product in stock before placing the order, and whether the manufacturer can ship it by an overnight service.

Truck charges are usually collected in cash or certified check upon delivery, and the additional expense is a real factor to consider when ordering very heavy items from a firm that's located far away. Truckers usually make "dump deliveries," meaning they unload the goods on the sidewalk in front of your home or business. For an additional fee (usually $10 to $20), you can usually have the goods delivered inside your house or apartment. Additional fees may be incurred if your order happens to be the only one the trucker is picking up from the firm that day or if the driver has to notify you of delivery. Before ordering an item you know will have to be trucked, get the price *plus* trucking charges and compare it to the cost of the same item if bought locally and delivered.

SHIPMENTS FROM FOREIGN COUNTRIES

After your payment has been authorized or has cleared the bank, the firm should ship your order. Depending on the dimensions and weight of the package, it may be shipped by mail or sent by sea or air freight.

Mailable Orders If the package weighs up to 20kg (about 44 pounds) and has a length of up to 1.5m (about 59") and a length/girth measurement of up to 3m (about 118") for surface mail or up to 2m (about 79") for airmail, it can be mailed. Almost everything you can buy from the non-U.S. firms listed in this book will be mailable, but you may have a choice of air or surface shipment. Mailed packages will be delivered by your postal carrier, regardless of the service used by the company, and duty will be collected on delivery.

Airmail is the most expensive service; airmailed packages generally take a week to ten days to arrive after they're dispatched, although some firms ask you to allow three weeks for delivery.

Surface mail, which includes both overland and boat shipment, is the cheapest service, but orders can take up to two months.

Nonmailable Orders In the unlikely event your order exceeds mail weight and/or size restrictions, it will have to be sent by an air or ship carrier.

Air freight is the best choice when the item or order just exceeds mail restrictions. Charges are based on the weight and size of the order, as well as the flight distance. The firm arranges to have the order sent to the airport with a U.S. Customs office that's closest to your delivery address. You pay the firm for air-freight charges, it sees the order to the airport, and sends you a Customs declaration form and invoice. When the airport apprises you of arrival, get right over with the forms, since most airports will charge a holding fee on goods still unclaimed five to ten days after delivery. In addition, you should make arrangements to have the package trucked to your home if it's too large to transport yourself. Once you clear Customs you can take the goods home or release them to the truckers you've hired and they'll make the delivery.

Sea freight is much less expensive than air, but it can take months for an order to reach you. If you live near a port, you may want to handle Customs clearance yourself and hire a trucker to deliver the goods to your home. You can also hire an agent (customs broker) to clear Customs and arrange inland trucking. This service will cost from $75 to $125, but it's the only practical way to deal with the process if you live far from the docking site and the foreign firm that sent the goods doesn't have arrangements with a U.S. agent who could take care of these details for you.

The procedure is similar to that of clearing an air shipment: You present the forms the firm has provided to the shipper and Customs officer, pay duty charges, and transport the goods home or release them to the truckers you've hired.

For information on duty rates, trademark regulations, and shipment of problematical or prohibited goods, see "Duty," page 551. For information on payment of duty on mailed goods, see "Deliveries from Foreign Firms," page 558.

HANDLING

Some firms charge an extra fee for processing or packing your order (usually $1 to $5), which is often waived on orders over a certain dollar amount. The handling fee helps to cover the costs of labor and materials used in processing your order, and it, like the shipping fee, may be taxed in certain states.

INSURANCE

Packages shipped by UPS are automatically insured for up to $100; you shouldn't have to pay extra insurance on those orders. (If you're buying from a firm that delivers via UPS but has a preprinted charge for insurance on the order form, don't pay it.) UPS charges 30¢ for each additional $100 in value on the same package—a fee usually covered in the shipping charge. The USPS does not insure automatically, so if you're having your package delivered by mail, not UPS, be sure to request insurance. Charges for postal insurance range from 70¢ for goods worth up to $50, to $5.00 for package contents worth from $400.01 to $500.00. Goods valued at more than $500 but under $25,000 must be registered as well as insured, and some goods can't be insured. If the item you're buying is uninsurable, have the firm arrange shipping with a carrier that will insure it. If you're not sure whether the firm will insure your goods, ask—*before you order.* The small fee is a worthwhile expense, something you know if you've ever had an uninsured order go awry. (See "Accepting Deliveries" for more information.)

Most insurance claims arise as a result of damage to or loss of goods. Procedures for claiming and reimbursement vary according to the carrier's rules and the firm's policy, but contact the firm as soon as you discover any damage to your shipment and ask the customer service department what to do. If there is documentation (signature of receipt on the UPS carrier's log or USPS insurance receipt), the claim can be verified and processed, and eventually you should be reimbursed or receive replacement goods. If there is no documentation and the worst happens—the goods never arrive—the firm may absorb the loss and send a replacement order. It may also refuse to do so, especially if its records indicate that the order was shipped. In such cases, it might be nearly impossible to prove that you didn't receive the order. (If you paid with a credit card, you may be able to get a chargeback. See "The Fair Credit Billing Act," page 569, for more information.) But if repeated entreaties for a refund or duplicate order meet resistance, state your case to the agencies listed in "Obtaining Help," page 568. And be sure to tell us—see "Feedback, " page 572, for more information.

SALES TAX

You're supposed to pay sales tax on an order if you're having goods delivered to an address in the same state in which the mail-order firm, a branch office, or representative is located, and when the goods ordered are taxable under the laws prevailing in the area. Most states require payment of sales tax on handling, packing, and shipping charges.

Those are the general rules. The right of a state to create its own definition of "doing business" in that state, or "establishing nexus," rankles consumers who have to pay tax on what they perceive as out-of-state orders, and businesses that have to be tax collectors for 50 states. The issue of nexus is no stranger to the Supreme Court; one energetic individual took on both Sears and Montgomery Ward over 40 years ago and lost, and other mail-order firms have done battle with state governments and lost as well.

State governments are now trying to collect tax on *all* mail-order purchases delivered to residents of their states, calling such a tax a "use" tax (the actual sale takes place out of state, at the seller's place of business). Mail-order companies envision an accounting nightmare, and consumers stand to lose one of the benefits of shopping out-of-state: no sales tax on their purchases (unless nexus exists). The court cases being decided now are running in favor of the tax department, which means you could see changes—and start paying more—quite soon. But until the issue is resolved, keep paying sales taxes according to previously established guidelines.

DUTY

Orders from foreign firms are usually charged duty, which can't be prepaid. Duty is paid to the postal carrier who delivers your package or the Customs agent if the order is delivered by air or sea freight.

Assessment of Duty U.S. duty is calculated on the transaction value, or actual price, of the goods being imported, on an *ad valorem* (percentage) or *specific* (per-unit) basis, and sometimes a combination of the two. Some goods—such as certified antiques, postage stamps, truffles, and original paintings—are imported duty-free. Check your local U.S. Customs office for current regulations, since rates and classifications are subject to change.

Prohibitions and Restrictions Some goods can be imported only under certain conditions, and others are prohibited outright. You can't import narcotics, pornography, fireworks, switchblade knives, absinthe, poison, or dangerous toys. If you wish to import animals, animal products, biologicals, petroleum products, plants, or seeds, you must make prior arrangements with certain agencies for the necessary permits. And if you want to buy name-brand goods, be sure to check trademark restrictions. The manufacturers of certain goods register the trademarks with Customs, limiting the number of those items that an individual may import. Sometimes the manufacturer requires removal of the trademarked symbols or names, which is done by the Customs agent or the firm selling the goods. Goods that often fall under trademark restrictions include cameras, lenses, optics, tape recorders, perfumes, cosmetics, musical instruments, jewelry, flatware, and timepieces. Many foreign firms offer trademark-restricted goods in their catalogs, but don't inform you of U.S. regulations—find out before you buy.

Obtaining Information If you want to know more about duty rates and classifications, import restrictions, permits, and prohibitions, request the free booklet "Rates of Duty for Popular Tourist Items" from the Office of Information and Publications, Bureau of Customs, 1301 Constitution Ave., N.W., Rm. 6303, Washington, DC 20226. Use it as a general guide only—contact your local Customs office for the latest rates. Provide a description of the goods you're ordering (materials, composition, and decoration or ornamentation), since the classification of goods is more specific than is indicated by the brochure.

If you want to import fruits, vegetables, or plants from abroad, write to Quarantines, Department of Agriculture, Federal Center Building, Hyattsville, MD 20782, and ask for an import permit application.

For more information on related matters, see "Ordering from Foreign Firms," page 540; "Paying for Goods from Foreign Firms," page 544; "Shipments from Foreign Countries," page 549; and "Deliveries from Foreign Firms," page 558.

SHIPMENTS ABROAD

Shipments to and from Canada: The U.S.–Canada Free Trade Agreement The Free Trade Agreement (FTA) is a pact between the U.S. and Canada intended to promote trade and expand and enhance markets in both countries by removing some restrictions. The linchpin of the FTA is the mutual elimination of duties by 1998. Duties are being reduced in three ways: Some were eliminated when the FTA went into effect January 1, 1989; others are being reduced 20% a year over five years; and all others are being phased out over ten years. This tripartite formula permits industries that are ready for the increased competition to benefit from the new policy immediately, while protecting others that might be destabilized by the rapid abatement of tariffs.

The FTA affects an enormous range of raw materials and consumer goods—from fish and computers to ferrous alloys and plywood—but only those goods that are *produced* in the U.S. or Canada are entitled to free-trade treatment. (Tariffs on products of other countries are unaffected by the FTA, which is intended to benefit the U.S.–Canadian market.) The pact permits restrictions and quotas on products of certain industries and includes provisions dealing with "dumping" of goods at below-market prices and special considerations for government-subsidized products of both countries.

Despite the scope of the Free Trade Agreement, it's worth noting that *prior* to its enactment, more than 75% of the goods traded between the U.S. and Canada were exempt from tariffs. It may take a number of years for the effects of economies of scale and specialization to be discerned in the marketplace. Since only domestically produced goods are covered and phase-in periods may apply, mail-order shoppers must consult the nearest office of U.S. Customs or the Customs and Excise Office in Canada for rates and current information.

Shipments to APO/FPO Addresses Most of the firms listed in this book will send goods to APO and FPO addresses. Finding out which is easy: Look for the *stars and stripes* next to the maple leaf on the line with the dollar signs and phone symbol.

Mail-order firms generally ship orders via the USPS's PAL (parcel airlift) to the military mail dispatch center, where they are shipped overseas via SAM (space available mail). The size restrictions are 60" in combined girth and length, and 30 pounds in weight. Firms sometimes charge additional handling fees for shipping to APO/FPO addresses, so read the catalog carefully and write for a shipping estimate *before* ordering if instructions aren't clear. Please note that neither UPS nor Federal Express makes APO/FPO deliveries, and that the USPS does not offer C.O.D. service to APO/FPO addresses.

Shipments Worldwide Many of the companies that ship to Canada and U.S. military personnel also ship orders worldwide. (This is noted in the "Special Factors" section at the end of each listing.) If you're planning to have goods delivered to Japan, Israel, Europe, or any other address not in the U.S. or Canada, see the catalog (if available) for details on the firm's shipping policy. If it's not clear, or if the firm sells on a price-quote basis, write or call the company before sending any funds and request a shipping quote. Since the employees of firms listed in this book are unlikely to be familiar with import restrictions and duty rates in other countries, check *before* placing your order to avoid unpleasant surprises. Most firms request payment in U.S. funds; this may be most easily handled by charging your purchase to your credit card, but before ordering check with your issuing bank for rates and charges that may apply to converting funds. And note that "The Complete Guide to Buying by Mail" has been compiled for readers who are having goods delivered to U.S. addresses, and will not apply in all parts to non-U.S. deliveries.

RECEIVING YOUR ORDER

What do you do when your order arrives? And if it doesn't? The following section details your basic rights and responsibilities:

ACCEPTING DELIVERIES

When the postal or UPS carrier or trucker delivers your order, inspect the carton, bag, or crate before signing for it. If you're having someone else accept the package, ask that person to do the same. If the packaging is extensively damaged, you can refuse to sign for or accept the goods. This is not recommended, for reasons explained in "Returns," in this section.

If the box, bag, or carton is in good condition, accept it and open it as soon as possible. Unpack the goods carefully, putting aside the packing materials and any inserts until you've examined the contents. Most firms include a copy of your order form or a computerized invoice itemizing the order. If it's a printout or there's no invoice at all, get your copy of the order and check to make sure you got what you requested. Check the outside of the box, since some firms insert the invoice with the packing slip in a plastic envelope affixed to the top or side of the carton.

Check your order for the following: damaged goods, short shipments, unauthorized substitutions, wrong sizes, colors, styles, or models; warranty forms if the products carry manufacturers' warranties; missing parts; and instruction sheets if a product requires assembly. Make sure ensembles are complete—that scarves, belts, hats, vests, ties, ascots, and other components have been included. Test electronic goods as soon as possible to make sure they function properly, and *do not* fill out the warranty card until you've tried the product and are satisfied that it is not defective. Try on clothing and shoes to make sure they fit. Check printed, engraved, or monogrammed goods for accuracy. If you decide to return a product, see "Returns" for more information.

If the goods are damaged, contact the seller immediately. Describe the condition of the goods and what you'd like done to correct the problem. If the firm asks you to file a complaint with the delivery service, request shipping information from the seller (the seller's shipping address, day of shipment, seller's account number, applicable shipment codes, and other relevant data). File the complaint with the delivery service, documenting your claim with photographs, if it seems necessary, and send a copy of the complaint to the seller. If you charged the purchase on a card with an extended warranty program, contact the issuer about the matter. Be persistent but reasonable.

If you receive a short shipment (one or more items you ordered are not included in the package), the firm may have inserted a notice that the item is being shipped separately or an option notice if it's out of stock. (See "The Option Notice," page 556, for more information.) Some companies don't back order, and will include a refund check with the order or under separate cover when a product is out of stock, or bill your account with the adjusted total if you used a credit card. If your shipment is short and there's no explanation, first check the catalog from which you ordered to see whether that item is shipped from the manufacturer or shipped separately by the firm. If there's no mention of special shipping conditions or delays in shipment in the catalog, contact the firm immediately.

DELAYED SHIPMENTS

What constitutes a real delay in receiving an order? What should you expect from the company if it has to delay shipping your order? The following section details your basic rights and responsibilities in this event:

The FTC Mail Order Rule The Federal Trade Commission's "Mail Order Rule" addresses one of the biggest problems in the mail-order industry: late delivery. Mail-order shoppers should understand principles of the Rule, know what types of transactions are exempt from its protection, and understand what actions they're obliged to take to ensure protection under the regulations.

Please note: When a state or county has enacted laws similar in purpose to the functions of the FTC Mail Order Rule, the law that gives the consumer the most protection takes precedence.

General terms of the Rule: The Rule specifies that a firm, or "seller," must ship goods within 30 days of receipt of a *properly completed order,* unless the firm asks for more time in its catalog, advertisement, or promotional literature. The operative term here is "ship"—the firm does not have to have *delivered* the goods within 30 days under the terms of the Rule. And it must have received a *properly completed order:* Your check or money order must be good, your credit must be good if you're charging the order, and the firm must have all the information necessary to process the order. The 30-day clock begins ticking when the firm gets your check or money order made out in the proper amount, but stops if it's dishonored. If you're paying with a credit card, it begins when the firm charges your account. (An amendment to the Rule has been proposed under which the clock would begin ticking when data sufficient to process the order—credit card number, expiration date, etc.—are received.)

If your check or money order is insufficient to cover the order total or is dishonored by the bank, if your credit card payment is refused authorization, or if you neglect to include data necessary to the processing of your order (which could include size or color information, your address, etc.), the 30-day clock will not start until the problems are remedied—the firm receives complete payment, payment is honored by the bank, the credit card purchase is authorized, or you supply the missing data.

Exceptions to the Rule: The 30-day limit applies only when a firm does not ask you to allow more time for shipment. (Most qualifiers request extra time for *delivery,* which only confuses the issue.) Certain kinds of goods and purchases are not protected by the Rule. These include: mail-order photo finishing; seeds and growing plants; C.O.D. orders; purchases made under negative-option plans (such as book and record clubs); magazine subscriptions and other "serial deliveries," except for the first issue; and orders placed by phone that are paid by credit card. Genuinely "free" items don't fall under the Rule, but catalogs for which payment or compensation is requested are protected. The typical phone order is not protected by the Rule. See "The Rule and Phone Orders," following, for more information.

Assuming your order is covered under the Rule, the firm from which you're ordering must follow a specific procedure if it's unable to ship your order within 30 days. You must respond under the terms of the Rule if you want to retain all of your rights. Read on.

The option notice: If a firm is unable to ship within 30 days of receiving your properly completed order, or by the deadline it's given in its literature, it must send you an option notice. An option notice written in compliance with the Rule will tell you that there is a delay in shipping the item and may include a revised shipping date. If it does, and that date is up to 30 days later than the original deadline (either 30 days or a date specified by the firm), it should offer you the option of consenting to the delay or canceling the order and receiving a refund. The option notice must also state that *lack of response* on your part is *implied consent* to the delay. If you decide to cancel the order, the firm must receive the cancellation *before* it ships the order.

If the new shipping deadline is over 30 days after the original date, or the firm can't provide a revised shipping date, the option notice must say so. The notice should also state that your order will be automatically canceled unless the firm receives consent to the delay from you within 30 days of the original shipping date, and unless it's able to ship the order *within* 30 days after the original deadline and has not received an order cancellation from you as of the time of shipping.

The firm is required to send notices by first-class mail and to provide you with a cost-free means of response—a prepaid business-reply envelope or postcard. Accepting collect calls or cancellations over WATS lines is acceptable as long as the operators are trained to take them. If you want to cancel an order, get the response back to the firm as quickly as possible after you receive the option notice. Photocopy the card, form, or letter, and send it "return receipt requested" if you want absolute proof of the date of delivery. (If the firm ships your order the day after it received your cancellation, and you can prove it, you have the right to refuse delivery, have the order returned to the firm at its expense, and claim a prompt refund or credit.)

The renewed option notice: When a firm is unable to meet its revised shipping deadline, it must send you a renewed option notice in advance of the revised deadline. Unlike the first notice, second and subsequent notices must state that if you don't agree *in writing* to a new shipping date or indefinite delay, the order will be canceled. And the consent to a second delay must be received before the first delay period ends, or the order must be canceled, according to the Rule.

If you consent to an indefinite delay, you retain the right to cancel the order at any time before the goods are shipped. And the firm itself may cancel the order if it's unable to ship the goods within the delay period, and *must* cancel the order under a variety of circumstances.

The Rule and refunds: Under the terms of the Rule, when you or the firm cancel the order, you're entitled to a prompt refund. If your order was prepaid, the firm must send you a refund check or money order by first-class mail within seven working days after the cancellation. If you paid with a debit card, inform the firm when you cancel or when it notifies you that it's canceling the order that it must treat the payment as if it were cash, a check, or a money order, and reimburse your account within seven working days or send you a refund check. If you used a credit card, the Rule states that refunds must be made within one billing cycle. (We assume that these "refunds" are credits to your account, which will void the charge made for the goods.) The firm is *not* permitted to substitute credit vouchers for its own goods instead of making a reimbursement.

The Rule and phone orders: As mentioned previously in "Phone Orders," orders placed by phone and paid by credit card are not protected by the Rule. When the Rule was promulgated in 1975, phone orders were a much smaller part of the direct-mail industry than they are today.

The FTC is aware of consumers' concern and in 1990 entered the hearings phase of the rulemaking process on the Telephone Marketing Amendment, which is the proposed change to the Mail Order Rule that would protect transactions taking place by phone and via such newly developed technologies as interactive cable. Until changes are legislated, check to see if your state has laws protecting phone orders. If you order goods by phone and charge a deposit or partial payment to your credit card, but finalize the sale (complete payment) by *mailing* a check, money order, or credit card information to the company, the purchase is protected. (This practice is common in the furniture industry.) But you can't trigger protection by confirming a phone order in writing after you've called it in.

See "Complaint Procedures," page 567, for help in dealing with unresolved delivery problems.

DELIVERIES FROM FOREIGN FIRMS

The general guidelines outlined in "Accepting Deliveries," page 554, apply to deliveries from foreign firms. Please note that *most* FTC regulations do not apply to shipments from non-U.S. firms.

The delivery procedure for foreign orders is determined by the shipping method the firm has used. For a complete discussion of carriers, see "Shipments from Foreign Countries," page 549.

You usually pay duty, or Customs charges, when you receive your order. The amount you pay is based on the value, type, and origin of the goods. See "Duty," page 551, for more information.

Most orders from foreign firms are mailable and are delivered by your postal carrier. Before your order reaches you, it's sent through Customs. Orders processed with the least delay are those with goods designated as duty-free because they qualify under certain provisions of Customs laws, or those worth under $50 that are marked "unsolicited gift." Some firms mark orders as gifts to save you money; this is not in keeping with Customs regulations, unless the order originates outside the U.S. Please don't ask a firm to send your order as an unsolicited gift, which can create problems.

The clearance procedure on dutiable goods includes entry, inspection, valuation, appraisal, and "liquidation," another term for determination of duty. Provided the necessary permits and entry papers have been filed with U.S. Customs and shipment of the goods violates no regulations, the Customs department will attach an entry form listing a tariff item number, rate of duty, and the amount of duty owed on the goods to the package. It will be sent to the post office and delivered to you by your postal carrier. He or she will collect the amount of duty and a "Customs Clearance and Delivery Fee," currently $3.25, as "postage due." Some foreign firms are annoyed by this term, since customers assume that the charge is for insufficient postage and complain to the company. Postal authorities have told us that the handling fee is not charged unless the order is assessed duty. But even if your order has dutiable goods, you may not have to pay any Customs charges—a high proportion of small orders are delivered fee-free.

If your parcel is held at the post office and you don't collect it within 30 days, it will be returned to the firm. If you disagree with the duty charge, you can challenge it within 90 days of receiving the order by sending the yellow copy of the mail-entry form to the Customs office named on the form, along with a statement explaining your reasons for contesting the charge.

DELAYED SHIPMENTS FROM FOREIGN FIRMS

You can reasonably expect your goods to arrive within six to eight weeks, provided you sent the order by air, are having it shipped by airmail or air freight, didn't order custom-made goods, and paid the correct amount—and as long as the country concerned is not at war. If you sent the order via surface mail and/or are having the goods shipped that way, are having any custom work done, or the country is in turmoil, don't hold your breath. We've been told that the delay for orders sent by surface mail averages three to six months.

Transactions with foreign firms generally come under the jurisdiction of international law. If your order doesn't arrive, write to the company, including photocopies of your order and proof of payment, and send the letter by registered airmail. Allow at least one month for a response, then try again. Put a stop on your check, or a tracer and a stop on a money order, if you paid with one. If the check or money order has been cashed, go to the post office and fill out an "International Inquiry" form. It will be sent to the postal service in the country concerned, which should investigate the matter. Notify the firm of your actions, and keep copies of all correspondence related to the affair, since you may need them at a later date.

If you paid with a credit card and you have not received your order, follow the querying procedure outlined above. If you don't hear from the company, but find that your credit card has been charged for the order, dispute the charge immediately under the provisions of the Fair Credit Billing Act. You may do this only if you have not received the goods at all and if the bank issuing the credit card is a U.S. bank. For more information, see "The Fair Credit Billing Act," page 569.

For more information on resolving problems with foreign companies, see "Complaints About Foreign Firms," page 571.

RETURNS, GUARANTEES, AND WARRANTIES

Your right to return goods is determined by the policy of the firm, the problem with the order, the conditions under which you make the return, and state and federal laws. See "Return Policies" and "Accepting Deliveries" for general information. Product warranties, whether written or implied, apply to many goods bought by mail. "Guarantees and Warranties," following, provides a comprehensive discussion of all types of warranties.

RETURNS

Return policies are often extensions of a firm's pledge of satisfaction. The policy determines how quickly you must return the product after receipt (if there's a time limit), acceptable causes for return, and what the firm will do to remedy the problem. Some companies will take anything back, but most exclude custom-made goods, personalized items, special orders, intimate apparel, bathing suits, and hats. Some also exempt sale items. Even a no-frills policy usually makes provisions for exchanges when the firm has erred or if the product is defective. It's important to read "Implied Warranties" for information on laws concerning product performance and rights you may have that are not stated in the catalog.

Obtaining Authorization Before returning a product for any reason, check the inserts that may have been packed with the order, as well as the catalog, for instructions on return procedures. If there are no instructions, contact the firm for authorization to return the item. State the reason for the return, the item price and order number, date of delivery, and what you'd like done. Depending on the firm's policy, you may request repairs or replacement of the item, an exchange, a refund check, credit to your charge account, or store credit for future purchases from the firm. Keep a photocopy of the letter for your files, or notes of your phone conversation.

Restocking Fees Some firms impose a charge on returned goods, to offset the labor and incidental costs of returning the item to inventory. Restocking fees, usually 10% to 15% of the price of the item, are most commonly charged by firms selling furniture, appliances, and electronics. Restocking fees are not usually charged when you're returning defective goods, or the item was shipped incorrectly.

Sending the Item Follow the mailing procedure outlined in the catalog, order insert, or authorization notice from the firm. When you send the goods back, include a dated letter with your name and address, the order number, authorization number or name of the person approving the return (if applicable), and a statement of what you want—repair, exchange, refund, or credit. Depending on the circumstances, you may have to enclose the invoice or sales slip. Keep file copies of your letter and invoices.

Pack the item in the original box and padding materials if requested, and insure it for the full value. Allow the firm at least 30 days to process the return or respond before writing or calling again.

Refunds and Credits If you want your charge account credited for the return, provide the relevant data. Not every firm will issue a refund check or credit your account; some offer replacement or repair of the product, an exchange, or catalog credit only.

Exchanges If you're exchanging the product for something entirely different, state the catalog code number, size, color, price, unit, etc. of the item you want in the letter you enclose with the return, or on the authorization form.

Postage Reimbursement Some firms accept returns sent postage-collect, or will reimburse you for the shipping and insurance charges on a return. Most will not. Businesses are not required by federal law to refund the cost, even when you're returning goods as a result of the firm's error. State and local laws, however, may make provisions for this; check to see whether they do.

GUARANTEES AND WARRANTIES

Although the terms "guarantee" and "warranty" are virtually synonymous, they're distinguished here for the sake of clarity. In this book, a "guarantee" is the general pledge of satisfaction or service a firm offers on the sales it makes. Guarantees and related matters are discussed in "Return Policies," "Returns," and "Implied Warranties." A "warranty" is used to mean the written policy covering the performance of a particular product. Both guarantees and warranties are free; paid policies (including "extended warranties") are *service contracts.*

Warranties are regulated by state and federal law. Understanding policy terms will help you shop for the best product/warranty value; knowing your rights may mean the difference between paying for repairs or a replacement and having the firm or manufacturer do it.

The Magnuson-Moss Warranty—Federal Trade Commission Improvement Act Also known as the Warranty Act, this 1975 law regulates warranties that are in print. Oral "warranties"—the salesperson's assurance of product performance and pledge of satisfaction—are worthless unless they're in writing.

The Warranty Act requires that warranties be written in "simple and readily understood language" that states all terms and conditions. If the product costs more than $15, a copy of the warranty must be available *before* purchase. In a store, it should be posted on or near the product, or filed in a catalog of warranties kept on the premises with a notice posted concerning its location. Mail-order firms comply with the law by making copies of warranties available upon request.

The Warranty Act requires the warrantor to use the term "full" or "limited" in describing the policy. A single product can have several warranties covering different parts, and each can be labeled separately as "full" or "limited." For example, a TV set may have a full one-year policy on the set and a limited 90-day policy on the picture tube. Generally speaking, the conditions stated here apply to warranties on goods costing over $15.

Full warranties provide for repair or replacement of the product at no cost to you, including the removal and reinstallation of the item, if necessary. The warranty may be limited to a certain length of time, and must state the period of coverage. Full warranties can't be limited to the original purchaser—the warrantor must honor the policy for the full term even if the item has changed hands. *Implied* warranties (see page 563) may not be limited in duration by the terms of the full warranty, and in some states may last up to four years.

The item should be repaired within a "reasonable" length of time after you've notified the firm of the problem. If, after a "reasonable" number of attempts to repair, the product is still not functioning properly, you may invoke the "lemon provision." This entitles you to a replacement or refund for the product.

Registering your product with the warrantor under a full warranty is voluntary, a fact that must be stated clearly in the terms. You can send the registration card to the firm, but this is at your discretion and not necessary to maintain the protection of the warranty.

Limited warranties provide less coverage than full warranties. Under them, you can be required to remove, transport, and reinstall a product; to pay for labor if repairs are made; and to return the warranty card to the firm in order to validate the policy. The warrantor can also limit the warranty to the original purchaser and give you prorated refunds or credits for the product. (The "lemon provision" doesn't apply to a limited warranty.)

Warrantors may also limit implied warranties (see the following section) to the length of *time* their policies run, but no less. If they limit the implied-warranty time, they must also state: "Some states do not allow limitations on how long an implied warranty lasts, so the above limitation may not apply to you." The warrantor may not limit the *extent* of protection you have under implied warranties, however.

Other provisions of the Warranty Act include the following:

- If you complain within the warranty period, the firm must act to remedy the problem within the terms of the warranty.
- If a *written* warranty is provided with the product, the warrantor can't exclude it from protection under implied warranties.
- A warrantor can exclude or limit *consequential damages* (see the following section) from coverage under both full and limited policies as long as the warranty states: "Some states do not allow the exclusion or limitation of incidental or consequential damages, so the above limitation or exclusion may not apply to you."
- All warranties must include information on whom to contact, where to bring or mail the product, and the name, address, or toll-free phone number of the warrantor.
- All warranties, full and limited, must state: "This warranty gives you specific legal rights, and you may have other rights that vary from state to state."

Implied Warranties Implied warranties are state laws that offer protection against major hidden defects in products. Every state has these laws, which cover every sale unless the seller states that no warranties or guarantees are offered; that goods are sold "as is." But if a particular product sold by a firm with a no-guarantee policy carries a *written* warranty, the *implied* warranty of the state is also valid on that item. The terms of implied warranties differ from state to state, but many have similar sorts of provisions.

The warranty of merchantability is a common implied warranty. It means that the product must function properly for conventional use—a freezer must freeze, a knife must cut, etc. If the product does not function properly and your state has a warranty of merchantability, you're probably entitled to a refund for that item.

The warranty of fitness for a particular purpose covers cases in which the seller cites or recommends special uses for the product. For example, if a seller says that a coat is "all-weather," it should offer protection in rain and snow. If it claims that a glue will "bond any two materials together," the glue should be able to do that. When a salesperson makes these assurances, check the printed product information to verify the recommendation or call the manufacturer. While the salesperson may have a direct incentive—commissions—to inveigle you into buying a product, the manufacturer should be more committed to your satisfaction and return business.

Consequential Damages Incidental or consequential damages occur when a product malfunction causes damage to or loss of other property. The FTC uses the example of an engine block cracking when the antifreeze is faulty. Less extreme is the food spoilage caused by a refrigerator breakdown or the damage resulting from a leaky waterbed mattress.

Written warranties usually entitle you to consequential damages, but warrantors are allowed to exempt this coverage under both full and limited warranties. If the warrantor excludes consequential damages from coverage, the warranty must state: "Some states do not allow exclusion or limitation of incidental or consequential damages, so the above limitation or exclusion may not apply to you."

Provisions for consequential damages entitle you to compensation for the property damage or loss, as well as repair or replacement of the defective product. In the engine block example, the exemption of damages must be considered as a definite disadvantage when evaluating the product/warranty value.

Evaluating Warranties Appraise the written warranty as thoroughly as you do the product's other features *before* you buy. In reading the warranty, bear in mind past experiences with products and warranty service from that manufacturer or seller, experiences with similar products, and your actual needs. Don't rush to buy the first model of a new product if you can wait. Later models are sure to be cheaper and better—just consider VCRs, CD players, and computers.

In evaluating a warranty, ask yourself these questions:

- Is the warranty full or limited?
- Does it cover the whole product, or specific parts?
- How long is the warranty period?
- Do you contact the manufacturer, seller, or a service center for repairs?
- Will you have to remove, deliver, and reinstall the product yourself?

- Do you have to have repairs done by an authorized service center or representative? If so, how close is the nearest facility?
- Will the warrantor provide a temporary replacement for use while your product is being serviced?
- Are consequential damages excluded? If the product turns out to be defective, could the consequential damages result in a significant loss?
- If reimbursement is offered on a pro-rata basis, is it computed on a time, use, or price schedule?
- Do you have the choice of a refund or replacement if the item can't be repaired?

Envision a worst-case scenario in which the product breaks down or malfunctions completely. What expenses could be incurred in consequential damages, supplying a substitute product or service, transporting the product to the service center or seller, and repair bills? Will returning the product be troublesome, and living without it while it's being repaired inconvenient? Your answers determine the value the warranty has for *you*. Consider that quotient along with the price and features of the product when comparison shopping to find your best buy.

Complying with Warranty Terms Understanding and fulfilling the conditions of a warranty should be simple, but we've outlined a few tips that may make it easier:

- Read the warranty card as requested.
- Read the instructions or operations manual before using the product, and follow directions for use.
- Keep the warranty and dated receipt or proof of payment in a designated place.
- If the manufacturer offers a rebate on the product that requires sending the proof of payment, photocopy the receipt and keep the copy with the warranty.
- Abuse, neglect, and mishandling usually void the warranty. Other practices that may invalidate the policy include improper installation, repair or service by an unauthorized person or agency, use of the product on the wrong voltage, and commercial use. If others will be using the product, be sure they know how to operate it.
- Perform routine maintenance (cleaning, oiling, dusting, replacement of worn components, etc.) as required by the manual, but don't attempt repairs or maintenance that isn't required or permitted in the warranty or guide.

If you have a question about maintenance or use, contact the manufacturer or service center. If you void the warranty by violating its terms, you'll probably have to absorb the costs of repairs or replacement.

Obtaining Service If the product breaks down or malfunctions, you'll find that you can expedite resolution if you follow these guidelines:

- Read the operating manual or instructions. The problem may be covered in a troubleshooting section, or you may find that you expected the product to do something for which it wasn't designed.
- Contact the warrantor, whose name, address, and/or phone number appear on the warranty, unless the seller offers service under warranty.
- Call, write, or visit as appropriate. State the nature of the problem, the date it occurred, and whether you want a repair, replacement, refund, and/or consequential damages. Bring a copy of the warranty and proof of payment when you visit, and include copies if you write. (Remember that your rights in respect to the nature and extent of compensation depend upon the terms of the warranty and laws prevailing in your area.)
- If you leave the product for repairs or have it picked up, get a signed receipt that includes the date on which it should be ready, an estimate of the bill if you have to pay for repairs, and the serial number of the product, if one is given.
- If you send the product, insure it for the full value. Include a letter describing the problem, the date on which it occurred, and how you'd like it resolved.
- After a call or visit, the FTC recommends sending a follow-up letter reiterating the conversation. Keep a photocopy, and send it by certified mail to the person or agency with which you spoke.
- Keep a log of all actions you take in having the warranty honored, including dates on which actions, visits, and calls were made, and a record of the expenses you incur in the process.
- If you've written to the seller or manufacturer concerning the problem and received no response after three to four weeks, write again. Include a photocopy of the first letter, ask for an answer within four weeks, and send the second letter by certified mail (keep a photocopy). Direct the letter to the head of customer relations or the warranty department, unless you've been dealing with an individual.
- If you've written to the manufacturer, it may help to contact the

seller (or vice versa). A reputable firm doesn't want to merchandise through a seller who won't maintain good customer relations, and a responsible seller knows that marketing shoddy goods is bad for business. Bilateral appeals should be made after you've given the responsible party an opportunity to resolve the problem.

- If you have repairs done, ask to see the product demonstrated *before* you accept it, especially if you're paying for repairs. If there are indications that the problem may recur (e.g., it exhibits the same "symptoms" it had before it broke or malfunctioned), tell the service representative—it may be due to something that wasn't noticed during the repair.
- If you're paying for repairs, ask for a guarantee on parts and/or labor so you won't face another bill if the product breaks down shortly after you begin using it again.
- If the product keeps malfunctioning after it's repaired and it's under full warranty, you can probably get a replacement or refund under the "lemon provision." Write to the manufacturer or seller, provide a history of the problems and repairs, plus a copy of the warranty, and ask for a replacement or refund. If the warranty is limited, the terms may entitle you to a replacement or refund. Write to the manufacturer or seller with the product history and a copy of the warranty, and ask for a new product or compensation.
- Explore your rights under your state's implied-warranty and consequential-damages laws. They may offer you protections not given in the product warranty.
- If you've been injured by a malfunctioning product, contact an attorney.
- If, after acting in good faith and allowing the manufacturer or seller time to resolve the problem, you are still dissatisfied, contact your local consumer-protection agency for advice.

You may also report problems to other agencies and organizations. For more information, see "Obtaining Help," following.

COMPLAINTS

COMPLAINT PROCEDURES

A formal complaint is justified if you've notified the firm of a problem and asked for resolution, following procedures outlined in the catalog, warranty, or this guide, with unsatisfactory results. Give the firm one last chance to remedy the situation before asking for help from outside agencies. If your problem concerns nondelivery or dissatisfaction with a product and you paid with a credit card, you may be able to withhold payment or ask for a chargeback under the Fair Credit Billing Act. See "The Federal Trade Commission," following, for more information.

The Complaint Letter State your complaint clearly and concisely with a history of the problem and all the appropriate documentation: photocopies of previous letters, proof of payment, the warranty, repair receipts, etc. Don't send original documents—use photocopies and keep the originals in your file. Make sure your letter includes your name and address, the order or product number or code and descriptive information about the product, and the method of payment you used. Type or print the letter, and please don't be abusive. Tell the firm exactly what you want done. Give a deadline of 30 days for a reply or resolution, and note that if you don't receive a response by that time, you'll report the firm to the U.S. Postal Service, Better Business Bureau, Direct Marketing Association, Federal Trade Commission, or other appropriate agency. (See "Obtaining Help," following, for information.)

If the firm doesn't acknowledge the request or you're not satisfied by the response, take action.

OBTAINING HELP

There are several agencies and organizations that can help you with different types of problems. Some undertake investigations on a case-by-case basis, and others compile files on firms and act when the volume of complaints reaches a certain level.

When you seek help, provide a copy of your final complaint letter to the firm, as well as the documentation described in "The Complaint Letter."

Consumer Action Panels (CAPs) CAPs are third-party dispute resolution programs established by the industries they represent. They investigate consumer complaints, provide service information to consumers, and give their members suggestions on improving service to consumers.

MACAP helps with problems concerning major appliances. Write to Major Appliance Consumer Action Panel, 20 N. Wacker Dr., Chicago, IL 60606, or call 800-621-0477 for information.

Better Business Bureaus (BBBs) Better Business Bureaus are self-regulatory agencies, funded by businesses and professional firms, that monitor advertising and selling practices, maintain files on firms, help resolve consumer complaints, and disseminate service information to consumers. BBBs also perform the vital service of responding to inquiries about a firm's selling history, although they can't make recommendations. Most BBBs have mediation and arbitration programs, and are empowered to make awards (binding arbitration).

Whether you want to check a firm's record before ordering or file a complaint, you must contact the BBB nearest the *company,* not the office in your area. You can obtain a directory of BBB offices by sending your request and a SASE to the Council of Better Business Bureaus, Inc., 4200 Wilson Blvd., Suite 800, Arlington, VA 22203. Write to the appropriate office, and ask for a "consumer complaint" or "consumer inquiry" form, depending on your purpose.

Direct Marketing Association (DMA) The DMA is the largest and oldest trade organization of direct marketers and mail-order companies in existence. Over half of its members are non-U.S. firms; this gives it some clout in dealing with problematical foreign orders placed with member firms.

The DMA's *Mail Order Action Line (MOAL)* helps to resolve nondelivery problems with any direct-marketing firm, not just members. Upon receiving your *written* complaint, the DMA contacts the firm, attempts to resolve the problem, notifies you that it's involved, and asks you to allow 30 days for the firm to solve or act on the problem. To get help, send a copy of your complaint letter and documentation to Mail Order Action Line, DMA, 11 W. 42nd St., New York, NY 10163.

Consumers may also have their names added to or removed from mailing lists through the DMA. Request an "MPS" form from Mail Preference Service, Direct Marketing Association, 11 W. 42nd St., P.O. Box 3861, New York, NY 10163-3861.

The Federal Trade Commission (FTC) The FTC is a law-enforcement agency that protects the public against anticompetitive, unfair, and deceptive business practices. While it doesn't act on "individual" complaints, it does use your complaint letters to build files on firms. When the volume or nature of problems indicates an investigation is justified, the FTC will act. Several levels of action are possible, including court injunctions and fines of up to $10,000 for each day the violation is occurring. Report deviations from FTC regulations; your letter may be the one that prompts an investigation.

The Fair Credit Billing Act (FCBA), passed in 1975 under the FTC's Consumer Credit Protection Act, offers mail-order shoppers who use credit cards as payment some real leverage if they have a problem with nondelivery. The Act established a settlement procedure for *billing errors* that include, among other discrepancies, charges for goods or services not accepted or not delivered as agreed. The procedure works as follows:

- You must write to the creditor (phoning will not trigger FCBA protection) at the "billing error" address given on the bill.
- The letter must include your name and account number, the dollar amount of the error, and a statement of why you believe the error exists.
- The letter must be received by the creditor within 60 days after the first bill with the error was mailed to you. The FTC recommends sending it by certified mail, return receipt requested.
- The creditor has to acknowledge your letter, in writing, within 30 days of receipt, unless the problem is resolved within that time.
- You do not have to pay the disputed amount, the related portion of the minimum payment, or the related finance charges while it's being disputed.
- If an error is found, the creditor must write to you, explaining the correction—the amount must be credited to your account and related finance charges must be removed. If the creditor finds that you owe part of the amount, it must be explained in writing.
- If the creditor finds that the bill is correct, the reasons must be explained in writing and the amount owed stated. You will be liable for finance charges accrued during the dispute and missed minimum payments.
- You may continue to dispute at this point, but only if your state's laws give you the right to take action against the *seller* rather than the creditor. Write to the creditor within ten days of receiving the justification of the charge and state that you still refuse to pay the disputed amount. If you continue to challenge, contact your local consumer protection agency, since the creditor can begin collection proceedings against you and the agency may be able to recommend other means of handling the problem that don't jeopardize your credit rating.

Disputes over the *quality* of goods or services are covered under the FCBA if state law permits you to withhold payment from a *seller*. This applies to credit-card purchases over $50 that are made in your home state or within 100 miles of your mailing address. (The limits do not apply if the seller is also the card issuer, as is often the case with department stores.) Contact your local consumer protection agency for advice before taking action.

The United States Postal Service (USPS) The USPS takes action on complaints and resolves about 85% of the problems. This may be because, under provisions of the U.S. Code, it can go to court, get a restraining order, and withhold mail delivery to a company. (This is a very serious action and is never undertaken simply at a private citizen's request.) A number of readers have reported that the USPS acts more swiftly, with better results, than do any of the other agencies we've cited here. You can send a copy of your final complaint letter and documentation to the Chief Postal Inspector, U.S. Postal Service, Washington, DC 20260—but readers have told us that writing directly to the Postmaster of the post office *nearest the firm* is what does the trick.

Bankruptcy Courts Bankruptcy courts may offer information, if no actual compensation, on errant orders and refunds. If you've written to the company and received no response and its phone has been disconnected, contact the U.S. Bankruptcy Court nearest the firm. Tell the clerk why you're calling, and ask whether the company has filed for reorganization under Chapter 11. If it has, get the case number and information on filing a claim. Chapter 11 protects a business against the claims of its creditors; all you can do is file as one of them, and hope. As a customer, your claim comes after those of the firm's suppliers, utilities, banks, etc. The "take a ticket" approach is no guarantee that you'll get anything back, but if it's your only shot, take the trouble to file.

COMPLAINTS ABOUT FOREIGN FIRMS

For general information on dealing with complaints about foreign firms, see "Delayed Shipments from Foreign Firms," page 559.

The DMA may be able to undertake an investigation on your behalf. See page 569 for more information on the organization and its address.

The Council of Better Business Bureaus has affiliates in Canada, Mexico, Israel, and Venezuela. If the firm is located in any of those countries, write to the Council for the address of the office nearest the company, and contact that office with the complaint. See page 568 for more information and the Council's address.

The foreign trade council representing the firm's country may be able to provide information that could prove helpful. Contact the council and briefly describe your problem. Ask whether the organization can supply the name of a regulatory agency or trade organization in that country that might be of help. The councils have offices in New York City, and directory assistance can provide you with their phone numbers.

We'll try to help resolve problems with firms listed in this book. See "Feedback," following, for more information.

FEEDBACK

Your suggestions, complaints, and comments help to shape each edition of *The Wholesale-by-Mail Catalog®*. When you write, please use the guidelines that follow.

Firms: If you'd like your company considered for inclusion in the next edition of WBMC, have your marketing director send a copy of your current catalog or literature with background information to me. Firms are listed at my discretion and must meet the established criteria to qualify for inclusion.

Consumers: If you're writing a letter of complaint, please read the sections of "The Complete Guide to Buying by Mail" that may apply to your problem, and try to work it out yourself. If you can't remedy the situation on your own, write to me, and please include:

- a brief history of the transaction
- copies (not originals) of all letters and documents related to the problem
- a list of the dates on which events occurred, if applicable (the date a phone order was placed, goods were received, account charged, etc.)
- a description of what you want done (goods delivered, warranty honored, return accepted, money refunded or credited, etc.)

Include your name, address, and day phone number in your cover letter. We'll look into the matter, and while we can't guarantee resolution, we may be able to help you.

If you just want to sound off, please feel free. And suggestions for the next edition of WBMC are welcomed. Send your postcard or letter to:

P. McCullough, Executive Editor
WBMC 1994
P.O. Box 150522, Van Brunt Station
Brooklyn, NY 11215-0006

SIZE CHART

CLOTHING SIZES

Women's Garments

U.S.A.	6	8	10	12	14	16	18	20
Great Britain	8	10	12	14	16	18	20	22
Europe	36	38	40	42	44	46	48	50

Women's Sweaters

U.S.A	XS	S	M	M	L	L
Great Britain	34	36	38	40	42	44
Europe	40	42	44	46	48	50

Women's Shoes

U.S.A	5	5 $\frac{1}{2}$	6	6 $\frac{1}{2}$	7	7 $\frac{1}{2}$	8	8 $\frac{1}{2}$	9	9 $\frac{1}{2}$	10
Great Britain	3 $\frac{1}{2}$	4	4 $\frac{1}{2}$	5	5 $\frac{1}{2}$	6	6 $\frac{1}{2}$	7	7 $\frac{1}{2}$	8	8 $\frac{1}{2}$
Europe	36		37		38		39		40		41

Men's Suits and Sweaters

	S	S	M	M	L	XL
U.S.A	34	36	38	40	42	44
Great Britain	34	36	38	40	42	44
Europe	44	46	48	50	52	54

Men's Shirts

U.S.A/Great Britain	14	14 $\frac{1}{2}$	15	15 $\frac{1}{2}$	15 $\frac{3}{4}$	16	16 $\frac{1}{2}$	17	17 $\frac{1}{2}$	18
Europe		36	37	38	39	40	41	42	43	44	46

Men's Shoes

U.S.A	7 $\frac{1}{2}$	8	8 $\frac{1}{2}$	9	9 $\frac{1}{2}$	10	10 $\frac{1}{2}$	11	11 $\frac{1}{2}$	12	12 $\frac{1}{2}$
Great Britain	6	6 $\frac{1}{2}$	7	7 $\frac{1}{2}$	8	8 $\frac{1}{2}$	9	9 $\frac{1}{2}$	10	10 $\frac{1}{2}$	11
Europe	39 $\frac{1}{2}$	40	40 $\frac{1}{2}$	41	42	42 $\frac{1}{2}$	43	44	44 $\frac{1}{2}$	45	45 $\frac{1}{2}$

COMPANY INDEX

Illinois Audio, Inc., 28
IMPCO, Inc., 80
Interior Furnishings Ltd., 312
International Association for Medical
    Assistance to Travelers (IAMAT),
    531
International Gem Corporation, 375
International Home Exchange
    Service/Intervac, 531
International Travel Card, 527
Interstate˜Music Supply, 409
The Itinerary, 531

J & J Products Ltd., 190
J & R Music World, 29
J-B Wholesale Pet Supplies, Inc., 7
Jackson & Perkins, 219
Jaffe Bros., Inc., 240
James River, 141
Le Jardin du Gourmet, 218
Jeffers Vet Supply, 8
Jerry's Artarama, Inc., 60
Jessica's Biscuit, 104
Johnson's Carpets, Inc., 293
The Jompole Company, Inc., 359
Justin Discount Boots & Cowboy Outfit-
    ters, 160

Kaiser Crow Inc., 360
Kaplan Bros. Blue Flame Corp., 327
Karen's Kitchen, 241
Kaye's Holiday, 520
Kennel Vet Corp., 9
Kennelly Keys Music, Inc., 410
Kettle Care, 276
Kicking Mule Records, Inc., 105
King's Chandelier Co., 293
Kitchen Etc., 327
E.C. Kraus Wine & Beermaking Supplies,
    242
Knapp Shoes Inc., 161

Don Lamor Inc., 312
Land O' Lakes Catalog, 263
Las Vegas Discount Golf & Tennis, 479
Leather Unlimited Corp., 382
Lee-McClain Co., Inc., 142
L'Eggs Hanes Bali Playtex Outlet Catalog,
    143
Harris Levy, Inc., 338
LIBW, 348
The Linen Source, 339
Lixx Labelz, 264
Loftin-Black Furniture Company, 313
Lone Star Percussion, 411

Leisure Pages, Inc., 479
LPI Discount Pool & Spa Co., 383
Luigi Crystal, 294
LVT Price Quote Hotline, Inc., 30
Lyben Computer Systems, Inc., 449
Lyle Cartridges, 31

M&E Marine Supply Company, Inc., 81
M.C. Limited Fine Leathers, 296
MacConnection, 449
D. MacGillivray & Coy., 207
MacWarehouse, 450
Mail Center USA, 426
Main Lamp/Lamp Warehouse, 295
Major Appliance Consumer Action Panel,
    20
Mandolin Brothers, Ltd., 412
Manny's Millinery Supply Co., 144
Manny's Musical Instruments & Acces-
    sories, Inc., 413
Manufacturer's Supply, 504
The Maples Fruit Farm, Inc., 243
Mardiron Optics, 124
Marion Travis, 319
Mark Sales Co., Inc., 313
Marlene's Decorator Fabrics, 295
Ephraim Marsh Co., 314
Marymac Industries, Inc., 451
Mass. Army & Navy Store, 494
Master Animal Care, 10
Masuen First Aid & Safety, 392
Medi-Mail, Inc., 393
Medical Supply Co., Inc., 392
MEI/Micro Center, 451
Meisel Hardware Specialties, 191
Mellinger's Inc., 220
Merryweather Imports, Inc., 42
Messina Glass & China Co. Inc., 361
Metropolitan Music Co., 413
Micro Warehouse, Inc., 452
Midamerica Vacuum Cleaner Supply Co.,
    31
Midwestern Sport Togs, 145
Mill Supply, Inc., 81
J.E. Miller Nurseries, Inc., 221
Miscellaneous Man, 43
Mr. Spiceman, Inc., 244
Model Expo, Inc., 192
Monarch, 348
Monterey Mills Outlet Store, 193
Mother Hart's Natural Products, Inc., 339
Mothers Work Maternity, 167
MSPCA, 2
Murrow Furniture Galleries, Inc., 315
Mystic Color Lab, 125

Weinkrantz Musical Supply Co., Inc., 416
Wells Interiors Inc., 303
West Manor Music, 417
West Marine, 85
Westcoast Discount Video, 35
Weston Bowl Mill, 267
Whole Earth Access, 510
Wholesale Tape and Supply Company,
    36
Wholesale Tool Co., Inc., 511
Wicker Warehouse Inc., 321

Wiley Outdoor Sports, Inc., 490
Wood's Cider Mill, 253
Woodworker's Supply, Inc., 512
World Abrasives Company, Inc., 513

Yachtmail Co. Ltd., 86
Yazoo Mills, Inc., 66
Richard Young Products, 456

Zabar's & Co., Inc., 331
Zip Power Parts, Inc., 514

PRODUCT INDEX

bicycle cushions, 132, 465
bicycles, stationary, 272–273, 468
bicycles and equipment, 469, 473
binoculars, 122, 123–124, 125–126, 128, 129, 465
birds, products for, 14, 16–17, 122
blackpowder (hunting) supplies, 382, 474, 486–487, 490–491
blood pressure measuring devices, 150, 272, 388, 392, 397
boating supplies and equipment, 76–78, 79, 81, 85, 86, 474, 480
  inflatables, 77, 81, 85, 86, 470
books
  academic press, 111, 113
  children's, 96–97, 101–102, 113
  cookery, 101–102, 104, 112, 223, 263, 325
  copyright-free, 101–102
  literary remainders, 101, 111, 113
  on art, 102, 107–108, 113
  on astronomy, 91, 126, 128
  on ceramics and pottery, 55, 107
  on country living, 112, 220–221
  on photography, 130
  on ships and model-building, 192
  on textile arts, 109, 181, 184, 198
  out-of-print, 102–103, 113
  remaindered, 93, 101, 113
  reviewers' copies, 113
  used, range of topics, 102–103, 106, 115
bow fishing supplies and equipment, 469, 486–487
bow hunting supplies and equipment, 469, 486–487
bowls, salad, 267–268
breast forms, 387
bridal accessories, 144
bridge-playing materials, 518
bulbs, flower, 213, 217, 221, 222, 225, 227–230
business cards, 421
buttons, 176–177, 185, 199

C.Z., see jewelry, cubic zirconia
calendars, 93
calligraphy supplies and tools, 60, 63, 64
camping gear, 470–471, 474–476, 484, 487–488, 490–491
candy, 233
canes, 388
car, see auto
carpeting, see rugs and carpeting
cards, greeting, 100, 110
cash registers, 259, 423

castanets, 411
caviar, 234–235
CB equipment, 259
CDs (compact discs), 93, 94, 96, 98, 109–110
ceiling fans, 281, 288–289, 295
cellos, 414, 417
cellular phones, 76
ceramics supplies and equipment, 54–55, 63
chain saws, 499, 505
  parts, 499, 503, 504, 505, 514
chair reweaving supplies and equipment, 177–178, 186
chandeliers and parts, 293–294
cheese, 236, 238–239
cheese-making supplies and equipment, 328–329
Christmas ornaments, decorations, and collectibles, 47, 55, 179–180, 263, 366
cider jelly, 253
cider-press liners, 260
cleaning and maintenance supplies, 253, 275, 326, 330, 434
clock-making supplies, 55, 178, 179, 191, 373
clocks, 259, 307, 319, 359, 356, 368, 380
clothing
  auto racing, 82, 83
  children's, 135, 165–166, 168–169
  cycling, 469, 473, 482
  hosiery, 135, 140, 143, 145–146
    support, 135, 145–146, 398
  infants', underwear and sleepwear, 135, 165–166, 168–171
  maternity, 140
  men's, 133–134, 135–137, 138, 141, 142, 145, 147–148, 149, 152, 153, 154, 207, 471, 474, 484, 486
  motorcycle, 145, 153
  nursing, 140, 143
  surplus, 494–495
  T-shirts, 135, 143, 149, 151, 478
  uniforms, 150, 151–152
  women's, 133–134, 135–137, 143, 145–147, 149, 152, 154, 207, 263, 484, 489–490
  work, 134–135, 148, 153
coffee, 235, 238–240, 243, 245, 250
comforters, down, 334, 336, 339–340
conservation supplies, 57, 461
construction tools and equipment, 511
consumer publications, 97–98, 114
  in Spanish, 97–98

Consumer Reports Auto Price Service, 68–69
contact lenses, 389, 394, 397
cookware, commercial, 326, 330–331
copiers, 29, 30, 32, 434
cottages, collectible, 42–43, 46, 367, 368
crafts projects, kits, and plans, 178, 179–180, 191, 199, 204
crafts stuffing, 175–186
crops, 226, 227
cruises, discount, 526
crutches, 388
cycling, *see* bicycling

diabetics, products for, 387–388, 397
diamonds, custom-cut, 372
diapers and covers, *see* clothing, infants'
display materials, 462
doll-making supplies, 179–180, 190, 194, 195, 199
draperies, hardware and supplies, 190, 302
drugs, prescription, 256, 267, 390, 393, 395
drums, *see* musical instruments, percussion
dyes, fabric, 181

educational programs for seniors, 528
effects boxes, *see* electronics, musical
electronics
    aviation, 79–80, 84
    marine, 76–77, 470, 480
    musical, 403–405, 407, 410, 412–413
embossing powder, 201
embroidery floss, 139, 172–173, 180, 194
envelopes, self-addressed with postage, 419
exercise equipment, 259, 272–273, 468, 483
extracts, flavorings, 234, 242–243, 244
eye guards, sport, 478
eyeglasses
    prescription, 391, 396–397
    reading (nonprescription), 388, 396

fabric, 139, 181, 182, 183, 195, 200, 203
    cashmere, 190
    crewel, 299–300
    cutaways, 193, 195, 199
    decorator, 182, 195, 200, 282, 284, 285–288, 290–292, 295–298, 301–302, 307, 335
    deep-pile ("fun fur"), 193, 195
    ikat, 188

lining, 190, 197, 207
    painting supplies, 56–57, 60, 63, 181, 200, 203
    tartan, 207
    tweed, 207
    wool flannel, 190
facsimile (fax) machines, 29, 30, 32, 430, 432, 434
factory repair manuals
    Corvair, 75
    motorcycle, BMW, 72–73
    tractor, 74
fax, *see* facsimile machines
feather boas, 187
feathers, 187
ferrets, supplies for, 6, 16
figurines, collectible, 46, 47, 354, 360, 363, 365, 367
film, 125, 126
filters, coffee, 245, 250
fire extinguishers, 83, 428, 499
first-aid kits, 148, 392, 499
fish, products for, 3, 5, 13–14
fishing tackle, 470, 474
flatware (silverware), 261, 328, 353–368, 377–378
    replacement (discontinued patterns), 353–355, 357
flooring, 283, 293, 303, 345, 349
    slate, 349
food
    bulk-packaged, 236, 240–241, 252–253, 266
    camping, 476, 487–488
    gourmet, 219, 237–238, 244, 250, 325, 331
    Mexican, 247
    Middle Eastern, 251
    organic, 236, 240, 252–253
food-handling supplies, 460
footwear
    athletic, 161, 162, 478, 482–483, 484
    cowboy boots, 153, 160–161, 162
    men's, 134, 137, 139, 141, 158–159, 160, 162
    moccasins, 132, 136, 137, 153, 162, 471
    motorcycle boots, 162
    nurses' shoes, 150, 159, 162
    women's, 158–159, 160, 162, 399
    work, 134–135, 139, 153, 160–161, 162, 471, 487
forms, business, 430, 434
frames, *see* picture frames
fruit, dried, 233, 240, 242, 243, 252–253
fruit crate labels, 44

furniture
  art, 41
  nursery, 321
  unfinished, 186, 313

games, 251, 259, 261, 268, 374
  lawn, 220, 259
garbage disposers, 345
garden carts, 505
Garden Way bulletins, 112
gardening supplies and equipment,
    220–221, 223
  hydroponic, 221
gas masks, 488
gemstones, loose, 373–375
gerbils, supplies for, 12, 16
gift boxes, 459, 462
gift wrapping and ribbon, 100, 265, 266,
    462
globes, 259
gloves, 136, 145, 148, 392
  driving, 145
  food handling, 148
  shooting, 145
  work, 148
go-cart parts, 504, 505
gold-panning equipment, 476
golfing clubs and gear, 259, 466, 476,
    477, 479, 488, 489
gongs, 411
grasses, 226, 227
greenhouses and supplies, 212, 221,
    228–229, 344
guinea pigs, supplies for, 16
guitars, 403–405, 407, 410, 412, 417
gun cabinets and safes, 259, 432, 437,
    474

hamsters, supplies for, 12, 16
hand trucks, 509
harmonicas, 408
hatboxes, 175
hats, women's, 144
hearing aids, 388
  batteries, 388, 397
herbs and spices, 238, 239, 241, 244, 246,
    247–249, 251
  plants, 215–216, 219, 221
hoof softener, 4
horses, products for, 4, 7–9, 11
hot tubs, 468
hotels, see accommodations
hunting supplies and equipment, 469,
    470, 472, 474, 490–491
hydraulics, 493, 495

incontinence products, adult, 392–393,
    398–399
ironing supplies and equipment, profes-
    sional, 173–174, 197

jewelry
  antique, 39
  boxes, presentation, 462
  cubic zirconia, 372, 376–377
  findings, 372, 373
  Masonic, 259
  men's, 138, 259
  religious, 259
jewelry-making supplies, 179

karaoke, 403–404
kilns, 54, 55, 63
kilts, custom-made, 207
kitchen cutlery, 259, 261, 267, 269, 328–
    331, 362
kneeboards, 466, 480–481

labels
  return-address, 257, 264–265, 426, 430
  woven (name tapes), 194
lampposts, 350
lapidary supplies, 372–373
laser discs, music, current, 96
lawnmowers, 259
  parts, 504, 514
layette items, 135, 139
leather conditioner, 4, 80, 392
leather hides, 296, 382
leather tanning and coloring services, 145
leatherworking supplies and equipment,
    54, 382
lighting fixtures, 281, 284, 288–289,
    293–295, 317, 320, 321, 432
linen, crib and juvenile, 336, 339
livestock supplies, 4, 8, 11
logging supplies and equipment, 499,
    505
luggage, 380–381, 383–384, 432

macrame supplies, 54, 179
magazines, by subscription, 108
mailing tubes, art, 66
mandolins, 407, 412
maple syrup, 241, 243, 246, 252, 253, 325
marine supplies, see boating supplies and
    equipment
meat, naturally raised, 236
metal detectors, 259
metronomes, 409, 415, 416, 417
microscopes, 259

millinery supplies, 144
minibike parts, 505
mirrors, 307, 311–314, 319–321
models (hobby) and supplies, shipbuild-
    ing, 192
moisture meters, 509
mosquito netting, 260, 495
motels, *see* accommodations
motorcycle parts, 504
    BMW, 72–73
    covers, 465
    seat cushions, 465
motors, 493, 495, 505
moving pads, 509
music boxes and supplies, 178, 191
music stands, 409, 414
musical instrument accessories
    bows, 414, 416
    mouthpieces, 409
    reeds, 406, 409
    strings, 405, 408, 414, 416
musical instruments
    esoteric, 403
    keyboard, 403, 413
    percussion, 411
    vintage, 407, 412, 413, 416

neon signs, 427–428
newel posts, 350
nurses' shoes, 150, 159
nutritional supplements, *see* vitamins
nuts, 233, 237, 243

onyx carvings 374
organic gardening supplies, 221
organizers and agendas, 428
organs, 402
ostomy supplies, 387–388
ovens
    commercial, 326, 327, 330
    conventional and microwave, 24, 27,
        30, 32, 33, 259

paint, house, 61
panel systems, office, 422, 424, 429
paperweights, 46
papyrus, 64
park benches, 420
party goods, 266, 517, 520–523
patio door panels, 344
patio and outdoor furniture, 259, 307,
    310, 313, 317, 319–321, 347
patterns, 194
    doll, 194
    ethnic and costume, 382

pens, fine, 29, 61, 259, 359, 365, 368, 380,
    381
perfume, 207, 271, 273, 277–279
pet food, 9
phones and phone machines, 25, 26, 29,
    33, 434
phonograph cartridges, styli, 31
photo processing, range of services,
    123–126, 128–130
photo storage supplies, acid-free, 436,
    461
piñatas, 522
pianos, 402
picture frames and framing supplies, 51,
    52, 57, 58, 59, 60, 61, 63, 64, 65,
    66, 180, 354, 358, 359
pillows, 175–176, 180, 182, 195, 296, 338
ping pong equipment 478
plants
    ground-cover, 224
    sweet potato, 218
plastic bags, 459–460
plumbing fixtures and supplies, 346, 348,
    501
post-surgical supplies, 487–488
posters
    astronomy, 91
    custom (photo), 128–130
    movie, 40, 43, 45
    reproduction, 40
    vintage (original), 40, 43, 45
potpourri ingredients, 199, 215–216, 247,
    249
printing presses and printing supplies,
    201, 435–436
punch embroidery supplies, 180

quilt batts, 175–176

rabbits, supplies for, 12, 16
racquetball supplies and equipment, 478
radar detectors, 29, 30, 32
radiator enclosures, 348
records, 45's, 103–104, 109
refrigerators, commercial, 326, 330
reloading supplies, 472, 474
roofing slate and tools, 349–350
roses, 219–220
    miniature, 222, 224
rototillers, parts, 504, 505
rug-making supplies and equipment, 63,
    189, 195, 205, 206
rugs and carpeting, 132, 283, 293,
    298–299, 303, 307–308, 312
safes, 259, 428, 432, 437

safety gear
ear plugs and muffs, 148, 499
glasses and goggles, 148, 392
respirators, 148
sailboarding, *see* windsurfing
saunas, 468
scales, 272, 330, 435
scarves, undyed silk, 181, 200, 203
screen doors and windows, 346–347
scuba-diving supplies and equipment, 467
sculpting equipment and supplies, 55, 65–66
security equipment, 25–26, 259
seed saving, 211
seeds
flower, 219, 221, 223
herb, 218, 221, 227
open-pollinated, 214–215, 227
vegetable, 214–215, 221, 223
sewing machines and sergers, 26–28, 33–35, 173–174, 197, 202, 259
sewing supplies and notions, 173–174, 176–177, 189–190, 194, 195, 197, 202
shallots, 218–219, 244
sheet music, 404, 415–416
shipping supplies, 428, 433, 434, 459, 461
art, 66
shrink art supplies, 204
shutters, wood, 351
shutter hardware, 351
silk flowers, supplies, 174, 204
silkscreening supplies and equipment, 54, 56, 201
silver chests, 259, 261
skates, inline, 473
skylights, 344
slate, roofing, 349–350
slide storage supplies, 436
slides, astronomy, 191
smoked fish, 235, 331
snorkeling supplies and equipment, 480
snow thrower parts, 504
snowmobile parts, 504
soccer equipment and theme items, 485
soil test kits, 210
sound systems, 403, 405, 409, 412
sphygmomanometers, *see* blood pressure measuring devices
spinning supplies and equipment, 184, 198, 205
spotting scopes, 124, 126, 128, 475
squash supplies and equipment, 478
stage lighting, 403, 409, 410

standby travel, 526–527
stationery
business, 257, 426, 430
children's, 100, 257
novelty, 100
personal, 100, 110, 257
wedding, 257
stencils, 178, 180, 204
stethoscopes, 150, 388
sumi supplies, 53, 57, 60, 181
sunglasses, 79, 82, 368, 389, 391, 396, 467, 471, 478, 486, 494
supports and braces, medical, 387–388, 398
surveying equipment, 510
survival guides and equipment, 488, 494
swimming accessories, 482–483
swimming pool supplies, 346, 479–480

table pads, 308, 311, 313
tape duplicating services, 36
tea, 238, 240, 242, 243, 245, 249, 250
telephones, *see* phones
telescopes and accessories, 122, 124, 125–126, 128, 259
tennis supplies and equipment, 428, 479
textile arts supplies, 181
thread, 139, 183–184, 190, 194, 197, 202
tires
auto, 72, 78, 84
lawnmower, 504
radial, 72
RV, 84
truck, 84
van, 84
toy-making parts, 178–179, 190, 191, 194, 195, 199, 500
toys, 135, 169, 259, 263, 264, 520–523
tractor and combine parts, 73, 505
trains, 259
travel
accessories, 432, 533–534
agents, discount, 526
consolidators, 525
educational, 528, 529
guides, 529–534
medical assistance abroad, 531
newsletters, 532
standby, 526–527
student discounts, 529
U.S. State Department information on, 531–532
with disabilities, 531
treadmills, 468